Advertising Media Planning

THIRD EDITION

Advertising Media Planning

Jack Z. Sissors
Lincoln Bumba

 NTC Business Books
a division of *NTC Publishing Group* • Lincolnwood, Illinois USA

Contents

Foreword by *Leonard S. Matthews*   ix

1   **An Introduction to Media Planning**   1
What Is a Medium?   1
What Is Media Planning?   1
Classes of Media   4
General Procedures in Planning Media   6
Problems in Media Planning   13
Questions for Discussion   18
Selected Readings   19

2   **The Relationship between Media, Advertising, and Consumers**   21
Media and Consumer Choice   21
How Consumers Process Information   22
The Need for a Good Media Vehicle Measurement   23
Steps People Take in the Buying Process   24
Exposure: The Basic Measurement of Media Audiences   25
Measurements of Responses to Advertising in Vehicles   27
Questions for Discussion   28
Selected Readings   29

3   **Basic Measurements and Calculations**   31
How Media Are Measured   31
General Uses of Vehicle Audience Measurements   33
Various Concepts of Audience Measurements   34
Measurements of Message Weight   51
Measures of Cost Efficiency   55
Questions for Discussion   57
Selected Readings   58

4   **New Media Measuring Tools**   61
People Meters   61
Single Source Data   67
Geodemographic Measurements   69
Other New Measurement Ideas   69

Conclusions   70
Selected Readings   70

5 Reach and Frequency 73

What Is Reach (in Broadcast Media)?   73
What Is Reach (in Print Media)?   78
Frequency in Broadcast and Print Media   79
Questions for Discussion   85
Selected Readings   85

6 Effective Frequency and Reach 87

The Underlying Need for Effective Frequency   87
The Essence of Effective Frequency   88
What Is Effective Reach?   90
A Brief History of Effective Frequency   91
Research That Underlies the Effective Frequency Concept   92
Problems with the Effective Frequency Concept   95
Where Effective Stands Now in Media Planning   98
Questions for Discussion   100
Selected Readings   101

7 Marketing Strategy and Media Planning 103

What a Media Planner Needs to Know   103
The Marketing Strategy Plan   104
Competitive Media Expenditure Analysis   114
Sources of Marketing Data   127
Questions for Discussion   131
Selected Readings   131

8 Strategy Planning I: Who, Where, and When 133

Using Index Numbers to Analyze Markets   134
Selecting Advertising Targets   137
Using Psychographic Analysis   142
Where to Advertise   146
When to Advertise   159
Questions for Discussion   161
Selected Readings   161

9 Strategy Planning II: Weighting, Reach, Frequency, and Continuity 163

Geographical Weighting   163
Reach and Frequency   172
Continuity, Flighting, and Pulsing   181

Questions for Discussion   187
Selected Readings   188

10   Selecting Media Classes: Intermedia Comparisons   189
Review of Consumer Media   190
Intermedia Comparisons for Nonmeasured Media   205
The Media Mix   206
Questions for Discussion   208
Selected Readings   209

11   Evaluating and Selecting Media Vehicles   211
Determining Media Values   211
Target Reach and Cost Efficiency   211
Strategic Impressions   213
Other Media Values   214
The Qualitative Values of Media   221
Ad Positions within Media   225
Questions for Discussion   227
Selected Readings   227

12   Putting a Media Plan Together: The Mechanics   229
Organizing the Plan of Action   229
Determining Media Objectives   230
Determining Media Strategies   236
Creative Media Strategy   238
Considerations in Strategy Planning   240
Assemblying Elements of a Plan   242
The Media Flowchart (or Schedule)   248
Questions for Discussion   253
Selected Readings   253

13   An Annotated Media Plan   255
Brand X Media Plan (Next Year) Summary   256
Marketing and Copy Background   258
Marketing Objective/Rationale   260
Media Strategy/Rationale   260
Description of Media Plan   266
Recommended Plan   266
Gross Impression Analysis   272
Media Rationale   274
Comparison of Plan with Strategy   278
Spot Television: Market Selection Methodology   282
Spot Television: Buying Strategy   290
A Final Note   290

14 Media Costs and Buying Problems   293
Some Considerations in Planning and Buying   294
A Discussion of Media Costs   297
Media Buying Problems   306
Questions for Discussion   311

15 Setting and Allocating the Budget   313
Setting the Budget   314
Allocating the Advertising Budget   328
Conclusion   334
Questions for Discussion   334
Selected Readings   335

16 Testing, Experimenting, and Media Planning   337
Tests and Experiments   337
What the Media Planner Should Know about Test
    Marketing   340
Media Testing   348
Media Translations   352
Conclusions   355
Questions for Discussion   356
Selected Readings   356

17 Use of Computer in Media Planning   359
What Does a Computer Do?   359
Media Models   360
Three Well-Known Media Models   361
Other Uses for Computers in Media Planning   369
Thoughts on the Use of Computers in Media Planning   382
Questions for Discussion   384
Selected Readings   384

18 The Future   387
Population Changes   387
Advertising after 1990   390
Media Planning   402
Changing Dynamics   403
Summary   406
Selected Readings   407

Glossary   409

Index   445

Foreword

Few people are better qualified to author a definitive book on media planning and strategy than Jack Sissors. Jack and I first met when I was in charge of the media department at the Leo Burnett Company. The lure of academe pulled Jack away from a promising career. Leo Burnett's loss was Northwestern University's gain.

Jack's close association with practitioner collegues has kept him current in the field of media planning. He created Northwestern University's annual "Media Symposium" for planners, and works on the Advertising Research Foundation's media research committees. In addition, he created and runs the *Journal of Media Planning*, a periodical written especially for media planners, which has made its mark in our business.

Jack's coauthor has a fine reputation at the Leo Burnett Company and in the media world, in general. He is Lincoln J. Bumba who is Senior Vice President and International Media Director at Burnett. Linc has worked in the media department for twenty-nine years, and brings to the book a wealth of media knowledge and experience acquired by working for sophisticated clients such as Procter and Gamble, Kellogg's, Pillsbury, McDonald's; and other leading marketers.

Sissors and Bumba have written the most comprehensive text I have seen on the complex world of modern media planning. Very few areas of the communications business have changed more in the past ten years than media, as mass media has given way to targeted media. Students and practitioners alike will find this book up to date; it leaves few, if any, questions unanswered. As media planning becomes more complex, the need to have a firm grasp on changing concepts and practices becomes more important than ever. This new edition is must reading for anyone who wants to understand the theory and practice of advertising media planning.

Leonard S. Matthews
Former President of the Leo Burnett Company,
and Past President of the American Association
of Advertising Agencies

Preface

This book is an introduction to the subject of planning media that are used to deliver advertising messages to consumers. The emphasis is on planning for consumer media—not buying or selling media, or planning other specialized media, such as those used in industrial advertising.

Planning for consumer media involves the selection and usage of media alternatives to achieve marketing as well as media goals. As a result, *Advertising Media Planning* has both a strong marketing and media foundation.

Originally, the text was written for college students majoring in advertising, but now it also has been written for professionals in the fields of advertising, marketing, and communication. As authors, our continuing goal is to explain media planning concepts and techniques as practiced by the leading media departments in American advertising agencies.

Emphasis is on media planning concepts, rather than on techniques or skills better learned on the job. Nevertheless, it is important to demonstrate how concepts are put into practice. We feel that unless readers know how concepts are implemented, their knowledge of the subject may be incomplete.

In this third edition, we have not only updated material from other editions, but have also added three new chapters (2, 4, and 6) that reflect the changing nature of media planning. We have included a basic discussion of ''people meters'' because they have become a widely used new tool for measuring television audiences. Other new measuring tools, such as ''single source data,'' market zip-code analysis, and the development of a passive people meter are also discussed.

The concept of effective frequency was first introduced in about 1973. Today, the concept itself has changed; for instance, there are new considerations that may determine how high frequency levels should be, and how these levels should be used. Chapter 6, in particular, addresses itself to these changes.

Creative media planning, an idea which comes into play after all the quantitative media evaluations are finished, is also discussed in this new edition. The complete media plan sample (Chapter 13) has been updated, arranged in an easier to understand format, and better explained.

All of these changes indicate that the practice of media planning is evolving and will continue to do so. Readers of this text should keep in mind that despite the fact that techniques change, basic media planning concepts have not changed very much. Therefore, the value of this book is closely tied to its explication of these basic concepts and is not diminished by changes in technique per se.

Finally we would like to thank the many media professionals who have contributed to the body of knowledge and thinking contained in these pages. We are deeply indebted to them.

Jack Z. Sissors
Lincoln Bumba

1

An Introduction to Media Planning

What Is a Medium?

The two most basic words in media planning are *medium* and *vehicle*. A *medium* is a carrier and deliverer of advertisements; media such as newspapers, magazines, radio, or television carry and deliver news, entertainment, and information to audiences. But they also deliver advertisements. The term *vehicle* generally is used to refer to a specific carrier within a media category—the *New York Times* is a vehicle within the newspaper medium—although some persons use the terms medium and vehicle interchangeably. Contemporary usage, however, seems to be settling on rather limited uses of the two terms:

Medium—a broad, general category of carriers such as newspapers, television, radio, magazines, direct mail, or outdoor

Vehicle—a specific single carrier within a medium, such as the *New York Times, Reader's Digest,* or a television program, such as the late news

What Is Media Planning?

Media planning consists of the series of decisions made to answer the question for advertisers: "What are the best means of delivering advertisements to prospective purchasers of my brand or service?" (Advertisements are delivered by media such as newspapers, magazines, or television.) While this definition is rather general, it provides a broad picture of what media planning is all about.

Some specific questions that a media planner attempts to answer are:

- How many prospects (for purchasing a given brand of product) do I need to reach?
- In which medium should I place ads?

1

- How many times a month should prospects see each ad?
- In which months should ads appear?
- In which markets and regions of the United States should ads appear?
- How much money should be spent in each medium?

These are only a few of the questions that must be asked. Each one requires a specific answer and decision.

When all questions have been asked and decisions made, the recommendations and rationales are organized into a written document called a *media plan*. The plan, when approved by the advertiser, becomes a blueprint for the selection and use of media. Once the advertiser has approved the plan, it also serves as a guide for actually purchasing the media.

It would be a mistake, however, to think of media planning as nothing more than finding answers to a list of questions about media. Such a view is too narrow to provide the necessary perspective. Rather, it is better to assume that each question represents certain kinds of problems that need to be solved. Some problems are relatively simple, such as, ''On which day of the week should television commercials be shown?'' Other problems, however, are much more difficult, such as, ''In which media will ads most affect the prospect's buying behavior to result in sales?''

Media planning should be thought of as a process or a series of decisions that provides the best possible answers to a set of problems. A planner may find that a solution to a given problem does not guarantee that it will work when other factors are considered. Finding the *best* solutions to a set of problems represents the main task of planners, and this is what makes media planning such an intellectually challenging activity.

The Changing Role of Media Planners

The role of media planners has changed in advertising agencies. Today, media planning ranks in importance with marketing and creative planning, but in the early days of advertising agency operations media planning consisted of simple, clerical-type tasks. There were fewer media available in those days, and little research on media audiences had been done to guide planners in decision making.

Planning today is an executive function because it has become so much more complex and important than it was years ago. Today's planners must have a greater knowledge base from which to formulate media plans. The planners must not only know more about media, which have increased tremendously in number, but also know more about marketing, research, and advertising than did their predecessors. Most important, planners are called upon not only to make decisions, but to defend those decisions as the best that could be made after considering the many alternatives.

What brought about this change? Foremost was the rise of the marketing concept, which changed media planning from an isolated activity to one closely related to marketing planning. In fact, one way to evaluate a media plan is to measure how effectively it helps to attain marketing objectives. Another cause of the change was the development of new and more definitive media audience research techniques.

As a result, there are more research data available to help planners choose from among a myriad of alternatives.

The change was also due to the increase in advertising expenditures by companies with smaller profit ratios to selling expenses. Quite simply, companies of all sizes now spend many more dollars for media. Also, the prices for purchasing ads in the various media have accelerated rapidly—media are very expensive to buy. As a consequence, company managements want better proof than ever before that their money is well spent. The media planner is the one who is responsible for providing detailed and valid explanations for the media decisions.

Media planning, then, is not so much a matter of being able to answer such relatively simple questions as where to place advertisements or how many advertisements to run each week, as it is a matter of proving that optimal decisions were made under a given set of marketing circumstances. Advertisers demand such explanations, and media planners must be able to provide them. Today's media planners have changed as requirements for planning have changed. The new planner must have breadth of knowledge, marketing understanding, research familiarity, creative planning awareness, and media acumen to do the job competently. It is within this framework that media planning now takes place.

Changes in the Media Planning Industry

Not only have media planners changed, but so has the media environment in which the planner works. One major change has been the creation of new media. Another change is the development of new kinds of audience measurement tools. Still another is new concepts of measuring audiences. The following is a quick overview of these exciting changes. More details about them will be found in Chapters 3 and 6.

New Media. Almost everyone has heard about cable television. Cable offers advertisers new opportunities for reaching more and different kinds of consumers. But other new media such as videotex (or two-way television) may allow media planners to use media in ways never before possible, such as to allow audience members to buy football or concert tickets, to do banking, to buy clothes and gifts, all without leaving home. Video cassettes and other new media offer many different kinds of planning opportunities.

People Meters. At least three companies have competed for the approval of media planners in measuring who watches what on television. Electronic measurements of viewers, it is hoped, will not only replace diaries that only indicate which TV programs are "tuned in," but will also tell planners which people are watching. And some people meters may be coordinated with product purchasing measurements (single source data) to provide a correlation between television watching and purchasing. The three main companies were A. C. Nielsen, through its Media Research Group (MRG); AGB Research (Audits of Great Britain); and Arbitron's Scan America. At present, only A. C. Nielsen measures audiences with people meters.

New Methods of Proving Advertising's Effects on Sales. A number of companies are measuring what consumers purchase through use of UPC scanners. One company will have members of a consumer panel show identification cards when they check out their purchases, and the data will be combined into a sample that shows which brands are being purchased, which sizes, and, it is hoped, which commercials and/or promotions affected purchases. This data can be correlated with television watching from the same sample. The A. C. Nielsen Company calls its service ERIM (Electronic Research for Insights into Marketing). Another company, IRI (Information Resources, Inc.), calls its technique Behaviorscan.

Classes of Media

Mass Media

Mass media, such as newspapers, magazines, radio, and television are especially well suited for delivering advertisements—as well as news, entertainment, and educational material—to a widespread general audience. (See Figure 1–1.) Planners find mass media valuable because (1) such media may be able to deliver large audiences at relatively low costs, (2) they can deliver advertisements to special kinds of audiences who are attracted to each medium's editorial or programming, and (3) they tend to develop strong loyalties among audiences who return to their favorite medium with a high degree of regularity. If a planner wants to reach a special kind of audience repeatedly within a certain time period, some media vehicles will be better suited for this purpose than others. Recent research suggests, for example, that certain types of broadcast programs create higher degrees of viewer interest than other program types, thus offering better environments for commercials.

Media planners, however, also know that mass media (like other media) have their limitations in delivering advertising messages. The most serious is that mass media audiences do not see, hear, or read a medium solely because of the advertising content. Media vary in their ability to get both editorial and advertising material exposed.

Newspapers have news, entertainment, information, and catalog values for their readers. A newspaper generally has excellent readership of both editorial and advertising material, serving as a buying guide for readers who are looking for many different kinds of products. Housewives, for example, often check newspaper ads immediately before their regular food shopping day to find the best grocery bargains. For frequently purchased products, where prices are prominently displayed, newspapers can be a very effective selling medium.

Magazines, on the other hand, are much different in their ability to get ads read. Although some people buy a magazine because they are looking for specific product information on a car or a piece of furniture, most magazine readers are looking for interesting editorial material rather than product information.

Broadcast media, such as radio and television, and the new media are least sought out by consumers for the advertisements alone. Broadcast commercials have

FIGURE 1-1.   Media Most Often Used for Advertising

There are many options open for delivering advertising messages to potential buyers. Some of these media have been widely used for many years, such as "Traditional Media." Others however, either are very specialized, or are so new that they have not been widely used, but are being considered.

Traditional Media

Print media
 Newspapers
 Magazines
 Supplements (newspaper distributed magazines)
 Shoppers (local newspapers carrying mostly ads)
 Direct mail
 Handbills
 Freestanding inserts (FSI) in newspapers and magazines

Broadcast media
 Television programs (network or local)
 Spot television (commercials placed between programs or in local programs)
 Radio programs (network or local)
 Spot radio (commercials placed between programs or in local programs)

Other
 Outdoor (printed, painted)
 Car cards and smaller posters

Specialized Media

Yellow pages of phone books
Business publications (including professional journals)
Directories and membership listings
Event programs (including concert, theater, and sporting programs)
Handbills
Catalogs

The New Media [*]

Some of these media are already being used by advertisers (such as cable), but others are still being evaluated for the future (such as pay cable, VCRs, etc.).

Cable (basic)
Pay cable (or pay for view) not accepting advertising as of now
Videotape players and video discs (cassettes)/recorders (VCRs)
Videotex/teletext and Qube (these are interactive media where audiences can respond to messages)
Personal computers
Multipoint Distribution System (MDS; an over-the-air signal delivery system sending programs from a closed-circuit microwave transmitter to an empty TV channel)
Direct Broadcast Satellites (DBS; signals sent from satellites directly to homes that have a receiving dish–earth station; uses a scrambled signal that must be unscrambled with a decoder)
Subscription TV (STV; a scrambled signal is broadcast from a UHF TV station to a home that has an unscrambler decoder)
Low power TV (LPTV; stations whose signal covers about 10 to 20 miles)
Picturephones (telephones that show pictures of persons making calls)
Satellite-Fed Master Antenna TV (SMATV; a minicable system for large buildings that picks up signals from a satellite and transmits them to individual apartments)

*Kaatz, Ronald B., *Cable Advertiser's Handbook,* Lincolnwood, Illinois. National Textbook Co., 1985, p. 32.

an intrusive character, breaking into the play or action of a program and compelling some attention to the advertising message. Whether any given viewer will or will not watch a particular commercial is determined more by the ingenuity and value of the message than by its appearance on an interesting program. Videotex, teletext, and Qube could be the exceptions. Audiences could seek them out for making buying decisions, and complete the sale via the media.

The effectiveness of the commercial or advertisement to communicate obviously affects the impact it will have on the consumer, and the number of consumers who will read, see, or hear it. This is true regardless of which medium is used.

Specialized Media

Special interest consumer magazines appeal to specific reader interests such as skiing, money management, photography, or antiques. These magazines are read as much for their advertising as they are for their editorial content. Therefore, these magazines often attract readers who purchase the magazine not only for the editorial material, but also for information on the kinds of products advertised.

A large category of media also exists to meet the specialized needs of industrial manufacturers, service companies, wholesalers, retailers, and professional workers such as physicians, attorneys, and teachers. These media may take the form of publications that contain editorial matter, as well as advertising, pertaining to the specialized market, but they may also include films, trade shows, convention exhibits, and phonograph records.

Other specialized media exist exclusively for the purpose of delivering advertising messages. They carry no editorial matter and are not sought after by readers as are other forms of media. Such advertising-oriented media include handbills, direct mail, outdoor billboards, car cards that appear on buses or trucks, and free-standing inserts in newspapers (called FSI).

Another special medium is the catalog. Although catalogs are often requested by consumers, they may not be looked at with the same degree of frequency as are mass media. Therefore, the advertising value of catalogs is somewhat limited. A special form of catalog is the telephone book, which carries advertising but also carries editorial matter—telephone numbers. Plumbers, for example, might justifiably use telephone book advertising exclusively because plumbers aren't needed until emergencies arise. On such occasions, the consumer will search ads in the Yellow Pages to find a plumber, but probably will not notice such ads at any other time.

General Procedures in Planning Media

Marketing considerations must precede media planning. Media planning never starts with answers to such questions as "Which medium should I select?" or "Should I use television or magazines?" Planning grows out of a marketing problem that needs to be solved. To start without knowing or understanding the underlying marketing problem is illogical, because the use of media is primarily a tool for implementing the marketing strategy. So the starting point for a media plan should be an analysis of a marketing situation. This analysis is made so that both marketing and media planners can get a bird's-eye view of how a company has been operating against its competitors in the total market. The analysis serves as a means of learning what the details of the problem are, where possibilities lie for its solution, and where the company can gain an advantage over its competitors in the marketplace.

After the marketing situation has been analyzed, a *marketing strategy and plan* is devised that states marketing objectives and spells out the actions to accomplish those objectives. When the marketing strategy calls for advertising, it is usually to communicate some information to consumers that affects the attainment of a marketing objective. Media are the means whereby advertisements are delivered to the market.

Once a marketing plan has been devised, an *advertising creative strategy* must also be determined. This consists of decisions about what is to be communicated, how it will be executed, and what it is supposed to accomplish. A statement of advertising copy themes and how copy will be used to communicate the selling message is also part of that strategy. Media planning decisions are affected by advertising creative strategy because some creative strategies are better suited to one medium than to any other. For example, if a product requires demonstration, television may be the best medium. If an ad must be shown in high-fidelity color, magazines or newspaper supplements may be preferable. Creative strategy also determines the prospect profile in terms of such demographic variables as age, sex, income, or occupation. These prospects now become the targets that the planner will focus on in selecting media vehicles.

It should be noted that up to this point persons other than the media planner have been making decisions that will ultimately affect the media plan. The marketing or marketing research people were responsible for the situation analysis and marketing plan, though media planners are, at times, involved at the inception of the marketing plan. Copywriters and art directors are generally responsible for carrying out the creative strategy. Sometimes a marketing plan may be as simple as a memorandum from a marketing executive to the media planner, or even an idea in an advertising executive's mind. In such informal situations, media planning may begin almost immediately with little or no marketing research preceding it. Figure 1–2 summarizes the preplanning steps.

The media planner begins work once a marketing strategy plan is in hand. This plan sets the tone and guides the direction of the media decisions to follow.

The first thing to come out of such a plan is a statement of media *objectives*. These are the goals that a media planner believes are most important in helping to attain marketing objectives. Goals include determination of which *targets*—those persons most likely to purchase a given product or service—are most important, how many of those targets need to be reached, and where advertising should be concentrated at what times.

Media strategies develop out of objectives. A media strategy is a series of actions selected from several possible alternatives to best achieve the media objectives. Media strategies will cover such decisions as which kinds of media should be used, whether national or spot broadcast advertising should be used, how ads should be scheduled, and many other decisions.

FIGURE 1–2.   The Scope of Media Preplanning Activities

After the strategy is determined, the implementation of the media plan begins. Some planners call all these subsequent decisions *tactics*. Whatever they are called, many decisions still have to be made before tactics culminate in a media plan. As indicated in Figure 1–3, these decisions might include the selection of vehicles in which to place ads, the number of ads to be placed in each vehicle, the size of each ad, and the specific position within each vehicle that an ad will occupy.

Media decisions need to be creative. Yet many of the decisions involved in media planning are based on quantitative analysis of research data, such as audience sizes, costs, product usage habits, and broadcast ratings. But a media plan does not totally depend on such numbers. It must also have a degree of creativity and good judgment. Although the research analysis may lead to fairly clear alternatives, the planner's judgment may modify these alternatives in some way. For that reason many advertisers who sell the same kind of product use widely differing media to advertise their brands. What is the correct decision for one brand may be incorrect for a competing brand. A dramatic example of this occurred some years ago when Shell Oil Company selected newspapers exclusively to deliver its ads, while all other major oil companies used a combination of television, radio, magazines, billboards, and newspapers.

The effectiveness of a plan depends to a great extent on the amount of creativity the planner uses. An example of how such creativity might be applied to a media/marketing problem was provided by Leonard Matthews, then vice president of marketing services of Leo Burnett Company, Inc., in Chicago:

> A couple of years ago, we introduced a new product on a regional basis, achieving national distribution in about an 18-month period. . . . Our problem was to advertise in 10 or 12 key market areas and to put extra advertising weight against a very selective local audience in these areas—for exam-

FIGURE 1-3. **Kinds of Questions That Lead to Decisions about Media Objectives and Strategies**

The following is an overview of some of the many questions that lead to media objectives and strategies. Note that strategies grow out of objectives.

Media Objectives	Media Strategies
What reaction should we take as a result of media used by competitors?	Should we use same media mix as competitors? Should we allocate weight as competitors? Should we ignore competitors?
What actions should we take as a result of our brand's creative strategies?	Which media/vehicles are best suited? Any special treatments? (Gatefolds, inserts?) Which dayparts?
Who should be our primary and secondary targets?	Which product usage patterns should we consider? Heavy/medium/light users? What distribution of strategic impressions? Which dayparts?
What balance of reach to frequency is needed?	What levels of reach and frequency? What levels of effective reach/frequency?
Do we need national and/or local media?	What proportions should go into national media? What proportion in local media?
What patterns of geographical weighting should we use?	Should we weight by dollars or GRPs? Where should we place weights? When should we weight (weeks/months)? What weight levels for each market?
What communication goals (or effectiveness goals) are needed?	Which criteria of effectiveness should we use?
Which kind of scheduling patterns suits our plans? Continuity/flighting/pulsing?)	Should we use one or the other? When should we weight more heavily?
Does media have to support promotions? How?	What proportion of the budget should be used? What media mix?
Is media testing needed? How should it be used?	How many and which markets? How should we translate (Little USA or As Is)?
Is budget large enough to accomplish objectives?	Do we need to set priorities? Which must we achieve, which are optional? Do we need more money than available?

ple, the factory worker in Columbus, Ohio. All local media are mass in their approach. There are no local magazines beamed at the blue collar worker.

The media planner on this account came up with what I believe was a creative solution to a fairly knotty problem. He isolated the major factory locations on a map of each market involved. He did some research on where these people lived in relation to where they worked. He worked out an outdoor poster showing which was tailored to the traffic pattern of the factory workers going to and from work. In some cases, he caused boards to be erected opposite plant gates or in plant parking lots.

An obvious idea? A simple idea? Sure. But the outdoor plants, the National Association of Outdoor Advertising, and the client all thought it one of the most creative uses of local media planning they had ever seen.[1]

The decision-making process for media involves not only the use of research as an aid, but judgment and creativity to make the decisions effective. Matthews summed up this combination of talents as follows:

Judgment, then, is the catalyst, the homogenizer which creates a media strategy out of an everglade of facts and opinion. Good judgment is the prime requisite for a good problem solver, and a good problem solver is a good media planner.[2]

Good judgment will still be required of the decision maker, even as better media measurement techniques and data become available.

Principles of Selecting Media Vehicles

Of all the media decisions made, one of the most important is selecting individual vehicles. Planners tend to select one or more vehicles that effectively reach an optimum number of prospects (a) with an optimum amount of frequency (or repetition), (b) at the lowest cost per thousand prospects reached (called cost efficiency), (c) with a minimum of waste (or nonprospects), (d) within a specified budget.

These principles apply most when selecting vehicles for mass-produced and mass-consumed products such as food, clothing, or automobiles. Yet even though they may be more difficult to execute, the principles should be the same in selecting vehicles for such products as noncommercial airplanes or yachts where prospects are distributed unevenly throughout the population. It may be less cost efficient to reach those prospects than it would be to reach prospects for mass-consumed products, because planners may have to select vehicles that contain large amounts of waste to reach such selective markets. There are other times when the principles may have to be modified. For example, if a creative strategy calls for certain kinds of media such as those that produce ads in high-fidelity color, then cost or waste may have to be disregarded in favor of meeting creative goals. Most often, however, these principles are followed consistently in planning.

When planners apply media selection principles, they use media delivery statistics as one piece of evidence that they have achieved the reach required. *Delivery* simply means the number of audience members reached by, or exposed to, a vehicle or a combination of media vehicles.

---

1. Matthews, Leonard S., "The Role of Judgment in Media Planning," in *How to Put Media Research Into Proper Perspective in Media Planning. Papers from the American Association of Advertising Agencies, Regional Conventions,* New York: AAAA, 1960, pp. 32–33.

2. Ibid.

With the goal of obtaining the highest possible exposure, the planner starts by looking among the many media alternatives that will reach prospects. A planner does this through using media audience research data for individual vehicles. The data are in the form of numbers classified by audience types, and the numbers listed for each medium may be used as proof of audience delivery. In other words, the planner may use this statistical evidence to prove that the best vehicle(s) for reaching the targeted prospects has been selected. Obviously there are other considerations in making this decision. Costs of media may be so high per prospect reached that the planner may have to reject the first choice in favor of other media that reach smaller numbers of prospects but at lower costs.

Once audience delivery numbers have been found, they are related to the total number of prospects in the market. If a market consists of 35 million women in the United States who purchased a given kind of product within the last month, then the size of the market is 35 million. The planner may select certain magazines that reach $17^1/_2$ million purchasing women, or 50 percent of the market. Is 50 percent enough? It depends on the marketing objectives. If it isn't enough, the planner may select one or more other media vehicles to increase the percentage reached. Because no decision is made in a vacuum, the planner must also take into consideration the creative, promotional, and executional goals of the marketing strategy while evaluating the vehicle's ability to deliver prospects.

Media Plans Are Custom Tailored

A media plan is designed expressly to meet the needs of an advertiser at a given point in time for specific marketing purposes. Today's media plan is usually not a copy of last year's plan, nor is it simply a blank form with spaces that can be filled in quickly with selected dates or times for running ads. Each media plan should be different from preceding ones for the same product.

Why, then, are plans custom tailored? The answer is that the marketplace is a dynamic center of activity that is rarely the same from year to year. Competitors rarely stand still in their marketing activities. They may be changing their messages, changing their marketing expenditures, introducing new brands, or discontinuing distribution of old brands. Consumers, too, change—moving to different geographical areas, getting new jobs, retiring, getting married, adopting different leisure-time activities, or buying new kinds of products.

As a result, the marketing situation of an advertiser presents new opportunities as well as new problems. The result is a need for a tailor-made media plan to fit a specific marketing situation.

Media planning is not a science with hard and fast rules that can be easily implemented. Because marketing situations change, new approaches to planning are constantly needed to keep up with, or ahead of, competitors. Media planning is also affected by the new kinds of research or analysis needed to keep abreast of a changing business world. Media planning requires a great sensitivity to change. See Case Study 1–1.

CASE STUDY 1–1
Is There a Best Media Strategy?

Problem:

Because there are basic principles by which media strategies are devised, it might seem that these principles would apply to many different marketing situations. The result would be that most media strategies would be alike and that almost every media plan would have about the same strategy.

The following data are presented to study such a situation. They represent media expenditures for the insurance market.

Percentage of Media Dollars Spent by Selected Insurance Companies (1985)

Company	Total Spent	Total Percentage of Advertising Budget	Percentage of Advertising Dollars by Medium								
			Maga-zines	Sunday Maga-zines	News-papers	Network TV	Spot TV	Network Radio	Out-door	Cable TV Network	Spot Radio
Aetna	8,405.5	100.00			9.29	86.94	0.72				3.06
Allstate	28,406.6	99.99	12.46	2.67	4.61	48.34	19.19	5.02		1.32	6.38
Metropolitan	20,333.0	100.00	27.09		8.24	29.55	34.00		0.19	0.09	0.84
Liberty Mutual	11,625.1	100.00	15.37		5.29	71.59		7.42	0.10		0.23
Prudential	33,980.3	100.00	19.48		3.05	66.43	5.39		0.32	3.61	1.72
State Farm	19,482.2	99.90	7.16		1.90	44.77	9.71	28.84	1.11	1.80	4.70

Source: Schnorbus, Paula, ''Premium Positioning,'' in *Marketing and Media Decisions*, February 1987, p. 85. Reprinted by permission.

Comments:

1. From the data above, one can see certain parts of strategies common to all brands shown and certain other parts that differ. For example, all brands spent heavily in network television. But the amounts varied from a high of 66.4 percent (or $22,572,800) for Prudential, to a low of 29.6 percent (or $6,008,100) for Metropolitan Life. But Metropolitan spent much more for spot TV than did Prudential (34% vs. 5.4%).

2. The implications of these data are that media strategies differ for each company because each sees the marketplace in a somewhat different manner. One must remember that the marketplace represents a battleground where brands vie for high-ranking positions. Some brands may be content to hold their own and not slip in their battle with competitors. Others want to move up the ladder. The strategies they devise are related to their marketing goals.

3. In essence, there is no ''best'' strategy for everyone. What is best for one company may not work best for another.

Problems in Media Planning

Although media planning has become very important within advertising agency operations, it is not performed as efficiently as one might suppose. The planner is faced with many different kinds of problems that make it difficult to arrive at objective decisions.

Insufficient Information

Media planners almost always require more data about markets and media than are available. Some data never will be available, either because audiences cannot be measured or the data are too expensive to collect. For example, no continuing research service measures the audience exposure to outdoor advertising, or to AM or FM radio listening in every market in the United States, or to portable television viewing. Why? Because such services are too costly to provide and because there is no adequate way of measuring these audiences. Both outdoor exposure and local radio listening have been measured—but not on a continuing basis in all cities so as to give the planner comprehensive and up-to-date information. There are also inadequate research data showing the amount of money that competitors spend yearly for outdoor advertising, for local radio advertising, and for newspaper ads.

In television planning, measurements of the audience size for commercial messages are not available. Most television rating services measure the audience size only in terms of individuals or homes tuned in to programs. This does constitute exposure measurement even though there is no assurance that those who press people meter buttons are paying attention to a program. Even if there is an audience in front of the television sets watching a given program, there is no guarantee that they would watch the commercials. How, then, can the media planner know with any degree of certainty how many people will view or hear a commercial on any given program?

Furthermore, while it may be possible to estimate the size of the audience for a given commercial, there is no way to measure the degree of attention audiences pay to that commercial. As the Audience Concepts Committee of the Advertising Research Foundation pointed out in a report titled *Toward Better Media Comparisons:*

> Television presents . . . difficult problems. . . . Exposure to television, unlike exposure to billboards, is not public and cannot be publicly measured. It is not conceivable that we shall be able to obtain any objective measure of the number of people whose eyes are confronted by a television commercial.[3]

If such data were available, the planner would be able to make decisions about television with a greater degree of confidence than is now possible.

Another problem in television planning is that decisions about the future performance of television programs must be based on data that represent past performance. If the future is radically different from the past, then the data on which a

---

3. Audience Concepts Committee Report, *Toward Better Media Comparisons,* New York: Advertising Research Foundation, 1961, p. 18.

decision is based may be worthless. William E. Matthews, former director of media relations and planning at Young & Rubicam, explained the problem as follows:

> Take spot broadcast ratings. The rating assigned to a station-break spot is an artificial quantity, a sort of average of preceding and succeeding program ratings, which become inapplicable the moment adjacencies change. Suppose you are buying spots in August for late September scheduling. You have no record for the fall because that is in the future, programming is not fully set, new shows are involved, and you are dealing with a radically different group of factors from those on which you have measurements.[4]

As a result, a decision made on the basis of past data is no more than a rough estimate of what the planner hopes to achieve in the future.

The problem of obtaining sufficient information is especially acute for small advertisers, many of whom cannot afford to buy research data. These companies often do not know how large their own retail sales are because they sell only to distributors or wholesalers. The media planner, then, must guess at the client's sales position in any given market.

Measuring how people read newspapers and magazines is another problem. How much of any given magazine or newspaper is read? How many advertisements are read? How thoroughly are they read? What is the value of placing an advertisement in one vehicle versus another? How does each vehicle affect the perception of an advertisement that it carries? Answers to these and many other questions are not available on a continuing basis, so the media planner must make decisions without knowing all the pertinent facts.

Time Pressures

A problem that affects media planning in an entirely different way is that of the time pressure involved in making decisions. When the agency and advertiser are ready to start their advertising program, the planner often is faced with a lack of sufficient time to solve problems thoroughly. For example, in many cases the planner requires competitive media expenditure analyses showing how much each competitor spends in major markets throughout the country. Gathering such information is a time-consuming task for media analysts, and the planner may have to bypass this investigation in order to write a media plan quickly.

Another time-related problem is the limited number of broadcast times and programs available to be purchased by advertisers at any given time. This problem is compounded if the client is slow to approve the budget, in which case the most desirable broadcast time periods and/or programs may be spoken for before the advertiser enters the marketplace.

In other situations, new research data are so plentiful that there is neither per-

---

4. Matthews, William E., "There's Always Another Set of Numbers You Don't Have," in *Hidden Media Values, or Going Beyond the Numbers, Papers from the American Association of Advertising Agencies Regional Conventions,* New York: AAAA, 1961, p.39.

sonnel nor time to analyze them. This is especially true for the large amounts of computerized data on media audiences and brand usage. The computer is able to produce masses of cross tabulations at lightning speeds, but often such data may go unused because there is insufficient time to analyze them.

External Influences on Media Decisions

There are at least two external influences on media planning decisions besides the directions that numbers provide. Whether these influences result in *better* media plans is not clear. But because of their subtle nature, there is a danger that they could exert negative influences on the best judgments of planners. Those who favor these kinds of influence think otherwise. The two influences are:

The Pressure to Produce "Creative" Media Plans. An established tradition in most advertising agency media departments is to provide clients with statistical proof that media decisions are the best alternative action that could be taken under budget and other constraints normally required for media planning. Therefore media plans are usually given to clients in statistical formats, composed of many pages of numbers.

But it seems as if a growing number of planners are developing an antagonism toward these kinds of plans. Some persons have a feeling that media plans for brands within the same product category are beginning to look too much alike. Media plans that are similar may tend to nullify each other's best efforts at reaching and communicating with consumers. Therefore, a brand may suffer.

Alan Goldin, media director, House of Seagram, and Kathy Neisloss, advertising director of *Vanity Fair,* wrote about young assistant media planners who are CPM driven. They grow weary of numbers-only accusations and look for opportunities to accelerate their rise in the profession by standing out and supporting some "out-of-ordinary" media opportunities. But their motivation may be further inspired by agency and account managers who dread the typical, mundane media plans. They "continually encourage something new in the name of imagination, creativity, or innovation."[5]

A better way to proceed, these planners suggest, is to make media plans "creative." This approach may suggest that quantitatively based plans are not creative, which is questionable. The definition of what creative means, however, is not universally agreed upon. On one hand, a plan that is different from other plans would probably be called creative. On the other hand, some planners would object, saying that "just being different" is not enough. The latter persons feel that the term "creative" means innovative, or doing things in novel and unusual ways.

One problem with the creative idea, therefore, is that the meaning of "creative" may need better definition. In fact, at least two approaches to achieving a "creative" media plan exist. First, some planners prefer a media plan that starts with a sound basic set of quantitative data, and then proceeds beyond the data in-

---

5. Goldin, Alan and Neisloss, Kathy, "Evaluating Print Qualitatively: A No-Nonsense Guide," in *Inside Print,* November 1986, pp. 27–29.

novatively, at no extra cost. Placing a pet food commercial within a TV program that features pets might be one example. Second, other planners feel that the numbers are relatively unimportant and that decisions for or against vehicles simply have to be innovative. These people might want a plan that is much different than plans for other products in the category, one that stands out because it represents an innovative way to communicate with people.

How many planners in this country support the concept of "creative" media plans? There are no data available. But there is a feeling that the idea is growing. The subject has been part of speeches given at various media planning conventions. Planners have discussed the need for creativity in their speeches and articles. One speech that was very well received in the industry was made by Philip Gerber, media director of Tatham-Laird, Kudner, Chicago.[6]

Another reason for a call for creativity is the feeling that media numbers are not as precise as many people assume them to be. Numbers such as ratings and audience sizes are not measures of everyone in the universe; they are projections based on samples. But once numbers get printed on paper, especially computer paper, or appear in plan reports, they seem to have a credibility that may not be warranted. In the last analysis, they are only estimates, and perhaps rough estimates at that.

In addition, "creative" media plans may be used by advertisers and their agencies in an attempt to reach increasingly fragmented and difficult-to-target audiences. The increasing number of working women, for example, may force more creative and selective daypart/program selection or add a nontraditional publication to a "women 25–54 schedule" which typically would consist only of daytime TV and women's service books.

The call for creativity in planning also comes from some media salespeople who do not have the largest or most acceptable media audience numbers for their vehicles as compared to their competitors', and who ask planners to make decisions on a subjective rather than objective basis. Perhaps the vehicle they are selling, has a "something" that can't be measured very well. Therefore, these people tend to be among the groups advocating more planning on a subjective and creative basis.

The need to be different also seems to have its roots in more than a simple rejection of quantitative values. It may be related to planners' performance as persons in need of self-expression. Media planners who work on the same product group team with creative people may be stimulated by the apparent freedom that the latter people have and wish they too could have that opportunity. Creative media plans may be an avenue for self-expression.

Goldin and Neisloss argued for a balanced point of view when they wrote that

> there is no such thing as a purely qualitative media opportunity. Everything can and must be accompanied by some supporting data or sound reason and logic. Every recommendation should be prudent, not frivolous, defendable, not impulsive.

---

6. Gerber, Philip, "Looking Behind the Numbers," speech given at the 1985 Media Symposium, Northwestern University, June 1985.

A media pro who goes only by the numbers *or* by ''gut'' feelings is no pro at all.[7]

It seems self-evident that both sources of influence need to be studied in greater detail so that we can speak more authoritatively about them than we can at present.

Institutional Influences on Media Decisions. One of the less obvious sources of influence on media decisions is the effect of client pressures to use or not use certain media vehicles, or to use them in certain ways. Often these pressures are well known by everyone working on a client's account; the client may continually remind everyone of the restrictions. But there are times when these influences are known by relatively few persons, perhaps only those who regularly visit the client and are constantly communicating directly with him or her.

But there are other subtle influences that affect planners. There may be people, such as directors or assistant directors in the media department, or in account executive positions, who may in some way, influence decisions.

The problem with these institutional influences is that little or no information is available concerning the extent to which they exist, or how much they affect decisions. These influences probably vary from client to client, too.

Lack of Objectivity

One of the continuing problems in media decision making is the sterility of thinking about strategy. Planners are not always objective. For example, an overdependence on numbers may affect objectivity. Media executives often feel that when a decision is substantiated by numbers, such as television ratings, the decision must be valid because the numbers prove it so. It is often difficult to argue with decisions proved by numbers, yet the numbers can be misleading. The methods of measurement may be imprecise, the sample size may be too small, the technique of measurement may be biased or too insensitive to really measure what it is supposed to, or there may be a set of numbers of major significance not available to the media planner—all of which may affect the objectivity of the decision maker. Uncritical acceptance of numbers can be a dangerous practice and may lead to a decision that common sense indicates is wrong. The planner should be wary of overreliance on numbers.

Objectivity is also affected when a planner accepts relative data as absolute. For example, the sizes of television audiences reported through ratings are not absolute measurements. When a television rating service shows that 15 million homes tuned in to a given television program, this does not necessarily mean that precisely 15 million homes actually tuned in to the program. Since the sample of homes measured was only about 1,700, projections from 1,700 to a total of about 86 million homes means that the margin of error may be quite large. It may be plus or minus a

---

7. Goldin and Neisloss, ''Evaluating Print Qualitatively,'' p. 27.

million homes. Such data are to be used for relative purposes only, and the data merely show that Program A probably has a larger audience size than Program B.

On the other hand, a planner cannot ignore the numbers and make decisions entirely on the basis of experience. Clients are certain to challenge the basis upon which media decisions are made.

Measuring Advertising Effectiveness

Because there is no valid way of measuring advertising effectiveness, it is often difficult to prove that media decisions were effective. Consequently, decision making has not been able to advance to the point where there is always substantive proof that one medium is much better than another. Often a media planner has biased preferences in favor of one media class over others and will favor that medium regardless of what statistics or other objective evidence might indicate.

Notwithstanding these problems, decision making is improving and will undoubtedly improve as long as the people in charge realize there are problems that need solutions and make attempts at improving the situation. The Advertising Research Foundation (ARF) and the Association of National Advertisers (ANA) have attacked some of the more pressing problems of research data and methodology. Furthermore, new and more highly qualified personnel within both agency and client organizations have shown a dissatisfaction with traditional methods of decision making and have demanded new and better evidence for decisions. They are critical of the misuse of statistics and have a broad enough background in research, marketing. advertising, and media to set high standards of performance. The era of accountability in which many large companies now operate also will act to improve the decision-making function by demanding better research data and the removal of major obstacles that stand in the way of such data.

QUESTIONS FOR DISCUSSION

1. Why is there a growing demand for "creative" media plans?
2. What are the conspicuous changes in the media today?
3. Why do most large advertisers prefer to use mass, rather than specialized, media to deliver their messages to their markets?
4. Explain why the media vehicle that reaches the largest number of people is not necessarily the best vehicle for every advertiser.
5. What is meant by the concept of *waste* in media planning?
6. At times a media planner may have to disregard waste in planning. Under what conditions might this happen?
7. Why does media planning require good judgment if the research data on media audiences is considered valid and accurate?
8. What conditions brought about the need to tailor make each media plan for each advertiser?
9. What is meant by "interactive media"?
10. What is meant by *accountability* as it pertains to media planning and marketing?

SELECTED READINGS

Advertising Age, "Ostrow on Media: Support Refocus from CPMs: Human Judgment Is the Key," October 16, 1987, p.96.

Advertising Age, "Editorial: "The Human Element in Media Planning," September 25, 1978, p. 14.

Banks, Allen, "Clutter in the Era of Control, in *Marketing and Media Decisions,* January 1987, pp. 51–52.

Deckinger, E. L., "Media Strategy and Accountability," *Perspectives in Advertising Management,* Association of National Advertisers, 1969, pp. 159–72.

Deckinger, E. L., "The Magnitude of the Media Problem and What to Do about It," *Papers from the American Association of Advertising Agencies Regional Conventions,* 1960, pp. 1–14.

Drexler, Mike, "How to Stay Ahead," *Media Decisions,* August 1978, p. 62.

Greenberg, Joseph, "The Proverbial Forbidden Fruit: Creativity," *Marketing and Media Decisions,* July 1981, pp. 170ff.

Gudrian, H. D., "How to Evaluate and Select Business Media for More Effective Advertising," *Industrial Marketing,* November 1972, pp. 119–20.

Jones, Richard P., "Quiet Revolution in Media Planning," *Media Decisions,* September 1967, pp. 36–40.

Kemp, Frank B.; Rush, Holton C.; and Wright, Thomas A., Jr. *Some Important Things I Believe a Young Account Representative Should Know about Media,* Committee on Client Service, American Association of Advertising Agencies, December 1963.

Keshin, Mort, "The Illusion of Numbers," *Media/Scope,* March 1966, p. 12ff.

Liddel, Robert, "Advertising Doesn't Work Overnight," in *Papers from the American Association of Advertising Agencies Regional Conventions,* 1960, pp. 29–36.

Maneloveg, Herbert, "How Media Men Buy Media—Six Factors for a Good Plan," *The New World of Advertising, Advertising Age,* November 21, 1973, p. 62.

Martin, Steve, "Taking the Guesswork Out of Media Planning," *Marketing and Media Decisions,* May 1981, pp. 196, 198.

Matthews, Leonard, "The Role of Judgment in Media Planning," in *How to Put Media Research into Proper Perspective in Media Planning, Papers from the American Association of Advertising Agencies Regional Conventions,* 1960, pp. 23–33.

Matthews, William E., "There's Always Another Set of Numbers You Don't Have," in *Hidden Media Values, or Going Beyond the Numbers, Papers from the American Association of Advertising Agencies, Regional Conventions,* 1961, pp. 37–42.

Sales Management, "Systematize the Logic of Media Planning," December 1, 1970, pp. 42–43.

Selwitz, Robert, "Clients Are Taking a More Active Role in Deciding Where Their Advertising Dollars Should Go," in *The Buck Stops (and Starts) Here,* in Madison Avenue, May 1985, pp. 72–76.

Surmanek, Jim, "Solid Research Begets Sound Ads," *Advertising Age,* January 18, 1979, pp. 51–52.

Surmanek, Jim, "More to Media Buying Than Numbers," *Advertising Age,* May 21, 1979, pp. 64ff.

Surmanek, Jim, "And Now a Word from Our Sponsor," *Chicago Tribune/Sun-Times Supplement,* October 26, 1980, p. 11.

Vladamir, Andrew, "No Magic Formula for Media Mix," *Stores,* June 1973, pp. 28–29.

Zeltner, Herbert, "Assumptions, Logic and Media Planning," *Media/Scope,* August 1963, pp. 8–10.

2

The Relationship between Media, Advertising, and Consumers

The purpose of this chapter is to help the reader think about the relationship of media, advertising, and consumers. This relationship affects the manner in which consumers perceive media as well as advertising. It also affects the manner in which media is measured, planned, and delivered. This chapter sets the stage for Chapter 3, "Basic Measurements and Calculations."

Media and Consumer Choice

Most advertising is delivered to consumers by mass media such as newspapers, television, or magazines. Consumers, however, are not standing by idly waiting for mass media to come to their doors. They have many other activities to participate in on a typical day. If they choose to look at a medium, they do so because it meets some need. If they reject it, it is because other needs may have higher priorities. When they do select a *medium* to watch, read, or listen to, it is because that medium offers them some specialized entertainment or information. Media that don't supply the right kind of entertainment or information usually are either ignored or rejected, at least for a time.

When consumers choose a vehicle of one medium or another to attend to (such as a television program), they may like it so much that they develop strong loyalties to it and return with varying degrees of regularity. But loyalty to the program does not necessarily equal receptivity to advertising carried in the program. In the same way, many consumers subscribe to a magazine, but, because of the press of other activities, they do not make a conscious effort to read advertising carried within it. Some consumers may have back issues of a magazine that have not been read on an end table, or nightstand. A consumer may be asked, "Why haven't you read these issues?" The answer may be something like, "Well, I intend to get around to them one of these days.'' But such days may never come, and eventually, if enough time passes, the magazines may be thrown out, given to someone else, or stored away indefinitely.

Knowledge of these possibilities is important to media planners who may have assumed that because audience measurement data that shows how many audience members read a given magazine is available, they now know how many of the audience will see a given ad in that magazine. Most planners know that audience measurement data does not indicate the relationship of media audiences to advertisements at all. Yet one of the major tasks of media planners is to not only deliver advertisements, but to help get them seen, heard, or read.

Media planners, on the other hand, also know that some consumers may choose to be involved with a mass medium not primarily for entertainment or general information, but *because of its advertising*. When consumers are in the market for a product that meets some want or need, they may begin to search media, using them as buying guides in attempting to find the right products or brands to help solve a particular problem. In such instances, media have a catalog value. This is more true of print than broadcast media.

Finally, many consumers do use media, and the advertising contained within, without any specific purpose in mind. Sometimes, a consumer will watch a television commercial with no intent of buying or even learning about a brand. At other times, consumers may watch commercials as a means of biding their time waiting for something else to happen. For example, a consumer's favorite program could be telecast from 7:00 to 7:30 P.M., and his or her next favorite program may not come on until 9:00 P.M. That consumer may watch the intervening programs and their commercials with no particular intent on finding brand information. At times serendipity takes place, and consumers discover a product or brand that meets a latent need that may have been forgotten for some time. Most often, consumers forget the advertising they have seen during these times because of the way they process information.

How Consumers Process Information

Much of the advertising information received by consumers is placed in a memory storage system called *short-term memory*. Such information, like the last few words of a sentence just heard, read, or seen, or a telephone number that may be remembered for a few minutes until it is dialed, is recalled for a very short time, and then forgotten. Advertisers have observed this response through a special kind of advertising research—a *telephone coincidental survey* of advertising messages that appear in a broadcast program. Even though consumers tell interviewers that they have just seen a commercial, they often cannot recall the name of a brand, nor the key selling point. Of course, if consumers should want to remember an advertising message, they can do so by expending the necessary time and effort. They may repeat the message again and again mentally until it is learned. In fact, if the repetition occurs often enough, the message may be remembered and transferred to another memory storage system in the brain called *long-term memory*.

The point is that media often do not do any more than deliver advertising to consumers. Media planners sometimes may be called on to help consumers remember a message by arranging for it to be repeated many times within a given time period. If consumers do not want to remember, however, they can reject the repetitions and simply choose not to pay attention. In the study of information processing, this is called *selective attention*.

Can a media planner do any more to deliver advertising messages? There is widespread disagreement among media experts about the answer to this question. Some say much can be done by strategic media planning, that by careful media selection, careful media timing, by placing ads in markets where sales opportunities are best, by repeating the advertising, and by other strategic activities, a planner can help the advertiser achieve his goals. Others say that a media planner's job is done when the message is delivered to the right targets, at the right time, and in sufficient quantities. (This subject will be discussed again later in the chapter on the media planning process.)

It is also clear that media work with the creative message and the nature of a product to get the advertising message through to the consumer. Media is supposed to deliver the message to the right consumer, in the right quantity, at the right time. Then the creativity of the advertising message takes over. If an ad is interesting, consumers will continue to pay attention to it, simply because it is so. But if the product is not important to the consumer at the time the ad is received then nothing else may make a difference. Consumers may simply not pay attention.

It seems clear, however, that media planners should know more about consumers, their needs, and perceptions, than they have known. Planners may have to use their knowledge of consumer behavior research findings in addition to traditional planning techniques in order to do a competent job.

The Need for a Good Media Vehicle Measurement

Meanwhile, planners need a measurement that can help them find the best medium or vehicle to help sell a client's product brand or service. If it could be shown that one medium sells more of a brand than any other media, and if the cost were not prohibitive, then that medium would be the one in which to place advertising. Unfortunately, there is no measurement available today that can provide precisely that kind of information. There are planners who have conducted custom-made research to guide them in finding a medium that has the greatest sales potential. The problem with that kind of research is that it is difficult to parse out a medium's contribution to a sale.

After all, media are not the only factors contributing to sales. Every element of the marketing mix may contribute a little, and some contribute a great deal. For example, sometimes the thing that is most responsible for selling a product is a reduced price. Media that carry news of the price reduction in an ad play a secondary role in the sale, while the price, and the advertising message, play a major role. Other media mix factors that contribute to a sale are distribution, positioning, personal selling, sales promotion, public relations, and packaging. (It is assumed that the most important element in the selling of a brand are its product quality and uniqueness.)

Another impediment to measuring the contribution of media to a sale is the spending activity of competitors. When competitors intend to spend heavily for a brand, a planner may not be able to react to a change quickly enough in order to meet the competition.

Steps People Take in the Buying Process

It is also assumed that the power of media to deliver and provide influence and impact for advertising messages may also depend on where in the purchasing process a consumer happens to be. If we use the Engel/Kollats model of the buying process we will find that the order of purchasing looks somewhat like the following:

1. Problem recognition (e.g., auto needs new tires, or individual wants a new suit of clothes).
2. Search for alternatives to solve a problem (e.g., consumer reads advertising, talks to a friend about the problem, or goes shopping looking for product or brand).
3. Alternative evaluation of different brands (e.g., consumer has found two or three brands that could solve a problem. Which one should be chosen?).
4. Purchases made through choice of "a brand." This is the buying action.
5. The consumer evaluates whether the product and brand meets expectations of solving the problem. This is the postpurchasing evaluation.
6. Feedback to the brain about how satisfying the purchase was. Unsatisfactory purchases may be returned, or consumer may keep the product/brand and look for confirmation that a "good" buying decision was made. Frustration in the quality of the purchase may result in anger, or indignation against the brand, or the store in which the purchase was made.[1]

If, on one hand, consumers do not perceive that they have a problem, then presumably, they will not react very much to either media or advertising. On the other hand, when consumers do have a problem they may be very receptive to both. Some problems are very simple, such as finding that there is no catsup in the house when hamburgers are being served; others, such as buying a new home, or deciding on a new career, are complex. The latter two problems may require great attention to media and, thus, advertising.

---

1. Engle, J. F., and Blackwell, R. D., *Consumer Behavior*, Chicago: Dryden Press, 1982, pp. 25–33.

TABLE 2-1.   Various Ways That Media Vehicles Could Be Measured

Media Measurement	What It Measures	What It Means
Vehicle exposure	Exposure to TV or print media	Open eyes facing a vehicle (or opportunities-to-see ads)
Print media circulation	Number of copies distributed	People/families receiving newspaper vehicles (no exposure counted)
Advertising exposure	Number of ads exposed per issue	A gross (or crude) counting of total number of ads exposed in a vehicle
Advertising perception	Number of ads that consumers remember having seen in a vehicle	The smallest amount of communication remembered of ads in a vehicle
Advertising communication	The total amount of recalled material from ads in a vehicle	Counts the feedback from ad messages in vehicles
Response function: *media effectiveness*	The number of responses to advertising in a vehicle	Measures the effects of advertising on consumers of responses such as sales, brand awareness, attitude change, and recall of messages

Source: Audience Concepts Committee. Modified from *Towards Better Media Comparisons,* Advertising Research Foundation, 1961, p. 18.

When consumers are trying to decide which brand to buy to resolve a problem they also tend to be receptive to both media and ads. Certain media measurement techniques have, at one time or another, been considered as possible means for comparing the audience sizes of media so that the best vehicles can be selected on behalf of a client.

Table 2-1 shows that there are a number of alternative ways that media audiences could be measured. However, the one that has been used for over twenty-five years is vehicle "exposure."

Exposure: The Basic Measurement of Media Audiences

Industry leaders have chosen a measurement of media audiences—exposure—that is less than desirable, but one that can differentiate media vehicles on the basis of their audience size. The audiences also can be measured at a reasonable cost.

Technically speaking, the meaning of exposure is "open eyes (or listening ears) facing the medium." Practically (as will be explained in detail in Chapter 3), it is a measurement of people who either say they are sure that they have looked into a vehicle; or say they read a vehicle within a given time period (yesterday, for newspapers; within the last thirty days, for a monthly magazine); or that they were looking in the direction of the TV set or listening to the radio, when a program was being telecast.

Exposure measurements are different for each medium. In magazines, for example, persons exposed to a publication are counted if they say they read the publication. But persons exposed to a television program are counted only if they press a button on a people meter measuring device. Not every home will have such a device. But even when the device is available, and even though a person may be watching a program, the failure to press a button on the device will mean that a viewer is not counted. (See Chapter 4 for explanation of people meters.)

People Exposed to Vehicles Do Not Necessarily Read, See, or Hear Ads

It should be noted that these measurements do not include any indications that audiences saw any of the ads within the medium or vehicle that is being measured. The reason for not measuring advertising responses in media is based on the fact that people have different degrees of ability to remember. Some individuals have excellent memories of advertisements they have seen within any month. Others remember so little that they would be missed in any measurement, and their lack of representation would radically distort the size of an audience exposed. It is much easier to remember whether or not one has seen a particular issue of a magazine.

Of course, there is an assumption that if a vehicle was exposed, then at least some of the ads were seen (or also exposed), but anyone who thinks about it for a minute can remember looking at a newspaper or a magazine, or viewing a television program and *not* being able to remember seeing any particular ads. The assumption that vehicle exposure automatically results in advertising exposure is usually wrong.

The measurement of media exposure may be rather confusing to those who work in media but are uninitiated in its complexities. It is often fashionable to talk about the number of readers or viewers or listeners who were exposed to a medium because audience research reports use such terms. These terms should not be taken literally because they are misleading. For example, how many pages of a magazine must an individual read to be counted a reader? No one knows. Or, how much of a television program must be seen before one is counted as a viewer? These are difficult questions to answer. As a consequence, media planners have accepted a measurement of audiences that represents a minimum relationship between consumers and media. There is no guarantee that audiences have seen advertising. Yet, there is some guarantee that exposure measures a minimal relationship with a medium. Nonetheless, exposure measurements are really quite significant, and this fact should be remembered by media planners who use audience measurement data.

There is a great deal of difference between someone who was exposed and someone who was not. Those exposed have *an opportunity to see ads*. An "opportunity to see" (OTS) means that audiences have an opportunity to learn something from ads. OTS represents an opportunity for advertisers to communicate with audiences. When audiences have not been exposed, advertising cannot work. Therefore, the total number of exposures to a vehicle by an audience composed of a precise demographic identification, constitutes a vehicle's target audience. (When each audience member is counted only once within a given time period, the total number of exposures has another name, *reach*. The average number of times the target audience was exposed to the vehicle within a given period of time is called *frequency*. See Chapter 5 for a more detailed discussion of reach and frequency.)

CASE STUDY 2-1
How Consumers Could React to Our Media and
Our Advertising

How can a planner think about the effect of a media plan in terms of the ultimate sales response? One answer that may help is to estimate what happens after the ads appear in the media vehicles. The following is a hypothetical example of such an estimate:

		Target Audience
1. Number of targets in the U.S.		10,000,000
2. Percent of U.S. targets that were exposed to media vehicles (this is the *reach* of our media plan)	50%	5,000,000
3. Percent of those reached who saw any ad in vehicles (called ad exposure)	25%	1,250,000
4. Percent of targets who saw any ad, who read ''our'' ad(s)	25%	312,500
5. Percent of those who read our ads who bought our brand because of our ad(s)	10%	31,250
6. Percent of those who bought our brand once, who also bought it a second time (a rough measure of brand loyalty)	10%	3,125

Question at This Point: Is there anything that a media planner can do through planning procedures, to increase the size of responses?

Two considerations should be made about these estimates:

1. These criteria are not the only ones that could be developed. Various stages of information processing could be incorporated into the model, and estimates could be made for each.

2. There is no precise way to make all these estimates, but experience with a brand over time should help planners improve their accuracy.

Measurements of Responses to Advertising in Vehicles

Some media planners believe that vehicles are nothing more than passive carriers of ads to consumers. A simple measurement such as exposure, therefore, may be considered adequate for comparing audience sizes of media vehicles. In other words, the vehicle (or vehicles) that deliver the largest number of exposed targets at the most efficient cost may be a good enough criterion for selecting media.

But many planners are dissatisfied with using exposure for media comparison purposes. They argue that media are *not* passive carriers of ads. Each medium has some power to affect an audience in some way, and this power should be measured. In technical terms, this power may be called the *response functions of media*.

Table 2–1 shows a response function called *effectiveness*. Measurements are called *effective frequency or effective reach*. These measurements use exposure as a basis for, first of all, determining a vehicle's audience size. Planners then modify exposure, using research to determine how many exposures to ads (or vehicles) to bring about such things as increased brand awareness and attitude change.

At this time, the use of *effective* frequency and reach are not objectively measured; they usually represent response data extrapolated from media comparisons. In other words, general research on responses to advertising may be used as if it applied to a particular brand being advertised. Many times this practice is not valid. If research were done on responses to ads for television sets, it may not be applicable to ads for margarine, or cake mixes.

Although there is disagreement in the industry about how to use this frequency and reach information, it is used a great deal. Special research for specific product categories is being done in an attempt to make this measurement valid and lay better theoretical foundations for it. In any case, effective frequency and reach are relatively new measurement ideas for the media planner's use. (See Chapter 5 on ''Reach and Frequency'' for further discussions on this subject.)

It is important to note that media planning should not be a mechanistic activity limited only to delivering media. Good media planners perceive consumers' needs and wants, and how consumers view advertising as an aid in helping them make buying decisions. As time goes on, media planners will expend additional efforts to better know and understand consumers. (See Case Study 2–1.)

QUESTIONS FOR DISCUSSION

1. How much of a magazine would an individual have to read to be considered a reader of the magazine?
2. What is the significance of opportunity-to-see (OTS) measurements for media planners?
3. Why is it so difficult to measure the number of consumers who bought a particular brand of product because of television commercials?
4. Do consumers ever use media as a catalog? Explain.
5. Explain why audience measurement research does not show how many people were watching advertisements?
6. Why is exposure a crude measurement for comparing veicles?
7. What kind of measurement would be better than exposure?
8. Media are considered to be ''active'' and ''passive.'' Explain in what ways they are active.

SELECTED READINGS

ADFORUM, "An Overview of TV Commercial Impact Studies," September 1982, pp. 50–52.

Audience Concepts Committee, *Toward Better Media Comparisons*, Advertising Research Foundation, 1961.

Banks, Seymour, "The Need for New Multi-Dimensional Measurements of Media," *Advertising Research Foundation 5th Annual Conference Proceedings,* September 1959, pp. 39–42.

Banks, Seymour, "Media Performance vs. Copy Performance," *Media/Scope,* August 1961, pp. 53–56.

Caffyn, J. M., *Qualitative Aspects of Reader Data*, Institute of Practitioners in Advertising, London, April 1964.

Dodge, Sherwood, "Dodge and Simmons Debate Recognition and Exposure," *Media/Scope,* May 1961, p. 51.

Finley, John A., "Reading," *Presstime,* September, 1984, pp. 18–25.

Fuchs, Douglas A., "Two Source Effects in Magazine Advertisng," *Journal of Marketing Research*, August 1964, pp. 59–62.

Gerhold, Paul E., "Predicted Advertising Yield ARF Proposes an Outline of How Advertising Works," *Advertising Research Foundation, 15th Annual Conference Proceedings,* October 1969, pp. 46–50.

Gomer, Frank J., and Vedder, Blair G., "Another Look Beyond the TV Ratings," from Association of National Advertisers Television Advertising Workshop Paper, June 1964, pp. 1–24.

Grass, Robert C., "Satiation Effects of Advertising," *Advertising Research Foundation 14th Annual Conference Proceedings,* October 1968, pp. 20–28.

King, Charles W., and Summers, John O., "Attitudes and Media Exposure," *Journal of Advertising Research*, February 1971, p. 26.

Krugman, Herbert E., "Answering Some Unanswered Questions in Measuring Advertising Effectiveness," *Advertising Research Foundation 12th Annual Conference Proceedings,* October 1966, pp. 18–23.

Krugman, Herbert E., "The Measurement of Advertising Involvement," *The Public Opinion Quarterly*, Winter 1966–67, pp. 583–96.

Krugman, Herbert E., "Brain Wave Measures of Media Involvement," *Journal of Advertising Research*, February 1971, pp. 3–10.

McConnell, J. Douglas, "Do Media Vary in Effectiveness?" *Journal of Advertising Research*, October 1970, pp. 19–22.

Media Decisions, "Beyond Demographics," February 1968, pp. 19–26.

Pitts, Robert E., "Commercials in Context," *Marketing and Media Decisions*, October 1986, p. 176.

Politz, Alfred, "Media Performance vs. Copy Performance," *Media/Scope*, November 1960, pp. 61–63.

Politz, Alfred, "What Is Essential to Know from Magazine Research?" *Media/Scope*, April 1959, pp. 39–44.

Sibley, Dawn, "Impact: Breaking Through the Clutter," *Marketing and Media Decisions*, October 1984, pp. 108–112.

Vitt, Sam B., "Editorial Environment" *Hidden Media Values or Going Beyond the Numbers*, Papers from the 1964 American Association of Advertising Agencies Meeting, pp. 17–28.

Warrous, Charles C., "The Awareness Myth," *Market and Media Decisions*, January 1987, pp. 55–56.

Wood, Wally, "The Race to Replace Memory," *Marketing and Media Decisions*, July 1986, pp. 166–68.

Wood, Wally, "How to Measure Exposure Quality," *Marketing and Media Decisions*, February 1987, pp. 130–38.

3
Basic Measurements and Calculations

The purpose of this chapter is to describe and explain basic measurements and calculations used in media planning. These explanations serve as the foundation by which media strategy decisions, to be discussed later, can be understood. The measurements and calculations discussed in this chapter are by no means all that are available. They simply represent those used most frequently. Throughout the chapter, the reader also will be introduced to media terminology not generally found in everyday speech. Terms such as *reach, gross rating points (GRPs), or cost per thousand* are examples of unique media language.

The importance of understanding how media audiences are measured and what those measurements mean should be obvious. Media planners can, and sometimes do, make strategy decisions without using measurement data as a guide, but such decisions may be difficult to defend because they tend to be too subjective. Measurement data, on the other hand, provide a degree of objectivity that is hard to refute.

How Media Are Measured

Most media audiences are measured through sample surveys, using data about a small group to find out about a larger universe. The chief reason for measuring samples rather than a vehicle's entire audience is that samples are less expensive to measure. But even if a vehicle's entire audience could be measured, it is doubtful that it would produce data that would justify the extra cost and time.

Sample sizes may vary from as little as 200 to as many as 30,000 individuals. Measurements are usually made at specified intervals, not every day of the year.

Network television audiences are measured through national samples of households whose program preferences are recorded by an electronic meter. At present seventeen markets are measured by electronic meters with plans to expand to about twenty. The A. C. Nielsen Company calls these devices Storage Instantaneous Audimeters. These meters automatically record the time of day, day of week, and channel numbers tuned in. One meter can record the tune-in data for as many as four different television sets in the same household. The meters are connected by a special telephone line to a computer that gathers and tabulates the data.

The value of data from metered households is somewhat limited since it shows only the basic tune-in information for a given program. Planners also want to know who the individuals were who viewed these programs. The answer to *who* is viewing comes from diaries: daily journals in which is recorded additional demographic information such as age and sex of the viewer.

Completed, the diary is mailed to the Nielsen Company, which tabulates the results. Findings from the electronic meters and diaries are then combined into a broad base of information about the audience size and composition for individual television programs.

Local television viewing is also measured through viewer diaries, but the sample size is relatively small, and the findings of these measurements are reported much less frequently than those of network television. The most frequently used data from both network and local market measurements are ratings (to be described later).

Radio measurements are also made through the use of diaries. However, the number of markets measured is smaller than for television. Furthermore, only large markets are measured relatively often (about 70 percent of the time).

At least three different techniques are commonly used to measure newspaper and magazine audiences. They are:

Through-the-book technique for magazines. A sample of readers is selected and interviewed personally. The interviewer shows each respondent a *stripped-down copy*—one in which all the ads have been eliminated, leaving only editorial material—of the magazine to be measured. After qualifying the respondent by making sure that he or she remembers having seen the cover page, the interviewer slowly turns the pages and asks whether each story looks interesting. The ostensible purpose of asking whether a respondent is interested in each article is to subtly determine whether the respondent really did read (or was exposed to) the magazine in question. After examining each article, the interviewer eventually asks, ''Now that we have gone through the entire magazine, are you sure that you have looked into it?'' Only those respondents who still say that they were sure they had looked into the book are counted. Those who are not quite sure and those who reply that they had not looked into the magazine are not counted. Those who say they are sure they have looked into the magazine are then asked demographic questions.

Recent-reading technique for magazines. A sample of respondents is visited by an interviewer who has a specially designed procedure to elicit responses. On individual cards are pasted the logotypes of magazines. Respondents are shown one card at a time and then asked if they read the magazine within the last month and where they read it. After this questioning, respondents are asked for demographic information. The interviewer also leaves behind a questionnaire that asks respondents to fill out details about various products they have used and how often they used them.

The interviewer returns later to pick up this special questionnaire. On this second visit, the interviewer again asks questions about which magazines have been read over a period of time.

Yesterday-reading technique for newspapers. Respondents in a selected sample are asked which newspapers they read yesterday. The procedure is much the same as the recent-reading magazine technique. Because there are relatively few newspapers read in any given market, this interview is relatively short.

These techniques are not used equally. The through-the-book and recent-reading techniques for magazines have been combined in the Simmons Market Research Bureau (SMRB) Report. Mediamark Research Inc. (MRI) uses recent reading.

Outdoor advertising audiences are measured by asking a sample of drivers to trace their day's travel on a map, indicating routes traveled and destinations. Then a plastic overlay sheet is placed on top of the respondent's map to indicate which billboards have been passed. Tabulations are made showing the numbers and demographics of audiences. These measurements are simply exposures to, or opportunities to see, the billboards.

Planners are always looking for better ways to measure audiences. Changes in measuring technology are continually being made as new ideas or methods are developed.

General Uses of Vehicle Audience Measurements

The ultimate purpose of media audience measurements is to enable planners to compare one vehicle with another on the basis of target audience sizes. The objective is to find the best vehicles for delivering the advertising message. Usually, so many different vehicles are available to be used in any advertising campaign that planners depend on measurement data to differentiate one from another.

The result of all these attempts at measurements is a large volume of numerical data, produced at regular intervals. However, the effect of such a quantity of data on media planners and others involved in marketing/media operations may sometimes be to provide a sense of confidence that is perhaps unwarranted. Despite the quantitative aspect, media planning is not scientific in the same manner that physics is. Media audience numbers are the best that can be attained at a reasonable cost, but they do not represent the kind of measurement data planners would ideally like to have, such as information about which media vehicle produces the most sales. Because the numbers may take on an importance that is not warranted, users of measurement data are warned that while the numbers are necessary, they are not absolutes, but rough estimates that need interpretation.

Planners use audience measurement data for the following comparative purposes:

1. To learn the demographics of product or brand users
2. To learn the audience demographics of various kinds of media vehicles—who reads, sees, or hears the vehicles

3. To learn the way purchasers use a product or brand (Are they heavy, medium, or light users?)
4. To learn whether audience members of a particular media vehicle are heavy, medium, or light users of the product
5. To learn how many people were exposed to vehicles

All of the above information has one basic purpose: to help the planner match media with target markets. The market for any product, from margarine to automobiles, can be identified in terms of certain demographics. What the planner wants is to find media vehicles that best reach the demographic target. Two main concepts guide planners in their use of measurement data. The first is to find vehicles that reach the largest numbers of prospects for a product category or a brand within that category. But planners do not always select the vehicle that delivers the largest number of prospects; sometimes they choose the vehicle that delivers the optimum number of prospects. An *optimum number* means that the number of prospects reached is sufficiently high to achieve some marketing/media goal and yet at the same time allow the planner to attain another goal, such as frequency. The vehicle that delivers the largest number of prospects represents large target reach, while the vehicle that provides a sufficient level of reach with a desired level of frequency would be the optimum. (For a more detailed discussion of the relationship of reach to frequency, see Chapter 6.)

Table 3–1 shows how media might be matched with a market using measurement data. Which medium is best according to the matching process of Table 3–1? A tentative answer is the one with the largest audience of prospects. Later analysis may or may not confirm this conclusion, because cost, as well as audience size, is also a consideration. But the first step in making a selection decision will probably center on the matching process.

Various Concepts of Audience Measurements

One of the difficulties in matching markets with media is that no single measurement can be used to determine the audience sizes for all media. Therefore, it is difficult to make intermedia comparisons (such as comparisons between the audi-

TABLE 3–1.   An Example of Matching Media with Markets (Cola Market)

Key Demographics (Adults)	Time		Reader's Digest		Popular Mechanics		Demographic Base
	Readers (000s)	Coverage	Readers (000s)	Coverage	Readers (000s)	Coverage	
Ages 18–34	10704	15.6%	11663	17.0%	2233	3.2%	68803
Live in metro suburban	11315	14.5%	17691	22.6%	2644	3.4%	78160
Regular cola drinkers	14695	13.7%	22886	21.3%	3784	3.5%	107451

Source: Simmons Market Research Bureau, 1986. Reprinted by permission.

ence sizes of a television program and a magazine). Audience size numbers do not mean the same thing from medium to medium because they are measured on different bases.

Actual or Potential Audience Size Measurements

Those who use media audience research should be careful not to confuse data that show the actual size of a vehicle's audience with other data that look similar, but show only potential audience size. The division of audience measurement data into classifications of actual versus potential, or vehicle distribution versus vehicle exposure, is the result of new measuring techniques. Before statistical sampling was widely accepted, media owners simply used distribution counts of their vehicles as evidence of audience size. Circulation of print media is one of these older measurements. It represents only potential audience size of the measured vehicle because it does not measure how many people will actually read a given copy of the periodical. As media research techniques have become more scientific, print media have been able to define their readership in terms of numbers of people who actually read the publication, in addition to just pure circulation or distribution counts.

Print Measurements

Print Circulation Measurements. Measurements of circulation are available for most newspaper and magazine vehicles, but these data are of limited use in selection decisions because the data do not provide the planner with precise enough information.

Circulation data also do not accurately reflect the number of readers in a vehicle's audience. One unit of circulation means one copy of the periodical distributed, but for every copy distributed, there may be as many as six different readers. One cannot know the size of a vehicle's audience simply by looking at its circulation, yet it is the audience size that is one of the major considerations in print media selection. Furthermore, circulation data tell the planner nothing about the demographics of the audience—crucial information when planning is based on reaching precise demographic targets.

As a result, circulation data are seldom used alone in selecting magazines in which to place ads. However, such data still are often used in making decisions about newspapers because little other audience data are available. Circulation data, while admittedly limited, are still valuable.

When circulation data must be used, measurements verified by the Audit Bureau of Circulation (ABC), as shown in Figure 3–1, are the most reliable. The accuracy of ABC audits is widely accepted throughout the advertising industry. The ABC is a nonprofit, cooperative association of about 1,100 advertisers and advertising agencies; and 2,800 daily and weekly newspapers, business publications, magazines, and farm publications in the United States and Canada. It audits and reports circulations of these publications at regular intervals.

ABC data will include paid circulations categorized for newspapers by city zone, trading zone, and outside areas. In addition, circulation is categorized for newspa-

Figure 3–1.   Audit Bureau of Circulation Audit Statement, Better Homes and Gardens

CLASS, INDUSTRY OR FIELD SERVED: A home and family service magazine serving husbands and wives who have a serious interest in home and family as the focal point of their lives and providing the service in the form of ideas, help, information and inspiration to achieve a better home and family.

AVERAGE PAID CIRCULATION FOR 6 MONTHS ENDED JUNE 30, 1986

Subscriptions:	7,496,702
Single Copy Sales:	515,333
AVERAGE TOTAL PAID CIRCULATION	8,012,025
Advertising Rate Base	8,000,000
Average Total Non-Paid Distribution	164,875

AVERAGE PAID CIRCULATION of Regional and Metro Editions

Better Homes and Gardens offers regional advertisers regional editions in each monthly issue based on Section Center (abbreviated S. C. below) as defined by U. S. Postal Service, as well as the total circulation. Regional editions may vary as to advertising and editorial content. Advertising for regional editions is sold separately or in combination of editions. Average paid circulation by editions is shown below. Counts for all three-digit Regions and Metro Markets are included in counts for two-digit Regions.

REGIONAL EDITIONS

Edition & number of issues		Edition & number of issues	
Region	11–Maine (6)	42,116	
Region	12–New Hampshire (6)	40,876	
Region	13–Vermont (6)	20,185	
Region	14–Massachusetts (6)	212,062	
Region	15–Rhode Island (6)	31,786	
Region	16–Connecticut (less S C 068 069) (6)	117,216	
Region	51–Delaware (6)	22,422	
Region	52–Maryland (less S C 206, 209) (6)	88,948	
Region	53–District of Columbia (plus S C 206, 209 220, 227) (6)	124,853	
Region	54–Virginia (less S C 220, 227) (6)	123,888	
Region	55–West Virginia (6)	52,860	
Region	56–North Carolina (6)	200,478	
Region	57–South Carolina (6)	91,634	
Region	21–New York State (plus S C 068 069) (6)	527,495	
Region	58–Georgia (6)	170,682	
Region	59–Florida (6)	357,211	
Region	211–New York less Metro (6)	241,214	
Region	22–New Jersey (6)	261,286	
Region	221–New Jersey less Metro (6)	72,673	
Region	61–Kentucky (plus S C 471 less 410) (6)	106,291	
Region	23–Pennsylvania (6)	417,201	
Region	231–East Pennsylvania (6)	265,510	
Region	62–Tennessee (plus S C 386, 723, 724) (6)	165,518	
Region	232–West Pennsylvania (6)	151,691	
Region	63–Alabama (6)	118,561	
Region	31–Ohio (plus S C 410, 470) (6)	429,480	
Region	64–Mississippi (less S C 386) (6)	59,253	
Region	32–Indiana (less S C 463 464, 470, 471) (6)	173,621	
Region	71–Arkansas (less S C 723, 724) (6)	58,311	
Region	33–Illinois (plus S C 463, 464, less 612, 620, 622) (6)	389,965	
Region	72–Louisiana (6)	100,708	
Region	73–Oklahoma (6)	109,847	
Region	331–North Illinois (6)	323,528	
Region	74–Texas (6)	449,688	

METRO MARKETS

Edition & number of issues		Edition & number of issues	
Albany (6)	45,933	Louisville (6)	68,228
Alexandria Shreveport (6)	45,574	Madison (6)	35,334
Amarillo El Paso (6)	61,091	Memphis (6)	56,169
Atlanta (6)	111,707	Milwaukee (6)	110,620
Austin Temple (6)	33,726	Minneapolis St. Paul (6)	77,820
Bakersfield (6)	36,233	Montgomery (6)	142,620
Baltimore (6)	88,498	Nashville (6)	43,280
Birmingham (6)	75,280	New Orleans (6)	51,324
Boston (6)	179,348	New York (6)	53,135
Buffalo (6)	62,318	Oklahoma City (6)	474,894
Cedar Rapids Waterloo (6)	42,653	Omaha (6)	63,892
Charlotte (6)	118,887	Philadelphia (6)	48,463
Chicago (6)	266,890	Phoenix (6)	252,579
Cincinnati (6)	70,923	Pittsburgh (6)	95,233
Cleveland (6)	175,831	Portland (6)	151,691
Colorado Springs Pueblo (6)	28,624	Providence (6)	104,811
Columbus (6)	92,291	Raleigh (6)	31,786
Corpus Christi (6)	19,820	Richmond Norfolk (6)	81,591
Dallas Fort Worth (6)	167,242	Roanoke (6)	74,186
Davenport Rock Island Moline (6)	24,844	Rochester (6)	49,675
Dayton (6)	43,559	Sacramento (6)	48,405
Denver (6)	95,779	Saginaw Traverse City (6)	94,774
Des Moines (6)	65,930	St. Louis (6)	42,603
		Salt Lake City (6)	115,477
			55,491

Region		Region		City		City	
Region 332–South Illinois (6)	66,437	Region 81–Montana (6)	33,027	Detroit (6)	188,418	San Antonio (6)	42,377
Region 34–Michigan (less S C 498, 499) (6)	345,900	Region 82–Idaho (6)	35,005	Evansville (6)	16,533	San Diego (6)	75,022
Region 35–Wisconsin (plus S C 498, 499, less 540) (6)	202,097	Region 83–Wyoming (6)	18,305	Fort Wayne So. Bend (6)	46,141	San Francisco Oakland (6)	195,091
Region 41–Minnesota (plus S C 540) (6)	186,454	Region 84–Colorado (6)	124,403	Grand Rapids (6)	76,088	Scranton Wilkes-Barre (6)	47,625
Region 42–Iowa (plus S C 612 less 515, 516) (6)	133,427	Region 85–New Mexico (6)	38,343	Green Bay (6)	45,615	Seattle Tacoma (6)	122,093
Region 43–Missouri (plus S C 620, 622 less 640, 641, 644, 647, 653) (6)	166,902	Region 86–Arizona (6)	95,233	Harrisburg (6)	60,402	Spokane (6)	40,134
Region 44–North Dakota (6)	26,234	Region 87–Utah (6)	55,491	Hartford New Haven (6)	117,216	Springfield, MA (6)	32,714
Region 45–South Dakota (6)	27,098	Region 8–Nevada (6)	28,450	Houston (6)	125,349	Syracuse (6)	84,558
Region 46–Nebraska (plus S C 515, 516) (6)	77,193	Region 91–Alaska (6)	16,272	Indianapolis (6)	110,947	Tallahassee Pensacola (6)	30,992
Region 47–Kansas (plus S C 640, 641, 644, 647, 653) (6)	168,298	Region 92–Wshington (less S C 986) (6)	162,227	Jacksonville (6)	55,837	Tampa (6)	157,800
		Region 93–Oregon (plus S C 986) (6)	117,009	Kansas City (6)	103,859	Toledo (6)	46,876
		Region 94–California (6)	788,481	Kearny Hastings (6)	28,730	Tulsa (6)	45,955
		Region 941–North California (6)	326,659	Knoxville (6)	58,025	Washington, D.C. (6)	124,853
		Region 942–South California (6)	461,822	Lansing (6)	38,791	Wichita Hutchinson (6)	64,439
		Region 95–Hawaii (6)	25,671	Lexington (6)	37,070	Focus V (6)	4,987,057
				Little Rock (6)	58,311	Super Spot (6)	1,179,443
				Los Angeles (6)	350,566		

PAID CIRCULATION by Issues

Issue	Subscriptions	Single Copy Sales	Total Paid	Issue	Subscriptions	Single Copy Sales	Total Paid
Jan.	7,531,203	403,000	7,934,203	Apr.	7,413,895	470,000	7,883,895
Feb.	7,575,309	495,000	8,070,309	May	7,399,772	610,000	8,009,772
Mar.	7,477,485	514,000	7,991,485	June	7,582,549	600,000	8,182,549

ANALYSIS OF TOTAL NEW AND RENEWAL SUBSCRIPTIONS

Sold during 6 Month Period Ended June 30, 1986

AUTHORIZED PRICES:

(a) Basic Prices: Single Copy: U.S. $1.50; outside U.S., $1.75. See Par 11(a).
Subscriptions: In United States and U.S. Poss. only. 1 yr. $12.97; 2 yrs. $23.97; 3 yrs. $34.95 to March 18, 1986; thereafter 1 yr. $14.00; 2 yrs. $26.00; 3 yrs. $38.00. In Canada, Pan American countries and all other foreign countries, 1 yr. $24.97 to March 18, 1986; thereafter, 1 yr. $26.00.

(b) Higher than basic prices: None 408,161
(c) Lower than basic prices: See Par. 11(b) 2,779,900
(d) Association subscription prices .... None

Total Subscriptions Sold in Period 3,188,061

(continued)

Figure 3-1 (continued)

DURATION OF SUBSCRIPTIONS SOLD:

(a)	One to six months (1 to 6 issues)	3,717
(b)	Seven to twelve months (7 to 12 issues)	1,299,221
(c)	Thirteen to twenty-four months	1,869,680
(d)	Twenty-five to thirty-six months	12,886
(e)	Thirty-seven to forty-eight months	1,645
(f)	Forty-nine months and more	912
	Total Subscriptions Sold in Period	3,188,061

CHANNELS OF SUBSCRIPTION SALES:

(a)	Ordered by mail and/or direct request	3,016,504
(b)	Ordered through salespeople:	
	1. Catalog agencies and individual agents	13,489
	2. Publisher's own and other publishers' salespeople	8,672
	3. Independent agencies' salespeople	27,159
	4. Newspaper agencies	1,400
	5. Members of schools, churches, fraternal and similar organizations	120,819
(c)	Association memberships	None
(d)	All other channels, See Par. 11(c)	18
	Total Subscriptions Sold In Period	3,188,061

USE OF PREMIUMS:

(a)	Ordered without premium	3,188,061
(b)	Ordered with material reprinted from this publication	None
(c)	Ordered with other premiums	None
	Total Subscriptions Sold in Period	3,188,061

ADDITIONAL CIRCULATION INFORMATION

POST EXPIRATION COPIES INCLUDED IN PAID CIRCULATION (PAR. 1):

(a) Average number of copies served on subscriptions not more than three months after expiration ... None

COLLECTION STIMULANTS: ... None

BASIS ON WHICH COPIES WERE SOLD TO RETAIL OUTLETS:

Fully returnable ... 100.00%

U.S. PAID CIRCULATION BY ABCD COUNTY SIZE based on Febuary, 1986 Issue

Total paid circulation of this issue was 0.73% greater than average total paid circulation for period.

County Size	No. of Counties	% of U.S. Population	Subscription Circulation		Single Copy Circulation		Total Circulation	
			Copies	% Total	Copies	% Total	Copies	% Total
A	177	41%	2,864,337	38.17	191,461	42.64	3,055,848	38.42
B	408	30%	2,383,240	31.76	138,252	30.79	2,521,492	31.71
C	496	15%	1,213,576	16.17	70,794	15.81	1,284,550	16.15
D	1,993	14%	1,042,592	13.90	48,308	10.76	1,090,900	13.72
	3,074	100%	7,503,795	100.00	448,995	100.00	7,952,790	100.00
Alaska–Hawaii	27		38,171		4,077		42,248	
TOTAL U.S.	3,101		7,541,966		453,072		7,995,038	

EXPLANATORY:

Latest Released Audit Report Issued for 12 months ended June 30, 1984
Variation from Publisher's Statements

Audit Period Ended	Rate Base	Audit Report	Publisher's Statements	Difference	Percentage of Difference
6-30-84	8,000,000	8,012,499	8,022,675	− 10,176	− 0.13
6-30-83	8,000,000	8,028,427	8,055,510	− 27,083	− 0.34
6-30-82	8,000,000	8,035,464	8,056,589	− 21,125	− 0.26
6-30-81	8,000,000	8,017,567	8,043,351	− 25,784	− 0.32
6-30-80	8,000,000	8,092,836	8,077,518	+ 15,318	+ 0.19

Source: *Better Homes and Gardens*. Copyright 1986 by the Meredith Corporation. Reprinted by permission.

pers by Metropolitan Statistical Areas (MSA), making it possible to determine how the distribution of circulation matches selling and marketing areas of advertisers.

Magazine data from ABC show circulation categorized by size of metropolitan areas, by states and regions of the United States, and by other geographical divisions, all aimed at helping the planner choose the medium that best reaches geographical targets. No demographic data of the reading audience are available from ABC.

Print Audience Measurements. Measurements of the actual size of print audience vehicles can be made by first sampling readers to find an average number of *readers per copy*. This figure then is multiplied by the circulation to provide an estimate of the total audience of readers. Most media planners are not interested in the total audience, but only in the numbers of those demographic targets who are the best prospects to purchase their products.

The Concept of Audience Accumulation

Audience accumulation is the buildup of total audiences over time. The time element, however, varies by medium. A major part of the accumulation concept is that audience members are counted only once, no matter how many additional times they are exposed to a particular vehicle. This is called *reach*. Another measurement, called *frequency*, accounts for repeat exposure. Both reach and frequency will be discussed in more detail in Chapter 5.

Audience Accumulation in Magazines. In magazines, audience accumulates in three ways:

1. Over the issue life of the publication, as the magazine is read by more and more people, passing it along from one reader to another
2. When advertising is placed in successive issues of the same magazine
3. When advertising is placed in the same month's issue of different magazines

The first method of audience accumulation is measured by various researchers who report on the *total audience* of the average issue of a publication. The amount of time it takes for this audience buildup has no bearing on the measurement. A person reading a magazine a month or more after its issuance is counted as a reader to the same extent as the person who reads the magazine the first day it is issued.

The second method of accumulation takes place over different issues. New readers may read a given issue each time it appears.

Quick accumulation is possible when the same ad is run in a given month's issues of different magazines. Some who read one magazine will not read others.

Within a magazine's total audience, researchers distinguish between *primary readers* (those who have purchased the magazine and the members of the purchaser's household), and *pass-along readers* (those not in the purchaser's household). Typical pass-along readers are the purchaser's friends, and/or people reading in doctors' offices, beauty salons, and on airplanes.

In addition to the type of reader (primary or pass along), a second designator of exposure is also researched: *place* of reading. Syndicated research companies provide data showing where people read magazines. Simmons Market Research Bureau and MRI cite in-home and out-of-home readership for all the publications in their reports.

Several isolated research studies have indicated that the in-home reader, whether a primary or pass-along reader, reads more pages of a magazine and spends more time reading than the person outside of the home. Media planners sometimes use this information to give different values, or weights, to each type of reader in order to compare one media vehicle to another.

Audience Accumulation in Broadcast. Audiences also build in broadcast media. Although the concept of accumulation is the same as with magazines, the mechanics differ widely. A television program, with the exception of those recorded on a video cassette recorder, does not have a life beyond its broadcast time. Unlike tangible magazine copies, once a TV or radio program is broadcast, it is finished. Those people who viewed/listened to the show are the only audience the program will have. There is no pass-along audience as with magazines. Time *is* a major element in broadcast accumulation.

Nevertheless, TV and radio programs do accumulate audience in three ways:

1. Within the program while it is being broadcast
2. With successive airings of the same program within a four-week period
3. With the airing of different programs within the same four-week period

TV viewers are counted if they press the buttons designating them as viewers of a given program. If new viewers watch a program after the first telecast, they are added to those who viewed it previously. Radio listeners are so designated if they listen to five minutes or more of the program. Therefore, if ten people are viewing a program during the first five minutes, then an additional ten people tune in the program in the next five minutes and stay tuned for at least five minutes, the program has accumulated a total audience of twenty people.

Each week that a program is aired, new audience members will tune in for the first time, and thus the accumulation grows. Another way accumulation grows is by advertising on different programs that appeal to the same audience such as women aged 18–49.

In the real world, people tune in and tune out programs at different times during the program broadcast. While ten people might tune in a particular program in the first five minutes, some of them will tune out and some new people will tune in. This phenomenon occurs throughout the program.

Table 3–2 shows how the accumulated total audience of a single episode varies for several programs compared with the audience who viewed the program during an average fifteen-minute segment. The tune-in audience in every case is greater in number than those who tuned out. The bucket, therefore, was being filled faster than it was being emptied. This results in a gradual buildup of audience over the entire program.

TABLE 3-2. Comparison of Program Ratings: Average Quarter Hour versus
            Total for Entire Program

		Households Viewing (%)	
Program	Day of Telecast	Average Quarter Hour	Total Program
60 Minutes	Sunday	24.1	31.8
Dallas	Friday	21.8	25.8
ABC Monday Night Movie	Monday	12.2	20.3

Source: Nielsen Media Research, NTI, January, 1987. Reprinted by permission.

The Coverage Concept

Audiences can be analyzed in two broad ways: in total numbers of people (e.g., the evening news audience) and as a percentage of the demographic universe of which they are a part (e.g., all women aged 35–49). One might compare the audience size of ten magazines or television programs on the basis of which delivers the greatest number of people in a target audience, or on the basis of which delivers the highest percentage of the total population in that target audience. Either method will reveal the same relative differences between the media vehicles.

Coverage is a convenient statistical term used to assess the degree to which a media vehicle delivers a given target audience. The higher the coverage, the greater the delivery. Coverage is usually expressed as a percentage of a market reached.

To calculate coverage, the delivery of a specific demographic group (or target audience) by a given media is divided by the total population of that demographic group (the market size). If Magazine X, for example, is read by $2^1/_2$ million women 35–49, and the total population of women 35–49 is 25 million, then Magazine X has a 10 percent coverage of this target audience.

Unfortunately, the term *coverage* may be confusing because it is used in different ways for different media forms. See Table 3–3 for a summary of its meanings.

In magazines, coverage is used in an ideal manner. If there are 12 million households in the United States that own cats and Magazine A reaches 6 million of them, then Magazine A's coverage is 50 percent. This 50 percent represents actual exposure to the vehicle.

But in newspapers and television, coverage may only represent potential degree of exposure, not actual exposure (or reach).

Because coverage can mean a number of different things, it is important for anyone who uses this term to know and understand its alternative meanings. Following is a discussion of how coverage is defined in specific media.

Newspaper Coverage. Most newspapers measure the number of copies sold or distributed and call this "circulation." Newspaper coverage represents the number of copies circulated compared to the number of households in the circulation area.

If the circulation of a newspaper is 500,000 and the number of households in the area is 2,000,000, then the coverage is 25 percent. The assumption is made that each unit of circulation equals one household covered. Coverage represents potential rather than actual exposure since everyone who receives a copy of a newspaper does not read it. No exposure to the medium is necessarily assumed. So coverage based

TABLE 3-3. Different Meanings of the Term "Coverage"

Kind of Coverage	Meaning	Uses
General Concept (more accurately called "Market Coverage")	The number of prospects delivered (exposed) by a given medium. Coverage expressed as a percent of the universe of prospects.	Serves as a goal in planning. Used to determine whether media selected are delivering enough prospects.
Newspaper Coverage	The number of circulation units as a percent of the number of households in an area. If the audience of newspapers in a local market is measured, then coverage is the number of readers in a demographic segment (such as men 18–24) as a percent of all men 18–24 in the local market.	For local markets. A goal to determine whether enough households are reached with one or more newspapers. This represents *potential* audience size.
Magazine Coverage (sometimes called "Reach")	Same as the general concept. Prospects are demographically defined.	Same as the general concept. This represents *estimated actual* audience size.
Spot TV and Radio Coverage (local market)	The number of TV (or radio) homes within the signal area of station that can tune in to that station.	Serves as a basis for potential delivery in planning. Indicates the maximum size of the *potential* audience of radio or TV homes.
Spot TV Coverage for a national campaign (also for spot radio)	Total number of TV homes in selected markets that are part of a campaign, that can tune in (or can be reached).	It can show how much of the country's TV homes may be *potentially* delivered by a spot plan. Maximum number and percent of potential exposure.
Network TV Program Coverage	The number and percent of all stations in a network carrying a given program compared to total TV homes in U.S.	An indication of the maximum *potential* of TV homes that a TV program can reach.
Outdoor Advertising and Transit Coverage	The number of people who pass, and are exposed to a given showing of billboards in a local market, expressed as a percent of the total of all people in the market.	To determine the size of an audience that might look at each showing of billboards.

on circulation is only a rough comparison of newspaper audience size related to the market size as measured by the total number of households in that area.

Coverage in newspaper planning, therefore, is not the same as for magazines and other media. The limiting factor is the kind of research that is available.

When using newspaper coverage, planners sometimes suggest that a minimum coverage level in any individual market should be no less than 50 percent. If it can be assumed that not all persons in all households will be exposed to any given edition of a newspaper, then 50 percent is the lowest level that seems practical. Perhaps only two-thirds of that 50 percent will be exposed. Some media planners often set much higher limits on local market coverage, such as no less than 70 percent. In such situations, it may take two or even three newspapers in that community to attain a 70 percent unduplicated coverage.

TABLE 3-4. **Market Coverage of Paper Napkin Users of Selected Magazines** *

Used Paper Napkins within Last Month	Number (thousands)	Coverage (%)
Total Users	44,939	100.0
Family Circle	11,459	25.5
Ladies' Home Journal	8,348	18.6
McCall's	9,959	22.2

Source: Simmons Market Research Bureau, 1979. Reprinted by permission.
* For adult female household heads.

When a newspaper has research on its readership and provides a breakdown of that audience by demographic segments, then coverage will mean something different. It will mean the number of individuals exposed to newspapers compared to the total number of *individuals* (rather than households) in the market. Because such measurements are not always available on a regular basis, newspaper coverage usually means potential exposure.

Magazine Coverage. Magazine coverage, already defined, is the simple ratio of the number of prospects delivered compared with the size of a target market. An example of magazine market coverage is shown in Table 3-4. In Table 3-4, the market is defined as all female household heads who used paper napkins within the last month, or 44,939,000 women. Each magazine reaches a proportion of that market, representing its market coverage. If a market is defined demographically, then coverage by a magazine represents a proportion of a demographic segment base.

Another way to look at magazine market coverage is to look at total users of a given product class. If, for example, one of the syndicated research companies reported that 44,939,000 female household heads used paper napkins within the last month, then that figure would represent the size of the total market. If 9,959,000 readers of *McCall's* used paper napkins within the last month, then that number would represent 22.2 percent market coverage by *McCall's*.

It should be clear from the preceding discussion that planners may define market sizes differently. A market may be defined as all female homemakers aged 18–49, or it may be defined as all product users. The subject of defining markets will be discussed in Chapter 7.

Local Television and Radio Coverage. For local radio and television, coverage means the number (or percent) of homes with radio or television sets within the signal area of a given station that *can* tune in to that station because they can pick up the station's signal. Whether or not they choose to tune in depends on a number of factors such as (a) whether the programming of the station is interesting enough to attract them; (b) the power of the station, since more powerful stations can cover more homes than weaker stations; (c) the height of a station's antenna and the height of the home's antenna, which affect reception of signals; and (d) the number and nature of obstructions that may prevent the signal from being received, such as bridges, tall buildings, or mountains.

Television stations produce an engineering contour map based on their signal strength in a market to indicate how wide an area the station's signal covers. The strongest signal is designated "Grade A" (or one that covers the primary market

TABLE 3-5.   Coverage of Top U.S. Markets by Using Spot TV

Markets	Coverage (%)
Top 10	31
Top 20	44
Top 30	53
Top 40	60
Top 50	66
Top 60	72
Top 70	76
Top 80	80
Top 100	86

Source: Leo Burnett 1986 Media Costs and Coverage.

area surrounding the station). The next strongest signal is "Grade B" (or secondary area coverage). These measurements, however, are not as useful in determining coverage as those that estimate the number of homes covered regardless of whether they are in Grade A or B areas. Research has also shown that some homes outside of the A or B areas can and do receive certain stations.

In order to learn the coverage of a station, research companies send out mail questionnaires to a carefully selected sample of homes located inside and outside the A and B signal areas. These questionnaires ask respondents to list the stations they view regularly. From the returns, estimates are made of how many homes in each county are covered by a station's signal. Such measurements are the starting place for determining the maximum potential audience for a given station. The criterion for being included in a station's coverage statistics is that the home must be able to receive the signal.

Spot Radio or Television Coverage in Multiple Markets. An advertiser who buys spot announcements in a number of markets located in various geographical regions of the United States may be interested in knowing what percentage of all television (or radio) homes in the country the commercial may potentially reach. Perhaps a planner has selected fifty of the largest markets in the country in which to advertise. In order to determine the percentage of coverage, it is only necessary to learn the coverage of each station in a plan and add the figures to find the coverage of the entire plan. For example, by buying spot announcements in the fifty markets, planners can potentially reach nearly 70 percent of the television homes in the country. The planner knows, then, that the maximum audience size (expressed in terms of homes than can tune in to a station's signal) is no larger than 70 percent. Since not everyone in those fifty markets will see the commercials, the exposure will be lower than 70 percent. Table 3–5 lists the percentage coverages of the largest markets.

Network Television Coverage. In network television, coverage is defined as the number and percentage of all U.S. television households that are able to receive a given program. The degree of coverage is affected by the number of stations in a network lineup. The more stations, the more coverage. Table 3–6 indicates the coverage of several network programs.

In broadcast, the term *circulation* is sometimes used to mean the same thing as coverage, but properly used it has a different meaning. Circulation means the num-

TABLE 3–6.   Network Program Coverage

Network	Program	Household Coverage (%)	No. of Stations in Lineup
CBS	60 Minutes	99	209
ABC	Monday Night Movie	93	178
NBC	News Digest	77	148
CBS	Dallas	99	208

Source: Nielsen Media Research, NTI, January, 1987. Reprinted by permission.

ber of radio or television households that *can* and *do* tune in to a station a minimum number of times, whether once a month, once a week, or once during a part of the day. Therefore, circulation describes the potential audience size of a network or a station over a period of time. Circulation is a potential audience measurement in that the minimum tune-in required for counting is generally spread over a broad time period, rather than a specific day and time. It is important, then, to remember that both coverage and circulation are measurements of the gross potential audience. *Gross* refers to a crude estimate, and *potential* means that the numbers deal with opportunities rather than actual audience tune-ins to a program. Opportunities for tune-in vary by time of day.

Out-of-Home Media Coverage. Out-of-home media include all media that are located outside a person's home, such as billboards, posters in shopping malls, advertisements in and on buses, and so forth. Coverage for out-of-home media is the percentage of the population that *passes* the advertisement. Coverage for out-of-home media, therefore, represents the potential for advertising exposure.

Out-of-home media, such as billboards, are generally purchased by advertisers on the basis of daily GRPs. GRPs are equivalent to a 100 showing in thirty days. A *100 showing* is the number of billboards needed in a given market to produce the equivalent of 100 percent coverage of the market potentially exposed in a single day. Suppose a market has 100 different billboards erected in and around the city, each of which is passed by an average of 1,000 people each day. If an advertiser purchases ten of these billboards, the equivalent of 10,000 people will pass these boards. If the market has a population of 10,000, then these ten boards would constitute 100 GRPs, or a 100 showing. Other showing sizes can also be purchased, such as a 75 (comprising 75 percent as many boards as in a 100 showing), a 50 showing (half as many boards), and so on. They may also be expressed as 100, 75, 50, and 25 GRPs.

The outdoor medium is able to generate very high coverage, and therefore reach, over time. Table 3–7 shows the accumulated reach over a thirty-day period for different size outdoor showings.

TABLE 3–7.   Reach and Frequency of Outdoor Showings for Adults

100 Showing		50 Showing		25 Showing	
Reach	Frequency	Reach	Frequency	Reach	Frequency
87.8%	28.4	83.5%	15.0	77.0%	8.1

Source: Simmons Market Research Bureau, Inc., 1986. Reprinted by permission.

Households Using Television (HUT)

One important television measurement that is frequently used in planning is *households using television* (HUT). It is a coverage figure and represents the percentage of homes tuned into television at a given point in time. Because it includes a *time* consideration, HUT may be classified as a measurement of *net* potential audience size.

Modifying Coverage Data by HUT Data. Coverage data in television represent only audience potential. If a station covers 1,410,000 TV homes, this does not mean that an advertiser will reach all of those homes with a commercial on that station. But what determines how many homes will be reached? To a great extent, the HUT at any time of day will provide a clue to the possible tune-in. As a measure of the net potential audience, HUT indicates what percentage of households with a television set have it turned on at any given time of day, such as morning, early afternoon, late afternoon, prime time, or late evening. The statistics are reported by fifteen-minute segments to allow a closer examination of tune-ins during various times of the day. Figure 3–2 shows how audience sizes vary by time of day.

Television viewing is affected by living habits. In the morning, tune-in tends to be low, with many men and women at work and children in school. Primary viewers are mothers and small children. When children return home from school about 4:00 p.m., the tune-ins rise dramatically, and after 6:00 p.m., when many people have returned home from work, the rise in tune-ins is even greater. After 10:00 p.m., viewing drops again. Table 3–8 (p.48) indicates the variations in viewing for different time periods, as well as by seasons of the year.

The planner can study HUT data and estimate potential audience size better than by studying coverage figures alone. In the evening hours there are more viewers available than at any other time of day, since both children and adults are usually at home. But there are variations in viewing not only during a single day, but during a given week, and month. During the summer, for example, when persons spend more time out-of-doors, television viewing is much lower in some viewing periods than it is in winter. These variations affect the size of audience that can be obtained.

The media planner, knowing that variations in viewing patterns exist, refines the coverage data to learn the approximate size of an audience that can be reached at various times. Table 3–9 (p.49) gives an example of how the potential audience size in the Chicago area may vary by county and by time period.. The advertisers who selects Station A can never hope to reach all of the 2,825,250 households at one time because some of them will prefer other local stations.

From Nielsen or Arbitron, however, it is possible to determine how large the net potential audience is. Table 3–10 (p.49) shows these data for Station A. These figures would probably be lower if the planner were studying data for the months of July or August, because fewer persons watch television during these months. Furthermore, there are also differences between the net potential audience of Station A and other Chicago stations. In any case, these figures help the advertiser learn about his potential audience size.

After potential audience sizes are examined, program ratings are used to learn the estimated audience size for a given program.

FIGURE 3-2.   Hour-by-Hour Percentage of TV Usage among Households (Jan.–Feb. 1986)

Source: *Nielsen Newscast*, No. 3, 1986, p. 14. Reprinted by permission of Nielsen Media Research.
Black = _____ ;   All Other = --------------

TABLE 3-8.   Variations in Viewing by Daypart and Season

Daypart	Total TV Households Tuned In (%)			
	Spring	Summer	Fall	Winter
Daytime (Mon.–Fri.)	25	26	26	29
Early Fringe (Mon.–Fri.)	39	38	47	49
Prime Time (Mon.–Sun.)	55	53	62	64
Late Fringe (Mon.–Fri.)	26	27	28	26

Source: Nielsen Media Research, Households Using TV Summary Report, 1979. Reprinted by
permission.

TABLE 3–9. Potential Audience Size in Chicago Metropolitan Area for Station A

Chicago Metro Area Counties	Daytime (Mon.–Fri.)		Prime Time (Mon.–Sun.)	
	Avg. Qtr. Hr. Households	Percent of County	Avg. Qtr. Hr. Households	Percent of County
Cook (Illinois)	209,772	11.0	278,080	14.6
DuPage	20,360	7.6	40,277	15.1
Kane	6,916	6.3	15,554	14.2
Lake	12,568	7.9	24,060	15.2
McHenry	4,447	7.7	9,599	16.6
Will	10,030	8.9	21,470	19.0
Lake (Indiana)	24,632	14.3	27,435	15.9
Porter	3,439	8.0	5,666	13.2

Source: Nielsen Station Index, County Coverage Study, 1988. Reprinted by permission.

Broadcast Ratings

A *broadcast rating* (television or radio) represents an estimate of the size of the audience that has viewed a program, or has tuned in during a specific time period. This rating is determined through sampling procedures. It is financially and physically impossible to measure the viewing habits of every person in the United States, but it is possible to measure a small sample of viewers. This information, however, is only an *estimate* of the size of the actual viewing audience.

These estimates are reported in the form of percentages of an audience base. For households tuned in to a network television program, the base figure usually includes all households in the United States that have at least one television set. For local television markets, the base is all TV households in the metropolitan area, or some other specially designated area.

Ratings are made for both households and individuals. The people base for network television consists of all persons of a given age group in network television households. For example, for women aged 18–49, the network program base would be all women aged 18–49 in television households in the United States.

A local radio rating is usually expressed in the form of an average quarter-hour tune-in, and as a percentage of either the people in the Metropolitan Statistical Area (MSA) or some other specific geographical area.

Rather than talk about a rating of, for example, 18 percent, it is common practice to talk only about a program having an 18 rating. The fact that a rating is a percentage is always assumed to be understood.

The Average Audience Rating. The A. C. Nielsen Company provides an average audience rating, obtained through a people meter device, which represents the percentage of homes (and people) tuned in to the average minute of a program. Data provided in the Nielsen Television Index shows average audience ratings tuned in for each half-hour or quarter-hour segment.

TABLE 3–10. Average Number of Homes Reached at Least Once by Station A

Morning (Mon.–Fri.) 6:00 A.M.–12:00 P.M.	Afternoon (Mon.–Fri.) 12:00 M–7:00 P.M.	Evening (Sat.–Sun.)	
		7:00–10:00 P.M.	10:00–10:30 P.M.
1,135,000	1,465,000	2,647,000	1,920,000

Source: Nielsen Station Index, Viewers in Profile, November 1987. Reprinted by permission.

TABLE 3-11.   Computing an Average Audience Rating

Minutes in a Program	1	2	3	4	5	6	7	8	9	10	11	12	13	14	15
Percent Tuned in	30	30	30	31	31	31	31	32	32	32	33	33	33	33	33

Total Tuned in for 15 minutes = 475
475 ÷ 15 = 31.7 (the average percentage tune-in for 15 minutes)

To learn how many households (or people) have tuned in to a program one need only multiply the rating times the total number of TV households in the United States. This is called a "projection." For example, if a program had a 16.0 average audience rating, and the total number of households in the United States were 88,600,000, then 88,600,000 x .16 = 14,180,000 households tuned in. On a local market level, the base would be relatively smaller, but the procedure for projection would be the same.

Table 3-11 illustrates the method by which the average audience rating is calculated for a fifteen-minute segment of a program.

Share of Audience Rating. The *share of audience rating* reflects the percentage of homes tuned in to a program based only on those homes that had their sets turned on, rather than on all television homes, as in the average audience rating. If all average audience ratings for a fifteen-minute time period were added together, the sum would represent the HUT, which always is a proportion of all television homes and is always less than 100 percent. But the sum of all share of audience ratings represents only those homes tuned in at a particular time and theoretically equals 100 percent since homes that had their sets turned off are never figured in the base. The formula for computing share is as follows:

$$\text{Share} = \frac{\text{Rating}}{\text{HUT}}$$

A comparison of share data with average audience ratings is illustrated in Table 3-12. In Table 3-12, 40 percent of the sets were *not* turned on. When this 40 percent is added to the HUT, the total is 100 percent. Share was computed by dividing the average audience rating by the HUT. The sum of all average audience ratings equaled the HUT, or 60 percent. But the sum of share of audience ratings is 100 percent.

The value of a share statistic is that it enables the media planner to compare two programs broadcast at radically different times of the day, week, or year, or any time where the HUTs for different programs are radically different. To illustrate the use of share data, Table 3-13 shows ratings for a sample program and its shares at different

TABLE 3-12.   Difference between Average Audience Rating and Share

Programs Being Broadcast during Same 15-Minute Period	Average Audience Rating (%)	Share of Audience Rating (%)
A	20	33.3
B	10	16.7
C	30	50.0
Total	60 (HUT)	100.0

TABLE 3–13.   Program X, Ratings versus Share

Month of Year	Average Audience Rating	HUT	Share of Audience Rating
January	15.2	66.5	22.9
April	14.6	63.6	23.0
July	12.5	49.8	25.1

times of the year. If a media planner had made decisions about Program X based only on the average audience rating, he or she might have concluded that this program was losing its audience. After all, ratings were declining. But a study of HUTs shows that they, too, were declining, as might be expected when comparing HUTs for January and July. When shares were computed, however, the numbers showed that the program was not only doing well, but actually improving from January to July.

Share is best used when making comparisons based on radically different HUTs. In other words, when the bases for ratings differ, share may be the most appropriate measure.

Figure 3–3 (p.52) show sample pages from Nielsen Television Index to illustrate the various kinds of ratings used by media analysts. The reader should note the ''Average Audience'' and ''Share'' for each program listed.

It is important to remember that while ratings may be reported for households, they are also reported for people viewing programs. Such ratings usually are broken down by various demographic groups such as age and sex. Furthermore, Nielsen also shows viewer data of programs cross-tabulated by sex and age and other demographic breakdowns. These cross-tabulations allow a media planner to have a better perception of who views each program so that it is possible to better match markets with media.

Measurements of Message Weight

When planners want to know the audience size for a single TV commercial, they use either a program rating or a calculation of the number of viewers exposed to the program. For a single ad in a magazine, they use either a target audience measurement, or a percent coverage of the market figure. But many times, planners want to discuss audience sizes for more than one commercial or ad. To do that they simply add ratings or audience size numbers and disregard the duplication that results.

The sum of ratings is called *gross rating points*. The sum of audience sizes for more than one ad is called *gross impressions*. Both numbers are *duplicated*, that is, they are sums of other measurements that may overlap. Gross rating points are often called GRPs.

Using gross rating points, or gross impressions, enables the planner to use a single number to describe the effect of *message weight*. Message weight is a number that quickly tells the planner the duplicated audience sizes for many commercials or ads within a given time period. In spot television, planners often deal with the number of gross rating points per week or per month. But one also can discuss the mes-

FIGURE 3–3. **Nielsen** National TV Audience Estimates—Eve. Tue. Mar. 22, 1988

TIME	7:00	7:15	7:30	7:45	8:00	8:15	8:30	8:45	9:00	9:15	9:30	9:45	10:00	10:15	10:30	1
HUT	56.8	59.4	59.7	61.2	62.6	64.3	64.8	65.5	63.7	63.7	63.3	63.2	59.4	56.6	54.4	5

ABC TV

		Who's the Boss?		Wonder Years		Moonlighting (PAE)				Thirtysomething (PAE)			
Average Audience	{	19,310		17,280		16,300				13,380			
(Hhlds (000) & %)		21.8		19.5		18.4	17.9*		19.0*	15.1	15.5*		1
Share Audience %		34		30		29	28*		30*	27	27*		
Avg. Aud. By 1/4 Hr. %		20.7	23.0	19.5	19.6	17.8	18.1	18.8	19.1	15.9	15.1	14.8	

CBS TV

		Trial & Error		My Sister Sam		Coming of Age		Frank's Place (PAE)		Cagney & Lacey			
Average Audience	{	4,520		6,110		6,730		6,110		9,480			
(Hhlds (000) & %)		5.1		6.9		7.6		6.9		10.7	10.6*		1
Share Audience %		8		11		12		11		19	18*		
Avg. Aud. By 1/4 Hr. %		5.3	5.0	6.6	7.2	7.5	7.6	6.7	7.0	10.3	10.8	10.8	

NBC TV

		Matlock				In the Heat of the Night				Crime Story			
Average Audience	{	17,010				14,880				10,540			
(Hhlds (000) & %)		19.2	18.4*		20.0*	16.8	16.7*		17.0*	11.9	12.2*		:
Share Audience %		30	29*		31*	26	26*		27*	21	21*		
Avg. Aud. By 1/4 Hr. %		18.0	18.8	20.1	20.0	16.7	16.6	17.1	16.9	12.7	11.7	11.5	

INDEPENDENTS
(Incl. Superstations)

Average Audience	16.1	14.3	11.5	11.5	12.1	11.1	10.5	8.4
Share Audience %	28	24	18	18	19	18	18	16

SUPERSTATIONS

Average Audience	4.5	3.8	2.8	3.3	3.7	3.6	2.8	2.1
Share Audience %	8	6	4	5	6	6	5	4

PBS

Average Audience	1.8	2.5	3.0	2.7	3.8	4.1	3.0	2.5
Share Audience %	3	4	5	4	6	6	5	5

CABLE ORIG.

Average Audience	6.1	6.4	6.0	6.4	7.0	6.6	6.8	5.8
Share Audience %	10	11	9	10	11	10	12	11

PAY SERVICES

Average Audience	1.5	2.0	2.6	3.1	3.1	3.1	4.1	4.3
Share Audience %	3	3	4	5	5	5	7	8

U.S. TV Households: 88,600,000

sage weight of an entire year using either gross rating points or gross impressions. The user of these numbers, however, must always remember that they represent duplicated audiences.

Gross Rating Points in Broadcast Media

In planning for television, gross rating points are often used to describe the message weight of a week or a month. Shown below is an example of commercials that constituted 90 gross rating points a week:

$$
\begin{array}{rcl}
\text{Two commercials each with a 15 rating} & = & 30 \text{ GRPs} \\
\text{Five commercials each with a 10 rating} & = & 50 \text{ GRPs} \\
\text{Two commercials each with a 5 rating} & = & 10 \text{ GRPs} \\
\text{Total weekly GRPs} & = & 90
\end{array}
$$

For television planning, one might also want to know how many GRPs per month would be needed to attain a 70 reach. There are appropriate tables and formulas to make such reach estimates once the number of GRPs is known.

Gross Rating Points in Other Media

In recent years, planners have extended the GRP concept to other media such as magazines, newspapers, and outdoor. In magazines, for example, gross rating points equal the percent of market coverage of a target audience times the number of ad insertions. An example would be as follows:

$$
\begin{array}{rcl}
McCall's \text{ target reach of paper napkin users} & = & 22.2\% \\
\text{Number of ads to be placed in } McCall's & = & \times\ 5 \\
\text{Gross rating points} & & 111
\end{array}
$$

Another way of using gross rating points for magazines (or newspapers) is to add the target coverage for one insertion in a number of magazines as shown below.

$$
\begin{array}{lcl}
\text{Target coverage for } McCall's & = & 22.5\% \\
\text{Target coverage for } Good\ Housekeeping & = & 20.6 \\
\text{Target coverage for } Time & = & 14.2 \\
\text{Target coverage for } Woman's\ Day & = & 22.5 \\
\text{Gross rating points} & = & 79.8 \text{ (rounded to 80 GRPs)}
\end{array}
$$

One last way to calculate GRPs is to multiply reach times frequency for a given time period.

In January 1973, the Outdoor Advertising Association of America adopted as its basic unit of sale the term ''100 gross rating points daily.'' This basic standardized unit of poster sales is the number of poster panels required in each market to produce a daily effective circulation equal to the population of the market. Other units of sale would be expressed as fractions of the basic unit: 75 gross rating points daily, 50 gross rating points daily, and 25 gross rating points daily. This change in no way alters the thirty-day period of sale, and measurement.

Gross Impressions

Gross impressions would be useful in a situation where a planner wants to know, for example, the total weight of four television programs that are being considered for commercials. The audiences of each program (for targets of women 18–49) are as shown:

Program A:	5,160,000
Program B:	6,990,000
Program C:	4,320,000
Program D:	6,180,000
Gross impressions	22,650,000

Another use of broadcast gross impressions might occur when someone wants to know the weight of nine commercials that may be purchased on any one program. The gross impressions for nine commercials on Program A (above):

$$9 \quad \times \quad 5,160,000 \quad = \quad 46,440,000$$

The use of gross impressions for print media is much the same as it is for broadcast. The following examples shows how total gross impressions would be calculated for three magazines with varying numbers of ads:

Magazine	No. of targets reached	No. of ads to be purchased	Gross impressions
A	5,000,000	× 5	= 25,000,000
B	2,100,000	× 3	= 6,300,000
C	7,000,000	× 2	= 14,000,000
Total gross impressions			45,300,000

The number of impressions delivered by a media plan usually runs into the millions, and because the number is so large, it is called a *boxcar* figure. Its value, however, is debatable. Alone, gross impressions have limited meaning. But if they can be related to some measure of campaign effectiveness such as sales volume, brand awareness levels, or competitive media plan effectiveness, they can be used to compare media.

How Gross Impressions Are Used in Planning

Gross impressions are useful in comparing the weight given to geographic areas or demographic segments of a market. For example, if the planner wants to be sure that a given media plan reaches a number of different geographic areas in the correct proportions, the gross impressions could be added for each vehicle in the plan and then the proportions of each compared with a weighted goal. Table 3–14 gives an example of how this works. This table indicates that the gross impression distribution of the vehicles selected comes fairly close to the goals set for the plan. It may not be worth extra effort to make the gross impression totals come any closer to the stated goals.

Another impression analysis could have been made for targets by age, sex, income, or any other demographic segment desired.

TABLE 3-14. Distribution of Gross Impressions in Media Plan for Brand X

County Size	Gross Impressions Delivered (thousands)				Target (%)	Goal Set for Plan (%)
	Vehicle 1	Vehicle 2	Vehicle 2	Total		
A	308,582	246,972	471,342	1,026,896	51.0	47.0
B	276,980	151,370	471,342	582,331	24.1	26.7
C	187,752	72,764	78,798	339,312	17.3	15.5
D	156,150	60,016	18,796	234,962	7.6	10.8
					100.0	100.0

Measures of Cost Efficiency

One of the principles of media planning stated earlier was that media should be selected on their ability to reach the largest audience of prospects at the lowest unit cost. Matching markets with media helps accomplish one part of this principle. The search for media with large audiences of prospects rather than large total audiences recognizes that media costs are too high to permit advertising to those individuals who are not likely to buy the product.

But the other portion of the principle is equally important. This requires that media be selected that reach the largest number of prospects at the most efficient cost. Cost efficiency simply means that audience size must be related to media costs.

Cost per Thousand

Rather than compute a single unit cost, the advertising industry prefers to compute a cost per thousand. Cost per thousand may be computed for a printed page or broadcast time, and the audience base may be either circulation, homes reached, readers, or number of audience members of any kind of demographic or product usage classification.

Cost per thousand is a comparative device. It enables the planner to compare one medium or media vehicle with another to find those that are the most efficient, and it may be used for either intramedia or intermedia comparisons.

Shown below are various formulas that may be used for making comparisons on the basis of cost per thousand (abbreviated as CPM):

1. *For print media (when audience data are not available)*

$$\text{CPM} = \frac{\text{Cost of 1 page (black-and-white)} \times 1000}{\text{Circulation}}$$

Because many print media do not have audience research data, this formula is often used. But it tells nothing about the audience.

2. *For print media (when audience data are available)*

$$\text{CPM} = \frac{\text{Cost of 1 page (black-and-white)} \times 1000}{\text{Number of prospects reached}}$$

3. *For broadcast media (based on homes reached by a given program or time period)*

$$\text{CPM} = \frac{\text{Cost of 1 unit of time} \times 1000}{\text{Number of homes reached by a given program or time period}}$$

4. *For broadcast media (when audience data are available)*

$$\text{CPM} = \frac{\text{Cost of 1 unit of time} \times 1000}{\text{Number of prospects reached by a given program or time period}}$$

5. *For newspapers (when cost of ad is known)*

$$\text{CPM} = \frac{\text{Cost of ad} \times 1000}{\text{Circulation}}$$

6. *For newspapers where only circulation is the base, and the agate line rate is used to establish the milline rate*

$$\text{Milline rate} = \frac{\text{Cost of 1 agate line} \times 1 \text{ million}}{\text{Total circulation}}$$

The procedure for using any of the above formulas is to compare media on the basis of the two variables: audience and cost. The lowest cost-per-thousand medium is the most efficient, other things being equal. It is obvious that wherever precise demographic classifications of the audiences are available, these data should be used in the denominator of the formula. Generally, the medium (or media) with the lowest cost per thousand are selected, but not always. Whenever a very special kind of target audience is required, and there are few or no media which reach them exclusively, then the cost-per-thousand comparisons may be ignored. In the latter situation, media selections are based on the principle of reaching the largest number of targets, regardless of cost.

For example, there are times when individuals with very high incomes (over $100,000 annually) are target audiences. A few media vehicles reach a small proportion of these audiences, but even if many such vehicles were used, the total number of persons reached might be relatively small. On the other hand, a very large number of these persons might be reached with mass media such as a network television program or a national magazine. It is obvious that either of these two media would also include a large amount of waste, so that when costs per thousand are computed, they will seem unduly high. Yet the waste and the high costs per thousand might have to be ignored in order to maximize the size of target audiences reached.

Mass produced and consumed products, such as cigarettes, breakfast cereals, and automobiles, usually have target audiences for whom media are selected primarily on a cost-per-thousand basis. Specialized products such as yachts, private airplanes, and classical phonograph records have specialized target audiences that may require that less attention be paid to cost efficiencies and more to audience sizes.

Cost per Rating Point

Another method of comparing the cost efficiency of vehicles is that of the *cost per rating point* (CPRP). Essentially, a CPRP is a method of comparing alternative broadcast vehicles; relating cost to a rating rather than to an audience number such as in a cost-per-thousand comparison. Both are measurements of relative value, but each uses a different base. The formula for calculating CPRP is as follows:

$$\text{Cost per rating point} = \frac{\text{Cost of a commercial}}{\text{Rating}}$$

If the cost of a prime-time spot commercial was $1,000 and the rating for that spot was 10, then the CPRP would be $100.

How does a CPRP compare with a CPM for the same station and commercial? The following shows the differences:

CPRP	CPM
Cost of thirty-second commercial: $110	Cost of thirty-second commercial: $110
Metro rating, 2:00 P.M.: 8	No. H.H. delivered, 2:00 P.M.: 77,000
$110 ÷ 8 = $13.75	$110 × 1000 ÷ 77,000 = $1.43

Is there any preference for using one over the other? Generally, cost per thousand is most often used to compare any vehicle efficiency, while CPRP is a tool most often used for quick cost comparisons in broadcast planning.

QUESTIONS FOR DISCUSSION

1. An advertiser is considering using the top newspaper in a given market, but finds that it only has 40 percent household coverage. Why might he conclude that 40 percent is not enough?
2. A planner finds that a television program has 98 percent coverage nationally. Can the planner assume that because the program has a large coverage, it will also have a large audience? Briefly explain.
3. A planner intends to buy 100 gross rating points a week in a given market. Why do 100 gross rating points not equal 100 percent reach in that market?
4. If a planner is considering the use of a magazine that reaches 65 percent of a target market, and intends to buy only one ad, how many gross rating points does that total?
5. What, precisely, is the meaning of the following? "We will have a 75 percent coverage in a spot television buy, if we buy the top sixty markets in the United States."
6. What is the relationship between GRPs and gross impressions?
7. Why are television ratings not an accurate measurement of the audience size for commercials broadcast within a program?
8. Is it proper to talk about the four-week reach of *Reader's Digest*? Briefly explain.
9. Of what value is it to know the readers per copy of a magazine?
10. Briefly explain why HUT figures for a given time period (such as a Monday evening in February) do not change very much from year to year.
11. Many newspaper columnists who are television critics tend to disparage broadcast ratings

with a statement such as, "Well, no one ever called me to ask which program I was watching." Is this statement valid? Briefly explain.

12. In comparing alternative television program ratings, when is the most appropriate time to use share calculations for comparison?

13. What is the value of having circulation audited by the ABC?

SELECTED READINGS

Bogart, Leo, "Isn't It Time to Discard the Audience Concept?" *Journal of Marketing,* January 1966, pp. 47–54.

Broadcast Rating Council, *Maintaining Ratings Confidence and Credibility,* July 1972.

Brooks, Hugh L., "B&W: Still Too Many Unknowns in Magazine Audience Research," *Advertising Age,* July 26, 1976.

Darmon, Rene Y., "Determinants of TV Viewing," *Journal of Advertising Research,* December 1976, pp. 17–20.

Edelstein, Art, Samuels, Gabe, and Tommaney, James J., "Audience Research Debate: Who's Got the Answer?" *Media Decisions,* May 1978, pp. 72–75.

Ephron, Erwin, "Good Media Plans Grow Out of Great Research," *Media Decisions,* October 1970, p. 40.

Ephron, Erwin, "Confused? Six Commonly Held Beliefs about Media Planning That Are Not So," *Media Decisions,* August 1972, pp. 48–102.

Faber, Neil, "Efficiency Is Not Really That Unless Based on Target Demographics," *Media Decisions,* October 1978, p. 84.

Gerhold, Paul, "Seven Fallacies in Audience Measurements," in *Papers from the American Association of Advertising Agencies Regional Conventions,* 1960, pp. 15–22.

Greene, Jerome, "Personal Media Probabilities," *Journal of Advertising Research,* October 1970, pp. 12–18.

Hall, Robert W., *Media Math,* Lincolnwood, Ill.: National Textbook Company, 1987.

Hope, John, "Gross Rating Points Become Official for Outdoor Showings," *Media Decisions,* February 1973, p. 82.

Keller, Paul, "Patterns of Media Audience Accumulation," *Journal of Marketing,* January 1966, pp. 32–37.

Lucas, Darrell, "How Valid Are Media Measures?" *Media/Scope,* January 1960, pp. 40–43.

Maneloveg, Herbert, "Media Research Future: Is There Any?" *Advertising Age,* July 15, 1974, p. 23.

Media Decisions, "Rating Points for Newspapers," April 1971, pp. 44–47.

Media Decisions, "What Is Best for Buying—CPGRP or CPM?" February 1973, pp. 48–49.

Media Decisions, "Media Research: Where It Stands Today," January 1977, pp. 55–59.

Papazian, Edward, "Setting Priorities," *Media Decisions,* December 1973, pp. 16–18.

Papazian, Edward, "Some Questions about TV Ratings," *Media Decisions,* September 1977, pp. 14–16.

Rutens, W. S., "A Guide to TV Ratings," *Journal of Advertising Research,* February 1978, pp. 11–18.

Samuels, Gabe, "A New Proposal for Judging the Goodness of the Data," *Media Decisions,* September 1978, p. 88.

Shiffman, Phil, "A Research Quandary: Problems of TV Audience Measurement through Nielsen," *Media Decisions,* August 1978.

Shocker, Alan D., "Limitations of Incremental Research in Media Selection," *Journal of Marketing Research,* February 1970, pp. 101–3.

Simmons, W. R., "We Can Believe *Most* of the Numbers *Most* of the Time," *Media/Scope*, September 1967, pp. 46–49.

Smith, Stewart, "Criteria for Media Comparisons: A Critique," *Journal of Marketing Research,* November 1965, pp. 364–69.

Stanton, Frank, "A State of the Art Appraisal of Advertising Research Measurements," *Perspectives in Advertising Management*, April 1969, Association of National Advertisers, pp. 237–45.

Surmanek, Jim, *Media Planning: A Quick & Easy Guide*, Chicago, Ill.: Crain Books, 1980.

Surmanek, Jim, "Coming to Terms with New Media Jargon," *Marketing Communications*, May 1981, p. 6.

Weinblatt, Ira, "Too Much Research?" *Media Decisions*, May 1976, p. 74.

Yergin, Jim, "TV Meters vs. Diaries," *Media Decisions*, December 1978, pp. 122–24.

4
New Media Measuring Tools

This chapter covers the subject of new media measuring tools that may radically change the way media planning is done in the future. Because these tools are so important, a special discussion of what they are, how they work, and what implications they may have for the future is presented here.

People Meters

Probably no new measuring tool in media history has generated as much interest and discussion as people meters. Essentially, a *people meter* is an electronic device for measuring the number and kinds of people who are watching television programs; they do not measure the audience size for commercials. There have been three major companies vying for adoption of their systems to measure national TV audiences in the United States: the A. C. Nielsen Company, Audits of Great Britain (AGB), and ScanAmerica (a joint venture, Arbitron and Time, Inc.). At present, only the A. C. Nielsen people meter is in full-scale operation in the United States.

For many years, television-viewing information was gathered in two ways: (a) Data were gathered by electronic meters attached to television sets. These meters would record a channel number and the time of day and the day of week for each program that was viewed. (b) A diary was also used to record who, demographically, was viewing. These two measurements were combined to provide data about audience sizes and demographics.

How People Meters Work

A people meter is an electronic measuring device. A. C. Nielsen's people meter consists of a box (about half the size of a cigar box) that sits on top (or at the side of) a television set. It has eight pairs of red and green lights on it and a button for each member of the family (up to eight members. A special unit containing sixteen buttons is available for larger families).

Before the unit is ready for use, a field representative collects demographic data about age and sex of each family member. These data are recorded in a control unit. Each button must be pressed at the beginning and end of each viewing. Visitors must key-in their sex and age on two special buttons. There is also a small key-pad for people to make viewing entries from across the room. (See Figure 4–1.)

The AGB meter is also in the form of a small box that sits on top of the television set. It is an audience monitor. It has a series of seven push buttons on it—one button is assigned to each family member. It comes with a separate hand-held device, about the size of a package of cigarettes, with buttons on it that must be pressed to indicate viewing. When viewers press a button on this pad to indicate that they are viewing, a light goes on in the box. They must also press a button to indicate when to stop viewing. That box also flashes when the set is turned on so that people will be reminded to press the buttons of the smaller unit. Also, at intervals, all the lights in the box on top of the set flash to remind viewers to cooperate. A basic metering unit can measure up to four television sets and can even monitor VCRs.

ScanAmerica has a device that flashes a question mark in the left-hand corner of the screen. Family members who are watching have a small handheld device which allows them to move a pointer on the TV screen to an identification number. Then they move the pointer over to an X to indicate that they are watching.

Information from these meters are returned over telephone lines to a centrally located computer. The demographics of each family member are already stored in the computer's memory, and are combined with viewing data to provide program ratings of people's viewing. Meters are supposed to be kept by a sample of homes for a period of five years, when the sample is replaced.

The Need for People Meters

Ratings based on diary measurements have long been considered inadequate. But for years, there was no technique available to improve them. A list of diaries' inadequacies includes the following:

1. Most of the measurements were limited to a seven-day period. Therefore it was not possible to measure the cumulative tune-in for a four-week period of a demographic audience segment (for example, women aged 18–49). Of course, estimates could be, and were, made to provide this kind of information.

   Nielsen, for example, required a sample of viewers to fill out diaries for one week only, only about a fourth of its entire sample. This data was then unified into a four-week figure. On a nationwide basis, Nielsen collected demographic data for only thirty-nine weeks of a year, making it difficult to know the cumulative audience for certain time periods.

2. It was found that the last days of diary measurement were not necessarily as accurate as the first days in a seven-day period.

FIGURE 4-1.   Nielsen's People Meter (with Hand-Held Remote Unit)
Reprinted courtesy of Nielsen Media Research.

3. Diaries tended to provide higher ratings for higher-rated shows. This indicates that respondents of diary samples may have reported their "typical" (rather than actual) viewing habits when filling out the diaries, thereby inflating the ratings of the more popular higher-rated shows.

4. People who can neither read nor write (or whose literacy skills were poorly developed) were not likely to fill out diaries. Some estimates of their number run as high as 20 percent of the total U.S. population.

5. Children and older people were not likely to fill out the diaries completely, to do it accurately, or to return them.

6. Diaries tended to inflate the number of viewers per viewing households in a sample. Therefore, the costs per thousands were lower than they should have been.

7. Ratings from cable TV homes tended to be lower than they should have been, presumably, because there were too many stations for diary keepers to remember, or it simply took too much time and attention to detail to fill out diaries.

8. Many diaries were not completed, and of those that were, only half may have been usable. Therefore the returns were nonrepresentative of the universe being measured.

Advantages of People Meters

The advantages of people meters for media planning purposes are as follows:

1. People meters are easier to use than diaries because no writing is necessary. Presumably, this fact may make measurements of TV watching more accurate than diaries.

2. Because writing is not necessary, the sample size and the characteristics of the universe being measured tend to be more representative than a diary sample.

3. Cable viewing may be much more accurately measured than it was in the past because viewers must only press buttons in order to record their cable viewing.

4. Measurements of cumulative viewing over a period of consecutive weeks result in reach and frequencies of demographic segments of target audiences that are measured directly. This direct measurement was not previously possible.

5. Reports of viewing can be made much more quickly because there are no long delays caused by the time taken to mail in diaries, edit and tabulate them.

6. People meters can measure movement of people in and out of the viewing room. If there is excessive movement, it may indicate that less attention is being paid to the program.

Potential Problems with People Meters

When considering the use of people meters as a media planning tool, a number of potential problems must be considered:

1. Will people cooperate fully? Americans are a very private group of people. Will they look at people meters as an invasion of privacy? If one or more groups perceive the meters as an invasion of privacy, the representativeness of the sample may be biased and the results invalidated.
2. Will people keep pressing the buttons accurately? Diaries are kept for only seven days. Meters may require people's attention for much longer periods of time. Will there be a point of diminishing returns when people simply tire of pushing buttons?
3. Will people who participate in this data-gathering process have to be replaced more frequently than the two-year time period agreed to because they tire of "button pressing"?
4. Will people be affected by the constant button pressing and thereby change their viewing habits? Older electronic meters were unobtrusive and tended to be forgotten after the initial viewing period was over. But the presence of meters will always be obvious.
5. Can meters tell whether people are watching commercials?
6. Will children, in particular, be inclined to play with key-pads and perhaps distort rating data? Perhaps mothers will have to push buttons for their children and themselves.
7. Will all the measuring companies be consistent in their definition of "viewing"? There seems to be some question about whether one needs only to be in the room when a TV set is on to be counted, or whether one must either watch or listen. The question focuses on who is to be counted, and is related to a more important question: namely, even if meters count people who are watching, are these people paying attention, especially to commercials?

Some answers to these questions are available from the tests that each company have already run in their testing periods, but more may be learned after extensive usage for national samples in varying geographic locations.

Practical Problems That Have Developed

Some practical problems have arisen. One of them occurred when the A. C. Nielsen Company reported on people meter ratings made for some television programs broadcast from November 10 to 23, 1986. These ratings were all lower than the Nielsen Television Index ratings that were measured for the same period. For example, the Bill Cosby show had a 27.4 Nielsen Television Index rating, but a 24.4 people meter rating for adults aged 25–54, about a 11 percent loss. Other network television shows had losses from 5 to 15 percent.

Nielsen began measuring television audiences using only people meters in September 1987. It was not altogether surprising that ratings obtained from these new measurements were different from those measured by a combination of diaries and audimeters. The new ratings are similar to the test ratings of November 1986. Many are lower than they were using the older system. Children's ratings also have suffered an average of 35 percent decline. Steps are being taken to address whatever problems and complaints there are in use of the ratings.

Early estimates of differences between the older and newer ratings were known, but the major implication of verified losses is that agencies initially took the negotiating posture that they wanted to base new advertising rates on the people meter ratings alone. If they had been successful, the prices of the networks' programs would have been lower. But networks resisted such cuts. They took the position that even if people meter ratings were lower, pricing is determined by demand rather than a change in audience measurement.

In the final analysis, then, because television is a commodities marketplace, the prices are set by supply and demand regardless of whether the old or new rating systems are used. An adjustment period may be necessary, but pricing will reflect market conditions just as it has in the past. For instance, should demand remain constant and unit prices stay relatively steady, even if people meters show lower ratings than the old Nielsen Television Index did, costs per thousand will continue to rise.

In the meantime, some networks would like Nielsen to continue to merge demographic data taken from diaries with household viewing data taken from passive meters as was done before people meters were used.

The importance of ratings is related to the manner in which networks charge for television programs. The networks, using projections based on past Nielsen data, guarantee advertisers that a given show (or group of shows) will attract a certain number of demographic targets for a specific, negotiated price on long-term, fifty-two-week purchases. If the program or package does not meet that figure in the season, the network compensates the advertiser with free compensatory (or make-good) commercials.

Some network executives have suggested that networks ought to do away with guarantees that were used in the past. These suggestions have met with considerable resistance from advertisers and agencies. At present, it appears that guarantees will remain a key factor in long-term buy negotiations—at least for the forseeable future.

An Evaluation

People meters, then, seem to be here to stay. Undoubtedly, they will be improved, and most of their inadequacies will be remedied. Some, perhaps, like the problem of monitoring little children, or very old people may remain troublesome.

There is consensus among media people that the industry will not support three companies selling the same kinds of information. Presumably, the company with the least perceived accuracy will be the one to go. Regardless of which research companies provide the people meter service, sample sizes will be higher than the previous diary samples. Nielsen's household sample size was 1,700, but the people meter sample size will be 2,000 initially, and it will be expanded to 4,000 in September

1988. In fact, as of August 1988, the AGB Company announced that it would discontinue people meter measurements in the United States because the operation was unprofitable. However, it plans to return in a somewhat different format. Plans call for a "single source" monthly measurement that would combine AGB's TV ratings with Mediamark Research Incorporated's product research information.

In terms of the advantages that people meters may hold for media planners, they include the following: the promise of calculating demographic reach and frequency, the expectation that lower network ratings may result in lower network prices, and the hope that advertising commercial effectiveness can be controlled. Therefore, planners will use people meter data, and the media planning and buying industry will make significant advances in its operations.

The Passive People Meter

The R. D. Percy Company of Seattle has developed a device for measuring the size of a television commercial's audience. It uses an "active" push-button people meter that records viewing, and a "passive" Voxbox that employs a heat sensor to record who is actually looking at the TV set during the time commercials are being broadcast. Some initial measurements have found that a pet dog may register on the passive meter. This problem is being attended to by installing a video camera in homes to make sure the sensor was working properly.

The device is being tested in the hope that it can help planners learn not only which commercials are being watched, but also whether audience members are "flipping" the TV dial in search of program substitutes in lieu of watching commercials. The system focuses on commercials rather than program audiences and measures second-by-second viewing.

After investing heavily in start-up costs for two years, Percy ceased operations in August 1988 due to their inability to attract support within the industry or from outside investors.

The Nielsen Company is now reported to be developing passive people meters to be tested for possible use as national audience measurement.

Single Source Data

Nielsen, ScanAmerica, AGB, and Information Resources Incorporated are also measuring product purchases and correlating television viewing with purchasing. The technique, called "single source," is measured from the same source, for instance, as an individual family. A single measurement is valuable because it should be more accurate than data obtained from two separate measurements. (See Figure 4–2.)

In the past, television audience data and sales responses were measured separately, and planners had to match people data with market data. Single source data, therefore, should be a more valid measurement, providing planners with evidence of which television programs have the greatest effect on sales. It is hoped that single

FIGURE 4–2.   **A Diagram of How Monitor-Plus Records Data**

Reprinted courtesy of Nielsen Media Research.

source data will go even further and measure exposure to other media such as newspapers, magazines, and radio.

Both ScanAmerica and AGB require people to wave a wand over products and thereby measure recent purchases. The wand picks up the Universal Product Code (UPC) printed on each package. By using such techniques, these services have been able to correlate purchasing and television program viewing patterns.

In its first sixteen-week test in Denver, ScanAmerica, found that the product measurement technique (using the wand) produced results that compared very favorably with actual purchase data measurements produced by SAMI.

Information Resources Inc. (IRI) also has developed a technique for combining measurement of television viewing with purchasing. IRI has installed special electronic instruments in 10,000 homes to monitor each TV set's audience, using devices that record whether a TV set is on, and the channel which is being viewed. Measurements are made every five seconds throughout a broadcast day, making it possible to know how many households are viewing a program being broadcast. With this data, gathered on a family-by-family basis, manufacturers and their agencies can learn which dayparts are most popular, and which programs are most related to product purchasing. It may also be possible to determine to what extent program choice and daypart are related to purchasing a given brand when manufacturers offer promotional deals.

Nielsen has developed a single source database called ERIM TESTSIGHT. This is a controlled testing environment that automatically measures consumer reactions to new products and new marketing strategies. The technique that Nielsen uses involves data gathered through electronic monitoring of grocery and drug sales at the retail level, consumer panel purchasing, and television viewing. In testing, various media weights from the same sample can be used at different times to determine what consumer reactions occur. Two test markets are compared with one another on the basis of sales produced showing the effects of altering the GRP levels of advertising media in different markets. The effects of media weights are known more quickly and more accurately using this technique. Testing precision, then, may be enhanced.

Geodemographic Measurements

A technique that is about twenty years old, and is still being developed, is that of correlating precise geographic and demographic data with media audience data. The idea behind this kind of measurement is that people with the same life-styles and income tend to live in the same geographic vicinity. Areas can be identified by zip codes and product purchases. They also can be identified by correlating purchasing data with census tract data in areas as small as a city block. Therefore, a media planner can select media that will reach them precisely, with little or no waste. If measurements are not available for every single block or zip code area, then mathematical procedures are used to refine the data.

Some of the companies who are involved in selling this kind of information are Nielsen's NTI PRIZM, using zip code data; C.A.C.I. Company's ACORN, which analyzes life-styles on a census block; and Arbitron, which has a measurement called Product Target AID. Much of the analysis made by these companies, including charts, maps, and tables, is made by computer.

To this date, geodemographic measurements have not been widely used, at least not by advertising agencies. Some clients, however, have used these techniques with varying degrees of success. Questions have been raised about whether it is economically possible to upgrade data as time passes; whether television programs, for example, can be classified by life-styles; and whether data collected over time, will be valid.

Other New Measurement Ideas

The Weinblatt Measurements

This era seems to have spawned many ideas for measuring media in ways unthought of before. Lee Weinblatt, chief executive officer of the Pretesting Company, Englewood, New Jersey, has created a wristwatch and a pair of reading glasses that measure magazine and television audiences. The watch measures readership by recording transmissions from microchips placed in magazine ads. The glasses, coupled with an infrared transmitter in the TV set, can record who is watching television.

These two are called "passive" measuring devices because the wearer does not have to respond in any way. No buttons need be pushed, and no records made by writing.

The wristwatch looks like any other wristwatch, but is equipped with a recorder that reads signals from the microchips embedded in ads that are to be tested. When the watch comes within nine inches of the magazine, it begins recording the name of the magazine, and how long the respondent looked at it. It stops when the respondent puts the magazine aside.

The glasses require a recorder that sits atop a TV set and tells whether a respondent is looking at the screen. When the user looks away, it stops recording.

The A.C. Nielsen Company is testing the idea at present. Both devices are so new that no records of adoptions have been recorded at this time.

Conclusions

All of these new measurement ideas should have some effect on the quality of media planning because they can provide better insights into media audiences; some of these measurements even provide insights into the consuming behavior of these audiences. In fact, it seems clear that what media planners want more than anything is to be able to prove that any medium chosen will sell more of a product than any other medium. This idea goes back to the Audience Concepts Committee of the Advertising Research Foundation's 1961 model of the ultimate media comparison: to show that there *is* a direct relationship between a media vehicle and sale. Perhaps these new measurements won't quite reach the ultimate comparison; certainly they will move media planning closer to the goal than it has ever been before.

Ron Kaatz, formerly senior vice president and director of media resources and research at J. Walter Thompson, and now a professor of advertising at Northwestern University's Medill School of Journalism, asked an assembly at Chicago's marketing and Media Workshop, "While a move to people meters would improve our national TV rating system, in the long run, would product usage ratings be a more useful improvement?" The response to this question was that 64 percent agreed and 36 percent disagreed. This result suggests that planners want both improvements, but some want something more than better ratings.

The implication for students and those entering the world of media planning is that it is important to know what is going on in the area of new measurements, and to be prepared to use innovations in the most efficient ways.

SELECTED READINGS

ACORN, *ACORN Market Segment Descriptions*, C.A.C.I., Market Analysis Division, 1982, pp. 1–18.

Broadcasting Staff, "1987 Ushers in the People Meter Era," *Broadcasting,* January 5, 1987, pp. 59–63.

Cebrzynski, Gregg, "New Research Tools Provide 'Accurate' Attention Data," *Marketing News,* April 11, 1986, p. 5ff.

Gay, Verne, "Automatic Metering Service Signs JWT," *Advertising Age,* November 17, 1986, p.6.

Gay, Verne, "AGB May Resurface: Percy Stops Service," *Advertising Age,* August 8, 1988, pp. 2, 43.

Gullen, Phil, and Johnson, Hugh, "Relating Product Purchasing and TV Viewing," *Journal of Advertising Research*, December 1986/January 1987, pp. 9–19.

Kaatz, Ron, "Mediology: Feedback '85," *Marketing and Media Decisions*, November 1985, pp. 88–89.

Papazian, Edward, "More People-Meter Games: What Constitutes Viewing?" *Media Matters,* September 1986, p.5.

Papazian, Edward, "Reservations about Single Source," *Marketing and Media Decisions*, October 1986, p.104.

Phelps, Stephen P., "Media Planning . . .

The Measurement Gap," *Marketing and Media Decisions*, July 1986, pp. 148–149.

Staff, "ScanAmerica Tells You Precisely Who's Watching, Who's Buying," *Beyond the Ratings* (Arbitron), March 1986, p.7.

Staff, "Can Geodemographics Simplify Media Planning?" *Marketing and Media Decisions*, August 1984, pp. 66–82.

Staff, "Reducing Costs and Increasing Efficiency with ERIM TESTIGHT," *Nielsen Researcher*, No. 2, 1985, pp. 2–7.

Staff, "Networks and Ad Agencies Battle over Estimates of TV Viewership," *Wall Street Journal*, January 7, 1987, p.1.

5
Reach and Frequency

The preceding chapter introduced the concept of audience accumulation along with other measurements. This chapter amplifies the subject of accumulation in terms of reach and frequency, two of the most important considerations in planning media. Reach and frequency are parts of strategy planning and can be manipulated to attain certain marketing and media objectives. Generally, when broad message dispersion patterns are needed, then high levels of reach will be planned. But when a great deal of repetition is needed, then high frequency levels will be planned. Sometimes planning will have to attain both high reach and high frequency.

What Is Reach (in Broadcast Media)?

Reach is a form of audience accumulation. It is a measure of how many different households or audience members were exposed at least one time to one or more media vehicles over a period of time (usually four weeks). Reach may be expressed as a raw number, or as a percentage of some universe. (A *universe* is a particular demographic group, such as women aged 18–49, or all employed persons.)

Reach differs from gross rating points in that the latter is a duplicated figure, whereas reach is not. The following example illustrates the difference:

> A weekly television program has an average weekly rating of 25. Therefore its four-week gross rating points are 100 (25 × 4 = 100). The same television program may have a four-week reach of 65 percent (or 65). Since reach is unduplicated, that number will be smaller than the gross rating points. To find this reach, the audience of the television program would have to be measured.

The reason that audience members are counted only once in a reach measurement lies in the history of media research. When early planners were trying to decide what kind of measurement ought to be used to count the size of a vehicle's audience, some felt that an audience member would have to be exposed about three times to a vehicle before ads within that vehicle would have any effect. Other planners disagreed, saying that it could not be known how many exposures would be required. Planners decided to compromise and to count one exposure to a vehicle as evidence of reach, because whether or not the ad was seen, there was a large difference between being exposed and not being exposed. To be exposed at least once meant that audiences then had an opportunity to see ads within the vehicle. There obviously would be no opportunity to see ads if there were no exposure.

Another historical reason for the development of reach concerned the invention of a statistic for radio and television that would parallel the audience reach of a monthly magazine. Planners realized it would be unfair to compare a one-week broadcast rating with the reach of a monthly issue of a magazine. Obviously the magazine reach would be higher. But by using a four-week reach for broadcast media, the planner now had a statistic that was fairly comparable to that of a monthly magazine in terms of audience size.

Table 5–1 illustrates the measurement of reach, using a sample of ten persons. The sample size for measuring reach is actually much larger, but ten was used to simplify the concept. While four weeks is the usual measuring period, reach can be measured for almost any period of time. Four weeks happens to have become a standard measuring unit, easily conforming to a monthly accounting period.

Table 5–1 is interpreted this way. Persons 3, 5, 8, and 9 saw the program in Week 1, so the one-week reach is four, and the rating is 40 or four out of ten. Because Person 7 was the only new viewer in Week 2, the two-week reach is five. Again in Week 3 only one new viewer, Person 6, was added, making a three-week reach of six; and the same applies to Week 4, when Person 10 was added, bringing the four-week reach to seven. Program X, then, had a reach of seven (out of ten) or a 70 percent reach. Note that Persons 3, 5, 6, and 9 viewed the program more than once in the four-week period, but they were counted only once for the purpose of calculating reach. Also note that the first week of viewing is unduplicated, so it is correct to speak of a one-week reach, although current usage refers to this first-week measurement as either a rating or an audience size statistic.

Kinds of Reach

There are two different kinds of reach that a planner would like to know about in broadcast planning: (a) the four-week reach of an individual vehicle such as a television program, or (b) the combined reach of four or five television programs that would be used as a single package in an ad campaign.

No matter which the planner is interested in, the same principles apply, namely, that audience members are counted only once, no matter how many times they may see the vehicle within a four-week period. In situation (b) where four television programs are being considered for one campaign package, some audience members may be exposed three or four times to only one television program, while other audience members may be exposed to all four television programs a different number of times. But if they see any one of the four programs at least once, they are counted as having been reached in a four-week period.

TABLE 5-1.   An Example of a Four-Week Reach Measurement for Program X

Person	Week 1	Week 2	Week 3	Week 4
1	—	—	—	—
2	—	—	—	—
3	⊕	×	—	×
4	—	—	—	—
5	⊕	—	×	—
6	—	—	⊕	×
7	—	⊕	×	—
8	⊕	—	—	—
9	⊕	×	—	×
10	—	—	—	⊕
Ratings Each Week	40	30	30	40

For a weekly evening program: × = Viewed the program;   ⊕ = Counted in reach measurement.

Suppose, for example, that the reach of four programs was 35 million men, aged 18–34. This means that if the planner places a commercial in each of the four television programs, it is estimated that 35 million men, aged 18–34, will have an opportunity to see at least one of those four vehicles and, ideally, one of the four commercials within the vehicles. The word "ideally" is a reminder that reach is concerned only with vehicle exposure, not ad exposure. Other measurements can provide ad exposure, but they are not yet available on a syndicated basis.

Table 5-2 shows how the reach of four television programs is calculated. Eight people viewed one of the four programs at least once in a four-week period. A person is counted only once regardless of how many programs were viewed. Therefore Person 1, who watched both Programs A and B, is counted only once, as is Person 7, who watched all four programs. The combined reach of the four programs is 8 or 80 percent. Each of the programs also had a reach of its own for the four weeks. The combined reach of all four programs is more properly known as the *net reach* of the four. Other terms that are sometimes used to describe the net reach of four television programs are "cumulative audience," or "audience accumulated by four television programs," or "net unduplicated audience." Each is correct, but in popular usage people are more likely to say, "The reach of four programs is. . . ."

TABLE 5-2.   Calculating the Combined Reach of Four Television Programs

Person	Program A	Program B	Program C	Program D	Total (four programs)
1	⊕	×	—	—	⊕
2	⊕	×	—	×	⊕
3	—	—	—	⊕	⊕
4	—	⊕	×	×	⊕
5	—	—	⊕	—	⊕
6	—	—	⊕	—	⊕
7	⊕	×	×	×	⊕
8	—	—	—	—	—
9	⊕	×	—	×	⊕
10	—	—	—	—	—
Reach	40%	50%	40%	50%	80%

× = Viewed program at least once;   ⊕ = Counted in reach measurement.

TABLE 5–3.   How to Use the Terms Reach and Coverage

Use Reach	to express a whole number or percentage of different people actually exposed only once to a media vehicle or combination of vehicles. Example: Television program X reaches 9 million men aged 18–34 within a four-week period. Example: Magazine Y has a reach of 25 percent of men aged 18–34 with an average issue.
Use Coverage	to express the potential audience of a broadcast medium *or the actual audience* of a print medium exposed only once. Example: A network television program may have a coverage of 95 percent of TV homes in the U.S. Example: Magazine Y has a 25 percent coverage of men aged 18–34. (Means same as reach.)

Relationship of Reach to Coverage

Students and others are sometimes confused about whether to use the term coverage or reach when referring to audience accumulation data. The terms can be interchangeable because coverage sometimes is synonymous with reach. A better answer is that coverage and reach are quite different because coverage could mean *potential* to be exposed to the advertising, while reach refers to those people who *actually are* exposed. (See Chapter 3 for complete explanations of coverage for each advertising medium.)

Popular usage of these terms provides the basic answer. Coverage *usually* refers to potential audience for broadcast media and to actual delivered audience for print media. Reach *always* refers to the audience actually delivered by any advertising vehicle. Table 5–3 treats the distinction in capsule form.

How Reach Builds Over Time

Reach for television programs accumulates, or builds, in a fairly consistent pattern over time. The first time a program is telecast, it accumulates the largest number of viewers. The second time it is telecast, most of the viewers are repeat viewers, although some new viewers are accumulated. The third and subsequent telecasts accumulate even fewer new viewers. If viewing over a four-week period were plotted on a graph, the curve drawn would look similar to that in Figure 5–1. If the same program were telecast over a long period of time, the curve eventually would flatten out and become almost horizontal, though it would never become perfectly horizontal because there would still be some persons, somewhere, tuning in the program for the first time.

An interesting aspect of the reach curve is that when the curve for any single program is compared with that for another program, the curves are similar in shape even though one curve may be higher or lower on a graph than another. Figure 5–2 shows reach accumulated for two television shows over a period of four consecutive telecasts.

Study of the reach curves for multiple television programs or commercials over a period of twenty-six weeks shows basically similar curves with only slight variations.

FIGURE 5-1.   The Shape of a Typical Reach Curve

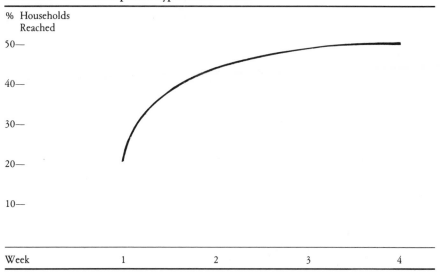

FIGURE 5-2.   Reach Curves of Two Television Programs

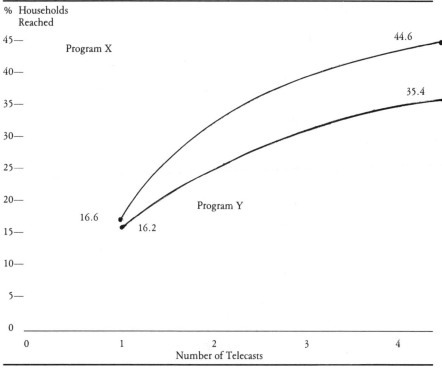

Source: Nielsen Media Research, Program Cumulative Audiences Report. Reprinted by permission.

FIGURE 5-3. Net Reach Curves of Multiple Programs for Twenty-Six Weeks*

Source: Nielsen Media Research. Reprinted by permission.
KEY: ─────── Prime time; ─ ─ ─ ─ ─ Monday–Friday Daytime.
*Heavy weights of GRPs are used in each.

Figures 5–3 and 5–4 plot reach curves for a period of twenty-six weeks for different parts of the day (called *dayparts*) and for different weight (GRP) levels.

What Is Reach (in Print Media)?

An issue of a magazine or newspaper, not time as in broadcast media, provides the basic measuring unit for reach measurement in print media. One does not usually speak of the four-week reach of Magazine A, although there are measurements that estimate audience accumulation over time for an average issue of a magazine. Generally speaking, monthly magazines have a longer issue life than weeklies and general content magazines a longer life than news-oriented magazines.

Magazine reach can be expressed in a number of ways:

1. Audience reach of one issue of a magazine, for example, the reach of the July 1 issue of *Newsweek* (may also be called the total audience of *Newsweek*)
2. Target audience reach of multiple issues of the same magazine, for example, the reach (or net unduplicated audience) of the July 1, July 8, July 15, July 22, and July 29 issues of *Newsweek*
3. Target audience reach of single issues of different magazines within the same month, for example, the reach (or net unduplicated audience) of July issues of *McCall's, Ladies Home Journal, Reader's Digest*, and *TV Guide*
4. The reach of single or multiple issues of different magazines occurring throughout the advertising campaign, for example, the reach of *Popular Mechanics* in June and August, *Field & Stream* in July and August, and *Sport* in June and July

FIGURE 5-4   Net Reach Curves of Multiple Commercials for Twenty-Six Weeks with Different Weight Levels*

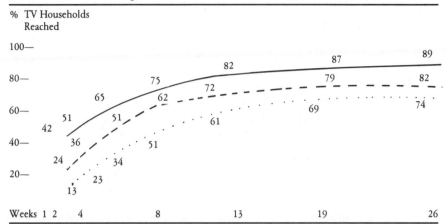

Source: Nielsen Media Research. Reprinted by permission.
Note: The more messages telecast, the more gross rating points they will accumulate. Therefore there is a direct relationship between the number of gross rating points achieved in a four-week period, and the degree of frequency that develops.
KEY: Light Schedule ············8 Messages/4 Weeks; Moderate Schedule ––––––––– 16 Messages/4 Weeks; Heavy Schedule ––––––––––– 48 Messages/ 4 Weeks.
*Monday–Friday daytime schedules only.

Because there are many qualities expressed in a reach measurement, it becomes important to know them all. Table 5–4 summarizes these qualities.

Frequency in Broadcast and Print Media

Frequency is a companion statistic to reach that tells the planner the average number of times that audience members were exposed to a broadcast program within a four-week period, or were exposed to issues of different print media. Reach is a measure of message dispersion, indicating how widely the message may be received in a target universe. Frequency is a measure of repetition, indicating to what extent audience members were exposed to the same vehicle or group of vehicles. Both reach and frequency are valuable decision-making tools because they give the planner different options for arranging message delivery in a media plan.

Frequency is usually calculated from measurement data. The formula is the same for broadcast and print media:

$$\text{Frequency} = \frac{\text{GRPs or total duplicated audience}}{\text{Reach}}$$

Example in broadcast: Program X telecast once each week has an average rating of 20 for each week. It has a four-week reach of 43. The frequency is as follows:

$$\text{Frequency} = \frac{20 \times 4}{43} \quad \text{or } 1.9$$

TABLE 5-4.   The Meaning of Reach, Summarized

Reach is
1. A measurement of audience accumulation
2. An unduplicated statistic
3. Measured, although it can sometimes be estimated
4. Measured for a single vehicle, or a group of different vehicles
5. Measured for subsequent issues of the same magazine, e.g., the seven-issue reach of *TV Guide* is . . .
6. Reported for a four-week period of television watching
7. Reported for almost any period of time in broadcast measurements
8. Reported by the issue in print media
9. Reported either as a raw number or as a percentage of some universe
10. Reported for households, or for individuals in a demographic category
11. Another term for coverage in print media
12. Measured on the basis of exposure to a vehicle or vehicles
13. Not measured on the basis of exposure to ads in vehicles
14. A measurement that tells how many people had an opportunity to see ads in vehicles

Example in Print: *TV Guide* has a reach of 54 for six consecutive issues. Its one-issue reach is 29.5.

$$\text{Frequency} = \frac{29.5 \times 6}{54.0} \text{ or } 3.3$$

Frequency Distribution

Persons who use measurement data sometimes forget that frequency is an average and not an absolute number. It is subject, therefore, to the characteristics of all statistical averages. Averages, for example, are affected by extreme scores in a distribution. A few very high numbers may bring up the average of all other scores while a few very low ones may drag down the average. The only way to guard against being deceived by a frequency statistic is to look at a frequency distribution and see whether some segments of a sample are getting disproportionately more frequency than others.

Table 5-5 shows a sample divided into fixed quintiles and each group's reach and frequency. (*Fixed quintiles* means that the sample of audience members exposed was divided into five equal groups, each with 20 percent of the total number exposed.) The distribution of frequency is obviously unequal in Table 5-5. Some of the quintiles received much more frequency than others. This phenomenon is known as *skew*.

TABLE 5-5.   Quintile Analysis of Tune-ins for Program X

Divisions of Viewer Sample	Reach (%)	Frequency	GRPs
Heaviest 20%	17	11	187
Next 20%	17	6	103
Third 20%	17	5	85
Next 20%	17	3	51
Lightest 20%	17	1	17
Totals*	85	5.2 avg.	443

*Reach of entire sample, 85; frequency of entire sample, 5.2; gross rating points, 443.

FIGURE 5-5.   Frequency Distribution for Program X

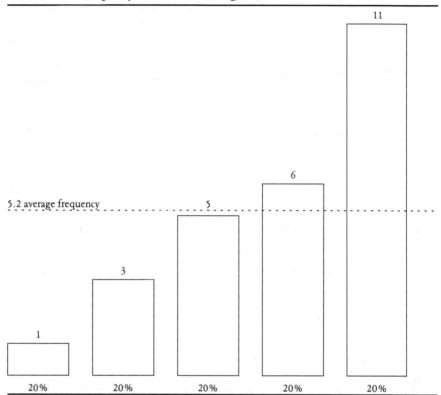

Note: The average number of times each group tuned in to Program X is shown at the top of each column.

Figure 5–5 dramatizes the skew by showing the frequency distribution in graphic form. While Program X had a 5.2 average frequency in Figure 5–5, some segments were receiving more frequency than others. The average frequency of 5.2 does not indicate the disparity. The planner may be deceived by the average frequency level of Program X, thinking that every home in the sample tuned to the program 5.2 times during a four-week period. The illustration shows otherwise. Frequency distributions with a large skew are called *unbalanced*.

Frequency distributions can be arranged according to quintiles, but they can also be arranged according to single increments of exposure, giving the planner a more detailed picture of exposure. Table 5–6 shows a frequency distribution of exposure for all media in a given plan. Subtracting the number reached from the universe size shows that 8,227,000 of the universe of 29,356,000 did not see any of the vehicles used. Some 3,125,000 were exposed only once out of the twelve opportunities for exposure, and 2,269,000 were exposed to any two out of the twelve exposures. The number exposed at any frequency is unduplicated, meaning that these people are counted only once. A person receiving twelve exposures would not be counted at any other frequency level.

Frequency distributions therefore provide planners with a method of determin-

TABLE 5-6. Frequency Distribution of a Media Plan

		Frequency of Exposure	Number Exposed (thousands)
		0	8,227
		1	3,125
		2	2,269
		3	3,632
Reach	71.97	4	5,235
Frequency	4.01	5	2,474
Gross Impressions	84,749	6	1,201
Number Reached	21,129	7	1,462
Universe	29,356	8	771
		9	622
		10	135
		11	104
		12	98
			21,129 = 71.97%

ing the pattern of repetition that the plan provides. Alternative plans may provide more or fewer repetition patterns. More important, however, is that the distribution will show whether repetition is spread widely, or only among a very few prospects.

The example in Table 5–7 shows how a frequency distribution can help a media planner decide among alternative plans. Plan A has a 4.0 frequency and Plan B, a 3.6. If frequency is important, then Plan A would seem to be the better plan.

Upon studying a frequency distribution such as the one in Table 5–7, however,

TABLE 5-7. Four-Week Reaches and Frequencies of Two Media Plans

Frequency of Exposure	Plan A	Plan B
1	24%	20%
2	16	15
3	9	12
4–5	6	13
6–8	5	10
9–12	5	4
13 +	5	1
Average Frequency	4.0	3.6
Total Reach	70	75
Reach at 3 + Frequency	30	40

TABLE 5-8. Comparison of Frequencies for Two Different Kinds of Programs

	Daytime Soap Opera (broadcast twenty times a month)	Nighttime Drama (broadcast once a week)
Total Audience Rating per Telecast	9.7*	19.4
Four-Week Reach	25.4	40.0
Frequency	7.6	1.9
	$\dfrac{9.7 \times 20^*}{25.4} = 7.6$	$\dfrac{19.4 \times 4}{40.0} = 1.9$

*The 9.7 rating is the average rating for a program broadcast 5 times each week (from Monday to Friday) and 4 weeks a month, or 20 telecasts.

FIGURE 5-6. Difference between Roadblock and Scatter to Build Reach *

Reach %	114	111	104	104	101	101

```
90—              ROADBLOCK                                    86      88
                                                    83
80—                              79                          85      87
                                                    80
70—
                         69            76          ↑
60—
                               62              SCATTER
50—          50
                                
40—          44

30—

20—
        Frequency:
10—     Roadblock      1.0      1.5      2.0      2.5      3.0      3.5
        Scatter        1.2      1.7      2.1      2.6      3.0      3.5
```

GRPs	50	100	150	200	250	300

Source: Nielsen Media Research (Prime time, Nov.–Dec. 1977). Reprinted by permission.
*Roadblock indexed to scatter.

the planner learns something that could change the decision: Plan A delivers more audience members at exposure levels 1 and 2. But for exposures 3–8, Plan B is superior. Plan B reaches more persons than does Plan A at the 3 or higher exposure level. If the advertising effort requires that people receive high levels of exposures (higher levels of frequency), then Plan B is the obvious choice. But only a frequency distribution made it possible for the planner to see why B was better than A.

The Relationship of Reach to Frequency

It is necessary to understand that reach and frequency occur at the same time, but at different rates and in an inverse relationship. Within a given number of gross rating points, as one goes up, the other goes down. Let us first look at the mathematics to understand how these companion terms relate to each other:

$$Reach \times Frequency = Gross \ Rating \ Points$$

An advertising schedule composed of a 50 reach with a 2.0 frequency yields 100 GRPs. If these same 100 GRPs were obtained in a different mixture of media, the reach might increase, but the frequency would decline. Conversely, a 100 GRP schedule in still other media mixtures might produce higher frequency, but less reach.

Seymour Banks, formerly vice president of Leo Burnett Company, explained the dynamics of reach and frequency relative to rating size and number of telecasts, as follows:

Reach is not directly proportional to either ratings or the number of telecasts. Rather, as ratings increase or as the number of telecasts used increases, reach also rises but at a decreasing rate. This is more easily understood when we consider that the companion of reach is frequency. And when the rating or the number of telecasts increases, some of this increase goes towards boosting reach, while some of it contributes toward an increase in frequency.[1]

Up to a certain point, it is relatively easy to build reach. By selecting television programs of a different nature in which to place commercials, it is possible to reach different kinds of people. But there is a point of diminishing returns, where each attempt to build more reach by selecting more and different kinds of programs results in reaching the same persons over and over again, with an increase in frequency rather than in reach. Some homes may never tune in their television sets over an entire month, so they are impossible to reach with TV in that month. Reach will increase as ratings and number of telecasts increase, but it will begin to decline in rate (not total) over time.

The point of diminishing returns mentioned in the previous paragraph occurs at about 70 percent and varies somewhat because some target audiences are easier or more difficult to reach. Then frequency begins to rise much faster than reach as additional media vehicles are added to the schedule. The problem can be seen in the following illustration:

Suppose that a media planner has devised a plan requiring the attainment of an 80 percent reach level. The planner selects a number of media vehicles, with a net reach of 75 percent. The question now facing the planner is how to reach the remaining 5 percent. When another vehicle is added to the list, reach may go up perhaps 1 percent, while frequency may go up a great deal. So it may take a large number of additional vehicles to reach the total of 80 percent. Meanwhile, as vehicles are added, frequency rises very fast because every new vehicle adds only a miniscule amount to reach and a large amount to frequency.

To summarize: reach and frequency are inversely related. As reach rises quickly, frequency tends to be low. Conversely, as frequency rises quickly, reach tends to be low.

Programs That Develop Reach or Frequency

Programs that develop reach are those whose contents tend to change during a given telecast or from week to week. As the contents change, so do audience types. When movies are broadcast, with a drama one week and a comedy the next, two different audiences are likely to develop (with some overlap, of course). Movies, therefore, tend to develop more reach than frequency. But a soap opera broadcast five days a week, or twenty times a month, will tend to draw a relatively smaller audience but one with greater frequency of viewing. An increase in the number of messages delivered also increases the potential for higher frequency.

---

1. Banks, Seymour, "How to Estimate Reach and Frequency," Leo Burnett Company, 1960, p.5.

Table 5–8 indicates that the drama had a much larger reach than did the soap opera, but the soap opera had a much larger frequency than did the drama. Part of the reason for the larger frequency was the frequency of telecasts. The more often a program is broadcast, the more likely it is that it will have a higher frequency.

Roadblock versus Scatter Plan

Planning media to build reach can be accomplished in the ways just discussed, but there are two other ways: (a) purchasing commercials on all three networks during the same half hour, called a *roadblock*, or (b) buying a *scatter plan* that places commercials within a number of different program types and time periods, thus bringing in new audience members. Figure 5–6 (p. 83) shows the differences. The chart shows that when the number of GRPs is low, the roadblock produces more reach. When the number of GRPs is high, either technique will produce about the same reach.

Chapter 6 will discuss how to use reach and frequency in planning.

QUESTIONS FOR DISCUSSION

1. If a planner wanted to build reach quickly using magazines alone, which of the three methods of building reach should be used?
2. Which kinds of magazines tend to develop large reach, and which develop large frequency?
3. Why can't one add the ratings for each week in a four-week period to find that program's four-week reach?
4. Which kinds of television programs tend to develop more reach than frequency?
5. Which kinds of television programs tend to develop more frequency than reach?
6. Why is it likely that a television program with a high initial rating (in Week 1) will probably also have a high four-week reach?
7. Why is *unbalanced frequency* possibly a poor media strategy?
8. Briefly explain: Is a rating for one telecast of a television program equivalent to a one-telecast reach?
9. If a television program were measured for fifty-two weeks (consecutively) what would the shape of the reach curve for that program probably look like?
10. Briefly explain: Of what value is a frequency distribution analysis of a television program?

SELECTED READINGS

Aaker, David A., and Brown, Phillip K., "Evaluating Vehicle Source Effects," *Journal of Advertising Research*, August 1972, pp. 11–16.

Agostini, J. M., "How to Estimate Unduplicated Audiences," *Journal of Advertising Research*, March 1961, pp. 11–14.

Barz, Edward, "A Fresh Look at Cumulative Audiences," *Advertising Research Foundation, 15th Conference Proceedings*, 1969, pp. 8–12.

Bass, K. M., Pessemier, E. A., and Tigert, D. J., "A Taxonomy of Magazine Readership Applied to Problems in Marketing Strategy and Media Selection,'' *Journal of Business,* July 1969, pp. 337–63.

Cannon, Hugh M., ''Reach and Frequency Estimates for Specialized Markets,'' *Journal of Advertising Research*, June/July 1983, pp. 45, 53.

Cole, Don, ''Hidden Reach,'' *Marketing and Media Decisions*, June 1986, p. 92.

Ephron, Erwin, ''Are the People You Want Watching?'' *Media/Scope,* October 1967, p. 46.

Forman, Stan, ''A Theory of Audience Accumulation,'' *Journal of Advertising Research*, February 1976, pp. 21–25.

Friedman, Lawrence, ''Calculating TV Reach and Frequency,'' *Journal of Advertising Research*, August 1971, pp. 21–26.

Headen, R. S., Klompmaker, J. E., and Teel, J. E., ''Increasing the Informational Content of Reach and Frequency Estimates,'' *Journal of Advertising,* January 1976, pp. 18–21.

Joyce, Timothy, *A Better Way to Measure Magazine Audiences*, Axiom Marketing Research Bureau, Inc., 1973.

Kaatz, Ronald B., ''Improving Agostini's Formula for Net Audiences,'' *Journal of Advertising Research*, September 1963, pp. 43–44.

Kamin, Howard, ''Advertising Reach and Frequency,'' *Journal of Advertising Research*, February 1978, pp. 21–25.

Keshin, Mort, ''Ins and Outs of TV Audience Cume,'' *Media/Scope,* May 1968, p.11.

Mayer, Martin, ''A Writer Looks at TV Ratings,'' *Journal of Advertising Research*, October 1972, pp. 3–10.

Media/Scope, ''Cox's Case for Cume,'' September 1968, pp. 99–140.

Mills, Martin, ''How to Estimate Network TV Audiences,'' *Media/Scope*, March 1966, pp. 90–93.

Lucas, Darrell B., ''Can Total Magazine Audience Be Ignored?'' *Media/Scope*, November 1964, pp. 64–72.

Marketmath, Inc., ''Advertising Reach and Frequency in Magazines,'' *Reader's Digest*, 1967.

Papazian, Edward, ''The Sixth Quintile,'' *Media Decisions*, September 1973, pp. 12–16.

Sprague, Jeremy D., ''Estimating Newspaper Turnover Rates,'' *Journal of Advertising Research*, June/July 1983, pp. 9–14.

Towers, Irwin M., Goodman, Leo A., and Zeisel, Hans, ''What Could Nonexposure Tell the TV Advertiser?'' *Journal of Marketing,* July 1963, pp. 52–56.

Twyman, W. A., ''A Technique for Measuring Program vs. Commercial Audiences—New Findings from British Television,'' *Advertising Research Foundation, 15th Annual Conference Proceedings, 1969, pp. 32–38.*

6

Effective Frequency and Reach

One of the most significant changes in media planning in recent years is the development of the concepts of *effective frequency and reach*. These concepts help planners understand a number of important facts that affect media planning such as which of two plans is better, or how much repetition is needed to achieve communication objectives. Strategically, these concepts are also attempts by planners to go beyond and improve regular reach and frequency data (as described in Chapter 5).

This chapter explains in detail what effective frequency and reach are, how they are used, some continuing problems with both the theory and practice, and a discussion of the role that both may play in the future.

The Underlying Need for Effective Frequency

For many years advertising practitioners have been trying to answer some important questions about advertising repetition, questions, such as the following, whose answers are all related to the effective frequency concept.

1. How much advertising is enough?
2. How many times must an advertising message be repeated for it to effectively communicate?
3. How much reach and frequency are ideal for a media plan?
4. How can planners improve the art of media planning?

Most of the research on these questions was directed toward answering the second question.

The Essence of Effective Frequency

Effective frequency may be defined as the amount of frequency (or repetition) necessary for advertisements to be effective in communicating. The underlying assumption, of course, is that average frequency used in most media plans is *not* effective. Therefore, effective frequency represents a great improvement over ordinary reach and frequency numbers used in traditionally created media plans.

The problem with ordinary reach and frequency is that they are not directly related to the effects that media plans may produce. They do not help a planner determine the adequacy of alternative plans. An ordinary reach number simply represents opportunities for audiences to see advertisements. There is no guarantee that those who are reached actually see any of the ads because exposure measurements used to compare media do not cover exposure to ads. Even if audiences see ads in a vehicle, there is no way to know whether the ads were effective or not simply by noting the reach of a media plan. Ordinary frequency generated by a plan is an average number of target audiences exposed to the media vehicles selected. Average frequency, too, is not related to the plan's effectiveness.

But planners who use effective frequency attempt to correct both situations by estimating the number of repetitions that are needed to attain communication goals such as achieving brand awareness, attitude changes, brand switching, and recall of messages, to name a few.

If, for example, someone sets a communication goal of building 70 percent brand awareness, a media planner should ask, how much repetition will help accomplish the task? Through test marketing, or studying responses to advertising done in the past, an estimate may be made of the vehicle frequency level needed. One unusual aspect of making an effective frequency decision is that it represents a technique of media planning that is different from those used in the past.

In the first place, building brand awareness is usually thought to be a communication goal—not a media goal. So by using effective frequency, planners are enlarging the scope of their work, combining media and creative activities. That combination in itself is a relatively new idea in media planning.

Second, there often is no data by which to determine objectively how much repetition is necessary to accomplish the task. Therefore the answer to the planner's question mentioned earlier may have to be based on either experience, or specialized research. If experience is used as a basis for the answer, then it may be rather subjective, because it is difficult to parse out a media vehicle's contribution to building brand awareness.

If research is used to find the answer to the awareness problem, then it will take both time and money, and the end result may not be conclusive, because it is difficult to prove conclusively.

The key point to be made is that it is not easy to prove the relationship between effective frequency and a 70 percent goal of brand awareness; the relationship is not an obvious one.

FIGURE 6-1: S-Shaped Response Curve

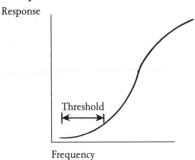

Response Curves and Effective Frequency

An important point in understanding the meaning of effective frequency is that the number at which point frequency is called "effective" is based on ideas of how much repetition is needed to communicate with consumers. This number has been found or estimated by observing what has happened at varying repetitive levels to achieve communication goals in the past. The results, plotted on a graph, have been called "response functions" or "response curves."

A response function is a measurement of advertising effect (as is a response curve). Over a period of many years, practitioners have hypothesized about how advertising works. Most have felt that advertising does not work immediately. According to Herbert Krugman, author of the "three hit theory," the first time an advertisement is perceived may result in audiences raising questions about the brand such as, "What is it?" After audiences have perceived the same ad a second time, they may ask, "What of it?" The second exposure, then, is where consumers react to the commercial by "personal responses ane elevations—the 'sale' so to speak—occurs," according to Krugman. The third exposure is a reminder of the other two, and is the beginning of a time where consumers pay little or no attention. Krugman hypothesized that when audiences are in the market to buy a product, they may return to that second repetition. Therefore, effective frequency begins after the second repetition, but only when a consumer is ready to buy a given product.

Many other practitioners have hypothesized that audiences begin to respond to advertising at about the third repetition. Beginning with the third repetition, the number of responses begin to grow with each additional repetition. In fact, response rises, but at a declining rate. If this hypothesis is plotted on a graph it will have an "S shape." (See Figure 6-1.) The first two repetitions are a "threshold" which audiences have to pass before advertisements become effective.

Most researchers of advertising responses curve, however, have not found the S-shaped curve to occur very often. In fact, a different kind of curve, often called a "convex-shaped" or "convex" curve, has been found more often. Nevertheless, many media planners, who have adopted the effective frequency concept, believe that a convex curve represents a graphical picture of how repetition works in advertising. (See Figure 6-2.)

FIGURE 6-2: Convex Response Curve

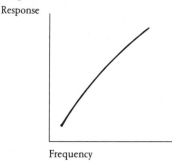

Effective Frequency Numbers

Effective frequency is expressed as a number. This number may vary from one repetition to as many as ten or more. Some planners, at first, thought the optimum effective frequency number was from three repetitions on. This was called the "three-plus" concept. Later, however, there was much agreement that the optimum effective frequency number could be as low as one or as many as nine (or more), or that the number could even be a range, such as a frequency level from two to seven. To date, this question has not been resolved, and more research on response functions may be needed to settle the argument.

What Is Effective Reach?

Effective reach is the second part of the concept. It represents the percent of a vehicle's audience reached at each effective frequency increment. If the effective frequency is believed to be from two to seven repetitions, then the reach is the sum of individual reach percentages for each frequency level. This can best be seen by the example in Table 6-1.

This table shows that the effective reach number is dependent on effective frequency numbers. In this example, because effective frequency is defined as being from a three to a six frequency, then effective reach is found in the sum of percent-

TABLE 6-1.   How Effective Reach Is Calculated*

Frequency, or Number of Impressions	Percent Reached at Each Frequency Level		Percent Reached at Least One or More Times
1	19.4		67.2
2	13.9		47.8
3	10.4 ⎫		33.9
4	7.8 ⎬		23.6
5	5.8 ⎭	28.1%**	15.8
6	4.1		10.5

*A frequency distribution for a reach of 67.2 and a frequency of 3.1.
**If effective frequency is from 3 to 6 repetitions, then effective reach is sum of all percentages reached from 3 to 6 or, in the example, 28.1%.

ages in the second column for frequencies 3, 4, 5, and 6, or 28.1 percent. Both effective frequency and reach are a necessary part of the same concept. They are not independent of each other.

A Brief History of Effective Frequency

Effective frequency, as an idea, existed prior to being given that name. In 1957, Brown, Lessler, and Weilbacher, in their book *Advertising Media,* wrote:

> It should be pointed out that there exists for every brand or product, a theoretical number of impressions required to convert each individual prospect into a purchaser.[1]

The authors gave an example of what their version of effective frequency was when they wrote:

> In order to maintain cigarette brand loyalty, it is necessary for the average smoker to receive sixteen television commercial messages for his usual brand, if the competitive copy claims are all roughly equivalent.

> And even though the notion of an average number of impressions required for action may be abstract, it does indicate the direction in which measurement must develop.[2]

This kind of measurement did not exist in 1957, but researchers ran many different kinds of experiments to learn if there was an optimum amount of repetition that could be called "effective."

Two British researchers, S. Broadbent and S. Segnit, contributed to the development of effective frequency when they won a prize for a paper entitled, "Response Functions in Media Planning," as part of the 1967 Thomson Medals and Awards in London. They devised a technique for evaluating media plans by using response function data. They offered ideas on how alternative media plans might be compared on an effective frequency basis, even if they did not use the terms effective frequency. They also hypothesized about the nature of response curves.

In the United States, the person who first started to publicize the need for effectiveness measures in media planning was Alvin Achenbaum, who was then director of corporate planning and marketing services at J. Walter Thompson, New York. Achenbaum did not advocate the use of effective frequency as we know it now, but recommended the use of effective rating points (ERPs). ERPs were a combination of effective frequency and reach as a replacement for gross rating points (GRPs).

Probably the greatest impetus to establishing the concept in this country was the publication, in 1979, of *Effective Frequency: The Relationship between Frequency*

---

1. Brown, Lyndon O., Lessler, Richard S., and Weilbacher, William M., *Advertising Media,* New York: The Ronald Press, 1957, p. 343.
2. Ibid.

and Advertising Awareness by Michael J. Naples.[3] This book, published by the Association of National Advertisers, became required reading for almost every planner in this country. After 1979, the concept spread throughout advertising agency media departments in the United States and is now used widely. Much of the background research that had been done on the concept was summarized in Naples's book. What follows is a brief summary of material in Naples's book covering significant research on the effective frequency concept.

Research That Underlies the Effective Frequency Concept

General Findings

The studies cited by Naples were performed by different persons for different reasons, but, in essence, they concluded that it takes at least two to three repeated exposures for a message to be learned. Some studies, like that done by Robert C. Grass for DuPont, found that some messages were effective from the third to the eighth exposure per month. Krugman's ''three hit'' theory was also discussed in these research projects. Most of the studies found that the effect of frequency increases, but at a declining rate. In essence, their conclusions correspond to the convex response curve. One of the studies, that done by Ogilvy & Mather, found that at the one frequency level, advertising effectiveness during different dayparts was relatively the same, but a higher frequency level at night was more effective than it was during other dayparts. Product category and brands also made a difference in frequency effects. Two researchers (Appel and Jacobovits) found that too much frequency had negative effects, although they did not indicate how much repetition brought these effects about.

The McDonald Study

The most significant study reported by Naples in terms of motivating media planners to adopt the concept was done by Colin McDonald in 1971.[4] The study, commissioned by the London office of J. Walter Thompson, was analyzed and reported by Colin McDonald of the British Market Research Bureau. A report on that study appeared in Naples's 1979 book. The subsequent widespread publicity helped it become one of the leading pieces of research that underlie the effective frequency concept.

The methodology used in this study involved having a panel of consumers in Great Britain keep two kinds of records: the number of television, magazine, and newspapers that they were exposed to each day for thirteen weeks, and the number

---

3. Naples, Michael J., *Effective Frequency*, New York: Association of National Advertisers, Inc., 1979.

4. McDonald, Colin, ''What Is the Short-Term Effect of Advertising?'' in *Effective Frequency*, pp. 83–104.

TABLE 6–2. Relationship of Frequency Levels and Purchasing the Same Brand Again

	Media Exposure (various number of repetitions)			
	0	1	2	3
Percent of brand's purchases repeated at the next purchase	54.4	58.4	62.6	63.1
Percent of gain		+ 4.0	+ 4.3	+ .04

of brands (in nine product categories) they had purchased in the same time period. The specific time unit that was analyzed, the purchasing cycle for nine brand categories, ranged from an average of $1^1/_2$ to $2^1/_2$ weeks. The media exposures that McDonald measured were really vehicle exposures or opportunities to see (OTS) and not exposures to advertisements. In Naples's book, McDonald used terms that seemed to indicate that advertising exposure was being measured, but subsequent explanations made it clear that it was really OTS.

McDonald counted the panel's OTS for every brand in each purchase interval, and compared this with purchasing behavior, noting whether successive purchases at the beginning and end of each interval were of the same brand or a different brand.

On one hand, Jeremy Elliott, senior associate director of J. Walter Thompson, London, commenting on McDonald's study, wrote that "the first OTS increased retention of advertising and that a second OTS increased it as much again."[5] But the third and any additional OTS in the purchase interval had little effect. (See Table 6–2.)

On the other hand, Elliott noted that OTS also had a different effect, the second OTS was about twice as effective as the first in bringing about brand switching. Elliott noted that brands that had two or more OTS in a purchasing interval were making gains at the expense of brands that had only one OTS. He concluded that "it takes greater stimulation to overcome inertia and change behavior than it does to maintain it."[6] Nevertheless, the third OTS still had no incremental value. (See Table 6–3.)

McDonald's study was important because it showed that it took at least two OTS to bring about brand switching, and that media plans ought to have at least as many to make frequency effective. Of course, the study was also well done, and that contributed further to its acceptance. Elliott also pointed out that J. Walter Thompson

TABLE 6–3. Relationship of Frequency Levels and Purchasing of Different Brands

	Media Exposure (various number of repetitions)			
	0	1	2	3
Percent of competitive purchases in which consumers switched to a different brand at the next purchase	17.2	20.91	27.4	27.9
Percent of gain		+ 3.7	+ 6.5	+ 0.5

5. Elliott, Jeremy, "How Advertising Frequency Affects Advertising Effectiveness: Indications of Change," in *ADMAP*, October 1985, pp. 512–515.

6. Ibid., p. 511.

has undertaken another study, similar to McDonald's, to determine which levels of frequency are effective. The results of this study concluded that effective frequency should be defined as four-plus coverage.[7]

Naples's Conclusions about Effective Frequency Studies

After presenting many research studies that supported the idea of effective frequency, Naples arrived at some conclusions about the implications for media planners. The following is a summary of each of his conclusions:

1. One exposure of an advertisement to a target consumer group (within a purchase cycle) has little or no effect.
2. Because one exposure is usually ineffective, the main thrust of media planning should be on emphasizing frequency rather than reach.
3. Most of the research studies suggested that two exposures within a purchase cycle is an effective threshold level.
4. Three exposures within a purchase cycle, however, is felt to be optimal.
5. After three exposures within a purchasing cycle, advertising becomes more effective as frequency is increased, but at a decreasing rate. If this were drawn on a graph, it would appear as a convex curve rising from a zero point.
6. Wear-out of an advertising campaign is not caused by too much frequency *per se*. It is caused by copy and content problems.
7. Generally, small and less well-known brands will benefit most by increased frequency. Larger and well-known brands may or may not be helped by increasing frequency "depending on how close they are to advertising saturation levels."
8. Different dayparts on television are affected by different frequency levels. A similar idea applies to thin versus thick magazines, with the thinner ones having better response effects than the thicker ones.
9. Frequency responses are affected by the amount of money an advertiser spends as a percentage of the product category total. Those brands with the greatest proportion of exposures within their categories should also gain great effect when frequency is increased.
10. The responses due to increased frequency are not affected by different media. What is true for one medium is true for others.
11. Each brand may require a different level of frequency of exposure. One cannot generalize from a given brand's experiences to some other brand. Specialized research is required to find the unique frequency level for a brand.

---

7. Cullen, Phil, and Johnson, Hugh, "Relating Product Purchasing and TV Viewing," in *Journal of Advertising Research,* December 1986–January 1987, pp. 9–19.

12. Two brands spending the same amount of money for advertising may
have different responses to their frequencies.[8]

Problems with the Effective Frequency Concept

When McDonald's study was published in Naples's book it was widely accepted
among media planners. But as time went on, a number of questions began to be
asked, not only of McDonald's study, but of other aspects of effective frequency
research. These problems are summarized and discussed in the following paragraphs.

The Need for Product Category Differentiation

One of the major problems of effective frequency research was that most of it did
not show much difference between frequency effects for various product categories.
This lack of differentiation tended to mislead planners into thinking that effective
frequency is the same for all product categories. Now, a growing number of planners have said "that idea cannot be correct." There *should* be differences between
various product category frequency levels.

Unfortunately, no measurements exist to show just which levels are needed for
different kinds of products. Until this problem is resolved, media planners will have
to make subjective decisions about how much frequency is necessary. There is, however, some speculation that high-involvement products may need less frequency
and low-involvement products may need more. The same idea may apply to frequency levels between interesting and noninteresting products. The role of frequency, then, may be to help break through the perceptual inertia of consumers for
certain kinds of products.

Is There a Threshold?

Another problem with the concept is whether or not a "threshold" always exists
before consumers begin to respond to advertising messages. Most of the research
on the subject suggested that there were relatively few responses to the first few
impressions of an advertising campaign. Advertising began to work with the second or third impression. Those who believed in the three-plus frequency concept
felt that advertising began to be effective with the third impression. But many
direct marketing practitioners objected, noting that, in their business, the first
impressions often drew tremendous responses. Gus Priemer, director of advertising service and media at S. C. Johnson, also noted that in his experience of new
product introductions, the first impression had been able to generate noteworthy
responses.

---

8. Naples, Michael, *Effective Frequency: The Relationship between Frequency and Advertising Effectiveness,* New York: Association of National Advertisers, 1979, pp. 63–82.

Members who attended a "Symposium on Effective Frequency" held in April, 1986, at Northwestern University also questioned whether a threshold was realistic. The consensus at that meeting was that most response curves are convex, not S-shaped. The S-shaped curve was the one that indicated there was a threshold. Nevertheless, many planners still believe in a threshold.

The Relationship between Good Advertising and Effective Frequency

There have been a great many questions asked about whether effective frequency could be affected by the quality of advertising messages. Why, for example, shouldn't the ad message play a more important role in determining how much frequency is effective? Dull, uninteresting copy may require a great deal more frequency than scintillating creative messages. But most of the research did not address that question. In fact, some planners believe that the role of media frequency in bringing about consumer responses has been grossly overstated.

Does Advertising Wear Out When There Is Too Much Frequency?

Some of the research cited by Naples showed that there were negative responses that occurred after using too much repetition. Some consumers may even forget an advertising message because of high levels of frequency. The research of Valentine Appel and L. Jacobovits (also reported in Naples's book), suggested that. (The shape of a wear-out curve was considered to be like an inverted U.) But there seems to be no wide-ranging concern about this potential problem among media planners.

In 1968, Robert C. Grass of DuPont, through his research, found that there were satiation effects on attention and learning levels as a result of increased advertising frequency.[9] After two or three exposures, attention and learning declined. Nonetheless, Grass also found, through a different piece of research, that favorable attitudes toward a company developed because of increased advertising frequency, and there were no diminishing returns.

The main problem, then, is when, and under what circumstances, does frequency affect wear-out? It should be remembered that those who use the three-plus concept assume that there is no wear-out, at least no wear-out caused by too much repetition. But some persons in the industry feel that there may be a range of wear-out, and after the range has been passed, wear-out begins. Achenbaum said that the range may be from three to ten, or perhaps, from two to seven, but he could not say with assurance (based on existing research) where the optimal range was.

Thus the problem exists. Planners will simply have to use judgment in answering this question until research provides a more definitive answer.

---

9. Grass, Robert C., and Wallace, Wallace H., "Satiation Effects of TV Commercials," in *Journal of Advertising Research,* September 1969, pp. 3–8.

TABLE 6–4. Differences between Homes Tuned-in, Viewing, Exposed, and Recalling Commercial Content in St. Louis and Chicago

	St. Louis Index	Chicago Index
Homes tuned in to program	100	100
Homemakers viewing program	59	50
Viewers possibly exposed to commercial	36	38
Viewers recalling content of commercial	16	20

Source: Gomer, Frank G., and Vedder, Blair B., "Another Look Beyond the TV Ratings," A. N. A. Television Advertising Workshop, New York, June 17, 1964.

How Much Vehicle Exposure Equals Advertising Exposure?

One of the difficult things to know about effective frequency is how to translate vehicle exposures into advertising exposures. Much research on effective frequency has been based on advertising exposure. But media planners still use vehicle exposure as a basis for planning. Certainly, there is no one-to-one relationship between the two. The number of advertising exposures is assumed to be less than vehicle exposures simply because every audience member does not look at every advertisement. During a television program broadcast, people do many other things than watch commercials. Perhaps the best known research studies on the differences between vehicle and advertising exposure were done by the Foote, Cone & Belding and Needham, Louis & Brorby agencies in 1962 and 1963.

As Table 6–4 shows, the number possibly exposed is considerably fewer than the number who viewed the program, and the recall level is even less than that, for both Chicago and St. Louis. If the "possibly exposed" group is considered the equivalent of "exposed" (and there is no reason to disagree with that assumption), then there is strong evidence that vehicle and audience frequency are very different.

The effective frequency concept for media planners relates most importantly to this point: How much media vehicle frequency is necessary to achieve the advertising exposure frequencies found in most of the research studies? Radio and television ratings and magazine audience exposures represent only exposures to vehicles. To go beyond vehicle frequency, we need research that either relates vehicle frequency to advertising frequency, or directly shows the effects of vehicle exposure frequency to a given response. Some research studies have tried to do the latter, but more research is obviously needed.

Some research, such as McDonald's, was devised to get around this problem by measuring opportunities to see correlated against purchasing and brand switching. But it is doubtful that media planners can assume that McDonald's findings are directly translatable to a media plan based on vehicle reach and frequency. Members who attended the 1986 Effective Frequency Symposium recommended that media planners use rules of thumb in converting vehicle exposure to advertising exposures. One might, for example, reduce television vehicle exposures to 35 percent of the total because various research studies done over the years have suggested that of those who were exposed to a television program, an average of 35 percent would see the commercials within the program.

Such generalized rules of thumb tend to make media planning less accurate than it is now, and their use is obviously going to raise more questions about the validity of effective frequency than are being raised now. Adjustments of vehicle exposure cannot be a simple mathematical computation because marketing creative, media, and sales promotion strategies are too different for each brand to make such generalizations.

Should Media Planning Be Based on Purchasing Cycles?

Historically, a considerable amount of media planning was based on a four-week period. Today, reach and frequency are typically expressed in terms of periods of advertising and for the total media plan. But one of Naples's recommendations about effective frequency is to use the purchasing cycle instead. McDonald's study found purchasing cycles to be important in analyzing his data. Therefore, purchasing cycles have been recommended by McDonald and others as well.[10]

If they are used in media planning, reach and frequency may have to be calculated for time periods as short as one or two days, such as the cycle for milk, or for as long as one year, for products such as tire chains and grass seed. This practice could be problematical because the time span between purchases for any individual may not match the span for all the people who are product category users. If, for example, a product has a purchase cycle of one month, one individual may buy that product at the first day of the month, and others at the last. The average user may buy somewhere in between. Therefore an advertiser, trying to use a purchase cycle in media planning, would have to advertise all during the month in order to maximize opportunities for consumers to see advertisements for a given brand. What then would be the advantage of using a purchase cycle?

At present, there have been relatively few attempts to plan reach and frequency on the basis of purchase cycles, although some attempts have been made experimenting with flighting patterns.

Where Effective Frequency Stands Now in Media Planning

Despite all the problems and questions that have been raised about effective frequency as a technique for media planning, it seems as if it is here to stay. Often it is used in its most simple form, the three-plus version. At other times, it is imaginatively used.

The consensus seems to be that even though there are problems with the concept, it is worth using. It is, potentially, very useful to planners. If it is used moderately, over time, as more research becomes available, the concept will be improved a great deal. As a result, media planning will also be improved. Therefore its use ought to be continued.

Case Study 6–1 shows one approach to using effective frequency. (See Chapter 9 on how to set effective frequency levels.)

---

10. McDonald, Colin, "Individual Respondent Analysis Made Better with Complete Single Source Records," in *Effective Frequency: State of the Art,* New York: Advertising Research Foundation, 1982, pp. 181–194.

CASE STUDY 6–1
Using the Effective Frequency Concept to
Determine the Impact of Alternative Media Plans*

The following is a practical example of how effective frequency might be used to judge the impact of three alternative media plans. Impact is defined as providing the largest number of responses to advertising at various frequency levels.

1. Reach, frequency, and target GRPs of three media plans:

	Monthly GRPs	Reach	Frequency
Daytime only plan	296	52	5.7
Nighttime only plan	142	71	2.0
Day + magazine plan	296	80	3.7

2. Subjective judgments are made about effectiveness of three media:

Daytime network TV	65 index of value
Nighttime network TV	100 index of value
Women's magazines	50 index of value

3. GRPs are multiplied by index of values:

Daytime plan $\quad\quad\quad\quad$ $296 \times .65 = 192$ net delivery
Nighttime plan $\quad\quad\quad$ $142 \times 1.00 = 142$ net delivery
Day $\quad$ (157 GRPs) $\quad$ $157 \times .65 = 102$ net delivery $\left.\vphantom{\begin{matrix}a\\b\end{matrix}}\right\}$ Total: 172
Magazine (139 GRPs) $\quad$ $139 \times .50 = 70$ net delivery

4. Gross reach and frequency are converted to net delivery:

Example: Daytime network TV

Gross Delivery			Net Delivery		
GRPs	Reach	Frequency	GRPs	Reach	Frequency
296	52	5.7	192	48	4.0

Effective frequency has been determined to be from 2 to 7 exposures. Therefore, a frequency distribution has been given an index of effective response for every frequency level. These indices are subjectively made here, but they could be objectively measured in test marketing situations.

5. Subjective judgments about indices of responses:

Frequency levels	Index of Response
From 1 to 3 exposures	50
From 4 to 7 exposures	100
From 8-plus exposures	100

A frequency distribution (from computer analysis) is now performed to show percentage of net delivery reach for each frequency level. These reaches are multiplied by the index of responses.

---

*Source: Fine, Jules, *Sex and Sanity in Media Planning,* A.N.A., March 21, 1979.

6. *Frequency distribution* × *Index of Responses:*

Example: Daytime network TV

Frequency Levels	Net Reach	×	Index of Responses	=	Net Impact
1 to 3 exp.	28.8%	×	50	=	14.4
4 to 7 exp.	11.8	×	100	=	11.8
8 + exp.	7.2	×	100	=	7.2
Totals	47.8%				33.4

7. *Now, all net impacts for three alternatives are calculated:*

Media Plan Alternative	Net Impact	Original Gross Reach	Frequency
Daytime plan	33	52	5.7
Nighttime plan	39	71	2.0
Day + magazine plan	39	80	3.7

8. *Results:*

1. The nighttime plan and the day plus magazine plan are equivalent in impact. This was not evident by studying reach and frequency alone.
2. The daytime plan is clearly the one with less impact potential.
3. The most critical points in these analyses were the subjective judgments of media values, and index of responses.

   These judgments can be improved by taking a consensus vote and averaging scores of a number of media experts within an organization. Or, they can be measured objectively through test marketing where variable weights can be determined.
4. Although this technique seems somewhat arbitrary, especially in the value judgments that have to be made, such judgments are usually made in media planning outside the confines of the data. In other words, data is collected on reach and frequency, cost-per-thousand, etc., but eventually someone has to make judgments about their values. This technique formalizes the judgment process.

QUESTIONS FOR DISCUSSION

1. Explain whether all advertising has a threshold that it must go through before it becomes effective.
2. Why did so many media planners adopt the ''three-plus concept'' in their everyday media planning?
3. Can too much frequency in advertising have negative consequences?
4. What are probably the most significant problems with the effective frequency concept?
5. Explain why effective frequency is felt to be superior to average frequency, normally used in past media planning.
6. Explain the meaning of a response curve. Which response curve is found most often in advertising research?

7. What was different about Cohn McDonald's research on effective frequency as compared with previous studies?
8. Joseph Ostrow recommended guidelines for using effective frequency in which three areas of marketing and advertising?
9. Explain how effective frequency might be used to compare two alternative media plans.
10. Explain how a media planner can convert "vehicle" reach and frequency data into advertisement reach and frequency data.

SELECTED READINGS

Achenbaum, Alvin, "Effective Exposure: The Subversion of a Useful Idea," *Journal of Media Planning,* Fall 1986, pp. 11–12.

Appel, Valentine, "On Advertising Wearout," *Journal of Advertising Research,* pp. 11–14.

Batra, Rajeev, and Ray, Michael L., "Situational Effects of Advertising Repetition: The Moderating Influence of Motivation, Ability, and Opportunity to Respond," *Journal of Consumer Research,* March 1986, pp. 432–45.

Behrmann, William V., "Putting Effective Frequency Strategies to Work in Media Planning," in *Effective Frequency: The State of the Art,* New York: Advertising Research Foundation, 1982, pp. 103–28.

Benz, William, "The Road to Better Use of Effective Frequency," *Journal of Media Planning,* Fall 1986, pp. 13–16.

Broadbent, S. R., and Segnit, S., "Response Functions in Media Planning," in *The Thomson Medals and Awards for Advertising Research,* London: 1967, pp. 35–86.

Brown, Lyndon O., Lessler, Richard S., and Weilbacher, William M., *Advertising Media.* New York: The Ronald Press, 1957, p. 343.

Caffryn, J. M., *Qualitative Aspects of Reader Data,* London: Institute of Practitioners in Advertising, 1964.

Cannon, Hugh and Goldring, Norman, "Another Look at Effective Frequency," *Journal of Media Planning,* Fall 1986, pp. 29–36.

Clunies–Ross, C. W., "The Practical and Theoretical Problems and Effects of Introducing Explicit Theories of Response Functions into Media Planning," in *Thomson Medals and Awards for Advertising Research,* London: 1967, pp. 125–30.

Douglas, Stephen A., "The Integrated Metered Data Base: Why Is It Needed?" *Journal of Media Planning,* Fall 1986.

Elliott, Jeremy, "How Advertising Frequency Affects Advertising Effectiveness: Indications of Change," *ADMAP,* October 1985, pp. 512–515.

Evanson, Donald, "Media Plans Frequently Don't Effectively Use Effective Reach," *Journal of Media Planning,* Fall 1986, pp. 43–46.

Jacobovits, L., *Semantic Satiation and Cognitive Dynamics,* a paper delivered to the American Psychological Association, September 1966.

King, Charles W., and Summers, John O., "Attitudes and Media Exposure," *Journal of Advertising Research,* February 1971, p. 26.

Knowlton, Archa, "Effective Frequency: Why Is It Important?" in *Effective Frequency: The State of the Art,* New York: Advertising Research Foundation, 1982, pp. 1–12.

Krugman, Herbert E., "The Measurement of Advertising Involvement," *Public Opinion Quarterly,* Winter 1966–67, pp. 583–96.

Krugman, Herbert E., "Next Steps—A Productive Approach to Measuring Effective Frequency," in *Effective Frequency: The State of the Art*, New York: Advertising Research Foundation, 1982, pp. 129–38.

Leckenby, John D., and Kishim Shizue, "How Media Directors View Reach and Frequency Estimation," *Journal of Advertising Research*, June/July 1982, pp. 64–69.

Lonning, Stephen, "Effective Frequency: A Planner's Perspective," in *Journal of Media Planning*, Fall 1986, pp. 47–50.

McDonald, Colin, *What Is the Short Term Effect of Advertising?*, Marketing Science Institute, 1971.

McDonald, Colin, "Individual Respondent Analysis Made Better with Complete Single Source Records," in *Effective Frequency: State of the Art*, New York: Advertising Research Foundation, 1982, pp. 181–94.

Naples, Michael J., *Effective Frequency*, New York: Association of National Advertisers, Inc., 1979.

Ostrow, Joseph W., "Setting Frequency Levels," in *Effective Frequency: The State of the Art*, New York: Advertising Research Foundation, 1982, pp. 89–102.

Papazian, Edward, "The Frequency Fracas," *Marketing and Media Decisions*, June 1986, pp. 85, 86.

Priemer, August, "New Alternatives to Effective Frequency in Media Planning," *Journal of Media Planning*, Fall 1986, pp. 25–28.

Rothman, L. J., "The Role of Response Functions: A Discussion and an Alterna-

tive," in *Thomson Medals and Awards for Advertising Research*, London: 1967, pp. 89–122.

Samuels, Gabe, "Why This Approach Will Produce Better Inputs than Awareness to GRP Models," in *Effective Frequency: The State of the Art*, New York: Advertising Research Foundation, 1982, pp. 155–66.

Schloss, Ira J., "How Important Is Effective Frequency to Advertisers and Media Planners?" in *Effective Frequency: The State of the Art*, New York: Advertising Research Foundation, 1982, pp. 13–20.

Schultz, Don E., and Block, Martin, "Empirical Estimation of Advertising Response Functions," *Journal of Media Planning*, Fall 1986, pp. 17–24.

Sissors, Jack Z., "Advice to Media Planners on How to Use Effective Frequency," *Journal of Media Planning*, Fall 1986, pp. 3–9.

Spaeth, James, "An Industry Data and Information Bank: How to Make It Work," in *Effective Frequency: The State of the Art*, New York: Advertising Research Foundation, 1982, pp. 139–54.

Steiner, Robert L., "Point of View: The Paradox of Increasing Returns to Advertising," *Journal of Advertising Research*, February/March 1987, pp. 45–52.

Time, Inc., and Seagram, Joseph E. & Sons, Inc., *A Study of the Effectiveness of Advertising Frequency in Magazines*, 1982.

7
Marketing Strategy and Media Planning

There are many ways to start the media planning process, but the best way is by analyzing the situation of a brand in the marketplace. The reason for making such an analysis is to learn how successful a brand has been against its competition, with the objectives of finding "opportunity" areas to exploit or "problem" areas to correct. Ultimately, the findings of a situation analysis should lead to the establishment of marketing objectives and strategies, which in turn lead to the establishment of media objectives and strategies. Although the responsibility for making a marketing situation analysis usually does not rest with a media planner, someone from the agency media department, such as a media researcher, may be involved to some extent in the research activities. Media planners often are involved in the marketing situation analysis, particularly the examination of the consumer, the competitive weight, and geographic and seasonal sales analysis.

What a Media Planner Needs to Know

To develop a successful media plan the planner must know as much as possible about the marketing background of the brand being advertised. This background includes product quality, product use, pricing, distribution, packaging, sales promotion, personal selling activities, public relations, and advertising. From a practical standpoint, planners may not need to know every detail, but they should know those pieces of information that contribute to the best planning. Those elements in a marketing situation analysis that most interest a planner are:

> **History of the market.** This deals with sales of all brands in the market, including the brand for which planning is to be done. The analysis includes geographic sales distribution, market size in dollars/units, market shares,

seasonal effects, and price effects. The goal is to find out where brands are now in terms of share of market and how they got there. An important item, for example, might be pricing history. What happened to prices for various brands over the years, and how did these price manipulations affect sales? Another concern might be an analysis of cost history and profit related to sales, both for the brand under consideration and for competitors' brands, if known.

Distribution channels. The objective here is to learn how a brand and its competitors distribute products. This includes the following information about each distribution channel: shelf-facings, inventories held, out-of-stock situations, methods of selling, display and advertising allowances, and how and why promotions are used. Problems of selling are sometimes caused by poor distribution, not advertising. Distribution information often affects media strategy because it may help the planner decide where to advertise.

The consumer of the product. This profile of users of the generic product type includes personal demographics such as age, sex, income, and occupation, as well as geographic location. Psychographics—life-styles and attitudes—should also be included. A consumer profile of those who buy a specific brand versus those who buy competing products is important. Buying habits should also be analyzed in terms of when products are purchased; in which kind of retail outlets; and which sizes, models, and colors are purchased most often. How and when consumers use these products also ought to be known. Finally, it would be helpful to know about the *buyer,* the *user,* and the *persons who motivate buyers/users.* All of this information helps the media planner select targets for media.

The product. A history of the product and how it was developed is included in the product section of the analysis. When and why product changes were made and the effects of such changes on each competitive brand could be important. Consumer perceptions of the values of various brands are also important background information for the media planner.

Advertising and media analysis. An analysis of media expenditures for competing brands would probably be the most important information that a media planner would like to know. This would include media classes used, names of individual vehicles, number of ads used, when advertising ran, and dollar and percentage allocation to each medium and market.

The Marketing Strategy Plan

Once the facts about a marketing situation have been gathered, the data then should be analyzed to learn where problems and opportunities lie. An *opportunity* may be defined as a marketing activity which, if adopted, may result in an advantage over the competitor. Such an opportunity might take place in a situation in which a manufacturer has improved a brand so that it is superior to competing brands, but this advantage may be known by only 10 percent of the potential consumers. If the manufacturer is able to communicate this advantage to 50 percent or more of potential consumers, increased sales may result.

Problem areas, on the other hand, are those that demand some action to correct the situation. A problem area might be a situation in which a brand does not have a competitive advantage or one in which a brand has been steadily losing its share of market for any number of reasons. Finding the causes for the decline is a first step toward changing the situation. Most situation analyses turn up more problem areas than opportunities, but the delineation of each problem area is a necessary preliminary step to marketing and media planning.

Marketing strategy planning consists of planning marketing actions that will solve the major problems and take advantage of the opportunities. In effect, a *marketing strategy and plan* is a blueprint for action geared to selling the product, with the ultimate goal of gaining an advantage over a competitor who, in a sense, is the enemy.

Perhaps the weakest part of many advertising campaigns is the lack of a sound selling strategy. Arthur Tatham, formerly chairman of the board of Tatham-Laird & Kudner advertising agency, once said, ''Brilliant copy and art will never make a weak selling strategy succeed. But . . . once there is a sound selling strategy, then good copy and art will multiply its effectiveness.'' Tatham's statement also applies to media selection and use. Without a sound selling strategy, media planning may represent wasted effort. Media planning does not exist as an activity unrelated to marketing; it is a service function of marketing and selling. The fact that media are often selected and used without being based on a sound selling strategy demonstrates poor logic and inefficient modes of operation. Selling strategy is the heart of a marketing strategy and plan.

In summary, the major goals in a marketing strategy and plan are as follows:

1. Setting objectives that will help solve existing problems and take advantage of opportunity and problem areas
2. Deciding how the product should be sold
3. Determining to whom the main selling effort should be directed
4. Determining what role various elements of the marketing mix should play in the sale of a brand
5. Determining what adjustments should be made in package shapes or sizes
6. Determining how much should be spent

Most often, the marketing plan is written by someone other than the media planner. Yet, even though the latter may not be directly involved in drawing up the plan, there are a number of reasons why the marketing strategy plan is a significant document to media planners.

The foremost reason is that the marketing plan serves as a unifying and organizing force for all activity within an agency on a given brand's marketing and advertising plans. This means that the market researchers, account executives, and creative people, as well as media planners, are all working from a single source of information. Thus, the plan serves to coordinate all efforts toward the same goals. Large advertising agencies often have so many persons working on so many different accounts that communication becomes difficult. The media planner, especially, needs to know that his or her decisions will be directed toward the same objectives as those of others on the agency team.

Once the plan has been written, it becomes easier to visualize the whole scheme of operations for a given brand. All proposed plans can be evaluated for their logic and completeness to avoid information gaps or contradictions. If a marketing plan exists only in someone's mind or in bits or scraps of memoranda, then errors are hard to locate because no one has an overview of the entire operation.

Perhaps the key to the success of a marketing plan is the degree to which all tactics are spelled out. Herbert Zeltner, marketing consultant, cautioned that many marketing plans are "either glossed over in the rush of hammering together a marketing program, or merely slapped together as a collection of ponderous cliches." He noted:

> To be truly useful, the market strategy statement should not merely reflect some happy generalities about an increase in volume or share of market for the coming fiscal period.

> But establishing the requirement that a specific percent volume increase is to be achieved—through the expenditure of a precise sensible sum of money—and that this increase can most realistically be expected through more aggressive development of certain stated territories or segments of the market . . . is the type of statement which gives a properly astute media planner the challenge he needs to create both a perspective and workable media recommendation.[1]

The media planner needs specific direction, explicitly stated, in order to begin decision making. The media plan grows directly out of the marketing strategy whenever it requires that advertising be used. The various segments of the strategy statement, however, are not all equally significant to the media planner. Foremost in importance are the marketing objectives, the basic selling idea, sources of business, overall sales strategy, and spending strategy. Each of these will be discussed in more detail on the following pages. Figure 7-1 shows an outline of a basic strategy statement.

Marketing Objectives

The marketing goals that the company and agency agree upon may, if achieved, result in the solution of a marketing problem. Marketing goals are measurable in most cases and provide a means of determining whether the strategy employed has been effective. For the media planner, the objectives will undoubtedly affect the

---

1. Zeltner, Herbert, "Marketing Strategy Statement," *Media/Scope,* August 1964, p. 10.

FIGURE 7-1. Outline for Basic Marketing Strategy Statement

Advertiser _____ Brand/Product _____

I. *Major Strategy*
This should be the briefest possible statement of the major one or two strategies you are going to recommend for the planning period, with just enough statement of the problem to explain the strategy.
If you can write this section in one or two sentences or paragraphs, do so. If it takes you more than a single-spaced page, it is probably too long.

II. *Basic Objectives*
A. Short Term (applies to next fiscal twelve months, unless otherwise stated, e.g., six months):
  1. Increase share of total market
  2. Arrest decline in share
  3. Develop added volume
  4. Increase total market
  5. Profit goal
  6. Reduce losses
  Translate objectives into approximate sales and/or profit goals.
B. Long Term (applies to any prescribed period beyond the next planning period):
  1. Increase share of total market
  2. Increase total market
  3. Increase profits
  4. Position goal, i.e., gain leadership
  5. Develop and establish a brand or corporate image
  6. Expand line of service or products
  Translate objectives into approximate sales and/or profit goals.

III. *The Basic Selling Idea*
A one- or two-sentence statement of the key selling idea. This is the base from which the creative strategy evolves.

IV. *Presentation of the Basic Selling Idea*
This is the creative strategy in its briefest form.

V. *Use or Uses for Which the Product Will Be Advertised*
A. Major
B. Minor

VI. *Sources of Business and Relative Importance of Each*
A. Consumer Sources—What are the characteristics of the people who are the best prospects?
  1. Regional factors
  2. City size
  3. County size
  4. Income groups
  5. Age of housewife
  6. Occupation of head of household
  7. Family size
  8. Seasonal
  9. Sex—men, women, children
  10. Who is principal purchaser?
B. Dealer Sources—What is relative importance of various types of outlets?
C. Competitive Sources—Important competitive brands or companies—national, regional, local

VII. *Overall Sales Strategy*
A. Relative importance of price
  1. To the consumer
  2. To the trade

Source: Reprinted by permission of the Leo Burnett Company, Inc.

(*continued*)

FIGURE 7-1.   (Continued)

   B. Relative importance of personal salesmanship
   C. Relative importance of dealers
   D. Relative importance of advertising
   E. Relative importance of promotion
   F. Relative importance of publicity

VIII. *Product Strategy*
   A. The need for product improvement—Analysis of product superiorities and weaknesses compared to competitive products
   B. The need for related products
   C. The need for adding new sizes or deleting unprofitable sizes
   D. The need for improving:
      1. Packaging
      2. Package design

IX. *Spending Strategy*
   A. Is there a need for higher or lower margins? What effect will this have on price, quality, quantity of the product?
   B. What is the proper amount to spend:
      1. On introduction?
      2. On re-introduction?
      3. On on-going basis?
   C. Is an extended payout plan indicated, and if so, what is the optimum time?

X. *Facts and Documentation*
   The pertinent facts needed to define the problems and to document the strategies outlined in the strategy sections

---

kinds of media selected and how media is used. In a sense, then, marketing objectives serve as controls for media planning.

Most marketing objectives relate directly to achieving share of market for a brand; others relate to communication objectives. Here is a sample of marketing objectives for different brands (taken from various strategy statements):

- To increase share in an expanding segment of the X market
- To regain lost volume—increase sales a maximum of 5 percent and, in turn, shoot for a 14 percent share of market
- To acquire a 20 percent share of market the first year after national introduction, 25 percent the second year, and 30 percent the third year
- To introduce the product so that we have at least 5 percent share in each sales division
- To increase share of market and increase the morale of the sales force in the face of many competitive new product introductions
- To find and persuade new customers for our product
- To maintain national coverage
- To provide regional and local impact where two-thirds of sales are made
- To increase the overall visibility of the product name against the potential customers and the trade across the country

Whenever marketing objectives require advertising in specific geographical areas, then media must be selected that best reach those areas. Sometimes the objectives call for added promotional effort in a geographical region such as the West Coast, or the East Central part of the country. Other times, the objectives may call for a special advertising effort in a given market such as Los Angeles or Cincinnati. Such objectives may limit media choices because few media vehicles are available in some specified areas. The marketing objectives provide direction for the planner in selecting media, but it is up to the planner to find media that best *deliver* the target audience specified.

When marketing objectives call for increases in share of market with special effort directed only at prospects, the media planner may be called upon to increase the number of messages to known prospects. In such cases, media selection becomes secondary to methods of using media. One such method may be to increase the frequency of exposure of advertising messages to prospects.

Occasionally, objectives deal with some area other than market share; for example, the requirement may be "to increase the image of authority among adults." In this situation, it might be felt that adults, especially those aged 21–44, are good prospects, yet they are not buying the product. The marketing objective influences the selection of adult-appeal media, such as magazines and Sunday supplements, and perhaps the use of well-known, authoritative television announcers whose personality images are strong in the 21- to 44-year-old age group.

The Budget

Once the marketing objectives have been stated, it is necessary to know how much money will be required to attain them. It is not realistic to make a grandiose marketing plan and then find that the advertiser is unwilling or unable to provide sufficient funds to make the plan successful. (Budgeting and allocations to markets and media will be discussed in a later chapter.) At this point, the media planner may be called in to help estimate the costs of the marketing strategy plan even before the main portion of the media plan has been started. If enough money is not available to accomplish a given set of objectives, then the objectives may have to be reduced or revised.

Estimating the cost of a marketing plan usually involves two separate activities: estimating media costs and estimating production costs. Media costs may be ascertained by checking published reference books that show media rates or by phoning media representatives to obtain general costs. Production costs may be estimated either by arbitrarily allocating a given percentage of the total budget for that purpose or, if the advertising is relatively simple, by obtaining estimates on specific kinds of production pieces that are needed, such as art work, typography, videotape, or film. Generally, the media planner is responsible for estimating only the media cost portion of the marketing plan.

The main problem in estimating marketing costs is determining whether any given amount of money spent for advertising will accomplish a given set of objectives. Marketing and media planners most often rely on their experiences with other brands and products as a basis for making these estimates. But other factors also enter in. A new product introduction may require very heavy investments to get it off the ground. Competitors' advertising—where and how much—also may influence the marketing budget. Brands that have to defend their shares of market against the inroads of competitors, or those that aspire to increase market share, may have to spend heavily. Determining the exact amount is by no means a scientific matter. It is based mostly on experience, although there are mathematical models that "predict" the effect of various spending levels. Past experience may show, for example, that an advertiser increased its national share of market by three percentage points by spending $10 million. It could then be roughly estimated that it would cost $3,333,333 to raise the share one percentage point. This linear relationship of spending and share of market, however, is seldom witnessed in the real world.

Sometimes the planner recommends spending an amount of money beyond the means of the advertiser. In such cases, either the objectives have to be changed or the advertiser must realize that spending the available budget will not produce the results desired. Sometimes, no matter what sum is recommended, the advertiser has a preconceived notion of the maximum amount that can be profitably spent and will not entertain requests for larger amounts. It behooves the planner, therefore, to establish budget parameters *before* full media plans are devised.

Creative Strategy

A major part of the marketing strategy plan is an explanation of how the product will be sold or a statement of the basic selling idea. From that basic selling idea comes the creative strategy, possibly the single most important influence on the planner during the media selection process. Many times the creative strategy directs the planner in choosing one medium over another or in selecting a combination of media.

Where color is an integral part of the creative strategy, then magazines, direct mail, newspaper supplements, or color television may be required. Newspapers accepting free-standing color inserts (FSIs) offer additional alternatives to the media planner. Where the creative strategy calls for the use of cartoon characters, then either comic strips or television may be most appropriate. Again, direction is given to the selection process.

Where a strategy calls for demonstration, one might first think of television; yet it is possible to demonstrate the use of a product in print media through the use of sequential panels showing the various steps in the use of the product. Radio also is capable of demonstration through the use of words that play on the listener's imagination.

Sometimes the creative strategy may call for the use of an announcer or salesperson who can exude a feeling of warmth and sincerity. Either television or radio may be required here, because each excels at conveying emotional impact.

If the creative strategy calls for music, media choices may be limited to radio or television. An alternative is to record the music and advertising message on thin vinyl records and have them inserted into magazines. In this case, however, the creative strategy may have to give way to the budget, which may not tolerate the expense of recording and inserting the record.

Occasionally, creative strategy calls for large and dominating illustrations. This suggests billboards to the media planner, although direct mail or a two-page center spread in newspapers or magazines may be equally acceptable.

Some advertising messages may seem to have more impact on consumers in one medium than they do in another. It should be noted, however, that *impact* is a hazy concept. It is generally assumed to mean that advertising does something to audience members, such as make the message memorable, change attitudes toward the brand, impart significant bits of information, or perhaps serve as a motivating factor in buying. The assumption is not always valid, because there is often little proof that what is claimed to happen actually does. In any case, where creative strategies call for traditional media because of their perceived impact, the planner may find it difficult to break tradition.

So, the creative strategy is an integral part of media planning, perhaps the most important of all. The planner cannot start work without first knowing what is to be said and how it is to be presented to consumers. Only then can media alternatives begin to be considered.

Dealers and Distribution

A major factor in media decision making is distribution to dealers, as it only makes sense to limit advertising to areas where the product is distributed. To do otherwise is to waste effort and money. There are, of course, exceptions, such as when a manufacturer will advertise in an area where the product is not distributed in an effort to "force" distribution on the dealers in that area. Perhaps dealers have refused to handle a new brand because they feel they already have too many similar products on their shelves. Some grocery chains even practice a *one-for-one policy* in which they refuse to take on a new brand unless the manufacturer removes an existing brand from the shelves. By advertising in an area where a product is not yet distributed, the manufacturer hopes that the advertising will create such a demand for the product that the dealers and distributors will be forced to carry the brand. This strategy, however, might sometimes backfire, because consumers who seek the brand and cannot find it might be alienated as future consumers of the brand.

For most products, however, advertising is limited to areas where the product is distributed, and even then, only to the markets that produce the most sales or have the greatest potential for sales.

Because dealers are important sources of business, the ability to select media that best communicate with dealers represents another aspect of the planner's job. Most frequently used is the trade press, but a planner may also choose to communicate with dealers through direct mail or trade shows and conventions.

In some cases, the major problem in selling a product is not advertising to consumers, but to dealers. Such a case was discussed by T. Norman Tveter, a marketing expert:

> The problem was to sell a top-quality model train to fathers through boy salesmen, or the sons of those fathers. A sales analysis by the media director, based on sales for the two previous years, was the basis for planning advertising and promotion. Only then did strong points as well as weak show up concerning such factors as availability and rate of sales.

> Using a state-by-state breakdown of two boy age groups . . . as measures of potential, the analysis showed that sales were radically out of line with market potential. Also a breakdown in dollars of shipments to various

outlets—such as department stores, specialty chains, and premium distributors—showed that 50 cities accounted for 78 percent of the shipments. Seventeen better-producing cities alone accounted for 62 percent of the shipments, and the two best producing areas, 28 percent to 30 percent. This left about 135 metropolitan areas accounting for approximately 22 percent of the shipments, simply because there were not enough dealers handling the product.

From this it was concluded that more effective use of media to develop dealers' business was needed. Fewer publications with larger, dramatic advertising to impress dealers was indicated. There were more than 100 metro areas where just one act of getting the right dealer with the proper cooperation could swing all negative factors to positive and score many hundreds of thousands of dollars in new retail sales. In other words, an impressive, primary dealer merchandising campaign in general media was indicated to take precedence over smaller-copy, more frequency, straight-consumer type of sell.[2]

This case illustrates the role of dealers in getting products sold, and also indicates how media can be used in communicating with dealers.

Dealers also influence media decisions because they are so important in selling at the local level. They are at the firing line and often know which medium works best in their markets. At times they may communicate with the agency indirectly through distributors, wholesalers, or salespeople. Their influence may be very important for their own markets. Furthermore, they often dislike agency media choices, feeling that the media planner is too distant from the scene of action to know which local or national medium works best. In any case, the media planner must pay a great deal of attention to both dealers and importance of distribution in the media plan.

Overall Sales Strategy

The media planner should examine each element of the marketing mix to determine how it might affect media selection and use. Foremost, of course, is the role to be played by advertising. Although one can conceive of a situation where sales promotion, for example, might be more important in attaining objectives, advertising usually plays a significant role in the marketing strategy, and its role should be defined. The more specific this definition is, the better the media planner can plan strategy. Generally, advertising is assigned a communication task that must be accomplished before a product can be sold effectively.

When pricing tactics are important in marketing strategy, a special media effort may be needed either to announce the price or keep the news in front of the consumers. Special prices to dealers may require special trade media selections and use.

---

2. Tveter, T. Norman, "What the Media Expert Gains from Studying Markets," *Media/Scope,* May 1964, pp. 96, 100.

Sales promotion, too, has special significance to media planners. Many promotions call for inserts in magazines or newspapers, such as coupons, booklets, samples of fabrics, tinfoils, or even vinyl records. All of these inserts require careful planning, especially in estimating their cost and timing. Marketing or creative plans might also require gatefolds, diecuts, or special inks, all of which require additional media considerations. Furthermore, the media planner must often select media to announce and keep a special promotion in front of consumers. Contests, cents-off deals, and premiums may lose their impact if they are not noticed by consumers. The general media strategy in such a case is to buy media so as to get the largest reach possible.

For other promotions, it may be necessary to tie in local store information with national advertising so that the audience in any given market knows where to buy an advertised national brand. The names and addresses of stores carrying the product are usually listed at the end of commercials or next to or near newspaper or magazine ads.

Other parts of the marketing mix such as personal selling, public relations, or packaging are of less importance in media planning. But the planner should know as much as possible about the whole marketing strategy to maximize the effectiveness of media decisions.

Test Marketing

Whenever a marketing strategy plan calls for test marketing, there is likely to be media involvement. For example, a test marketing situation might use three markets to test whether the following objectives can be attained: (a) to gain a substantial share of each market's sales, (b) to determine whether the total market for the product can be expanded, (c) to determine how many repeat purchases will be made, (d) to accomplish the above objectives within a reasonable length of time at a reasonable profit. Special media planning will be required in this situation.

To carry out the test, the new brand may be introduced in each of the three markets using different marketing tactics. In Market A, 50 percent of the households may be given a free sample; in Market B, 100 percent of the households may be given a free sample; while in Market C, local newspapers could carry a coupon redeemable for a free sample at local stores. In each case, local advertising may be required to call attention to the offers, especially to the coupon offer. Measurements of sales would then be made and compared market by market to see which performed best.

As another example, test marketing could affect media planning if media weight varied in each of the three test markets. (*Weight* refers to the number of dollars spent, or GRP levels, in each market.) Market A might receive 100 television GRPs per week; Market B, 150 per week; and Market C, 200 per week. Sales would then be measured to see how the different weights affected volume.

Still another way to test media weights in several markets would be to give each market a specified advertising weight for a limited period of time. Sales would be measured for that period, then a heavier weighting might be applied to each market equally or in different proportions and sales again measured. (Test marketing strategy affects media planning in ways ranging from simple dissemination of advertising to special testing situations within all or portions of the test markets. For more details on test marketing, see Chapter 16.)

In summary, then, the marketing strategy plan will affect the media planner's operation in many ways. The media plan itself will grow out of a marketing plan. It is inconceivable for the media planner to operate without first having some kind of marketing strategy as a basis on which to select and use media. The ideal situation occurs when the marketing strategy plan is written and available for all personnel who work on a product or brand within the agency. The plan then serves as a unifying force and directs action toward a common goal.

Competitive Media Expenditure Analysis

Once the planner has scrutinized the marketing strategy plan to determine how media will be involved, it is time to consider the kinds of media and the way they are used by competition. Sometimes competition varies so much that the planner may have to sort out local and regional competitors as well as those on the national level. The planner's first job is to know just who the competitors are, and, his or her second, to know to what extent competitors affect sales.

There is little problem in finding such information if the advertiser or agency subscribes to Nielsen, SAMI, MRCA market data, or various other syndicated research sources. But there is quite a problem in discovering who competitors are when such research services are not purchased. Some information may be obtained from competitive media expenditure analysis, but products produced and sold locally may not be identified very well, especially if they do not advertise much. Other sources of information may be the trade press, local media salespeople, media representatives, local media research departments, or the company's own sales staff.

In determining the effect of competitors' media plans and devising strategies to counter such effects, the key piece of information is the share of market held by each competitor as compared with the advertiser's brand. Brands that lead or are close behind the advertiser may pose a threat. As far as media planning is concerned, the question is: "Should we use the same media our competitors use, or make special efforts to use different media?" Another question is, "How much advertising should we put into a market to counter competitors' advertising effects?"

The answers to these and other questions about competitors depend to a great extent on an advertiser's marketing objectives and an evaluation of what effect competitors may have in preventing the attainment of such objectives. Each situation may be different. Whether to use the same media competitors use may not be as important as answering the question, "Which medium or combination of media best reaches the kind of prospects who are likely to buy my brand?" The media that best reach prospects for "my" brand may happen to be identical with the media used by competitors. But the media planner, although considering competitors, should not necessarily imitate them simply because they happen to have larger shares of markets.

Planners should try to assess weaknesses in competitors' media tactics. Perhaps a competitor is not using a medium properly, or has dissipated advertising money in too many media, or is missing an important segment of the market. These errors represent opportunities in media selection and use and should be exploited. The analysis of a competitor's activities and its effects on a brand is not done in order to copy its tactics, but rather to assess its strengths and weaknesses in light of the marketing objectives. Plans for attaining objectives are made on the basis of problem as well as opportunity situations.

In essence, then, the planner must know at least the following information about competitors before making plans:

- Which media are used? Which are most significant?
- How much is spent in each medium?
- In which markets are media concentrated?
- How much weight is placed in each market?
- Which issues, broadcasts, times are used? In other words, when do competitors use various media and how are they used?

We will see in the next section that the compilation of competitive media information is very much an inexact science.

Major Expenditure Data Sources

Media spending information can be purchased from regular reporting services, although these services have limitations. They do not provide a perfect picture of competitive media expenditures because it is economically unfeasible to measure every dollar spent in every medium for every product. The task is simply too great. Expenditure analyses are therefore never quite complete. Furthermore, such analyses are not precise, because the dollars reported do not incorporate the discounts earned when each competitor purchased space or time. There may be large variations between what the syndicated services report and what competitors actually spent. Finally, competitive reporting companies often do not accurately break down spending allocations when two or three brands appear in a single ad. In other words, the entire cost of the ad may be credited to one of the three brands to the exclusion of the other two. The best way to assess the accuracy of competitive media use reports is to compare the findings of these reports to the actual media use for the product you have planned and placed in media.

These limitations do not render competitive media expenditure analyses invalid, but the data are not to be interpreted literally. Coupled with other marketing and media information, such data will help provide a more complete picture of a competitor's spending activities than would be possible otherwise.

Following is a brief description of the information provided by major media expenditure data sources. It should be noted that the data generally report expenditures of large national advertisers only; neither small national advertisers nor retail advertisers of any size are represented. Users of such data should be aware that often they may be missing significant information simply because it is not reported by any of the services. In such cases, it would be necessary to estimate spending.

Media Records (Expenditures in Newspapers). Media Records reports advertising expenditures in 202 daily and Sunday newspapers, in seventy-three cities. Actual measured advertising has been multiplied by the one-time rate (general open inch rate) of every newspaper measured. It also uses rates for premium space portions of a newspaper such as group supplements *(USA Weekend* and *Parade)*, preprinted inserts, colored comics, and rotogravure and color advertising.

The contents of a typical Media Records report are divided into five separate sections as follows: (a) category investments, showing product category expenditures (See Figure 7-2.); (b) ten leading brands in each classification, ranked for year-to-date, showing both dollars and percentages; (c) top fifty brands/products in all product categories are ranked on year-to-date expenditures; (d) alphabetical advertiser index, which is a summary of all advertisers, brands, and products in the book, listed in alphabetical order for easy reference, as well as the brand's ranking within a category, and the page number location of a brand's full activity in the fifth section; (e) categories and brands—Media Records reports three total investment figures for each brand/product. Every brand spending $15,000 or more is listed in alphabetical order in its category. Detailed spending data includes monthly, quarterly, and cumulative spending.

Because most daily newspapers in this country have converted to standard advertising units (SAUs) from agate lines, it becomes necessary to make conversions from one to the other. Media Records measures advertising in agate lines, but reports this information in SAU inches. The technique they use is as follows:

1. Measure a printed page, both width and depth in inches.
2. Calculate the square inches (multiply width times depth).
3. Divide the square inches by 2.0625 (2.0625 equals agate lines in an SAU inch).
4. Measure total agate lines of a page by multiplying one column depth in agate lines times the number of columns on a page.
5. Calculate the factor for converting agate lines to SAU inches by dividing the total agate lines for a page by the MRCS/SAU inches on a page.

Leading National Advertisers (LNA)—BAR/LNA Multimedia Service. The Leading National Advertisers publishes multimedia reports that cover seven media: magazines, supplements, network television, spot television, network radio, cable television networks, and outdoor. (See Figure 7-3.)

These reports are prepared quarterly and are available eighteen weeks after the end of a quarter. The brand data is derived from BAR, PIB, and LNA Outdoor.

1. Ad Summary lists brands, and shows total spending in seven media, including parent company and classification codes.
2. Company/Brand shows companies, and dollars spent for the year to date (YTD) in the seven media. A seven-media total is also shown.
3. Class/Brand YTD shows brands grouped by PIB classes. Within each class, brands are listed by their parent companies. Data includes dollars spent for the year to date in seven media.
4. Class/Brand QTR shows brands grouped by PIB classes. Brands are

FIGURE 7-2. Media Records (Expenditures in Newspapers)

CITY	NEWS PAPER	OCT.	NOV.	DEC.	QTR.	TOTAL
*** TOURS & TRAVEL SERVICE***						
VACATION OUTLET						
BOSTON	G S	3236			3236	13361
BOSTON	H M	7022	2809		9831	13623
BOSTON	S					3320
TOTAL ACCOUNT EXPENDITURES -			QTR	$13067	YTD	$30304
TOTAL EXPENDITURE EXCL. SUPPLEMENTS				$13067		$30304
PROJECTED 125 MARKETS EXCL. SUPPLS.				$16334		$37880
VACATION TRAVEL CONCEPTS						
NEW YORK	T S					16715
TOTAL ACCOUNT EXPENDITURES -			QTR		YTD	$16715
TOTAL EXPENDITURE EXCL. SUPPLEMENTS						$16715
PROJECTED 125 MARKETS EXCL. SUPPLS.						$17384
VACATION TRAVEL INC						
AKRON	BJ S					1370
CHICAGO	T S	971			971	971
HOUSTON	P M					1731
HOUSTON	P S					1683
MIAMI	H S	4770	3625		8395	18507
MILWAUKEE	J S	4569			4569	19705
ST LOUIS	PD S					960
TOTAL ACCOUNT EXPENDITURES -			QTR	$13935	YTD	$44927
TOTAL EXPENDITURE EXCL. SUPPLEMENTS				$13935		$44927
PROJECTED 125 MARKETS EXCL. SUPPLS.				$23593		$72611
VACATION VALUES						
AKRON	BJ S					479
CLEVELAND	PD S					36226
PITTSBURGH	P E					1140
PITTSBURGH	PG M					1140
TOTAL ACCOUNT EXPENDITURES -			QTR		YTD	$38985
TOTAL EXPENDITURE EXCL. SUPPLEMENTS						$38985
PROJECTED 125 MARKETS EXCL. SUPPLS.						$46392
VACATIONS TO GO						
AKRON	BJ S			822	822	5479
ATLANTA	J&C S			1891	1891	28797
BALTIMORE	S			1621	1621	18954
BOCA RATON	N S			161	161	1202
BOSTON	G S		2856	2665	5521	47918
BUFFALO	N S			1487	1487	15658
CHARLOTTE	O S			1010	1010	15229
CHICAGO	ST S	2321	2321		4642	24602
CHICAGO	T S		4855	9710	14565	43442
CINCINNATI	E S	1251		1251	2502	11835
CLEVELAND	PD S			1596	1596	14245
COLUMBUS	D S			886	886	10563
DALLAS	N S	1432	1432	2974	5838	38742
DENVER	P S			2525	2525	14571
DENVER	RMN S			1187	1187	14794
DETROIT	FP S	3297		4946	8243	31559
DETROIT	N S					42804
FORT WAYNE	JG S			512	512	512
FT LAUDERD	NCSS S	2934		2934	5868	32071
GRNWCH/STF	A S			194	194	194
GRNWCH/STF	T S			194	194	194
HARTFORD	C S	5853		1238	7091	10130
HOUSTON	C S	1347	1243	1451	4041	52634
HOUSTON	C AD			1251	1251	1251
HOUSTON	P S	1287		1386	2673	44253
INDPLS	S S			1256	1256	12790
LEXINGTON	HL S			633	633	7846
LONG ISL	N S					6749
LOS ANGELS	T S	4333	4333	4667	13333	104952
MIAMI	H S	2289		2480	4769	26818
MILWAUKEE	J S			1856	1856	22347
MINNPLS	ST S			1795	1795	20163
NASHVILLE	T S			1020	1020	16918
NEW YORK	T S					50145
NEWARK	SL S			1949	1949	1949
OAKLAND	T S			797	797	6010
PHILA	I S	3239		3239	6478	79485
PHOENIX	AR S	1539		1733	3272	18784
PITTSBURGH	P S	1987		1987	3974	17769
PROVIDENCE	J S			1149	1149	1149
SAN ANT	EN S	1900		950	2850	2850
SAN ANT	L S					15177
SAN DIEGO	U S	962	1923	962	3847	16202
SAN FRAN	E&C S	2586	2586	2586	7758	63500
SAN JOSE	MN S			993	993	10651
ST LOUIS	PD S			1455	1455	18941
ST PAUL	PPD S			3106	3106	11979
TOLEDO	B S			644	644	644

CITY	NEWS PAPER	OCT.	NOV.	DEC.	QTR.	TOTAL
VACATIONS TO GO (CONTINUED)						
WASHINGTON	P S	7388	3694	7388	18470	100873
WICHITA	EB S			710	710	3767
YOUNGSTOWN	V S					378
TOTAL ACCOUNT EXPENDITURES -			QTR	$158435	YTD	$1160469
TOTAL EXPENDITURE EXCL. SUPPLEMENTS				$158435		$1160469
PROJECTED 125 MARKETS EXCL. SUPPLS.				$215597		$1609304
VAGABOND TRAVEL SERVICE INC						
ASBURY PK	P E					1095
ASBURY PK	P S					1760
BOULDER	C M					514
BOULDER	C S	204		219	423	1356
MILWAUKEE	J E		1887		1887	3574
MILWAUKEE	J S	11423	27273	11852	50548	178142
MILWAUKEE	S M	480			480	1054
TOTAL ACCOUNT EXPENDITURES -			QTR	$53338	YTD	$187495
TOTAL EXPENDITURE EXCL. SUPPLEMENTS				$53338		$187495
PROJECTED 125 MARKETS EXCL. SUPPLS.				$72006		$252804
VALLEY TRAVEL						
BALTIMORE	S E	59			59	59
BRIDGEPORT	P S	601	743	601	1945	7744
LA/SFV	N M	833	555	611	1999	9219
LA/SFV	N S					344
SAN DIEGO	T E					112
SAN DIEGO	U S					148
TOTAL ACCOUNT EXPENDITURES -			QTR	$4003	YTD	$17626
TOTAL EXPENDITURE EXCL. SUPPLEMENTS				$4003		$17626
PROJECTED 125 MARKETS EXCL. SUPPLS.				$4644		$20424
VALUE TRAVEL						
DENVER	P S					952
DENVER	RMN M					1274
DENVER	RMN S	1826	2100	365	4291	17899
TOTAL ACCOUNT EXPENDITURES -			QTR	$4291	YTD	$20125
TOTAL EXPENDITURE EXCL. SUPPLEMENTS				$4291		$20125
PROJECTED 125 MARKETS EXCL. SUPPLS.				$5794		$27169
VALUE VACATIONS						
ATLANTA	J&C S					582
BOSTON	H S					255
FT LAUDERD	NCSS S	1467	2257	1128	4852	21152
TOTAL ACCOUNT EXPENDITURES -			QTR	$4852	YTD	$21989
TOTAL EXPENDITURE EXCL. SUPPLEMENTS				$4852		$21989
PROJECTED 125 MARKETS EXCL. SUPPLS.				$9510		$42918
VANISHING TEXAS RIVER CRUISE THE						
SAN ANT	L S	1949	2549	1499	5997	20303
TOTAL ACCOUNT EXPENDITURES -			QTR	$5997	YTD	$20303
TOTAL EXPENDITURE EXCL. SUPPLEMENTS				$5997		$20303
PROJECTED 125 MARKETS EXCL. SUPPLS.				$10257		$34718
VARIETY VACATIONS						
FT LAUDERD	NCSS S	2934	2031		4965	16952
TOTAL ACCOUNT EXPENDITURES -			QTR	$4965	YTD	$16952
TOTAL EXPENDITURE EXCL. SUPPLEMENTS				$4965		$16952
PROJECTED 125 MARKETS EXCL. SUPPLS.				$9731		$33226
VAVOLIZZA TOURS						
LOS ANGELS	T S					5667
NEW YORK	T S					15648
TOTAL ACCOUNT EXPENDITURES -			QTR		YTD	$21315
TOTAL EXPENDITURE EXCL. SUPPLEMENTS						$21315
PROJECTED 125 MARKETS EXCL. SUPPLS.						$22338
VEGAS FUN BUS						
PHOENIX	AR S	3197	4664	3732	11593	57892
PHOENIX	G E	1497	1650	2048	5195	25020
TOTAL ACCOUNT EXPENDITURES -			QTR	$16788	YTD	$82912
TOTAL EXPENDITURE EXCL. SUPPLEMENTS				$16788		$82912
PROJECTED 125 MARKETS EXCL. SUPPLS.				$28370		$140121
VEGAS TRAVEL						
BOSTON	G S	2475	952		3427	26339
HONOLULU	SB E					251
HONOLULU	SB&A S					223
MIAMI	H S			382	382	382
NEW YORK	N S	2139	6064	1654	9857	65468
NEW YORK	P AD					2223

Source: *Media Records Green Book* 1987. Reprinted by permission.

FIGURE 7-3.   BAR/LNA: Multi-Media Service (9 Media Expenditures) *

BAR/LNA MULTI-MEDIA SERVICE

AD $ SUMMARY
BRAND INDEX   January - December 1987

BRAND/PARENT COMPANY	CLASS CODE	9-MEDIA YTD $ (000)	MEDIA USED	BRAND/PARENT COMPANY	CLASS CODE	9-MEDIA YTD $ (000)	MEDIA USED
DAUPHIN DEPOSIT BANK & TRUST CO DAUPHIN DEPOSIT CORP	B151	107.3	S	EIR SPORTSWEAR MEN & WOMEN EIR SPORTS	A115-3	12.5	M
DAUPHIN DEPOSIT BANK & TRUST CO CS DAUPHIN DEPOSIT CORP	B151	51.6	O	EJ GITANO SPORTSWEAR CHILDREN JOIA EVA INC	A115-2	36.5	M
DEUTSCHE BANK AG INTERNATIONAL DEUTSCHE BANK AG	B151	652.4	M	ELLEN TRACY SPORTSWEAR WOMEN ELLEN TRACY	A115-2	222.2	M
DEUTSCHE BANK CAPITAL CORP BUS SVC DEUTSCHE BANK AG	B151	17.2	M	ELLESSE SPORTSWEAR MEN & WOMEN ELLESSE SPA	A115-3	81.7	MO
DEUTSCHE BANK CAPITAL MKTS LTD SEC OFF DEUTSCHE BANK AG	B151	6.2	M	ELLESSE SPORTSWEAR WOMEN ELLESSE SPA	A115-2	62.2	M
DG BANK INTERNATIONAL DEUTSCHE GENOSSENSCHAFTSBANK	B151	59.7	M	EMANUEL UNGARO SPORTSWEAR & COATS MEN GFT USA CORP	A115-1	43.7	M
DICKIES WORKCLOTHES MEN WILLIAMSON-DICKIE MFG CO	A115-1	198.0	M	EMANUEL UNGARO SPORTSWEAR & COATS WOMEN EMANUEL UNGARO	A115-2	125.7	M
DICKIES WORKCLOTHES MEN & WOMEN WILLIAMSON-DICKIE MFG CO	A115-3	445.2	C	EMANUEL UNGARO SPORTSWEAR MEN GFT USA CORP	A115-1	50.3	M
DIME SAVINGS BANK OF NEW YORK DIME SAVINGS BANK OF NEW YORK	B151	4.1	O	EMANUEL UNGARO SPORTSWEAR WOMEN EMANUEL UNGARO	A115-2	92.8	M
DIME SAVINGS BANK OF NEW YORK CS DIME SAVINGS BANK OF NEW YORK	B151	9.4	O	EMANUELLE MOUSTACHE SPORTSWEAR MEN & WOM AMEX FASHIONS INC	A115-3	321.7	M
DINO VALIANO SPORTSWEAR WOMEN VALIANO DINO FASHIONS INC	A115-2	65.8	M	EMIGRANT SAVINGS BANK CONSUMER SERVICES EMIGRANT SAVINGS BANK	B151	32.1	M
DODGE CARAVAN CHRYSLER CORP	T121	7,938.8	MONSC	EMPIRE BANK EMPIRE BANK	B151	59.9	O
DODGE CARAVAN & PLYMOUTH VOYAGER WAGONS CHRYSLER CORP	T121	11,404.4	MPWN	ENRICO COVERI APPAREL MEN COVERI ENRICO	A115-1	27.5	M
DODGE COMPACT TRUCKS CHRYSLER CORP	T121	504.0	MS	ENRICO COVERI SPORTSWEAR MEN & WOMEN COVERI ENRICO	A115-3	43.3	M
DODGE COMPACT TRUCKS & RAM VAN CHRYSLER CORP	T121	46.2	S	ENRICO COVERI SPORTSWEAR WOMEN COVERI ENRICO	A115-2	44.9	M
DODGE COMPACT TRUCKS & VANS CHRYSLER CORP	T121	257.6	S	ENRICO COVERI SPORTSWEAS & SWMWEAR WOMEN COVERI ENRICO	A115-2	18.0	M
DODGE DAKOTA COMPACT TRUCK CHRYSLER CORP	T121	23,496.1	MONSYC	EQUIBANK PITTSBURGH EMPIRE OF AMERICA FSB	B151	640.6	S
DODGE DESPARADO COMPACT TRUCK CHRYSLER CORP	T121	10.5	S	EQUITABLE TRUST BANK BUSINESS SERVICES EQUITABLE BANCORPORATION	B151	3.9	O
DODGE EASTERNER COMPACT TRUCK CHRYSLER CORP	T121	782.4	S	EREZ SPORTSWEAR & DRESSES WOMEN EREZ	A115-2	49.2	M
DODGE IMPORT RAIDER COMPACT TRUCKS CHRYSLER CORP	T123	2,273.2	MNSC	ERREUNO SPORTSWEAR MEN ERREUNO	A115-1	9.6	M
DODGE IMPORT RAM 50 COMPACT TRUCK CHRYSLER CORP	T123	1,959.1	M	ERREUNO SPORTWEAR WOMEN ERREUNO	A115-2	42.9	M
DODGE MINI RAM VAN CHRYSLER CORP	T121	1,398.0	M	ESCADA SPORTSWEAR WOMEN SRB FASHION INTERNATIONAL INC	A115-2	195.6	M
DODGE RAM COMPACT TRUCKS CHRYSLER CORP	T121	6,161.9	MONSC	ESPRIT SPORT SPORTSWEAR WOMEN ESPRIT DE CORP	A115-2	150.9	M
DODGE RAM VAN/WAGON CHRYSLER CORP	T121	1,357.7	M	ESPRIT SPORTSWEAR CHILDREN ESPRIT DE CORP	A115-4	223.4	M
DODGE RAM VANS CHRYSLER CORP	T121	472.5	MS	ESPRIT SPORTSWEAR MEN & WOMEN ESPRIT DE CORP	A115-3	117.3	M
DODGE RAM VEHICLES CHRYSLER CORP	T121	18.1	S	ESPRIT SPORTSWEAR WOMEN ESPRIT DE CORP	A115-2	3,213.8	MPW
DODGE RAMCHARGER COMPACT TRUCKS CHRYSLER CORP	T121	468.7	MS	ESPRIT SPORTWEAR FAMILY ESPRIT DE CORP	A115-3	461.7	MO
DODGE TRUCKS CHRYSLER CORP	T121	6,674.8	ONSR	ESSENCE SPORTSWEAR WOMEN ESSENCE COMMUNICATION INC	A115-2	134.6	M
DODGE TRUCKS & VANS CHRYSLER CORP	T121	517.6	S	EUROPEAN AMERICAN BANK & TRUST CO CS EUROPEAN AMERICA BANCORP	B151	7.7	M
DODGE TRUCKS RAM 50 PICKUP CHRYSLER CORP	T121	3,922.2	NSC	EVA JOIA SPORTSWEAR CHILDREN JOIA EVA INC	A115-4	57.9	MPW
DOLLAR DRY DOCK SAVINGS BANK CONS SVC DOLLAR DRY DOCK SAVINGS BANK	B151	144.9	OS	EVAN-PICONE SPORTSWEAR WOMEN PALM BEACH INC	A115-2	565.4	MPW
DONEGAL II SPORTSWEAR MEN DONEGAL II	A115-1	15.5	M	EXCHANGE NATIONAL BANK OF CHICAGO EXCHANGE INTERNATIONAL CORP	B151	780.6	S
DONNA PARKER SPORTSWEAR WOMEN TRANS-ATLANTIC LTD	A115-2	52.6	M	F & M BANCORP F & M BANCORPORATION	B151	8.4	O
DRESDNER BANK AG GENERAL PROMOTION ASSOCIATED BANKS OF EUROPE CORP	B151-8	218.4	M	F & M BANK & TRUST CO TULSA F & M BANCORPORATION	B151	45.6	S
DRESDNER BANK AG INTERNATIONAL ASSOCIATED BANKS OF EUROPE CORP	B151	546.4	M	F & M BANK MENOMONEE FALLS F & M BANCORPORATION	B151	33.6	S
DRIVER SPORTSWEAR MEN & WOMEN DRIVERS JEANS	A115-3	11.4	M	FABE SWEATERS WOMEN FOREIGN MARKET	A115-2	41.6	M
DUAL CONTROL SPORTSWEAR MEN GOBUTY SPORT	A115-1	64.5	M	FABRICE SOLIVERES SPORTSWEAR MEN PROMASTER	A115-1	5.8	M
DUNHILL SPORTSWEAR MEN DUNHILL ALFRED	A115-1	274.7	MPW	FARAH SPORTSWEAR MEN FARAH MANUFACTURING CO	A115-1	100.4	M
E JOVEN SPORTSWEAR MEN FARAH MANUFACTURING CO	A115-1	103.7	M	FARM CREDIT BANKS CS FARM CREDIT ADMINISTRATION	B151	7.3	OS
EASTERN BANK BUS SVC EASTERN BANK	B151	15.7	M	FARMERS & MERCHANTS BANK FARMERS & MERCHANTS BANK	B151	39.3	O
EDWIN JEANS MEN EDWIN JEANS	A115-1	70.8	M	FARMERS FIRST BANK FARMERS FIRST BANK	B151	48.9	S
EDWIN JEANS WOMEN EDWIN JEANS	A115-2	13.3	O	FARMERS STATE BANK ARCHER DANIELS MIDLAND CO	B151	2.2	O
EILEEN WEST SPORTSWEAR WOMEN SAN FRANCISCO MERCANTILE	A115-2	27.5	M	FARMERS TRUST CO FARMERS TRUST CO	B151	14.8	O

Source: Broadcast Advertisers Reports, and Publishers Information Bureau. Copyright 1987. Reprinted by permission.
*M = magazines; P = newspaper supplements; W = newspapers; A = all; O = outdoor; N = network TV; S = spot TV; Y = syndicated TV; C = cable TV networks; and R = network radio.

listed by parent company, and data shows dollars spent for the current quarter in the seven media, plus totals for the seven.

The main advantage of these reports is that brand spending information is available in one source. Newspapers and spot radio, however, are not shown.

LNA Outdoor Advertising Service. This is a service that reports national and regional poster and painted outdoor signs in markets with a 100,000 population or more. Brand market-by-market expenditure data represents gross sales volume for those plant operators who participate. (See Figure 7–4.)

The service has four reports as follows:

1. Outdoor Contributors by Market shows which plant operators have contributed advertising expenditure data for each quarter's report.
2. Classification Totals shows expenditures listed by industry, major, subclass, and special classes.
3. Brand Index lists all brands that bought outdoor during the reporting period. It also shows parent company and classification code.
4. Parent Company Index summarizes spending by quarter for each brand and parent company.
5. Outdoor Brand Detail shows brands by parent company within classification subclasses and total dollars spent for the year to date and each quarter.

Publisher's Information Bureau (PIB/LNA)—Publisher's Advertising Reports (PAR). This is a monthly report showing expenditures in over 100 magazines and two supplements (*Parade* and *U.S.A. Weekend*). PIB publishes three volumes. The first two volumes cover expenditures by brand within specific product classes. (See, for example, Figure 7–5, p.121.) The third volume covers total revenues by magazine and product class. It also covers parent companies and brand expenditures.

Costs are estimated by using the one-time rates for each insertion. Seasonal rates are used if all the usual frequency and volume discounts are earned by an advertiser. Regional one-time rates reflect discounts for use of more than one edition, where applicable. Advertisers who buy a great deal of magazine advertising may show overspending because they earned volume discounts that were not reported. Not all magazines are covered.

Broadcast Advertisers Reports (BAR). Broadcast Advertisers Reports monitors advertising expenditures of competitors for network television, radio, and cable. The following reports, showing brand, product and parent company, schedule detail and estimated expenditures, are prepared:

- Network TV (Figure 7–6, p.123)
- Cable TV Networks
- Network Radio
- National Syndicated TV
- BARCUME, National Spot TV (Figure 7–7, p.124)
- BARCUME, Retail/Local Spot TV

FIGURE 7-4.   LNA Outdoor Advertising Service (Expenditures in Outdoor)

OUTDOOR ADVERTISING SERVICE
BRAND DETAIL
January - December 1987

CLASS COMPANY BRAND STATE - MARKET	CURRENT QUARTER $ (000)			YEAR-TO-DATE $ (000)		
	TOTAL	POSTER	PAINT	TOTAL	POSTER	PAINT
F310 BEER (CON'T)						
ANHEUSER-BUSCH COS INC						
ANHEUSER-BUSCH BEERS (F3100)						
CA SAN FRANCISCO-OAKLAND-SAN JOSE METRO	15.3	15.3	0.0	15.3	15.3	0.0
DC WASHINGTON	24.3	0.0	24.3	24.3	0.0	24.3
GA SAVANNAH	0.0	0.0	0.0	10.6	10.6	0.0
MA NEW BEDFORD-FALL RIVER	11.7	11.7	0.0	11.7	11.7	0.0
MI DETROIT	11.6	11.6	0.0	11.6	11.6	0.0
NB OMAHA	0.2	0.2	0.0	0.2	0.2	0.0
NY ALBANY-SCHENECTADY-TROY	1.0	1.0	0.0	1.0	1.0	0.0
OH CANTON	3.5	3.5	0.0	3.5	3.5	0.0
COLUMBUS OH	1.6	0.0	1.6	4.1	0.0	4.1
DAYTON	0.0	0.0	0.0	8.0	0.0	8.0
PA PHILADELPHIA	26.9	26.9	0.0	26.9	26.9	0.0
TX LAREDO	2.4	2.4	0.0	2.4	2.4	0.0
BRAND TOTAL	98.6	72.6	25.9	119.6	83.2	36.4
ANHEUSER-BUSCH COS INC GENERAL PROMOTION (F3108)						
GA SAVANNAH	0.0	0.0	0.0	5.3	5.3	0.0
MO ST LOUIS	12.6	5.0	7.6	12.6	5.0	7.6
BRAND TOTAL	12.6	5.0	7.6	17.9	10.3	7.6
BUDWEISER BEER (F3100)						
AL BIRMINGHAM	0.0	0.0	0.0	10.4	0.0	10.4
GADSDEN	1.5	1.5	0.0	1.5	1.5	0.0
MOBILE	0.0	0.0	0.0	13.9	1.9	12.0
MONTGOMERY	0.5	0.5	0.0	12.5	12.5	0.0
AZ PHOENIX	17.3	7.2	10.2	65.4	24.8	40.7
CA FRESNO	6.9	6.9	0.0	16.8	16.8	0.0
LOS ANGELES METRO MARKET	2.9	2.9	0.0	345.4	345.4	0.0
MERCED COUNTY	0.0	0.0	0.0	3.9	3.9	0.0
MODESTO	0.3	0.3	0.0	1.2	1.2	0.0
OXNARD-SIMI VALLEY-VENTURA	36.3	36.3	0.0	36.3	36.3	0.0
SACRAMENTO	4.5	4.5	0.0	40.9	40.9	0.0
SAN DIEGO	6.4	0.0	6.4	16.6	0.0	16.6
SAN FRANCISCO-OAKLAND-SAN JOSE METRO	10.5	2.4	8.1	107.3	90.9	16.5
STOCKTON	0.0	0.0	0.0	3.0	3.0	0.0
CO COLORADO SPRINGS	0.0	0.0	0.0	2.6	2.6	0.0
DENVER-BOULDER	0.0	0.0	0.0	94.6	94.6	0.0
FL JACKSONVILLE	8.3	0.0	8.3	41.7	0.0	41.7
LAKELAND	5.5	0.0	5.5	18.1	0.0	18.1
MIAMI	0.0	0.0	0.0	28.2	0.0	28.2
ORLANDO	20.5	0.0	20.5	83.7	0.0	83.7
PANAMA CITY	0.0	0.0	0.0	2.7	2.7	0.0
PENSACOLA	3.9	0.0	3.9	23.8	9.5	14.3
TALLAHASSEE	0.0	0.0	0.0	10.8	0.0	10.8
TAMPA-ST PETERSBURG	19.8	0.0	19.8	91.6	4.0	87.6
GA ALBANY	0.0	0.0	0.0	8.0	8.0	0.0
ATHENS	0.0	0.0	0.0	7.2	5.6	1.6
ATLANTA	23.5	11.0	12.4	95.5	11.0	84.4
IA DAVENPORT-ROCK ISLAND-MOLINE	0.0	0.0	0.0	23.8	1.2	22.7
IL CHICAGO	86.8	0.0	86.8	290.1	0.0	290.1
PEORIA	0.0	0.0	0.0	1.5	1.1	0.4
ROCKFORD	3.2	0.0	3.2	5.3	0.0	5.3
SPRINGFIELD	0.0	0.0	0.0	4.6	0.0	4.6
IN GARY-HAMMOND-E CHICAGO	2.5	2.5	0.0	2.5	2.5	0.0
SOUTH BEND	0.0	0.0	0.0	2.7	2.7	0.0
KY LEXINGTON-FAYETTE	7.7	0.0	7.7	27.5	2.0	25.5
PADUCAH	0.0	0.0	0.0	1.5	1.5	0.0
LA BATON ROUGE	13.8	11.9	2.0	51.2	44.0	7.2
MONROE	0.1	0.0	0.1	2.5	2.4	0.1
NEW ORLEANS	0.0	0.0	0.0	20.4	15.6	4.9
MA NEW BEDFORD-FALL RIVER	0.0	0.0	0.0	11.7	11.7	0.0
MD BALTIMORE	0.0	0.0	0.0	35.2	35.2	0.0
WINCHESTER-FREDERICK	0.0	0.0	0.0	0.4	0.4	0.0
MI ANN ARBOR	0.0	0.0	0.0	5.7	5.7	0.0
BATTLE CREEK	2.1	2.1	0.0	4.2	4.2	0.0
DETROIT	75.9	13.4	62.6	299.4	70.2	229.2
GRAND RAPIDS	6.6	6.6	0.0	36.0	26.4	9.6
JACKSON	0.0	0.0	0.0	6.8	6.8	0.0
LANSING-EAST LANSING	0.0	0.0	0.0	0.3	0.3	0.0
MONROE MARKET	0.3	0.3	0.0	1.2	1.2	0.0

FIGURE 7-5. PIB/LNA: Magazine Service (Expenditures in Magazines)

LEADING NATIONAL ADVERTISERS
1987 BRAND DETAIL REPORT
AS OF DECEMBER 31

- Full-time Spot TV Monitor (conducted in six markets: New York City, Los Angeles, Chicago, Philadelphia, Dallas, and Atlanta)

In addition, BAR has a "Checking Service" that reports commercial placement irregularities, such as product conflicts, overcommercialization, and multiple spotting, to subscribing agencies.

Specific program and brand information is obtained by audiomagnetic tape recordings, made continuously during the broadcast day, every day of the year. Cable network and nationally syndicated programs are also videotaped directly from satellite feeds. Spot TV is monitored continuously during a broadcast day in 337 stations in the top seventy-five markets, directly from broadcast. In sixteen markets, recordings are made continuously by videotape.

To estimate brand spending, BAR assigns a dollar value to each program and applies this rate to each brand television commercial monitored. Network costs estimates are developed from information provided by the networks and by some advertising agencies. Syndicated program rates are based on cost data supplied by advertisers and agencies. Spot TV rates are provided by a few agencies and buying services and are adjusted to agree with station revenue information compiled by the Television Bureau of Advertising. The entire reporting process is done manually.

Recently, BAR and MediaWatch, a competitor, merged. The result is that both may begin to use MediaWatch's technique of computerized pattern recognition. One of BAR's competitors, Nielsen's Monitor-Plus, uses a pattern recognition system (described in Chapter 3).

Gathering and Assembling the Data

The first of two major tasks involved in studying competitive expenditures is to gather and assemble the data. The second task is to analyze them.

What kinds of data should the media planner seek? The most obvious answer is to find the amount of money that each competitor spends annually in each medium. Such data provide a bird's-eye view of the competitor's media activities. To make such data more meaningful, the planner should analyze expenditures for individual brands, rather than total expenditures for a company. Because each brand is competing with others for a proportion of total market sales, specific expenditures by brands are most meaningful. In gathering expenditure data by brand, it is advisable to include the planner's brand as well as competitors' brands so that all are compared on the same basis.

Furthermore, in analyzing expenditure data, it is important not only to show dollars spent in each medium, but what percentage that comprises of each competitor's annual expenditures. (See Table 7–1, p. 125.) The proportion of each competitor's total expenditures in each medium makes comparisons easier, though problems can occur in making comparisons on the basis of percentages when the bases differ widely. Ten percent of one brand's total budget spent in newspapers, for example, may not be equivalent to a competitor's 10 percent spent in newspapers if the base of one was $3,000 and the base of the other, $3,000,000.

FIGURE 7-6. Barcume: Network TV Expenditures

SECTION 2 BRAND DETAIL WITHIN PARENT COMPANY

PARENT COMPANY BRAND/PRODUCT PROGRAM	NETWORK AND DAY	CLASS CODE & TIME	OCTOBER NO OF COMM.	MINUTES SECONDS	DOLLAR EST.(000)	NOVEMBER NO OF COMM.	MINUTES SECONDS	DOLLAR EST.(000)	DECEMBER NO OF COMM.	MINUTES SECONDS	DOLLAR EST.(000)	4TH QTR & YEAR TO DATE NO OF COMM.	MINUTES SECONDS	DOLLAR EST.(000)
GENERAL MILLS INC --------- CONT														
TODAY SHOW	N M-F	700A	3	1:30	60.0	3	1:30	63.0				6	3:00	123.0
M/F DAYTIME TOTALS			18	9:00	198.3	17	8:30	218.6				35	17:30	416.9
SUNDAY TODAY	N SUN	800A				1	:30	7.0				1	:30	7.0
						1	:30	7.0				1	:30	7.0
S/S DAYTIME TOTALS														
PRODUCT TOTALS			26	13:00	1176.4	28	14:00	1307.1				54	27:00	2483.5
PRODUCT TOTALS YTD												54	27:00	2483.5
YOPLAIT FOOD-REGULAR YOGURT ----- F131														
GOOD MORNING AMER	A M-F	700A		:30	17.1							1	:30	17.1
M/F DAYTIME TOTALS			1	:30	17.1							1	:30	17.1
PRODUCT TOTALS			1	:30	17.1							1	:30	17.1
PRODUCT TOTALS YTD												141	70:30	6285.8
YOPLAIT FOOD-SOFT FRZN YOGURT ----- F131														
PRODUCT TOTALS YTD												66	16:30	1170.1
PARENT CO. PRIME TIME TOTALS			99	41:00	8421.1	66	27:00	5492.1	83	35:45	5738.3	248	103:45	19651.5
PARENT CO. M/F DAYTIME TOTALS			429	183:00	5466.1	274	113:00	3275.5	207	77:15	2031.8	910	373:15	10773.4
PARENT CO. S/S DAYTIME TOTALS			169	79:22	3769.1	67	31:45	1467.2	100	49:30	1245.5	336	160:37	6481.8
PARENT CO. E/L FRINGES TOTALS			87	37:45	3203.3	59	23:00	2153.8	77	33:15	2806.7	223	94:00	8163.8
PARENT CO. TOTALS			784	341:07	20859.6	466	194:45	12388.6	467	195:45	11822.3	1717	731:37	45070.5
* PARENT CO. PRIME TIME YTD												825	357:30	63501.0
* PARENT CO. M/F DAYTIME YTD												2914	1224:45	32212.9
* PARENT CO. S/S DAYTIME YTD												1114	536:37	16165.8
* PARENT CO. E/L FRINGES YTD												823	346:00	21844.7
* PARENT CO. TOTALS YTD												5676	2446:52	133724.4
GENERAL MOTORS CORP ********														
A C DELCO PDTS-BATTERIES ---- T111														
NFC FOOTBALL POST-SUN	C SUN	715P				1	:30	67.1				1	:30	67.1
PRIME TIME TOTALS						1	:30	67.1				1	:30	67.1
COLLEGE FTBL PRE-FRI	C FRI	230P				1	:30	8.0				1	:30	8.0
M/F DAYTIME TOTALS						1	:30	8.0				1	:30	8.0
COLLEGE FTBL GAME-SAT	C SAT	208P	2	1:00	74.4	2	1:00	70.0	1	:30	44.8	5	2:30	189.2
COLLEGE FTBL GM 1-SAT	C SAT	120BP				4	2:00	140.0				4	2:00	140.0
COLLEGE FTBL GM 2-SAT	C SAT	330P				2	1:00	78.6				2	1:00	78.6
NFC FOOTBALL GAME-SAT	C SAT	358P							2	1:00	174.8	2	1:00	174.8
NFC FOOTBALL GAME-SUN	C SUN	125BP	1	:30	80.1	1	:30	139.3	1	:30	132.5	3	1:30	351.9
NFC FOOTBALL GM 1-SUN	C SUN	125BP				1	:30	139.3	1	:30	265.0	2	1:00	404.3
NFC FOOTBALL GM 2-SUN	C SUN	415P				1	:30	103.8	1	:30	104.9	2	1:00	208.7
NFC FOOTBALL POST-SUN	C SUN	405P				1	:30	67.1				1	:30	67.1
NFC FOOTBALL PRE-SUN	C SUN	1230P	1	:30	48.0	2	1:00	97.6	4	2:00	162.4	7	3:30	308.0
AFC FOOTBALL PRE-SUN	N SUN	1230P	1	:30	32.0							1	:30	32.0
PBA FALL TOUR	N SAT	200P	1	:30	15.0							1	:30	15.0
SPORTSWORLD-SATURDAY	N SAT	330P	1	:30	23.0							1	:30	23.0
S/S DAYTIME TOTALS			7	3:30	272.5	14	7:00	835.7	11	5:30	884.4	32	16:00	1992.6
NFC FOOTBALL POST-SAT	C SAT	720P							1	:30	37.8	1	:30	37.8
E/L FRINGES TOTALS									1	:30	37.8	1	:30	37.8
PRODUCT TOTALS			7	3:30	272.5	16	8:00	910.8	12	6:00	922.2	35	17:30	2105.5
PRODUCT TOTALS YTD												67	23:30	3062.8
A C DELCO PDTS-OIL & AIR FILTERS ---- T154														
COLLEGE FTBL GAME-SAT	C SAT	237P	1	:30	37.2							1	:30	37.2
NFC FOOTBALL PRE-SUN	C SUN	1230P	2	1:00	96.0							2	1:00	96.0
S/S DAYTIME TOTALS			3	1:30	133.2							3	1:30	133.2
PRODUCT TOTALS			3	1:30	133.2							3	1:30	133.2
PRODUCT TOTALS YTD												62	31:00	2332.2
A C DELCO PDTS-SPARK PLUGS ---- T154														
COLLEGE FTBL GAME-SAT	C SAT	238P	2	1:00	74.4							1	1:00	74.4
NFC FOOTBALL GAME-SUN	C SUN	125BP	2	1:00	160.2							1	1:00	160.2
S/S DAYTIME TOTALS			4	2:00	234.6							4	2:00	234.6
PRODUCT TOTALS			4	2:00	234.6							4	2:00	234.6
PRODUCT TOTALS YTD												57	28:30	2303.7
A C DELCO PDTS-VARIOUS ---- T154														
SPORTSWORLD-SATURDAY	N SAT	330P		:30	23.0							1	:30	23.0
S/S DAYTIME TOTALS			1	:30	23.0							1	:30	23.0
PRODUCT TOTALS			1	:30	23.0							1	:30	23.0
PRODUCT TOTALS YTD												5	2:30	120.5
BUICK AUTOS-CENTURY ---- T111														
PRODUCT TOTALS YTD												41	20:30	1578.2
BUICK AUTOS-ELECTRA ---- T111														
NFL MONDAY NIGHT FTBL	A MON	900P							2	:30	199.0	2	:30	199.0
HOMECOMING	C THU	900P							2	1:00	33.2	2	1:00	33.2
PRIME TIME TOTALS									3	1:30	232.2	3	1:30	232.2
NBC NIGHTLY NEWS	N WED	630P							1	:30	38.9	1	:30	38.9
E/L FRINGES TOTALS									1	:30	38.9	1	:30	38.9
PRODUCT TOTALS									4	2:00	271.1	4	2:00	271.1
PRODUCT TOTALS YTD												18	9:00	749.6
BUICK AUTOS-GEN PROMO ---- T111														
PRODUCT TOTALS YTD												13	6:30	403.2
BUICK AUTOS-LE SABRE ---- T111														
PRODUCT TOTALS YTD												11	5:30	658.7
BUICK AUTOS-REGAL ---- T111														
20/20	A M-F	1000P	1	1:00	160.0				1	:30	80.7	2	1:30	240.7
ABC FRIDAY NIGHT MOVIE	A FRI	800P	1	:30	85.4							1	:30	85.4
ABC SUNDAY NIGHT MV	A SUN	900P							1	:30	94.4	1	:30	94.4
BUCK JAMES	A SUN	1000P	1	1:00	188.7							1	:30	188.7
DOLLY	A SUN	900P				1	:30	125.2				1	:30	125.2
HOOPERMAN	A WED	900P				1	1:00	281.4	1	:30	170.1	2	1:30	451.5
MACGYVER	A MON	800P				1	1:00	176.8				1	1:00	176.8
NFL MONDAY NIGHT FTBL	A MON	900P	2	1:00	342.8	3	1:30	609.3	4	2:00	796.0	9	4:30	1748.1
PERFECT STRANGERS	A WED	800P	1	1:00	276.2							1	1:00	276.2
WHO'S THE BOSS-NITE	A TUE	800P	1	:30	197.6							1	:30	197.6
CBS SUNDAY NIGHT MOVIE	C SUN	902P							1	:30	94.4	1	:30	94.4
FRANK'S PLACE	C MON	800P	3	1:30	300.9							3	1:30	300.9
JAKE AND THE FATMAN	C TUE	900P	1	1:00	183.0	3	1:30	265.5	1	:30	67.4	5	2:30	449.9
LAW & HARRY MCGRAW	C TUE	1000P	1	:30	76.0	2	1:00	150.0				4	2:00	293.4
MURDER, SHE WROTE	C SUN	804P	1	1:00	281.1	2	1:00	312.2				3	2:00	593.3
NEWHART	C MON	800P	3	2:00	594.5							3	2:00	594.5
AMER. LGE CHAMP GAME 2	N THU	831P	2	1:00	230.0							2	1:00	230.0
BEVERLY HILLS BUNTZ	N THU	930P							1	:30	120.0	1	:30	120.0
COSBY SHOW	N THU	800P							1	:30	210.0	1	:30	210.0
L.A.LAW-NITE	N THU	1038P	1	:30	205.0							1	:30	205.0
MATLOCK	N TUE	800P				1	1:00	222.0				1	1:00	222.0
MIAMI VICE	N FRI	900P	2	2:00	686.0							2	2:00	686.0
MY TWO DADS	N TUE	844P	2	1:30	567.0							2	1:30	567.0
NAT'L LGE CHAMP GM 1	N TUE	822P	1	:30	115.0							1	:30	115.0
NAT'L LGE CHAMP GM 4	N SAT	441P	2	1:00	230.0							2	1:00	230.0
NAT'L LGE CHAMP GM 6	N TUE	817P	2	1:00	230.0							2	1:00	230.0
NAT'L LGE CHAMP GM 7	N WED	815P	1	:30	115.0							1	:30	115.0
NIGHT COURT	N THU	1000P							1	:30	276.5	2	1:00	276.5
ST. ELSEWHERE	N WED	1000P				1	:30	131.0				1	:30	131.0
PRIME TIME TOTALS			30	19:00	5066.2	15	9:00	2273.4	12	6:00	1909.5	57	34:00	9249.1
CBS MORNING NEWS	C M-F	600A	1	:30	3.0	1	1:00	5.8				2	1:30	8.8
NAT'L LGE CHAMP GM 2	N SAT	300P	1	1:00	38.0							1	1:00	38.0
NBC NEWS AT SUNRISE	N TUE	600A				1	1:00	14.0				1	1:00	14.0
TODAY SHOW	N M-F	700A	2	1:30	101.0	2	1:30	63.0				4	3:00	123.0
M/F DAYTIME TOTALS			4	3:00	101.0	4	3:30	82.8				8	6:30	183.8
AMER. LGE CHAMP GAME 3	N SAT	100P	1	:30	59.5							1	:30	59.5
SUNDAY TODAY	N SUN	800A	1	1:00	7.0	1	:30	7.0				2	:30	21.0
S/S DAYTIME TOTALS			2	1:30	73.5	1	:30	7.0				3	2:00	80.5
CBS EVENING NEWS	C M-F	630P	4	3:30	353.5	2	1:00	100.8	2	1:00	104.0	8	5:30	558.3
CBS EVENING NEWS-SUN	C SUN	600P	1	:30	24.1	2	1:30	68.4				3	2:00	92.5
CBS NEWS/SUMMIT-LATE	C TUE	1130P							1	:30	9.2	1	:30	9.2
NBC NIGHTLY NEWS	N M-F	630P	4	3:30	357.7	3	2:30	272.5	4	2:00	221.3	11	8:00	851.5
NBC SATURDAY NGT NEWS	N SAT	630P				2	1:30	123.0	1	:30	41.5	3	2:30	164.5
E/L FRINGES TOTALS			9	7:30	735.3	9	6:30	564.7	8	4:00	376.0	26	18:00	1676.0
PRODUCT TOTALS			48	31:00	5976.0	29	19:30	2927.9	20	10:00	2285.5	95	60:30	11189.4
PRODUCT TOTALS YTD												111	71:30	13318.0
BUICK AUTOS-RIVIERA ---- T111														
PRODUCT TOTALS YTD												9	4:30	259.5
BUICK AUTOS-SKYHAWK ---- T111														
PRODUCT TOTALS YTD												18	9:00	1075.0
BUICK AUTOS-SKYLARK ---- T111														
PRODUCT TOTALS YTD												18	9:00	728.8
PARENT COMPANY CONTINUES														

Source: Broadcast Advertisers Report. Copyright 1988. Reprinted by permission.

FIGURE 7-7.   Barcume: National Spot TV Expenditures

SECTION 2 BRAND/PRODUCT MARKET EXPENDITURES

BRAND/PRODUCT MARKET(S)	OCT	NOV	DEC	QTR
F132				
CHEESE				
************ CONTINUED ************				
CHEEZ WHIZ CHEESE SPREAD-------------CONT				
KNOXVILLE	.8			.8
LITTLE ROCK			.6	.6
MINNEAPOLIS		1.5		1.5
NEW YORK	2.2			2.2
OMAHA			.1	.1
PHILADELPHIA	1.0	1.3	.5	2.7
PITTSBURGH	.1			.1
SACRAMENTO		.6		.6
SAN ANTONIO	.3			.3
SCRANTON	.5			.5
SEATTLE	.8			.8
SPOKANE	.8			.8
TOTALS	6.8	3.5	2.4	12.7
COLEMAN DAIRY-COTTAGE CHEESE-------				
LITTLE ROCK			1.1	1.1
COUNTRY FRESH DAIRY-COTTAGE CHEESE-----				
GRAND RAPIDS	.8			.8
COUNTY LINE CHEESE-------				
ATLANTA	30.1	27.2	18.3	70.6
CHICAGO	79.0	38.6	28.6	146.2
DALLAS	39.8	36.5	25.9	102.2
DETROIT	19.4	15.2	14.5	49.1
FLINT		14.2	13.7	27.9
HOUSTON	36.4	22.6	16.6	75.7
JACKSONVILLE	16.5		14.3	30.8
MIAMI	45.4	28.7	21.7	95.9
SAN ANTONIO	28.9	23.3	28.5	80.6
SCRANTON	25.2		14.6	39.8
TAMPA		52.6		52.6
TOTALS	320.7	234.6	268.1	823.3
CRYSTAL CREAM DAIRY-COTTAGE CHEESE----				
SACRAMENTO		18.4		18.4
DAIRYLEA DAIRY-CTTG CHEESE&SOUR CRM-----				
ALBANY	21.6	14.0		35.6
SYRACUSE	18.6	10.9		29.5
TOTALS	40.2	24.9		65.0
EMMENTALER SWISS CHEESE--------				
NEW YORK		5.7		5.7
GOLDEN GUERNSEY DAIRY-COTTAGE CHEESE-----				
MILWAUKEE		3.0	2.1	5.1
HELUVA GOOD DAIRY PDTS-CHEESE&DIPS-----				
NORFOLK		30.5		30.5
RICHMOND		3.1		3.1
TOTALS		33.6		33.6
KAUKAUNA CHEESE----				
GREEN BAY		2.6		2.6
KRAFT FOOD-CHEESES-----				
CHICAGO	1.1			1.1
SALT LAKE CITY	27.9			27.9
WASHINGTON	1.0	1.6	1.3	3.9
TOTALS	30.0	1.6	1.3	32.9
KRAFT FOOD-GRATED CHEESE-----				
SCRANTON		18.4	11.9	30.3
KRAFT FOOD-SHREDDED CHEESE-----				
WASHINGTON		1.0	.6	1.6
WICHITA	.3			.3
KRAFT FOOD-SINGLES CHEESE SLICES-----				
CHICAGO		.5		.5
DALLAS		.6		.6
HOUSTON		.5		.5
MINNEAPOLIS		.2		.2
NEW YORK	4.4		4.4	
ST LOUIS	1.1		1.1	
WASHINGTON	1.0		1.0	
TOTALS	8.1	8.1		
LAUGHING COW CHEESE----				
NEW YORK	41.0	55.5		96.5
LORRAINE CHEESE-----				
BUFFALO	10.0	9.8		19.9
MIAMI	38.7	37.5	38.7	114.8
MILWAUKEE	31.1		22.4	53.5
ST LOUIS		28.1	2.2	30.3
TOTALS	79.8	75.4	63.2	218.4
LOUIS TRAUTH DAIRY-COTTAGE CHEESE-----				
GRAND RAPIDS			.3	.3
MCCAINS FOOD-CHEESE-----				
BUFFALO	14.7			14.7
PHILA BRAND-CREAM CHEESE-----				
BOSTON		1.1	.5	1.6
CEDAR RAPIDS	.1			.1
CHAMPAIGN	.1			.1
CLEVELAND	.1			.1
DALLAS	.1			.1
DETROIT	.2			.2
GRAND RAPIDS		.5		.5
GREENVILLE	.6			.6
HOUSTON	.6	.3	.1	1.0
LOUISVILLE	.4			.4
MIAMI	.6			.6
MINNEAPOLIS	.2			.2
MOBILE	.1			.1
NEW YORK	.5			.5
OMAHA	.1			.1
PHILADELPHIA	1.3	.5	.2	1.9
PITTSBURGH		.3		.3
PORTLAND OR	2.6			2.6
ROCHESTER	.2			.2
SEATTLE	.1			.1
SYRACUSE	.1			.1
WASHINGTON	.1			.1
WICHITA	.1			.1
TOTALS	9.0	7.7	2.2	12.0
PHILA BRAND-LIGHT CREAM CHEESE-----				
ALBANY	.7			.7
BIRMINGHAM	.2			.2
BOSTON	.5	.2		.7
BUFFALO	.2			.2
CEDAR RAPIDS	.1			.1
CHICAGO	.4	1.8		2.1
CINCINNATI			.4	.4
CLEVELAND	.1	.4	.6	1.1
DALLAS		.5		.5
DETROIT	.2		.6	.8
FRESNO	.1			.1
GREEN BAY	.1			.1
HARRISBURG	.1			.1
HOUSTON	.1			.1
INDIANAPOLIS	2.2			2.2
JACKSONVILLE			1.1	1.1
LITTLE ROCK			.5	.5
LOS ANGELES	.6	.1	1.4	1.5
LOUISVILLE	.9			.9

BRAND/PRODUCT MARKET(S)	OCT	NOV	DEC	QTR
MEMPHIS	.1			.1
MIAMI	.4	.2	.2	.7
MINNEAPOLIS	.4	.9	.1	1.3
NASHVILLE	1.0			1.0
ORLANDO	.3			.3
PHILADELPHIA	.5	.3	.5	1.3
PHOENIX	.5			.5
PITTSBURGH	.1			.3
PORTLAND ME	.1	.3		.3
RALEIGH	.5			.5
ROANOKE	.1			.1
SALT LAKE CITY	.3			.3
SAN ANTONIO		.5		.5
SAN DIEGO		1.1		1.1
SAN FRANCISCO	.3	.3	.2	1.1
SCRANTON	1.1			1.1
SEATTLE		.4		.4
SHREVEPORT		.1		.1
SPOKANE		.1		.1
ST LOUIS		.9		.9
TAMPA			1.1	1.1
WASHINGTON	.2	.2		.5
WEST PALM BCH	.2			.2
WICHITA		.2		.2
TOTALS	7.9	13.6	6.6	28.3
POLLY-O DAIRY PDTS-CHEESE SNACKS-----				
BALTIMORE	53.2			53.2
BOSTON	60.4	24.6	2.9	87.9
HARTFORD	1.7			1.7
MIAMI	9.3	6.9		16.2
NEW YORK	58.7	52.3		111.0
PHILADELPHIA	45.2	15.3		60.5
WASHINGTON	56.5	16.5	2.5	75.6
TOTALS	284.9	115.7	5.4	406.1
SARGENTO CHEESE-GRATED-----				
JACKSONVILLE	.9			.9
SARGENTO CHEESE-SHREDDED-----				
ALBANY	11.8	13.8		25.6
ATLANTA	21.2	16.9	1.2	39.3
BOSTON	37.8	46.5	3.4	86.7
BUFFALO	2.1	20.2		22.3
CEDAR RAPIDS	5.5			5.5
CHARLOTTE		4.8		4.8
CHICAGO	51.0	39.9	6.3	97.2
CINCINNATI	15.0	27.4		42.4
COLUMBUS	34.1	32.0		66.1
DENVER	16.6			16.6
DES MOINES	7.7			7.7
GRAND RAPIDS		.2		.2
GREEN BAY	1.2	4.0		5.2
GREENSBORO	10.9			10.9
INDIANAPOLIS	40.4	50.4		90.8
JACKSONVILLE	5.0		1.3	6.3
KANSAS CITY	21.7	14.0		35.8
MIAMI	25.8	30.9		56.7
MILWAUKEE	8.4	11.8		20.1
MINNEAPOLIS	17.8	19.2		37.0
OMAHA		1.1		1.1
ORLANDO	28.7	27.4		56.1
PROVIDENCE		.2		.2
ROCHESTER		.2		.2
WEST PALM BCH	14.1			14.1
TOTALS	374.6	360.2	12.2	749.2
SARGENTO CHEESE-SHREDDED&GRATED-----				
CINCINNATI		3.2		3.2
SUPREME CHEESE-----				
PROVIDENCE		4.8		4.8
SWITZERLAND SWISS CHEESE-----				
ST LOUIS		.1	.1	.2
VELVEETA FOOD-CHEESE SPREAD-----				
PHILADELPHIA		1.9		1.9
RALEIGH	2.1			2.1
WASHINGTON		.3		.3
TOTALS	2.1	2.2		4.4
VELVEETA FOOD-SHREDDED CHEESE-----				
DALLAS	22.2	19.8		42.1
KANSAS CITY	8.3	9.1		17.4
MEMPHIS		4.7	5.7	10.4
OKLAHOMA CITY	6.8	6.7		13.5
TULSA	7.0			7.0
WICHITA	4.2			4.2
TOTALS	48.6	40.3	5.7	94.6
WISCONSIN CHEESE-----				
DENVER			36.1	36.1
F133				
ICE CREAM, SHERBETS & FROZEN NOVELTIES				
ANDERSON ERICKSON-ICE CREAM-----				
DES MOINES	4.8	2.0	2.6	9.4
ARCTIC FRUIT ICE-----				
DALLAS	.5			.5
BARRICINI ICE CREAM-----				
DALLAS	38.9			38.9
HOUSTON	15.0			15.0
TOTALS	53.8			53.8
BLUE BUNNY DAIRY-ICE CREAM-----				
DES MOINES	5.5		7.4	12.9
KANSAS CITY	11.2	1.5		12.7
LITTLE ROCK			6.0	6.0
MINNEAPOLIS	4.5	5.4	4.6	14.5
OKLAHOMA CITY	15.4	8.3		23.7
OMAHA	13.0	10.6	1.7	26.4
TULSA	6.9			6.9
TOTALS	56.4	25.8	19.6	96.9
BLUE BUNNY DAIRY-ICE MILK-----				
MINNEAPOLIS	2.1			2.1
BORDEN FOOD-ICE CREAM-----				
ALBUQUERQUE			2.6	2.6
CINCINNATI	2.3	.8		3.1
CLEVELAND	.1			.1
TOLEDO	.4			.4
TOTALS	2.8	.8	2.6	6.2
BREYERS-ICE CREAM-----				
LITTLE ROCK	13.4			13.4
PORTLAND OR	2.4			2.4
TOTALS	15.8			15.8
BREYERS-MARBLE CLASSIC ICE CRM-----				
JACKSONVILLE	22.6			22.6
MIAMI	52.6			52.6
TOTALS	75.1			75.1
COLEMAN DAIRY-ICE CREAM-----				
LITTLE ROCK	6.4			6.4
CREAMLAND OLTY CHCK-ICE CREAM-----				
ALBUQUERQUE			2.0	2.0
CRYSTAL LIGHT-FROZEN BARS-----				
PROVIDENCE	.2			.2

BRAND/PRODUCT MARKET(S)	OCT	NOV	DEC	QTR
DEERING ICE CREAM-----				
BOSTON		9.7	3.7	13.3
PORTLAND ME		67.3	67.3	
TOTALS		9.7	71.0	80.6
DISNEY FROZEN TREATS-----				
WASHINGTON			.5	.5
DOLE FOOD-FRUIT N CREAM BAR-----				
DALLAS			16.4	16.4
HOUSTON			19.5	19.5
JACKSONVILLE			4.9	4.9
LOS ANGELES			79.5	79.5
MIAMI			17.3	17.3
NEW ORLEANS			8.3	8.3
NEW YORK			33.1	33.1
ORLANDO			10.8	10.8
PHOENIX			16.9	16.9
SACRAMENTO			23.9	23.9
SAN ANTONIO			6.5	6.5
SAN DIEGO			25.9	25.9
SAN FRANCISCO			37.5	37.5
TAMPA			17.1	17.1
TOTALS			317.7	317.7
DOLE FOOD-FRUIT N JUICE BARS-----				
MIAMI			.4	.4
DOLE FOOD-FRZN FRUIT SORBET-----				
DALLAS			16.7	16.7
HOUSTON			17.8	17.8
JACKSONVILLE			5.9	5.9
LOS ANGELES			46.1	46.1
NEW ORLEANS			4.8	4.8
NEW YORK			29.3	29.3
ORLANDO			10.9	10.9
PHOENIX			22.9	22.9
SACRAMENTO			16.3	16.3
SAN ANTONIO			11.1	11.1
SAN DIEGO			35.1	35.1
SAN FRANCISCO			45.4	45.4
TAMPA			16.7	16.7
TOTALS			304.6	304.6
DOVEBAR ICE CREAM-----				
DENVER			.8	.8
SAN FRANCISCO		1.9		1.9
TOTALS		1.9	.8	2.7
DRUMSTICK ICE CREAM TRTS-----				
LOS ANGELES	169.0	66.0		235.0
SACRAMENTO		43.0		43.0
SAN FRANCISCO	109.3	32.4		141.6
TOTALS	278.2	141.4		419.6
EAGLE BRAND-ICE CREAM-----				
CINCINNATI			4.0	4.0
CLEVELAND	.1	.1		.2
COLUMBUS	.7			.7
EDY'S LIGHT ICE CREAM-----				
KANSAS CITY	86.1	45.4		131.5
MINNEAPOLIS	31.9			31.9
TOTALS	118.0	45.4		163.4
FITZGERALD ICE CREAM-----				
ALBUQUERQUE		10.0	10.4	20.7
FOREVER YOURS ICE CRM SN-----				
SAN FRANCISCO	64.1	50.9	12.8	127.8
FRUSEN-GLADJE-ICE CREAM-----				
CHICAGO	35.4	11.7	28.3	75.4
GOLD RUSH-ICE CREAM BARS-----				
DALLAS	1.5			1.5
SAN DIEGO	1.9			1.9
ST LOUIS	2.1			2.1
TOLEDO	.7			.7
WASHINGTON	3.0	.4		3.4
TOTALS	9.2	.4		9.6
HOMEMADE BRAND-ICE CREAM-----				
CINCINNATI		25.6		25.6
DAYTON		15.0		15.0
INDIANAPOLIS		37.0		37.0
LOUISVILLE		14.1		14.1
TOLEDO	1.4	13.0		14.4
TOTALS	1.4	104.7		106.1
HOOD DAIRY-LITE ICE CREAM-----				
BALTIMORE		42.7	2.2	44.9
WASHINGTON		37.9		61.4
TOTALS	23.5	80.6	2.2	106.4
HYGEIA DAIRY-ICE CREAM-----				
HOUSTON	33.1			33.1
ICEE ICE CONFECTION-----				
HARRISBURG	.7			.7
JELL-O-FRZN GELATIN POPS-----				
MIAMI			5.1	5.1
JOHNSONS DAIRY-ICE CREAM-----				
CHARLESTON	1.5	1.4		6.4
KEMPS DAIRY-ICE CREAM-----				
MINNEAPOLIS			6.4	6.4
KINNETTS FRZN TREATS-----				
ATLANTA	5.9	5.0	3.8	14.7
KLONDIKE-ICE CREAM BAR-----				
PHILADELPHIA	10.7			10.7
WASHINGTON	7.5			7.5
TOTALS	18.2			18.2
KLONDIKE-ICE CREAM NUGGETS-----				
NEW ORLEANS	4.5			4.5
KLONDIKE-ICE CREAM SANDWICH-----				
FLINT		8.6	27.9	36.5
GRAND RAPIDS		25.1		25.1
GREEN BAY	9.0	18.7		27.8
MILWAUKEE	13.5	40.9		54.4
PITTSBURGH		46.4	22.8	69.3
TOTALS	101.6	110.3		211.9
LA SALLE ICE CREAM-----				
NEW YORK	5.3	9.2		14.5
LADY BORDEN-ICE CREAM-----				
ALBUQUERQUE			1.0	1.0
LIGHT N LIVELY FOOD-ICE MILK-----				
BOSTON	30.4			30.4
HARTFORD			30.5	30.5
TOTALS	30.5			30.5
MCARTHUR T G LEE-ICE CREAM-----				
ORLANDO	11.1			11.1
MCDONALDS DAIRY-ICE CREAM-----				
FLINT	1.4	10.9		12.3
MELODY FARMS DAIRY-ICE CREAM-----				
DETROIT	.1			.1
MORADE-FRZN CHEESECAKE/STICK-----				
CHICAGO		85.2	30.6	115.8
MY FAVORITE ICE CREAM-----				
BUFFALO	57.4	18.0		75.4
NESTLE FOOD-CRUNCH ICE CREAM BAR-----				
NEW YORK		.9		.9
PITTSBURGH	.3			.3
WASHINGTON	.4	.9		1.3
TOTALS	.4	.9		1.3

Source: Broadcast Advertisers Report. Copyright 1988. Reprinted by permission.

TABLE 7-1. Competitive Media Expenditure Analysis for a Product Class

Brands	Magazines (%)	Supplements (%)	Newspapers (%)	Network TV (%)	Spot TV (%)	Outdoor (%)	Totals (%)
A	9.8	12.8	50.3	19.8	—	7.3	100
B	36.7	11.5	43.1	8.7	—	—	100
C	0.5	5.9	47.8	45.3	—	0.5	100
D	5.4	2.9	5.9	80.6	5.2	—	100
E	0.5	—	9.6	20.2	69.6	—	100

The study of annual expenditures is only one approach in analyzing competitors' marketing and media strategies. Another useful analysis may be made by comparing expenditures of a brand with its competitors on a market-by-market basis. This technique may be helpful in learning which markets were most important to competitors, and the analysis may serve as one basis for weighting media in a given market. It is easy to locate these markets in Media Records but difficult in LNA Network Television Service or LNA Magazine Analysis Service. It may be possible, however, to estimate which markets were used and the relative weights placed in these markets.

Still another kind of analysis may be made of the dollars spent in each medium by a brand and its competitors, correlated with the audience delivered for the dollars spent. This technique makes possible a quick analysis of the relative delivery effectiveness of competitors' media expenditures. Plans for a brand's reach and frequency often come from such an analysis.

Finally, it is important to learn how much was spent in each medium during each month of the year. Most brands have peak selling seasons and vary the weight of their advertising accordingly. This kind of analysis helps to establish timing and scheduling plans for the media selected later in the planning process.

Analyzing the Data

One worthwhile use of media expenditure figures is to examine spending by advertisers who lead in share of market. Those with smaller shares might want to learn which media, markets, and audiences are most important to the leaders. Sometimes it is possible to find that leading competitors ignore one or two media entirely. In such a case, it may be possible for those with lesser shares to preempt a medium for themselves. For example, all of the share leaders may emphasize network television. Then, a planner may select radio as a medium in which a brand could be very significant because no others are using radio. The planner should keep in mind, however, that if a competitor avoids a medium, there may be good reason to conclude that the medium is not appropriate for the product's advertising.

There are, of course, problems in analyzing media expenditure data. Most such data are incomplete, do not show any discounts earned in a medium, and cover only large advertisers. An additional problem is the age of the data. It is rare that any data are less than one month old, and, as a result, the nature of the data is historical rather than contemporary. The question arises whether such data have very much meaning, especially if a competitor is not currently using the same media in the same ways as in the past. Yet if a competitor uses media in a predictably consistent pattern, then additional data may be of little value. Probably the best use of an expenditure analysis is as part of an organized intelligence system including other kinds of marketing information to provide a clear picture of competitors' strategies. Although some advertising agencies tend to deprecate the use of expenditure analysis as not being worth the investment in money or time, most large agencies feel that it is valuable if used properly as an indication of spending strategy.

Probably the greatest danger in analyzing expenditure data may come from simply copying the leaders in a blind fashion. If a leading share competitor places 10 percent of its budget in Market A, then other competitors may follow the leader. But the followers' products and market strategies may not lend themselves to such weight in Market A. Furthermore, the share leader may establish its weight proportions for reasons quite different from those that followers ought to use.

An expenditure analysis is helpful as a means of knowing what competitors have done, but not necessarily as a means of knowing what to do as a result. These analyses may show, for example, that a competitor is test marketing a product, and this information may call for a revised market strategy to combat the situation. Intelligently used, expenditure data may be well worth the time and money invested.

Using Competitive Media Expenditure Analyses

Following is a list of uses of a competitive media expenditure analysis devised by the staff of *Media Decisions.*[3] It reviews the most important uses and values to be obtained by completing such an analysis:

1. The expenditure figures can show you the regionality and seasonality and how these factors are changing for all competitive and potentially competitive brands.
2. The data can give you a fix on ad budget size and media mix market by market.
3. You can use the data to spot new product tests and to track new brand roll-outs.
4. You can infer from where the money is being spent how competitors view their target audiences, how they profile their brands, and where they seek to position themselves in your marketplace.
5. You can watch spending patterns of the opposition—TV flighting, radio station rotation, position practices in magazines, or day of week in newspapers.
6. Once you have complete knowledge of what your enemies are up to, you can make better decisions as to where to meet them head-on and when to outflank them.
7. In new-product and line-extension planning, expenditure data are es-

3. *Media Decisions,* "Do You Know Your Competitive Brand Data?" August 1975, p. 60.

sential to estimate how much it will cost to get into a market, who's already there, and which competitive product types are growing fastest in the new product's market segment.

Sources of Marketing Data

Size and share of market for a brand and its competitors, and other information that comprise a situation analysis, may be obtained from a number of syndicated research services. Other data may be obtained from periodicals, association reports, government, and media.

Major Data Services

The most widely used syndicated research services are those of the A. C. Nielsen Company, the Market Research Corporation of America (MRCA), Audits and Surveys, Inc., Selling Areas-Marketing, Inc. (SAMI), Mediamark Research, Inc. (MRI), and the W. R. Simmons Company (SMRB). Numerous other research companies also exist.

The A. C. Nielsen Company. Nielsen provides a national brand, store-audited service covering almost every product sold in food and drug stores. Each of these product categories is audited in a national sample of retail stores every sixty days. The service provides share-of-market data based on sales to consumers at the retail level, in addition to average retail prices, wholesale prices, inventory, out-of-stock, dealer support (displays, local advertising, and coupon redemption), and major media advertising. The sample data are then projected in order to obtain national and regional data. The figures are further broken down by county size, store type (chain and independent), brand, package size, and product type.

The method of making an audit is to count a store's inventory of a given product no matter where it is stored. Sales for a given period are found by subtracting the total stock on hand at the close of a period from the total available for sale at the beginning. Because only a sample of stores is audited, it becomes necessary to project average per store sales to a national figure and to geographical regions, city-size groups, and so forth.

Market Research Corporation of America. MRCA maintains a consumer panel of 7,500 families who keep continuous diaries of their purchases. The panel members record food, grocery, and personal care items purchased during any given week and then mail their diaries to the company for tabulation. Diaries include quantities purchased, package sizes, prices paid, and the kind of retail outlet through which purchases were made. Other information includes effects of promotional activities such as coupons, one-cent sales, or combination sales of different products. Through such tabulations it is possible to learn the share of market for many different brands and varieties of food products.

Audits and Surveys, Inc. This service measures the national total market based on a sample of the client's product class distribution. The sample of stores to be audited is drawn only from the types of outlets in which the client has distribution. Information is provided on sales, inventory, distribution, out-of-stock, and the number of days stock is on hand. These data are projected to the total U.S. and the client's sales regions. Audits and Surveys telephones a flash report to the client at the close of the audit followed by a formal report two weeks later, compared to Nielsen's forty-five to sixty days for reports to reach a client.

Selling Areas-Marketing, Inc. (SAMI). This company reports warehouse withdrawals to food stores in defined marketing areas. Specifically, SAMI provides information on the sales movement of all dry grocery and household supplies. Frozen food, health and beauty aids, fresh meat, perishables, milk, bread, and soft drinks are not included. An "Executive Review" is especially important because it summarizes individual brand shares for all SAMI markets and provides category sales volume and brand share for the total U.S. market.

Mediamark Research, Inc. (MRI), and W. R. Simmons (SMRB). These companies provide marketing as well as media data on a regular basis. Each company reports how often products and/or brands are used so that a planner can identify heavy and light users demographically. In addition, each company reports how heavy and light users were exposed to either network television programs or national magazines. As a result, the planner can select media that not only have the largest audiences, but the largest audiences of heavy users of a given product or brand. Special studies are also available on a custom basis.

Zip Code Marketing. There are two major concerns in this area: PRIZM and ACORN. PRIZM provides marketing data at every microgeographic level including zip codes, census tracts, census block groups, compiled list cells and postal carrier routes.

ACORN provides a classification for residential neighborhoods. It classifies all U.S. neighborhoods into forty-four distinct, homogeneous, "life-style" types or market segments, for example, "middle-income, post-war suburbs, older populations, etc." (For further discussion, see Chapter 4, "New Measuring Tools.")

Other Sources of Data

The preceding sources of data provide specific and pertinent data for a situation analysis, but are relatively expensive. The cost may be too high for many small manufacturers or agencies, so it becomes necessary to find substitute sources of data. There are a number of relatively inexpensive sources, though they do not provide the same amount of detail, especially about competitors' sales and distribution practices. When the information is incomplete, assumptions will have to be made about the missing data. These assumptions, however, can often be checked by astute observers of the marketing action of both their own company and competitors. The following list, meanwhile, may be helpful in locating data for the situation analysis.

Sales & Marketing Management's Survey of Buying Power. Marketing and media planners often find the *Sales & Marketing Management Survey of Buying Power* a convenient source of three kinds of data about markets:

1. Population and household data for all major geographical markets in the United States.
2. Effective buying income and spending statistics about markets.
3. Retail sales data by broad product classes. The classes reported are: (a) food stores; (b) eating and drinking places; (c) general merchandise stores; (d) automotive dealers; (e) furniture, home furnishings, and appliances; (f) drugstores; (g) apparel and accessory stores; (h) gasoline service stations; (i) building materials and hardware stores.

No individual brand sales are shown, and there are no classifications of consumers other than by population and income. However, the periodical is convenient in locating and evaluating geographical markets by state, by Metropolitan Statistical Area, by county, or by city. Furthermore, the three factors (population, income, and retail sales) have been combined into a multiple factor index number for each market that makes comparisons among markets easier. Convenient tables ranking markets by sales potential also facilitate comparisons by each of the nine retail product categories. A user trying to find and evaluate markets for a drug product, for example, will find a table that ranks markets from best to poorest on the basis of sales of drugs. *Sales Management & Marketing Survey of Buying Power* is published annually.

Standard Rate and Data Service (SRDS). The Standard Rate and Data Service publishes media rate books for all major media. In its local media books (newspaper, spot radio, and spot television) are market data sections similar to those in the *Survey of Buying Power.* SRDS also shows geographical markets by state, Metropolitan Statistical Areas, counties, and cities, but not in as much detail as the *Buying Power* book. Retail sales, too, are shown by seven different categories: (a) food, (b) drugs, (c) general merchandise, (d) apparel, (e) home furnishings, (f) automotive, and (g) service stations. Ranking tables are also provided, showing markets for the seven product types. Local media rate books are published monthly, and the market data are revised annually.

Editor and Publisher Market Guide. This annual publication contains geographical market data similar to that of the preceding two. Markets are also ranked by population, total income, total retail sales, total food sales, and by household income. The text also provides individual descriptions of markets.

Census Data. The U.S. Department of Commerce publishes many census analyses that are helpful in marketing planning. Most useful have been the "Census of Business" and "Census of Population." But other census data, too numerous to list here, are available for special industries. The *Statistical Abstract,* published once a year, has been considered helpful as a quick source of data for media market planning.

Media Studies of Special Markets. Often local and national media conduct special market studies that may be quite helpful in learning about geographical as well as special markets. Although the purpose of these reports is to show a given medium in a favorable light, the researcher should not assume that all such studies are biased. Often a medium will sponsor a study that represents a significant contribution to the understanding of markets and media. Many times the only research available on a special market or medium is to be found in these studies.

Among the most widely used sources of market data and among the few that show brand share of markets are brand preference studies conducted by local newspapers and provided free of cost to agencies. Different newspapers use different names for these studies, but they are essentially home inventories of the many different product brands that have been recently purchased. The *Milwaukee Journal* has one of the most well-known of such studies; reports on brands of face soaps, coffees, packaged meats, and almost one hundred other items. The data are tabulated and the percentage of total sales that each brand has is computed so that, in effect, one may have a share of market for a given brand in that area. Because there are many such studies in existence, it is possible to get some idea of the relative share of market for a brand in various parts of the country by comparing data from a composite selection.

Unfortunately, most studies are conducted only once a year and some newspapers do not repeat their studies each year. Furthermore, there may be differences in the degree of control exercised in the collection and reporting of such data, so that it is difficult to know how precise the data are. Then, too, because the data are collected only once a year, there is no measure of total volume purchased, because an individual may just happen to have purchased a given brand only at the time the study was made.

There are a number of publications that offer market and media data on a regular basis. The more useful ones are: *Advertising Age, Marketing and Media Decisions, Marketing Communications, Adweek, Broadcasting, Editor & Publisher, Magazine,* and *Television/Radio Age.* Information can be obtained from the publications by either subscribing to them or by contacting their libraries to determine what studies were published in their past issues.

Associations. There are many trade associations that report market data for their members. In some cases, these data show sales by brands, but others tend to be rather general. Because there are so many different trade associations in the country, it is advisable to determine whether they can be of aid in compiling the situation analysis.

Miscellaneous Sources. There are yet other sources of data that are available at relatively low cost to the market/media planner. Federal, state, and local governments all produce various kinds of research that may be helpful. Federal data may be found by writing to the Government Printing Office in Washington, D.C.

Chambers of Commerce, both national and local, may be helpful in finding the right kinds of data needed for marketing situation purposes. Obviously this kind of data will be rather general but may be useful for preliminary portions of the analysis.

Finally, for analysis of products and product values, both *Consumer Reports* (published by the Consumer Union of U.S., Inc.) and *Consumer Bulletin* (published by Consumer Research, Inc.) provide monthly and annual publications for a small cost. Both of these organizations put various brands of products through rigorous tests to determine quality and the best buy for the money. Not all brands or models are tested, but many of the most popular brands on the market are analyzed. Ordinarily, this kind of information is difficult to obtain except by special research services, so these two publications make the job of finding product values relatively easy.

In conclusion, then, the situation analysis is a very important document in the media planning area. To the extent that it is done thoroughly and accurately, it can help the media planner make more effective decisions by providing a complete picture of the marketing situation not only for the client's brand but for the competitors'.

QUESTIONS FOR DISCUSSION

1. Briefly explain the role of a marketing strategy plan in media planning.
2. Give some examples of marketing objectives and some related marketing strategies that could be used to attain each objective.
3. What is the difference between a marketing objective and the basic selling idea in a marketing strategy plan?
4. Why may it be advisable to place more dollars in markets where a brand has been selling well, rather than in a new undeveloped market?
5. Why can't a manufacturer of cereals look at its sales records and know how well the brand is selling at any local (retail) level?
6. Why may it not be a good idea for a national advertiser to select local markets in which to advertise only on the basis of shipments to those markets?
7. Should media planners use the same media that most of their competitors use? Briefly explain.
8. How can an advertiser ''force'' distribution sometimes in a market where its brand is not distributed?
9. In what ways does a sales promotion plan affect media planning?
10. Suppose that a planner feels that television is best for a given brand, but the creative people insist that an ad appear only in four colors in print. Whose judgment will probably be more significant?

SELECTED READINGS

Advertising Age, ''Bolte Tells of 12 Criteria to Check Marketing Approach,'' May 16, 1966, p. 98.

Advertising Age, ''Know Market Goals, Then Pick Media, AMC Exec Says,'' May 8, 1972, p. 32.

Blair, William, ''Does Profile Matching Work?'' *Media/Scope,* September 1965, pp. 82–86.

Bogart, Leo, ''Relating Media Strategy to Sales,'' *Sales Management,* November 1, 1971, p. 26.

Bruno, A. V., *et al.,* ''Media Approaches to Segmentation,'' *Journal of Advertising Research,* April 1973, pp. 35–42.

Chait, Lawrence, *Targeted Marketing,* Lawrence G. Chait & Co., Inc., 1965.

Clancy, Kevin J., ''The Failure of Marketing Programs," *Marketing and Media Decisions,* May 1986, p. 160.

Colley, Russell H., *Defining Advertising Goals for Measured Advertising Results,* Association of National Advertisers, Inc., 1961.

Garfinkel, Norton, "New Measurements of the Value of Marketing Targets and Media Vehicles." Speech delivered to the Advertising Research Foundation, 12th Annual Conference, 1966.

Greene, Jerome D., "Media Exposure as a Demographic," *Media/Scope,* November 1966, pp. 116–18.

Honomichl, Jack J., "How Research Relates to the Marketing Process," in "The New World of Advertising," *Advertising Age,* November 21, 1973, pp. 52ff.

Journal of Small Business Management, "Guidelines for Advertising Media Management," January 1978, pp. 34–40.

Joyce, Timothy, "Target Weighting Gives Boost to Consumer Studies," *Advertising Age,* July 15, 1974, p. 27.

Lodish, L. M., "Considering Competition in Media Planning," *Management Science,* February 1971, pp. 293–306.

Media/Scope, "How Media Strategy Is De-

veloped in the Marketing Concept," May 1960, pp. 45–48.

Meyers, Edward H., "Media Market Planning," *Grey Matter,* Vol. 41, May 1970 (Speech).

Ostrow, Joseph, "Let's Become Objective," *Media Decisions,* May 1972, p. 64.

Peckham, James O., "Can We Relate Advertising Dollars to Market Share Objectives?" Advertising Research Foundation, 12th Annual Conference, 1966, pp. 53–57.

Setar, John W., "How to Solve the Problem of Problem Markets," *Television Magazine,* September 1959, p. 56.

Sissors, Jack Z., "Matching Media With Markets," *Journal of Advertising Research,* October 1971, pp. 39–43.

Staff, "Marketing's New Look," *Business Week,* January 26, 1987, pp. 64–69.

Surmanek, Jim, "More to Media Buying than Number Review," *Advertising Age,* May 21, 1979, pp. 64, 66.

Wolfe, Harry D., "The Dimensions of Media Audiences," in *Evaluating Media,* National Industrial Conference Board, Business Policy Study No. 121, 1966, pp. 31–41.

8

Strategy Planning I:
Who, Where, and When

Among the most important decisions that must be made early in the media planning process are:

1. To whom should we advertise?
2. Where, geographically, should we advertise?
3. When should we advertise?

The answers to these questions comprise three of the most important parts of media strategy. Other parts of strategy will be discussed in subsequent chapters.

Once made, these decisions will control other decisions. For example, if it has been agreed that advertising should be directed primarily to women 18–34, then media alternatives such as sports magazines or TV programs directed primarily to men would not be appropriate. (Obviously there are some exceptions—but not many.) To control later decisions, target decisions must be made early.

Sometimes the media planner makes these decisions alone, but more often the process includes creative and marketing planners as well as input from the client. It is most often a team process.

Answers to each of the three big questions rely most heavily on numerical analysis of marketing and media data, but they also involve judgment and subjective appraisal. Numbers that are evaluated literally may be subject to error. One must know where the numbers came from—how they were obtained or calculated. The best planners know the value of research methodology as well as how to analyze the numbers. The search for objectivity in planning requires both abilities.

In analyzing numerical data, there are three commonly used bases: raw numbers, percentages, and index numbers. Raw numbers are used least often because they are so large and because it is difficult to compare the raw numbers of one brand with those of another brand, each of which may have radically different bases. Percentages are a

TABLE 8-1.   Use of Ground Coffee by Age Segment

Age Segment	No. of Homemakers in U.S. (thousands)	U.S. Homemakers (%)	No. of Homemaker Users (thousands)	Homemaker Users (%)
18–24	9515	11.6	4204	8.9
25–34	19317	23.5	10588	22.5
35–44	15210	18.5	9526	20.2
45–54	11398	13.9	7397	15.7
55–64	11663	14.2	7278	15.5
65 +	15171	18.4	8102	17.2
Total	82274	100.0	47095	100.0

Source: Simmons Market Research Bureau, 1985. Reprinted by permission.

way to equalize the bases of numbers from two or more companies and thus are usually preferred over raw numbers. For ease and quickness in seeing the relationships among many numbers, index numbers are preferred over the other two.

Using Index Numbers to Analyze Markets

As used most often in marketing and media analysis, an index number is a number that shows a relationship between two percentages or between two raw numbers. Generally index numbers are expressed as whole numbers, though they can be expressed as percentages. The value of an index number is that it relates population demographics to sales or product usage for many different demographic segments, enabling one to have a convenient common method for comparison. If the population segment is considered to be "average," then an index number for sales tells how much above or below average sales are, in absolute terms. An average index number is 100, while 125 is 25 percent above average, and 80 is 20 percent below average. An example of how index numbers may be used is shown in Tables 8-1 and 8-2.

Which demographic segments should be selected as target markets for media to reach? The usual answer is: Select those demographic segments with the largest volume of sales, or the largest number of users. In other words, advertise where the brand has a history of success. According to the traditional point of view, then, three age segments of homemakers in Table 8-1 might be the prime targets for ground coffee—those aged 25-34, 35-44, and 45-54. Of course, 45-54 and 55-64 are also relatively high. Obviously, income, occupation, education, and other demographic categories would also have to be checked before a final decision could be made.

TABLE 8-2.   Calculating Index Numbers (based on Table 8-1)

Age Segment	Calculation	Index
18–24	8.9 ÷ 11.6	77
25–34	22.5 ÷ 23.5	95
35–44	20.2 ÷ 18.5	109
45–54	15.7 ÷ 13.9	113
55–64	15.5 ÷ 14.2	109
65 +	17.2 ÷ 18.4	93

However, there is another way to look at the data in Table 8–1, and that is to compare the percentage of usage in each age segment to the percentage of population in that segment. (One could compare the raw numbers of usage and population distribution in each segment, but such comparisons are more difficult than those made using percentages.)

When the percentage of usage is compared with the percentage of population distribution in each segment, an index number may be calculated to make the comparisons easier to analyze. The formula for calculating such numbers is as follows:

$$\text{Index number} = \frac{\text{\% of users in a demographic segment}}{\text{\% of population in the same segment}} \times 100$$

Using the formula to calculate index numbers for the data in Table 8–1 yields the index numbers in Table 8–2. The index numbers in Table 8–2 show how much the product is being used compared with the potential (or population proportion) for use in each segment. An index number above 100, as seen in the 35–44, 45–54, and 55–64 age groups, indicates higher than average usage. Now one can see that the potential for usage has shifted a bit to older age segments. In this sense, index numbers more accurately indicate potential for usage or sales. One cannot easily see this kind of relationship, however, without first calculating the index numbers.

It may be helpful to think of index numbers as measures of central tendency, just as "averages" or "means" are in the statistical world. An average does not describe any one person in a group, only the group as a whole.

Likewise, an index number over 100 means that the usage of the product is proportionately greater in that segment than one that is average (100) or below average (any number below 100). Segments with index numbers over 100 do not necessarily have numerically more users in them than in other segments; they may only have proportionately more. Theoretically, the segment with the highest index number represents the best potential for usage. In analyzing marketing data, one should calculate index numbers for all demographic groups such as age, sex, income, occupation, and education. Combining the index numbers for all demographic groups will produce a market profile similar to the one shown in Figure 8–1.

Although the technique of calculating index numbers shown in Table 8–2 can be used, there is a simpler way of computing the numbers that is often preferred by planners. This method is shown in Table 8–3. Briefly stated, the method starts with a measurement of the total number of users in a market. A percentage of the universe is then computed. This percentage indicates that of the total population, X percent are users. The number of users is compared with the number of individuals in each population segment and percentages are calculated. Finally, each of these segment percentages is divided by the total percentage of users. Note that the index numbers obtained by this method are identical to those obtained in Table 8–2.

A note of caution about using index numbers: One may be easily misled into believing that the demographic segment with the highest index number *always* represents the best potential. This is not true. Aside from the fact that one segment may have some other qualification that is of great marketing value, there is also the possibility that a segment with a high index number may have a low degree of prod-

FIGURE 8-1.   Profile of a Market

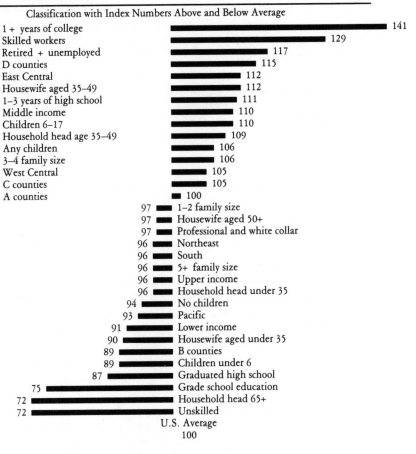

Classification with Index Numbers Above and Below Average

Classification	Index
1 + years of college	141
Skilled workers	129
Retired + unemployed	117
D counties	115
East Central	112
Housewife aged 35–49	112
1–3 years of high school	111
Middle income	110
Children 6–17	110
Household head age 35–49	109
Any children	106
3–4 family size	106
West Central	105
C counties	105
A counties	100
1–2 family size	97
Housewife aged 50+	97
Professional and white collar	97
Northeast	96
South	96
5+ family size	96
Upper income	96
Household head under 35	96
No children	94
Pacific	93
Lower income	91
Housewife aged under 35	90
B counties	89
Children under 6	89
Graduated high school	87
Grade school education	75
Household head 65+	72
Unskilled	72

U.S. Average
100

TABLE 8-3.   Another Method of Calculating Index Numbers

Step One: Find the total number of users compared with the total population in the market as follows:

  a. Total number of users in all segments: 21,500,000
  b. Total number of homemakers in the U.S.: 72,924,000
  c. Percentage of total homemakers that are users: 29.5%

Step Two: Find the percentage of users in each demographic segment (from Table 8–1):

18–24	3,204 ÷ 9,565	=	33.5%
25–34	5,238 ÷ 16,151	=	32.4
35–44	3,582 ÷ 11,812	=	30.3
45–54	3,457 ÷ 12,028	=	28.7
55–64	2,990 ÷ 10,687	=	28.0
65 +	3,029 ÷ 12,681	=	23.9

Step Three: Divide each of the percentages in Step Two by the percentage in Step One:

18–24	33.5 ÷ 29.5	=	114 index
25–34	32.4 ÷ 29.5	=	110 index
35–44	30.3 ÷ 29.5	=	103 index
45–54	28.7 ÷ 29.5	=	97 index
55–64	28.0 ÷ 29.5	=	95 index
65 +	23.9 ÷ 29.5	=	80 index

TABLE 8-4. An Example of Misleading Index Numbers

Age Segment	Population in Each Segment (%)	Product Usage in Each Segment (%)	Index
18–24	11.1	15.0	134
25–34	19.3	17.8	92
35–49	30.2	29.2	97
50+	39.4	38.0	96
Total	100.0	100.0	

uct usage or sales or a low population size for that segment. If so, the segment with the highest index number may not represent the best potential for continued usage.

To illustrate, Table 8–4 shows marketing data for a fictitious brand, showing that, although the 18–24 age segment has the highest index number (134), it also has the lowest percentage of product usage and the lowest population percentage of any segment. It would not be very meaningful, therefore, to limit the selection of media to those reaching the 18–24 segment and ignore the other segments, especially since 85 percent of the usage is in the 25 and older segment.

One should first examine the volume of usage or sales in each demographic segment to determine whether the volume warrants inclusion as a media target. Only then will index numbers help locate good potential target segments.

Selecting Advertising Targets

The answer to the question: "To whom should we advertise?" implies that not everyone should be the target for advertising. Some individuals are more likely than others to buy a given product or brand. The goal is to identify the targets—those who are most likely to buy. Targets will most often be identified on the basis of one or more of the market's demographic characteristics. Which demographic characteristics? Those typical of consumers who have purchased the product/brand in the past and who resemble past purchasers in terms of age, income, occupation, education, and so forth. One source used frequently to gather demographic information is Simmons Market Research Bureau. (An example of Simmons' data is shown in Figure 8–2.) Custom-made research can also provide this kind of information, but it is usually quite expensive and time-consuming.

The planner must consider a number of factors in analyzing how consumers buy certain products. The first is to find those demographic segments that use the product most. Other considerations include: (a) whether any segment of product users ought to be singled out for special treatment, such as heavy users only, medium users, light users, or combinations; (b) whether users of the advertised brand differ from users of the product category in general; (c) whether the creative strategy positions the brand to appeal more to one demographic segment than another; and (d) whether some other kind of target identification, such as psychographics, should be used instead of or in addition to demographics.

FIGURE 8–2. Page from Simmons Market Research Bureau [*]

CAFFEINATED INSTANT & FREEZE-DRIED COFFEE: USAGE ON AVERAGE DAY IN LAST 30 DAYS
(FEMALE HOMEMAKERS)

	TOTAL U.S. '000	ALL USERS A '000	B % DOWN	C % ACROSS	D INDX	HEAVY USERS FIVE OR MORE A '000	B % DOWN	C % ACROSS	D INDX	MEDIUM USERS TWO-FOUR A '000	B % DOWN	C % ACROSS	D INDX	LIGHT USERS ONE OR LESS A '000	B % DOWN	C % ACROSS	D INDX
TOTAL FEMALE HOMEMAKERS	82531	24347	100.0	29.5	100	6022	100.0	7.3	100	10760	100.0	13.0	100	7565	100.0	9.2	100
18 - 24	8060	1943	8.0	24.1	82	*393	6.5	4.9	67	968	9.0	12.0	92	*582	7.7	7.2	79
25 - 34	19731	5571	22.9	28.2	96	1441	23.9	7.3	100	2355	21.9	11.9	92	1776	23.5	9.0	98
35 - 44	16107	4660	19.1	28.9	98	1081	18.0	6.7	92	2284	21.2	14.2	109	1295	17.1	8.0	88
45 - 54	11491	3386	13.9	29.5	100	948	15.7	8.2	113	1384	12.9	12.0	92	1054	13.9	9.2	100
55 - 64	11584	3698	15.2	31.9	108	934	15.5	8.1	111	1555	14.5	13.4	103	1208	16.0	10.4	114
65 OR OLDER	15558	5089	20.9	32.7	111	1223	20.3	7.9	108	2215	20.6	14.2	109	1651	21.8	10.6	116
18 - 34	27791	7514	30.9	27.0	92	1834	30.5	6.6	90	3322	30.9	12.0	92	2357	31.2	8.5	93
18 - 49	49721	13752	56.5	27.7	94	3256	54.1	6.5	90	6301	58.6	12.7	97	4195	55.5	8.4	92
25 - 54	47328	13618	55.9	28.8	98	3471	57.6	7.3	101	6022	56.0	12.7	98	4125	54.5	8.7	95
35 - 49	21930	6238	25.6	28.4	96	1421	23.6	6.5	89	2979	27.7	13.6	104	1837	24.3	8.4	91
50 OR OLDER	32810	10595	43.5	32.3	109	2766	45.9	8.4	116	4459	41.4	13.6	104	3371	44.6	10.3	112
GRADUATED COLLEGE	12730	3694	15.2	29.0	98	673	11.2	5.3	72	1642	15.3	12.9	99	1380	18.2	10.8	118
ATTENDED COLLEGE	14775	4351	17.9	29.4	100	1031	17.1	7.0	96	1764	16.4	11.9	92	1555	20.6	10.5	115
GRADUATED HIGH SCHOOL	34358	9468	38.9	27.6	93	2231	37.0	6.5	89	4378	40.7	12.7	98	2859	37.8	8.3	91
DID NOT GRADUATE HIGH SCHOOL	20668	6834	28.1	33.1	112	2087	34.7	10.1	138	2976	27.7	14.4	110	1771	23.4	8.6	93
EMPLOYED	42595	12198	50.1	28.6	97	3091	51.3	7.3	99	5380	50.0	12.6	97	3728	49.3	8.8	95
EMPLOYED FULL-TIME	34314	10059	41.3	29.3	99	2605	43.3	7.6	104	4584	42.6	13.4	102	2870	37.9	8.4	91
EMPLOYED PART-TIME	8281	2139	8.8	25.8	88	*485	8.1	5.9	80	796	7.4	9.6	74	858	11.3	10.4	113
NOT EMPLOYED	39936	12149	49.9	30.4	103	2931	48.7	7.3	101	5380	50.0	13.5	103	3838	50.7	9.6	105
PROFESSIONAL/MANAGER	11254	3339	13.7	29.7	101	756	12.6	6.7	92	1312	12.2	11.7	89	1271	16.8	11.3	123
TECH/CLERICAL/SALES	20325	5887	24.2	29.0	98	1407	23.4	6.9	95	2786	25.9	13.7	105	1694	22.4	8.3	91
PRECISION/CRAFT	1151	**157	0.6	13.6	46	**9	0.1	0.8	11	**113	1.1	9.8	75	**35	0.5	3.0	33
OTHER EMPLOYED	9865	2815	11.6	28.5	97	919	15.3	9.3	128	1170	10.9	11.9	91	727	9.6	7.4	80
SINGLE	10026	2800	11.5	27.9	95	633	10.5	6.3	87	1275	11.8	12.7	98	892	11.8	8.9	97
MARRIED	51804	14546	59.7	28.1	95	3682	61.1	7.1	97	6385	59.3	12.3	95	4479	59.2	8.6	94
DIVORCED/SEPARATED/WIDOWED	20700	7000	28.8	33.8	115	1706	28.3	8.2	113	3100	28.8	15.0	115	2194	29.0	10.6	116
PARENTS	32158	9187	37.7	28.6	97	2433	40.4	7.6	104	4112	38.2	12.8	98	2642	34.9	8.2	90
WHITE	71508	20857	85.7	29.2	99	4985	82.8	7.0	96	9111	84.7	12.7	98	6761	89.4	9.5	103
BLACK	8998	2960	12.2	32.9	112	821	13.6	9.1	125	1432	13.3	15.9	122	707	9.3	7.9	86
OTHER	2025	**530	2.2	26.2	89	**215	3.6	10.6	146	**217	2.0	10.8	83	**97	1.3	4.8	52
NORTHEAST-CENSUS	17924	6186	25.4	34.5	117	1348	22.4	7.5	103	2879	26.8	16.1	123	1959	25.9	10.9	119
MIDWEST	20733	5525	22.7	26.6	90	1332	22.1	6.4	88	2328	21.6	11.2	86	1865	24.7	9.0	98
SOUTH	28151	8443	34.7	30.0	102	2360	39.2	8.4	115	3826	35.6	13.6	104	2257	29.8	8.0	87
WEST	15723	4193	17.2	26.7	90	982	16.3	6.2	86	1727	16.1	11.0	84	1485	19.6	9.4	103
NORTHEAST-MKTG.	18407	6470	26.6	35.1	119	1402	23.3	7.6	104	3134	29.1	17.0	131	1934	25.6	10.5	115
EAST CENTRAL	11926	3835	15.8	32.2	109	1100	18.3	9.2	126	1414	13.1	11.9	91	1321	17.5	11.1	121
WEST CENTRAL	13778	3297	13.5	23.9	81	716	11.9	5.2	71	1478	13.7	10.7	82	1104	14.6	8.0	87
SOUTH	24337	6965	28.6	28.6	97	1892	31.4	7.8	107	3186	29.6	13.1	100	1888	25.0	7.8	85
PACIFIC	14084	3780	15.5	26.8	91	913	15.2	6.5	89	1549	14.4	11.0	84	1319	17.4	9.4	102
COUNTY SIZE A	34003	10266	42.2	30.2	102	2277	37.8	6.7	92	4625	43.0	13.6	104	3364	44.5	9.9	108
COUNTY SIZE B	24568	6906	28.4	28.1	95	1579	26.2	6.4	88	3096	28.8	12.6	97	2231	29.5	9.1	99
COUNTY SIZE C	12690	3838	15.8	30.2	103	1253	20.8	9.9	135	1578	14.7	12.4	95	1007	13.3	7.9	87
COUNTY SIZE D	11270	3338	13.7	29.6	100	913	15.2	8.1	111	1461	13.6	13.0	99	964	12.7	8.6	93
METRO CENTRAL CITY	25244	7807	32.1	30.9	105	1621	26.9	6.4	88	3773	35.1	14.9	115	2412	31.9	9.6	104
METRO SUBURBAN	37633	10659	43.8	28.3	96	2506	41.6	6.7	91	4570	42.5	12.1	93	3583	47.4	9.5	104
NON METRO	19654	5881	24.2	29.9	101	1894	31.5	9.6	132	2417	22.5	12.3	94	1570	20.8	8.0	87
TOP 5 ADI'S	18670	5525	22.7	29.6	100	1292	21.5	6.9	95	2459	22.9	13.2	101	1774	23.5	9.5	104
TOP 10 ADI'S	26125	7906	32.5	30.3	103	1862	30.9	7.1	98	3705	34.4	14.2	109	2339	30.9	9.0	98
TOP 20 ADI'S	37308	11147	45.8	29.9	101	2458	40.8	6.6	90	5088	47.3	13.6	105	3602	47.6	9.7	105
HSHLD INC. $60,000 OR MORE	6423	2123	8.7	33.1	112	*532	8.8	8.3	114	805	7.5	12.5	96	786	10.4	12.2	134
$50,000 OR MORE	10293	3276	13.5	31.8	108	*802	13.3	7.8	107	1345	12.5	13.1	100	1129	14.9	11.0	120
$40,000 OR MORE	19142	5628	23.1	29.4	100	1331	22.1	7.0	95	2532	23.5	13.2	101	1765	23.3	9.2	101
$30,000 OR MORE	32190	9295	38.2	28.9	98	2101	34.9	6.5	89	4177	38.8	13.0	100	3017	39.9	9.4	102
$30,000 - $39,999	13048	3666	15.1	28.1	95	771	12.8	5.9	81	1644	15.3	12.6	97	1252	16.5	9.6	105
$20,000 - $29,999	17313	4934	20.3	28.5	97	1271	21.1	7.3	101	1995	18.5	11.5	88	1668	22.0	9.6	105
$10,000 - $19,999	18416	5475	22.5	29.7	101	1358	22.6	7.4	101	2519	23.4	13.7	105	1598	21.1	8.7	95
UNDER $10,000	14612	4643	19.1	31.8	108	1291	21.4	8.8	121	2070	19.2	14.2	109	1282	16.9	8.8	96
HOUSEHOLD OF 1 PERSON	12984	4008	16.5	30.9	105	956	15.9	7.4	101	1711	15.9	13.2	101	1341	17.7	10.3	113
2 PEOPLE	26960	7830	32.2	29.0	98	1717	28.5	6.4	87	3452	32.1	12.8	98	2661	35.2	9.9	108
3 OR 4 PEOPLE	31657	9225	37.9	29.1	99	2263	37.6	7.1	98	4235	39.4	13.4	103	2727	36.0	8.6	94
5 OR MORE PEOPLE	10930	3285	13.5	30.1	102	1085	18.0	9.9	136	1362	12.7	12.5	96	837	11.1	7.7	84
NO CHILD IN HSHLD	47582	14409	59.2	30.3	103	3337	55.4	7.0	96	6358	59.1	13.4	102	4714	62.3	9.9	108
CHILD(REN) UNDER 2 YRS	7212	2028	8.3	28.1	95	*495	8.2	6.9	94	902	8.4	12.5	96	*632	8.4	8.8	96
2 - 5 YEARS	12718	3434	14.1	27.0	92	964	16.0	7.6	104	1526	14.2	12.0	92	944	12.5	7.4	81
6 - 11 YEARS	16339	4826	19.8	29.5	100	1269	21.1	7.8	106	2142	19.9	13.1	101	1416	18.7	8.7	95
12 - 17 YEARS	15697	4569	18.8	29.1	99	1234	20.5	7.9	108	2118	19.7	13.5	103	1217	16.1	7.8	85
RESIDENCE OWNED	56505	16723	68.7	29.6	100	4099	68.1	7.3	99	7333	68.2	13.0	100	5291	69.9	9.4	102
VALUE: $60,000 OR MORE	29835	8845	36.3	29.6	100	2151	35.7	7.2	99	3786	35.2	12.7	97	2909	38.5	9.8	106
VALUE: UNDER $60,000	26670	7878	32.4	29.5	100	1949	32.4	7.3	100	3548	33.0	13.3	102	2382	31.5	8.9	97

(continued)

Source: Simmons Market Research Bureau, 1987. Reprinted by permission.

FIGURE 8–2. (continued)

*How to Read This Data:

Top Row: There were an estimated 82,531,000 female homemakers in the U.S.

Second Row: There were an estimated 8,060,000 female homemakers who are aged 18–24 in the U.S.

Column

A—24,347,000 homemakers used caffeinated instant and freeze-dried coffee (within the last 30 days).

A—1,943,000 homemakers used caffeinated instant and freeze-dried coffee.

B—Column A represents 100% of users.

B—8.0% of all users are aged 18–24 (1,943,000 ÷ 24,347,000 = .079 or 8.0%).

C—29.5% of all homemakers used caffeinated instant and freeze-dried coffee (24,347,000 ÷ 82,531,000 = 29.5%).

C—24.1% of all homemakers aged 18–24 are users (1,943,000 ÷ 8,060,000 = 24.1%).

D—The index of usage (users compared to the population base) is 82 (24.1% ÷ 29.5% × 100 = 82). This means that female homemakers aged 18–24 drink 18% less than the average female homemaker (100 equals average).

Defining Target Audiences

The problem of defining target audiences primarily involves the use of demographic data, though other information may also be considered. The planner will want to know as precisely as possible which demographic segments of the market should be considered targets. There are usually many options from which to choose. Broad categories include age, sex, income, occupation, and education. These categories, however, can be broken down into more specific segments. The age category, for example, might be broken down into such segments as 18–24, 18–49, or 34–49. But age is only one way to define a target group. The planner might opt for an income segment such as upper or lower; or an education segment such as "attended college" as opposed to "high school graduate." Or the planner could combine segments from age, sex, income, and occupation. A caution, though—it becomes unwieldy to select too many demographic segments for target definition. Three or four segments usually represent an optimum number for planning. If too many are selected, the planner may find media selection difficult because alternative media vehicles must be compared on too many different bases. Using one segment, however, is usually too restrictive to result in good planning.

Another consideration in target definition is the source of the information. There are at least three: the client's own past research; custom-tailored research, where a special study is designed and commissioned to delineate present and future users; and syndicated research studies such as those provided by the Simmons Market Research Bureau or MRI.

If possible, cross-tabulated demographic data should be used to determine a target group. With cross tabulations the planner is able to define a target in multi-demographic terms, such as men 18–34 in households with $20,000 or more income; or women 35–49 with a college education who have children under 18 living

TABLE 8-5.   Brand X—Incidence of Usage by Age

Age Segment	U.S. Population (%)	Usage of Brand (%)	Index
18–24	15	17	113
25–34	24	21	88
35–49	26	32	123
50–64	18	20	111
65 +	17	10	59
Totals	100	100	

at home. The more precise the definition, the better. However, the more precise (or narrow) the target, the more unreliable are raw numbers insofar as the sample base in the research source is smaller.

Determining Product Usage Potential

In using market research data, the planner usually begins by studying usage habits for the product category that the designated brand is a part of. Examples of these categories may include food products such as instant coffee, automotive products such as tires, or drug products such as aspirin. Sometimes a product category may not be measured by Simmons, MRI, or other research services. In such a situation, the planner may have to buy custom-made research or simply guess who the targets are.

Determining which targets to choose may be among the first steps in the analysis. Should the planner look for buyers, users, or those who influence buyers? Such decisions must come from research about who is the most influential person in the buying process. For example, the planner may have to decide whether to reach all adults, men only, women only, or female homemakers.

In making the analysis, the planner usually begins by studying percentages and index numbers of all demographics for users of the product category, and then for the specific brand. The search will be for the demographic segments that have the highest percentages and index numbers. Table 8–5 shows part of such an analysis— brand usage by age.

Table 8–5 shows that the greatest usage is found in the 35–49 age segment. It so happens that the same age segment also has the highest index number: 133. Examination of other data may show that the segment with the highest index number does not have the greatest degree of usage. In such a situation, the planner will have to decide whether to target advertising against the high index group, the high usage group, or both.

Another aspect of these data to study is whether the targets should be limited only to the 35–49 year age segment. Should the 25–34 year age segment be added, to broaden the age segment? Should yet another age segment be combined? Age segments that are too narrow will be difficult to reach; yet if they are too broad, they may be meaningless. If a strategy decision is made to use television later, it may be difficult to reach narrow groups because television is so much a mass medium. Decisions such as these require the experience and judgment gained by working with media planning over a period of time.

TABLE 8-6.   Brand X—Incidence of Usage by Age/Sex

	Age Segment	U.S. Population in Each Segment* (%)	Users of brand (%)	Index
Adults	18–34	39.1	57.8	148
	35–49	26.1	20.5	78
	18–49	65.2	78.3	120
Men	18–34	19.7	30.2	153
	35–49	12.8	14.4	113
	18–49	32.5	44.6	137
Women	18–34	19.4	27.6	142
	35–49	13.3	6.1	46
	18–49	32.7	33.7	103

*Base: 179,600,000.

Some situations present a multifaceted problem. Should the target be adults? Males or females? At which age levels? Table 8–6 shows one way to analyze the data in such a situation. The table indicates that age segment men 18–34 is the one with the most potential (index 153). But both adults and women 18–34 also have potential (indices of 148 and 142). Perhaps adults with a slightly smaller index number can cover both males and females? In reading this table however, it should be remembered that other marketing and/or media information might temper the decision about which segment to choose, so that some other targets would be selected.

After a usage study is made of the brand in question, another study may be made of actual sales volume by the same categories. The question to be answered here is: Are the segments who *use* the brand the same as the segments who *buy* the brand? These data may help narrow the decision. Here, too, the data should be examined for all demographic segments, not simply age, as illustrated in Table 8–7.

The search for a target audience, however, is not yet finished. A planner may also want to study purchasing influences. It is well known that wives or husbands, for example, have more or less influence in buying certain products, suggesting that advertising should be targeted to one or the other. But special research is needed to determine the relative influence of each.

Table 8–8 shows how the influence differs for three product categories. The data suggest that the target audience definition ought to take wives and husbands into consideration in varying degrees for different products. For purchases such as wine, both husbands and wives should be considered targets, while wives should be the primary target for dishwashing detergents and husbands for gasoline. This informa-

TABLE 8-7.   Brand X—Incidence of Sales by Age

Age Segment	U.S. Population in Each Segment (%)	Current Sales (%)	Index
18–24	15	14	93
25–34	24	25	104
35–49	26	36	138
50–64	18	17	100
65 +	17	8	100
Total	100	100	

TABLE 8-8.   Purchasing Influences by Husbands and Wives for Three Product Categories

Category	Purchasers (%)		Direct Brand Influence (%)	
	Husbands	Wives	Husbands	Wives
Gasoline	58	42	70	30
Wine	48	52	54	46
Dishwashing detergents	20	80	10	90

tion should be added to demographic segment information to form a composite target picture.

Selecting Usage Groups

Another consideration in determining the target audience is whether to target one or more special-usage groups instead of the more general "all-user" category. The answer is more a matter of judgment than of following a formula. If the heavy-user segment is specially targeted, it may be difficult to reach because the segment members are so widely dispersed throughout the population. Research about the buying habits of a group, however, may be of help in target selection. For example, some product categories may have heavy users who tend to purchase lower-priced brands more often than premium-priced brands. Or, research may show that light users tend to switch brands more often than other user groups. Sometimes, one or more groups may be more persuadable than others and therefore deserve special targeting. But when none of this guidance is available, the planner is likely to select the all-user category rather than any special group.

Table 8-9 is an analysis of all users versus heavy users of orange juice (in bottles, cans, or cartons). There are dramatic differences between these two groups on the basis of index numbers. The largest differences are in ages 35-44, households with 1-2 members, 5 + household members, and those who did not graduate high school. Most other demographic categories do not show much difference.

Using Psychographic Analysis

The term *psychographic* is an adjective used to describe psychological characteristics of consumers. Psychographics are used to differentiate among prospects with the same demographic characteristics.

Psychographic descriptions of purchasers are sought because demographic descriptions do not discriminate well enough between consumers. For example, a janitor may be in the same income class as a college professor, but their lives and purchasing habits are likely to be vastly different. Two adults may have graduated from college, but their life-styles could be radically different. Two men may be working in the same profession, but demographic analysis would not show that they tend to buy different kinds of products. Market researchers, therefore, have long felt that the best way to go beyond demographics is to use some kind of psychological description of consumers.

TABLE 8-9.   Demographic Data for All Users versus Heavy Users of the Orange Juice Market (Bottles, Cans, or Cartons)

	All Users/Index	Heavy Users/Index
Total Female Homemakers	100	100
Age:		
18–24	97	81
25–34	99	102
35–44	106	126
45–54	108	113
55–64	99	89
65 +	92	81
Household income		
Under $10,000	105	112
$10,000–24,999	97	102
$25,000+	100	103
Household size		
1–2 members	95	66
3–4 members	107	116
5+ members	113	163
Education		
Did not graduate high school	108	127
High school (but not college	102	105
College (attended)	94	73
County size		
A	95	95
B	104	100
C	108	104
D	99	110

Source: Simmons Market Research Bureau, 1985. Reprinted by permission.

In the past, many different kinds of psychological descriptions were tried and discarded. Social class categorization was one of the first attempts at psychological-sociological discrimination, but it was only minimally helpful. Later researchers used findings from various psychological tests to help find better discriminators, but without success. Even intelligence quotients (IQs) were tried. In addition to the attempts of market researchers to find psychological discriminators, media publishers also sought a similar measure as a means of differentiating media audiences. *Better Homes & Gardens* conducted some well-known research in 1956 showing that the magazine's audience contained many venturesome persons—those who were first in a social group to try new products. Yet researchers were generally dissatisfied with most attempts to provide psychological descriptions of consumers.

Another method of psychological analysis called *life-style research* has caught the attention of many marketing and media planners. Joseph T. Plummer, of the McCann-Erickson advertising agency, is one of the leaders in this research. Plummer describes life-style research as follows:

Lifestyle is designed to answer questions about people in terms of their activities, interests, and opinions. It measures their activities in terms of how they spend their time in work and leisure; their interests in terms of what they place importance on in their immediate surroundings; their opinions in terms of their stance on social issues, institutions, and themselves; and finally, basic facts such as their age, sex, income, and where they live.[1]

In order to find consumers' life-styles, samples of individuals are selected and administered questionnaires which ask respondents to check such things as:

_____ I like gardening.
_____ I do not get enough sleep.
_____ I enjoy going to concerts.
_____ A news magazine is more interesting than a fiction magazine.
_____ There should be a gun in every home.
_____ Instant coffee is more economical than ground coffee.
_____ I stay home most evenings.
_____ There is a lot of love in our family.[2]

These questions cover activities, opinions, and interests as well as media usage and preferences, and product and brand usage. Life-style analysis has shown that media audiences differ a great deal and can be used to predict who will prefer one medium over another.

Simmons Market Research Bureau also reports psychographic data as well as demographic research. To obtain a psychographic breakdown of users, Simmons asks each respondent to evaluate a list of fourteen personality traits in terms of "how you would like to be." Then each respondent is asked to indicate from the same list "how you feel you are." Each of these fourteen characteristics is cross tabulated for each product category, for heavy users (in those categories where usage rates are 10 percent or higher), for magazine audiences, and for demographics. Listed below are the fourteen characteristics:

Trait	Meaning
Energetic	Usually energetic, active, and on-the-go
Courteous and cooperative	Always courteous, polite, and cooperative
Self-controlled	Cool-headed, even-tempered, and calm
Venturesome	Adventurous and willing to risk trying new things
Happy and outgoing	Cheerful, happy, and outgoing
Pragmatic	Practical, down-to-earth, and well-organized
Not anxious	Not worried or distressed
Influential	Able to persuade, convince, and influence others to accept your ideas
Benevolent	Always considerate, sympathetic, and kind
Not domineering	Not bossy, domineering, or stubborn
Inquisitive	Intellectually curious about others' opinions

1. Plummer, Joseph T., "Life Style Patterns," *Journal of Broadcasting*, Winter, 1971–72, p.79.
2. Plummer, p.81.

Self-confident — Self-assured and poised
Spontaneously decisive — Able to make decisions on the spur of the moment
Not egocentric — Not self-centered, egotistical, or conceited

One way in which such data may help planners in selecting target markets is to compare regular with heavy users. Table 8–10 shows some psychological differences between regular and heavy users of cigarettes. One might weigh this information subjectively using the demographic information already obtained to get a more definitive picture of regular versus heavy users. Or one might evaluate media selected on the basis of demographic segments on their ability to reach desired psychographic segments in order to find which media provide the best reach of both targets. The special needs of planners may also dictate other uses for psychographics.

Media planners who are looking for better target audience definitions will certainly find psychographic definitions radically different from those of demographics. But being different does not necessarily make psychographics better. The important question is: How useful are psychographic target definitions?

The answer is that psychographics can be used in media planning when certain conditions are met. If a market has been identified demographically, yet there is reason to believe that the demographics do not segment the market precisely, then psychographic analysis may discover new dimensions of the target audience. If such new dimensions are found, however, it is important to have available an analysis that shows which alternative media reach large numbers of the psychographic categories that are shown to be important for the given brand. This may be difficult, because syndicated research services such as Simmons provide only a limited analysis of psychographic categories. It may mean that the planner will require custom-made research in order to find which alternative media reach the required psychographic categories. If the data are available and if categories such as those provided by Simmons give the planner more insight about who the best target is, then psychographics may play a large role in media selection.

After the data have been analyzed, the planner should decide on one or more demographic and psychographic segments that constitute the target audience. If the planner has access to a computer, it may be possible to have as many as three or four demographic segments all cross tabulated as a single target audience. An example of a cross tabulated single target is women 18–49 years of age whose

TABLE 8–10. Some Psychographic Differences between Male Regular and Heavy Smokers

	Regular Smokers			Heavy Smokers*		
Traits	Index Self-Image	Index Ideal Image	Total	Index Self-Image	Index Ideal Image	Total
Energetic	96	101	197	144	88	232
Courteous and cooperative	97	112	209	119	169	288
Not anxious	127	106	233	156	50	206
Benevolent	98	89	187	181	113	294
Not domineering	96	105	201	75	50	125

Source: Simmons Market Research Bureau. Reprinted by permission.
*Heavy smokers—11+ packs per week.

TABLE 8-11.   Cross Tabulation of User Demographics for a Product Category

	Adult Female Usage Patterns			
	Average No. Times Used per Week	Women in Group (%)	Total Usages per Week (%)	Index of Usage
Total U.S.	4.95	100	100	100
Household size 1–4; children 6–17 or none; B, C, D counties; college; $3,000+ income	6.54	6.2	8.2	132
Household size 1–4; children 6–17 or none; B, C, D counties; grade or high school; $8,000+ income	6.18	7.2	9.0	125
Same as above except income $3,000–$7,999	5.30	13.0	13.9	107
Household size 1–4; children 6–17 or none; income $3,000+ ; A counties	5.14	22.0	22.9	104
Household size 5+ ; high school or less	4.83	18.2	17.8	98
Household size 1–4; children 6–17 or none; income under $3,000	4.58	14.4	13.4	93
Household size 1–4; children under 6	4.27	13.1	11.2	86
Household size 5+ ; some college	3.03	5.9	3.6	61

Source: Reprinted by permission of J. Walter Thompson Company.

household incomes are more than $25,000 a year, who have achieved a high school or higher level education, and whose households consist of five or more people.

If such cross tabulation is not available, the planner will then have to take the top two or three mutually exclusive segments as targets and determine to what extent each is to be reached in the media plan. The reason for requiring mutually exclusive segments is to enable the planner to reach each segment separately, and then measure gross impressions delivered to each without the confusion of one segment being part of another. For example, women 18–49 is an exclusive segment. But once one adds the demographic segment "total women with incomes of more than $25,000 a year," there is bound to be some duplication. Some women will be earning less than $25,000 but still be in the 18–49 category, and some will be earning more than $25,000 who are not aged 18–49.

Only cross-tabulated data can bring the two segments together. Table 8–11 shows an example of cross tabulation.

Where to Advertise

There are a number of answers to the question of where to advertise. The simplest, of course, is to advertise wherever the brand is distributed. Obviously, it is usually a waste of money to advertise in a geographical market where the brand is not distributed. Occasionally, however, the objective may be to "force" distribution by creating a demand for a brand through advertising, even though the brand is not distributed in the market. When the planner has this objective, it makes sense to advertise before distribution is available.

Beyond the obvious answer, however, is the question of whether it is better to advertise in geographical markets where sales for a given brand have been good, or where sales *have not* been good.

Some planners feel that to advertise where sales have been good is a good defensive strategy—one should protect what one has and also try to build on it. Additionally, one should ask, Have sales in the good markets been fully exploited? If not, why not spend more money there, rather than going to some other market where the risks would be greater? After all, many customers like the brand well enough to buy it repeatedly and their word-of-mouth influence may well prompt sales to people who have not purchased the brand in the past.

Choosing where to advertise is really a matter of risks. Despite the observation that "it is always good sense to fish where the fish are," is an advertiser missing productive new markets by placing most advertising in the best markets? Yet can the advertiser afford the risk of losing the best markets to sound out new, unknown markets? The "defensive strategy" minimizes risks and maximizes potential.

Advertising in markets where a brand's sales are low is called an "offensive strategy" because success may require heavier advertising expenditures than previously used. Again, the risks must be carefully weighed. If competitors have been selling well in these markets but the brand in question has not, the question is, why? Is it due to poor distribution? Is it due to insufficient advertising expenditures in the market? Some other reason? Can these problems be corrected?

A planner selecting a market with a low-sales history should be able to answer the following question: Is there any evidence that increased advertising in this market will produce a corresponding increase in sales? This is a difficult, but necessary, question. Students in practice exercises often want to increase advertising because they believe that "advertising sells." But they usually cannot find any other strong reason for doing so except that competitors are selling well in the market. One must understand, however, that once a competitor becomes entrenched in a market with a good brand that meets the needs of consumers, there may be no reason for consumers to switch brands. In fact, it may be impossible to get them to switch brands, unless the new brand has some superior attribute that, if publicized, will cause consumers to switch. The risks of trying to exploit such a market are great and the likelihood of success is, at best, indeterminable.

Finally, the greatest risk is to select new markets where neither the designated brand nor competitive brands have been exploited through advertising. These markets may have great sales potential, but may also be difficult places to sell a given product. It also might be assumed that if these markets really had great potential, competitors would have known about it too, and would have made efforts to exploit them.

Aside from these basic guides for market selection, there are other factors that should be taken into consideration. One of the foremost involves selecting one or perhaps more markets in each of the client's sales territories. Almost all companies with nationally distributed products divide the country into sales territories, and these in turn may be subdivided into smaller groups. The names of such territories vary somewhat from company to company. Some use the terms "divisions and districts," others use "regions and divisions" or other designations. No matter what they are called, it may be necessary to include at least one market in each of these

TABLE 8–12. Comparison of Geographic Divisions

4As Media Audience Research Committee Divisions	Nielsen's Basic 10 Territories	Census Bureau's Nine Divisions	Census Bureau's Four Regions
1. North East	1. New England	1. New England	1. Northeast
2. North Central	2. Middle Atlantic	2. Middle Atlantic	
3. South	3. Metro New York	3. East N. Central	2. Midwest
4. Pacific	4. East Central	4. West N. Central	
	5. Metro Chicago	5. South Atlantic	3. South
	6. West Central	6. East S. Central	
	7. South East	7. West S. Central	
	8. Metro Los Angeles	8. Mountain	4. West
	9. South West	9. Pacific	
	10. Remaining Pacific		

divisions, depending on the needs of the company. The *weights* (or quantity of advertising used) in these areas may vary a great deal, however, so that the better markets receive more dollars of advertising than the poorer markets.

Thus, to answer the question of where to advertise, planners study distribution, sales records, or brand/product usage. Simmons provides data on usage, while Nielsen and other similar companies provide data on sales.

Classification of Geographical Areas

Sales should be analyzed by different geographical patterns, from the largest, that is, regions of the country, to the smallest, neighborhoods, although analysis by neighborhood may not be possible because of the lack of research data. The idea behind geographical analysis at all levels is to learn precisely where prospects live. This information serves as a guide in media selection. The following are the most commonly used geographical categories:

- Regions
- States
- Counties
- Metropolitan or nonmetropolitan areas
- TV market delineation such as DMA (designated market area), or ADI (area of dominant influence)

In studying marketing and media research data, the analyst will find a number of different methods used to divide the country geographically. The Census Bureau divides the country into four regions and nine divisions. The Media Audience Research Committee of the American Association of Advertising Agencies recommends that the country be divided into four areas. The A.C. Nielsen Company, however, uses a division consisting of ten geographical territories, although it will divide the country in almost any way most suitable for a specific client. A comparison of these divisions is shown in Table 8–12. Figure 8–3 maps the states in Nielsen's ten territories.

What is a local market to a media planner? A *market* is a group of people living

FIGURE 8-3. Nielsen Territories

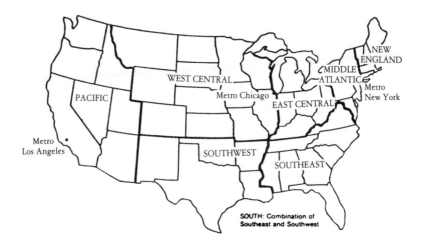

Source: Reprinted by permission of Nielsen Media Research.

in a certain geographic area, who are likely to buy a given product or brand. But that definition is unsatisfactory for planners when it comes to determining the nature of a local market because definitions vary depending on the research company providing the data for a given area. Different research companies define markets differently to meet the needs of their users. A local retailer who advertises exclusively in newspapers in a given city may prefer to think of its market as a *retail trading zone* which includes the central city and surrounding suburbs. But a national advertiser who uses all media may prefer that a market be defined in terms of the entire metropolitan area, and would use the Census Bureau's Metropolitan Statistical Area definition. Another manufacturer who uses television almost exclusively, however, may prefer to use Arbitron's area of dominant influence. Each of these local market definitions is somewhat different.

As a result, it becomes important for the planner to know the various definitions of what constitutes a local market when planning media. Which definition is most suitable? There has been some agitation from media planners to standardize definitions, but without much success. Until standardization becomes acceptable, the differences should be clearly understood. The following list explains the most often used definitions:

Area of Dominant Influence (ADI). All counties in which the home-market stations receive a preponderance of total viewing hours. This definition was conceived by Arbitron. The ground rules for the ADI allocations are relatively simple. Once the estimated total viewing hours for a county and the percentage of such estimated total for each station are known, Arbitron adds up the station percentages by market of origin. The market of origin having the largest total percentage is deemed by Arbitron to be the ''dominant influence'' in the county under consideration, and thus the county is allocated to that market for ADI purposes. The total number of ADI markets in the country may change from year to year as research on them is updated.

Designated Market Area (DMA). This definition, used by the A. C. Nielsen Company for a television market, includes counties in the metropolitan area of a market provided that at least one station in that area is estimated to have the largest average quarter-hour audience share from 9:00 A.M. to midnight, plus the remainder of counties in which this market's station are estimated to have the largest average quarter-hour share.

Metropolitan Statistical Area (MSA). The MSA has replaced the Standard Metropolitan Statistical Area definition used in the past. An MSA is a population area with a large nucleus at the center and adjacent areas that have a large degree of economic and social integration with the center. The MSAs may be classified on the basis of the following levels:

Level A—population of 1,000,000 or more
Level B—population of 250,000 to 999,999
Level C—population of 100,000 to 249,999
Level D—population of less than 100,000

Note the difference between the SMA classifications and A. C. Nielsen's classifications on page 152.

PMSAs and CMSAs. Within the metropolitan areas of one million or more population, separate component parts of an MSA are defined if certain criteria are met as follows:

Primary Metropolitan Statistical Area (PMSA)—The MSA defined by counties

Consolidated Metropolitan Statistical Area (CMSA)—Large metropolitan complexes that contain PMSAs

The following analysis is shown to better explain how these new designations would look for the Chicago SMA:

Chicago PMSA
　Cook County
　Du Page County
　McHenry County

Chicago, Gary, Ind., Lake County Ill., Illinois, Indiana, Wisconsin CMSA
　Chicago, Ill., PMSA
　Aurora, Ill., PMSA
　Gary-Hammond, Ind., PMSA
　Joliet, Ill., PMSA
　Kenosha, Wisc., PMSA
　Lake County, Ill., PMSA

City Zone and Retail Trading Zone. These terms are used by newspapers in defining their markets. A *city zone* represents the corporate city limits plus heavily populated areas adjoining a city in which the newspaper is sold, as designated by an agreement between the publisher and the Audit Bureau of Circulation. A *retail trading zone* is an area beyond the city zone from which retailers draw sufficient customers to warrant spending advertising dollars to reach them. This area is also determined by the agreement of the publisher and the Audit Bureau of Circulation.

Newspaper Designated Markets. This is another newspaper classification and covers the geographical area in which the newspaper provides primary editorial and advertising services. Decisions about which areas are to be included and the boundary lines are made by the Audit Bureau of Circulation in consultation with the publisher. Publishers who report their circulations by newspaper designated markets usually eliminate city and retail trading zone circulation data.

Newspaper market definitions may also be made by counties in which coverage percentages are computed. Data show where newspapers have at least 50 percent coverage, 20 percent coverage, and so forth.

To illustrate how market definitions vary, even within one geographical market, a map of the city of Chicago and outlying areas is shown in Figure 8–4. It shows the ADI (with nineteen counties in Illinois, Wisconsin, Indiana, and Michigan), the MSA (three counties), and the newspaper designated markets of the *Chicago Tribune* (with eight counties in Illinois and Indiana).

Sales Analysis

After sales volume information about a brand and its competitors has been gathered, it is possible to start making decisions about where to advertise. One approach is to select geographical markets on the basis of sales or market share produced in the past. In this situation, the volume of past sales, rather than the index of potential sales, is the deciding factor. Without a doubt, the volume of sales produced by a geographic market in the past has to be the first consideration in making the selection. The question of whether to go to high-index potential markets depends to some extent on whether sales have been optimized in the existing high-volume markets. Perhaps an increase in advertising in current markets will result in an equivalent increase in sales.

Table 8–13 (p. 153) shows the sales of a company and its competitors reported on the basis of seven regions, plus three large metropolitan areas: New York, Chicago, and Los Angeles. In this table, index numbers were computed by comparing sales percentages for each brand with total industry sales by region.

Does Table 8–13 tell the planner precisely where to advertise? No, but it tells where the brand is doing well as compared with competitors: in New England, East Central, West Central, Chicago, and the Southwest. Obtaining, and understanding, this kind of information is necessary before the planner proceeds to more specific information that will help pinpoint markets in which to advertise.

Sales analysis by regions usually is followed by a county analysis that provides another dimension for the media planner to consider in selecting media to reach markets.

To deal with county sizes conveniently, Nielsen and Arbitron use an A, B, C, D classification system:

A counties—all counties located within the twenty-five largest metropolitan areas

B counties—all counties not included under A that have more than 150,000 population

C counties—all counties not included in A and B that have more than 40,000 population

D counties—all remaining counties

FIGURE 8-4.   ADI, MSA, and Newspaper Designated Markets of Chicago—by Counties

TABLE 8-13.   Sales of Brand X and Competitors—by Regions

Region	Total Industry Sales — U.S. House-holds (%)	Sales (%)	Index	Brand X — Sales (%)	Index	Brand Y — Sales (%)	Index	Brand Z — Sales (%)	Index
New England	5.8	3.4	59	3.5	103	3.5	103	2.4	71
New York	8.4	5.0	60	4.6	92	4.5	90	6.5	130
Middle Atlantic	11.4	10.8	94	11.0	102	10.1	94	12.9	119
East Central	15.8	17.6	111	19.5	111	16.8	95	18.3	104
West Central	14.0	16.0	115	17.5	109	16.2	101	16.4	103
Chicago	3.7	5.4	144	7.1	131	5.4	98	5.3	98
Southeast	15.7	13.3	85	13.1	98	12.1	91	14.0	105
Southwest	9.9	8.8	89	9.4	104	9.2	105	7.5	85
Los Angeles	5.1	7.0	138	4.7	67	9.1	130	5.8	83
Remaining Pacific	10.2	12.7	124	9.6	76	13.2	104	10.9	86
Total	100.0	100.0		100.0		100.0		100.0	

Source: Data provided by a major advertiser.

Table 8–14 shows a sales breakdown by county size for liquid and powdered forms of a given product. For the total market, county size C has the best potential. The same is true for the liquid market segment with the addition that county size A also shows above average potential. But for the powdered market segment, C counties have the best potential. Once again, note the potential for sales shown by index numbers and the actual sales volume shown for the total market and its segments. In all cases, county size A has the highest percentage of sales. Both volume and potential will have to be weighed before a decision is made.

Heavy User Data

Although a geographic analysis may be a start in answering the question of where to advertise, an examination of heavy user data may provide additional insights. Often, a small percentage of heavy users account for the largest percentage of product usage. This is true for many product categories, but not for all.

Studying heavy users gives a different dimension of where the market is located. If the marketing strategy calls for heavy users, then their whereabouts becomes important. Table 8–15 shows that heavy users of international flavored instant coffee

TABLE 8-14.   Sales of Total Market and Segments—by County Size

County Size	Population Distribution	Total Market Sales (%)	Index	Powdered Market Segment Sales (%)	Index	Liquid Market Segment Sales (%)	Index
A	41.4	42.3	102	39.1	94	45.4	110
B	27.2	26.9	99	27.6	101	26.2	96
C	16.3	19.2	117	20.6	126	17.9	109
D	15.1	11.6	76	12.7	84	10.5	70
Total	100.0	100.0		100.0		100.0	

Source: Data supplied by a major advertiser.

TABLE 8-15.   Heavy and Light Users of International Flavored Instant Coffee

	Index			
	All Users	Heavy Users	Medium Users	Light Users
Metropolitan (central city)	103	127	103	94
Metropolitan (suburban)	107	104	88	120
Nonmetropolitan	81	60	118	70

Source: Simmons Market Research Bureau, 1986. Reprinted by permission.

tend to be in metropolitan central city areas, whereas light users are within the metropolitan suburban area.

The Brand Development Index (BDI)

One of the most useful tools available to a media planner in deciding where to advertise is the *brand development index (BDI)*. The BDI is quite simple in structure, and calculated from data for each individual market in which the brand is sold according to the following formula:

$$\text{BDI} = \frac{\% \text{ of a brand's total U.S. sales in Market X}}{\% \text{ of total U.S. population in Market X}} \times 100$$

Here's an example of how the BDI would be calculated for a brand in Seattle:

$$\frac{\text{Sales of the brand in Seattle (\% of U.S.)}}{\text{Population in Seattle (\% of U.S.)}} \quad \frac{3.09}{1.23} \times 100 = 251$$

The BDI is an index number representing sales potential. It conforms to the same basic characteristics of index numbers discussed earlier. The larger the sales in a market relative to population percentage the higher the BDI in that market.

The Category Development Index (CDI)

The *category development index (CDI)* is similar to the BDI except that it is based on the percentage of sales of a product category in a given market rather than a brand. The method of calculating the CDI is as follows:

$$\text{CDI} = \frac{\% \text{ of a product category's total U.S. sales in Market X}}{\% \text{ of total U.S. population in Market X}} \times 100$$

Example of the CDI in Seattle:

$$\frac{\text{Category sales in Seattle (\% of U.S.)}}{\text{Population in Seattle (\% of U.S.)}} \quad \frac{2.71}{1.23} \times 100 = 220$$

Both the BDI and CDI are useful in decision making. One tells the planner the

FIGURE 8-5.   BDI/CDI Relationships

	High BDI	Low BDI
High CDI	High share of market Good market potential	Low share of market Good market potential
Low CDI	High share of market Monitor for sales decline	Low share of market Poor market potential

relative strengths and weaknesses for the brand and the other, the relative strengths and weaknesses for the category. Any market where the brand is sold should have these indices calculated for it.

The following are the possible results (see Figure 8-5):

High BDI and high CDI.   This kind of market usually represents good sales potential for both the brand and the category.

High BDI and low CDI.   Here the category is not selling well, but the brand is. Probably a good market in which to advertise, but surely one to watch to see if the brand's sales decline in time.

Low BDI and high CDI.   This kind of market shows potential for the category but demands that someone study the reason why the brand is not doing well here. Is it because of poor distribution? Not enough advertising dollars, GRPs, or reach in the market? To advertise in this market without knowing the answer would be a risk.

Low BDI and low CDI.   This kind of market represents a risk for any brand. Here, too, a planner might want to know why the category doesn't sell well. Such a market would probably not be a good place to advertise under most circumstances.

In using the BDI/CDI data for each market in decision making, the planner has a number of ways to proceed. One is to set arbitrary parameters for each market. For example, a planner could decide that for a market to be selected it would have to meet at least one of the following requirements:

- It would have to have a BDI of 125 or higher.
- It would have to have a BDI at least ten points higher than the CDI.
- It would have to have a certain percentage sales increase over a previous year in that market, and/or a sales volume of X dollars in the market.

Market selection on such a basis may seem arbitrary, but it could be based on the experience of a planner who, over a period of years, simply knows which market characteristics have been the most profitable.

Weighted BDIs and CDIs. Another method of selecting markets might be to weight the BDI and CDI to arrive at a single combined index. Before this weighting is done, however, a marketing strategy decision must be made to guide the media planner in the proper weighting of the two indices. A marketing strategy that calls for X dollars of advertising spending in direct proportion to sales (a basically defensive posture) requires that the BDI be used exclusively in allocating media expenditures to each market. At the other extreme, a marketing strategy that requires that brand advertising be allocated only on the basis of category development (a basically offensive posture that is generally used for new brands that have not developed a sales pattern) would force the media planner to use only the CDI in deciding spending by market. Any mixture of these two strategies requires a mixture of weights for the BDI and the CDI. For example, if the marketing strategy states that brand sales should be protected in all high sales areas, but that spending should be increased where category development is high and brand development is low, the planner might elect to weight the BDI 75 percent and the CDI 25 percent. The following illustrates how the calculation would be made in a typical market:

$$BDI = 165 \times .75 = 124$$
$$CDI = 140 \times .25 = 35 \quad 124 + 35 = 159 = \text{Weighted BDI/CDI}$$

All markets would be evaluated on the basis of a similar weighting and only those that reach a certain level would be selected. Weighting, however, may be a risky procedure unless the planner knows exactly what each weighting signifies. A safer procedure might be to weight the BDI and CDI 50 percent each and then combine them. Nevertheless, some kind of arbitrary decision would have to be made. The cut-off point might be set at 125. Any markets indexed at over 125 would be selected and any under 125 rejected, at least until experience dictates otherwise.

Using Buying Power Indices

There are times when an advertiser may not know its product's sales volume in each geographical market, possibly because the advertiser sells through distributors and wholesalers. Although many manufacturers in the food, drug, and appliance fields know, from their own records, how large their sales are to wholesalers or distributors, they often do not know how well sales are going at the retail level. The factory is separated from the consumer by what is called the *pipeline* (composed of wholesalers and retailers). What happens at the consumer level is eventually reflected in activity at the factory, but the time lag can be exceedingly long. Sales to wholesalers may be high, but wholesalers may have large inventories in their warehouses because the product hasn't been selling well at the retail level.

Furthermore, even if a manufacturer should eventually learn how consumer sales are going, this information may not be indicative of a brand's share of total sales compared to its competitors'. The best that these advertisers can do is to examine the number of wholesale shipments into each market and prepare their media plans on such a basis. The weakness of this technique should be apparent, though; the relative number of shipments into a given market may not be equivalent to the sales potential of that market. Lack of sales volume and share, market by market, handicaps the media planner in deciding where to place advertising. Nevertheless, many small advertisers simply cannot afford to purchase sales volume and share data from the syndicated research services. Shipments or sales potentials determined through other ways may then have to be used.

One source available to almost all advertisers and agencies is *Sales & Marketing Management*'s "Survey of Buying Power," which can help determine the sales potential of geographic markets. The "Survey of Buying Power" is published annually and is available to anyone at a relatively low cost. The data are based on census measurements plus updated projections.

The survey uses a multiple factor index that is computed for every major metropolitan area in the country. A *factor* is a market quality that affects sales. Therefore, it is possible to examine the general sales potential of every geographical market. Generally, the more people there are in a market, the greater the sales potential; so population is a factor. Effective buying income based on total income after taxes (similar to disposable income), is another market factor. A third factor in the survey's index is total retail sales.

The three factors are arbitrarily weighted to indicate that some factors are more important than others in making sales. Population is weighted twice, total retail sales are weighted three times, and effective buying income is weighted five times.

On one hand, the indices described help the planner determine the relative value of each market. These values in turn may be used to determine budgets or media weights. On the other hand, the indices may be too general for certain kinds of products. Some specialized products may need additional or more specific marketing data. However, the information in the "Survey of Buying Power" may be used with data from other sources to provide a better and more selective index. The market for air conditioners could be used as an example. It would be possible to combine survey data with information on average maximum annual temperature and average annual humidity to create a special index number for each market. Furthermore, factors could be weighted in any way necessary to get a better perspective of the relative value of each market.

One can use the buying power indices for a quick evaluation of alternative geographic markets.

The question of where to advertise is based on an analysis of sales and product usage or general sales potential, plus consideration of whatever marketing objectives must be met. The users of the buying power data will find that the index numbers are an easy way to compare a large number of categories. If raw numbers or percentages are needed, they are usually provided so that users need not make any further preliminary calculations.

Determining Cut-Off Points

In selecting markets for advertising, it is often difficult to judge at which point to drop markets that are at the bottom of the list. The place at which the list is divided into those markets that are selected and those rejected is called the *cut-off point*.

One way to establish a cut-off point is to select markets on the basis of some arbitrary number, usually in multiples of 10, 25, or 50. This is a widespread practice in industry. So whatever markets are listed as Number 51 or lower may be eliminated. Yet most media planners would agree that there isn't always much difference between the 50th market and the 51st market.

A more logical way to cut off is to determine how much weight (in terms of dollars) should be assigned to the best markets. Once these dollars have been allocated, then all remaining money may be distributed to the poorer markets based on a weighting system. Usually such weighting would be based on spending a minimum amount of money in a market. If a market's potential does not justify such an expenditure, then it may not be worthwhile to advertise. Weighting systems divide markets into groups titled A, B, C, and so on. A markets might receive a given number of dollars of advertising, B markets receive somewhat less, and C markets receive much less.

At times a system of gross rating points is used to determine how much money will be spent in a market. The money is allocated from the top of the list down, until it runs out, thereby automatically establishing the cut-off point.

In many cases, media planners and client representatives have, through experience, developed a minimum number of markets that must be on any list. Additional markets may be added if there is money left after allocating money to the basic list.

One of the problems in establishing cut-off points is that often a small number of markets account for a very large percentage of sales. For example, twenty-five markets might account for 75 percent of a brand's sales. But the next twenty-five largest markets might only account for 8 percent additional sales. Usually media planners prefer to have fewer markets, but have enough money to fully exploit the selected markets.

Often, too, marketing objectives affect the length of a list. For example, if an objective is "to protect the brand's share of market from inroads of competitors," then more money may have to be put into markets where competitors are trying to sell against the brand. Usually these are a brand's best markets, so the list may have to be reduced somewhat in order to allocate extra money at the top of the list.

The whole process of selecting markets and determining cut-off points is not the responsibility only of the media planner, but may be shared by the account executive and a client representative. In such cases, decisions are made by compromise as well as by logic. One media planner explained:

> This give and take process between the account executive, the client, and myself is often logical, but sometimes ludicrous. For example, I'll have both Rochester and Albany on my market list. The account man may take Albany off but leave Rochester in. But the client puts Albany back in and removes Rochester. Why? Well it could be that we can't afford both, or the client feels that he has to back a stronger sales force at Albany. But the whole process of selecting markets is an "editing" operation, in which we each edit the others' recommendations until a market list takes shape.[3]

In summary, market lists and cut-off points are established on the basis of subjective factors as well as objective criteria. The most important criteria are the sales goals and the money needed to attain them in each market. Experience, compromise, and some arbitrary factors also influence the process at various times. Other, more sophisticated methods of selecting markets to receive advertising are discussed in Chapter 6.

---

3. Personal conversation with an agency media planner.

When to Advertise

Decisions about when to advertise depend on a number of important considerations such as (a) when sales are greatest or lowest, (b) budget constraints, (c) when competitors advertise, (d) the specific goals for the brand in question, (e) availability of the product, and (f) promotional requirements. Each of these points deserves individual discussion, though there is one point underlying them all: Advertise when people tend to buy the product in question, because it is difficult if not impossible to make them buy at any other time. Studying sales by product category over a period of twenty or more years shows that buying takes place at fairly regular intervals and not capriciously. Therefore, it is important to learn when people tend to buy and to capitalize on these buying habits.

Analyzing Monthly Sales

The most important consideration in deciding when to advertise is to know when sales peaks occur for the product category compared with when sales peaks occur for the brand. Table 8–16 shows category sales indexed to brand sales by month. Sales for the category in question tend to be rather flat month by month, but the brand tends to have rather clear-cut highs and lows. Theoretically, the brand should advertise more heavily in those months when its sales have been higher.

However, the answer may not be quite so clear-cut. It may be that the category sells well in a particular month, while the brand does not. Thus the dilemma. Should the brand advertise more heavily in those months when the *category* is selling well or in the months when the *brand* is selling well? Usually, one would advertise more heavily in the months when the category is selling well. Although other considerations may require a change in this strategy, some planners use only category sales as their guide in planning.

Usually a monthly sales analysis for a product category will indicate a seasonal effect. Thus a planner should keep in mind the effect of certain seasons on sales in studying monthly sales records. Back-to-school or graduation months certainly in-

TABLE 8–16.   Category and Brand Sales by Months

Month	Category Sales (%)	Brand Sales (%)	Index
January	8.5	6.9	81*
February	7.7	6.5	85
March	8.5	8.2	96
April	8.2	7.5	91
May	8.5	8.9	105
June	8.2	8.9	109
July	8.5	9.4	110
August	8.5	10.3	121
September	8.2	6.8	83
October	8.5	8.8	103
November	8.2	7.6	93
December	8.5	10.2	120

*6.9 ÷ 8.5 × 100 = 81.

fluence the sales of certain kinds of products, as do Christmas or Easter. January and August have become the "white goods" months to sell bed linens, towels, and tablecloths. If a brand belongs to a category that is affected by seasons, then monthly sales should be more carefully studied so as not to miss an opportunity.

Budget Constraints

Often the advertising budget is not large enough to permit year-round advertising. In such a situation, the planner will probably allocate the advertising dollars to the best selling months. Whether to maintain *continuity* (continuous advertising all year long) or *flights* (periodic advertising interspersed with no advertising) is dependent on other considerations that will be discussed later.

Competitive Activities

In planning a media schedule it is important to consider when competitors advertise. If their timing pattern is different than that of the overall category, then the planner will have to decide how important the difference is. Does it put the planner's own brand in a weaker position? If so, the planner may want to copy a competitor's timing. Most often, however, competitors tend to follow category sales patterns fairly closely.

Specific Goals for the Brand

At times a marketing or media objective is to react aggressively to competitive strategies. Perhaps such a strategy may be necessary to attain a market share increase. In such a situation, one might time heavy advertising to begin before most competitors start. As a result, a brand may achieve higher and quicker visibility before the normal buying season starts. Another specific goal may be to outspend competitors in some particular month. This may require withdrawing money allocated to the year-long advertising effort for the concentrated attack. Other marketing/media goals may also affect timing. New product introductions, for example, require a timing pattern of heavy initial advertising (first quarter of sales year) and relatively lighter weights later on.

Product Availability

In certain marketing situations, marketing demand outstrips a manufacturer's ability to supply the product. Even though a company may be building a new plant to keep up with demand, the added capacity may not be ready for some time. In such a case, the timing of advertising has to be related to production availability. Most often a problem with availability occurs when new products are introduced, but it occasionally happens when there is a surge in the sales of existing products.

Promotional Requirements

If an aggressive sales promotion campaign is planned for a brand preceding or during the brand's regular advertising when the campaign, this may affect timing. A cents-off deal, for example, may require an aggressive advertising when the campaign to announce the promotion starts.

QUESTIONS FOR DISCUSSION

1. Why are counties usually preferred to cities as a basis for analyzing markets?
2. If you knew that 11.1 percent of all housewives 18–24 had used a product within the last month, what other information would you need to compute an index number?
3. In searching for demographic target segments, is the demographic segment with the highest index number always the best target? Explain briefly.
4. What is the value of knowing a brand development index (BDI) number for a given market?
5. If 20 percent of the men who rented cars within the past year accounted for about 90 percent of all car rentals, should they be the only targets for advertising messages? Discuss.
6. In the *Sales & Marketing Management* "Survey of Buying Power" index, each factor is weighted differently. Briefly explain why.
7. How could the data from the *Sales & Marketing Management* "Survey of Buying Power" be used to create one's own index for outboard motors?
8. Percentages are easier to use than raw numbers in comparing sales or usage data for two brands. But why should the user pay special attention to the bases on which the two sets of figures were computed?
9. In studying sales or usage data, the planner will find that occasionally the research needed is not available. What does a planner do when necessary data are missing and the budget does not allow buying it?
10. Why might a manufacturer with national product distribution want to advertise only in the top seventy markets in the U.S.?

SELECTED READINGS

Advertising Age, "Newspaper Bureau Promotes Psychographics," September 10, 1973, p.6.

Committee on Research (Media Research Subcommittee), *Recommended Breakdowns for Consumer Media Data*, American Association of Advertising Agencies (revised), 1973.

Editor & Publisher, "Study Indicates Psychographic Data Are Weak Media Buying Tool," September 8, 1973, pp. 8–9.

Garfinkle, Norton, "The Marketing Value of Media Audiences—How to Pinpoint Your Prime Prospects," (Speech) ANA Workshop, July 19, 1965.

Maneloveg, Herbert, "Another Way to Look at Audience and Marketing Figures," *Advertising Age*, April 13, 1964, pp. 95–96.

Media Decisions, "How—Not Where," January 1968, p.22.

Media Decisions, "Beyond Demographics," February 1968, pp. 22–23.

Media Decisions, "Is ADI the One?" November 1969, pp. 42–45.

Media Decisions, "How Nestlé Uses Psychographics," July 1973, pp. 68–71.

Media Decisions, "What's the Competition Doing?" September 1973, p.64ff.

Media Decisions, "The Campaign That Psychographics Built," April 1974, pp. 64ff.

Media Decisions, "Timing," December 1978, p.140.

Media/Scope, "What's a Market to a Media Planner?" June 1966, pp. 64–72.

Nelson Alan R., "New Psychographics: Action-Creating Ideas, Not Lifeless Statistics," *Advertising Age*, June 28, 1971, pp. 1, 34.

Ostrow, Joseph, "Competitive Media Expenditure Analysis," *Media Decisions*, December 1971, p.52.

Papazian, Edward, "Buzz Words Like Psychographics," *Media Decisions*, October 1973, pp. 14–16.

Papazian, Edward, "Media Targeting: Like Pinning the Tail on the Donkey," *Media Decisions*, November 1977, pp. 14–16.

Peterson, Robert A., "Psychographics and Media Exposure," *Journal of Advertising Research*, June 1972, pp. 17–20.

Plummer, Joseph T., "Life Style Patterns," *Journal of Broadcasting*, Winter 1971–72, pp. 78–89.

Sales Management, "New Ways to Measure Markets," September 18, 1964, pp. 55–56.

Shiffman, Phil, "Psychographic Data Could Be the Base for Both Copy and Media," *Media Decisions*, August 1973, pp. 80–82.

Sissors, Jack Z., "What Is a Market?" *Journal of Marketing*, July 1966, pp. 17–21.

Sprague, Jeremy D., "Local Media Analysis through Marketing Considerations," *Journal of Marketing Research*, January 1964, pp. 49–53.

Strong, Edward C., "The Spacing and Timing of Advertising," *Journal of Advertising Research*, December 1977, pp. 25–31.

Teel, J. E., Bearden, W. O., and Durand, R. M., "Psychographics of Radio and TV Audiences," *Journal of Advertising Research*, April 1979, pp. 53–56.

Tveter, Norman T., "What the Media Expert Gains from Studying Markets," *Media/Scope*, May 1964, pp. 94–100.

Van Bortel, F. J., "Applying What We Know about Marketing Segmentation," *Perspectives in Advertising Management*, Association of National Advertisers, April 1969, pp. 103–12.

Wells, William D. (ed.), *Life Style and Psychographics*, Chicago: American Marketing Association, 1974.

Wells, William D., "Psychographics: A Critical Review," *Journal of Marketing Research*, May 1975, pp. 196–213.

9

Strategy Planning II: Weighting, Reach, Frequency, and Continuity

In Chapter 8 three major strategy decisions were discussed: target audiences, geographical market selection, and timing. These decisions must be made early in the planning process because they control other strategy decisions discussed in this chapter. This chapter also contains decisions that follow those in Chapter 8; a further discussion of geographical weighting, reach and frequency, and continuity versus flighting.

Geographical Weighting

Geographical weighting is the practice of giving extra consideration to one or more markets that have more sales potential—because of location or demographics or other reasons—than other markets. A record of good sales and/or good potential for sales for the product category and the brand being advertised may make one market more important than others. If all geographical markets had an equal record of sales and/or sales potential, then there would be no need to add extra advertising weight. But markets are rarely equal in value, so weighting is necessary.

There is another reason for weighting markets. Advertisers who buy national media usually find that the gross impressions delivered by a media plan do not match differences in local sales potentials. Market A may have good sales potential but receive relatively few impressions from national media, while Market B may have weak sales potential but receive many more impressions than required.

Table 9–1 illustrates the difference in gross rating points delivered by a nighttime network TV schedule in different markets. As the table shows, the delivery of GRPs by a national medium such as network television is generally distributed un-

TABLE 9-1.   How Network Television Delivery of Gross Rating Points Varies by Market

	Night Network GRPs
National Average	100
New York	90
Miami	110
Detroit	110
Chicago	100
Denver	80
Los Angeles	80

evenly among markets. If the delivery of these GRPs happened to match sales potential in each market closely, there would be no need for adjustment. Unfortunately, this rarely happens, so adjustments in advertising weight are required.

The final determination of the need for weighting is the wide variance in media costs—again, not necessarily in relation to sales potential. On one hand, a planner who allocates dollars on a proportional basis may be unable to buy as much advertising as required in the best markets because costs may be too high. On the other hand, one may be able to buy more impressions than needed in less expensive markets.

To illustrate the variation in media costs, Table 9–2 gives a cost-per-thousand analysis for several spot TV markets. The reader should recall that cost-per-thousand numbers reflect the relationship between target audiences delivered and the costs of media in delivering those targets. Table 9–2 shows that media costs per thousand for reaching women in various markets are not directly proportional to the size of each market. Smaller markets often have a higher CPM than larger markets to reach a given target audience.

Different Forms of Weighting

There are different techniques of weighting that will accomplish the same objectives. The simplest way, the *dollar allocation technique*, allocates proportionately more money to good markets. Therefore, if Market A accounts for 10 percent of total sales, it receives 10 percent of the advertising budget. This technique, however, does not take varying media costs into consideration.

A second technique, *gross impression weighting,* does take varying media costs into consideration. It allocates the budget on the basis of gross impressions desired: Good markets are budgeted to receive more impressions and weaker markets, fewer.

Table 9–3 illustrates the differences between the first and second weighting techniques. The table shows that when dollars are allocated proportionately, gross impressions vary; when gross impressions are allocated proportionately, dollars vary.

TABLE 9-2.   Cost-per-Thousand Analysis

City	Spot TV CPM Women
New York	$2.36
Hartford	5.65
Chicago	3.41
San Francisco	3.78
Baltimore	8.16

TABLE 9-3.   Differences in Weighting Methods

	Total Sales (%)	CPM	Dollar Weighting		Gross Impression Weighting	
			10% of Dollars	No. of Gross Impressions 10% Dollars Buy	10% of Impressions	Cost of 10% Impressions
Market A	10	$2.50	$100,000	40 million	32 million	$ 80,000
Market B	10	3.75	100,000	26 million	32 million	120,000
Total			$200,000	66 million	64 million	$200,000

Source: Ogilvy & Mather.

Why do these two techniques differ? Dollar allocation does *not* take media gross impressions into consideration. Therefore, 10 percent of the available dollars buys more impressions in Market A than Market B because cost per thousand is lower in Market A. So the dollar allocation technique leaves Market B with fewer gross impressions per year than Market A, even though sales potential is equal. To equalize the number of gross impressions in A and B, the planner will tend to favor gross impression allocation. Yet each technique has different values.

Dollar allocation tends to generate:

1. More impressions in cost-efficient markets (A cost-efficient market is one where the cost per thousand is relatively low.)
2. Fewer impressions in inefficient markets or high cost-per-thousand markets
3. The opportunity for good markets to develop their potential because more gross impressions are received in these markets, presumably generating more sales
4. A slightly unbalanced advertising weight-to-sales ratio

Gross impression allocation tends to generate:

1. Proportional communication pressure regardless of cost
2. Balanced reach and frequency based on sales potential (This means that the good markets get proportionately more reach and frequency than poor markets.)
3. The opportunity for good markets to develop their potential because more gross impressions are received in these markets, presumably generating more sales
4. A slightly unbalanced advertising-to-sales ratio

In deciding which weighting technique to use, the planner has to consider which best meets the marketing objectives. In many instances, gross impression weighting is considered better because it is more directly related to communication goals. One of the main goals of media strategy planning is to reach large numbers of target audiences with a certain amount of repetition. Within a given budget, gross impression weighting accomplishes this goal best because it takes media costs into consideration. In the dollar allocation technique, costs may be directly proportional to sales, but audiences may not be reached often enough or in sufficiently large numbers.

TABLE 9-4. How U.S. Dollar Allocation Matches Sales Distribution

Market	Sales (%)	Cost (thousands)	Dollar Allocation		
			Total Cost (%)	Gross Impressions That Can Be Bought (millions)	Total Gross Impressions (%)
A	45	$ 675	45	343	48
B	30	450	30	214	30
C	15	225	15	93	13
D	10	150	10	64	9
Total U.S.	100	$1,500	100	714	100

Source: Ogilvy & Mather.

Tables 9–4 and 9–5 provide another picture of the relationships of both processes. Table 9–4 shows again that even when dollars are matched perfectly against sales percentage, gross impressions do not match (except in Market B). Table 9–5 shows that when gross impressions are matched perfectly against sales percentages, dollar costs do not match (again, except in Market B).

Share of Voice (Message Weight Distribution)

A planning concept that is sometimes used in making media decisions is called *share of voice*. It is also more appropriately called *message weight distribution*. This concept requires a planner to determine how much advertising is being done for his brand relative to the amount being done for competitive brands. A share of voice is a percentage of total advertising weight for each brand.

The assumption underlying share of voice is that if a brand is not spending an amount equal to or exceeding the expenditures of competitors, then it may not be able to achieve its goals. This assumption is not necessarily valid because there may be many variables, other than media spending, that affect the success of an advertising campaign. The superiority of the brand, or the uniqueness of the copy, or the amount and quality of distribution, or frequency and quality of promotions are a few variables that may be more important. In fact, many planners do not use the share of voice concept at all, while others think of it as a general idea that may be of help in determining allocations and/or budgets.

If, however, one is inclined to determine share of voice, it is important to do so on another basis in addition to comparing the percent of dollars spent. "Dollars spent" do not buy a constant number of gross impressions or target rating points.

TABLE 9-5. How Gross Impression Allocation Matches Sales Distribution

Market	Sales (%)	Gross Impressions Planned For (millions)	Total Gross Impressions (%)	Cost of Gross Impressions Planned (thousands)	Total Cost (%)
A	45	318	45	$ 637	42
B	30	212	30	444	30
C	15	106	15	251	17
D	10	71	10	168	11
Total	100	707	100	$1,500	100

Source: Ogilvy & Mather.

TABLE 9-6.   Share of Voice (Message Weight Distribution) for Nine Competitors

Brand	Share of Market (%)	Share of TV dollars (%)	Share of TV Messages to Women 18–39 (%)
A	35	25	19
B	26	25	28
C	17	16	16
D	8	8	12
E	7	4	6
F	4	3	6
G	3	2	4
H	N/A	14	8
I	N/A	3	1
Total	100	100	100

Source: Roth, Paul, "How to Plan Media," *Media Decisions,* 1976, p. 26.

So, it would be better to first find how many gross impressions or target rating points can be purchased for a given number of dollars and then convert this information into percentages. Comparisons can be made, for example, on the basis of the actual number of messages (or commercials) delivered.

Table 9–6 shows the share of TV messages to women 18–39 for nine brands. It is important to note that the share of voice (TV messages) does not match share of TV dollars in the example shown.

It also analyzes nine competitors and their message weight deliveries. The table shows that Brand A has 35 percent of the market but spends only 25 percent of the total TV dollars and has a relatively lower percentage of message delivery than Brand B.

The planner should ask a number of questions to determine "why" Brand A has such a high ratio of market share to message share. Is Brand A inherently superior in quality to B? Does Brand A have better distribution? Better copy? Most other brands show a high degree of consistency between market share and message share. Additional message weight analysis should be made of individual markets to see how they, too, relate to market share.

Guidelines in Geographical Weighting

There is no one formula used to determine advertising weights applied in different geographic areas. Weighting decisions are usually a result of many factors. Using one or the other of the two techniques described earlier, a planner may weight advertising in geographic markets in a number of ways. The following guidelines comprise some of the more important considerations in weighting.

A general concept is to apply extra weight to markets where sales volume or market share is high. In a market-by-market analysis, a planner might look at the brand development index (BDI) and compare it with a category development index (CDI). At times, more weight is added to markets with high BDIs.

More often, however, when a CDI is high and a BDI is low for a given market, additional weight may be added to bring the market up to its potential (as shown in the CDI).

Market potential, as a basis for weighting, may depend on any one, or perhaps all, of the following considerations:

1. Past history of each market's responsiveness to advertising. If a local market has not responded well to advertising in the past, then additional weight may not help.
2. History of profitability. Although additional weighting in a local market may improve sales volume or market share, it may do so at an unprofitable level. There may be a point of diminishing returns relative to profit in adding extra weight to a market.
3. Pipeline problems. If distribution levels in a market are low, or difficult to increase, or there are other marketing channel problems, then these factors may influence the amount of extra weight to be applied.
4. Sales force input. Some companies use their salespeople as sources of marketing intelligence at the local level. Their information may affect the manner in which weighting is applied.
5. Local market idiosyncracies. Some local markets may have problems in communication and/or selling that may not be true of other markets. One advertiser may find that an equal number of GRPs applied to both large and small markets usually produces greater awareness in smaller markets, regardless of other factors. If such idiosyncracies exist, then they should be allowed for in the weighting decision.
6. Competitive noise levels. If competitors advertise heavily in a market, the net effect of the noise level may require heavier weight in that market.
7. Cost efficiency of advertising in the market. Additional weighting may cost too much or result in cost inefficiency.

Once these considerations are evaluated, the planner may want to decide on a course of action that could affect the final weighting. Does the advertiser want to defend strengths in good markets? Improve weaknesses in problem markets? Or develop opportunity markets? After this decision has been made and other factors considered, weighting decisions for local geographical areas can be made.

Case Studies 9–1, 9–2, and 9–3 are examples of how different advertisers have used weighting techniques.

CASE STUDY 9–1
Weighting Sales Branches on the Basis of Sales Potential

An advertiser who uses magazines almost exclusively has divided the country into eleven sales branches, with each branch composed of a number of counties.

In planning advertising weights, each sales force in each branch first estimates its dollar sales for the next year. These dollars then are converted into percentages of total sales for the entire country, which each branch is expected to deliver.

The circulations of all magazines in a media schedule for this company are broken down by counties to match the eleven sales branches. Weighting matches the number of dollars to be spent in each branch with sales potential percentages for that branch. The following example clarifies the process:

Branch	Sales Potential (% of total)	Advertising Expenditures in Magazines by Branches (%)
1	2.8	2.0
2	15.8	12.8
3	16.9	17.0
4	13.4	15.7
5	10.6	10.0
6	11.2	9.1
7	6.4	8.4
8	11.2	11.9
9	4.9	7.0
10	5.5	4.4
11	1.3	1.7
Total	100.0	100.0

Ideally, magazine weighting should follow sales potential weighting perfectly. In practice, however, this is difficult because of the manner in which advertising expenditures in magazines must be allocated. Magazine publishers do not charge for their space on the basis of cost-per-county-circulation delivered. Instead, they simply charge by the page—either nationally or regionally. The media planner must therefore take the national page cost and divide it by the proportion of its circulation that goes into any county. For example, if a page cost $50,000 and 0.67 percent of the magazine's national circulation went into County A, then $335 would be allocated to County A ($50,000 × .0067 = $335). When adding county costs of numerous magazines in a schedule, it is difficult to match cost percentages precisely with sales potential percentages. The only way to achieve a relatively close match is to purchase local (or city) magazines and/or newspaper supplements in addition to national and regional magazines.

CASE STUDY 9-2
Weighting Markets on the Basis of Minimum BDIs and CDIs

The previous chapter discussed how BDIs and CDIs are generally used in selecting target markets. These two evaluative statistics may also be used to weight markets on the basis of minimum standards.

In this method, sales goals are first set for each individual market. Then 5 percent of the budget is cut from each market and reallocated to problem and/or opportunity markets.

A problem market is one:

1. With at least 1 percent of brand sales
2. With a CDI and BDI less than 100
3. With an unfavorable sales trend

An opportunity market is one:

1. With at least 1 percent of brand sales
2. With a CDI over 100, but BDI lower than CDI
3. With client's brand showing an unfavorable sales trend, but the product category doing well

Note: When CDI is over 100, the category is doing well. A BDI under 100 usually indicates a brand is not doing well.

The 5 percent that was cut from each market's budget is now distributed to both problem and opportunity markets. The idea underlying this practice is that problem markets may be strengthened by additional dollars, while opportunity markets need extra dollars to optimize potential. But at the same time, all markets were allocated *some* money based on potential.

Note: All markets will receive some advertising weight through the use of network television or national magazines. The weights discussed in this case are added to national weights.

CASE STUDY 9-3
Weighting Markets by Combining Quantitative and Qualitative Values for Each Market

This technique was used by an advertiser who purchased network TV to provide national coverage, and spot TV to weight the best markets. The value of each market was determined as follows:

Step 1. Calculate the cost index. The cost index is simply the average CPM for all spot TV markets in the country, related to the CPM for each individual market. If the average CPM for the country was $2.50 and it was $3.50 for Market A, then the cost index would be 140.

$$\$3.50 \div \$2.50 = 140 \text{ cost index}$$

Step 2. Calculate the CDI/CPM value for each market. If Market A had a CDI of 120, then the CDI/CPM value for each market would be 86.

$$120 \div 140 = 86$$

Market A now has less value than it had before because the CDI/CPM value is so low.

Step 3. Determine each market's responsiveness to advertising. This is primarily a qualitative judgment. If sales last year rose by more than 15 percent in a market, that market could be described as responsive. If sales rose between 3 percent and 15 percent, it might be described as somewhat responsive. If sales rose less than 3 percent, it might be described as not responsive. (An alternative method for making this decision is at the end of this section.)

Step 4. Assign extra weight on the basis of the following criteria:
  Group A Markets (Receive 50 percent more weight than average)

  1. CDIs are high
  2. CPMs are reasonable
  3. Network delivery is low
  4. Responsiveness to advertising was good in the past
  Group B Markets (Receive 25 percent more weight than average)
  Combinations of those considerations above yield a lower number, but show that the market is important
  Group C Markets (No spot TV)
  All other markets

The following example shows three sample markets assigned extra weight as described earlier:

Weighting on the Basis of CDI and CPM

Markets	Share of U.S. Population (%)	Industry Sales	Network TV Delivery	CDI	CDI/ Spot CPM	Sales Trend Last Yr. (%)	Weighting Used
Chicago	4.0	4.7	97	117	158	+ 19	A—add 50%
Seattle	1.2	1.8	85	150	117	+ 6	B—add 25%
Indianapolis	1.1	1.2	109	101	83	− 1	C—None

Note: Responsiveness to advertising could be determined differently. For example, an advertising-to-rates ratio figure could be calculated as follows: If sales in Market A were $1,450,000 and advertising in that market were $340,000, then the A/S ratio would be 0.235 (340 ÷ 1450 = 0.235).

Then an index of advertising to sales could be calculated whereby the A/S index for Market A was divided by the A/S index for the entire country. For example: 0.235 ÷ 0.405 = 0.58.

These indices could be added to the CPM average for each market and the CDI for each market to provide a multiple factor index as follows:

	Market A
CDI/CPM Index:	86
CDI	120
A/Sales Index	58
Total	264
Average for Market A (264 ÷ 3 = 88)	88

Population of Market A: 5 percent of total U.S. × 88 average index = 4.4 percent of the total allocation for Market A.

This technique could be used to allocate spot dollars proportionately throughout the country.

The three case studies indicate that different advertisers use different methods of weighting. No single method is used to the exclusion of all others. Each technique meets the needs of individual advertisers.

Reach and Frequency

As explained earlier, *reach* refers to how many people are exposed to a vehicle at least once, while *frequency* refers to how often they are reached in a four-week period.

How Much Reach Is Necessary?

One of the most difficult decisions facing a media planner is setting the level of reach needed for a media plan. It is difficult because there is little hard evidence from research or experimentation that provides the necessary direction. What is known about how much reach to use is the product of tradition, experience, common sense, and research done for particular brands in certain market situations. But there is little evidence to indicate that a given reach level is "correct" for a given marketing situation. Therefore the guidance provided here, based as it is on widely held beliefs, has to be general. Even with all these qualifiers, there are some planners who may disagree with this approach.

It is generally held that high reach is necessary for new product introductions, the rationale being that few people know the name of the brand or what its value is. As many different people as possible need to be informed, thus the need for high reach. But determining just how much reach is necessary is difficult.

The purpose of high reach is to generate awareness of the new brand. The reach level may be decided to some extent by the brand awareness level that is needed. Is the goal to make 65 percent of the targets aware of a brand name? Some people will need only one exposure to a vehicle to become aware of that brand. Others will need multiple exposures, so a certain level of frequency will be needed in addition to reach. Some planners might opt for a reach level higher than the brand awareness level desired, on the assumption that not everyone exposed to a vehicle will be exposed to the ad and the brand name. Others will want reach *and* frequency, which for planning purposes can be expressed in gross rating points. Within a given number of gross rating points, the reach and frequency levels can be juggled to bring either one to a required level. Some available research attempts to relate GRP levels to brand awareness levels. For example, one piece of research conducted by a well-known advertising agency found that about 2,400 GRPs a year produced a 70 percent brand awareness.

Sales promotion activities also need a high degree of reach because consumers need to be made aware when certain deals or promotional options are available. In planning media to advertise a cents-off deal, a high level of awareness is a requirement and, again, the precise amount of reach needed cannot be expressed.

One media planning strategy might be to set a reach level equal to or surpassing that of competitors who are deemed to be vulnerable to attack. Presumably these competitors have products that are not as good as the brand in question, or perhaps they are not advertising enough, or to the right targets. Setting a reach level equal to or higher than that of certain competitors offers a potential advantage to the planner, and is a way to determine how much reach ought to be attained.

Another consideration in planning reach is the budget. No matter which media are chosen, a fixed budget size limits the amount of reach possible. All the planner has to do is to calculate the amount of target reach that each medium and vehicle will deliver, plus the amount of continuity desired, to set a reach level.

There is a media strategy that stretches media dollars and therefore also stretches reach. This strategy holds that by cutting ad unit sizes, more money will be available to buy new reach. (The same strategy can be used to buy more frequency.) If the planned ad unit is thirty-second commercials or full-page ads, it could be cut to ten-second IDs or half-page ads. But there are two penalties for cutting unit sizes. First, the cost of smaller unit sizes usually is not exactly proportional to larger sizes—a ten-second ID costs 55 to 65 percent of a thirty-second commercial; a half-page ad costs 55 to 65 percent of a full-page ad. Second, there is a possible loss in communication value from the smaller ad unit.

Probably the best level of reach is determined by looking at what levels were used previously. If a brand has successfully achieved certain marketing goals in the past with a given level of reach, this same level (or proportional adjustment) should probably be used again.

In essence, then, the amount of reach needed for a media plan is based more on judgment and experience than on research evidence. Since media plans almost always require a certain amount of frequency, the combination of reach and frequency can be calculated in terms of gross rating points. But research on GRPs and communication effects is weak, and the GRP level is also a matter of judgment and experience.

How Much Frequency Is Necessary?

The question of how much frequency is necessary is probably the most pressing problem facing media planners. It is more important than learning how much reach or how many GRPs are necessary. A great deal of thinking and research has gone into this subject, although no clear-cut breakthroughs are yet apparent.

Frequency is needed whenever repetition of a message is necessary. Most planners feel that there are practical reasons for needing more than minimum amounts of frequency.

The first reason for needing frequency is that not everyone hears or sees an ad the first time it appears. Why? Because so many ads bombard a person each day that it is impossible for anyone to pay attention to all of them. Even if an individual has seen an ad many times, little or none of the information may have been absorbed by the person. Therefore, one goal of frequency is to surpass the *threshold,* the first few exposures, so that the audience member will absorb the message. Research has shown that there are indeed threshold levels, although it isn't known precisely whether the threshold is one, two, three, or more exposures.

In some cases, one exposure may be sufficient. Gus Priemer, advertising director of S. C. Johnson Company, has proved through test-market research on a new product that the first impression of an ad was remembered for a certain product/brand at a given time. As he explained:

> My own evidence strongly suggests that the first ad exposure actually *can* stimulate a large proportion of total *advertising response,* even when a product is using TV where the viewer is not in control of the communication vehicle.
>
> My TV evidence comes from some 35 first-exposure tests of commercials done for 16 new products prior to test marketing.
>
> For five of these products, viewers had already memorized the new brand name at significant levels (7 to 9 percent of those exposed to the test commercial). Almost one in four had clearly understood the new product promise of the testing brands.[1]

Priemer was not, however, generalizing about all products or all brands. He simply pointed out that there are different thresholds for different brands.

Frequency in media is not the same as frequency of ad exposure. In media planning, the frequency sought is vehicle exposure. But not everyone exposed to a vehicle also sees the ads in that vehicle. So, any frequency expressed as part of a media plan overstates the size of frequency of exposure to ads in the vehicle chosen. Because there is no syndicated research measurement of ad exposure, a planner must plan for more frequency than seems necessary; this creates a cushion of loss of exposure to account for audience members who see the vehicles, but don't see the ads of a given brand.

There has been a feeling in the industry for years that high frequency (or repetition) represents a strong form of persuasion in selling a product. The more frequently a persuasive message is heard or seen, the more likely the consumer is to see the merits of the advertised brand and be convinced to buy. At least, that is a widely held assumption. Additionally, the higher the frequency and the longer the advertising effort, the better the opportunity to reach a person when he or she is most ready to buy the product.

Some feel that every media planner should try to learn how many impressions (meaning frequency of exposure) a consumer needs before being persuaded to buy a given brand. This number is part of a cause-and-effect relationship. Planners assume that a level of impressions that will directly affect sales exists for every brand. However, this level is probably somewhat different for every brand and must be determined by experimental research. Test marketing experiments may have to be

---

1. Priemer, Gus, "Are We Doing the Wrong Thing Right?" *Media Decisions,* May 1979, p. 64.

conducted, trying various frequency levels to determine which is the most productive. The Advertising Research Foundation is working on a massive study to tackle the question of how much frequency is necessary.

Even those planners who view frequency as not necessarily a direct cause of sales see it as a necessary requirement for communicating with large numbers of disinterested consumers, or consumers who miss advertising because they are inundated by the noise level of all the competitive ads. Frequency, therefore, is a means of "getting through" to the consumer. The following quotation, from over a hundred years ago, has often been cited as a generalization about how frequency affects communications, and eventually sales.

> The first time a man looks at an advertisement, he does not see it.
> The second time he does not notice it.
> The third time he is conscious of its existence.
> The fourth time he faintly remembers having seen it before.
> The fifth time he reads it.
> The sixth time he turns up his nose at it.
> The seventh time he reads it through and says, "Oh brother!"
> The eighth time he says, "Here's that confounded thing again!"
> The ninth time he wonders if it amounts to anything.
> The tenth time he thinks he will ask his neighbor if he has tried it.
> The eleventh time he wonders how the advertiser makes it pay.
> The twelfth time he thinks perhaps it may be worth something.
> The thirteenth time he thinks it must be a good thing.
> The fourteenth time he remembers that he has wanted such a thing for a
> long time.
> The fifteenth time he is tantalized because he cannot afford to buy it.
> The sixteenth time he thinks he will buy it some day.
> The seventeenth time he makes a memorandum of it.
> The eighteenth time he swears at his poverty.
> The nineteenth time he counts his money carefully.
> The twentieth time he sees it, he buys the article, or instructs his wife to do
> so.[2]

Many media planners believe that a plan should have a frequency level of at least four exposures a month. The thinking is that the first three exposures tend to be ignored, but the fourth is the threshold at which consumers begin to pay attention to the advertising message.

Other planners disagree. Some say that the frequency level must vary because certain situations may require higher or lower levels. The uniqueness of the advertising message, for example, can affect frequency. The more innovative and unusual the message is, the more likely that consumers will notice it and pay attention to it. The converse is also true. A rather ordinary ad message might need many more than four

2. Smith, Thomas, *Hints to Intending Advertisers* (London, 1885): quoted in Herbert E. Krugman, "An Application of Learning Theory to TV Copy Testing," *Public Opinon Quarterly,* vol. 26, 1962, pp. 626–34.

exposures to be seen and remembered. (In all discussions on frequency levels, the planner must be aware that creative executions vary from brand to brand, and the creative element can argue for more or less frequency than the competition uses.)

Another consideration affecting the frequency level is the perceived value of a brand as compared with the values of competitors' brands. When a brand has an important and easily perceivable benefit not shared by competitors, then less frequency may be called for. In other words, the brand has an easily exploited advantage over competitors. But when a brand is very much like all other brands in a product category, more frequency may be necessary for the message to be noticed or remembered.

The noise level in a product category also plays a role in deciding how much frequency is needed. On one hand, if many similar brands are being advertised simultaneously, consumers may find it difficult to recall the message for any one brand amid the confusion caused by the noise level of competitors. On the other hand, when few competitors advertise, less frequency may be required.

Some planners feel that a frequency level should be based on the level of that used by a brand's most serious competitive threat; or, that the competitor who is the most vulnerable to a brand's promotional attack efforts should be singled out. The frequency level of that competitor should be equaled or surpassed, with the objective of gaining an advantage.

Media values may also be used in conjunction with gross-rating-point planning to determine frequency (as well as reach) levels. Media value is simply the judgment that a given medium has been found, through experience, to be more effective for a brand and its creative message, thus justifying more frequency in that medium. The chief problem, however, in combining media evaluations and frequency levels is that of making too subjective an evaluation of each medium. Is daytime television always less than 35 percent as effective as prime-time television? To say that it is *always* less effective is an unreasonable assumption. For certain brands, in certain marketing situations, at certain times, the 35 percent differential may be true—but it is dangerous to generalize. The method is a good one, however, when research evidence can be used to back up a generalization about media values.

Frequency levels in media plans therefore range quite a bit. When the threatening or vulnerable competitor technique is being used, frequency levels may go to as high as fifteen average exposures a month. But these levels are not decided upon in a scientific manner in terms of a cause-and-effect relationship. Even when various frequency levels are tested in three or four local markets and one is found to be better than others, there is no guarantee that this level can be projected nationally. What is true in a test market may or may not be valid for every market. The experience of many national advertisers who have used test marketing for setting frequency levels varies from a few who have had excellent results to many who have had costly failures.

All of these considerations about where to set the frequency level are based primarily on common sense, and on unfortunately little research evidence. As a consequence, it is not surprising to find frequency levels being set somewhat arbitrarily, based on tradition plus common sense. In the future, the concepts and practices of *effective* reach and frequency may totally supplant present techniques.

One of the most important guidelines to remember in determining how much frequency is necessary is that vehicle frequency does not equal advertising frequency. The levels planned for media vehicles should not be confused with advertising frequency, which must also be planned.

Effective Frequency and Reach

The question of how to set effective frequency (and effective reach) levels cannot be answered very well, despite the fact that planners have been using the 3 + level in their plans for a number of years. There is enough agreement among the leading researchers and practitioners of media to agree that a 3 + level is not correct. The reason, as discussed in Chapter 6, is that it is oversimplified. There are too many variables in planning that the 3 + concept does not address.

However, these same people agree that there already are guidelines for setting effective frequency levels in an objective manner. We may not know objectively how much frequency is needed, but we can know that 3 + is not the correct level *unless* we have modified that number by the guideline criteria. Therefore, the best advice to date is to plan media in the same way that planners did *without* effective frequency. This procedure means that the first step in planning is to review the different variables that can affect the amount of frequency needed. Then, starting with a frequency level needed to account for these variables, add them to what is already known about effective frequency. In other words, considering all the variables that affect normal frequency, one might arrive at a 2 + level. Adding that to the 3 + level arrived at by some effective frequency research, brings one to a 5 + level. However, a planner could end up with a 1 + plan just as well, depending on these variables.

Joseph Ostrow spelled out the variables that planners should first consider in his talk at the Advertising Research Foundation Conference on Effective Frequency in 1982. (Ostrow's ideas are presented in Case Study 9–4, along with some numbers that could be applied for every consideration that Ostrow recommends which the authors have supplied.)

CASE STUDY 9–4
How to Set Effective Frequency Levels

One of the problems facing a media planner is that of deciding how much effective frequency a media plan should have. Although the research may be interpreted to suggest a 3 + level, there is great dispute about it.

One suggestion about how to set a frequency level was made by Joseph W. Ostrow, executive vice president of the Foote-Cone & Belding agency at the 1982 Effective Frequency Conference sponsored by the Advertising Research Foundation.* He specified a number of conditions that should influence the decision, based on

---

*Ostrow, Joseph W., "Setting Effective Frequency Levels," in *Effective Frequency: The State of the Art,* New York: Advertising Research Foundation, Key Issues Workshop, 1982, pp. 89–102.

marketing, media, and creative strategy considerations. He pointed out that "the right level of frequency for a media plan is the point at which effective communication takes place." For example, "getting consumers to understand the message; helping consumers become more positive about a product (or service) or influencing the purchase decisions directly."

The authors, however, have made some additional suggestions about Ostrow's model to help solve the problem of setting the correct frequency level, by asking the reader/user to add a certain amount of frequency points to a base, if the marketing, media, or creative condition meets the planner's needs. These additional frequency points are only suggestions; the user may opt for different ones.

The planner should use these additional points by starting with a base, such as a 3 + level, then adding or subtracting points as the situation dictates.

Here's an example of how to use these suggestions. Suppose a planner is faced with the following situations:

1. He or she is introducing a new product.
2. The introduction is in a highly competitive market.
3. The product has a short purchase cycle.
4. The brand will be among those that are less well known.
5. The product is not used daily.
6. Ad copy is somewhat complex.
7. Copy is more unique than competitors'.
8. Copy will be in large-size ad units.
9. There is high ad clutter in category media.
10. Media environment is compatible with product.
11. Advertising will be continuous.
12. Many media will be used.
13. There will be many opportunities for repetition.

The planner should now consult Ostrow's considerations and note the suggested point levels that may be added for setting effective frequency levels, as follows:

Marketing Factors That Affect Effective Frequency

Marketing Factors	Frequency Needed	Comments
Established brands	Lower	Repetition helps consumers learn a message. New brands need to be learned.
New brands	Higher	
High market share	Lower	High market share assumes that brand loyalty must be high. Thus less frequency needed.
Low market share	Higher	
Dominant brand in market	Lower	Large brands may not benefit from more repetition if the market is saturated. Smaller brands can benefit from more frequency.
Smaller, less well-known brands	Higher	

High brand loyalty	Lower	An inverse relationship usually exists between frequency and brand loyalty.
Low brand loyalty	Higher	
Long purchase cycle	Lower	Consumers may do more thinking about products with longer purchase cycles.
Short purchase cycle (High volume segments)	Higher	
Product used daily	Higher	Products used daily, or more than once daily probably need higher frequency.
Product used occasionally	Lower	
Needed to beat competition	Higher	In heavy-spending-categories, more frequency may be needed above the level that achieves effective communication.
Advertising to older consumers or children	Higher	Special targets may need higher frequency levels.

Copy Factors That Affect Effective Frequency

Copy Factors	Frequency Needed	Comments
Complex copy	Higher	Copy research augmenting good copy may be needed to determine how copy is perceived.
Simple copy	Lower	
Copy less unique than competition	Higher	The assumption is that copy uniqueness is an asset that translates to less frequency.
Copy more unique	Lower	
New copy campaign	Higher	Just as a new product introduction needs higher frequency, so does new copy.
Continuing campaign	Lower	
Image type copy	Higher	Image campaigns are deemed more complex and subtle, needing more frequency.
Product sell copy	Lower	
More different kinds of messages	Higher	This covers the question of how much message variation there is, and is tied to the number of commercials in a pool of commercials.
Single kind of message	Lower	
To avoid wearout: New messages Older messages	Higher Lower	The question here is: has advertising worn out? Measurements will need to be made to learn what the situation is.
Small ad units	Higher	Advertising units either in broadcast or print may need more or less frequency.
Larger ad units	Lower	

Media Factors That Affect Effective Frequency

Media Factors	Frequency Needed	Comments
High ad clutter	Higher	This is an oddity because high clutter requires more frequency that adds to the clutter.
Lower ad clutter	Lower	
Compatible editorial environment	Lower	An example of compatible environment would be a dog food ad appearing in a television pet show.
Non-compatible environment	Higher	

Attentiveness high	Lower	Some media vehicles have higher attentive levels than others.
Attentiveness low	Higher	
Continuous advertising	Lower	Interruptions in advertising, such as in pulsing or flighting, need more frequency.
Pulsed or flighted advertising	Higher	
Few media used	Lower	Each medium used may require a minimum level of frequency.
More media used	Higher	
Opportunities for media repetition	Lower	Certain media offer better and more opportunities for repetition, and these require less frequency.
Fewer opportunities for repetition	Higher	

Marketing Factors That Affect Effective Frequency

Established brands	$-.2$	$-.1$	$+.1$	$+.2$	New Brands
High market share	$-.2$	$-.1$	$+.1$	$+.2$	Low market share
Dominant brand in market	$-.2$	$-.1$	$+.1$	$+.2$	Smaller, less well-known brands
High brand loyalty	$-.2$	$-.1$	$+.1$	$+.2$	Low brand loyalty
Long purchase cycle	$-.2$	$-.1$	$+.1$	$+.2$	Short purchase cycle (high volume segments)
Product used daily	$-.2$	$-.1$	$+.1$	$+.2$	Product used occasionally
			$+.1$	$+.2$	Needed to beat competition
			$+.1$	$+.2$	Advertising to older consumers, or children

Copy Factors That Affect Effective Frequency

Simple copy	$-.2$	$-.1$	$+.1$	$+.2$	Complex copy
Copy more unique than competition	$-.2$	$-.1$	$+.1$	$+.2$	Copy less unique than competition
Continuing campaign	$-.2$	$-.1$	$+.1$	$+.2$	New copy campaign
Product sell copy	$-.2$	$-.1$	$+.1$	$+.2$	Image type copy
Single kind of message	$-.2$	$-.1$	$+.1$	$+.2$	More different kinds of messages
To avoid wearout: New messages	$-.2$	$-.1$	$+.1$	$+.2$	Older messages
Larger ad units	$-.2$	$-.1$	$+.1$	$+.2$	Small ad units

Media Factors That Affect Effective Frequency

Lower ad clutter	$-.2$	$-.1$	$+.1$	$+.2$	High ad clutter
Compatible editorial environment	$-.2$	$-.1$	$+.1$	$+.2$	Non-compatible environment
Attentiveness high	$-.2$	$-.1$	$+.1$	$+.2$	Attentiveness low
Continuous advertising	$-.2$	$-.1$	$+.1$	$+.2$	Pulsed or flighted advertising
Few media used	$-.2$	$-.1$	$+.1$	$+.2$	Many media used
Opportunities for media repetition	$-.2$	$-.1$	$+.1$	$+.2$	Fewer opportunities

Source: Ostrow, Joseph W. "Setting Frequency Levels," in *Effective Frequency: The State of the Art.* Copyright 1982. Reprinted by permission.

The next step is to determine how many additional points beyond 3 + that ought to be added to arrive at an effective frequency level. Ostrow's criteria are the source of these considerations, and the suggested points are the authors'.

	Suggested additional points
1. He or she is introducing a new product.	+ .2
2. The introduction is in a highly competitive market.	+ .2
3. The product has a short purchase cycle.	+ .2
4. The brand will be among those that are less well known.	+ .2
5. The product is used daily.	− .1
6. Ad copy is somewhat complex.	+ .2
7. Copy is more unique than competitors'.	− .2
8. Copy will be in large size ad units.	− .1
9. There is high ad clutter in category media.	+ .2
10. Media environment is compatible with product.	− .1
11. Advertising will be continuous.	− .2
12. Many media will be used.	+ .2
13. There will be many opportunities for repetition.	− .2
Sum of Points	+ .5

Effective Frequency Base	3.0 +
Additional Points	+ .5
Modified Effective Frequency Level	+ 3.5 or 4 +

The reader should note that not all of Ostrow's criteria may be applicable to a situation at hand. However, it is conceivable that a planner's own criteria may be added to the list to make it more relevant.

Continuity, Flighting, and Pulsing

An important part of timing advertising is scheduling it so that it appears at the most propitious selling times. A major objective of scheduling is to control the pattern of times when advertising appears by plotting advertising timing on a yearly flow chart. There are three major methods of scheduling advertising, each with a somewhat different pattern, as follows:

1. *Continuity* (sometimes called straight-through advertising)

◄———————— Yearly time period ————————►

This pattern is continuous, although there may be small gaps of time, at regular intervals, when no advertising is done. One continuity pattern may be to run one ad every day for 365 days. Another continuity pattern may be one ad a week for 52 weeks. The time gaps show up in a pattern of dashes on a flow chart.

2. *Flighting* (sometimes called bursting)

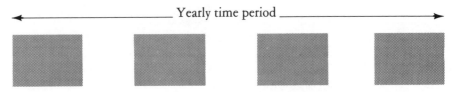

Flighting is an intermittent pattern where there are gaps of time when no advertising is done. If advertising were done once a month, this might be called flighting. Most often, however, flighting patterns are more irregular, with heavy concentrations of advertising at certain times interspersed with no advertising for shorter lengths of time.

3. *Pulsing*

Pulsing is a form of flighting and continuity combined—where an advertiser buys continuous advertising throughout the year and "heavies up" at various propitious time periods. Pulsing is sometimes mistakenly called flighting, and when planners use either term (pulsing/flighting), they should be sure that everyone using these terms understands them.

The media planner must decide, as part of the strategy, which pattern to use.

The first step in selecting a pattern is to examine purchasing patterns for the product category. Because most product categories have unique purchasing patterns, it is important to learn what they are before thinking about a scheduling pattern. An unusual example of a purchasing cycle is the market for Christmas trees. Trees are rarely purchased at any time of the year other than November or December. By the same token, typewriters are sold primarily during the spring, summer, and late fall as gifts or for students going back to school. Although some typewriters may be sold throughout the year, under ordinary circumstances it would not be advisable to advertise at times other than the three heavy selling seasons. But for a product such as face soap that is purchased throughout the year, though with heavier consumption in the summer, the best scheduling plan might be pulsing (year-round advertising with "heavy-up" in the summer).

TABLE 9–7. GRPs in Continuity versus Flighting

Week No. →	1	2	3	4	5	6	7	8	9	10	11	12	13	14	15	16	
Continuity pattern GRPs	40	40	40	40	40	40	40	40	40	40	40	40	40	40	40	40	Total 640
Flighting pattern GRPs	80	80	80	80					80	80	80	80					Total 640

Source: Ogilvy & Mather.

Continuity

Continuity is needed when an advertiser has a message that it does not want consumers to forget. Continuous advertising works as a reminder, keeping the message always before the consumer. That is one of the strongest arguments for continuity.

Another advantage of continuity is that the entire purchase cycle will be covered because there will be no gaping holes in time periods. This assures the planner that most of the customers are reached at all times, both when they will be purchasing and during times when they may not be buying.

Another reason for using continuity is that it makes it possible to take advantage of larger media discounts granted because so much advertising is purchased continuously. There may be cost efficiencies in such discounts, because the cost-per-target reached will tend to be lower than plans that do not contain such discounts. In addition, the advertiser may have an advantage in obtaining certain kinds of desirable positioning within media. Because the advertiser is buying a fairly large block of advertising, it may be easier to find the broadcast programs or times that are most favorable. There may also be positioning advantages in print where certain parts of the magazine or newspaper become more readily accessible to anyone who will buy a great deal of advertising over a long period of time.

Flighting

An advantage of flighting over continuity is that it allows the advertiser to meet competition better by placing advertising at the most favorable times relative to competition. Advertising can be concentrated in high-sales-potential periods, either in broadcast time or print space. Advertising can be timed precisely to reach the best purchasing cycle time periods with little waste when buying is slow.

Ostensibly, flighting is used when there are budgeting limitations or sharp sales fluctuations. The advertiser buys ads only when sales are growing and drops out when sales trends are declining. This tends to save money.

Furthermore, flighting allows the planner to support advertising in one medium by using another medium simultaneously. If an advertiser plans to use television as the basic medium, then flighting allows concentration of radio and newspaper support at the same time.

Finally, flighting allows a series of ads and commercials to appear as a unified campaign rather than as a series of unrelated ads. By concentrating them at certain times of the year, the ads will appear to the consumer to be part of a single communication entity.

By concentrating advertising, an advertiser can sometimes catch competitors off guard and gain an advantage over them, especially if the competitors tend to use continuity rather than flighting in their strategy. The advantage is simply that the advertiser buys much heavier weight than competitors for a relatively short time.

But there are risks in flighting, too. The first is that so much advertising may be concentrated in one time period that the commercials could wear out before the flight is over. Great amounts of flighting in concentrated time periods tends to build high frequency.

A second drawback of flighting is that consumers may forget the essence of the advertising message between flights if too much time elapses between them. However, the effectiveness of advertising does not stop the moment advertising is stopped. There is some carry-over.

Third, competitors may take advantage of the advertiser by placing heavy ad weights at precisely the time the advertiser is not advertising. So during those times, competitors have an advantage over the advertiser.

Pulsing

Pulsing represents the best of both techniques; it is a mixture of continuity and flighting. All of the advantages of continuity and flighting are now possible, with none of the disadvantages. Pulsing is the safest of the three because it covers different marketing situations. Not all advertisers, however, would be advised to use pulsing. It best fits those product categories that are sold all year round, but have heavier concentrations of sales at intermittent periods.

Both continuity and flighting can develop the same reach and frequency over a long period of time (such as sixteen weeks), as shown in Table 9–7 (p.183). However, there will be considerable differences of reach and frequency over the short run, as shown in Table 9–8. The table shows that, for a four-week period, the flighting pattern had a considerably larger reach than continuity had. The reason is the larger concentration of GRPs.

TABLE 9–8. Reach and Frequency of Continuity versus Flighting

	Continuity	Flighting
Monthly GRPs	160	320
Reach	57	76
Frequency	2.8	4.2

Frequency Distribution No. Times Reached	Cumulative Reach	
	Continuity	Flighting
1	57.1	75.8
2	39.1	61.5
3	25.8	49.4
4 or more	15.7	39.0

Source: Ogilvy & Mather.

Relationships among Reach, Frequency, Continuity, and Number of Markets

In planning strategy, there are usually four elements that are closely related: reach, frequency, continuity, and number of markets to be used. A person cannot plan for one of these elements without simultaneously considering the others, because of their close relationship. The relationship grows out of a fixed budget size, which means, in effect, that if any one of these elements is strongly emphasized, the others will, of necessity, suffer.

Each of these elements costs a considerable amount of money to attain. Reach, for example, usually means that advertising messages must be dispersed widely so that many different persons in the target audience will have an opportunity to see the messages. Generally, one single media vehicle, such as one television program or one magazine, will not deliver a high reach. Multiple vehicles are usually required, and the more that are purchased, the greater the cost. As the cost for reach goes up, the amount of money available for the other three elements becomes more limited.

The same holds true for continuity. If an advertiser wants to plan continuous advertising over 52 weeks, the cost will be high, leaving minimal amounts of money for the other three elements. Often as much as six or more months of advertising must be sacrificed in order for the reach to attain a high enough level in the remaining six months.

Likewise, the number of individual markets in a plan, where national media may be used in conjunction with local media, clearly affects overall costs. Even if only local media are used, the same concept prevails. The more markets used, the higher the cost, and the less money available for the other elements.

Figure 9–1 shows to some extent what happens when a planner tries to manipulate the four elements within the constraints of a fixed budget. The figure shows some ways to vary the weights of reach, frequency, continuity, and number of markets. Other possibilities, not shown, also exist. One part of a planner's job is to weight each of the four alternatives and decide which of the four needs more emphasis (usually at the expense of the others). Of course, if the budget size can be increased (unfortunately, it usually can't), then different emphases can be achieved. As a consequence of this dilemma, the planner needs some criteria for weighting the alternatives.

Weighting Alternatives

Reach and frequency are the two most important elements of a media plan. Because they occupy such an important position in a plan, they are usually considered before continuity or number of markets. When a media budget is very high, it may be possible to achieve both high reach *and* high frequency levels. But most often, the cost is too high to do both.

If high reach is planned, it will probably cause the frequency level to decline somewhat, because reach and frequency are inversely related. If, however, reach is very high (at the 90 percent level), then frequency can be increased by extra dollar expenditures because most of the money will go into building frequency and a very

FIGURE 9-1.   Alternative Strategies within a Fixed Budget

A

Reach	Frequency
Continuity	Number of Markets

Strategy A is a balanced strategy—reach, frequency, continuity, and number of markets were deliberately given equal weight.

B

Reach	Frequency
Continuity	Number of Markets

Strategy B was planned to emphasize reach and frequency at the expense of continuity and number of markets.

C

Reach	Frequency
Continuity	Number of Markets

Strategy C emphasizes frequency and number of markets, but reach and continuity have been reduced.

D

Reach	Frequency
Continuity	Number of Markets

Strategy D shows most emphasis on the number of markets with the others being downplayed.

small increment will go to building reach. This is the natural consequence of trying to reach new persons who have not already been reached by some other vehicle.

Higher reach will be necessary when the media plan calls for building brand awareness at significant levels. If a brand awareness level is now at 25 percent and an objective is to raise it to 75 percent, then higher reach will probably be required, and frequency will be sacrificed. Also calling for higher reach is the announcement of various kinds of promotions such as cents-off deals, special coupon promotions, or refund offers. Such promotions need to build a great deal of awareness so that consumers will take advantage of the offer. Still another high-reach situation occurs when changes in the brand or changes in the creative strategy are important. Finally, more reach may be needed when it becomes necessary to meet or exceed competitive reach levels. One goal could be to steal customers from a competitor by showing them that the advertised brand better meets their needs, in which case enough reach might be needed to equal or better the competitor's reach.

More frequency, at the expense of reach, may be needed when the brand awareness levels are already high due to the cumulative effect of past advertising. At that point, more frequency may be needed to meet or surpass frequency levels of competitors. When the advertising noise level of all competitors is already high, then more frequency also may be needed to meet or surpass frequency levels of competitors. There are certain marketing situations where a minimum frequency threshold must be passed before consumers start paying attention to the message. The effectiveness of the media plan may be directly related to high frequency. Sometimes a frequency level from three to ten must be achieved for the campaign to be considered effective.

Although brand awareness may be a campaign or creative objective, it may be necessary to advertise in a pattern that matches the purchasing cycle of a product class. Some products are not sold to any great extent at certain times of the year. Calculators, for example, require heavy media usage in spring, early fall, and at Christmas time. Reach levels also will probably be high at those times. On the other hand, in the case of beer—sold all through the year with summer peaks—reach levels may have to be sacrificed at some times of the year in order to have enough money to cover the year and, at the same time, spend heavily during summer. When high reach is necessary, it is sometimes necessary to sacrifice continuity. In some situations, advertisers may drop out of advertising for as long as six months, allowing the product to keep selling at lower volume levels, in order to have sufficient money to advertise at high levels during peak volume seasons.

The final variable affecting the budget allocation is the number of markets to be used. There are two methods of arriving at this number. The older method consisted of creating national media plans in which the number of markets would not be considered until after other strategies were decided. A newer technique starts with a market-by-market analysis and sets strategies for each market. Once communication goals are set for each market, then reach and frequency levels may be set after the number of markets has been decided. Still another approach is to determine the number of markets and minimum communication goals simultaneously—meaning that reach and frequency levels and degree of continuity are also determined simultaneously.

Setting Priorities

An important step in weighting the four elements is that of setting priorities. A planner should do this early so that it will be easier to decide which of the four elements is most or least important. Priorities come from media objectives, and some objectives are obviously more important than others. If there is any doubt, then a planner must not only state the priorities, but also explain why one objective is more important than another and how much more important. Once the priorities are clear, then the allocation of a budget to the four variables should be relatively clear.

QUESTIONS FOR DISCUSSION

1. Briefly explain why a media planner for Brand X who intends to use only network television in the plan, should be concerned about sales potential on a market-by-market basis.
2. Which form of weighting—dollars or impressions—should be used to reach communication goals more easily?
3. What is meant by a threshold level of three impressions in a media plan?
4. Is the frequency of a media plan equivalent to advertising exposure frequency? Explain.
5. Suppose that an advertiser plans a month-long promotion of a brand of soap, with three bars being sold for the price of two. Which would a media planner be most likely to adopt for this plan: reach or frequency? Explain.
6. How did one media executive arrive at an exposure level of three to ten to set effective reach levels?

7. Which will probably develop more reach: continuity or flighting? Explain.
8. Explain what a planner should do if the advertising budget is not large enough to reach the media objectives. (Assume that the planner cannot ask for more money.)
9. In what way can an advertiser's sales force contribute to the planning of geographic weighting in a media plan?
10. Suppose that we plan to run full-page ads in a media plan, but find that we need more reach. We cannot obtain more dollars to buy extra reach. What alternatives are available to possibly attain our reach goals?

SELECTED READINGS

Achenbaum, Alvin, "GRPs Can't Measure Effectiveness," *Media Decisions,* May 1977, pp. 64–65.

Adams, S. C., Britt, S. H., and Miller, A. S., "How Many Advertising Exposures per Day?" *Journal of Advertising Research,* December 1972, pp. 3–9.

Advertising Age, "High Cost of Advertising Got You Down? Try ERPs," November 7, 1977.

Cohen, Jack, "The Dollars & Sense of National Ad Rates," *Marketing and Media Decisions,* May 1986, pp. 119–21.

Geis, Robert H., and Jones, Richard P., *The Allocation of Advertising Funds: Put Your Money Where Sales Are,* New York: Association of National Advertisers Media Workshop, December 4, 1973, p. 14.

Haley, Russell I., "Sales Effects of Media Weights," *Journal of Advertising Research,* June 1978, p. 78.

Hill, Jack D., *Why Three Exposures May Not Be Enough,* New York: Association of National Advertisers Workshop, February 25, 1975, p. 9.

Kamen, Joseph M., "How to Get High Ratings and Sell Less," *Journal of Advertising Research,* April 1979, pp. 59–60.

Kingman, Merle, "Admen See Pulsing as Way to Beat Soaring TV Time Costs," *Advertising Age,* July 4, 1977.

Krugman, Herbert E., "Why Three Exposures May Be Enough," *Journal of Advertising Research,* December 1972, pp. 3–9.

Krugman, Herbert E., "Memory without Recall, Exposure without Perception," *Journal of Advertising Research,* August 1977, pp. 9–12.

Light, Larry, *Some New Ways of Allocating Media Dollars by Market,* Association of National Advertisers Advertising Research Workshop, New York, March 1977, p. 6.

Lippman, Stacey, "How Much Frequency," *Marketing and Media Decisions,* May 1986, pp. 116–17.

Moran, William T., *Media Scheduling Patterns (When to Run, When to Stop and Flight),* New York: Association of National Advertisers Advertising Research Workshop, March 1977, p. 10.

Naples, Michael, *Effective Frequency: The Relationship Between Frequency and Advertising Effectiveness,* New York: Association of National Advertisers, 1979.

Ostrow, Joseph W., "What Level Frequency?" *Advertising Age,* November 9, 1981, p. S-4.

Papazian, Ed, "How Much Frequency Is Enough?" *Media Decisions,* May 1976, p. 12.

Shifman, Phil, "Frequency Not Reach," *Media Decisions,* August 1975, p. 86.

Staab, Walter, "Are You Making Media Plans? Watch for Geographic Skew," *Advertising Age,* March 24, 1975.

Stevenson, Robert L., "The Frequency of Newspaper Readership," *American Newspaper Publishers Association News Research Report,* October 21, 1977.

10

Selecting Media Classes: Intermedia Comparisons

The two preceding chapters covered major strategy decisions comprising a part of the activities involved in media planning. This chapter and the next deal with the selection of media, covering decisions that usually follow strategy decisions. This chapter will discuss the selection of media classes—decisions on whether to use television, magazines, newspapers, or some other medium. Once media classes have been selected, then decisions about specific vehicles within classes will follow. (Vehicle choices are discussed in Chapter 11.)

To make decisions about media classes the planner must make *intermedia comparisons*—comparisons among different media. Comparisons among media vehicles in the same class, such as among magazines A, B, and C, are called *intramedia* comparisons. It is obvious that intermedia comparisons should be made before intramedia comparisons.

The main problem is whether or not it is logically correct to make intermedia comparisons on a statistical basis. Although it may be valid to compare media classes statistically in some cases, in most others it is not. The reason is that the numbers for one media class may not be comparable to another class. Comparisons of readers, viewers, and listeners may aptly be likened to the comparison of apples and oranges. The definition of a reader is so different from that of a viewer that comparisons of numbers may be misleading. For example, would it be correct to compare the cost-per-thousand viewers of a television program with the cost-per-thousand readers of a magazine? Only partially. If one vehicle delivers more audience at better cost efficiency than another in a different media class, the answer is correct to that point. But it is questionable whether a television commercial with its action and sound can be fairly compared with the static appearance of a four-color print advertisement. Yet the planner must make such comparisons whenever it is necessary to choose between two different media classes. Table 10–1 shows some of the differences between print and broadcast media.

TABLE 10-1.   Differences between Print and Broadcast Media

Print Media	Broadcast Media
Message must be read or seen.	Message must be heard, read, or seen.
Message can be read at the reader's convenience	Message is viewed/heard only when it is broadcast
Message does not interfere with editorial or entertainment content, although some articles are arranged in a format that does interrupt the reader	Message often interrupts editorial or entertainment content
A reader is defined as one who was exposed to the medium	A viewer is defined as one who has tuned in to the program
Messages can be reread as often as the reader wishes	Message appears only once and viewer has no idea when the same message will be rebroadcast
Generally, one pays full or partial attention to medium while reading or even scanning	It is possible to perform other tasks while program is on, so range of attention may be from none to full
Reader can search for products of interest	Viewer has little idea when a desired product will be advertised
Color fidelity is usually excellent	Color fidelity ranges from one extreme to another depending on the TV set
Medium can be read in almost any location	Viewing is limited by the size and portability of TV or radio set
Medium is sold in space units	Medium is sold in time units
Many production variables are possible, such as gatefolds, pop-ups, Day-Glo inks	Some kinds of production variables are possible such as split-screen, cartoons, stop-motion, cut-ins

Review of Consumer Media

Following is a brief review of reasons for and against using major measured consumer media: newspapers, magazines, television, radio, supplements, direct mail, outdoor, transit, and cable TV. The pros and cons of using a medium often grow out of a planner's perceptions and impressions rather than from objective evidence. So there are some media experts who might take exception to the reasons and/or limitations stated here.

Newspapers—Reasons for Using

Sense of Immediacy. Readers tend to perceive newspapers as being the most immediate medium in the market. Every day a newspaper contains something new and with the news come new advertisements. Newspapers may be thought of as having a *now* quality at all times. This quality is important when advertisers want to communicate something immediately. When manufacturers introduce new products to the market, they usually include newspapers as part of the media mix.

Local Emphasis. Almost all daily newspapers have a local quality that is important to advertisers. Although advertisers may use a national medium such as network television, they may also want to use a medium with local impact. All selling is local and the newspaper helps emphasize that fact by advertising local merchants' names and addresses.

Flexibility. Newspapers are geographically flexible because they may be used nationally, regionally, and locally in a media plan. Even when a manufacturer's markets are widely scattered throughout the country, it is possible to reach them by using local newspapers.

Production flexibility allows copy to be changed easily and quickly. For example, some national advertisers want to have different prices for the same products in different markets. There are also special production techniques available. Perhaps an advertiser wants to include preprinted inserts in newspapers in certain geographical markets. These and other production alternatives are possible.

High-Fidelity Color Inserts. Through the use of gravure-printed inserts, newspapers can compete favorably with magazines in given markets. Gravure printing gives the advertiser brilliant, life-like colors similar to those that enhance the brand's advertisement in magazines. Furthermore, any printing technique may be used on any quality paper to provide high-fidelity color.

Mass Reach. Because newspapers are read by so many individuals in each market, total reach per market may include many individuals in each family. When a product's target audience includes Mom, Dad, and the children, then newspapers may be an ideal medium.

Catalog Value. A newspaper may serve as a catalog for consumers who are doing comparison shopping. Often consumers search their daily newspaper before they go shopping. The effect of such a search is that they are often presold before they walk into a store to buy the product. Some readers even cut out ads and bring them along as a reminder.

Ethnic Appeal. Although newspapers are considered a mass medium, they have the power to reach selective ethnic classes as well. If the local newspaper does not reach these markets, then an ethnic newspaper may do the job.

Newspapers—Limitations

Variation in ROP (Run of Press or Run of Paper) Color and Black-and-White Quality. An advertiser buying advertisements printed in ROP color may find great variations in color fidelity from market to market. This variance means that the message may be more effective in one market than in another even though all markets have the same value.

High Cost of Buying National Coverage. Although newspapers are indeed a flexible medium, the cost of buying national coverage is very high and may be prohibitive for national advertisers with limited budgets.

National Advertising Rates Usually Higher than Local Rates. Most daily newspapers charge more for national advertising than they do for local. Of course, an advertiser who must advertise in a particular local market will pay the premium rate without question.

Small Pass-Along Audience. Newspapers are rarely passed along to other audiences as magazines are. This means that advertisements in yesterday's editions have a limited time value because relatively few other persons will see the newspaper after it is read by family members.

Magazines—Reasons for Using

Selectivity. Magazines are very successful in reaching certain kinds of selected audiences. There are an increasing number of magazines being started each year to meet the interests of special groups such as tennis or chess players, cooking enthusiasts, hobby fans, or those wanting to know more about investing in the stock market. In addition, some magazines have demographic editions such as a physicians' edition, a college students' edition, or one limited to those whose annual income is over $15,000. Finally, there are geographic editions that enable the planner to reach broad or narrow markets. This versatility and flexibility enable the planner to use magazines in many different ways.

Fine Color Reproduction. Many magazines are able to reproduce advertisements with excellent color fidelity. The necessity for fine color reproduction is obvious for certain kinds of product advertising such as food, clothes, and cars.

Long Life. Magazines usually have a long life, at least a week. But some last for more than a month and some for years. The effect of long life is that the advertiser can continue to build reach long after the present campaign has formally ended. Although the product featured in the ads may even have been discontinued after a number of years, the effect on a person who reads an ad years after it originally ran is to build brand awareness for long periods of time. Reach built over long periods of time, however, may not help the planner attain short-range goals.

Pass-Along Audience. Magazines usually have pass-along audiences that increase the reach. The size of the pass-along audience varies, however, from magazine to magazine.

Controlled Circulation. Because magazines are able to locate and meet the needs of special interest groups, it is possible for many of them to have controlled circulation. In a controlled circulation arrangement, the publisher is able to identify a special group of targets, mostly by profession or occupation, and then send each of these individuals the magazine free of charge. The publisher then informs advertisers that a circulation audience of a certain size can be guaranteed. Most controlled circulation magazines are in the business field.

Magazines—Limitations

Early Closing Dates. Some magazines require advertisers to have their artwork and type for four-color ads in the printing plant as much as two and a half months before the cover date. The consequence is that the marketing, creative, and production work on the campaign must be completed so far ahead of publication date that the advertiser may lose the advantage of timeliness. It is even possible for a marketing situation to have changed by the time the ad appears in print.

Lack of Immediacy. With the exception of weekly news magazines, most magazines lack a sense of urgency and immediacy. In other words, readers may not even look at the latest issue of a given magazine until some time after it has reached their homes. Even news magazines do not have the sense of immediacy that newspapers have.

Slow Building of Reach. Because some readers do not turn to their magazines quickly, reach tends to build slowly in this medium. Some readers read a small portion of a magazine immediately and then continue at later dates and times, whenever convenient. Active people who are always on the go sometimes will scan through a number of issues at one time to catch up with their reading. At other times, they just ignore a number of issues and will read only the most current one.

Newspaper Supplements—Reasons for Using

Local Market Impact with a Magazine Format. Newspaper supplements offer the advertiser the advantage of being able to reach local markets with a format that closely resembles magazines. Therefore, many of the qualities of magazines are also qualities of the supplement. Most important, however, is the ability of the planner to reach many local markets with a magazine format.

Good Color Fidelity. Newspaper supplements are usually printed on gravure presses and therefore have high color fidelity.

Depth of Penetration. Whereas magazines usually would have limited penetration in any given market, supplements have high penetration. The reason is that magazines, because of their specialized natures, might have relatively small numbers of readers in any local market. But the supplement, distributed with newspapers, would naturally have access to large numbers of individuals for whom the editorial features are of general interest.

Broadened Coverage Area. One bonus of using supplements is that it is possible to reach some markets normally covered by daily newspapers that do not carry the supplement. This is possible because large metro area newspapers will often have extensive area coverage far beyond the Metropolitan Statistical Area. Consumers in these bonus markets carrying the supplement may read their local newspapers on weekdays, but a large metro paper on Sunday.

Reach Prospects on Sunday Morning. When supplements are read, they will have little competition from other media, because Sunday mornings and afternoons typically offer freedom from other media. Many readers are more relaxed on Sundays and can spend more time reading than on other days.

High Readership. Because supplements have large penetration in individual markets, it is not surprising that they are widely read, especially by women. Working women especially tend to have the time to read this format, because it is available on Sunday, it is part of a newspaper, and because many features tend to cover women's interests.

Flexibility: Geographic and Production. It is obvious that supplements allow the planner to place advertising locally, regionally, or even nationally. But supplements also allow production flexibility such as the option of running a full-page ad in some markets, while at the same time running smaller ads in other markets.

Newspaper Supplements—Limitations

Early Closing Dates for Four-Color. Because supplements are printed by the gravure process, the material for ads must be in the printing plant as much as eight weeks before publication date. This deadline is even earlier than required for most magazines that are printed either by letterpress or offset process. Gravure is printed from copper cylinders that take an exceedingly long time to prepare. Furthermore, because it is so difficult to make corrections on gravure plates, greater care and time is taken in the preparation of the cylinders than is necessary for other printing processes.

Little Pass-Along or Secondary Readership. Because supplements come with weekend newspapers, they inherit some of the weaknesses of newspapers. One of these is that supplements rarely are passed along to others. They usually are thrown away after the family has read them. In addition, one rarely finds supplements in barber or beauty shops or doctors' or dentists' offices as one finds magazines.

Television—Reasons for Using

Sight and Sound for Dynamic Selling. Audiovisual demonstrations are one of the best teaching methods known. The combination of sight and sound gives the advertiser the benefit of a technique that comes closest to personal selling. Television selling is very dynamic. It is also one of the best methods of demonstrating the uses or advantages of a given product.

Flexibility. Network television offers broad national coverage, while spot television allows the planner to use markets in any number of combinations.

Reach of Both Selective and Mass Markets. Television may be used to attract both selective and mass markets through program selection. When professional football games are being broadcast, the audience is almost all male. Children's programming on Saturday mornings, or daytime television, tends to reach selected audiences. On the other hand, some programming such as movies, comedies, or special events will attract audiences consisting of many different kinds and ages of people.

Cost Efficiency. Television can be very cost efficient at times. Daytime television, for example, usually has low costs per thousand as does fringe time. Though the overall costs are high, the audiences are large.

Television—Limitations

High Total Cost. The cost of commercial time can be beyond the means of some advertisers. The change from 60- to 30-second commercial lengths to 15-second, and even 10-second commercials reflects the advertiser's needs for lower total cost.

Short-lived Messages. Although audiovisual messages may have the potential for high recall, the nature of television commercials is such that either viewers pay attention or they may miss the message. Therefore the commercial's life tends to be fleeting.

No Catalog Value. It is evident that viewers do not search for commercials when they are in the market for a product. Although they pay greater attention to a commercial they happen to see for a product in which they are interested, they usually have little idea of the exact time such commercials will be broadcast.

Limited Availability of Good Programs and Time Slots. Because television is a widely used medium, there is a limit to the number of programs with large audience following or time slots that are available and desirable.

Radio—Reasons for Using

Reach of Special Kinds of Target Audiences. Radio is able to reach certain kinds of audiences very well. Through programming specialization a radio station becomes known for its ''sound'' and attracts special kinds of audiences, such as men, women, teenagers, farmers, ethnic populations, blacks, the elderly and shut-ins. Many ethnic groups such as the Greek, German, Italian, Mexican, or Polish have programs dedicated to their interests. Religious groups, especially, have found radio to be an excellent communication medium.

A High Frequency Medium. Where a great deal of repetition is necessary, radio may be the ideal medium. The total cost is relatively low and there are usually many stations with time available to permit building a media plan with high frequency.

A Good Supporting Medium. Because of the low cost and good reach of special target markets, radio is often used as a supporting medium. Often when a plan uses print predominantly, radio can be added at low cost to bring sound into the plan.

Excellent for Mobile Populations. Because most Americans own and drive automobiles, radio becomes a means of reaching them while they are traveling. Many people drive long distances to and from work and the distances are getting longer as suburbs develop farther from cities. Listening to the radio in what is known as "drive time" has become a diversion to help pass the long commuting time and is an excellent means of reaching commuters.

But commuters aren't the only ones who travel every day. Homemakers often take their cars to shopping centers that may be located far from their homes. They, too, will often turn on the radio to help pass the traveling time. In fact, radio may be the last medium that homemakers are exposed to before they enter retail stores. Local retailers might very well carrry on a campaign to communicate with these customers before they arrive at the stores.

Summertime Exposure. Because we are a mobile population and so many people travel during the summer months, radio is an excellent medium to reach them en route. Some experts dispute this, however, claiming that radio tune-in is no higher in the summer than it is any other time. *When* listeners tune in, however, does change during the summer, especially among teenagers who are not in school during the day.

Flexibility. Radio, like television, may be used locally, regionally, or nationally. There are not too many production advantages to radio, however. Copy can be changed quickly, and added or eliminated from a program quickly, but radio is still not highly regarded for its great production flexibility.

Local Coverage Availability. Local radio is usually purchased because it reaches a given market very well. But radio signals may be carried far from the originating market into other geographical areas. This occurs at night when the Kennelly-Heaviside layer (a natural atmospheric phenomenon) broadly disseminates signals far beyond the local market. For the national advertiser who is trying to build brand awareness in many different markets, this added feature may be perceived as a bonus when a planner buys local radio.

Radio—Limitations

Many Stations in Any One Market. In many large metropolitan markets, so many radio stations are vying for attention that only a relative few reach a substantial audience. If one wants to build large reach via radio, it will be necessary to buy more than one station and, in some areas, many stations. In New York City, there are 27 AM and FM stations and another 41 in the greater metropolitan area. In Chicago, there are 27 stations in the city and another 26 in the greater metro area. And the numbers are constantly changing (SRDS, December 1987). Another consequence of the large number of stations available is the fragmentation of audiences caused by specialized programming. On the one hand, specialized programs do waste few exposures because the program structure is not attractive to everyone. But on the other hand, they may fractionalize the audience too much for an advertiser who wants a mass— not class—audience.

Fleeting Messages. Like television, but even more so, radio messages are fleeting and may be missed or forgotten if only partially heard.

Direct Mail (Direct Response)—Reasons for Using

Very Selective. Direct mail is the most selective of all media, provided that the names and addresses of a target audience are known, and the list is up-to-date and complete. When such a list is available, there may be minimal waste, so the advertiser pays only for targets that are reached.

Response to Advertising Is Easy to Check. It is relatively easy to learn whether a direct mail piece was effective. One simply counts the number of responses to an offer. The number of inquiries from direct mail may or may not be related to sales, but inquiries from direct mailings do constitute one form of measurement. Often alternative copy treatments are sent out by direct mail and the most effective one is easily checked. Although it is very difficult to measure response functions in most other media, the same cannot be said of direct mail.

A Personal Medium. Direct mail can be a personal medium when it bears a consumer's name and address. Most advertising is very impersonal because, in most media, it is impossible to address anyone by name. Direct mail, using specific names and addresses, comes closest to overcoming this problem. Of course, not all recipients of direct mail pieces appreciate advertisers calling them familiarly by name. But many people do appreciate seeing their names in print, and may pay more attention to the offer as a result.

Geographic and Production Flexibility. Direct mail is probably the easiest of all media to tailor precisely to the geographic marketing needs of an advertiser. The beauty of this flexibility is that direct mail can be adjusted to very small markets (as few as needed), and also can be adjusted to as large an area as needed.

The medium is also flexible in terms of production. Almost any size and kind of paper and any kind of ink or special printing technique is possible. Advertisers with special creative problems may turn to direct mail because it is so versatile. Samples of a product can be mailed with ads; special die cuts can be made; special kinds of foldings and special kinds of packaging are available only in this medium.

Long Life for Certain Mailings. Consumers tend to keep catalogs for long periods of time. Some educational materials also share this quality. If the educational matter has value, such as a chart showing how to administer first aid, or a booklet on how to eliminate stains on clothing, it may be retained for long periods of time.

Possible Savings When Direct Mail Is Inserted with Bills. No special envelope, special addressing, or extra postage is necessary when direct mail advertising is sent along with bills. The bills have to be sent anyway, so the addition of a direct advertisement may not even cost extra postage. Printing costs, however, must be borne. Even when the total weight of the advertising enclosed with a bill is greater than the bill alone, there may still be substantial savings because there are no extra envelope and addressing costs. The addition of the advertising may increase the total cost only slightly.

Direct Mail—Limitations

Possible Expense. There are two situations, at least, where direct mail is very expensive, perhaps more so than any other medium—when a production technique requires the use of very heavy enameled or other expensive papers or when some unusual method of engraving, artwork, or printing is used, or when very large mailings are made that cannot take advantage of bulk mailing privileges. It is unlikely that postage rates will decline in the future, and these high costs will continue to affect direct mail usage.

Inaccurate and Incomplete Lists. Without an accurate and complete mailing list, direct mail cannot do its best. In this era, when so many individuals move from one place to another, it may be too difficult or expensive to keep lists up to date or develop new ones. In the past, it was possible to buy large mass mailings at low cost and not be concerned about the accuracy of the list. But today's high postage and production costs require that accurate and complete lists be used.

Variance in Delivery Dates. Although a large mailing may be taken to the post office at one time, the pieces may be delivered to various individuals at widely different times. If time is not essential to the marketing objectives, then the lag doesn't matter. But timing of an advertising message is often critical and the direct mail user cannot control it very well. Compared with other media, direct mail comes off second best in respect to timing. When ads are placed in newspapers, they are printed on the day requested. When broadcast commercials are purchased, they are delivered not only on the day, but the hour requested. In comparison, direct mail delivery dates are unpredictable.

Outdoor—Reasons for Using

Wide Coverage of Local Markets. Outdoor advertising is able to build large local coverage of the mobile population in many markets in a thirty-day period. However, this coverage does not represent reading of the messages, only potential exposure to them.

High Frequency. Billboards also have high frequency in reaching the mobile population of a market. It is in this area that billboards may be strongest. Although the differences in reach of a 100 versus a 50 showing are not great, the frequency levels are quite different.

Largest Size Print Ad Available. Size is a powerful attraction. Outdoor allows the advertiser to buy the largest size print ad available. The use of attractive color printing plus dramatic lighting and, at times, moving portions, all offer the advertiser great attention-getting power.

Geographic Flexibility. Outdoor may be used locally, regionally, and nationally. Even within any given market, it is possible to add emphasis wherever desired. Movable billboards enable an advertiser to concentrate messages in many places, or to increase the potential for exposure.

High Summertime Visibility. Media plans often will include billboards in the summer, because they increase the visibility of a brand name at a time when many people are traveling. Warmer weather encourages people to take to their cars, and it is possible to reach them through billboards and other outdoor signs.

Around-the-Clock Exposure. Because many billboards on main thoroughfares are lighted, anyone passing at any time of day or night can see the messages. As long as there is a mobile population, these is an opportunity for exposures.

Good for Simple Copy Theme and Package Identification. When the message is relatively short and simple and the package is distinctive, outdoor can be an excellent way to attract attention and build frequency for the message. Building brand awareness is a strength of the medium.

Outdoor—Limitations

Limited to Simple Messages. The best use of outdoor is for a simple message; complex or long messages do not work very well. This restriction means that the medium cannot be used in precisely the same manner as other print media.

High Outdoor Reach Does Not Necessarily Mean High Recall of Messages. Though outdoor may provide high reach, and sometimes good recall of ad messages, it is not necessarily true that high reach means high recall. The creativity of the message is an important criterion in assessing the ability of the message to be recalled. But because of the nature of this medium, people may often look at billboards and be unable to recall what they saw.

A Relatively High Cost Medium. Although the cost per thousand is low, outdoor is a relatively high cost medium when compared to some other media. For a 100 showing nationally, the cost is more than a million dollars for a month. Considering that outdoor is a medium often in the background, that it requires very short messages, and that drivers' interests are primarily focused on the road ahead, this cost may be prohibitive for many advertisers.

Transit Media—Reasons for Using

Transit media involve interior and exterior displays on mass transit vehicles, and terminal and station platform displays.

Transit Provides Mass Coverage of a Metropolitan Area. When an advertiser wants to reach individuals in the heart of a market, then mass transit advertising may be desirable. It is primarily a vehicle for reaching adults either on their way to, or returning from, work. But its reach is extensive.

High Frequency. Because this medium takes advantage of normal travel patterns that are duplicated many days throughout the year, there is an opportunity for a great deal of repetition of message delivery.

Relative Efficiency. Based on potential exposures, this medium can deliver large numbers of individuals at low unit costs.

Flexibility. An advertiser can select transportation vehicles in which to place ads that reach certain kinds of demographically defined groups. The advertiser does not have to select all mass transit systems, only those that are known to have large numbers of targets.

Opportunity to Position Messages to Consumers on the Way to Their Points of Purchase. Local advertisers can buy messages that reach consumers on their way to their places of purchases. Therefore, it is possible that, for some consumers, the transit ads will be the last medium they are exposed to before making a purchase. (Note that radio is often credited with the same idea.)

Transit Media—Limitations

Limited Message Space. Most often, large or complex messages cannot be disseminated in this medium because there is not enough space available to carry such messages.

High Competition from Other Media and Personal Activities. Transit is not an intrusive medium—it competes for attention with other things such as the attractiveness of scenery, the nature of the transit vehicle, or other people. The person who travels to and from work on the same transportation vehicle may be tired, bored or interested in some other media vehicle. For exterior displays, something of extra creative pulling power is often necessary to attract attention, a requirement that may be difficult to achieve.

Cable Television—Reasons for Using

Cable television has grown a great deal since 1980 when it had only 23 percent penetration of U.S. households. As of this writing, it has 51 percent penetration. As each year passes, it is being used by an increasingly larger number of advertisers.

Cable television is transmitted via a local community antenna that sends programming to individual homes via cables. Individuals pay a fee for a basic service, and additional fees for other programming such as movies, sports, and so on.

Good for Reaching Homes That Have Difficulty Picking Up Local Stations. Cable provides a planner with an opportunity to add to an existing schedule television viewers who for different reasons cannot pick up signals from local stations. At present, this number is relatively small, but it is expected to grow.

Provides Some Reach for Special Pay Programming. Some cable operators have the ability to provide movies and special events, such as sports, for an extra charge to cable subscribers. This could provide a substantial audience, depending on the interest in the programming being broadcast.

Specialized Programming Allows Advertisers to Reach Selective Audiences. Most cable operators offer their subscribers specialized programming not available on broadcast stations. Many of these programs appeal to a small, and therefore selective audience, based on demographics or life-styles.

Low Out-of-Pocket Costs. Because cable is very localized and audiences are proportionately small in number, the cost to advertise is relatively low, on either a per commercial or total continuous campaign basis.

Availability of Unusual Commercial Lengths. Cable operators sometimes allow advertisers to use shorter or longer commercial lengths than local or network broadcasters usually allow. Therefore, a great deal of information can be placed within a commercial to meet the specific needs of different kinds of advertisers.

Ron Kaatz's Suggestions about *What Cable Can Do for You*

The following advantages of using cable TV were adapted from Ron Kaatz's *Cable Advertiser's Handbook*. (See pp. 68–69.)

Cable can:
1. Convey advertising messages in a more compatible environment and act as more than just a commercial carrier.
2. Serve as a means of having an advertiser "sponsor something and attain some real identity."
3. Provide enough time beyond thirty seconds (that may be all that is affordable) to tell a story.
4. Provide a medium with the advantages of both television and print.
5. Be a means of appealing to the special people who buy "my brand."
6. Provide high frequency that radio offers at affordable prices.
7. Provide ability to reach "upscale cable homes more frequently."
8. Provide the means to reach small towns where "my dealers are located."
9. Provide means to run a "dozen or more different commercials" but at affordable production costs.
10. Provide means to "experiment a bit and explore new commercial ideas" such as direct response.

Cable Television—Limitations

Relatively Weaker in Major Markets. At present cable penetration is relatively weak in large markets although it is growing. In "A markets (the largest 25 cities in the U.S.), eleven have less than 45% penetration of households."[1] On the other hand, smaller markets tend to have very high penetration.

Programming on Cable Tends to Duplicate That Provided by Networks and Local Stations. Although local cable operators have a great opportunity to create truly innovative programming that will pull specialized audiences to their stations, that

---

1. *Advertising Age,* April 11, 1988, p. S–2.

hasn't happened to any great extent. Cable programming so far tends to resemble that offered by free television broadcasting. This may change in the future, as more homes sign up for cable.

Home Video (VCRs)[2]—Reasons for Using

One of the ''new media'' mentioned in Chapter 1 was home video, otherwise known as video cassette recorders or VCRs. Currently, about 47 percent of TV households have a VCR. By 1990, the number will rise to 60 percent, with a forecast of 70 percent penetration by the year 2000.

This medium consists of either recording and playing back television programs, buying / renting videotape recording for playback, or recording from video camera for replay. The most common use is the recording and playback of TV programming:

Television programming	83%
Purchase/rental tapes	16%
Recording from video camera	1%
	100%

If viewers record entire programs for playback at some other time, there may be an opportunity for advertisers who had placed commercials in the original program to have their commercial seen again.

However, these same commercials can be avoided in two ways, zipping and zapping. Zipping occurs during the playback of recorded programs. *Zipping* involves pressing a button on a remote control device that activates the fast-forward part of VCRs to skip over the commercial. About 60 percent of the viewers zip by commercials when playing them back. Zapping occurs during the viewing of on-air television programming. *Zapping* takes place when the viewer switches channels to avoid a commercial or program. Viewers also zap commercials while recording on-air television programs. The viewer pushes the pause or stop button at the beginning of a commercial segment and then presses the pause or start button at the end of the commercial segment to resume recording. This type of zapping deletes the commercial segment when the program is played back. About half of VCR users zap most or all the commercials during taping.

Home video offers advertisers an opportunity to reach audiences that may be difficult to reach with other media, especially if the audience is actively seeking something in particular during playback. In addition:

- It is received in a home environment where viewers presumably are relaxed and paying attention.
- It has the potential to provide repeat exposures to targets.

---

2. Some observations for this section drawn from Ogilvy & Mather, Chicago, ''Zapping & Zipping the Time Away,'' (special report) February 4, 1987.

- It allows flexible length and format options.
- It has a low cost.
- It allows consumers to "timeshift" (record at one time and view at a later, more convenient time).

Home Video (VCRs)—Limitations

From the advertiser's viewpoint, the main problem with VCRs is that commercials can be avoided by zapping and zipping. These points will be discussed later in this section.

Measurement of VCR usage is also a big problem. Nielsen provides a weekly VCR analysis, which provides data on which homes watched a program either as it was aired, or recorded for possible later viewing. In this way advertisers can track the amount of VCR recording of network programming. Nonetheless, at this writing, Nielsen cannot answer the question, "How much recorded programming is played back and what happens to the commercials contained within?" However, they are in the process of completing a system that will soon provide an answer. At present, Nielsen only knows that a VCR was on and tuned to a network such as NBC on Thursday at 8:00 P.M. By knowing which program was on at that day and time, they know which program was recorded.

The new system will record the program code and the exact time on VCR tape. When a program is played back, Nielsen will then have a record of what has played. Furthermore, when the program is being played back, two time counters will start tracking. The first will record the length of the program. The second will record the amount of time actually spent viewing the show. By matching up the original length of the program with the length of the taped playback, Nielsen will be able to tell if some commercials were deleted by the viewer, but will not know which commercials were deleted. This system should be available by 1988.

Zapping. Viewers have been zapping commercials since the introduction of the remote control television unit. With the growth of VCRs and the ability to zap while recording, zapping has become an increasingly popular phenomenon.

Who zaps? "Zappers" tend to be younger (under age 34), college-educated, affluent males who have active life-styles. They comprise less than 10 percent of the average television program's audience. Children in homes where zappers live tend to zap more than children of nonzappers. Fifth- and sixth-grade children tend to zap more than their parents.

What do they zap? Under actual viewing conditions, this group uses the remote control device to zap the program itself nearly as often as they zap actual commercials. Sports gets zapped the most. Zappers are most likely to switch channels at commercial breaks within sporting events because they are trying to keep up with two or more games at the same time.

Daytime commercials get zapped the least. The reason for less daytime commercial zapping is that the viewers are involved in other activities while the set is on. Commercials that are placed between programs tend to get zapped more than those placed within programs because viewers know there is a three-to-five-minute break between the closing credits in one program and the opening scenes of another. Since this nonprogram time is available, zappers often take the opportunity to sample one or two other programs that may interest them.

Essentially, the main reason for zapping under live viewing conditions is to find out what is on other channels. Some viewers zap out of curiosity, some to reduce the boredom of a program, and some to follow the progress of two or more programs simultaneously. The main reason for zapping while recording is to have continuous programming, without commercial interruption, for playback. Those viewers who zap while recording are exposed to the commercials because they must press the stop and start buttons at the beginning and end of the commercial segment.

Zippers. Zippers fast forward over commercials during the playback of recorded programs. Almost 70 percent of VCR users are not watching the program as it is being recorded. The following are some measurements of what viewers are doing while recording:

The TV set turned-off	56%
Turned to the same channel	31%
Turned to a different channel	13%
	100%

Many of these viewers opt to zip through commercials during playback instead of zapping commercials during taping. About 80 percent of what is recorded is played back, but only 27 percent actually watch the commercials being replayed.

Who zips? "Zippers" are primarily male, college educated, urban, and upper-middle class. They zip to avoid commercials. Ogilvy & Mather suggests that the increasing number of commercials being broadcast at any one time may partly be responsible. They also found that two-thirds of all respondents in a study believe that commercials were boring or irritating. This caused the agency to observe that, "the consumer turns on TV with the perception for every hour in front of the tube, I must endure 10 minutes of unwanted commercials."

Zippers, however, may be at least partially motivated to save time, rather than to avoid commercials they dislike. An hour program can be viewed in less than fifty minutes. In addition, zipping also helps maintain a semblance of program flow.

How significant is zapping and zipping? The proportion of total households that own remote control TVs and VCRs is nearly 50 percent at this time. Despite this relatively high penetration, it is estimated that very little of a program's rating is lost due to zipping or zapping (perhaps $1/10$ to $2/10$ of a program rating point). In a program that attracts over 30 million people (like "The Cosby Show"), only 30,000 to 60,000 viewers are lost. Media planners, however, will be watching the progress of this TV phenomenon closely to track its effect on commercial audiences.

Intermedia Comparisons for Nonmeasured Media

Almost every medium in existence has some qualities that are useful for one or another advertiser. There are times when nonmeasured media are useful. A nonmeasured medium is one that is not measured regularly to find precisely who is exposed to it. Such media include car cards, telephone book advertising pages, theater or concert program advertising pages, and others. A planner who wants to use such media may have to rely on much more subjective judgments about audience sizes and/or demographics, especially when comparing nonmeasured to measured media.

Sometimes nonmeasured media will conduct research that may help the media planner in making intermedia comparisons. Unfortunately most such research is suspected of being biased in favor of the company that pays for it, because it has a vested interest in the outcome. As a result, it is difficult to make intermedia comparisons even on a subjective basis for nonmeasured media except in simple, obvious areas.

Recall Scores

One way to approach the dilemma of noncomparable measuring techniques for intermedia comparisons is to use response functions as a criterion of effectiveness. If it could be shown that an ad in one medium generates more recall than an ad in another medium, then one might assume that the medium with the higher recall is better. However, the ad or ads used for comparative purposes cannot be indiscriminately chosen. Nor can average recall of many ads be used in measuring recall of one medium versus another. The reason is that some products or brands may be inherently more interesting than others and therefore generate higher recall scores.

To prevent such bias, the same ad is usually measured in two different media. As a result, researchers hope that any variation in the recall scores is due to the effect of the medium rather than the ad. Although this procedure attempts to solve the problem, it is still questionable whether dual measurement represents a valid means of intermedia comparisons.

The reason is much the same as mentioned earlier: Comparing the differences in print and broadcast is like comparing apples and oranges. If a cola product were being tested on television and a similar ad were tested in a print medium, it would be difficult, if not impossible, to keep the copy and creative elements constant. A commercial for a cola drink usually features an announcer's voice, whether on or off camera. Most of the time the message features action and music rather than still scenes. Then, too, the audience sees the message on many different-sized televisions screens, some in black and white, but most in color.

If a similar cola ad were placed in print, the size of the ad would probably be constant from magazine to magazine, and there would be no sound of a well-known personality's voice and no music. Furthermore, if the print ad were placed in a magazine, there would be competition for attention from other ads, while the television program in which the commercial was placed would have no competition for attention at the same time (unless the viewer zapped a commercial while recording the program on VCR).

Therefore, any results of recall measurements could not be considered unbiased. Any one of the variables exclusive to the ad in a given medium could account for the greater or lesser recall scores. Although such techniques may be helpful for other purposes, they may not be entirely valid for use in intermedia comparisons.

Often a medium in one class, such as magazines, will spend a great deal of money to prove that it is better than a medium in another class. Although the results are interesting, they cannot be considered valid for intermedia comparative purposes because of the vested interest problem.

The Media Mix

In planning strategy, the planner may decide to use a single medium or a number of media. When more than one medium is used, the result is called a *media mix*, meaning that the plan mixes a number of media classes to reach certain target audiences. The planner must consider whether to use a single medium or a mix. Is one strategy better than another?

Generally, a planner uses a media mix because a single medium such as television cannot reach the target market in sufficient numbers or with sufficient impact to attain a media objective. When a planner does not define the target market narrowly, the targets represent such a broad spectrum of consumers that the only way to reach them is through multiple vehicles. Most planners narrow the definition of targets to reach *only* those with the best potential. Another situation that might call for a media mix strategy occurs when a planner has segmented targets into two key groups, each of which is about equal in importance.

A question that a media planner ought to raise when trying to decide whether to use a media mix is, What part of the market *cannot* be reached with a single medium? Generally, vehicles within one media class can reach a substantial part of a market, perhaps 90 percent. The percent of the market not covered may not be worth the extra cost of employing an additional medium. If 20 percent of the population accounts for 80 percent of product consumption, and this 20 percent is within the reach of a single medium, it may be inefficient to try to reach more with additional, but different, media. *Inefficiency* means that the additional media have substantially higher costs per thousand than the original medium.

John J. Meskill, senior vice president and director of media at Warwick, Welsh & Miller, Inc., has pointed out another consideration in the media mix question: There are times when a medium covers a market, but heavy users are only lightly exposed to the medium.[3] Generally, it is assumed that it is better to reach heavy users who are heavily exposed to a given medium under consideration.

---

3. Meskill, John J., "The Media Mix," *4A Media Letter*, January 1979, pp. 1–2.

When to Use a Media Mix

The following are some important reasons for using a media mix:

1. To extend the reach of a media plan. By doing so, the plan adds prospects not exposed by using a single medium.
2. To flatten the distribution of frequency so that there is a more even distribution of those who are exposed to a medium.
3. To add gross impressions, assuming, of course, that the second or third medium is cost efficient.
4. To reinforce the message—or help audience members remember the message by using different kinds of stimuli.
5. To reach different kinds of audiences, perhaps differentiated by lifestyle as well as demographics.
6. To provide unique advantages in stressing different benefits based on the different characteristics of each medium.
7. To allow different creative executions to be implemented.

Meskill, however, felt that the idea of using a media mix ought to be challenged more often than it has been, and that many times one medium will do the job.

Criteria for Media Selection beyond the Numbers[4]

Media selections usually are made by examining quantified data showing the abilities of alternative media to reach select target audiences. But comparisons are also made on an objective and subjective basis covering materials cited in this chapter. The latter two criteria deal with the strengths of media to do certain things better than others.

Unfortunately, these latter criteria are subject to debate, and sometimes are simply the perceptions of either a planner or the client who sees things a certain way.

DDB Needham Worldwide presents the following criteria as a means of promoting the message and the medium in making selection decisions. If a planner disagrees with these decisions, at least the chart will encourage more thought about just what it is that makes one more useful than another for achieving a client's objectives.

---

4. This illustration adapted from DDB Needham Worldwide promotion piece, ''Which Media Do It Best?''

	TELEVISION	MAGAZINES	NEWSPAPERS	RADIO	OUTDOOR
Demonstration					
Elegance					
Features					
Intrusion					
Quality					
Excitement					
Imagination					
Beauty					
Entertainment					
Sex Appeal					
Personal					
One-on-One					
Snob Appeal					
Package I.D.					
Product-in-Use					
Recipe					
Humor					
Tradition					
Leadership					
Information					
Authority					
Intimacy					
Prestige					
Bigger-Than-Life					
News					
Event					
Price					

QUESTIONS FOR DISCUSSION

1. Explain whether it is valid to compare cost per thousand for a commercial on radio with cost per thousand for an ad in a magazine.
2. What are the general advantages of a print medium versus a broadcast medium and vice versa?
3. Briefly explain the two kinds of flexibility that may be important in media planning.
4. Explain the reasons why cable television may not be a good medium in which to place advertising now. Also explain why, in the future, it may be an excellent medium for advertising.
5. What is the most important reason for a publisher choosing to have controlled, rather than paid, circulation for a magazine?
6. What advantages does a Sunday supplement have over a magazine and vice versa?
7. Why might a media buyer who wants to build very high frequency choose radio rather than television for a media plan?
8. If a planner wants a high level of brand visibility during the summer months, which medium is the likely choice?
9. Which medium is probably the most selective of all in reaching very selective target markets? What conditions must be met, however, before this medium can be called most selective?
10. If a motorist passes any outdoor billboard, is he or she covered by that showing for the month? Briefly explain.

SELECTED READINGS

Editor & Publisher, "CBS-TV Claims Newspaper Ad Reading Time Is Under 6 Seconds," September 5, 1970, pp. 9–10.

Forkan, James P., "Tele–Research Gives TV an Edge over Magazines in Latest Effectiveness Fight," *Advertising Age,* May 29, 1972, p. 6.

Goldstrom, Donald G., *How a Change in Media Mix Paid Off for Armstrong,* New York: ANA Media Workshop, December 4, 1973, p. 8.

Grass, Robert C., *Corporate Image Advertising: Print vs. Television,* New York: ANA Advertising Research Workshop, March 15, 1977, p. 15.

Greenburg, A., "Point-of-View: Intermedia Comparisons," *Journal of Advertising Research,* October 1972, pp. 47–49.

Grudin/Appel/Haley Research Corporation, "Advertising Recall in *Life* vs. Television," *Life,* 1970.

Kaatz, Ronald B., *Cable Advertiser's Handbook,* Lincolnwood, Ill.:National Textbook Company, pp. 68–69.

Kanner, Bernice, "TV vs. Print Study Finds Readers More Attentive," *Advertising Age,* August 7, 1978, p. 2.

Keshin, Mort, "Apples and Oranges Revisited," *Media/Scope,* June 1966, pp. 12–14.

Kinley, Daniel L., "Inter-media Comparisons," *Media/Scope,* September 1959, p. 28.

Krugman, Dean, "Cable Television and Advertising: An Assessment," *Journal of Advertising,* Fall 1978, pp. 4–8.

Life, "A Six-Step Inter-Media Comparison," Spring 1971.

Lodish, L. M., "Exposure Interactions Among Media Schedules," *Journal of Advertising Research,* April 1973, pp. 31–34.

Look, "Study of Advertising Communications," Cowles Publishing Company, 1962.

Maneloveg, Herbert, "Television Isn't Alone in Commercial Clutter—Magazines, Newspapers Have It Too," *Advertising Age*, October 11, 1971, p. 47.

Media Decisions, "The Clutter Crisis," December 1971, p. 40ff.

Media Decisions, "Update on Cable TV: Big Impact, Weak Numbers," January 1979, pp. 62–63.

Media/Scope, "No Simple Solution to Comparison of Media," March 1959, pp. 54–63.

Meskill, John J., "The Media Mix," *4A Media Letter*, January 1979, pp. 1–2.

Monosson, Judith, "Outdoor: New Users, New Uses," *Marketing and Media Decisions*, May 1986, pp. 121–22.

Newsweek, *Eyes-On, A Comparison of Television Commercial Audience with Magazine Page Audience*, New York: Audits & Surveys, 1978.

Orenstein, Frank, "When People Want to Know, Where Do They Go to Find Out?" *Media/Scope*, October 1967, pp. 61–68.

Roper Organization, *What People Think of Television and Other Mass Media 1959-1972*, Television Information Office, May 1973.

Shiffman, Phil, "Comparability—It's Still a Very Important Question," *Media Decisions*, December 1978, pp. 94–96.

Staff, "How Business Talks to Business," *Marketing and Media Decisions*, June 1986.

Surmanek, Jim, "Spot vs. Network TV," *Media Decisions*, October 1978, p. 78ff.

11

Evaluating and Selecting Media Vehicles

After selecting media classes, the media planner is ready to select media vehicles within classes. To some extent, previous strategy decisions will spell out criteria for this selection. These criteria grow out of an evaluation of relative media values. The discussion in this chapter covers the most important considerations.

Determining Media Values

An elementary principle for selecting media stated in Chapter 1 was to select those vehicles that reach a large number of targets at a cost-efficient price. Although this principle seems to suggest that this is all there is to the selection process, nothing could be further from the truth. A more advanced principle is to determine the full extent of each vehicle's value in terms of the desired criteria *and then* select from among those that best meet the criteria. Some of these criteria may be measured quantitatively and the numerical values of various criteria can be combined into a single number. Others are qualitative, and it is more difficult to assign numerical weights to these. But both should be considered in the selection process. Table 11–1 lists the most important objective and subjective criteria usually considered in magazine selection.

Target Reach and Cost Efficiency

The most important criterion in determining media values is a combination of two principles: (a) finding vehicles that reach a large number of targets, and (b) selecting from among these only those with the lowest cost per thousand. The logic of

TABLE 11-1.   Criteria for Determining Media Values

Primary objective criteria
   a. Delivery of demographic targets
   b. Cost efficiency of delivered targets
   c. Delivery of product-class user targets
   d. Delivery of strategic targets
   e. Delivery of psychographic targets

Secondary objective criteria
   a. Primary vs. pass-along readers
   b. Editorial features/content related to brand's image
   c. Special editions/issues/sections in print
   d. Media imperatives
   e. Color reproduction
   f. Circulation trends in print vehicles
   g. Geographic flexibility
   h. Production flexibility
   i. Positioning opportunities within print vehicles

Subjective (or qualitative) criteria
   a. Writing tone
   b. Reader respect
   c. Leadership in media class
   d. Believability

using these two principles in combination should be obvious. Advertising and marketing today are directed to certain demographic targets. Assuming that these targets can be identified precisely, it follows that media vehicles should be selected to reach the largest number of targets efficiently.

It should be noted, however, that the decisions to select or reject alternative vehicles do not always rest *only* on finding vehicles that reach large numbers of targets. Another variable in the decision process occurs when a given media strategy calls for high frequency. When frequency is needed, vehicles with less reach (and more duplication) may be preferred. Because reach and frequency levels are inversely related, the selection process may result in sacrificing some reach for more frequency. However, most planners have minimum levels of reach below which they will not go even to attain high frequency. For example, reach may not be allowed to go below 50 percent of a target base, such as women aged 18–34.

Some media planners tend to use the two criteria of high reach and low cost almost exclusively to define media values. Others, however, see that the selection process requires much more input on what constitutes value. Shown in Table 11–2 are four print vehicles compared on the basis of target delivery and cost per thousand. In the table it is obvious that the vehicle that delivers the largest number of prospects (targets) also has the lowest cost per thousand. Such is not always the situation, however. Note that the term *coverage* as used in this context is sometimes called *selectivity percentage*. Both terms mean essentially the same thing, but one advertising agency may prefer to use one term rather than the other.

If computer capability is available, it is possible to cross tabulate demographic segments to make composite analyses. For example, a computer makes it possible to find the best media vehicles to deliver women, aged 18–49, with over $25,000 annual income, who live in households of five or more persons.

Occasionally, a planner will find that the vehicles that deliver demographic tar-

TABLE 11-2.   Comparison of Four Print Vehicles on Targets Delivered and Cost per Thousand

Vehicle	Cost per Insertion	Targets Delivered Men 18–49 (thousands)	Selectivity or Coverage (%)	Cost per Thousand
A	$54,849	13,992	31.8	$ 3.92
B	25,641	2,772	6.3	9.25
C	10,696	484	1.1	22.10
D	15,382	3,344	7.6	4.60

gets most efficiently do not deliver the most users efficiently. When that situation occurs, the planner will have to decide whether demographic targets or users are the more valuable criterion. The planner may also compromise and select vehicles that deliver both kinds of targets.

Strategic Impressions

In evaluating alternative media vehicles, it may be necessary to reach different targets in certain proportions. In other words, a planner evaluating media vehicles in terms of ability to deliver certain kinds of targets does not want these targets delivered in a capricious pattern. If, for example, the planner felt that most advertising messages ought to go to women aged 18–49 and a much smaller number ought to go to men aged 18–49, then the desired proportions for each should be determined and appropriate vehicles selected to deliver these proportions. If the planner wants 60 percent women and 40 percent men, it would not be logically sound to have the delivery total reversed.

To decide on the relative proportions, a planner studies product usage and demographic data, then uses judgment to arrive at the desired proportions. If women are the primary decision makers in the purchase of a product, then they should be allotted a larger percentage than men.

In selecting media, then, the planner tries to select vehicles whose audiences are divided in roughly the same proportions as the desired target audience. Because media vehicles may not deliver audience segments in precisely the same percentages that the planner feels desirable, the division of gross impressions may not be precise, but approximate. For example, if the planner decides that women aged 35–49 should constitute 70 percent of targets delivered and women aged 18–34, 30 percent, then either a 65 percent/35 percent split or a 75 percent/25 percent split might be acceptable.

Table 11–3 shows strategic impressions from a media plan that delivers targets close to the proportions of 75 percent women and 25 percent men, aged 18–49. In studying Table 11–3, one should remember that the desired division of impressions was 75 percent/25 percent. But because of the difficulty of finding media vehicles with precisely the desired proportions, those vehicles that come close are usually accepted as satisfactory, as long as the impression proportions are not equal, or reversed.

The planner should also keep in mind that the same type of vehicle need not be

TABLE 11-3.   Impressions Delivered by a Simulated Schedule

| | Gross Impressions Delivered by Each Vehicle* | | |
	Men	Women	Total
Magazine A	1,500	15,000	16,500
Magazine B	1,500	14,000	15,500
Network TV Program C	5,540	7,000	12,540
Network TV Program D	4,000	9,000	13,000
Total Gross Impressions	12,540	45,000	57,540
Percent Total Impressions	21.8	78.2	100

*Goal: 75% women, 25% men.

used consistently in order to deliver the desired division of impressions. In Table 11–3, for example, all four media vehicles provide audiences that are concentrated among women (women account for the majority of adult delivery for each vehicle). A combination of male-oriented vehicles and female-oriented vehicles, combined possibly with dual audience vehicles, could also produce a net effect that divides total impressions according to objectives.

Other Media Values

Secondary Audiences

Secondary (or pass-along) audiences also must be considered in evaluating media vehicles. Because the primary audiences have a regular opportunity to see a given magazine and secondary audiences do not, then primary audiences should be more valuable to the media planner. A *Study of Printed Advertising Rating Methods* (PARM), conducted by the Advertising Research Foundation and Alfred Politz, Inc., found that primary readers were more valuable than secondary readers—not necessarily because they had a better opportunity to see the magazine, but because they paid more attention to advertisements than did secondary readers. Furthermore, the PARM study showed that, for the Gallup-Robinson (Aided Recall) Measuring Technique, fewer of the out-of-home pass-along readers were able to recall ads than other secondary readers. Table 11–4 shows some of the findings that support the conclusion that primary readers are more valuable than secondary readers. Although there were differences between Starch and Gallup-Robinson, each method found less recall among pass-along audiences than primary audiences. Audits and Surveys Research Company also conducted a study for *Look* magazine and found the differences between primary and secondary audience recall as shown in Table 11–5. Here again, fewer secondary readers were able to recall ads than were primary readers.

These research studies provide some clues about the value of secondary, pass-along audiences. If the secondary audiences are deemed less valuable, then it seems reasonable to discount them in some way. But few media planners would ignore them entirely.

Dr. Seymour Marshak, formerly manager of advertising and distribution research of the Ford Motor Company, felt that simply discounting the secondary audi-

TABLE 11-4.   Recall of Ads Using Starch and Gallup-Robinson

Type of Audience	Recall Using Starch (%)	Recall Using Gallup-Robinson (%)
Primary	20.0	3.2
Out-of-home pass-along	17.9	2.5

Source: Advertising Research Foundation and Alfred Politz Research, Inc., *A Study of Printed Advertising Rating Methods*, Vol. III, N.Y., 1956.

ence was not correct.[1] Instead it would be better to determine the value of a secondary reader on the basis of how important that individual was in the target audience and then determine what opportunities he or she had to see a given advertisement in a given medium. For example, secondary readers may be even more important than primary readers when they receive only one or two exposure opportunities compared to primary readers who might receive over twenty opportunities. This assumes that high frequencies (or many exposure opportunities) are not automatically good media strategy. Each marketing/media situation may be different. Foremost in this kind of evaluation is the assumption that secondary readers are the most important target audiences and have to be reached if the advertising message is to have the proper effect.

One method that could be used for discounting the pass-along secondary audience is simply to cut their numbers in half. If Medium A has a total audience of 37 million of which 75 percent is primary and 25 percent is secondary (out-of-home) readers, then the latter is discounted 50 percent.

Table 11-6 shows an example that first treats the secondary audience at full value and then at a 50 percent discounted value. The example is based on the total audience. Typically, media planners discount only the demographic group that comprises the target audience, such as men aged 18-34, or women who graduated from high school, for example.

Marshak cited examples of two different ways to determine the value of a pass-along reader:

1. The product is advertised in only one medium. The secondary reader has a regular source for obtaining the medium and he is a member of the target group. His value should be equal to the value of a primary reader.
2. The product . . . is advertised in many small circulation magazines (e.g., camping and fishing magazines plus others). The secondary reader, by chance, sees the ad for a product in medium Z while waiting in a pizza parlor. The reader has already seen, or had the opportunity to see, the ad in 20 other media. The value of this 21st exposure within a short time period may be very low.[2]

---

1. Marshak, Seymour, "Forum Question: Generally Speaking, What Value Do You Place on the Secondary or Pass-along Reader?" *Media/Scope*, February 1970, p. 26.
    2. Ibid.

TABLE 11-5.   Percent of Respondents Who Were Able to Recall Advertisements

Type of Audience	Verified Recall Average (%)
Subscribers (primary)	27.4
Nonsubscribers (secondary)	17.8

Source: Roth, Paul, "Why We Discount Out-of-Homes by 50%," *Media/Scope*, March 1967, p. 64.

Marshak, therefore, felt that the value of the secondary audience depends on a number of things: (a) whether it is possible to reach the target audience entirely through primary readers; (b) the relative importance of targets where, perhaps, one demographic group may be as much as three times as important as some other demographic target; and (c) whether the planner needs some other measurement on which to base a decision.

In conclusion then, there seems to be good evidence for not using secondary audience data at full value. The method of discounting the secondary audience should be based on logic and research evidence rather than on subjective judgment alone.

Editorial Environment

It is conceivable that vehicles that reach targets efficiently may not be well-suited to an advertiser's messages because the editorial environments of the vehicles under consideration are incompatible with the ad message. This concept is related to the need for psychographic data to fit demographic data discussed earlier. Two college graduates may be the same age and in the same income class, but lead radically different lives. Similarly, two media vehicles can reach the same demographic targets with about the same cost efficiency, but each may feature editorial material of interest to different kinds of readers. This difference may be important in determining a media vehicle's advertising value.

An example might occur when an advertiser for salad dressings is considering eight potential vehicles, each of which may reach the demographic targets fairly well. But the editorial environments may differ widely, as Table 11-7 shows. The editorial environment criteria in the table are: number of food pages printed in four colors, number of food photographs, number of recipes, and number of editorial lines dealing with salads. These criteria were arbitrarily selected by the planner, so others could be substituted or added to provide a composite evaluation of the media alternatives. If this evaluation is combined with criteria of target reach and cost efficiency, a better approach to evaluating media may be found. Based on the criteria shown, the data show that *Better Homes & Gardens* was found to be the best vehicle.

The only problem with this kind of evaluation is that the planner must have someone available to do the research, because it is not always readily available for

TABLE 11-6.   Two Bases for Analyzing the Audiences of Magazine A

Full Value Basis	Number (millions)	Out-of-Home Audience Discounted 50% Basis	Number (millions)
Primary audience	27.75	Primary audience	27.75
Out-of-home audience	9.25	Out-of-home audience	4.63
Total audience	37.00	Total audience	32.38

TABLE 11-7. Index of Editorial Environments for Salad Dressings

Magazine	Four-Color Food Pages	Food Photo-graphs	Number of Recipes	Editorial Lines Dealing with Salads	Average of Four Scores
Better Homes & Gardens	127	255	107	135	156
Good Housekeeping	138	56	89	192	119
Woman's Day	84	29	212	108	108
Sunset	12	165	102	121	100
Family Circle	136	83	105	59	96
Ladies Home Journal	115	85	81	51	83
McCall's	104	70	57	53	71
American Home	86	56	48	81	68

Source: Kaatz, Ronald B., *Dr. (un)Strangeperson, or, How I Learned to Stop Worrying (about Some Numbers) and Love My Magazine Plans!* Paper presented to the American Academy of Advertising Convention, April 1975, Knoxville, Tennessee.

every product class. Such research can be very expensive and time-consuming to collect. Furthermore, the research would have to be repeated year after year to determine whether or not any changes in editorial policies were taking place.

Special Opportunities in Magazines

Media planners who want to reach special or limited markets may find that magazines can be adapted to meet their needs. This is because special demographic or geographic editions have been devised by some media for just that purpose. Table 11–8 lists some of the demographic breaks that are available in major consumer and business magazines.

In addition to offering special demographic and geographic breakouts, most magazines offer two-way (and in some cases even four-way) copy splits. *Reader's Digest*, for example, can distribute special copy to one out of every four subscribers across the nation through the use of zip coding and computers. This trend toward increased flexibility and specialization is expected to continue.

TABLE 11-8. Some Demographic Editions of Magazines

Publication	Name of Edition	Target
Better Homes & Gardens	Super Spot	Upper income homes
Fortune	Manufacturing	Manufacturers
McCall's	V.I.P./ZIP	Upper income homes
Nation's Business	Industry	Top management in industry
Nation's Business	Leadership	Members—Chamber of Commerce
Newsweek	College Student	College students
Newsweek	Women	Women
Time	Student/Educator	Students and educators
Time	B	Business executives
Time	Doctors	Doctors
Time	T	Top management
Sports Illustrated	Homeowners	Homeowners
U.S. News & World Report	Blue Chip	Top management
Playboy	Military	Military

TABLE 11-9.   General Findings of Media Imperatives

Group	Population (%)	Magazine Reading (%)	Television Viewing (%)
Heavy Mag/Light TV	33	47	16
Heavy TV/Light Mag	39	20	57
Dual (Heavy TV/Heavy Mag)	15	29	23
Neither (Light TV/Light Mag)	13	4	4
Total	100	100	100

Source: Ogilvy & Mather.

Media Imperatives

A planner considering media vehicle alternatives must be aware that although some vehicles reach target audiences very well, the data on reach can sometimes hide important facts. For example, the planner may find that television best reaches a given target audience, but those reached may be light television viewers and heavy magazine readers. In other words, reach figures do not indicate the degree of exposure to a given medium. *Media imperatives* is a form of research that provides information on the degree of exposure to television and magazines. It is supplied by SMRB.

Television imperatives show that some targets are heavy television viewers and light magazine readers, while *magazine imperatives* show that some persons are heavy magazine readers and light television viewers. In addition, media imperatives can also show dual audiences (or heavily exposed individuals in both media, and lightly exposed individuals in both media).

So media imperatives are a means of comparing magazines and television based on the degree of exposure to each medium. It also shows how much of various product categories are purchased by the four groups measured. Table 11-9 provides a general analysis of heavy versus light exposure to magazines and television on the basis of the media imperative's data.

A study of media imperatives, then, may motivate a planner to shift spending into or away from either television or magazines. The data do not answer all questions, but add another quantitative dimension to help solve the selection problem, as well as the problem of allocating money.

Position Alternatives

Some print vehicles offer advertisers selected positions, such as front-of-book or next to editorial material, which, if accepted, may turn out to be advantageous in reaching the targets with more impact. Sometimes premium rates are charged for position, but other times, the cost may be relatively low. So the planner may consider the availability of favored positions as a factor in weighing one vehicle against another. Those that offer selected positions may be a better buy than those that do not.

Advertising Clutter and Product Protection

In both television and print media, it is possible to measure the amount of clutter that occurs. Presumably, the medium that reaches the maximum number of targets at the best cost efficiency, and at the same time, is the least cluttered, would be the most desirable. There are, however, exceptions to this assumption. For example, in certain magazine classes, such as fashion and shelter, readers look for many ads and they buy the magazine to shop through advertising. But, if all competitors are in the same magazine, and there are also many other ads in the magazine, it may be questionable whether that vehicle is the most desirable for a specific advertiser. Brands with a clear-cut competitive advantage over other brands should prosper when placed in close proximity to competitors. Other brands, perceived as less desirable, may suffer from such competition. Generally, clutter is undesirable and product protection is something to be sought. This means keeping competitive ads within the vehicle at a reasonable distance from the advertised brand.

In evaluating the effect of clutter in a print medium, one should consider the Starch studies that show that the readership of the average advertisement in a magazine declines as the number of ads in the vehicle increases.

In television and radio, product protection, although desirable, is no longer affordable for most advertisers.

Circulation Trends

An objective measurement of a medium's value is the trend of circulation over a period of at least a year or two. Because advertising is sometimes planned more than a year ahead of time, media planners might want to study the latest Audit Bureau of Circulation (ABC) circulation figures for the last twelve to twenty-four months to see what has been happening. If a magazine under consideration has shown a decline, it may be dropped from the list. On the other hand, magazines with increasing circulation trends may be considered valuable.

New Product Editorial Features

Some magazines are known for their editorial features on new products. It is assumed, therefore, that readers know this and when they want to learn about the existence of new products they turn to such a magazine in preference to another magazine.

Advertising Copy Checking

Some media have a reputation for examining the veracity of all advertising copy and claims and annually reject many dollars of advertising. They publicize this fact regularly. The assumption here is that readers, knowing of this practice, will prefer to read ads in such a vehicle in preference to others that do not publicize their censorship efforts. *Good Housekeeping*, many newspapers, and network television organizations are among those that check copy carefully.

Response to Coupons, Information, or Recipes

Measurements of the number of audience members who send in coupons or ask for information or recipes may provide a planner with the type of qualitative data that would allow him or her to differentiate one magazine from another. This is not public information, however, and may be difficult, if not impossible, for all magazines to obtain. In situations where an advertiser runs the same ad in more than one magazine, it is sometimes possible to learn which magazine pulled best.

Available Discounts

Sometimes the value of a medium is directly affected by the nature of the discounts that it offers. If a number of ads are planned for a calendar year in several vehicles that are otherwise about equal, that vehicle offering a substantial discount may represent the best value of all. However, it would seem obvious that discounts rank relatively low on the scale of criteria. Target reach and target cost efficiency, for example, are more important than discounts. Likewise, the vehicle with the larger number of product users is usually more important than the vehicle with a large discount potential.

Flexibility

Two kinds of flexibility can affect media value. One is the degree to which a medium can be used to reach geographically superior markets precisely, while at the same time avoiding relatively weak markets. Generally, local media such as newspapers, spot radio, spot television, and outdoor are considered flexible media in the geographic sense. Magazines have some flexibility with their regional and local market issues. But often there may not be a local edition for a market that the planner deems necessary, or a regional edition that covers an advertiser's sales divisions with much precision. A media vehicle that has the potential for geographical flexibility may be more valuable than one that is not flexible.

A second kind of flexibility concerns the ability of the medium to make quick changes in copy, that is, production flexibility. There could be many reasons why an advertiser might need to change an advertising message quickly. In some media, this is a relatively easy job; in others, it is not. Black and white ads in print media can usually be changed quite easily and quickly in many vehicles. When a print ad is to be run in four colors, however, it becomes more difficult to make changes because it may be necessary to remake four-color printing cylinders. Generally, print media printed by letterpress are easier to change than those printed by offset. Gravure-printed media are the most difficult to change, especially if the printing cylinders have already been prepared and are ready for printing. In broadcast, it is easier to change live or videotaped commercials than film commercials. So production flexibility may be a consideration in determining media value if changes in the advertising message are contemplated.

Color Quality

In print media, color quality can be important in determining media values. The problem of color quality is twofold. First, there is the problem of simply achieving the color quality of the original artwork planned for an advertisement. Some publications may find it difficult to attain this quality because of the kinds of ink and paper they use. A second problem concerns the maintenance of consistent color quality during the entire press run. Printing presses running at high speeds sometimes wear out printing plates because of the friction of metal on paper; certain colors will print heavier or lighter than required. The planner should know the printing abilities of the publishing organization. Some vehicles have a distinct production control advantage over others.

The Qualitative Values of Media

As stated earlier, media selection is based mostly on the ability of specific media vehicles to reach precise target audiences with high cost efficiency and little waste. Other considerations in planning include the total cost of the medium plus the reach and frequency to be generated. Before a final decision for or against any medium is made, however, the planner may want to consider the qualitative values of each medium and how important these values are for the plan.

What Is a Qualitative Value?

A *qualitative value* is some characteristic of a medium that enhances the chances that an advertising message carried within it will be effective. It is based on the assumption that media are not simply passive carriers of advertisements; they are active carriers. A media vehicle is an environment with a personality of its own which may rub off on its advertisements and make them more effective in disseminating their messages. Social Research, Inc., defined this environment as follows:

> Think of a magazine as similar to a geographic location, a neighborhood, or a section of town. There are certain meanings that are generally associated with the location, and these meanings usually are known and taken for granted by most people living in the community. When an advertiser buys a lot in that location, it automatically buys whatever connotations the neighborhood carries. The building erected on this site (or the ad placed in this magazine) is responded to in terms of its own merits. But the edifice is also thought of in connection with its location, and this will either add to or detract from the impression the building makes.[3]

A medium's environment, therefore, may represent a qualitative value that could affect each advertisement carried within it. William Weilbacher, former vice president of Dancer-Fitzgerald-Sample, defined a qualitative value more specifically, as follows:

> Qualitative media value is the total increment to advertising message effect contributed by the medium or media vehicle. This qualitative medium value includes such individual contributors . . . as the special characteris-

---

3. Social Research, Inc., *Advertising Impact and Business Magazines*, Chicago, 1959, p. ii.

tics of the audience attracted to the medium or vehicle, and whatever personality characteristics are attributed to it by its audience members.

Implicit in this usage of the term qualitative value is the notion, that, beyond individual and definable sources . . . such as demographic and attitudinal characteristics, the medium may also contribute completely undefined, even unanticipated, values to the advertising process.[4]

Weilbacher warned, however, that his concept of a qualitative value did not include such general media characteristics as the image and prestige of each medium because these, although easily measured, did not necessarily add to advertising effectiveness. He preferred to deal with qualitative values that specifically affect individual advertisements.

Weilbacher's warning, however, focuses attention on the kinds of problems planners face in using the concept of qualitative values in media planning. Because it is so easy to measure the image of a magazine, it is often done. One way to measure the image is to compile a list of adjectives that could describe a magazine and ask respondents in a study which best represents the medium being studied. Such adjectives might include interesting, learned, dynamic, timely, modern, and alert.

The problem with studies of magazine images is: What does one do with the results? Because one magazine has a different and presumably better image than another magazine, does this have anything to do with advertising effectiveness? There is very little evidence to suggest such a relationship. Therefore image studies, though a form of determining a qualitative value, have little importance in media planning.

Measuring Qualitative Values

The kind of research needed to prove that media have qualitative values is that which tests the effectiveness of the same advertisement in two or more media. If all variables are held constant, then differences in reactions to the same advertisements may be due to qualitative values.

Alfred Politz studied responses by women to twelve advertisements appearing in *McCall's* against responses to the same twelve advertisements placed in *Life* and *Look* magazines. In order to isolate the qualitative media effects of each vehicle, he first solicited responses from his sample with no exposure to the ads to determine what respondents knew about the brands without having seen the ads.

Then he exposed the ads to the respondents in all three magazines, after which he measured responses again. Any differences between no exposure and one exposure were attributed to the qualitative differences of the medium as they affected readership of ads within them.[5] Shown in Table 11–10 are some of Politz's findings. Not only were there differences in responses with no exposure between *Mc-*

4. Weilbacher, W. M., ''The Qualitative Value of Advertising Media,'' *Journal of Advertising Research*, December 1960, p. 14.

5. Politz, Alfred and *McCall's*, ''A Measurement of Advertising Effectiveness,'' November 1962, p. 11.

TABLE 11-10. Some Findings from the Politz Study

Respondents who:	McCall's (%)	Life/Look (%)
1. Were familiar with the brand		
a. With no exposure	16.3	15.0
b. With one exposure	20.6	18.2
2. Believed claims found in ads		
a. With no exposure	17.0	16.5
b. With one exposure	19.4	17.8
3. Considered advertised brand to be one of the "very highest quality"		
a. With no exposure	17.6	17.8
b. With one exposure	21.4	18.8
4. Were interested in buying the brand		
a. With no exposure	10.3	10.1
b. With one exposure	13.2	11.6

Source: Politz, Alfred, and *McCall's*, "A Measurement of Advertising Effectiveness," November 1962, p. 11.

Call's and *Life/Look*, but there were greater differences after one exposure between the two magazine measurements. Presumably these differences were the effect of the magazine.

Using Qualitative Values

Notwithstanding Politz's and others' research on qualitative values, there is still little consensus about the matter. The tendency in most advertising agencies is to rely very little on such evidence of qualitative values in media planning. When they do use such values, they are apt to prepare the following kind of statement for their plans: "We feel that Medium A reflects greater authority and prestige than other media and therefore recommend that we purchase X number of ads in it."

Other terms that are used in the same manner are impact, mood, believability, atmosphere, excitement, and leadership. In addition, print media are sometimes judged on the following qualitative values:

Reputation of media for attracting ads of only the highest quality products. It is assumed, therefore, that readers knowing this fact will be more favorably inclined toward products and brands advertised in these media than they would for products and brands advertised in other media.

Reading days. How many days, totally, are alternative magazines read? If a magazine is opened at any time on a given day, this constitutes a reading-day. If, for example, there is evidence that Magazine A is read more total days than Magazines B, C, D, and E, (all under consideration) then the planner has one more qualitative reason to select A. More reading days represent more opportunities to see ads.

Reading time. In a similar manner, it is possible to measure the total or average number of hours spent reading magazines. These measurements may indicate that the magazine with the largest number of reading hours is more attractive than others. It may be assumed that audience members have more opportunities to see ads if they spend more time reading.

Page openings. It is possible to measure the number of pages opened in alternative magazines. A technique in which a tiny spot of glue is applied to pages containing ads may be used. Respondents may be given specially glued magazines on a given day. On the next day (or two) the interviewer may return and pick up the special copies. The number of pages pulled open are then counted. Another variation of page-opening measurements is simply to count page traffic on all ad pages. Using a "recognition measuring technique" researchers count the number of pages where any ads on the page were noted by audience members who comprise a sample. Page traffic data is a measure of the net potential audience size of a magazine and may play a role in the final selection decision.

The above list is by no means complete, but it does show how media planners might use the qualitative values of various media in planning.

Probably the most misused of all media qualitative value terms is that of "impact." Print media executives often claim their magazine has more impact than other magazines. If they mean that an ad in their magazine will sell more of the product than an ad in any other magazine, this cannot be proved and is, therefore, conjecture on the part of the executives. It is generally not possible to determine the effect of a media vehicle and an advertisement on sales.

Conceivably, there could be a careful testing program conducted for one advertiser, with strict controls, to prove that more people recalled a given ad in one magazine than in any other. But recall and sales are quite different. How can one prove that it wasn't the price, the packaging, the distribution, or the sales promotion that sold the product? Some vehicles are better than others, but not on the basis of impact, which is too vague a concept to be used in media planning. Only when a clear-cut cause-and-effect relationship can be established for the brand and the vehicle on sales can the concept of impact be used.

Qualitative rationales for selecting media have a place in planning procedures. But there are some reasonable guidelines that ought to be kept in mind if they are used:

1. Qualitative, or subjective, rationales should never be a total replacement for quantitative substantiation.
2. Qualitative consideration should be used *after* quantitative analysis has been made and thereby modify numerical relationships.
3. If possible, more than one person should contribute to making the subjective analysis in order to reduce the possibility of individual bias.
4. Media sponsored research concerning qualitative values such as high impact, "liked most," and so forth, should be considered suspect. Much of this kind of research tends to be highly promotional rather than objective. It is very difficult to transfer the findings from one medium to another.

In conclusion then, qualitative values of media do exist, but they can't be used as the main criteria in media planning. They are simply not objective enough to be used alone for decision making. Perhaps ways will be found to prove that one medium indeed has more impact than others, but at present it cannot be proved. Experts can only agree that media are not passive carriers of ads. They do have qualitative values, and some can be used for planning purposes.

Ad Positions within Media

Assuming that media vehicles have been selected, the budget allocated, and a schedule worked out, in theory, media planning could end at this point.

In practice, however, there are still questions that are often asked by planners themselves and others interested in media. Is there nothing else that can be done to help in the advertising communication process? Are reach and frequency all there is? The problem is to find ways for the media planner to go beyond delivery and not only get vehicles exposed, but get ads within those vehicles exposed, and finally, get the ads read.

To a great extent, this last responsibility belongs to the creative people: planners, writers, and art directors who have special talents for getting advertising communication "through" to the reader. The copy people, for example, can write scintillating headlines and meaningful words. The art director can devise fascinating layouts. The creative people can ask for four-color ads, bleed pages, reverse printing, gatefold-size ads, two-page spreads; they can print ads on unusual stock such as acetate or aluminum foil; they can use unusual inks such as day-glo or perfumed inks. These are but a few of the many options open to the creative personnel in getting ads noticed and read.

What, then, can media planners do to help the situation? They can ask for certain positions within media that are felt to be better than other positions. This, however, leaves them open to questions about positioning research and strategy.

Problems of Positioning Research

There are a number of media positions that appear to be better than others. For example, the fourth cover of a magazine is generally conceded to be the best place in a magazine for an ad. In fact, research confirms that the fourth cover is one of the best positions. But many media experts question the research. Nonetheless, there is some logic, even without research, to suggest that a fourth cover position is a valuable position. There is not much agreement among experts about other media position. The research tends to be weak, and therefore inconclusive.

Perhaps the foremost problem of position research is that it is difficult to separate measurements of position from copy effects. Most research techniques that are used to establish the effects of position are really a mixture of copy and position. In some research studies, another dimension, that of size, is added. Then, too, averaging data for position effects that contain widely varying degrees of copy effectiveness may not truly represent the effects of position. Averaging tends to be unduly affected by extreme copy-effect scores. Some media experts question whether there is any copy measuring device that is totally valid. But assuming that most are valid, there is still no way, through present-day measurements, to know the effect of position alone.

A solution would be to design experiments involving ad copy that is held constant with the only variable being position. Because the same ads would be measured in different positions in different media vehicles, the effects of position alone could be found. However, there still is dissatisfaction with much research devised to measure position because it is not carefully controlled to eliminate bias. Research designs are often poor or nonexistent. Samples are often nonrandom and selected haphazardly. Questionnaire design and interviewing controls are not always the best. As a result, much position research is suspect.

Some Position Effects

What follows is a brief summary of position effects that some media planners accept. The reader is cautioned about accepting them as valid evidence. They are presented to show a sample of the kinds of positions that *may* affect the communication power of advertisements placed in vehicles.

Position in Magazines. (a) Fourth cover positions are usually considered better than any inside positions if Starch Adnorm data are used as a guide; (b) second cover and page one positions are about equal and are the next best to fourth cover positions; (c) front of the magazine positions (from page 2 to about page 20) are the next best positions; (d) righthand pages are somewhat better than lefthand pages, with some exceptions. Keep in mind that these are generalities based on the research findings across many different magazines. Specific magazines, which might have uncommon editorial layouts, might produce different readership patterns.

Position in Newspapers. (a) Ads near the front are considered better than those near the back, but the differences are small; (b) there is no significant difference between righthand and lefthand pages; (c) inside a newspaper section is better than the last page of the section; (d) there is little difference between ads above or below the fold; (e) editorial environment affects the readership of ads (ads for male products prove better on sports pages and ads for female products do better on women's pages); (f) preprint stuffers, while they cost about 4.6 times as much as ROP color, do about 3.8 times better in responses.[6]

Position in Television. (a) Attention to programs is greatest during late fringe and poorest in early fringe times; (b) mysteries, spy adventure programs, and movies do a little better than varieties and western programs in recall of messages; (c) daytime is about 50 percent to 80 percent as good as nighttime recall; (d) a thirty-second commercial has about 60 percent to 75 percent the recall value of a sixty-second commercial; (e) high-rated programs have higher attention levels than low-rated

6. Jain, Charman L., "Newspaper Advertising: Preprint vs. R.O.P.," *Journal of Advertising Research*, August 1973, p. 32.

programs; (f) in-program commercials do better in recall than between-program commercials. According to SMRB's *Television Attentiveness and Special Events Study,* attention levels are greatest during late fringe and prime time, and poorest during early morning.

Cost Considerations

A major consideration in deciding whether to use a special position in a vehicle is the premium cost. Some positions may not be worth the extra cost. Even if it seems to be worth the cost, it may be difficult to support a decision one way or the other because the research is questionable.

QUESTIONS FOR DISCUSSION

1. In planning media strategy, why does it make a difference whether a print vehicle reaches its audience slowly or quickly?
2. How important should the cost-per-thousand evaluation of vehicles be in comparison to other selection criteria?
3. Why do some media planners believe that the primary audience is more important than the secondary audience of print vehicles?
4. Explain how product protection is given to ads in a print vehicle. In a broadcast vehicle.
5. What kinds of marketing situations would require a media plan to have good geographic flexibility?
6. What is the value of having special demographic editions of print vehicles?
7. If a vehicle charges more for a special position, is it worth the extra cost? Discuss.
8. Suppose salespeople for a given publication point out that their vehicle has a better image than competitors. Is this fact alone enough to make a difference in the decision to buy or not buy that vehicle?
9. How does one decide what proportions of strategic impressions are needed for an effective media plan?
10. Why isn't editorial environment used more often as a criterion in making vehicle selections?

SELECTED READINGS

Banks, Allen, "How National Is National Network Television?" *Marketing and Media Decisions*, January 1986, pp. 86–88.

Carter, David, "Newspaper Advertising Readership: Thick vs. Thin Issues," *Journal of Advertising Research,* September 1968, pp. 39–42.

Davis, Laurie, "Sunday Comics: Not to Be Taken Lightly," *Marketing and Media Decisions*, December 1985, p. 95–96.

Frankel, Lester R., and Solov, Bernard M., "Does Recall of an Advertisement Depend on Its Position in the Magazine?" *Journal of Advertising Research*, December 1962, pp. 28–32.

Graphic Communication Weekly, "Study Shows Reader Conflicts," March 12, 1968, p. 13.

Hamilton, Jerry, "15-Second Effectiveness," *Marketing and Media Decisions*, November 1986, pp. 90–93.

Jain, Charman L., "Newspaper Advertising: Preprint vs. R.O.P." *Journal of Advertising Research,* August 1973, pp. 30–32.

Joyce, Timothy, "Target Weighting Gives Boost to Consumer Studies," *Advertising Age,* July 15, 1974, p. 27.

Marder, Eric, "How Good Is the Editorial Interest Method of Measuring Magazine Audiences?" *Journal of Advertising Research,* March 1967, pp. 2–6.

Maneloveg, Herbert, "The Total Audience Concept for Magazines—Good if Understood," *Advertising Age,* October 14, 1963, pp. 84–85.

Marsteller, Rickard, Gebhardt and Reed, Inc., *Qualitative Media Measurements,* Chicago, 1959.

Martin, Stephen H., "Fear of Radio," *Marketing and Media Decisions,* June 1986, p. 98-99.

McGuire, Dennis F., "Buying Radio: A Primer," *Marketing and Media Decisions,* January 1986, pp. 92–93.

Media Decisions, "How Ayer Applies Weights to Media Plans," September 1972, p. 48.

Media Decisions, "When JWT Picks Magazines, Numbers Aren't Everything," June 1975, pp. 65–69.

Media/Scope, "Position in Broadcast Advertising," No. 1, August 1962, p. 50; No. 2, September 1962, p. 41; No. 3, October 1962, p. 48; No. 4, November 1962, p. 46.

Media/Scope, "Timing in Broadcast Advertising," September 1962, p. 46.

Media/Scope, "How Important Is Position in Consumer Magazine Advertising?" June 1964, pp. 52–57.

Media/Scope, "Forum Question: Generally Speaking, What Value Do You Place on Secondary or Pass-along Readers?" February 1970, p. 26.

Newspaper Advertising Bureau, Inc., and the *Minneapolis Star and Tribune* (Facts), *The Influence of Position, Size, Color, Creativity on Newspaper Advertising Readership,* 1972.

Ostrow, Joseph, "Some Problems in Profile Matching," *Media Decisions,* November 1972, pp. 72–74.

Papazian, Ed, "Qualitative Comparisons —a Necessary Ingredient in the Planning Process," *Media Decisions,* January 1979, pp. 16–18.

Papazian, Ed, "TV's Qualitative Values," *Marketing and Media Decisions,* December 1985, pp. 89–90.

Rice, Roger, and Severance, Dick, "Who's Winning the War of Imperatives?" *Media Decisions,* December 1978, pp. 64–65.

Roth, Paul, "What Is the Value of the Pass-along Audience?" *Media/Scope,* November 1963, pp. 84–87.

Roth, Paul, "Why We Discount Out-of-Home by 50%," *Media/Scope,* March 1967, pp. 63–68.

Roth, Paul, "How to Plan Media," *Media Decisions,* 1974.

Shiffman, Phil, "Special Significance of Newsstand Sales Data on Magazines," *Media Decisions,* July 1973, p. 82.

Starch, Daniel, "Do Inside Positions Differ in Readership?" *Media/Scope,* February 1962, pp. 44–46.

Starch, Daniel, "Is Preferred Position Worth It?" *Printers Ink,* August 25, 1961, pp. 43–44.

Swan, Carroll J., "In Magazines—Selectivity within Within," *Media/Scope,* July 1968, p. 33.

Weilbacher, William, "The Qualitative Values of Advertising Media," *Journal of Advertising Research,* December 1960, pp. 12–17.

Wheatley, John J., "Influence of Commercial's Length and Position," *Journal of Marketing Research,* May 1968, pp. 199–202.

Wiener, Norman, "What's Wrong with Newsstand Distribution of Magazines?" *Advertising Age,* October 16, 1972, pp. 59–60.

12
Putting a Media Plan Together: The Mechanics

The last four chapters have dealt at length with the important decisions that go into media planning. This chapter explains how to pull these elements together into a document, the *media plan*. The chapter analyzes the writing of media objectives and strategies, as well as the organization of the media plan.

Organizing the Plan of Action

It is possible, and often probable, that media planning is done in such a way as to end with a series of decisions only remotely related to each other or to the original problem. One might find, for example, that media were selected on the basis of cost per thousand for target audiences reached, while neglecting the reach or frequency that resulted. Or, the media selected might have little to do with the marketing objectives. Or, a series of media decisions might represent a loosely organized plan of action. Sometimes, media are selected first, and then scheduled. Following this, a strategy may be devised. Such practices are inefficient.

It is important, therefore, for a planner to organize media planning in such a way as to be logical and efficient. The goals should be as follows:

1. All media decisions should be based on marketing objectives and strategies. The goal of the planner is to select and use media to help attain some one objective or to carry out the overall strategy.
2. The first step in media planning should be to create media objectives, whose purpose is to implement the marketing objectives and strategy.
3. Media strategy should be created after the objectives have been written. It should consist of a series of broadly conceived decisions directly aimed at fulfilling specific media objectives. The reason media strategy should

TABLE 12-1.   Logical Progression of Steps in Media Planning

1. Marketing Objectives	2. Marketing Strategies	3. Media Objectives	4. Media Strategies	5. Decisions Implementing Strategies (Tactics)	6. Media Buying
A number of marketing goals for a given brand, presumably, based on best opportunities for sales or solving other marketing problems.	A number of broadly conceived marketing decisions, organized into a unified plan of action aimed at attaining marketing objectives.	A number of media goals, all related in some way to helping attain marketing objectives, or related to marketing strategy.	A number of broadly conceived media decisions, organized into a unified plan of action aimed at attaining media goals.	A number of very specific decisions that implement the media strategy. In many instances, these decisions serve as a basis for media buying.	Actual purchasing decisions involving the selection and use of media.

Examples

1. Marketing Objectives	2. Marketing Strategies	3. Media Objectives	4. Media Strategies	5. Decisions Implementing Strategies (Tactics)	6. Media Buying
Goal: increase brand share of market by 5 percent over last year, nationally.	Concentrate on stealing customers from competitors by using ads that show ways in which our brand is better than theirs.	Goal: plan media selections so as to deliver at least 80 percent of both our and competitors' target markets (targets are defined demographically).	Frequency goal: 4.5. Use network TV, day and late fringe, spot TV in top 30 markets. Use: 30s. Buy 600 GRPs in spot markets.	Eliminate newspapers, spot radio, spot TV, and billboards from consideration. Use network TV or magazines. Find which gives 80 percent net reach of targets at lowest CPM.	Make purchase of best alternative media according to the specifications laid down in strategy and tactical plans, and according to any other specifications (such as creative requirements).

represent broad (or general) media decisions in that it is logical to proceed from the general to the specific. Thus, the strategy should serve as the basis for the next step in planning: tactics or implementation, which in turn leads to media buying.

Table 12-1 presents the relationship between the various steps in media planning. Table 12-2 summarizes some of the most important variables that may be manipulated in planning, and Table 12-3 shows some of the marketing objectives and strategies that may affect media variables.

Determining Media Objectives

The best way to plan media is to decide what goals are most important and then to find ways to achieve them. *Media objectives,* the group of goals designed to enable

TABLE 12–2.   Variables That May Be Manipulated in Media Planning

1. *Constraint variables*	d. Weighting proportions:
a. Budget size	By geographical markets
b. Creative strategy	By demographic targets
c. Nature of the product	By heavy-user targets
d. Nature of the brand	By season
e. Past use of media	By gross rating point levels
f. Competitive uses of media	e. Schedule length
g. Competitive spending in media	f. Schedule patterning
	g. Cost efficiency standards
2. *Media plan objective variables*	h. Discounts
a. Reach (or market coverage) needed	i. Allocation of budget to media or markets
b. Frequency needed	or both
c. Continuity patterns needed	j. Number of ads or commercials to be run
	k. Number of different media to be used
3. *Media strategy variables*	l. Number of different markets to be used
a. Strategy concept variables:	
Concentration	4. *Other variables*
Media dominance	a. Size of ads or lengths of commercials
Flighting	b. Kind of sponsorship in broadcast media
b. Levels of reach needed	c. Use of qualitative factors
c. Levels of frequency needed	d. Availability of media units

marketing goals to be met, serve the purpose of helping planners decide where they want to go, while the media strategy serves as the means of getting there.

Because media objectives are not ends in themselves, but are aimed at implementing either marketing objectives or strategies, it is necessary to study both marketing antecedents. But it may not be obvious how such a study can lead to media objectives, nor is it possible to find an easy-to-use formula for creating media objec-

TABLE 12–3.   Some Marketing Variables That Affect Media Strategy Variables

1. *Introduction of new products*	7. *Increases in the advertising budget*
a. Roll-out patterns	*caused by*
b. Key market patterns	a. Movement into new markets
c. Broad-scale national introductions	b. New product introductions
	c. Need for any changes in
2. *Increasing market share requirements*	communication
a. Steal from competitors	
b. Get present users to consume more	8. *Changes in sales promotion strategy*
c. Expand the entire market	a. New relationship between sales
	promotion and advertising
3. *Changes needed in brand image*	b. New or different sales promotion
a. Requiring new creative strategy	techniques required
b. Requiring new timing strategy	
	9. *Test marketing situations*
4. *Changes in corporate image*	a. Testing various budget levels in
a. Requiring new creative strategy	different markets (same media)
b. Requiring new timing strategy	b. Testing various budget levels in
	different markets (different media)
5. *Changes in brand positioning*	
a. Requiring new creative strategy	10. *Changes in the life cycle of a product:*
	growth, maturation, decline
6. *Reductions in the advertising budget*	
caused by	11. *Meeting competitive marketing strategies*
a. Attempts to increase profits	*head on*
b. Attempts to cut losses	
c. Production problems of all kinds	

tives. Perhaps the best direction that could be given to a media planner who wants to create objectives would be to first answer the following question as thoughtfully as possible: "In what ways can I use media to help implement either a marketing objective or strategy?"

The answer to this question must come from a thorough knowledge of media, research, and marketing, along with good judgment. Furthermore, there may not be one answer to the question, but a number of alternatives, each of which may be important to a greater or lesser degree. If, for example, one of the marketing objectives is to introduce a new brand of soap to a market, then a number of alternative media objectives might be considered.

1. Use media that reach heavy users of soap.
2. Use media that other soap manufacturers have used most often in the past (assuming, of course, that such media will reach heavy soap users).
3. Spend at least as much money in the same media as the manufacturer of the number one brand in market share does.
4. Try to reach as much, or more, of the market as the manufacturer who has the number one brand share.

Which should become *media* objectives? The answer may depend on what the other marketing objectives are, the relative importance of each, and what marketing strategy has been devised. After such considerations, perhaps one or all may be adopted as media objectives.

Sometimes, however, media objectives are based on marketing strategy rather than marketing objectives. If, for example, the objective is to introduce a new brand to the market, and the marketing strategy is to use a roll-out pattern of introduction, then the media objective would specify the geographical areas where media would be used first. Sometimes a roll-out pattern might be limited to the states in the northeastern United States; only after the brand sells well would it be introduced gradually to adjacent western states. Media objectives could clearly indicate which states should receive media and when such media might be used.

It is not possible to explain precisely how media objectives should be created. Instead, the idea of a "relationship" between media objectives and marketing objectives or strategy should serve as a guide in planning.

Budget Constraints

Even though the relationship of marketing objectives to media objectives is clear, a number of constraints often temper the planner's decision. The size of the budget, if known ahead of time, is one such constraint. Many times, the marketing budget is set before any media planning takes place. In such a situation, the media objectives will have to be written with the budget in mind.

If no budget is available, then media objectives may well serve as a guide to setting a budget, at least as far as the cost of time or space is concerned. Once planners have a general idea of their goals, they are in a position to estimate what it will cost to achieve them. Sometimes, a budget cannot be set at the media objectives stage, but must wait until the strategy has been worked out. In such cases, media objectives may have to be rewritten later to accommodate the size of the budget. Perhaps a series of marketing/media priorities may have to be set so that the planner achieves those goals that are most pressing, while secondary goals may have to wait for another day. The size of a budget recommended by a media planner might be reduced by the client after examining marketing/media objectives and strategy.

Creative Constraints

Creative strategy can be a constraint in setting media objectives. The role of creative strategy in planning media was discussed earlier. Suffice it to say that a media planner should first study creative strategy before writing objectives.

Reach and Frequency

When planners select media they are, in effect, choosing those that will deliver a given number of target audiences. Delivery, however, is nothing more than exposures. Because all research data represent measurements taken in the past, the data therefore represent only "estimates of exposures." The future may be somewhat different.

But the number of estimated exposures contracted for in a media plan may be patterned in such a way as to maximize either reach or frequency, or to attain effective reach and frequency. Media objectives should be set so as to obtain whichever goal is sought. Brown, Lessler, and Weilbacher called this pattern the "message basket."[1] They meant that, without clear-cut, deliberate planning, all of the potential exposures planned may produce only a confused basket of numbers, some of which may even represent contradictory goals. Therefore, media objectives should be written in such a way as to bring control and order out of the chaos in the basket.

More explicitly, media objectives should state whether reach or frequency is to be the goal, and explain why each is or is not needed. In addition, the levels of reach and frequency should become objectives. Here, too, an explanation is needed to justify, logically, why any given level is desired.

Continuity

It should be apparent that media objectives will affect the kinds of strategies that later evolve. One important goal that will affect the timing of advertising during weeks and months of a year is continuity. *Continuity,* as previously described, is the consistency of advertising placement. Like reach and frequency, continuity may result in many contradictory patterns of placement if not controlled.

One placement pattern, for example, may consist of advertising appearing every day of the year; another may be limited to placing ads once a month. Which is better? The answer depends on a number of factors. What are the brand market-

---

1. Brown, Lyndon O., Lessler, Richard S., and Weilbacher, William M., *Advertising Media,* Ronald Press, New York, 1957, p.118.

ing goals and strategy? Do they require a given pattern? Does the creative strategy require a different pattern? (For example, if the creative strategy includes a very complex message in television commercials, will audiences be able to grasp the meaning if the commercials are shown once a month or will a pattern of frequent showings be required?)

Therefore media goals will have to be based, to some extent, on continuity.

Market Coverage Levels

Coverage (or reach) levels desired should be stated in the media objectives, if possible. As it was previously defined, *coverage* is the percentage of a target market, that a combination of all media will reach. It is important to set that level carefully, keeping in mind how much coverage is needed to attain a given marketing or media objective.

It is also a good practice to explain why a given level of coverage is required. In other words, if a media plan is supposed to deliver 75 percent of the market, the planner ought to be able to explain, reasonably, why 75 percent was chosen. Why not 65 percent or 85 percent? Budget limitations, frequency, and marketing objectives probably constitute the main considerations in determining coverage levels. A coverage level gives the market/media planner a given number of potential consumers, many of whom, it is hoped, will be turned into buyers through exposure to the advertising message.

Media Targets

To whom will advertisements be directed—users, persons who influence users, or both? The more specific a planner is in identifying targets by demographic or other means, the easier it will be to find media that will reach those targets. Most media targets are defined demographically. Occasionally, some other description such as psychographics (the psychological descriptions of targets) is used. The goal, however, is to be as specific as possible, because a vague description may mean exposures wasted on individuals who never buy a given product or brand under any circumstances. Once media targets have been specified, then all subsequent decisions can be checked to see whether the correct targets are being reached by the media selected.

Media objectives usually include a statement indicating where targets are located geographically. Sometimes this information is stated in the strategy portion, rather than the objectives portion, of the plan.

Cost Efficiency

Cost-per-thousand maximum levels may or may not be a part of media objectives. Usually, cost-per-thousand targets are needed to discriminate between media. In past years, when media planning was often based on large audience figures (sometimes called *box-car figures*) representing crudely identified media audiences, maximum cost-per-thousand levels were usually stated in media objectives. For example, one media objective might have been written to warn buyers not to buy any medium that had a cost per thousand over $5 for total audiences. But at the present, and most likely in the future, maximum levels of cost per thousand may be meaningless, because cost-efficiency formulas are now used mostly to help discriminate between the ability of various media to deliver prospects at the lowest unit cost. But even the lowest CPM among all alternatives may be high.

Examples of Media Objectives

The actual practice of writing media objectives often results in statements that are mixtures of both objectives and strategy. The probable reason for this is that there are too few objectives, so both objectives and strategy are planned about the same time. Often there is little difference between the two.

The following are examples of media objectives (with some strategy statements intermixed) taken from various advertising agency media plans.

Media Objectives from Plan A. Television will continue to be X's primary medium because of its ability to provide efficiently:

1. Audience: the desired woman, or heavy user, reorganizing the role of women as the decision maker regarding X type of food.
2. Effectiveness: demonstration of X's palatability, via sight, sound, and motion.
3. Schedule and pressure variation—based on need for:
    a. Continuity—year-round support that can reasonably be expected to reach a significant number of established customers on a regular basis.
    b. Impact—heavy pressure during certain flight periods affording the brand the opportunity to reach a large audience with a frequency substantially above the continuity level, the purpose being to help stimulate new trial.
    c. Flexibility—to capitalize on geographic variation in existing market potential and to support major promotions.

Media Objectives from Plan B. Based on the outline of the problem, the specific objectives of the media plan are:

1. To reach large families with special emphasis on the homemaker, who is usually the chief purchasing agent.
2. To concentrate the greatest weight of advertising in urban areas where prepared foods traditionally have greater sales and where new ideas normally gain quicker acceptance.
3. To provide advertising continuity and a fairly consistent level of impressions throughout the year except for extra weight during the announcement period.
4. To deliver advertising impressions over the entire country in direct relation to food store sales.
5. To use media that will help to strengthen the copy strategy and put major emphasis on convenience, ease of preparation, taste, and economy.

6. To attain the greatest possible frequency of advertising impressions consistent with the need for broad coverage and the demands of the copy plan.

Because, as we have pointed out, the regional strategy normally stems from the national plan, we will outline first the campaign that is proposed for Phase II when full national distribution will have been attained.

Media Objectives from Plan C.

1. Coverage of all homemakers, with special emphasis on those in larger urban markets, in middle and lower-middle income groups, and in larger families.
2. Maximum frequency, within budgetary limits, to match the relatively frequent pattern of purchase in this category.
3. Adequate time or space for a complete, thorough, multiseason sales message.
4. The opportunity to punctuate a continuous level of coverage with two crescendos of special weight, one in the summer in the south and one in the winter in the north.
5. Maximum efficiency for every advertising dollar spent—to combat higher competitive per-pound expenditures by buying more impressions per dollar than competition.
6. A corollary requirement, if it can be realized, is dominance of advertising weight in Brand X's markets to appear more important than any competitor.
7. To reach homemakers as close as possible to mealtimes; early morning, noon, and dinnertime.

Determining Media Strategies

A strategy is a series of actions, usually planned far ahead of time, to accomplish specific and stated goals. Whenever there are alternative ways of accomplishing a goal, then there is the need for a strategy. In media planning, there are many opportunities to use strategy, and inevitably a problem arises in trying to find a way to know, objectively, which course of action will be optimal. The mental process of weighing media strategy alternatives, however, presents a formidable task because there are many alternatives to think about at any one time. While thinking about audience sizes, a planner must, at the very same time, be thinking about cost efficiencies, availabilities of media units, discounts that could change the whole plan, the effect of competitors, the creative strategy and execution, the amount of money that is available, and the time available to accomplish objectives—and this is only a partial list.

Generally, no single strategy comprises a media plan. Instead, there are a number of strategies, with varying priorities, that constitute the essence of a plan. There may be a weighting strategy, a spending strategy, a reach and frequency strategy, and so forth. Each strategy should be clearly stated and defended. Usually, strategy statements are organized so that the most important strategies come first.

Although a selected strategy may represent the best of all alternatives, the net total of a number of strategies to be included in a single plan may not represent a unified or coordinated plan. A unified plan is an objective of good strategy planning. Perhaps the term "orchestrated" better describes how all media actions work together for the attainment of media and marketing goals. Contradictory or incomplete actions have no place in good strategy.

It is important to place media strategies into a frame of reference so that one can see what position each occupies relative to other parts of a plan. Strategies are neither the beginning, nor the end, of planning. Media objectives precede them, and media selections usually follow them. Selection decisions are sometimes called the "tactics" of a plan.

How is strategy judged? The answer is that, eventually, the strategy will be evaluated on what happens as a result of the planning. Someone will have to answer a question such as, "Were the marketing and media objectives attained as a direct result of the strategy or in spite of the strategy?" Such questions really comprise a post evaluation, however, and they are far removed from the immediate problem of evaluating strategy in the short run.

There are several ways to evaluate strategy *before* a plan is implemented. One way is to determine the risks of doing or not doing something. This requires subjective judgment plus the experience of having tried various strategies and finding them not worth the risk. Another evaluation technique is a weighing of economy of effort and time. If a strategy takes too much effort, or is too time-consuming to execute, it may not be worthwhile. If it costs more than the budget provides, then a question arises, Can one be sure that the extra money is worth the risk?

Another method of evaluation is based on estimating the probabilities of success. Unfortunately, beginners have no way of knowing whether a plan will succeed, especially if the marketing situation is unique or new. But there may be strong clues. One clue is the experience of others in an organization who have created plans or know of plans that are similar to the one proposed and have been successful. Another clue may be found in published reports of competitors' strategies that have succeeded. The planner will have to determine whether their experience is directly translatable to the present situation.

Sometimes marketing and/or media consultants may have to be hired to provide expert opinion on whether a strategy will work. At other times testing and experimenting may be necessary to provide the answer. In addition, journals of marketing and advertising often provide information and/or theories that can be adapted to fit the needs of a given situation.

Finally, there is no substitute for good reasoning and logic. Even if the evidence is not available, the planner can make assumptions about how the marketing/media environment is operating. But the better planners go beyond making assumptions. They first attempt to check the validity of their assumptions by observing what happens after a strategy has been tried—whether or not the strategy has been successful and if its assumptions were valid. Secondly, good planners are always challenging their own assumptions and changing them if necessary, as time progresses.

Once strategies have been devised, it is the responsibility of planners to prove that the media choices are the best of all alternatives. Planners should be able to defend their decisions with as much evidence as possible, plus good judgment.

Creative Media Strategy

In Chapter 1, we discussed the *creative media plan* as a problem to be solved. In this chapter, we make suggestions on how to implement a creative media strategy that will help solve this problem to a great extent.

Our first recommendation is that the media planner understand what is meant by the term *creative media strategy*.

It must first be pointed out that there is no universally agreed-upon definition of this term. However, in general, we believe a creative media strategy to be one that is innovative enough to secure for an advertised brand some advantage over competitors' brands. Such a strategy may accomplish this by helping the advertising stand out against competitors' advertising, giving the messages a better chance of being absorbed. Many advertised brands in product categories (margarines, or TV sets, for example) tend to use similar media strategies. If all products in a category are also similar, then consumers may have difficulty distinguishing one brand from another. Perhaps a creative media strategy will help solve the problem.

More specifically, however, we offer five guidelines criteria for implementing a creative media strategies:

1. *Be sure that the media strategy is different from and more innovative than competitors' media strategies.* It is very important to realize that simply being different is not enough. There is no evidence that a plan that is different from competitors' plans will accomplish anything. But, there is the testimony of media and marketing planners that truly innovative plans can accomplish key goals and attain competitive advantages.

   The key elements in the *innovative* are ideas that make a brand's advertising stand out from the competitors' advertising. This assumes that advertising messages have something to say that is meaningful to consumers. What this also means is that the media dollars being spent are supposed to return more than they would if the plan was based on a typical brand's media strategy.

2. *The ability to be creative should not depend on additional dollars spent for media.* Innovative strategies that could cost more than what is considered normal are not considered valuable unless there is evidence that the increased spending will result in superior returns.

3. *Media strategy should start with quantitative proofs of the best media choices and usages. . .but then go beyond numbers.* A creative media strategy is not a substitute for quantitative proof that the best media have been selected and used. Without measures of reach, frequency, effective frequency, and other kinds of useful numerical data, a planner would have to rely on gut instinct. It is difficult to convince clients who

are spending large amounts of money for media to rely on gut instincts as proof. But when a plan is built on good quantitative proof, and a good creative strategy, the combination may be just what is required.

4. *A good creative media strategy should be dramatic rather than ordinary.* It is the drama of the innovation that can make a strategy stand out from all the others and secure special benefits for a brand.

5. *A creative media strategy should be relevant to the problems that the advertised brand has.* Being creative is sometimes interpreted as being "off-beat" or "new." It is important to make a creative media plan relevant to the marketing situation and not just "different."[2]

It is important to understand that a media planner should be the person to make contributions to the overall marketing plan with creative media strategies. Planners typically are thought of as "number crunchers," or "people with only quantitative skills." Both stereotypes ought to be dismissed. When given an opportunity to be creative, a media planner should be able to think of innovative ways to solve problems.

Examples of Creative Media Strategies

Listed below are some examples of creative strategies used by various advertisers to achieve special attention to their messages:

Chrysler introduced its new styles of automobiles in 1988 with a twenty-page, four-color insert in *Newsweek* magazine, showing the new models. It was arranged to be pulled out by readers for more careful inspection.

Transamerica and Merit Cigarettes both used three-dimensional ads that pop out of a two-page spread to stop and hold readers as they paged through magazines.

Continental Baking Company needed to build brand awareness in a local market, but did not have a budget to attain its goals, so it rented seven buses, painted them in the colors and shapes of "Wonder Bread," and had each travel through the market for a limited amount of time.

These are but a few examples of what creative strategies may look like. There are many more opportunities available to planners. The essence of being creative is to be "innovative." The media planner who first does a job of providing the best numbers lays a groundwork. It is the creative planner who goes beyond the numbers to make a media plan stand out and do something extra for a brand.

---

2. Recommendations (1), (2), and (5) were made by Prof. Ron B. Kaatz, in various speeches and lectures on Creative Media Planning. (Medill School of Journalism, Northwestern University, 1987)

Considerations in Strategy Planning

The first consideration in planning media strategy is to take a close look at the entire marketing/media situation, with special attention to competitors' marketing and media strategies. Perhaps one of the first steps should be to answer the question, "To what extent do I copy competitors' media strategies?" At times in planning media strategy, there may be the temptation simply to implement media objectives without first considering the strategies of competitors. But such temptations should be subdued by the realization that no brand exists in a vacuum, so strategy will have to be based, in some part, on what competitors are doing.

The Competitive Situation

What should the planner look for in considering competitors? Perhaps the most important consideration is market-share position. What rank does the brand in question have in the market? If a brand has the greatest share, then it deserves special study. Does it have the best product in its class? Is its distribution outstanding, its creative efforts in advertising superior, or its selection and use of media better than others? The final answer may grow out of a combination of these and other considerations. In any case, brands with smaller shares cannot ignore the leader if they intend to make inroads against competitors' shares. If the leaders tend to limit their media choices to spot and network television, then brands below the leaders must take this fact into consideration in planning their media strategies. One of the most important questions relating to competitors' media selections may have to be, "Should I fight it out with competitors in the media they use, or shall I seek media they don't use?"

The answer to this question depends on how much money a brand has budgeted to fight competitors. If a brand has a much smaller budget than its competitors, then its advertising may be lost among that of competitors who can buy much more advertising. But even if a brand has about the same budget as that of a leading competitor, another strategy consideration arises. It is possible that the brand in question is perceptively superior to the competitor's brand. Is it possible to demonstrate its superiority in advertisements? If so, the brand may not require as much money as its competitor because its superior qualities are so obvious. Advertisements may not have to work so hard to communicate essential information. Perhaps there may even be word-of-mouth advertising.

Still another consideration is whether a brand's advertising targets are the same as its competitiors'. If the targets are different, then strategy can be worked out using media different from that of competitors. If, however, a brand's targets are identical to competitors', then the brand's planner may have to use the same or similar media.

Finally, in considering competitors' strategies, it may be necessary to determine whether competitors are using their media effectively. If they are not, then even though a brand may have a smaller budget, it may succeed in the same media. For example, if a brand reaches the correct targets, but with not enough frequency to be optimally effective, another brand may use the same media more effectively if it can match or surpass its competitor's frequency.

Strategies When Budget Size Is Too Small

The size of the budget, as mentioned earlier, gives the planner a frame of reference regarding what can be done to attain a media objective. Media planners know what it costs to buy a low- or high-impact level in 25 or 150 markets for spot television, or for a lineup of 200 stations on network television. They know about how much it takes to buy a full-page ad and 100 GRPs in the top sixty markets, or 100 GRPs in outdoor billboards in fifty markets. The number of dollars available affects the choice of media and the depth of impact needed.

What strategies are available when there are insufficient funds to attain media objectives? There are at least four different courses of action, and possibly more.

1. Marketing objectives may have to be changed toward more modest and realizable goals for the amount of money allotted.
2. A series of priorities may have to be set up in which the greater part of the budget will have to be allocated to the most pressing priorities. Minor priorities will have to be ignored until more money is available.
3. It may be possible to obtain large discounts from media, which will spread a small amount of money farther. This may be done by limiting advertising to one medium. In addition, the flighting strategy could be used to spread a small amount of money over a longer period of time.
4. Finally, the client may be advised not to advertise until there is enough money. The media planner is often responsible for giving this advice. If the agency proceeds to buy media with a budget that is known to be inadequate, the client may later blame the agency for poor advertising performance.

Attempting to attain objectives with an inadequate budget is like fighting a war without enough troops, ammunition, or troop carriers. A high degree of realism is necessary to make a plan work.

Flexibility Needs

One factor that can affect the strategies and objectives of a media plan is the need for flexibility. It is often necessary to change media at the last minute because the marketing situation has changed or because new opportunities in different media become available. But this isn't possible unless care has been taken to select media that are flexible. Generally, local media such as newspapers, spot radio, and spot television are flexible because they can be purchased in many different ways and at different times. For example, spot television may be purchased nationally, regionally, or locally. Furthermore, it can be purchased in very small amounts (such as two or three spots a week), or it may be possible to buy the large volumes of time needed for a saturation campaign within a given market. Then too, spot television often can be cancelled at short notice, and sometimes reinstated (if there are time slots available).

Flexibility is needed most when the marketing situation is liable to change, requiring subsequent changes in media selection or use. Media selection for some large-budget products such as automobiles, however, may achieve flexibility in different ways. Instead of limiting themselves to local media, such advertisers can buy network television time or national magazine space in what is called an *umbrella pattern:* Through these two classes of media they reach a national audience, but they achieve flexibility through additional purchases of local media where they can make changes easily and relatively inexpensively. In most cases, however, advertisers cannot afford to buy both national and spot media and must limit themselves to those that are the most flexible.

Authority and Prestige

Authority and prestige are qualitative aspects of media that are difficult to measure but which, experts feel, have some effect on audiences' awareness or perception of advertising. Some media such as the *New Yorker* or *Fortune* are felt to have considerable amounts of both qualities, but because research in this area is so meager it isn't known precisely just how these, or other media, affect audience reaction to advertisements. That research has not been able satisfactorily to measure prestige, however, does not mean prestige is not a factor. While authority and prestige may not be the most important factors in media planning, they often become quite significant in helping the planner make a decision about two or more media vehicles that are very much alike.

Seasonal Impact on Media Effectiveness

In considering whether to use a medium, one might also look at how it performs during all seasons of the year. Summer months, for example, are a problem when planners use television because so many people are out-of-doors or on vacation and may miss advertising. Similarly, winter months may not be as effective for outdoor advertising. Newspaper and magazine reading, too, may vary to some extent during the summer months. Furthermore, there may be differences in the year-round effectiveness of local media. In some parts of the country, where there are extremely hot or cold temperatures, reading habits, as well as viewing or listening habits, influence local media effectiveness. So, in planning media, the degree to which media effectiveness fluctuates during key selling seasons becomes an important consideration.

Assembling Elements of a Plan

What information belongs in a media plan, and in how much detail? Where do various kinds of information belong? These questions can best be answered by using checklists that serve as the planner's reference. Checklists 12–1 and 12–2 which follow will help the reader understand what belongs in a media plan and where it should appear. The first is a subject checklist that simply calls attention to the contents of a plan. The second is an operational checklist showing how to proceed in the actual planning process. Chapter 13 is devoted to the presentation of an actual media plan prepared by a professional in a large advertising agency. This plan is a concrete example that shows how the contents appear and explains what has been done and/or why. The explanations appear in the form of notations after each major section.

Before preparing a media plan, planners must have a broad perspective on what they are trying to accomplish. A plan is more than a list of media selected and a schedule sheet. It is really part of the solution to a marketing problem—that part that will be solved through the selection and use of media. It is more than a listing of actions to be taken; it should be proof that the planner has made the best of all possible decisions, given the constraints of a budget, a creative strategy, and a brand whose qualities have been perceived by consumers to such an extent that the brand now occupies a given position in the marketplace.

It is, first of all, necessary to make sure that all important information, whether numerical data or text, is presented so as to show how the planner intends to use media to solve the problem(s). The reader of a plan should not have to ask too many questions about what is recommended or why. Second, each piece of information must be presented within an organizational framework that represents a logical progression from the most important decisions to the least important. Third, the document must be organized in such a way that it is easy to read and understand. Such organization may require the use of subheads in appropriate places, and the careful heading of all tables, charts, graphics, or whatever else is presented. Sources and dates of research should be noted.

Some advertising agencies place most of the statistical details in an appendix, while others place data in a logical position next to text. This is probably a matter of individual preference. It is also a good idea to provide a summary to give the busy executive a quick overview of decisions. The details can follow.

Although there is no one form for presenting media plans, there are similarities among all well-presented plans. The main goal is always that of achieving good communication, which will lead to good decision making.

CHECKLIST 12–1. Media Planning Subject Checklist

The following checklist shows the major considerations in planning media. It is a means of checking to see that everything of importance is included.
  I. Marketing Objectives
    A. Restatement of the marketing objectives in media terms
    B. If plan is for a new product, differentiation between introductory and sustaining periods (duration of each).
    C. Relative need for reach, frequency, impact, continuity (including seasonal aspects)
    D. Broad indication of how media strategy and creative strategy support each other:
        1. Are copy considerations necessary in media planning, such as need for sound, motion, demonstration, color?
        2. Will "word pictures" be enough?

        3.Is the story emotional or rational?

        4.Is the story complicated? Is there a need for space and time to tell the story? Will short messages be sufficient? Or, is some combination of short and long better?

  E. Brief indication of how merchandising and promotion strategy and media strategy support each other

  F. The consumer profile

      1.For the product class

      2.For the brand

  G. The profile of the brand's target audience

  H. Is the media strategy flexible, in terms of markets, timing, or ability to switch from medium to medium on short notice?

II. Media Summary

  A. Summary of proposed budgeting by media for the company's fiscal year

      1.By product

      2.By major company division

      3.By sales districts

  B. Where appropriate, differences with preceding year, with reasons for differences

  C. Sales objectives

  D. Media investment per unit of sales

      (For C and D, show for past year and for projected year. Sales projections should be reasonably conservative, so that there is a reasonable chance that they will be met and probably exceeded.)

  E. Reasons, in broad terms, for major media recommendations. How do major elements in the media plan meet the specified media objectives?

  F. Is it possible to test media program in each major medium or market area?

  G. Merchandising support that might be expected of media

  H. Does the media program have any marks of originality, inventiveness, ingenuity?

III. Stand-by Plan

  A. What should be done, if during the year:

      1.Sales expectations are not being met. How should plans be changed or reduced?

      2.Sales expectations are being exceeded. How should advantage be taken of this situation?

      3.A major competitor takes some serious anticipated action, such as introduction of a new and improved product, with certain predictable results.

IV. Media History

  A. Media history over at least the past five years, showing comparison with sales trends

      1.By product

      2.For competition

  B. Information on media tests previously conducted

      1.Nature of tests

      2.Products

      3.Places

      4.Dollars invested, actual and per thousand population (indicate regular media used during that period)

      5.Results

V. Commentary for Subject Brands

  A. For each medium logically a candidate for brand advertising:

      1.Advantages for subject product (document as necessary)

      2.Disadvantages (document)

  B. Indication as to how chosen media contribute to attainment of objectives, and where each falls short (document)

  C. How composite media mix meets brand objectives (document)

  D. For major rejected media, the reasons for rejection (document)

VI. Media Specifics

  A. Business publications

      1.Editorial

      2.Circulation

      3.Total market potential

      4.Advertiser acceptance

      5.Space cost

      6.Services available to advertisers

  B. Consumer magazines

      1.Audience buying potential

2. Advertiser acceptance
3. Space cost
4. Services available to advertisers
5. Editorial
6. Circulation and audience
7. Audience composition—characteristics
C. Direct mail
1. Source of names
2. Set-up of list
3. Filing method
4. Maintaining accuracy
D. Newspapers
1. Market and economic factors
2. Circulation
3. Reader characteristics
4. Editorial
5. Advertiser acceptance
6. Newspaper services available
E. Outdoor advertising
1. The outdoor plant
a. Distribution and coverage, visibility of showing, traffic and circulation, rates and costs, etc.
b. Type of panels: twenty-four-sheet, junior panels, painted bulletins, rotary plan, lighting, embellishments
2. The market
a. Size of market, economic factors, special market characteristics
F. Point of purchase
1. Marketing factors
2. Planning, including materials to be used
3. Merchandising and distribution
4. Technical considerations and finding the right producer
G. Radio
1. The market—area, size, economic factors, special market characteristics
2. The station—coverage, audience characteristics, programming and ratings, station identification, policies, facilities, time cost, advertiser acceptance, station services available
H. Television (network)
1. Day vs. night
2. Program ownership vs. participation
3. Children vs. teens vs. adults
4. Type of program: drama, comedy, documentary, etc.
5. Time period
a. Sets in use
b. Seasonal variation
c. Lead-in and lead-out program
d. Competitive programs
e. Cost per thousand
f. Length of commitment
6. Details (by season where appropriate)
a. Period of sponsorship
b. Name of program, if known
c. Number of commercials per week
d. Expected ratings (household, adult male, adult female, etc.)
e. Expected cost per thousand
f. Expected reach, frequency
g. Expected net coverage of a given schedule over a four-week period
7. Market lists
a. Markets covered and not covered
b. If necessary, markets where coverage is expected to be weak, because of delayed broadcasts or other reasons
c. Necessity of supplemental coverage
d. Whether markets over a certain size are covered by originating market or from outside

    I. Television (spot)
       1.The market
         a. Market area and size
         b. Economic factors
         c. Special market characteristics
       2.The station
         a. Coverage / audience characteristics
         b. Programming and ratings
         c. Station identification, policies, facilities
         d. Time cost
         e. Advertiser acceptance
         f. Station services available
    J. Transit advertising
       1.The market—size, economic factors, special characteristics
       2.The medium—circulation and traffic, audience characteristics, the system, advertiser acceptance, operating procedures and policies, reproduction of car cards and posters
    K. General considerations in respect to media
       1.Investments by market in each medium
       2.Cost per thousand for estimated noters, or thousand exposures, or thousand households reached, or other measure appropriate to the medium
       3.Conversion of medium's audience into units of consumption of advertised product and medium's cost per unit of product
       4.Relationship of proposed schedule to audience objectives
       5.Use of local media—what coverage is also obtained from national media
       6.Competitive advertising—budgets and media used

CHECKLIST 12-2. Media Planning Operational Checklist

Some elements in the subject checklist often are not pertinent for a given media plan. The *operational* checklist shows what is most likely to be required for a typical media plan and in about what order items should appear.

    I. Marketing Objectives and Strategies That Relate to Media
        These are usually summarized rather than being presented in detail. Presumably, they already have been explained in detail in another document, the marketing plan.
    II. Copy Strategy Statements and How Media Will Support or Relate to Them
        A copy strategy is not always a part of a media plan. If there is any special reason for including it, such as to clarify decisions of media selected, or media used in a certain way, then it belongs here.
    III. A Summary of the Entire Plan
        This section allows an executive a quick overview of what actions are recommended so that the full scope of the plan is visible. Often the details occupy so many pages that it is difficult to get an overview of the plan easily.
    IV. Media Objectives
        A. A clear statement of each objective is necessary, using enough words to make them meaningful
        B. Statements should show precisely how media objectives relate to marketing objectives and / or strategies
        C. Objectives should cover the following topics as a minimum:
            1. Specification of target audiences (in demographics and psychographics if pertinent)
            2. Budget available and any restrictions on its use
            3. Reach and frequency needed
            4. Effective reach levels needed
            5. Continuity needed
            6. Pattern of monthly and yearly continuity
            7. Special geographic weighting needed
            8. Merchandisability of media if necessary
            9. Flexibility needed
           10. Degree to which media will have to support promotions

         11. Creative strategy implications

    D. A rationale for decisions must be included

V. Media Strategy

    A. Each strategy must be stated clearly

    B. Each strategy should be related to one (or more) media objectives

    C. Why certain other obvious strategies were *not* used should be explained

    D. Strategies should include (as a minimum):

        1. Media classes selected (e.g., network television, or magazines)

        2. Strategy for allocating the budget to geographic areas (roll-out vs. national introduction; spot only or national plus spot heavy-up)

        3. Allocation of budget to media classes (dollars and percentages of total)

        4. Allocation of budget by months and/or quarters of year; introductory vs. sustaining period strategy

        5. Reach and frequency levels desired by months and/or quarters of the year

        6. Effective reach and frequency levels per typical month

        7. Size of the primary and secondary target markets

        8. Weighting of strategic targets

        9. Geographical weighting requirements that must be used

      10. Cost-per-thousand standards, if required

      11. Explanations of why a strategy is different from previous ones

      12. Specifications of the size of media units to be used (15-, 30-, or 60-second commercials; full or fractional pages)

      13. Criteria to be used for selecting or scheduling media (need for flighting)

      14. Relationship of strategy to that of competitors, with special emphasis on certain key brands that must be dealt with specifically

      15. A rationale for each strategy statement

VI. Media Plan Details (and Documentation)

    A. A statement of criteria for determining media values

    B. Proof that vehicles selected are the best of all alternatives (using media value criteria) and for the budget (data plus words)

    C. Data showing net reach and frequency for targets reached by a combination of all vehicles, including frequency distributions

    D. Data showing gross impressions for a combination of all vehicles, especially for target audiences

    E. Costs per thousand shown for all vehicles selected or considered

    F. Cost summary tables showing each vehicle, number of times used per month, cost per insertion, and total cost per month

    G. Yearly cost summary

    H. Yearly flow chart (or schedule) showing vehicles, weeks of insertions, reaches, frequencies, and costs per month for the year

    I. Any other data that will help buyers implement the plan

VII. Overview

    A. Is the plan well organized? Is it easy to find specific information desired?

    B. Are topics delineated with appropriate headings?

    C. Are all tables of data headed properly so as to explain precisely what the data are about?

    D. Is there a Table of Contents with page numbers?

    E. Is there a review of key marketing objectives and/or strategies?

    F. If data are voluminous, have some been relegated to a special documentary section?

    G. Are there any weaknesses in the logic or reasoning of the plan?

The Media Flowchart (or Schedule)

Special consideration ought to be given to the flowchart (also called a schedule sheet) of a media plan. A *flowchart* is a graphic presentation of all major actions that comprise a media plan. It is presented in notation form (or a form of shorthand) enabling the planner to place a great deal of information in a small amount of space.

The most important purpose of a flowchart is to provide everyone involved—the planner, the media buyer, the account executive, the client—with a bird's-eye view of the entire plan of action. Elsewhere in the plan are myriads of details explaining what actions are to be taken and why, but the flowchart places all actions in a single, easy-to-see frame of reference showing the flow of media purchases throughout the year. Some planners refer to this flow as a *pattern* of media delivery. The pattern is clearly discernible and makes it relatively easy to compare one part with another.

It is important, then, to make this flowchart understandable and not to omit anything that is essential to this bird's-eye view. For example, it would overly complicate a flowchart to list the number of targets reached in raw numbers, but it is useful to show the reach and frequency in percentages. It is not necessary to show the dollars spent in media each week of the year, but it is useful to show how much will be spent by each month or quarter of the year. If quarterly figures are not important, then monthly figures should be shown.

Essentials of a Flowchart

Although different advertising agencies may organize their flowcharts differently, there are some basic elements that are common to almost every flowchart:

1. The name of the brand and the year the plan covers should be at the top.
2. All months of the year should be aligned across the top of the page, usually placed horizontally on the page so that more space will be available. Some media planners prepare their flowcharts on large sheets of paper and reduce them photographically to an $8^1/_2$'' x 11'' size so that they can be assimilated easily in a bound document.
    a. The month that is shown first is usually the first of the fiscal, or financial, year. Some companies have fiscal years that begin with months other than January. At times, the first month listed may be the month in which the first media vehicles are to be bought. This is purely a matter of judgment.
    b. The months may be divided by quarters if the planning is done on a quarterly basis. If not, each of the months is listed next to each other across a page.
3. Each week of the year should be given a separate column under each month. Months with five weeks should contain five columns instead of four. It is debatable whether or not each week should be numbered from 1 to 52, or numbered on the basis of the first day of each week. Some media plans do not show any week numbers.

4. The left side of the page should contain media information.
    a. Each medium class used (by daypart if pertinent).
    b. Length of commercial or size of page and color (for example, thirty-second commercial, or $1/2$ page/four color).
    c. If spot television is used, each market group should be shown, and the number of markets in each group. (This number will refer to a market list that appears elsewhere in a plan.)
    d. If market groups receive different GRPs or TRPs (target rating points), this fact should be listed at the left or in a prominent place.
    e. A row labeled *reach*, and one underneath labeled *frequency*, should appear somewhere, often placed at the left side, bottom. If gross rating points or target rating points are important, then this information should appear below reach and frequency rows. If different geographic areas are to receive varying weights, then each area should be listed with a row underneath for reach, another for frequency, and another for the appropriate gross rating points (if important).
    f. At the bottom there usually is a row showing media expenditures by month and/or quarter of the year. At the extreme right side, these should be summed.
    g. At the very bottom, percentages of total media expenditures are usually shown by month and/or quarter with a 100 percent total at the extreme right.
5. Each week of advertising should be blocked-in. Some agencies eliminate all the column lines from their flow chart, so their flowcharts would show the number of weeks of advertising as a rectangle. Inside the rectangle should be the number of GRPs or TRPs to be used per average week. The length of the rectangle should cover the number of weeks of advertising required. Some planners place a small numeral above the rectangle to show how many weeks of advertising will occur. Such a numeral is not needed if the length of time covers the entire year.

The reader should study Figures 12–1, 12–2, and 12–3 for examples of different kinds of flowcharts prepared for different kinds of media plans. No matter which format is used, it should contain all the essential details. Above all, it should be easy to read and understand without the use of excessive explanatory symbols or other notations.

FIGURE 12–1.   A Sample Media Plan Flowchart for Television

Network Television

Day

25 Women
18–49
TRPs/wk
24 Weeks

Cost: $1,323.6

Late Fringe

43 Women
18–49
GRPs/wk
24 Weeks

Cost: $4,281.3

TOTAL
COST: $5,604.8

FIGURE 12-2. A Sample Media Plan Flowchart for Magazines

Total Year 75/4.2

*Adults 18-49 with household income $15,000 +

FIGURE 12–3.   A Sample Media Plan Flowchart for Specialized Publications

QUESTIONS FOR DISCUSSION

1. Briefly explain why it is so important to relate marketing objectives and strategies to media objectives.
2. What are the consequences of writing very short, general statements of objectives versus detailed, specific objectives?
3. Briefly explain the difference between a media objective and a strategy.
4. It is widely believed that not all media objectives and strategies are of equal importance. How should a planner take these inequalities into consideration and note them in the plan?
5. What strategies might be used when there are insufficient funds available to meet media objectives?
6. Why do many media planners prepare alternative media plans to show a client, if their first plan is presumed to be the best of all alternatives?
7. In preparing a flowchart, which month should be listed first on the chart (usually placed to the extreme left)? Why?

SELECTED READINGS

Advertising Age, "Pulsing Schedules of Ads an Effective Technique," October 20, 1969, p. 270.

Frankel, Lester R., "Where Does Effective Exposure End and Irritation Begin?" *Media/Scope,* November 1957, pp. 40–41.

Gomer, Frank J., "Problems in Media Planning and How to Solve Them," *Media/Scope,* October 1963, pp. 49–73.

Greene, Jerome, "Using Media Research to Help Build and Appraise the Media Plan," *Perspectives in Advertising Management,* Association of National Advertisers, Inc., April 1969, pp. 173–77.

Hays, Henry, "How to Have More Fun Writing a Media Plan," *Marketing and Media Decisions,* December 1986, pp. 91–94.

Jones, Richard P., "Building and Appraising the Media Strategy," *Perspectives in Advertising Management,* Association of National Advertisers, Inc., April 1969, pp. 185–95.

Kanner, Bernard, "Building and Appraising the Media Strategy," *Media/Scope,* September 1965, pp. 157–65.

Krugman, Herbert, "What Makes Advertising Effective?" *Harvard Business Review,* March–April 1975, pp. 96–103.

Maneloveg, Herbert, "How Media Men Buy Media—Six Factors for a Good Plan," in "The New World of Advertising," *Advertising Age,* November 21, 1973, p. 62.

McCann-Erickson, *A Point of View on Advertising Strategy* (White Paper I) October 1972.

Media Decisions, "Why Reach for Frequency?" June 1969, pp. 36-37.

Media Decisions, "The Name-Callers," April 1973, p. 66.

Ochs, Malcolm B., "The Fight for Awareness," *Media/Scope,* July 1966, pp. 58-61.

Papazian, Edward, "Creative Media—A Time and Place for Everything," *Media Decisions,* March 1973, p. 12.

Papazian, Edward, "Structuring Media Plans for Maximum Effect," *Media Decisions,* March 1974, pp. 12-14.

Papazian, Edward, "Bottom Up Planning," *Media Decisions,* August 1978, pp. 16-18.

Ray, Michael, Sawyer, A. G., and Strong, E. C., "Frequency Effects Revisited,"

Journal of Advertising Research, February 1971, pp. 14–20.

Roth, Paul, *How to Plan Media,* Media and Market Decisions (Publisher), 1974.

Surmanek, James, "Let Reps in on Media Planning," *Advertising Age,* September 11, 1978, p. 78.

Vedder, Blair, "Smart Media Buying Begins with a Plan," *Media/Scope*, October 1960, pp. 49–56.

Vedder, Blair, "An Outline for Media Plans," *Media/Scope*, August 1961, pp. 69–71.

13

An Annotated Media Plan

This chapter is intended to help readers visualize a media plan as created by a professional planner in a large advertising agency. It is assumed by this time that the reader will know the concepts and terminology used in planning and therefore be able to easily follow and understand the plan. Because this plan was made for a brand product in a highly competitive market, a number of changes were made in it to keep certain proprietary information confidential: the brand is called X, the product category is not identified, and certain pieces of information have been eliminated, such as a creative strategy statement. (Note that network and spot television costs reflect 1986–87 trends.)

All other essentials are included and explained in annotated remarks on the corresponding facing pages. The plan has been divided into more parts than the original plan contained, but these parts should help the reader more easily understand the underlying thinking that went into the planning. In addition, each notation has been coded with a number which refers back to the same number in the plan.

PLAN

[1] ## PART 1
Brand X Media Plan (Next Year) Summary

[2] ### A. TASK
1. Maintain the current strength of Brand X franchise

[3] ### B. AVAILABLE FUNDS

Total advertising budget	$15,370,000
Less production	1,420,000
Working media budget	$13,950,000

[4] ### C. MEDIA PLAN
1. Objectives
   a. Direct advertising toward current users
   b. Maintain current share
   c. Encourage ongoing use of the brand
[5] 2. Strategy
   a. Direct impressions toward all women proportionate to their Brand X volume contribution, with emphasis on the primary targets: women aged 35-plus, living in $15,000-plus households, in A counties.
   b. Allocate media dollars in proportion to current Brand X sales volume by market, while maintaining competitive levels in high-volume Brand X areas.
   c. Achieve at least a 75 reach with an average frequency of 5 among total women in key areas. Concomitantly, seek a reach of 50 among women exposed at least three times within any given four weeks of advertising.
   d. Distribute advertising pressure according to quarterly volume contribution.
   e. Maintain financial and geographic flexibility.
   f. Provide continuous support within the quarterly investment allocation once the reach/frequency goals are met.

NOTES

Notes on Part 1—Summary

(Numbers refer to same numbers in plan)

[1] This summary is a quick overview of the entire plan. In a typical media plan, the exact year would appear in place of the phrase "next year."

[2] This states one important marketing objective: to maintain the current strength of the Brand X franchise. The term *franchise* is not used here to mean a franchising business, such as McDonald's hamburgers. Rather, it means "the brand's usage or financial position in the marketplace."

[3] The available funds statement breaks down the budget into media and production costs. Production costs can be estimated before media costs, if the creative strategy has been devised and the numbers of broadcast commercials and print ads have been spelled out. Television production costs normally include cost of studio time, sets, crew, director's fees, special effects, casting, editing, music, as well as initial talent fees and residual talent payments. It should also be noted that the budget is one of the most significant constraints on media objectives and strategy and therefore must be discussed early in the planning process.

[4,5] Objectives and strategies have been reduced to simple declarative statements here. Later on, however, more will be said about each.

[4] It is important to note the nature of objectives. User demographics have been spelled out earlier. Although it usually is a part of marketing objectives, market share here is listed as a media objective, which is acceptable. Likewise, the encouragement of ongoing use of the brand (item C1c) is related to creative objectives and therefore might appear in a different place in other media plans.

[5] Strategies C2a to C2g are very specific and cover parts of the recommended media strategy.

[5] **C2a.** Media targets are identified first. Two kinds of targets are to be reached: one target is broadly based and consists of all women. A second target consists of those demographic segments that have greater sales potential because they purchase more. They will be given special treatment.

[5] **C2b.** While the targets in C2a were based on personal demographics, this category considers geographic demographics. The identification of both types of targets is usually necessary for media planning. Advertising impressions are to be delivered proportionately to sales potential in each area.

[5] **C2c.** Reach and frequency requirements in key market areas are spelled out here. A 75 reach and a 5 average frequency are to be attained. Although the planner did not specify the time period for such reach and frequency, it is presumed to be for a four-week period. The planner did specify an effective reach goal in a four-week period of 50 with a frequency of 3 or more. It is important to remember that this reach is for women targets only.

[5] **C2d.** This is an allocation strategy and explains that the budget is to be proportionately distributed according to the volume of sales made in each quarter of a year. If the first quarter of the year accounts for 27 percent of sales, it would receive about 27 percent of the advertising budget.

[5] **C2e.** The need for flexibility influences the strategy. Although reasons for wanting it are not given, presumably flexibility is needed to make quick media changes if sales opportunities or problems develop. Competitors' activities often cause a company to make changes in media plans after the plan has been devised. When the plan is flexible, it can be changed easily.

PLAN

g. Employ media vehicles that are compatible with the copy requirements and overall brand image.

6   3. Plan

	Dollars	Percent
Day Network TV	$3,960,000	28.3
Late Network TV	3,869,000	27.7
Fringe Spot TV	6,121,000	44.0
TOTAL	$13,950,000	100.0

7   D. DELIVERY
1. Demographics—Slightly underdeliver upper income category as a result of concentrating in television.
2. Geographics—Overspend spot TV markets by 11 percent in order to maintain competitive posture in key franchise areas.
3. National Effort—Network television represents 56 percent of total media budget.
4. Reach/Frequency—Delivery achieves goal in key markets.
5. Allocation Requirements—Generally follows the quarterly sales volume.

8   E. TASK ACCOMPLISHMENT
1. The plan accomplishes the task of providing support to maintain current franchise of the brand.
2. Minor deviations from demographic and geographic targets result from optimizing total plan delivery.

PART 2
Marketing and Copy Background

9   A. OVERVIEW
For the preceding year, Brand X had a severe business decline. Brand performance showed loss of momentum and was characterized by market share erosion, volume misses, and weakened distribution.

10   B. OBJECTIVE
Stabilize the franchise in key marketing areas.
    National share and volume objectives:

Share:	6.0
Volume:	3,606

11   C. MARKETING STRATEGY
1. Allocate marketing funds according to the brand's consumption.
2. Continue to place heavy emphasis on promotion, especially consumer.
3. Implement a program of case rates designed to put Brand X back in the feature cycle.

12   D. COPY STRATEGY
(Omitted for reasons of confidentiality)

NOTES

[5] **C2g.** Some media vehicles may not be suitable for a given copy strategy, even though they have a large number of targets in their audience. The brand image must be suitable to the media selected.

[6] This is an expenditure analysis in both raw dollars and percentages. Media plans must show expenditures in both forms to enable easy analysis.

[7] **D1.** Delivery analysis explains how well the plan's statistical data prove that the plan reaches the objectives set out for it. For example, D1 explains that the plan will slightly underdeliver upper-income targets. Slight underdelivery is not considered to be an error.

[7] **D2.** It also points out that the budget will be overspent by 11 percent in spot TV markets and why.

[7] **D3.** Network television accounts for 56 percent of the media budget.

[7] **D4. D5.** Reach and frequency are attained as planned, and expenditures follow sales volume by quarters, also as planned.

[8] This is an evaluation statement based on judgment. It explains that the plan accomplishes the tasks set for it and why there are minor deviations. It is important to note that the planner tries to anticipate questions and answer them before they can be asked.

Notes on Part 2—Marketing and Copy Background

[9] This is a brief overview of the marketing situation of Brand X for the past three years. Its market share was declining, its sales volume was not reaching goals set for it, and the number of stores distributing the product was declining.

[10] This is a marketing objective in terms of market share and sales volume. The number 3,606 refers to millions of units sold.

[11] Marketing strategies are stated here. Strategies C1 and C2 are obvious. Marketing strategy C3 is to build distribution and is to be accomplished by giving retailers a higher mark-up on cases purchased as an incentive for stocking the brand.

[12] The copy strategy has been omitted here because it would have revealed the name of the brand. But the categories in the copy strategy may be stated. They were: copy objective, definition of prime prospects, competitive stance, key benefits, support, copy tone, and manner of presentation. These are components of creative strategy.

PLAN

PART 3
Marketing Objective/Rationale

[13] Objective: Direct advertising toward current users to capitalize on current strengths.

Rationale: The goal is to maintain share and encourage ongoing use of the brand.

Next year is expected to be a year of intense competitive pressure when Brand A (Brand X's main competitor) dominates the product category with its key selling features and Brand B dominates consumer promotion activity.

At this time, no product improvements for Brand X are planned for next year.

[14] PART 4
Media Strategy/Rationale

[15] Part 4A—Prospect Definition

Direct impressions toward all women proportionate to their Brand X volume contribution, with emphasis on the primary Brand X targets.

Primary targets are women with the following characteristics:

1. Age 35-plus
2. In $15,000-plus households
3. Living in A counties

Demographic details are provided in Table 13–1.

TABLE 13–1.   [17] Demographic Targets

		U.S. Women[18] (%)	Brand X[19] Volume (%)	[20] Index
Total Women		100.0	100.0	100
Age: Total		100.0	100.0	100
	18–24	18.0	13.9	77
	25–34	20.4	17.9	88
	35–49	23.0	21.3	93
	50-plus	38.6	46.9	122
Nonworking		56.6	60.4	107
	18–24	8.4	6.0	71
	25–34	10.4	9.7	93
	35–49	11.1	11.0	99
	50-plus	26.7	33.7	126
Working		43.4	39.6	91
	18–24	9.6	7.9	82
	25–34	10.0	8.2	82
	35–49	11.9	10.3	87
	50-plus	11.9	13.2	111

[16] Source: MRCA Demographic Analysis.

(continued)

NOTES

Notes on Part 3—Marketing Objective/Rationale

[13] The main objective is to retain present users. Ordinarily, such an objective is listed as a creative responsibility or perhaps a marketing responsibility. Essentially, all that media can do to keep present customers is to deliver the message to the correct targets with a certain amount of repetition. However, because media do at least play some role in helping attain this objective, it may be considered appropriate here.

Another media objective is to capitalize on current strengths. The comment made earlier applies here as well. Media cannot capitalize on current strengths, but copy can.

The reader, therefore, has to recognize that the planner from this particular advertising agency is not following the recommendations of writing objectives as presented in this text. The planner's objectives are communication-oriented, and as such they are copy objectives rather than media objectives. An expected increase in competitive pressure is also mentioned here. Although detailed analysis is not provided, it is assumed that the media planner has completed a detailed competitive brand and category media/promotion spending analysis, and found sufficient data to warrant projected increase pressure from Competitor A.

Notes on Part 4—Media Strategy/Rationale

[14] This part of the plan consists of strategy details and rationale, much of it fairly obvious statistical data.

Notes on Part 4A—Prospect Definition

[15] This definition first appeared in the summary [5] but is spelled out in greater detail here. There are two bases for selecting media targets (prospects): (a) the volume of Brand X that was purchased (as shown in percentages in [19]), and (b) the index numbers that relate volume-usage to population distribution by demographics (as shown in [20]).

[16] The source of statistical data is at the bottom of Table 13–1.

[17,18,19,20] A study of demographic usage and index numbers shows some interesting data. The largest index of users is for women, aged 50-plus, with income of $15,000-plus, who live in A counties. Why, then, did the planner select women aged 35-plus instead of only those aged 50-plus? The reason is that the target market would have been too small (only 38.6 percent of U.S. women are age 50 or over). By increasing the primary target segment to all women over 35, the population base has now been increased to 61.6 percent (23.0 + 38.6 = 61.6 percent) and brand volume to 68.2 percent. Why also were *all* women considered a target? It is probable that the client wanted a very broad target rather than a narrow one, and all Brand X users are to be reached, even though there are proportionately fewer Brand X users in the younger demographic segments.

PLAN

TABLE 13-1.   (continued)

		U.S. Women[18] (%)	Brand X[19] Volume (%)	[20] Index
Household Income	Under $8,000	38.1	28.6	75
	$8,000–$14,999	34.5	33.0	96
	$15,000-plus	27.4	38.4	140
Household Size	1–2	39.9	38.0	95
	3–4	35.8	37.7	105
	5-plus	24.3	24.3	100
County Size	A	40.9	51.0	125
	B	26.2	24.1	92
	C	19.4	17.3	89
	D	13.5	7.6	56

[21] Part 4B—Media Allocation

Allocate media dollars in accordance with the current Brand X sales volume of each market.

The media budgets of the individual markets will be prorated to the estimated volume contribution of each area. However, in the interest of strengthening the Brand X franchise in key markets and also recognizing the competitive spending environment, additional weight will be placed in the following areas. To the degree affordable, the following minimum spending versus Competitor A will be sought:

Eastern Region	85%
Detroit District	85%
Chicago District	65%
Los Angeles District	65%

Table 13–2 shows in detail the geographic targets based on Brand X volume.

TABLE 13-2.   [22] Geographic Targets

	U.S.[23] Women (%)	Brand X[24] Volume (%)	Brand X[25] Development Index (BDI)
Eastern Region			
Boston	5.28	6.60	125
New York	9.42	13.04	138
Philadelphia	7.75	13.34	172
Syracuse	3.38	5.91	175
Youngstown	4.78	6.55	137
Total Eastern	30.61	45.44	148
Southern Region			
Charlotte	5.55	3.83	69
Atlanta	4.03	3.24	80
Jacksonville	3.89	3.08	79
Detroit	4.76	8.52	179
Cincinnati	5.44	4.42	81
Total Southern	23.67	23.09	98

Source: A. C. Nielsen Company.

(continued)

NOTES

Notes on Part 4B—Media Allocation

[21] This part of the media plan deals with strategies for weighting advertising by geographical area. The main strategy is to allocate the media budget proportionately to the sales volume contributed by each of four sales regions: Eastern, Central, Southern, and Western.

However, another part of the strategy is to add extra weight in those geographical markets that have done best in sales. A study of [25] shows that all markets in the Eastern Region have indices over 100 and therefore are among the best in the country. Detroit also has an index over 100. Chicago and Los Angeles do not have exceptionally high index numbers but do have large volumes of sales as shown in [24]. The planner, therefore, wants to add extra weight in these key markets. The goal is to add 85 percent more dollars than Competitor A in the Eastern Region and Detroit and 65 percent more in Chicago and Los Angeles. Although the planner does not show competitors' media expenditures, it is assumed that estimates are available. Also note that the extra spending depends on "the degree affordable." This means that the extra money can be spent if it is available after other priorities have been met.

[22,23,24,25] These figures show sales volume and Brand Development Indices. Such data provide the basis for the decisions in [21].

PLAN

TABLE 13–2.   (continued)

	U.S.[23] Women (%)	Brand X[24] Volume (%)	Brand X[25] Development Index (BDI)
Central Region			
Chicago	6.44	5.35	83
St. Louis	3.57	2.91	82
Memphis	4.65	2.89	62
Kansas City	3.92	2.46	63
Dallas	6.46	3.60	56
Total Central	25.04	17.21	69
Western Region			
Minneapolis	4.15	2.01	48
Denver	2.40	1.30	54
Portland	2.77	1.80	65
San Francisco	4.01	2.67	67
Los Angeles	7.35	6.48	88
Total Western	20.68	14.26	69
Total U.S.	100.00	100.00	100

Part 4C—Performance / Delivery Goals

[26] A. Total Reach / Average Frequency

Provide at least 75 reach with an average frequency of 5 among total women in the key areas.

B. Effective Reach

Concomitantly, seek a four-week reach goal of 50 among women who have been exposed at least three times.

	Four-Week Reach / Frequency Goals
Total Reach / Average Frequency	75 / 5.0
Effective Reach	50 / 3 +

[27] C. Distribute Advertising Pressure according to Quarterly Volume Contribution

Quarter	Volume (%)
April–June	24
July–September	23
October–December	26
January–March	27
Total	100

[28] D. Maintain Flexibility

It is recommended that all media activity be scheduled to run at the same time and that a substantial portion of the budget be placed in flexible media so the Brand can quickly react to:

1. Competitive activity
2. Key promotional events

NOTES

Notes on Part 4C—Performance/Delivery Goals

[26] Communication goals are listed in A as reach/frequency and effective reach.

In determining communication goals, it is important to note estimated competitive delivery levels that should be taken into consideration. Here again, category confidentiality prohibits explicit details, but it is assumed that the planner has a good understanding of competitors' delivery activity.

The use of the term *communication goals* tells the reader how the planner perceives reach and frequency. Both serve as controllers of message distribution: reach controls dispersion, while frequency controls the degree of repetition.

The reader should note that a reach of 75 and a frequency of 5 is for total women, in certain parts of the country only. It is for women in the key marketing areas mentioned in Part 4B—"Media Allocation." The levels of 75 and 5 have been arrived at on the basis of experience and judgment.

The *effective* reach and frequency is different: 50 and 3 + . These levels come from an analysis of a frequency distribution (see [37]). The reader should note that an effective frequency of three is based on a judgment about the specific needs of Brand X. So the reach percentages at a frequency of 3 + were determined (from the frequency distribution) to be 50.

[27] Quarterly distribution of sales volume is shown. Media planners use sales volume data by month or by quarter of the year in making budget allocation decisions. Most planners use both.

[28] The need for flexibility is explained here. Flexible media are usually local media such as spot television, spot radio, newspapers—media which can be purchased or cancelled quickly.

PLAN

[29]   E. Continuous Support within the Quarterly Investment Allocation Will Be Sought Once the Reach/Frequency Goals Are Achieved.

Continuous advertising is desirable for the following reasons: (a) there is sufficient evidence of advertising recall erosion among consumers during nonadvertising periods; (b) the daily traffic in stores includes Brand X purchases; (c) pressure against competition should be maintained. Therefore, as soon as reach/frequency goals are achieved, advertising periods will be extended within the boundaries of the quarterly investment allocation. A total of thirty-six weeks of advertising has been set as the minimum.

[30]   F. Employ Media Vehicles That Are Compatible with the Copy Requirements and Overall Brand Image.

A balance of highly efficient and effective media will be sought to ensure the most desirable combination of copy and media.

[31] ## PART 5
Description of Media Plan

[32] The next fiscal year, the Brand X media plan will use television as the sole medium for the following reasons:

1. The intrusive nature of the medium makes it the most effective vehicle for communicating the Brand X message.
2. It is highly efficient in reaching the target audience.
3. On judgment, at the current budget level, concentrating efforts on the primary medium should maximize the effectiveness of communication.

[33] Daytime network television will provide the base upon which other national and local media efforts will be structured. This medium is the most efficient vehicle for reaching a broad national base of adult women.

[34] Late night network television will be used to extend reach nationally and increase the delivery of women in the higher income category ($15,000-plus).

[35] Fringe spot television will be implemented to align media to targets and, tactically, to furnish additional support for Brand X's markets against competitive pressures.

Both network and spot television will be scheduled to run at the same time in order to maximize advertising pressure.

PART 6
Recommended Plan

Part 6A—Flowchart

The major recommendations of the media plan are summarized in a yearlong flowchart, as shown in Figure 13–1.

NOTES

[29] This part of the strategy discusses the use of continuity in relation to reach and frequency *per quarter*. The planner sets reach and frequency as a higher priority than continuity. But once the reach and frequency levels have been reached, good continuity should be attained within a thirty-six-week period. The flow chart located at [36] shows a flighting pattern of continuity in which there are five time periods in which a hiatus occurs, not counting the weeks before advertising starts and after it ends. These are brief, two-week hiatuses. So the pattern of continuity is fairly extensive within the thirty-six-week period, from May to the middle of March the following year.

[30] The requirement for the kinds of vehicles to be selected in the plan is clear: Use only those that best convey the copy and the brand image.

Notes on Part 5—Description of Media Plan

[31,32,33,34,35] The description of the media plan consists of statements about which classes of media and kinds of vehicles should be selected and the rationale for selecting each. Essentially, television—network and spot—is recommended with network being restricted to daytime and late night (fringe time).

PLAN

FIGURE 13–1. [36] Recommended Plan—Flowchart

Television	June Quarter			September Quarter			December Quarter			March Quarter			Total Year
	Apr.	May	June	July	Aug.	Sept.	Oct.	Nov.	Dec.	Jan.	Feb.	Mar.	
		9		1	4	4	5	4	4	5		4	
Day Network :30		35 WGRP/Wk.			35 W	35 WGRP/Wk.		35 W		35 W		35 W	
Late Network :30		14 WGRP/Wk.			14 W	14 W	25 W		25 W	25 W		25 W	
Combination Fringe :30 45.8% U.S. Women 62.2% Target		82 WGRP/Wk.			82 W	82 W	98 W		98 W	98 W		98 W	
Reach/Frequency													
Spot Area													
Total Women		81/5.1			81/5.1			84/5.9			85/5.8		
3+		53			53			59			60		
$15M+		77/4.5			75/4.3			80/5.3			80/5.2		
3+		47			44			53			52		
Remainder U.S.													
Total Women		57/3.4			57/3.5			61/3.8			63/3.7		
3+		27			27			32			33		
$15M+		51/2.9			51/2.8			56/3.5			56/3.4		
3+		21			21			27			27		
Day Network		$965.0M*			$867.1M			$1,069.0M			$946.2M		$3,847.7M
Late Network		718.3M			662.1M			1,471.0M			1,079.8M		3,931.2M
Comb. Fringe		1,399.7M			1,400.3M			1,686.5M			1,684.6M		6,171.1M
Total		$3,083.0M			$2,929.5M			$4,226.9M			$3,710.6M		$13,950.0M
Percent		22.1%			21.0%			30.3%			26.6%		100.0%

*M = 000.

NOTES

Notes on Part 6A—Flowchart

[36] Note carefully how this flowchart has been arranged. It is the source of a great deal of important information. These are its key components:

1. The year has been divided into fifty-two weekly segments, which in turn have been divided into quarters, with the first fiscal quarter (April–June) coming first. This first fiscal quarter could start in January or any other month, depending upon the client's fiscal year.

2. Vehicles that are to be used are shown at the left hand side, followed by the lengths of commercials, which are all :30s (or thirty-second commercials). The terms "Day Network," and "Late Network" mean that commercials will be purchased in these dayparts. "Combination Fringe :30" means early and late fringe daypart placements of commercials.

   The 45.8 percent (underneath "Combination Fringe :30") refers to the percent of total U.S. Women in primary markets, and 62.2 percent refers to the sales volume that these women account for. The reason these two percentages are listed is to remind those who read the flowchart that the planner wants to concentrate advertising in primary markets as a means of stimulating more sales. In other words, "sell where the product already has sold well." (See these data in their marketing context, on Table 13–6[51,52], No. 2, which follows.)

3. Next on the left, geographical targets have been divided into key markets and the remainder of the U.S. Then key target markets are indicated: total women and women with incomes of $15,000-plus a year and 3 + effective reaches.

4. The dollar expenditure per quarter is listed at the bottom for each category of vehicles used, and at the very bottom a percentage of the total is shown.

5. Advertising is shown by number of consecutive weeks followed by the number of women gross rating points (WGRP). The number of weeks during each flight is shown. For example, Day network (:30s) starts in the last week of April and continues for nine weeks in the June quarter plus one week in the September quarter. Then there are two more four-week schedules in the September quarter, and so on. The number of weeks per month is shown on the top of each rectangle as follows: 9, 1, 4, 4, 5, 4, 5, 4 = 36 weeks.

6. In the category of reach and frequency levels, note that the designation for total women in the June quarter is shown as 81/5.1 (81 reach and 5.1 frequency for total women). Reach of women with $15,000-plus income is shown in the same manner (77/4.5). But the designation for 3+ , referring to effective reach, comes from frequency distributions where the effective reach is 53 for total women for the average four weeks in the first quarter for spot area and 27 for the remainder of the U.S. See next section.

PLAN

Part 6B—Frequency Distribution Analysis

Going beyond the summary flowchart, the media planner has also provided a frequency distribution analysis (see Tables 13-3 and 13-4) that breaks down the reach and frequency, and total exposures, among all women in the selected spot TV markets and secondarily in the remainder of the United States.

TABLE 13-3. [37] **Total Women Frequency Distribution Analysis–Spot Area**

	June Qtr. May	Sept. Qtr. Sept.	Dec. Qtr. Oct.	Mar. Qtr. Jan.
Reach/Frequency	81.1/5.1	81.0/5.1	84.3/5.9	84.7/5.8
No. of Exposures				
1+	81.1	81.0	84.3	84.7
2+	65.8	65.7	70.8	71.1
3+	53.2	53.2	59.2	59.5
4+	43.0	42.9	49.5	49.5
5+	34.6	34.6	41.2	41.1
6+	27.8	27.8	34.2	34.0
7+	22.3	22.3	28.4	28.0
8+	17.8	17.8	23.5	23.0
9+	14.1	14.2	18.8	18.0
10+	11.2	11.2	15.9	15.4
11+	8.9	8.9	13.1	12.6
12+	7.0	7.0	10.7	10.2
Weekly Women				
Gross Rating Points				
Day Network	35	35	35	35
Late Network	14	14	25	25
Spot TV	54	54	65	65
Total	103	103	125	125

TABLE 13-4. [38] **Total Women Frequency Distribution Analysis–Remainder U.S.**

	June Qtr. May	Sept. Qtr. Sept.	Dec. Qtr. Oct.	Mar. Qtr. Jan.
Reach/Frequency	56.8/3.4	56.5/3.5	61.4/3.8	62.6/3.7
No. of Exposures				
1+	56.8	56.5	61.4	62.6
2+	38.5	38.5	43.5	44.4
3+	27.3	27.4	32.0	32.5
4+	19.7	19.8	23.9	24.2
5+	14.3	14.5	18.0	18.1
6+	11.5	10.7	13.6	13.5
7+	7.6	7.8	10.3	10.2
8+	5.5	5.7	7.8	7.6
9+	4.0	4.2	5.9	5.7
10+	2.9	3.1	4.4	4.2
11+	2.1	2.2	3.3	3.1
12+	1.5	1.6	2.5	2.3
Weekly Women				
Rating Points				
Day Network	35	35	35	35
Late Network	14	14	25	25
Total	49	49	60	60

NOTES

Notes on Part 6B—Frequency Distribution Analysis

[37,38] These are frequency distributions for determining effective reach. Since effective frequency is felt to be three or more impressions, the corresponding reaches are shown by quarter for the spot area [37] and the remainder of the U.S.[38]. The data come from computer analysis of television programs and time periods that were selected.

Note also that the weekly women gross rating points are shown at the bottom. This comes from the planner's desired GRP levels as shown in the bars on the flowchart.

PLAN

[39] PART 7
Gross Impression Analysis

Gross impression analysis, as detailed in Table 13–5, shows the duplicated weight of advertising to each target audience member.

TABLE 13–5.   Gross Impression Breakdown (thousands)

	Day[39,40] Network	Late[41] Network	Fringe[42] Spot	Plan[43] Total	% of[44] Plan	% of[45] Target	[46] Index
Total Women	929,464	531,122	722,917	2,183,503	100.0	100.0	—
Age							
18–24	156,150	86,573	108,438	351,161	16.0	13.9	115
25–34	177,528	104,631	137,354	419,513	19.2	17.9	107
35–49	198,905	142,872	170,608	512,385	23.5	21.3	110
50+	396,881	197,046	306,517	900,444	41.3	46.9	88
Household Income							
Under $8,000	448,002	195,984	261,696	905,682	41.5	28.6	145
$8,000–14,999	310,441	198,108	234,225	742,774	34.0	33.0	103
$15,000+	171,021	137,029	226,996	535,046	24.5	38.4	64
Household Size							
1–2	370,856	215,104	329,650	915,610	41.9	38.0	110
3–4	340,184	182,175	166,271	688,630	31.5	37.7	84
5+	218,424	133,843	226,996	579,263	26.6	24.3	109
County Size							
A	308,582	246,972	471,342	1,026,896	47.0	51.0	92
B	276,980	151,370	153,981	582,331	26.7	24.1	111
C	187,752	72,764	78,798	339,314	15.5	17.3	90
D	156,150	60,016	18,796	234,962	10.8	7.6	142

NOTES

Notes on Part 7—Gross Impression Analysis

[39] While the frequency distribution analysis shown in Part 6B gives the client an idea about how many different target members were reached an average number of times, gross impression analysis enables everyone to see whether or not advertising is distributed to these various targets in the correct proportions. Some planners may be inclined to call such data strategic impression analysis, implying that the distribution of impressions is not haphazard, but rather part of the strategy.

[40,41,42,43] The numbers shown in these columns are the duplicated impressions delivered by the various media. They are calculated by multiplying the average ratings for the vehicles by the audience base times the number of commercials telecast during the plan, or simply by multiplying the annual GRPs by the audience universe.

[44] This column indicates the strategic impression proportions. For example, women aged 18–24 are to receive 16.0 percent of total impressions for the age category, and households with incomes under $8,000 a year are to receive 41.5 percent of all impressions for that income level.

[45] This column, however, shows what proportion of impressions these demographic segments actually received.

[46] This is simply an index rating targets to delivery. For example, in the category of women aged 18–24, the index is calculated as follows: $16.0 \div 13.9 \times 100 = 115$, or 15 points higher than the goal.

A careful investigation of the impression analysis reveals that the percent of delivery for the three key target groups (women aged 35 + , in households with $15,000+ income, and in A counties) is slightly less than desired. As shown in Part 8 of the plan, the planner opted to purchase more impressions overall (through the purchase of daytime network) than to purchase fewer impressions but in the desired proportions. Also see Part 9 of the Media Plan.

PLAN

[47] **PART 8**

Media Rationale

[48] A. Daytime Network Television :30s

Daytime network television at a level of 35 WGRPs per week will be scheduled for thirty-six weeks beginning in April of next year.

1. It delivers the Brand X target audience more efficiently than other television dayparts.

Television Efficiency Comparison (:30)			
	Daytime Network	Prime Network	Late Night Network	Combined Fringe
Households	$2.78	$7.69	$4.43	$4.48
Total Women	3.25	9.59	6.94	6.63
Women 35 +	5.08	14.50	10.23	9.76
Women $15,000 +	7.85	16.94	12.73	12.55

2. It furnishes efficient national coverage while supporting the Brand X high-development areas. At comparable rating levels, the cost of day-time network is 1 percent less than day spot and delivers 34 percent more audience than using spot in the top sixty U.S. markets.

	:30 Cost	U.S. Women (%)
Day Spot		
10 WGRPs Top 60 Markets	$30,036 (100)	73 (100)
Daytime Network		
10 WGRPs	$29,280 (97)	98 (134)

3. Daytime television offers the greatest concentration of women viewers compared with the other television dayparts.

	% U.S. Adults	Daytime %	Daytime Index	Prime Time %	Prime Time Index	Late Night %	Late Night Index
Women Audience Composition							
Total Women	52	81	(156)	57	(110)	56	(108)

In addition on an equal dollar basis, daytime television furnishes the greatest absolute number of the Brand X target audience members.

Women Delivery (Equal Dollars)					
	Daytime Millions	Daytime Index	Prime Time Millions	Prime Time Index	Late Night Millions	Late Night Index
Total Women	43.4	100	18.6	43	24.9	57
Women 35 +	27.8	100	12.1	44	9.1	33
Women $15,000 +	8.0	100	4.8	60	6.6	83
Women in A Counties	14.4	100	7.1	49	11.7	81

NOTES

Notes on Part 8—Media Rationale

[47] This is an explanation (or rationale) for the decisions about which media are recommended. Although the rationale provided does not include reference to other daypart combinations, it is important to note that in the early stages of media planning, several alternatives are considered, the best of which is shown here. Further detail is provided in Table 13–6.

[48] Note that 35 women gross rating points (WGRPs) were chosen for daytime network television. Why 35 and not more or less? The answer is based on the planner's judgment that with a given budget and with the given goals, 35 WGRPs a week for thirty-six weeks are adequate, as explained in A4 of the plan.

A1. This section shows relative cost per thousand for the three key targets for alternative television classes. The plan consists of daytime network and a combination of late night and fringe network times. But the cost-per-thousand figures also show prime-time and late night television alone as alternatives. The latter two alternatives are shown to be fairly efficient in reaching some targets, but on balance, the selected alternatives are better.

A2. The planner is trying to show in this paragraph that another alternative to daytime network TV might be considered. Is this alternative better? The planner proves that daytime network TV, when compared to an alternative of daytime spot TV in sixty markets, would deliver more targets at a lower cost. The method employed was to take 10 WGRPs in each alternative, cost them out, and see which delivered the most women. The proof is that daytime network TV both costs less and delivers 34 percent more women (100 vs. 124 index numbers).

A3. The purpose of this section is to compare deliveries of primetime and late night television with daytime network television in reaching target groups. Index numbers for daytime are all 100, while alternatives are shown to be less capable of reaching targets (with index numbers less than 100).

PLAN

4. Thirty-five women gross rating points weekly are judged to be a desirable level of daytime network for Brand X. That level provides adequate women delivery nationally and also serves as a strong base upon which to build other national and local advertising efforts.

	Total Women
Reach	42.0
Average Frequency	3.2

49 **B.** Late Night Network :30s

Late night network television will be implemented for thirty-six weeks at a level of 14 WGRPs per week for the first two quarters of the fiscal year. This will provide one announcement a week on each of the three networks. For the balance of the year, 25 WGRPs weekly will be used in recognition of the brand's quarterly volume contribution.

1. Late night network extends the reach nationally among the $15,000-plus household income group.
2. Late night television usage is not affected by seasonal variations as much as other dayparts. This gives the daypart excellent reach opportunities even during the summer months.

	Index of Homes Using TV				
	Average	Spring	Summer	Fall	Winter
Daytime	100	96	96	100	107
Prime Time	100	95	89	107	111
Early Evening	100	92	85	110	113
Late Evening	100	100	100	96	104

50 **C.** Combined Fringe/Spot Television :30s

A combination of one-third early and two-thirds late fringe will be implemented at varying levels for thirty-six weeks in thirty-two Brand X markets.

1. This permits the opportunity to align the allocation of expenditures in accordance with the anticipated business opportunities in these markets.
2. The use of this medium further increases advertising pressure in key markets.
3. The flexibility of spot TV allows quick reaction to competitive activity.
4. Spot television improves the delivery of the Brand X target audience in A counties.

	Total Audience Delivery			
	Day Net	Prime Net	Late Night Net	Spot TV
A Counties	33.2%	38.1%	47.0%	65.3%
Index	100	115	142	197

NOTES

[49] This explains why late night network television was selected.

[50] This explains why a combined early and late fringe pattern for spot television was recommended.

PLAN

[51] **PART 9**
Comparison of Plan with Strategy

This section explains how the proposed media plan meets the designated strategy and objectives. Table 13–6 outlines this comparison in detail.

TABLE 13–6.   Comparison of Plan with Strategy

Strategy	Plan
[51,52] 1. Concentrate impression delivery among the primary Brand X demographic targets.	1. The recommended plan furnishes the best delivery among the target audience (women 35-plus, living in A counties) than alternative plans investigated.

	Total U.S. Women (%)	Target (%)	Index		Impressions (%)	Indices Women	Indices Target
Age							
18–24	18.0	13.9	77		16.0	89	115
25–34	20.4	17.9	88		19.2	95	107
35–49	23.0	21.3	93		23.5	102	110
50–plus	38.6	46.9	122		41.3	107	88
Household Income							
Under $8,000	38.1	28.6	75		41.5	109	145
$8,000–$15,000	34.5	33.0	96		34.0	99	103
$15,000–plus	27.4	38.4	140		24.5	89	64
Household Size							
1–2	39.9	38.0	95		41.9	105	110
3–4	35.8	37.7	105		31.5	88	84
5-plus	24.3	24.3	100		26.6	109	109
County Size							
A	40.9	51.0	125		47.0	115	92
B	26.2	24.1	92		26.7	102	111
C	19.4	17.3	89		15.5	80	90
D	13.5	7.6	56		10.8	80	142

In terms of absolute impressions delivered, the recommended plan furnished about 10 percent more impressions than Alternative III delivers (day net, prime net, fringe spot plan).

Women	Recommended (thousands)	Prime Net Alternate (thousands)	Index
35–plus	1,412.8	1,318.9	107
$15,000-plus	535.0	481.3	111
A Counties	1,026.9	932.4	110

NOTES

Notes on Part 9—Comparison of Plan with Strategy

[51] This part of the plan explains how the plan as outlined achieves the objectives set for it. The strategies are listed at the left and the proof that the strategies were fulfilled is shown at the right in statistical form. For example, look at women aged 50-plus. The plan delivers 41.3 percent of its impressions to women 50 years and older. This is less than desired as shown by the index of 88 to the target (41.3 ÷ 46.9) but more than needed to concentrate among older women in the population (41.3 ÷ 38.6).

[52] Note that at the end of the demographic analysis of delivery there is a statement about a plan titled Alternative III. Alternative III was one of three media plan alternatives devised for the client to provide other options in media strategy. The manner in which these options are compared is through gross impression analysis. In [52] the planner points out to the client that the recommended plan (Alternative I) delivered about 10 percent more gross impressions than Alternative III, which consisted of a strategy of day network television, prime network, and fringe spot. The big difference between Alternatives I and III was the use of late night network in I and prime network in III. Alternatives II and III were omitted from this text, since much of both plans consisted of similar kinds of data and strategies as Alternative I.

PLAN

2. Allocate dollars according to current Brand X sales volume while trying to stimulate development in high volume areas.

	U.S. Women (%)	Volume (%)	Index
Primary Markets	45.76	62.16	136
Remainder U.S	54.24	37.84	70
Total U.S.	100.00	100.00	100

2. The recommended plan provides a 111 index of investment among the primary Brand X markets.

Investment (%)	Index (Vol. = 100)
69.06	111
30.94	82
100.00	100

3. Provide at least a 75 reach with an average frequency of 5 among total women in key areas. Concomitantly, seek a reach goal of 50 among women who have been exposed at least three times.

	R/F Goals
Total Reach/Frequency	75/5.0
Frequency Distribution	50/3 +

3. The reach/frequency goals were achieved in the key areas that provide Brand X with 62 percent of its volume.

	Volume (%)	Low	High
Key Markets	62		
Reach/Frequency		81/5.1	85/5.8
Frequency Distribution		53/3 +	52/3 +
Remainder U.S.	38		
Reach/Frequency		57/3.4	63/3.7
Frequency Distribution		27/3 +	33/3 +

4. Distribute advertising pressure according to quarterly volume contribution.

Quarter	Contribution
June	24
September	23
December	26
March	27
	100

4. The plan follows the contribution pattern.

Quarter	Contribution
June	22
September	21
December	30
March	27
	100

5. Flexibility should be maintained.

5. The plan is sufficiently flexible to permit a reallocation of funds from one geographic area to another or from one quarter to another. About 45 percent of the budget is invested in spot TV.

6. Provide as many weeks of activity as affordable within the quarterly investment allocation once the reach/frequency goals are met.

6. The plan provides for thirty-six weeks of activity in flights ranging from four to ten weeks in length with short (two weeks) durations of non-advertising periods after an initial hiatus of four weeks.

7. Employ media vehicles that are highly compatible with the copy requirements and overall brand image.

7. The plan uses television exclusively, capitalizing on the effectiveness of the medium in communicating the taste appeal of the product.

NOTES

PLAN

[53] **PART 10**
Spot Television: Market Selection Methodology

As stated in the strategy sections, media dollars are to be allocated to current Brand X sales volume by market while maintaining competitive levels in high-volume areas. The allocation of delivery to each market is on a dollar basis, following the philosophy of spending in those areas where business is best.

The dollar allocation is based on the brand's total budget, not just the spot television budget. By using the total budget (national and local), the contribution made in each local TV market by network television is included in the allocation.

The market selection procedure employs a computer system that allocates media budgets to each TV market based on a target percentage. Adding all of the targets for all markets in the U.S. equals 100 percent. The target is obtained by weighting various factors in each market: sales, Nielsen county size consumption indices, and population. Once the targets are obtained, the computer system then calculates delivery of the network television portion of the media plan as well as the amount of money to be spent in spot television.

The following explains how markets were selected to receive spot TV and how much spot TV is to be used in each market.

1. District sales are put into the computer. Example: Boston District sales = 6.6% of total U.S. sales.
2. Nielsen county size consumption indices are put into the computer (note that each Sales District has a different consumption index):

A counties	128
B counties	128
C counties	150
D counties	150

3. Each market's total women population by county size is weighted by (multiplied by) the brand's regional Nielsen county size consumption index:

Example: Boston TV Market

	Population (thousands)	Index	Weighted Population (thousands)
A counties	1,195.4	128	1,530.1
B counties	434.4	128	556.0
C counties	215.9	150	323.9
D counties	23.3	150	35.0
Total	1,869.0		2,445.0

NOTES

Notes on Parts 10 and 11—Spot Television Market Selection and Buying Strategy

[53] Whenever a media plan calls for the use of spot television, there must be some statement explaining how the markets that are part of the spot plan are to be selected. There are many ways to make market selections. The criteria for this plan are listed here.

PLAN

4. The weighted women populations are totaled by District and each market is assigned a percentage of the District total. These percentages are then applied to the appropriate District sales volume contribution of each market.

Boston District

Market	Weighted Women Population (thousands)	% of Total	% of Sales Target*
Bangor	159.1	3.17	0.20
Boston	2,445.0	48.79	3.22
Hartford	896.9	17.89	1.18
Portland	401.1	8.00	0.53
Presque Isle	43.5	0.87	0.06
Providence	770.0	15.38	1.02
Springfield	295.6	5.90	0.39
Total	5,012.1	100.00	6.60

*Obtained by multiplying the percentage of weighted women population in each market by the District sales percentage total of 6.6%.

5. In order to concentrate dollars in the most productive markets, a judgment was made to eliminate from spot television consideration any market that had less than 0.35 percent of U.S. sales. In the Boston District, two markets (Bangor and Presque Isle) were eliminated.

6. Network television expenditures are allocated to each TV market based on the local rating point delivery of the network programs that will be purchased. Total network dollars and specific dayparts have already been determined.

    (Note: As discussed in Table 9–1, a national medium such as network television does not produce the same level of gross rating points in each market. To allocate network TV dollars to each market, therefore, local GRP delivery of programs must be obtained. Local GRPs are then multiplied by a local market's population to yield impressions. Impressions are multiplied by the national cost per thousand of network TV, which results in the prorated local market dollar allocation of network TV. These calculations can be done by hand. For this media plan, the computer system automatically makes all these calculations.)

	Network Budget	% of Total TV Budget
Boston TV Market	$ 157,645	1.13
Total Network Budget	7,829,000	
Total TV Budget	13,950,000	100.0

Note that the network delivery in the Boston TV market comprises 1.13 percent of the total TV budget of $13,950,000. An additional 2.09 percent investment is required to align the expenditures with the target percent of the total budget.

NOTES

PLAN

7. Supplementary spot television weight is added as required to align total market expenditures with market targets.

	Boston TV Market	
	Dollars	% of Total TV Budget
Network TV	$157,635	1.13
Spot TV	291,255	2.09
Total	$448,890	3.22

8. Insofar as markets with less than 0.35 percent of sales contribution were eliminated from spot television consideration, the total spot TV budget of $6,121,000 was not completely allocated. The remaining spot TV budget is therefore re-allocated proportionately to each selected TV market based on the target percentage. This results in an increase of spot TV expenditures in each market.

	Boston TV Market	
	Dollars	% of Total TV Budget
Network TV	$157,635	1.13
Spot TV	309,690	2.22
Total	$467,325	3.35

9. Spot TV dollars are converted to gross rating points per week by using individual market cost per rating point data. It had been predetermined to schedule a minimum of thirty-six weeks of activity with spot television:

Boston Market	
Spot TV Budget	$309,672.00
Cost per GRP	158.04
Total Affordable GRPs	1,959
Weekly GRPs (for thirty-six weeks)	54

10. Adjustments in spending were made after the initial computer calculations to recognize both competitive pressures and minimum GRP levels:
    a. It was decided, in light of competitive pressures and the brand's development, to further increase support in spot TV markets in the Chicago and Los Angeles districts.
    b. Four markets—Hartford, Johnstown, San Diego, and Phoenix— were scheduled to receive less than a minimum amount of weekly GRPs (over thirty-six weeks). Rather than construct a separate spot TV market group for these four markets (with less than thirty-six weeks of activity), it was decided to increase spending in these areas until a full thirty-six weeks of activity was affordable.

Table 13–7 shows the spot TV market list for Brand X that shows GRP delivery for network TV and spot TV, as well as the dollar allocation to each TV market.

NOTES

PLAN

TABLE 13-7.   Spot TV Market List—Brand X

District/DMA	Pop. (%)	Tgt. (%)	BDI	Day Net.	Late Net.	Spot TV	Total
				\multicolumn{4}{c}{36 Week Average WGRP/Week}			
Boston							
Boston	2.61	3.22	123	32	10	54	96
Hartford/N.H.	.95	1.18	125	32	12	45	89
Portland	.39	.53	132	39	12	85	136
Providence	.83	1.02	123	35	20	75	130
Spgfld./Holyoke	.32	.39	123	39	8	53	100
Total Markets	5.10	6.34	124	33	12	55	100
Total District	5.28	6.60	125				
New York	9.42	13.04	138	32	20	160	212
Syracuse							
Alb./Sch./Troy	.60	1.10	182	32	14	103	149
Buffalo	.89	1.58	178	35	18	109	162
Burlington	.25	.37	149	46	10	58	114
Rochester	.44	.77	175	35	20	73	128
Syracuse	.60	1.10	183	35	10	130	175
Total Markets	2.78	4.92	177	35	15	98	148
Total District	3.38	5.91	175				
Philadelphia							
Baltimore	1.12	1.91	170	32	8	82	122
Harr./Lanc./York	.60	1.03	172	32	18	104	154
Philadelphia	3.47	5.91	171	39	18	113	170
Washington, D.C.	1.86	3.22	174	28	8	114	150
Wilkes-Barre	.62	1.09	176	46	22	67	135
Total Markets	7.67	13.16	172	35	14	102	151
Total District	7.75	13.34	172				
Youngstown							
Cleveland	2.01	2.82	140	35	14	130	179
Johnstown	.52	.41	79	49	18	50	117
Pittsburgh	1.67	2.30	138	42	22	69	133
Youngstown	.33	.46	139	35	20	65	120
Total Markets	4.53	5.99	132	39	18	88	145
Total District	4.78	6.55	137				
Detroit							
Detroit	2.33	4.35	187	35	14	156	205
Flint	.56	.95	171	42	14	191	247
Fort Wayne	.29	.48	170	35	16	67	118
Grand Rapids	.64	1.11	174	39	10	126	175
Lansing	.26	.46	176	39	8	89	136
Toledo	.48	.83	173	46	28	84	158
Total Markets	4.56	8.18	179	38	15	130	183
Total District	4.76	8.52	179				
Chicago							
Chicago	4.07	3.48	86	32	32	84	148
South Bend	.37	.43	117	39	18	141	198
Milwaukee	.90	.69	77	32	26	54	112
Total Markets	5.34	4.60	86	32	30	82	140
Total District	6.44	5.35	83				
Los Angeles							
Los Angeles	4.98	4.81	97	25	18	59	102
San Diego	.67	.57	86	21	10	30	61
Phoenix	.71	.55	78	28	12	31	71
Total Markets	6.36	5.93	93	25	16	47	88
Total District	7.35	6.48	88				
Total Key Markets	45.76	62.16	136	33	18	90	141
Total Key Districts	49.16	65.79	134				
Rem. U.S. Key Markets	54.24	37.84	70	37	22	—	59
Rem. U.S. Key Districts	50.84	34.21	61				
Balance U.S.	100.0	100.0	100	35	20	—	—

Day Network	Late Network	Spot TV	Total	Dollars (%)	Index
		Budget			
91,872	65,773	309,672	467,317	3.35	105
33,660	27,856	124,848	186,364	1.34	114
16,632	10,059	50,796	77,487	.56	105
31,680	35,981	80,784	148,445	1.06	105
13,464	5,803	37,944	57,211	.41	105
187,308	145,472	604,044	936,824	6.72	106
196,812	148,182	604,044	949,038	6.80	103
325,512	430,617	1,145,440	1,901,569	13.63	105
23,364	20,118	117,504	160,986	1.15	105
35,640	35,594	157,896	229,130	1.64	105
9,504	4,642	39,780	53,926	.39	106
17,028	18,958	74,664	110,650	.79	110
21,384	11,993	126,684	160,061	1.15	105
106,920	91,305	516,528	714,753	5.12	105
135,828	115,296	516,528	767,652	5.50	93
40,392	21,666	217,260	279,318	2.00	105
21,384	22,827	104,652	148,863	1.07	105
144,540	135,028	578,952	858,520	6.15	105
58,212	34,821	373,320	466,353	3.34	105
31,284	30,178	96,084	157,546	1.14	105
295,812	244,520	1,370,268	1,910,600	13.70	105
297,792	246,455	1,370,268	1,914,515	13.72	104
76,032	59,195	274,176	409,403	2.93	105
21,780	14,702	26,316	62,798	.95	110
75,240	76,606	182,988	334,834	2.40	105
12,276	14,702	39,780	66,758	.48	105
185,328	165,205	523,260	873,793	6.26	105
197,604	180,295	523,260	901,159	6.46	98
90,288	76,606	463,896	630,790	4.52	105
25,344	16,249	97,308	138,901	1.00	105
10,692	9,285	48,348	68,325	.49	102
28,116	15,089	118,728	161,933	1.16	105
10,296	5,029	51,408	66,733	.48	105
22,572	27,856	69,768	120,196	.86	105
187,308	150,114	849,456	1,186,878	8.51	105
198,792	156,694	849,456	1,204,942	8.64	101
138,600	277,794	364,752	781,146	5.60	161
12,672	11,220	72,216	96,108	.69	161
34,056	48,749	74,052	156,857	1.12	162
185,328	337,763	511,020	1,034,111	7.41	161
232,848	394,251	511,020	1,138,119	8.16	153
140,976	195,384	438,192	774,552	5.55	115
16,632	14,315	89,964	120,911	.87	150
19,800	17,023	72,828	109,651	.79	144
177,408	226,722	600,984	1,005,114	7.21	123
208,296	248,002	600,984	1,057,282	7.58	117
1,650,924	1,791,718	6,121,000	9,563,642	68.56	110
1,793,484	1,919,792	6,121,000	9,834,276	70.50	107
2,309,076	2,077,282	—	4,386,358	31.44	83
2,166,516	1,949,208	—	4,115,724	29.50	86
$3,960,000	$3,869,000	$6,121,000	$13,950,000	100.00	100

PLAN

PART 11
Spot Television: Buying Strategy

Target audience	Primary—women aged 35-plus
	Secondary—total women
	Others—$15,000-plus household income
	A counties
Fringe Mix	$1/3$ early fringe
	$2/3$ late fringe
Buying Goal	Spend to budget
Spot TV Objectives	Spot television is being implemented to align impressions in accordance with the anticipated business opportunities in these markets. Spot TV is also being used to extend reach among the brand's target audience in key markets.

In general, high-rated shows with an above average concentration of women aged 35-plus are the most desirable. Implicit in high-rated shows are higher than average levels of attentiveness. In addition, in-show positions are preferable to those during the break.

The $1/3$ early, $2/3$ late dispersion of WGRPs is designed to place additional pressure among upper income women who are available in late fringe. It is also an attempt to capitalize on the higher attentiveness levels generated during late fringe. This dispersion, however, is directional and should not be construed as being inflexible.

A Final Note

Some readers may wonder why the names of individual television programs were not mentioned in this plan. The reason is that the selection of individual programs is part of the buying strategy. The buying strategy is always to select those programs which best fulfill the demographic profile stated in the media objectives. The plan shown on the preceding pages clearly specifies the kind and the number of television programs that need to be selected. After the plan has been approved, buying will begin through negotiation with network and spot time sales representatives.

NOTES

[54] When the media plan has been approved, it will be necessary for the spot television buyer to buy spots as the plan recommends. To make the buyer's job easier, specific criteria for buying have been listed here.

14

Media Costs and Buying Problems

One of the major tasks of a media planner is to match markets with the best media for reaching those markets at the most favorable cost to the client. Earlier chapters have discussed how markets are defined in terms of people and their product consumption, geographic distribution, and demographic characteristics. Those chapters also noted that individuals are exposed to media in varying degrees. On one hand, for example, full-time homemakers are more likely to watch daytime television shows and read women's service magazines than are teenagers or working men and women. On the other hand, men are more likely than women to read sports magazines or watch sports television programs.

Each of these media alternatives has a different cost. The final media plan emerging from the marketing strategy should effectively maximize the delivery of the designated marketing target in the most cost-efficient manner. Therefore, the media planner must be familiar with market definition, and be fully versed in how people utilize various media. In some instances, as is the case with television time, the cost of media varies with supply and demand. Other media, such as magazines and newspapers, tend to remain fairly constant in cost, thereby providing a high degree of predictability as planners develop costs for the media plan.

The costs that go into the final media plan are always in a state of flux. Estimating such costs is as much an art as a science; it depends heavily on the experience and professionalism of the media planner and the media buyer. If a plan is based on costs that are way out of line with marketplace realities, it can result in faulty media plan delivery. For example, if a planner estimates that 100 gross rating points of prime-time television can be purchased for $200,000, and the actual cost of that time is $300,000, the deliverability of the plan is seriously impaired. The client can then justifiably question the value of that media plan as well as the competence of the planner.

Estimating media costs is a complex task. In addition, different media have dif-

TABLE 14-1.   Average Four-Week Delivery Estimated for a $5 Million Budget

	Night Network	Day Network
Commercial unit	30 seconds	30 seconds
Total affordable GRPs		
Households	740	2,050
Women	570	1,680
Total fifty-two-week R&F		
Households	96/7.7	66/31.1
Women	89/6.4	60/28.0
Average four-week GRPs		
Households	57	158
Women	46	134
Average four-week R&F		
Households	44/1.3	47/3.4
Women	37/1.2	41/3.3

ferent problems connected with the buying process. This chapter will identify the importance of the planner's involvement in the media buying process and explain why this involvement requires familiarity with both the cost of media and the problems associated with purchasing different media types.

Some Considerations in Planning and Buying

The value of a media plan is related to how well it delivers the designated marketing targets at the lowest cost with the least amount of waste. The criteria for determining how well the plan accomplishes its mission are related to such concepts as reach, frequency, and target market impressions delivered. The gross number of target market impressions, coupled with the reach and frequency associated with those impressions within the designated budget, form the nucleus of an effective media plan. The media planner must go through a calculated process of matching the cost of various media alternatives with the delivery of the plan to arrive at the optimal relationship between cost and delivery.

For example, the cost per thousand of women 18 years of age and over for day-time network television is currently about $3.33 (:30 basis) while the cost per thousand for the same audience segment in nighttime network is approximately $8.70. Therefore, in terms of total impressions, daytime network will deliver three times more impressions to women 18 and over than will nighttime network. However, for a $5 million budget over a one-year period of time allocated to thirty-second commercials, it is estimated that the average four-week reach and frequency for nighttime would be lower than the same budget in daytime, as is illustrated in Table 14-1. However, the reach of nighttime will be higher than the daytime reach over the total fifty-two-week period. Conversely, the frequency in daytime will be higher than the frequency in nighttime over the total fifty-two-week period.

Two ways most often used to analyze media costs are to calculate cost per thousands on the basis of either gross impressions or net reach. Whichever method is used, the cost efficiency of media delivery is important. It may be found that the medium with the largest reach or the most gross impressions is not necessarily the best buy because its cost efficiency is so low. Table 14-2 shows a rough comparison of alternative media deliveries and cost efficiencies.

An examination of the table shows that different coverage levels are achieved by different media vehicles, with certain cost-per-thousand implications. The media planner's task is to fully combine a familiarity with media costs and delivery dynamics with the goals of the marketing plan to reach designated audiences. The planner must be careful to employ correct media cost assumptions in the development of the plan. Table 14-2 shows that, if inappropriate cost assumptions are used in estimating the costs of daytime network versus women's service magazines, it would be possible to include one media type in the plan to the exclusion of the other.

There are several ways media planners can help ensure correct and current media cost estimates. It should be noted that although we refer to media planners here, it is common for many companies to have media buyers, professionals trained in purchasing, make these decisions.

First, the planner must maintain close contact with media marketplace cost mechanisms. For example, pricing for print media such as magazines, newspapers, and newspaper preprints tends to be related to the cost of producing the product. As paper, ink, and wage costs increase, magazine and newspaper publishers will pass these costs on to the reader, to some degree, and to the advertiser. Generally speaking, magazine costs have tended to grow at a relatively modest annual rate compared with broadcast, as shown in Table 14-3 (p.295).

Conversely, broadcast media costs, particularly television, are importantly influenced not so much by the cost of the product as by the law of supply and demand. The media planner assesses supply and demand in broadcast by maintaining constant contact with broadcast suppliers, that is, the network and television station representatives. These contacts give the planner a feel for what is transpiring in the market and thus enable the forecasting of changes (upward or downward) in broadcast pricing.

Second, intelligent media planners will include media buyers in the development of media cost estimates. Many agencies and advertisers employ media buying specialists whose sole responsibility is the purchase of media. Such media buyers are in regular contact with the media suppliers with whom they do business on behalf of the agency/client. During the course of the numerous media buyer–seller transactions, the buyer acquires a familiarity with what is occurring in the marketplace. Such familiarity can assist the media planner in forecasting media price changes. Media buyers are expected to maintain good media supplier relations to facilitate this flow of information. Media planners should make it a point to maintain close communications with the media buyers so as to tap this source of media cost information.

Third, agencies develop expertise in estimating media cost changes based on the agency's total experience. Over a period of time, the agency can compile media cost information in various markets, or nationally, by generalizing from various specific buying experiences. It is not necessary to breach security within an agency in order to develop this information. Generalized experience is one of the reasons many agencies have gone to buying media by market as opposed to buying by brand. The indi-

TABLE 14–2.   Alternative Media—Cost and Delivery

Medium	Advertising Unit	Nat'l Equiv. Cost (000)	Women 18+ Number (000,000)	Women 18+ % U.S.	Women 18+ CPM	Men 18+ Number (000,000)	Men 18+ % U.S.	Men 18+ CPM
Night Network	:30	$ 89.3	10.3	11.3%	$ 8.67	7.3	8.9%	$12.23
Day Network	:30	14.3	4.3	5.0	3.33	1.2	1.5	11.92
Sports Network	:30	43.3	2.5	2.7	17.36	4.1	5.0	10.72
Late Night Network	:30	17.7	2.7	2.9	6.55	2.1	2.6	8.14
Early Network News	:30	39.1	7.3	8.0	5.36	5.8	7.1	6.74
General Magazines (gen. mag. avg.)	1P4/C	48.1		15.4	3.44	10.8	13.2	4.45
Women's Magazines (seven mag. avg.)	1P4/C	48.9	19.9	21.9	2.45	3.9	4.8	12.34
Newspapers	Full P B/W	2190.8	37.0	40.7	59.20	37.0	45.1	59.20
Network Radio	:60	2.4	1.1	1.2	2.25	1.1	1.3	2.25
Outdoor	100 Showing	104.3	47.8	52.6	2.18	46.2	56.4	2.26

Sources: Nielsen Media Research, *NAD Report*; Leo Burnett 1986 Media Costs and Coverage; Marketer's Guide to Media; RADAR, Fall 1985; Newspaper Advertising Bureau; Standard Rate & Data Service; Simmons Market Research Bureau, 1985; Institute of Outdoor Advertising.

TABLE 14-3.   Media Cost and Cost-per-Thousand Trends Index from 1975

	Prime-Time Network TV		Daytime Network TV		Consumer Magazines		Newspapers		Network Radio	
	Unit Cost	CPM	Unit Cost	CPM	Unit Cost	CPM	Unit Cost	CPM	Unit Cost	CPM
1975	100	100	100	100	100	100	100	100	100	100
1976	131	121	119	110	105	102	110	110	126	122
1977	153	143	145	145	116	114	117	115	141	136
1978	171	153	150	145	126	123	127	125	153	144
1979	203	176	174	159	138	139	132	130	174	161
1980	196	172	174	164	143	143	160	156	191	156
1981	225	203	198	183	157	162	176	170	208	148
1982	235	224	202	199	167	173	194	189	229	138
1983	260	241	226	200	181	189	213	207	246	142
1984	293	281	263	253	189	196	100*	100*	260	135
1985	306	280	265	258	197	199	111*	112*	303	130

Sources: Nielsen Media Research, NAC Cost Supplement, November, 1985; SRDS, June 1985, Editor and Publisher Yearbook; Marketing and Media Decisions, August 1986.
*Conversion from line to inch rates in 1984 makes indexing to 1975 impossible. Therefore, indices after 1984 are indexed to 1984 costs and CPMs.

vidual responsible for buying an individual market (or markets) is intimately acquainted with the media cost picture in those areas.

Once the media plan has been implemented and the schedules completed, the media planner should examine how closely the media cost estimates compare with actual costs. By conducting such a postbuy analysis, the planner can sharpen the capability to forecast costs by reviewing what went into the original estimates. Such trial-and-error devices assist the media professional in developing the personal art of media cost forecasting. Major variations between cost estimates and actual plan delivery cost may uncover flaws in understanding or thinking, or may be the consequence of significant media marketplace cost changes that could not have been anticipated. In any event, the media planner, in checking back over the implemented plan, should consider the exercise an important learning experience.

A Discussion of Media Costs

Table 14-4 shows national media expenditures by major consumer media types for 1986. The chart identifies the major media to which national advertisers direct their dollars. Note that television and magazines comprise nearly 74 percent of national expenditures. The magnitude and complexity of planning and buying these media require close attention to cost implications.

Within these broad media types, there are numerous alternatives available with which the media planner must be acquainted. In addition to understanding general media cost relationships, for example, between television and magazines, the professional media planner must be familiar with costs of network versus spot, and the different availabilities within the general broadcast medium as well as the changes over time—a complex and difficult assignment, but a necessary one.

TABLE 14-4.   National Media Expenditures (1985)

Media	Dollars Spent (MM)	Portion of Total (%)
Newspaper	3,629	13
Magazine	4,928	18
Newspaper supplements	401	1
Network TV	8,313	30
Spot TV	7,044	26
Network radio	443	2
Spot radio	1,440	5
Network cable	472	2
Outdoor	685	3
Farm publications	181	*
Total	27,544	100

Source: *Advertising Age,* September 4, 1986. Reprinted by permission of Crain Communications, Inc.
*Less than 1%.

Television Costs

Table 14–4 showed that television expenditures accounted for 56 percent of total advertising dollars spent in 1985. Most of the television investment was for consumer goods and services. However, there has been a growing use of the medium by industrial and business-related advertisers. In view of the magnitude of the investment in television, a media planning professional must be fully conversant with all phases of the medium. The major characteristic of television, insofar as media costs are concerned, relates to the "perishability" of the inventory. Generally speaking, there is a fixed amount of television time available for sale. Unlike a magazine or newspaper that can expand or contract the number of advertising pages available for sale in any given issue, a commercial minute that is unsold can never be recovered. The sellers of television time must contend with this perishability concept in selling the medium.

Although marketplace pricing conditions prevail at any given time, these prices are subject to change as advertisers' demand for that time increases or decreases. The stronger the demand and the earlier the sale in relationship to the program air date, the more likely that pricing will be higher. Less advertising demand close to air date can create lower pricing, assuming inventory availability. These interrelated conditions of perishability, demand, and inventory create a dynamic marketplace. The buyer of television time must, therefore, be alert to these changes by maintaining close contact with the marketplace.

Under the broad heading of television, there are basically two sub-categories, national network and local spot.

Network Television. Certain parts of the broadcast day are programmed by the national networks: the American Broadcasting Company, the Columbia Broadcasting System, the National Broadcasting Company, and the Fox network. Figure 14–1 illustrates the dayparts when network programming is usually made available to *affiliates* (the individual stations that comprise a network lineup). The number of stations serviced by a given network can vary from 150 to 225, depending on the strength of the network programming available. The networks sell commercial time

FIGURE 14–1. Daypart Programming Available for Network Use

6 7	8 9	10 11	12 1 2 3 4	5 6	7	8 9 10 11	12 1	2
AM			PM				AM	
LOCAL	Network	LOCAL	Network Daytime Programs	LOCAL	NETWORK	LOCAL · Network Prime-time Programs · LOCAL	Network Late Night Progs.	LOCAL

to advertisers to run within specific programs. These programs can appear throughout various parts of the day—for example, daytime network series, prime-time network, or late night (post-prime-time) segment.

Prime time (8:00 P.M. to 11:00 P.M. EST), because of the high HUT (homes using television), generally provides the highest ratings. This time period tends to deliver a family audience with high reach levels of most viewing segments. Media costs for prime time are generally the highest per commercial minute of all network time segments available for sale. The cost for thirty seconds in prime time, as indicated in Table 14–2, can be in the area of $89,300 (or higher for certain programs). Individual program costs will vary depending on rating level and the amount of inventory available for sale. As discussed earlier, the less inventory, generally, the higher the cost.

Daytime network (10:00 A.M. to 4:30 P.M. EST) is generally the least costly of the network dayparts. An average cost for thirty seconds will be somewhere in the vicinity of $14,300 with an average household rating of approximately 5.6. This results in an extremely efficient cost-per-thousand delivery of homes and women.

Late night (11:30 P.M. to conclusion EST) network programming tends to vary from network to network and over time. This time period is generally programmed with talk shows, movies, and different types of entertainment including drama, rock concerts, and comedy. Pricing for this time period, since fewer sets are in use than during prime time, tends to be about $17,700 for thirty seconds with an average household rating of 4.8. Although the rating levels for late night are comparable to daytime, there is a dual audience (both men and women) included in late night that is not generally the case in daytime. Thus, pricing for that dual audience tends to be somewhat higher than daytime.

Most network programming on weekends is in the sports and children's areas. Sports programming, for the most part, is the domain of the male-oriented advertiser. Such products as beer, male grooming aids, investment counseling, and automobiles are heavily represented on weekend sports programming. In general, there is a limited amount of broadscale sports programming compared with other network program time. Therefore, pricing tends to be relatively high on a cost-per-thousand basis for the higher interest sporting events. However, the value of identifying with a major high-interest sports event has distinct rub-off effects on brands associated with such programming.

Children's programs, often referred to as "kid TV," are the primary fare on Saturday mornings. Nearly all of this programming are cartoons, but there are some live-action shows, especially in the action/adventure area. The predominant audience is children, and the advertising, therefore, is highly child-oriented. Cereal, toy/game, fast food, and candy advertisers concentrate a significant portion of their advertising budget in kid TV.

The diversity of programming provided by the networks ranges from the all-family interest generated in prime time to highly selective shows of interest to perhaps relatively few households. Such diversity provides the media planner with rich opportunities for reaching broad national markets with programming aimed specifically to target market interests. Costs for such programming will change as marketplace demand changes so that the media planner must be ever alert to the buying implications of the programming selected for inclusion in the media plan.

Syndication is the development or packaging of programming that is sold directly to the advertiser and/or cleared on a market-by-market basis by the syndicator. Clearances for a syndicated property can range from a program run one time in a few markets to weekly series clearing in 70–90 percent of the U.S. for extended periods of time. Syndicated properties include first-run talk shows, specials, sports events, and game shows as well as off-network reruns of sitcoms and serials. Table 14–5 lists the top ten syndicated properties of February 1986. Nationalized ratings, percent coverages, and time period clearances are also listed.

There are four types of syndication deals: Straight Barter, Part Barter/Part Cash, Cash, and Scatter. *Straight Barter* involves the local station receiving the program and a percentage of the commercial time within the program for local sale in return for airing the show. *Part Barter/Part Cash* requires the local station to pay a license fee to broadcast the program. This arrangement allows local station control of most of the commercial time with a smaller percentage of the commercial minutes being sold to national advertisers by the syndicator. In a pure *Cash* syndication deal the local station pays cash for the syndicated property and can sell all the commercial time to both local and national advertisers on a market-by-market basis. *Scatter* syndication is a unique situation in which the stations are obligated to run national commercial spots for a specific syndicator. The local station can drop or retain the syndicated show, but if the station elects to run the show, it must run the program in a predetermined period of time. The time period restriction provides the syndicator with the means to guarantee national coverage by daypart for its national advertisers.

The costs and efficiencies of good syndicated properties are generally better than network program costs and efficiencies. Syndicated cost efficiencies, for example, generally run 20–40 percent better than network cost efficiencies.

Local Stations. Announcements can be purchased on local television stations, which are either affiliated with a network and carry network programming at certain times of the day or are independent stations, which do not have any network affiliation and thus must program the entire day on their own.

Costs for local announcements vary from market to market based on audience delivered. Generally speaking, the costs for scheduling announcements in markets

TABLE 14-5. Top 10 Syndicated Properties

Program	Nationalized Rank	Rating	No. of Markets	Percent of U.S. Cov.	M-F Daytime Cov.	Rank	M-F Fringe Cov.	Rank	M-SA Access Cov.	Rank	S/S Prime Cov.	Rank	S/S Late Night Cov.	Rank	Daytime Cov.	Rank	S/S Fringe Cov.	Rank
Wheel of Fortune	1	22.5	193	99.2	—	—	43.1	87	56.8	107	3.5	10	—	—	—	—	25.3	32
Jeopardy	2	13.4	172	96.7	6.6	9	67.8	100	32.1	69	2.1	7	.5	1	—	—	3.0	6
New Newlywed Game	3	11.2	170	94.4	.8	2	53.2	104	43.8	69	1.9	6	.2	1	—	—	.2	2
M*A*S*H	4	11.1	169	93.6	—	—	44.0	81	28.6	53	5.4	18	38.9	67	1.6	9	6.6	14
Three's Company	5	9.6	155	85.5	.4	2	60.2	102	19.4	40	2.4	11	8.2	15	2.9	8	11.6	10
People's Court	6	9.1	166	94.5	4.0	6	86.0	153	3.8	6	5.5	3	.7	1	—	—	—	—
Entertain. Tonight	7	9.0	145	91.2	—	—	32.7	60	42.6	53	2.5	6	19.6	36	—	—	—	—
Phil Donahue	8	8.5	180	97.7	89.9	166	9.3	16	—	—	.5	1	.7	1	—	—	.5	1
Different Strokes	9	7.9	127	84.2	1.7	3	80.1	115	1.7	7	.8	4	.2	1	2.6	5	7.5	8
Hee Haw	10	7.5	172	81.4	—	—	—	—	—	—	10.2	13	15.2	15	15.2	19	45.7	138

Source: Nielsen Media Research, NSI Report, February 1986. Reprinted by permission.

like New York, Los Angeles, and Chicago are higher than those for smaller markets because of the amount of circulation delivered by these stations. Time is made available for sale, whether the station is network-affiliated or independent, across almost the entire daypart. Even within daypart programming by the networks, such as in prime time, there are certain segments of time set aside for local sale. This means that it is possible for a local advertiser, for example in Chicago, to purchase a thirty-second announcement (if available) in a network-originated program, or between programs at the station break.

Because independent stations program for the entire day, there are numerous opportunities for the advertiser to select specific dayparts and programming to reach the target audience. In addition to adjacencies next to and, at times, within network programming, commercial time can be selected in what is termed *fringe time*. Generally speaking, the fringe dayparts and the programming contained therein might look something like the following:

Sample Schedule

Station	Local Time (EST)	Program
A	6:00 P.M.–6:30 P.M.	Local news
	6:30 P.M.–7:00 P.M.	Local news
	11:00 P.M.–11:30 P.M.	Local news
	11:30 P.M.–Conclusion	Movie
B	5:00 P.M.–5:30 P.M.	"I Dream of Jeannie"
	5:30 P.M.–6:00 P.M.	"Bewitched"
	6:30 P.M.–7:00 P.M.	"Andy Griffith"
	10:30 P.M.–Conclusion	Local movie

Pricing for dayparts and specific programs within dayparts will again vary based on audience delivery and availability of commercial time. It is difficult to generalize about pricing and relationships between dayparts, stations within a market, and between markets because of the diversity associated with purchasing local announcements. However, in general, spot television is a highly cost-efficient media vehicle for reaching specialized geographic markets. Such geographic selectivity enables the advertiser to concentrate dollars in markets representing the greatest sales potential.

Magazine Costs

The two major print advertising categories are magazines and newspapers. Advertising pricing for print space tends to be somewhat more stable than for broadcast media because magazines and newspapers can adjust upward or downward the number of pages they print on an issue-to-issue basis. Thus the cost of printing is somewhat variable in contrast to the fixed commitment of television and its resultant commercial time perishability. Newspapers and magazines generally issue rate cards that cover future costs with a high degree of certainty although recently a number of magazines have begun negotiating rates. A media planner constructing a plan for a year in advance can be relatively assured that the rate card costs will change little, if at all, during the course of the year, unless the magazines the buyer plans to use are among those negotiating their rates. In those cases, the buyer most make a judgment as to the rate to be used in the future media plan.

There is considerable diversity within the broad category of magazines. Some of the categories include the following:

General Interest (Dual Audience). Such publications as the *Reader's Digest, TV Guide*, and perhaps to some degree *Time* and *Newsweek*, are viewed as general interest magazines in view of the diverse audiences they reach. Their editorial content by nature does not exclude any potential reading group. Along with the large circulation delivered by these publications goes a commensurately high cost per page. As such, the costs per page for these dual-audience magazines take into account the audience they reach though their circulations vary.

	Cost per Four-Color Page	Circulation (thousands)
Reader's Digest	$104,600	17,657
TV Guide	95,900	17,000
Time	114,955	4,600
Newsweek	84,390	3,050
People	61,345	2,971

Women's Service Magazines. More editorially selective publications, such as *Ladies' Home Journal, McCall's, Good Housekeeping, Family Circle, Woman's Day*, and *Redbook* gear their interest primarily to women. The editorial content of these publications is designed to be informative and entertaining. However, male readership, as a percentage of total readership, is not very high compared with the general interest magazines. Following are sample costs for these selected magazines.

	Cost per Four-Color Page	Circulation (thousands)
Ladies' Home Journal	$61,300	5,235
McCall's	60,800	6,312
Good Housekeeping	80,025	5,000
Family Circle	75,250	6,600
Woman's Day	66,960	6,900
Redbook	55,255	4,094

Home Magazines. Other magazines segment their editorial target in a different way, namely by environmental considerations such as the home. Such magazines as *Better Homes & Gardens* speak to the interests and concerns of homeowners. By their editorial nature, these magazines tend to be adult and dual-audience oriented. Here again, selectivity of editorial content as well as audience gives the advertiser an opportunity to position a commercial message in a highly compatible environment. The costs for some of these magazines are as follows:

	Cost per Four-Color Page	Circulation (thousands)
Better Homes & Gardens	$95,400	8,060
House & Garden	21,960	592
House Beautiful	28,240	838
1001 Decorating Ideas	27,825	700
Sunset	28,787	1,408
Southern Living	42,250	2,150

Categorization of these magazines is somewhat arbitrary. One could argue that *Better Homes & Gardens* is a general interest publication based on the duality of the readership. In the final analysis, categorization is not nearly so important as the quantity and quality of the readership, compatibility of editorial with the sales message, and the cost of running the insertion—all of which must be taken into account by the media planner. A cost delivery relationship, however, is a good starting point in categorizing magazines from which to select those that then can be qualified based on the editorial content within which the message will appear.

Newspaper Costs

At the beginning of 1988, there were 1,645 daily newspapers in the United States, in addition to 7,498 weekly newspapers. Newspapers provide the distinct benefits of flexibility in adjusting efforts from market to market, quick closing dates, strong local market coverage, and individual market identification. As with other media, newspapers are also highly diverse in the ways they can be bought and the advertising units available for sale. The major categories include the following:

ROP (Run of Paper). ROP advertising can be purchased in virtually any size unit from full page down to just a few lines in both black and white and color. Generally speaking, color costs about 25 percent more than black and white.

Supplements. Preprinted newspaper distributed supplements can be purchased either on a syndicated basis (*Parade, USA Weekend*) or on an independent basis such as the *Chicago Tribune Magazine*. Preprinted supplements provide all the benefits of newspapers in today's market coverage with four-color magazine-type reproduction when desirable. Costs for independent supplements vary from market to market. Costs and circulation levels for the syndicated supplements are as follows:

	Cost per Four-Color Page	Circulation (thousands)
Parade	$260,400	25,169
USA Weekend	119,400	14,500

Custom Inserts. In addition to ROP and magazine supplements, newspapers provide for advertising inserts printed outside the paper and stuffed inside. These inserts may be used in many different forms. They may be printed on fine quality or inexpensive papers, in many different sizes, used as single sheets or booklets, and printed in many different ways. All of these alternative production techniques allow advertisers to create unique advertising that will communicate whatever they want and can afford. Costs for custom-tailored inserts obviously vary depending on how elegant they are. Each newspaper also may charge different prices for stuffing and carrying the inserts.

Radio Costs

Radio is offered both on a national network and individual local market spot basis.

Network Radio. Network radio programming available for advertiser sale includes news, music, sports, and drama. Costs are comparatively low for a network radio announcement. The average network charges $2,400 for a sixty-second announcement and delivers an average rating of 1.4 to men, 1.3 to women, and 0.7 to teenagers.

Spot Radio. Spot radio programming formats vary widely from market to market. In major markets, such as New York, Los Angeles, and Chicago, there are numerous radio formats appealing to a wide variety of listener interests. Programming ranges from talk shows to various kinds of music formats to total news. ABC–Contemporary, ABC–Direction, ABC–Entertainment, ABC–FM, ABC–Information, ABC–Rock, CBS, CBS RadioRadio, Mutual, Mutual PM, National Black, NBC, Satellite Music, Sheridan, The Source, Transtar, United Stations One, and United Stations Two.

As is the case with spot television, it is extremely difficult to generalize about costs because of the diversity of the medium. In overall terms, however, spot radio selectively purchased against designated target audiences can be an exceptionally cost-efficient medium for reaching these audiences.

Many station groups have developed and make available computerized reach and frequency programs that help planners measure the effect of different combinations of stations in delivering both gross impressions as well as reach and frequency estimates against selected audience segments.

Out-of-Home Media Costs

Out-of-home media come in a wide range of availabilities that differ dramatically in size and location. Out-of-home media are the most local of all media forms, inasmuch as one advertising unit can be purchased in one very specific location geographically. The more popular varieties of out-of-home media are the following.

Poster Panels. A *poster panel* is an outdoor advertising structure on which a pre-printed advertisement is displayed. The most widely used poster sizes are standard, junior, and three-sheet. The *standard poster,* or *thirty-sheet poster,* measures approximately 12 feet high by 25 feet long, but dimensions vary from one location to another. The *junior panel,* or *eight-sheet poster,* is about one-fourth the size of a standard poster. The *two-sheet poster* is used extensively at transit or train stop. It is 60 inches by 46 inches.

Poster panels are generally sold in packages of gross rating points. For example, a 100–GRP package will deliver in one day exposure opportunities equal to 100 percent of the population of the market. The cost for posters varies tremendously from one market to another, and often from one location to another in a given market. The cost to purchase a 100-GRP package for one month in standard posters in the top ten markets of the U.S. is approximately $1,065,000. The same purchase encompassing the top 100 markets is about $3,235,000.

Painted Bulletins. A painted bulletin is an outdoor advertising structure that is painted with the advertising copy. Paints are generally larger than posters and measure, on average, 14 feet high by 48 feet wide. "Paints" are sold both individually and in packages. There are basically two types of paint availabilities: permanent and rotary. In the case of a *permanent paint*, the advertiser buys the specific location for one or more years and the units may vary in size. A permanent paint is usually bought for the specific location's desirability and is priced accordingly. *Rotary paints* are sold individually or in packages. The rotary bulletin is moved from location to location within a market on a set schedule (either 30-, 60-, or 90-day cycles, depending on the market).

The cost for one painted bulletin can range from as low as $500 in smaller markets to more than $3,000 in larger markets for an average month.

Transit. Transit advertising is available on buses, taxi cabs, trains, and in carrier terminals (train stations, airline terminals, etc.) in selected cities. There are numerous sizes and shapes that can be purchased, with advertising costs varying depending on the market, the medium, the size of the advertisement, the length of the purchase, and the scope of the purchase.

Media Buying Problems

As indicated earlier, audience delivery and cost estimating represent major considerations in the development of a media plan. Once the plan has been approved, it becomes necessary to implement the budgeted effort in the most effective manner possible. Knowledge of how media sell their product is vital both for the development of the plan and its ultimate implementation. This section discusses some of the timing and buying implications associated with various media. Here again, as in the case with cost estimating, the major distinction rests between broadcast and print.

Network Television

Network television is a negotiated medium; it is bought and sold somewhat like a commodity on the commodities exchange. The network television market is a supply and demand market whose goods are highly perishable. A minute not sold is a minute wasted, and it results in lost revenue for the network. Consequently, the first problem the network television buyer must consider is timing. Incorrect timing and wrongly assessing when to buy can lead to severe implementation problems. For example, if the network buyer waits too long before committing the designated budget, all of the availabilities could be exhausted, thus leaving nothing to buy. Generally, the earlier the network buy is initiated, the more likely it is that desired programming in terms of audience delivery and stability will be obtained. The longer the buyer waits before committing to a buy for a specified period of time, the less likely it is that the most desirable programming will be available. There is, however, the increased possibility of lower pricing for the inventory that remains if demand is low. The ideal time to buy is when sellers are anxious to sell, just before others enter the market. In general, in a seller's year, an advertiser should buy early before prices rise and quality inventory is gone. In a buyer's year, an advertiser should buy as late as inventory is available and prices are likely to be favorable.

Network television time can be purchased in packages of shows or by the individual program. Packages, multiple programs with a few commercials per program during the course of the advertising schedule, provide maximum programming dispersion and thus tend to generate broader reach for the available budget. In addition, the risk of not delivering the specified weight levels is reduced, because the outcome of the buy is not based on one or two programs achieving their audience levels. Conversely, networks also make individual programs available for sale on a continuity basis. Commercials regularly appearing on one or two shows can be highly effective when the planner can identify the specific audience values in those shows that achieve the objectives of the media plan.

Three factors are key in determining network costs: (a) demand by advertisers, (b) estimates by both buyer and seller of audience delivery and cost per thousand, and (c) network overhead and expenses in doing business. By far, advertiser demand is the most important determinant of network costs. Seasonal demand and the strength of the network and its programming best illustrate the effect of supply and demand on the network television marketplace. During the time of the year when an advertiser's sales are expected to be greatest, advertising time is in great demand and as a result, network prices are high. For example, for toymakers, the pre-Christmas season, the fourth quarter of the year, is a time of great seasonal demand. In addition, advertisers generally prefer high-rated, popular programming in any given daypart. Such programming enables them to reach a large audience in a good commercial environment. This preference increases the price for that particular programming and in many cases increases pricing for an entire daypart on a network if that particular program dominates the daypart.

Estimates by both buyer and seller of audience delivery and cost per thousand are also key determinants of network pricing. In most major agencies, network TV buyers estimate delivery for all network programming prior to starting the negotiation process. These estimates are based on consistent tracking of audience shares from week to week to determine audience trends. Network buyers are also aware of any network scheduling changes, new programs, and program cancellations. The networks also project audience delivery. Network projections are usually higher than agency projections. If a substantial long-term network buy is made using the network projections, the delivery is normally guaranteed by the network. If the network does not meet its guaranteed projections it then must "make good" by offering compensatory units.

Finally, the network's expenses also affect network pricing. For example, the network will try to cover the cost of programming and business overhead. An expensive production may be priced at a premium to offset its costs. In addition, there are mechanical charges for national and regional advertisers. An integration fee is charged to place the commercial into its proper pod within the program reel. Additional mechanical fees are also charged to regional advertisers for regional feeds, program cut-ins, and regional blackouts.

Three Ways to Buy Network TV

There are three primary ways to purchase network television: upfront (or long-term), scatter (or short-term), and opportunistic (or last-minute) buys.

An *upfront network television buy* is the purchase of inventory for all four quarters of the coming broadcast year. Advertisers' dollars are committed upfront in the spring/summer for the following television season, which begins in September. Upfront network buying is also called long-term buying. Upfront buying usually involves a guaranteed audience delivery which is expressed as a guaranteed cost efficiency and consists of premium inventory. By committing dollars in the upfront market, the advertiser has insurance against sellouts but has little flexibility with regard to possible cancellation (contingencies out with ninety days notice). At best, networks will generally grant cancellation options on a portion of the last half of a long-term buy.

Scatter buying is the purchase of inventory within a specific quarter made prior to the start of that quarter. Scatter buys are negotiated on a quarterly basis and give the buyer a better fix on the marketplace, that is, the buyer knows pricing from the upfront market as well as pricing from the previous quarter. Scatter buys offer the advertiser more financial flexibility with dollar commitment required only one to two months prior to the air date. There are, however, inventory and efficiency risks involved in buying scatter, because the best inventory may be depleted and scatter has historically tended to be less efficient (priced higher) than the upfront market. Finally, scatter buys are usually not guaranteed by the networks.

Opportunistic buying involves the purchase of inventory on a last minute basis if the networks have any remaining inventory to sell. Although there is a high risk of sellout in opportunistic buys, these buys can sometimes be very efficient because the networks are trying to get rid of last minute inventory just prior to air date.

Network television programs are also occasionally purchased on a full or partial sponsorship basis. A full sponsorship involves purchase of all of the commercial time available in one or more telecasts of a program. Partial sponsorship requires purchase of at least three or four thirty-second units of commercial time in one or more telecasts of a program. In the early days of television, sponsorship was common. Today, however, very few hours of network television are sponsored. The advantages of sponsorships include the identification the sponsor has with the program, the additional exposure in the form of opening and closing billboards, use of the cast in commercials, and participation in high-quality programming. However, sponsorships are generally very expensive, and the advertiser takes a chance that the program will not do well. In addition, audience reach is limited with a single program as compared to spreading the buy over a variety of programs.

Special event network programming can also be purchased unit by unit or as program sponsorship. Specials provide a good environment for new product introductions and for seasonal advertisers because they frequently have mass audience appeal and high visibility. In general, special event programming carries a premium price.

Finally, network regional time is also available. In a regional network buy an advertiser buys only a portion of the country, with another advertiser or advertisers buying the remainder. Regional network availabilities can be beneficial to advertisers who seek certain types of programming identification, for products with less than national distribution, or for introducing new products to specific regions. Regional network time availabilities are generally very difficult to execute and involve considerable planning and discussions with the network sales departments.

Buying Syndication

Syndication is bought much like network television—the advertiser makes one national buy. However, unlike network television, syndication buys can include either packages of time on several shows or time purchased on one program. Here again, the percent of national coverage varies by syndicated property and pricing varies according to coverage and projected performance.

Spot Television

There are 209 Designated Spot Television Markets with 941 commercial television stations in the United States. The number of stations per market, which directly influences spot inventory, ranges from a high of 13 in Los Angeles to many markets with only one or two stations.

Major markets with multiple stations offer a considerable spot inventory from which to select. The multiplicity of spot commercial availabilities in such markets allows the buyer to be somewhat selective as far as programming and timing are concerned. Spot schedules are generally purchased two weeks to two months in advance of the start date of the schedule. Spot time can be bought for specified flight periods or on a continuing basis until canceled. Most station contracts call for cancellation notice to be given four weeks prior to the end of a schedule.

Magazines

Once the planner has designated which magazines will carry the approved schedule, the plan implementation has tended historically to be relatively mechanical. Most national publications accept space reservations guaranteeing that advertising space will be available in the desired issues. Space reservations can be made almost any time in advance of the issue. The final date for contracting to appear in a given issue is called the *closing date*, which varies by publication. Closing dates for monthly magazines will generally be from sixty to ninety days in advance of issue. Closing dates for weekly publications normally fall about three to seven weeks prior to issue.

There is a recent developing trend that deserves mention, as it may result in a standard pattern in future magazine buying—the trend toward negotiated rates. You will recall, this was mentioned previously in the "Magazine Cost" section. For many years, there was controversy in the magazine business over the possibility of rate concessions by some magazines. The situation became a public issue in the spring of 1987 when *McCall's* women's magazine publicly announced their intention to negotiate rates. Since then, the women's magazine field and some other magazine categories have been openly negotiating rates with agencies and advertisers. This trend should be watched carefully as many professionals believe it will become common practice in the U.S. as it has in many countries around the world.

National magazines provide regional and test market circulation breakouts for achieving coverage in specified geographic areas. The regional availability can include multiple states or just a limited area such as New York City. The remainder of the circulation carries either another advertiser or editorial material. Magazines also make available test market circulation breakouts that conform closely to television market coverage patterns, thus permitting test translations of national plans into local test areas. Costs and availabilities of such special breakouts must normally be secured from the magazines prior to order since they are subject to change.

Many magazines also make available what are called A and B *copy splits*. This means two different blocks of copy can appear in alternate copies of the magazine in the same issue. These copy splits provide opportunities to test alternative copy approaches or they can be used by different brands when national coverage is desired and half of the circulation is considered adequate for each brand. Some magazines also make available demographic breakouts. Such demographic breaks might include space only in copies going to physicians, or businessmen, or some other breakout provided by the publication.

Media planners, in the course of continuing their education, should keep abreast of the flexibilities provided by the ever-changing publishing industry.

Newspapers

Space closing for ROP space is only a few days before the actual issue. If a special unit is desired, such as a two- or four-color half-page, then additional time in ordering such space is generally required. However, the advance notice time to the newspapers is still relatively short compared with the longer closing dates of national magazines.

Newspapers have been very aggressive in developing special sections geared to various audiences and issues. For example, many food advertisers look for what is called the Best Food Day. Best Food Day in most markets is Wednesday or Thursday, the days that major food chains schedule their advertising. The advertiser is positioned adjacent to the special editorial sections that the consumer is likely to read before going to market. Positions within these sections are generally available at no extra cost.

Other sections that can be advantageous in reaching selected audiences include sports, business, and special features on fashion, good grooming, and home care. In addition to such regular opportunities for positioning, newspapers offer availabilities for special preprints such as hard stock inserts. In most cases, the advertiser provides the particular preprint to the newspaper. Such advertising units have to be ordered well in advance to ensure space availability.

Network Radio

Network radio programming tends to offer relatively few format types such as news and sports and some special events. Network radio is purchased in the same way as network television, that is, a contractual obligation for a specified number of commercials over a designated period of time.

Spot Radio

Spot radio provides different buying problems in view of the tremendous selectivity and diversity of programming and stations in many major markets. Rating information is available in most markets, but does not provide the total picture in buying radio. The number of men, women, and teenagers listening at various times to specific radio stations can be identified. However, the format, whether it be contemporary music, country western, stock market reports, music/weather, or sports, can be an important factor influencing station selection. The planner must rely heavily on the buyer's experience in executing a local market radio buy and ensuring a close match between the commercial copy, audience, and station format.

This chapter has examined the essential elements of media costs, accuracy, and related problems in implementing the media plan. There is a high degree of art in good media planning because the audiences of media and the pricing of advertising time/space are in a constant state of change. The professional media planner never stops inquiring and learning. The ability to form sound judgments about alternative media values requires intense concentration on the part of the planner. In the final analysis, those judgments are what distinguish a qualified media professional from a competent numbers manipulator.

QUESTIONS FOR DISCUSSION

1. Explain the main bases upon which broadcast and print media often set their prices.
2. What is the value of analyzing costs *after* a media plan has been implemented?
3. What is meant by the term "perishability of the inventory" in selling television broadcast time?
4. Why do print media costs tend to be more stable and less variable than broadcast media costs?
5. About how much more does it cost to print a four-color ad in newspapers than it does a black-and-white ad? Explain why color costs more.

6. How does cost efficiency of radio (in general) compare with other media? Briefly explain why this is so.
7. Why would an advertiser want to buy a magazine that makes available A and B copy splits?
8. What is meant by the term "availabilities" in the sale of spot television time?
9. In planning for preprints such as hard stock inserts, what costs other than typical space costs must be considered?
10. What are the advantages of buying network packages instead of buying time in a number of individual programs for commercials?

15

Setting and Allocating the Budget

One of the most difficult tasks facing advertising and agency planners is that of determining the optimum amount of money to spend for advertising. This is a problem that seems to defy solution despite the time and thought that have been given to attacking it. This amount is called the *appropriation* or the *budget.* We will use the latter term in this book. The main difficulty in determining the budget size is that no one knows precisely how a given amount of money spent for advertising will affect sales or other marketing goals. Media expert Herbert D. Maneloveg summarized the problem as follows:

> Our major problem, I believe, is that we really don't know how much advertising is enough. And we haven't done much about trying to find out. Not until lately. When someone asks about the amount of advertising pressure needed to make a potential consumer aware of the merits of a brand, we fumble and grope. When asked to justify an increase or decrease in advertising budget, we are lost because of an inability to articulate what would happen with the increase or decrease: if sales go up, we credit advertising; if sales go down, we blame pricing, distribution, and competition.[1]

In other words, there is no simple cause and effect relationship between the amount of money spent and the sales results that are supposed to occur because of the expenditure. Some manufacturers have been able to learn from experience how much money they should spend to obtain a desired share or sales volume at a given time. But even these manufacturers do not assume that the relationship will remain

---

1. Maneloveg, Herbert D., ''How Much Advertising Is Enough?'' *Advertising Age*, June 6, 1966, p. 130.

constant at all times. At some time or other, they and most other advertisers are in the same quandary about how much to spend on advertising.

What further complicates the matter is that each brand usually has a number of competitors whose changing activities make it difficult to anticipate correctly what they will do. The dynamic marketplace situation makes the task of budget setting— including having to estimate probable competitors' activities and allow a portion of money for contingencies—a difficult task for most advertisers.

Finally, advertising is not the only factor that contributes to the sale of a product. Other elements of the marketing mix, such as pricing, sales promotion, personal selling, and packaging, also play a role. But who can separate the precise contribution of advertising from the effects of the other marketing mix elements? Few, if any.

Despite these problems, advertising budgets must be established, and the task is performed based on as much knowledge as is available at the moment. This chapter outlines some of the major methods and problems of setting budgets, along with their advantages and disadvantages.

Setting the Budget

Ogilvy & Mather's Approach to Budgeting

The following, prepared by Olgilvy & Mather as an in-house presentation, is a brief introduction to the subject of advertising budgeting. It presents a frame of reference for thinking about budgeting and serves as a preparation for studying the various techniques of budgeting that follow.

> One of the most important and perplexing questions confronting advertisers is how much to spend on advertising. If too little is spent, the most brilliant campaign can fail. Conversely, if too much is spent on advertising, money will be wasted no matter how effective the campaign is.

> How much to spend on advertising is a strategic decision. The budget must be viewed as a function of the marketing and selling objectives of the brand or company. Modest budgets and ambitious goals are irreconcilable. Ambitious budgets for modest goals are inexcusable. One must clearly define the role of advertising and its task must be decided before settling on the budget.

> Until planners have positioned the advertising task, they cannot apply the necessary discipline and available techniques to determine how much money is required.

> Here are some factors to consider in determining an advertising/spending strategy:
> 1. In what market will the brand compete?
>   In the U.S., Mercedes-Benz decided to compete with the $10,000-plus luxury cars as well as luxury imports. This required an advertis-

ing budget many times greater. Had Mercedes decided to compete with the top-of-the-line Buicks, Chryslers, etc., even this budget would have been insufficient. Here are some points to remember:

a. Expanding a market usually requires higher advertising expenditures than gaining competitive share. The reason? It is usually far more difficult to induce consumers to switch to or try another brand.

b. The broader the market the brand competes in, the larger the advertising budget required. The reason? The brand must talk to more people and its competitive world is more diverse.

c. Precise definition of a marketing target can save the advertiser money. For example, advertising just to children requires less expenditure than reaching children plus parents; reaching women only can be done more efficiently than reaching all adults.

2. What is the brand's current market position?

When an advertiser has decided upon the market to compete in, the advertiser will know the product's relative strength compared with competitors. This will help define the planner's task. While all brands seek growth, the difficulty of achieving specific goals relates very importantly to a brand's position in a clearly defined market.

3. How does the advertiser evaluate the competition?

In evaluating a brand's requirements versus competition, the planner should bear in mind that the market leader can usually retain business by spending relatively less than the brand rated second, third, or fourth. A low-rated brand must spend proportionately more to stay in business. To increase competitive position, a planner should be prepared to spend proportionately more than the brands he or she wants to overtake.

4. Where will the brand be advertised?

Invariably, all brands have pockets of strengths and weaknesses across the country. Spending decisions must take these variations into consideration. The same rate of spending in every city or region will not produce the same results. Determining local spending policies requires a great deal of marketing homework. It is not sufficient to simply know the share of market. The planner must try to determine why that share of market exists. Quite often, poor share areas are a result of distribution deficiencies, pricing policies, or sales force weaknesses. Knowing the whys will help the planner judge the contribution that can or cannot be made by advertising. This in turn will help the planner determine spending policies. So it is important to determine the importance and ability of advertising to effect sales change.

Traditional Methods of Setting Budgets

There are a number of widely used methods of determining the budget. Those used most often tend to be simple to understand and quick and easy to compute.

Percent-of-Sales. In the *percent-of-sales* method, an advertising budget is determined by multiplying projected sales revenue for the year by a given percentage. The amount of money available for advertising purposes, therefore, is based directly on the sales achievement of the brand. As sales increase, so does the advertising budget. But as sales decline, the budget also declines.

The heart of this method is the *multiplier,* the percentage by which the sales base is multiplied. In determining which percentage to use, one must consider the cost of goods and the pricing policy of each industry. If a brand costs 15 cents to manufacture and distribute and sells for $1.25, a considerable margin is available for advertising, promotion, and profit.

The first step in setting a budget based on percent of sales is to determine the expenses incurred in manufacturing and distribution. The difference between this cost and the selling price helps determine the margin available for advertising, promotion, and profit. (There are, of course, other costs to be factored in, such as overhead.) Smaller margins may mean a smaller percentage available for advertising.

The key to this method of setting budgets is that of finding the best multiplier. Many times this multiplier is determined arbitrarily. At other times, industry standards may be used as a base. (See Table 15–1.)

Textbooks that discuss the percent-of-sales method of budgeting often give the impression, however, that the method is totally inflexible. This is not true. Often the percent of sales may be only the starting point. After the percentage is multiplied by gross sales, the total may be adjusted to compensate for special marketing situations. When there are special marketing needs, extra dollars are added. Some companies, instead of adding to the total, will raise the multiplier when they are introducing a new product or when they are faced with very heavy competition. In some instances, however, the percentage multiplier remains constant year after year no matter how much sales may vary. When this happens, the multiplier tends to become a historical figure that is rarely questioned.

The multiplier is also affected by product pricing. Sales of low-ticket products such as drugs or supermarket items depend heavily on advertising, while high-ticket items such as appliances, cars, and home furnishings are less dependent on advertising. A rule of thumb for determining whether the multiplier should be large or small is that the more advertising is used as a substitute for personal selling, the higher the multiplier (or the higher the margin to advertising).

Among the advantages of this method are that it is easy to manage and easy to understand. It is self-correcting as sales volume changes, and it may maintain a consistent profit margin. It also is suitable for both financial and marketing group needs.

However, there are many criticisms of the percent-of-sales method. It may well be illogical because advertising is based on sales rather than the other way around. When sales decline, less advertising money will be spent when perhaps more money should be spent. Also, unless the advertising-to-sales ratios are analyzed by area, better sales areas will tend to get better and weaker sales areas will get little relief. This technique also assumes that there is a direct linear relationship between advertising and sales, which is not always true.

Another criticism of this method is that it does not encourage companies to pro-

TABLE 15-1. 100 Leaders' Media Expenditures Compared in 1986 (in measured media only)

Category	Rank	Company	Total	Magazine	News Supplements	Net TV	Spot TV	Net Radio	Outdoor	Net Cable
						Percent of Total Dollars				
Airlines	62	UAL, Inc.	$145,000M	16%	X	48%	30%	3%	1%	2%
	88	Delta Airlines	94,020	2%	X	23%	50%	X	7%	18%
	91	Eastern Airlines	89,700	20%	X	2%	71%	X	6%	1%
Appliances, TV/Radio	24	GE/RCA	373,336	44%	4%	39%	9%	1%	1%	2%
	41	Tandy	186,861	13%	X	68%	8%	8%	X	2%
	57	GTE Corp.	153,606	13%	X	18%	69%	X	X	X
	94	Apple Computer	83,859	31%	X	66%	1%	1%	X	1%
Automobiles/Tires	5	General Motors Co.	779,000	28%	X	55%	13%	2%	X	2%
	7	Ford Motor Co.	614,600	32%	X	53%	10%	2%	X	X
	22	Chrysler Co.	393,400	30%	X	39%	26%	2%	1%	2%
	45	Toyota Motor Co.	172,035	13%	X	23%	58%	1%	2%	3%
	49	Nissan Motors Co.	162,566	17%	X	36%	45%	X	1%	1%
	55	Honda Motor Co.	156,475	25%	1%	57%	10%	3%	X	4%
	58	Goodyear Tire & Rubber Co.	149,305	27%	X	42%	18%	12%	X	1%
	65	American Motors Co.	126,000	29%	X	64%	4%	X	X	3%
	67	Volkswagen of America	123,000	41%	1%	39%	18%	X	X	1%
	85	Mazda Motors of America	101,743	33%	X	57%	8%	X	X	2%
Chemicals	31	American Cyanide Co.	266,189	18%	2%	50%	24%	1%	X	5%
	75	DuPont	112,184	57%	6%	30%	6%	X	X	1%
	77	Union Carbide	110,000	3%	1%	75%	16%	3%	X	2%
	82	Dow Chemical	105,000	15%	X	67%	15%	2%	X	1%
Communications/Entertainment	39	CBS Inc.	208,000	54%	12%	16%	13%	1%	1%	3%
	56	Time Inc.	156,918	41%	2%	3%	43%	X	X	11%
	63	Walt Disney Co.	140,000	19%	2%	6%	71%	X	X	2%
	66	Warner Comm.	124,165	5%	X	47%	38%	X	X	10%
	98	Capital Cities/ABC	72,247	84%	1%	X	11%	X	3%	2%
Drugs	37	Sterling Drug	224,940	10%	X	72%	13%	3%	X	2%
	48	Schering-Plough Corp.	169,383	33%	X	53%	5%	5%	1%	3%
	53	Pfizer Inc.	158,463	29%	X	65%	5%	X	X	1%
	78	Bayer AG	108,000	2%	X	80%	7%	10%	X	1%
Food	3	RJR Nabisco	1,093,000	28%	6%	31%	14%	*	17%	4%
	6	Beatrice	684,000	20%	X	53%	10%	2%	*	X

(continued)

Source: *Advertising Age*, 1986. Reprinted by permission of Crain Communications, Inc.
* = less than 1%; X = no spending.

TABLE 15-1.   (in measured media only) (continued)

Category	Rank	Company	Total	Magazine	News Supplements	Percent of Total Dollars				
						Net TV	Spot TV	Net Radio	Outdoor	Net Cable
	9	McDonald's	550,000	X	X	59%	38%	X	3%	X
	12	Ralston Purina	508,365	11%	1%	54%	31%	1%	1%	1%
	13	Darr & Kraft	489,349	17%	1%	52%	29%	X	X	1%
	14	General Mills	484,146	9%	X	41%	44%	1%	X	5%
	17	Pillsbury	473,220	2%	X	49%	48%	X	X	X
	25	Kellogg	364,299	X	X	74%	24%	X	X	2%
	29	Sara Lee	285,956	23%	1%	52%	21%	2%	X	1%
	32	H. J. Heinz	261,541	8%	X	56%	34%	X	X	2%
	36	Quaker Oats	245,997	11%	1%	64%	22%	1%	X	1%
	38	Campbell Soup	215,059	14%	1%	55%	24%	4%	X	2%
	69	American Dairy Assoc.	121,000	1%	X	72%	23%	2%	1%	1%
	72	Wendy's	115,000	1%	X	50%	46%	X	2%	1%
	100	George Hormel	70,702	13%	X	20%	39%	25%	2%	1%
Gum/Candy	30	Mars Inc.	275,504	4%	X	58%	27%	3%	X	8%
	28	Nestle SA	319,254	14%	X	48%	34%	2%	X	2%
	71	Hershey Foods Corp.	118,990	18%	X	48%	26%	5%	X	3%
	96	Wm. Wrigley Jr.	81,536	3%	X	64%	26%	2%	X	5%
Photographic equipment	35	Eastman Kodak	347,300	21%	1%	63%	11%	1%	1%	2%
	97	Canon Inc.	81,201	43%	X	40%	10%	2%	1%	4%
	64	Xerox	128,898	41%	X	58%	X	X	X	1%
Retail chains	4	Sears, Roebuck & Co.	800,000	9%	X	61%	17%	10%	X	3%
	8	K-mart Corp.	567,000	19%	X	29%	42%	8%	X	X
	15	J. C. Penney Co.	478,892	14%	X	62%	24%	X	X	X
Soaps, cleaners (and allied)	1	Procter & Gamble	1,600,000	10%	2%	54%	31%	2%	X	3%
	19	Unilever U.S.	413,623	8%	X	66%	24%	1%	X	1%
	20	Johnson & Johnson	401,217	15%	X	78%	5%	X	X	2%
	34	Colgate-Palmolive Co.	253,495	7%	2%	71%	18%	X	X	2%
	61	S. C. Johnson & Sons	146,146	24%	2%	57%	11%	5%	X	1%
	79	Clorox Co.	107,105	15%	3%	58%	17%	2%	X	5%
Soft drinks	16	Pepsico Inc.	478,372	1%	X	29%	65%	2%	1%	2%
	23	Coca Cola	390,000	4%	X	55%	36%	1%	2%	2%
Telephone service, equipment	11	ATT	521,318	28%	2%	53%	9%	7%	X	1%
	27	IBM	327,834	43%	29%	51%	2%	2%	X	X
	59	ITT	149,000	42%	1%	35%	15%	1%	3%	3%

Category	Rank	Company	Total	Magazine	News Supplements	Percent of Total Dollars				
						Net TV	Spot TV	Net Radio	Outdoor	Net Cable
Tobacco	2	Philip Morris	1,400,000	26%	2%	43%	18%	X	8%	3%
	51	American Brands	160,000	59%	1%	15%	12%	X	13%	X
	3	RJR/Nabisco	1,093,000	28%	6%	31%	14%	X	17%	4%
Toiletries/Cosmetics	18	Warner-Lambert Co.	469,339	9%	1%	53%	25%	10%	X	2%
	21	American Home Products	399,516	7%	X	81%	9%	X	X	3%
	26	Brystol-Myers Co.	344,293	16%	X	71%	10%	X	X	3%
	42	Beechan Group Plc.	186,322	4%	X	79%	15%	1%	X	1%
	50	Gillette Co.	161,000	14%	X	64%	19%	1%	X	2%
	52	Chesebrough-Pond's	159,792	26%	X	55%	7%	10%	X	2%
	54	Leows	156,918	54%	6%	X	3%	X	37%	X
	60	Revlon Group	147,215	41%	2%	42%	11%	3%	X	1%
	80	Noxell Corp.	106,128	28%	X	63%	6%	1%	X	2%
Wine, Beer, Liquor	10	Anheuser-Busch Co.	522,900	5%	X	57%	26%	3%	2%	7%
	74	Stroh Brewery Co.	113,000	3%	X	70%	18%	X	3%	6%
	83	Adolph Coors Co.	104,981	4%	X	31%	60%	X	2%	3%
	76	Jos E. Seagram Sons	110,183	40%	3%	21%	13%	1%	21%	1%
	87	Brown-Forman Co.	94,260	43%	10%	16%	19%	X	10%	2%
	89	Van Munching & Co.	93,388	32%	2%	27%	38%	1%	X	X
Miscellaneous	33	U.S. Government	259,050	31%	X	44%	15%	5%	4%	1%
	40	Mobil Corp.	195,262	16%	1%	28%	50%	X	1%	4%
	43	Grand Metropolitan	186,322	36%	5%	29%	20%	X	9%	1%
	44	Batus Inc.	176,749	35%	17%	X	15%	X	33%	X
	46	I. C. Industries	171,000	4%	X	39%	55%	2%	X	X
	47	American Express Co.	169,868	34%	1%	41%	20%	3%	X	1%
	68	Cosmair Inc.	122,149	32%	1%	53%	13%	X	X	1%
	70	CPC International	120,000	27%	2%	42%	29%	X	X	X
	73	Hasbro Inc.	114,849	6%	X	29%	64%	X	X	1%
	81	AMR Corp.	105,412	6%	X	54%	38%	2%	X	X
	84	Greyhound Corp.	102,604	13%	X	44%	8%	31%	X	3%
	86	MCA Inc.	98,360	2%	1%	72%	16%	1%	1%	7%
	90	Monsanto Co.	92,885	9%	X	72%	11%	7%	X	1%
	93	Mattel Inc.	85,092	6%	X	58%	32%	X	X	4%
	92	Matsushita Electric Co.	86,000	70%	X	3%	21%	1%	1%	4%
	95	Gulf & Western	82,101	11%	X	39%	38%	6%	X	6%
	99	Cotter & Co.	71,670	15%	X	32%	29%	20%	X	4%

vide the research money needed to find the relationship between advertising and sales. Marketing expert Alfred A. Kuehn offered this comment:

> Perhaps the best of these rules [methods of setting budgets] for an established brand is "budget a percentage of expected sales equal to the industry average." This rule is of particular interest since it is self-adjusting over time, and appears to be a low-risk policy for a firm which does not have a better understanding of the effects of advertising than does its competitors.[2]

On the other hand, if all competitive brands used this method and employed about the same percent multiplier, advertising budget sizes would be approximately proportional to market share, thus limiting investment spending for advertising warfare among competitors.

Competitive Spending. The *competitive spending* method depends on setting the budget in relation to the amount of competitive spending. The amount to be spent need not be precisely the same as that of competitors, though at times it is. At times, a brand that has a smaller market share than its competitor may be given an amount to spend equal to or greater than the competitor, as a means of improving the share position.

A major criticism of this approach is that it assumes that competitors know what they are doing or that competitors' goals are the same as one's own. It also assumes, incorrectly, that a simple increase in advertising expenditures will automatically increase sales and/or market share. The products of competitors may be different, or at least consumers may perceive them as different, so that a company's advertising may have to work much harder to make sales than competitors' advertising. Certainly, the marketing goals of one company are not the same as another, and the ability of advertising to create sales also is not the same.

Objective and Task. The *objective and task* method starts with someone setting specific marketing and/or advertising objectives that are then costed out. The total cost represents the budget. Objectives may be sales, share volume levels, revenues expected, income, or profit.

There are two main criticisms of this method. First, it is not always possible to determine how much money it takes to attain any given objective. Second, the method does not consider the value of each objective and the relationship to the cost of obtaining it. Is it really worth all of the money necessary to achieve any given objective?

Expenditure per Unit (Case Rate). This system is a variant of the percent-of-sales method. In the *case-rate* method, the budget is generated as a result of sales, but units sold, not dollar sales, are used as the base. Many of the same advantages and disadvantages of the percent-of-sales method apply also to this method. However, there are two additional disadvantages:

---

2. Kuehn, Alfred A., "A Model for Budgeting Advertising," *Mathematical Models and Methods in Marketing,* Homewood, Ill.: Irwin Publishing Company, 1961, pp. 315–16.

1. Unless the method is properly handled, there is a possibility that the control of profits may be lost. This is particularly true if the product or brand has a wide range of sizes or prices. Shell Oil Company, for example, has four types of gasoline ranging from Super-Regular (premium price) to Regular (lowest price). Profitability varies for each. Spending on a cents-per-gallon basis must take into consideration the mix of the line.
2. Working with units and fixed rates of expenditures will not take inflation into account. To overcome this, the case rate must be adjusted from year to year.

Subjective Budgeting. These budgeting systems involve decisions made on a subjective basis. Essentially, the executive whose responsibility it is to determine the budget size uses experience and judgment as a basis for decisions. This is not to say that such executives would not consider some objective factors as well, such as first determining the minimum job that advertising will be required to do, or perhaps considering available profit margins as a basis. But after such considerations, the final figure is decided upon rather subjectively.

One subjective budgeting method is known as "All We Can Afford." Although at first glance, this approach may seem illogical or crude, it may be quite realistic if the subjective decision is accurate. This method generally starts by setting a profit percent or dollar figure, then systematically analyzing the costs of doing business. The remaining figure, after all other costs are accounted for, is spent in marketing, a portion of which is advertising. A budget made on such a basis may be difficult to defend, especially when there is reason to believe that if more money had been appropriated, the result then would be higher sales and higher profits.

Newer Methods of Setting Budgets

Experimental Methods. A number of marketing and advertising professionals feel that the best way to determine the size of an advertising budget is by testing various levels of expenditures to see which will produce the most sales at the lowest total cost. The experimental designs for this purpose may range from a simple before-and-after test in one market to elaborate designs in which many markets are tested and compared with control markets. Although the details of such experiments are usually kept secret, occasionally some are publicized.[3,4]

Essentially, experimental tests involve trying different advertising expenditure levels in different markets. In one example, Anheuser-Busch used three sets of markets (each set consisting of nine individual markets) to test alternative expenditure levels and measure the effects on sales. In one set of markets, advertising expendi-

3. McNiven, Malcolm A., "Choosing the Most Profitable Level of Advertising" (case study), in *How Much to Spend for Advertising,* Association of National Advertisers, Inc., 1969.

4. Newell, Thomas M., "What Is the Right Amount to Spend for Advertising?" in *Papers from the 1968 American Association of Advertising Agencies Regional Convention,* Palm Springs, California, Oct. 6–9, 1968.

tures were reduced from 50 percent to 100 percent below the level that ordinarily would have been used in those markets. In another group of markets, the budget was increased by 50 percent to perhaps as much as 300 percent. A third group of markets were control markets where there was no increase or decrease in normal advertising expenditures to provide a base of comparison with the other market groups.

In some experimental situations, advertisers discover that they can reduce advertising expenditures without any effect on sales. In other situations, increases in advertising produce varying degrees of sales increases.

If the experimental method is indeed as effective as some individuals assume it to be, why then is it not used more often to determine budget size? There are a number of reasons. George H. Brown, former director of the U.S. Census Bureau and a marketing expert, cited two problems involved with this method. The first is the relatively high cost of conducting the experiment, which involves finding and measuring a fairly large sample. The second problem is the long time span, perhaps a year or more, that is required. By the time the experiment is completed, the marketing situation may have changed, making the final figures irrelevant. Brown also pointed out that, although the cost may not be considered too high if the payoff is accurate and valuable, the payoff may not be worth the cost.

At present, not many companies use the experimental method, though some who have used it are quite content with it. Unfortunately, most of these companies have not revealed the details of their methods so that no outside evaluation is possible.

The Hendry Method. The detailed mathematical description of this method is not publicly known because companies that want to use it must pay the Hendry Corporation for the privilege. However, some of the essential ideas have been made public. Stanley D. Canter, former senior vice president of Ogilvy & Mather, explained some of these ideas in a speech given to the Association of National Advertisers.[5]

When making a purchase, consumers tend to buy the products and brands they have purchased in the past. But their decision to buy based on past preference contains a degree of uncertainty. The nature of this uncertainty has not been explained, although it can be assumed that consumers may perceive buying as a risk and wish to minimize such risks. This uncertainty represents an opportunity to change purchase habits.

Canter noted that ''the degree of uncertainty is a marketing analogy to the properties of entropy in statistical mechanics. In marketing it becomes a measure of brand switching.'' Therefore, the degree of entropy may be considered the degree of probability that consumers will switch brands.

The relationship between consumers' preferences and their uncertainties can sometimes be shifted one way or another by various marketing strategies, one of

5. Canter, Stanley D., ''Exposition of the Hendry Advertising Analysis Model,'' presented at the Association of National Advertisers Workshop on Media Planning, New York, Sept. 30, 1971.

FIGURE 15-1.   The Concept of the Hendry Method

A brand's current share of market	=	That part of the brand's share due to all other factors *except* advertising	+	The brand's advertising expenditures / (The brand's ad expenditures + Sum of all expenditures of other brands in the category (weighted for effectiveness))	×	The probability of brand switching (entropy)

Source: Canter, Stanley D., *Exposition of the Hendry Advertising Analysis Model,* Association of National Advertisers Workshop on Media Planning, New York, September 30, 1971, p. 2.

which is advertising. However, other marketing strategies—price, distribution, and personal selling—may also play a role in influencing buying.

The additional share of market gained by a given brand due to advertising is equal to the share of advertising weighted by differences in the effectiveness, multiplied by the entropy of the brand. Figure 15-1 illustrates this.

If the probability of brand switching is zero, then advertising would have no effect on that brand's share of market, and its market share would be due entirely to factors other than advertising. "But as the probability of brand switching increases, the opportunity for advertising to work increases, and a greater proportion of a brand's share of market may be attributable to advertising," noted Canter.

As advertising is increased, profits may also increase to a maximum point beyond which profits will decline. Therefore it is important to look at the relationship between advertising, profits, and market share simultaneously, as shown in Figure 15-2. In this figure, advertising expenditures, profits, and market share are input data that are used for calibration purposes to help position the brand under current marketing conditions on a specific curve, out of a general family of curves describing a generalized relationship between the three variables. That curve is called the *profit profile.* Using the profit profile curve, the marketer can experiment to see how alternative advertising expenditures will affect potential market shares and/or profits. How one determines this curve, however, has not been explained publicly.

When a company comes to Hendry, the first step in determining the advertising budget size is to calibrate the three variables. The third variable may be direct advertising margins (gross sales minus the cost of producing the product).

Once this calibration has been made, Hendry, through its formulas and computer analysis, can then show the relationship between advertising expenditures and market share or profit for that brand. Hendry can also show what share of market and profits would result if the advertising level for a brand were increased or decreased. Allocations can be made by sales territories, and a client can learn how much to spend for new product introductions, or what impact advertising expenditures will have upon competitors' profits and share of advertising. Although the details of this method are not known, it is known that some large companies that have used the method have found it successful.

Andrew Kershaw, former chairman of the board of Ogilvy & Mather, has reported some findings using Hendry methods in about forty different analyses.

FIGURE 15–2.   Relationship between Expenditures, Market Share, and Profit

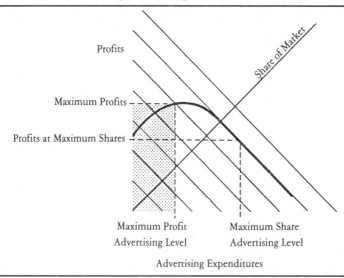

Source: Kershaw, Andrew, ''How to Use Our Media Dollars as a More Effective Marketing Tool,'' Association of National Advertisers Workshop on Media Planning, September 30, 1971, p. 10.

1. Advertising always makes a measureable contribution to share of market. On the average, one-quarter of market share points of a brand is attributable to advertising. Some brands depend entirely on advertising, but other brands' advertising contributes much less to share.

2. For every brand, there is a point where additional media expenditures do not result in an increase in market share. While some brands have spent more money than needed, others are getting less than 50 percent of the share they could attain if they spent more for advertising.

3. Maximum share of market never results in maximum profits. There is evidence that the advertising expenditures that yield maximum share of market do not maximize profits, so the rule would be to spend less than needed to achieve maximum share.

4. Many companies choose to advertise at less than maximum profits. Figure 15–3 shows that 56.5% of brands studied advertise at a budget level that results in maximum profits. More than four out of ten brands spend too little or too much money in advertising to achieve profit maximization.

5. Some product categories spend too much on advertising.

6. Some market definitions based on consumer usage are too narrow and the brand finds itself with a lower market share. This in turn may require more money to be spent to hold or increase market share.

7. It may be far more efficient to adopt a corporate media expenditure policy rather than a brand-oriented one. . . . Thus it is possible to shift

FIGURE 15-3. Proportion of Brands Advertising Below, At, or Above Level That Results in Profit Maximization

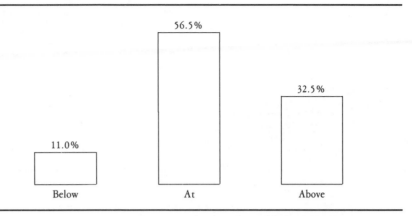

Source: Kershaw, Andrew, "How to Use Our Media Dollars as a More Effective Marketing Tool," Association of National Advertisers Workshop on Media Planning, September 30, 1971, p. 10.

media funds from one brand with a lower marginal advertising productivity to another brand with a higher rate of productivity.[6]

Theoretical Methods. An increasing number of theoretical budgeting methods have been discussed in journals of marketing and/or business. Most are based on rather complex mathematical formulas and none have found continuing acceptance in the everyday world of advertising and marketing. This text is not the appropriate place to discuss the alternative theoretical methods, but the reader who wants to know more about them should consult the selected readings at the end of this chapter.

Which Methods Are Used Most Often?

Table 15-2, compiled by Andre J. San Augustine and William Foley, gives some indication of the prevalence of methods currently in use.

Factors in Determining the Size of an Advertising Budget

Although it may not be possible to determine a budget size scientifically, it may be advisable to approach the task by weighting a number of factors that might affect the budget size. Setting a budget in this manner might be called "atomistic" in that one could think about each factor separately (like a collection of atoms), then assemble these factors into a final budget figure.

6. Kershaw, Andrew, "How to Use Our Media Dollars as a More Effective Marketing Tool," speech given to the Association of National Advertisers Workshop on Media Planning, New York, Sept. 30, 1971.

TABLE 15-2.   Methods 100 Executives Use to Set Advertising Budgets*

Methods	Consumer Product Companies		Nonconsumer Product Companies	
	Averages (%)	Rank	Averages (%)	Rank
Percent of anticipated sales	50	1	28	2
All that is affordable	30	2	26	3
Others (not specified)	26	3	10	5
Percent of past years' sales	14	4	16	4
Arbitrary approach	12	5	34	1
Unit anticipated sales	8	6	10	5
Objective and task	6	7	10	5
Unit past years' sales	6	7	4	6
Quantitative models	2	8	0	7
Don't know	2	–	2	–
Total**	156		140	

Source: San Augustine, A. J., and Foley, W. F., "How Large Advertisers Set Their Budgets," *Journal of Advertising Research,* October 1975, p. 12.
 *Sample consisted of two executives from each of 25 nonconsumer product companies, and 25 consumer product companies. One was a financial executive and the other an advertising executive. The averages are of two percentages representing two executives per company.
**Adds to over 100 percent because of multiple responses.

In weighting each factor, some will be found to be more important than others, suggesting that priorities for marketing the brand must be determined first. Furthermore, each factor must be judged on the basis of whether one should spend more than, the same as, or less than the previous year. Again this is a subjective decision, but it may help the executive arrive at a final figure more easily.

A brief discussion of these factors follows.

Assessing the Task of Advertising. Before deciding on any figure, it is reasonable to determine what role advertising is to play. Must it do the selling job alone, or will it be added to other marketing mix elements such as reduced prices and sales promotion? If advertising must do the selling job alone, the size of the budget may have to be substantial. If it works with other marketing mix elements, the size of the budget may be less.

Important in this consideration is an understanding of the power of advertising to sell the brand. Some brands simply are not sensitive to advertising; perhaps because they are so much like other brands on the market, because they do not have a unique selling proposition, or because it is difficult to be creative in presenting the message through print or broadcast media.

Long- and Short-Term Goals. To some extent advertising may have long- and short-term goals set for it, but when the objective is to build an image, then the budget should be treated as an investment rather than an expense (as one would treat the budget for short-term goals). If both goals are required at the same time, then more money may be required because advertising has been given a dual function. The advertising copy for immediate sales may differ markedly from the copy whose goal is to build an image.

In a sense, however, the concept of dividing an advertising budget into an expense for immediate sales and an investment for long-term image building may be invalid. The reason is that image-building advertising may not consist of special ads that are designed for that purpose. If the brand image is thought of as a "long-term investment in the reputation of a brand," then every ad that is run, no matter whether it opts for immediate or future image, contributes to the long-range goal.

The goals of the company and advertising's relationship with them, then, affect to some degree the amount of money to be spent. Companies may perceive this relationship somewhat differently, so no general principle can be extracted.

Profit Margins Affect Budget Size. There is an assumption in the industry that where there are larger profit margins there will be larger advertising budgets, and the converse is also assumed to be true. Profit margins may be a limiting factor in setting marketing and/or advertising goals—what one would like to do cannot be done simply because there isn't enough money available to do it. It may be ironic that when profit margins must be increased, advertising expenditures also should be increased, but there is little or no money available to do the job.

Degree of Product Usage. Products that are used widely throughout the country may require more money for advertising than those whose usage is limited to a relatively small geographic area. However, some local and regional advertisers may find it necessary to invest heavily in their marketing area due to heavy competitive spending, e.g., fast-food firms and automobile dealers.

Difficulty in Reaching Target Markets. Some markets are so unique that no single medium reaches them well, such as the market for expensive yachts. A number of different media may have to be purchased, requiring more money. Many times, targets are so spread out geographically that mass media may have to be purchased, resulting in enormous message waste. When this occurs, more money is needed to do a reasonable job.

Frequency of Purchase. It is assumed that brands and/or products purchased frequently will require more money for advertising than those that are purchased infrequently. However, an exception occurs when the advertising goals of infrequently purchased brands are such that they require more money to be spent for other reasons than frequency of purchase.

Effect of Increased Sales Volume on Production Costs. If there is a danger of demand exceeding supply because of advertising's power, the consequence may be that a new plant must be built. In that situation, the amount of money spent for advertising may have to be limited until the factory is built or a decision is made to the contrary. The advertiser may want to reduce advertising expenditures for awhile until it is possible to supply the demand.

New Product Introductions. It is widely held that new product introductions take a great deal of additional money to break into the market. How much more depends on the size of the market, the degree of competition, and the desirable qualities of the new brand. A rule of thumb is that it takes at least one-and-a-half times as much as is spent on established brands to introduce the new brand.

Competitive Activity. In markets where competitors are very active in advertising and sales promotion, it may be necessary to match, or even exceed, their expenditures, depending on the marketing goals of the brand in question. While the preceding factors do not indicate exactly how much to spend on advertising, they do serve as decision-making guidelines.

Allocating the Advertising Budget

Once the size of the advertising budget has been determined, then it must be allocated, or apportioned, in some reasonable way. When relating advertising to source of sales, advertising budgets are allocated to geographic areas. Many advertisers, however, particularly on a national level, allocate their budgets on the basis of national media selection with relatively little concern for geographical business skews.

Geographic Allocations

Perhaps the most often used budget allocation technique is to allot at least equal portions to the amount of sales produced by a geographical area. The reasoning behind this method is that one takes a minimal risk in allocating the most dollars to areas where sales are known to have been good. If previous budgets were successful in producing or at least contributing to sales, why would not more money (or an equal amount relative to sales) be equally effective? The concept is not only to keep the risk low, but to optimize whatever monies are available.

If a geographical area contributed 15 percent of total sales, then it may be assumed that it would get 15 percent of the budget. Of course, there may be a problem here. It is possible that it took much more than 15 percent of the previous year's allocation to produce 15 percent sales. In such a case, a different method of allocation could be used, one based on the amount of profit produced by the area in proportion to total profit nationwide. Allocating on the basis of profit is simply another method of distributing effort.

Other methods could be based on the market share contributed by each area, the anticipated sales produced by each area, or some number that would be a composite of a number of marketing variables, such as population, income, retail sales of the product class, plus other related variables.

In practice, formula methods of allocating budgets tend to be only the starting point, rather than the endpoint, of the allocating procedure. Adjustments usually have to be made to take into consideration special marketing problems. One such problem could be that the media in a particular area may cost much more, proportionally, than in any other part of the country. More money may have to be added to the initial allocation figure to compensate for this problem. Another problem could be that competitors have started to promote more heavily in areas that have been most profitable for the brand in question. Again special adjustments will have to be made to the original allocation.

TABLE 15-3.   A Budget Allocated Proportionately to Sales Made by Each Area

Sales Area	Sales Made by Each Area (%)	Budget Goal	Network Delivery* (%)
A	30	$1,500,000	25
B	15	750,000	15
C	10	500,000	20
D	10	500,000	10
E	35	1,750,000	30
Total	100	$5,000,000	100

Source: J. Walter Thompson Company, *Allocating Advertising Weight Geographically*, 1973, p. 9.
*Delivery is based on a number of selected network programs that cover targets.

Media Allocations

A budget allocated by geographic sales territories may not be sufficient to put a marketing/advertising plan into operation—a further allocation may have to be made to media. In fact, one could dispense with allocations to areas and start with allocations to media that reach demographic targets no matter where they are located geographically. Following is a simulated example of how a budget may be allocated to both area and media.

For purposes of illustration, assume that a manufacturer sells a product in five geographic areas of the country. Sales percentages for each of the five areas are shown in Table 15-3, as is a proportional allocation of the budget to each sales area. Also shown is the percentage of network television delivery in each sales area.

Table 15-3 shows that each area received a proportional amount of dollars equal to the percentage of sales made in the area. However, a close look at the relationship of sales and network delivery percentages shows some anomalies. For example, Area A delivered 30 percent of total sales but has only 25 percent of total network delivery. As a result, it may be necessary to allocate some of the budget to local television.

The problem that arises is how to divide the television budget between network and spot so that each area receives an equitable portion of the budget. Ideally, a planner would like the percentage of network television delivery to match sales percentages in each market. Therefore, if a market provides 20 percent of total U.S. sales, then it should receive 20 percent of the budget. Unfortunately, when advertisers use network television, the delivery in some markets is more than needed, while the delivery in other markets is less than needed.

For example, if sales in Market A are 30 percent and the percentage of total U.S. network program delivery is 20 percent, then some way must be found to bring television delivery up to the 30 percent level. This may be done by adding a certain amount of dollars to local spot television. However, if a market accounts for 10 percent of sales and network television delivery is 20 percent of the U.S. total, one cannot easily cut network, market by market. So a technique has been created to take dollars from network television in certain markets and add them to spot television to bring each market up to a percentage equal to its sales.

The technique outlined step-by-step applies to Table 15-4 in particular. The total U.S. budget was set by the client at $5 million.

   1. The planner should first calculate a budget for each individual market.

TABLE 15-4.   Allocation of Budget to Network and Spot TV

Sales Area	Sales Made by Each Area (%)	Budget Goal	Total Network Delivery (%)	Index: Network to Sales Delivery	Network Budget	Spot TV (Local) Budget
A	30	$1,500,000	25	83	$ 625,000	$ 875,000
B	15	750,000	15	100	375,000	375,000
C	10	500,000	20	200	500,000	—
D	10	500,000	10	100	250,000	250,000
E	35	1,750,000	30	86	750,000	1,000,000
Total	100	$5,000,000	100		$2,500,000	$2,500,000

Source: J. Walter Thompson Company, *Allocating Advertising Weight Geographically*, 1973, p. 9.

One technique for doing that is called the *pro-rata* (or proportional) method. This simply means that each market will get the same percentage of a budget that it produces in sales.

So, the planner first multiplies each percentage of sales by the total budget ($5 million). In Table 15-4, Market A accounted for 30 percent of total sales, so it received 30 percent of the $5 million budget, or $1,500,000.

2. The planner then determines how much each market is overdelivered by using network television. Planners must check local market rating books to see how many GRPs that network programs selected for a client are being delivered to each market. This is done by comparing the percent of sales made in each market, with the percent of network television audience delivered in the same market, and calculating an index of over-delivery.

This is the formula:

$$\text{Index} = \frac{\text{Percentage of network delivery in each market}}{\text{Percentage of sales in market}} \times 100$$

For example, from Table 15-4, Market C had a sales of 10 percent and a network delivery of 20 percent. Its pro-rata budget was $500,000. So $500,000 ÷ .20 = $2,500,000. The latter figure now becomes the basis for a *revised total network budget* leaving the other $2,500,000 for spot television.

3. Now, each market's percent delivery is multiplied by the revised network budget of $2.5 million. Market C still gets $500,000, but the other markets will get less. When all revised budgets are added they should total $2.5 million. For example, Market E had a network delivery of 30 percent. Therefore, multiplying .30 × $2.5 million would give Market E a revised network budget of $750,000.

4. To find how much ought to be spent in spot television, in each market, subtract the revised local budget for network from the pro-rata budget. The difference will be an estimate of how much to spend locally in each market. For example, Market A has a revised network budget of $625,000. Its pro-rata budget was $1.5 million. Subtracting $625,000

from $1.50 million equals $875,000, which is the estimated allocation for Market A in spot.

5. Note that Market C had a revised network budget of $500,000 and a pro-rata budget of $500,000. Therefore through subtraction, Market C gets no extra money for spot television. Why? Because it was the most overspent market in terms of network audience delivery. There is no need for adding spot TV because network TV is adequate.

Payout Planning

The Concept. Another kind of budgeting operation that media planners may be involved with is called payout planning. A *payout plan* is a budget used in new product introductions where more money than usual is needed to launch a brand. The extra dollars come not only from the sales made by the brand, but also from allocating the brand's profits to advertising, for a limited time.

The following data may be helpful in explaining the situation before studying the formal portions of a payout plan. A new brand may have the following costs and pricing:

	Per case
Selling price of brand by factory	$12.00
Costs of manufacturing, overhead, and selling the brand	7.00
Amount available for promotion and profit	$ 5.00
Normal amount available for promotion	$ 2.50
Normal amount available for profit	2.50
Full amount available for introducing the new brand: promotion + profit	$ 5.00

So, in new product introductions, the manufacturer may be willing to forego profits for a limited time and invest them in advertising, in addition to the usual advertising investment. This practice of investing both promotion and profit funds is called *full available*.

What is important to understand about this investment is that in the very first months, the brand does not earn enough money to pay for the extra heavy advertising investments that it needs. Therefore, the company, in a sense, invests money (or pays out of its own pocket) to the brand during the early periods of selling. But, as the brand begins to sell more and earn more money, it begins to be in a position to start paying back the investment that the company made. Finally, if everything goes well, the brand will be selling enough of the product to pay back the entire investment and stand on its own as a profit center. When that happens, the full available is divided so that part goes for profits and a portion for advertising.

Explanation of a Payout Plan. Following is an explanation of the payout plan shown in Table 15–5. Each paragraph is keyed to the number at the beginning of each row on the plan. Although payout plans are not generally calculated by media

TABLE 15-5.   A Three-Period Payout Plan

(1) Time Periods	Period 1	Period 2	Period 3	Total
(2) Size of total market in millions of cases	10	11	12	
(3) Average share for the brand	12%	18%	25%	
(4) Year-end total share for the brand	15%	25%	25%	
(5) Cases (millions) purchased by pipeline	0.4	0.2	0.1	
(6) Cases (millions) purchased at consumer level	1.2	2.0	3.0	
(7) Total shipments from factory (millions of cases)	1.6	2.2	3.1	
(8) Factory income @ $12 a case*	$19.2	$26.4	$37.2	
(9) Less cost @ $7 a case	$11.2	$15.4	$21.7	
(10) The budget (dollars available for promotion and profit)	$ 8.0	$11.0	$15.5	$34.5
(11) Reallocation of budget to place heavier weight in first period	$14.9	$11.7	$ 7.9	$34.5
(12) Percent of reallocated budget	43%	34%	23%	100%
(13) Allocation of budget to advertising and sales promotion				
To advertising (85%)	$12.7	$ 9.9	$ 6.7	$29.3
To sales promotion (15%)	$ 2.2	$ 1.8	$ 1.2	$ 5.2
Total	$14.9	$11.7	$ 7.9	$34.5
(14) Profit (or loss)	($ 6.9)	($ 0.7)	$ 7.6	—
(15) Cumulative investment	($ 6.9)	($ 7.6)	0	—

*All dollar figures are in millions. Thus 19.2 = $19,200,000.

planning personnel, the media planner should be aware of the mechanics insofar as they bear on the final advertising budget.

1. **Time periods**. Although three time periods are shown on the payout plan, more or fewer could have been used. Furthermore, these time periods could have varied from one to three years in length, or they could have been one to three six-month periods. The timing, therefore, is a matter of judgment and experience on the part of the planner who must estimate how long it will take to pay back the money necessary to get the brand launched in the marketplace.

2. **Size of total market in millions (MM) of cases**. A market may be described in any way most suitable to the advertiser. Some prefer to use cases. Others use pounds of the product, packages, or dollars. The data for the number of cases that will be sold is an estimate, based on trend analysis, modified by the judgment and experience of the advertising executive. If these estimates are wrong, then the payout plan will have to be adjusted accordingly.

3. **Average share for the brand**. As a new product is introduced and begins to be purchased by wholesalers, retailers, and consumers, it is obvious that the share of market could vary considerably from month to month. So this percentage represents the average for the year rather than the total. Either could have been used, but the more modest percentage is probably safer. Again, this is a crucial estimate which, if incorrect, would require the plan to be adjusted immediately.

4. **Year-end total share for the brand**. This figure is shown only as a guide to what the executive hopes to achieve at year end. It is not used in the

calculations, though it could be substituted for average share, as previously mentioned.

5. **Cases purchased by pipeline.** The first factory sales could be to pipeline companies such as wholesalers and distributors (depending on how the product is distributed). This group of companies represents a portion of total sales. The amount in the pipeline at any time can be estimated from past experience with similar types of products.

6. **Cases purchased at the consumer level.** This figure is calculated by multiplying the average share expected times the number of cases expected to be sold in the total market: ($10,000,000 \times 12\% = 1,200,000$ cases).

7. **Total shipments from factory.** Pipeline and consumer purchases are added here: ($400,000 + 1,200,000 = 1,600,000$ cases for Period 1).

8. **Factory income @ $12 a case.** Since the decision was to price a case at $12 each, then this figure is multiplied by the number of cases expected to be sold for each period. Period 1: ($1,600,000$ cases $\times$ $12 a case $= \$19,200,000$ income).

9. **Less cost of $7 a case.** Here $7 (the total manufacturing cost) was multiplied by the estimated number of cases that will be sold: (Period 1: $1,600,000 \times \$7 = \$11,200,000$ cost).

10. **The budget.** Since the budget is composed of dollars allocated both for promotion and for profit (or full available) it is necessary only to subtract the cost of cases sold per period from the selling price to learn what amount of money is available for promotion. Period 1: ($\$19,200,000 - \$11,200,000 = \$8,000,000$). The term promotion as used here does not mean sales promotion, but more broadly, advertising and sales promotion. As a result of the subtraction in each period, there is a given amount of money available in each, which when added together equals $34,500,000.

11. **Reallocation of budget.** Although $34,500,000 would be available for advertising and sales promotion, the budget as it is shown in paragraph (10) is allocated in a strict mathematical fashion, rather than with an understanding of advertising investment needs. Most of the budget occurs in the third period. On the other hand, most of the money is needed in the first period, where extra heavy expenditures usually are needed to launch the brand.

12. **Percent budget.** So the executive has reallocated the budget total ($34,500,000) in the manner felt necessary. As a result, the executive allocated 43 percent of the $34,500,000 to the first period instead of the 23.2 percent that would have been available if the budget were accepted as shown in paragraph 10: ($\$8,000,000 \div \$34,500,000 = 23.2\%$).

13. **Allocation of the budget to advertising and sales promotion.** This is an arbitrary allocation based on what the executive thinks is needed for each. Some other executive with a different marketing situation and product might think the proportions should be different.

14. **Profit or loss.** At this point, an investment in the brand must be made. Since the amount of money available for promotion in Period 1 is only $8,000,000 (paragraph 10) and dollars needed for the same period are $14,900,000 (paragraph 11), it will be necessary for the company to invest an additional $6,900,000, which represents a loss for the brand for Period 1. The brand now owes the company $6,900,000 for Period 1.

In Period 2, again the reallocated budget is more than the brand would earn for that period, $11,700,000 vs. $11,000,000. Again the brand loses money; only this time not so much, $700,000. If this amount is added to the amount already owed to the company from Period 1, the cumulative total for Period 2 is now $7,600,000. This means that the company has to give the brand $7,600,000 for the extra amount needed above sales dollars up to the end of Period 2.

However, in Period 3, the brand earns enough money ($7,600,000) to pay back the amount given to it by the company. At this point it has made a profit, paid back the money given to it by the company, and presumably will make a profit to keep it going in Period 4. When the brand makes a profit, it *pays out* money to the company. Not shown in this example, but what obviously should be included in real situations, is the inflation factor. Money "loaned" to a brand in Year 1 is worth more than face value in succeeding years.

Conclusion

Although media planners have begun to use more scientific tools in budgeting, many areas still require judgment. The area of planning that most seems to defy solution is how to determine the optimum size of an advertising budget. Methods described in this chapter have been used for many years. Though they are considered relatively crude, they are easy and quick to compute, and for that reason they have maintained their popularity over many years. Allocation techniques, on the other hand, can be characterized as logical and reasonable. Some involve decisions based on subjective judgments of what will happen in the marketplace, as the payout plan indicates. But in any case, allocation procedures are more advanced than previous budget-setting methods have been. Perhaps the greatest advances have come in theoretical model building on the relationship between advertising, sales, and share of market. None of these have found their way into everyday use, though the Hendry method may be the one most operational at this time.

QUESTIONS FOR DISCUSSION

1. What is the difference between setting a budget and allocating it?
2. Why is it so difficult to devise an advertising budget using scientific methods?
3. Why is the percent-of-sales method probably the most widely used method of budgeting, considering the fact that it has many limitations?

4. Discuss the question of whether a company that wants larger profit margins should increase or decrease its advertising budget.
5. Often markets are assigned proportions of budgets in direct relation to the amount of sales or market share they produce. Under what conditions might this practice not be advisable?
6. Although the objective and task method of budgeting is often considered to be one of the best methods, what limitations does it have?
7. What is the underlying concept of a payout plan?
8. Discuss the question of whether a planner with the third-rated brand on the market ought to copy competitors' budgets.
9. Where, in a payout plan, is it possible to make a judgmental error that could affect the outcome of the plan?

SELECTED READINGS

Blasko, V. J., and Patti, C. H., "The Advertising Budgeting Practices of Industrial Marketers," *Journal of Marketing,* Fall 1984, pp. 104–110.

Canter, Stanly D., "Exposition of the Hendry Advertising Analysis Model," speech presented to the Association of National Advertisers Workshop on Media Planning, New York, September 30, 1971.

Cheek, Logan M., *Zero-Based Budgeting Comes of Age,* Amacom (American Management Association), New York, 1977, 314 pp.

Dean, Joel, "How Much Should You Spend for Advertising?" *Advertising Plans: Preparation and Presentation,* Vol. III, 1957, Association of National Advertisers, pp. 92–107.

Friedman, Lawrence, "Game Theory Models in the Allocation of Advertising Expenditures," *Operations Research,* Operations Research Society of America, 1958, pp. 699–709.

Kelly, Richard S., and Ahlgren, Herbert A. (eds.), *The Advertising Budget,* New York: Association of National Advertisers, 1967, p. 289.

Kershaw, Andrew, "How to Use Our Media Dollars as a More Effective Marketing Tool," speech presented to the Association of National Advertisers Workshop

on Media Planning, September 30, 1971.

Kuehn, Alfred, A., "A Model for Budgeting Advertising," *Mathmatical Models and Methods in Marketing,* Homewood, Ill.: Irwin Publishing Company, 1961, p. 315.

Kropp, H. R., Ehrenberg, A. S. C., Butler, Ben, Sr., and Gross, I., "Setting Budgets and Allocating Advertising Efforts," *Advertising Research Foundation 19th Annual Conference Report,* New York, 1973, pp. 29-38.

Little, John D., and Ackoff, Russell L., "How Techniques of Mathematical Analysis Have Been Used to Determine Advertising Budgets and Strategy," Advertising Research Foundation *Fourth Annual Conference Report,* 1958, pp. 19–24.

Mansfield, Frank W., "Budgeting Your Advertising for Profit," *Advertising Plans: Preparation and Presentation,* Vol. III, Association of National Advertisers, 1957, pp. 108-14.

Mason, Kenneth, "How Much Do You Spend on Advertising? Product Is the Key," *Advertising Age,* June 12, 1972, pp. 41–44.

McCabe, Thomas B., "How Much to Spend for Advertising," *Perspectives in Advertising Management,* Association of National Advertisers, New York, 1969, pp. 113–23.

Newell, Thomas M., "What Is the Right Amount to Spend for Advertising?" *Papers from the 1968 Regional Conventions*, American Association of Advertising Agencies, New York.

Parrish, T. Kirk, "How Much to Spend for Advertising," *Journal of Advertising Research*, February 1974, pp. 9–12.

Peckham, James O., "Can We Relate Advertising Dollars to Market Share Objectives?" Advertising Research Foundation, *12th Annual Conference Report*, 1966, pp. 53–57.

Pyhrr, Peter A., *Zero-Based Budgeting*, John Wiley & Sons, New York, 1973, 231 pp.

Schaffir, Kurt H., and Orr, E. W., Jr., "The Determination of Advertising Budgets for Brands," *Journal of Advertising Research*, March 1963, pp. 7–11.

Weinberg, Robert S., "Are We Spending Too Much for Advertising?" Advertising Research Foundation, *14th Annual Conference Report*, 1968, pp. 29–36.

K. Weeks, "How to Plan Your Ad Budget," *Sales and Marketing Management*, September 1987, pp. 13–14.

16

Testing, Experimenting, and Media Planning

Most of this book deals with the statistical data and subjective judgment that a media planner uses to decide among strategy alternatives. Most of such data comes from syndicated research companies whose services are widely available. This chapter, however, deals with the use of custom-made research to help the planner in making decisions. Such research usually is not under the direct supervision of a media planner, but there are some important facts about research that every media planner should know.

Tests and Experiments

Most of the research used to evaluate alternative media strategies falls under the general heading of tests and experiments. Briefly defined, a *test* is a simple field study of some advertising variable. An *experiment* is a carefully designed study in which the researcher controls and manipulates conditions to see how an experimental variable may affect audience behavior. A more comprehensive explanation of the two kinds of research will be given later.

Why Test or Experiment?

There are a number of reasons why testing or experimenting is necessary. The most important reason was stated earlier: to help the planner make decisions. Often the planner is faced with alternatives that are seemingly equal, and there might be differences of opinion between the planner and others (such as account executives or clients) about whether to use a given alternative. A way to resolve these differences is through custom-made research.

Another reason for testing or experimenting is to avoid making costly errors; the rising cost of media time and space, plus the proliferation of many new media alternatives, makes this more necessary than ever. Furthermore, clients want more and better proof that they are getting their money's worth in media, and that optimum media strategies are being used.

Finally, although media planners use numerical data in making decisions, they often modify the data with their own judgment, based on personal experience. But often such personal experience may not be broad enough, or the current situation may be vastly different from what it was in the past. Research is needed to answer the question of which strategy may work best.

Tests a..d Experiments: How They Differ

Because both tests and experiments usually involve field studies, they may seem to be alike. But tests are quite different from experiments.

In advertising or marketing, a test is a simple piece of research in which one measures a variable (or treatment) introduced into the market to see what effect it has. Although advertising can be tested in one market, most often it is tested in at least two; each market is given a different treatment. For example, in one market $500,000 could be spent for advertising, while in the other $1 million could be spent, using the same medium in both markets. Results could be measured on the basis of which dollar amount produced the greatest sales.

When the test was over, it might be seen that the $1 million produced 10 percent more sales than did the smaller figure. Which treatment was better? The answer depends on the decision maker who, on the basis of experience, judgment, or a payout calculation, says one expenditure is better than another. The most important characteristic of the test is its simplicity and its minimal controls. Although some attempts may have been made to see that the two test markets were alike, the nature of testing is such that it is simple and not too much trouble is exerted to control extraneous factors that could affect its outcome. Such rough testing provides guidelines for decision making rather than yielding definitive and projectable results.

An experiment resembles a test in that similar markets are selected for treatments, but great care is exerted to make sure that the markets are equivalent in nature. Usually the same treatments are assigned to two or more test markets, and usually two or more treatments are used. Finally, the treatments must be assigned at random, by using a table of random numbers or, perhaps, in simple cases, the toss of a coin. Furthermore, in measuring the results that occur because of the different treatments, a random sample must be drawn from each test marketing unit, and two or more replications may be made of each advertising treatment.

Once a random sample has been drawn from each of the test markets, the samples are measured through normal survey techniques to determine the effects of the various treatments. Results from experiments are analyzed, however, in a much different manner than in test results. In tests, the percentage of change from one market to the other is probably the most sophisticated analysis made; in experiments, data are cast in the form of analysis of variance, or some other statistical technique that helps tell the experimenter whether there is a cause and effect relationship between the treatment and the result.

The difference between the test and the experiment is that a better basis for decision making exists in the experiment, as noted by Dr. Seymour Banks, former vice president at the Leo Burnett Company, Chicago, when he wrote:

> The importance of experimental design versus mere testing lies in the fact that the existence of an experimental error permits use of a whole system of logical inference about the meaning of the data. It may well be the case that a test will produce empirically useful information, but there exists no logically defensible system for evaluating results. A test may come up with the true answer, it may not; nobody really can tell which condition is true.[1]

Which Is Better: Test or Experiment?

There are advantages and limitations to both testing and experimenting. The experiment is preferable when the highest degree of objectivity is needed. In evaluating one against the other, the following should be considered:

Experiments are better controlled than tests. This means that special efforts usually have been taken to exclude from the study any extraneous variables that could seriously bias the findings. In addition, experiments are designed or planned to allow statistical inference to be used in making decisions, whereas tests usually are based on some one person's (or group's) judgment. Statistical inference is usually more valid than personal judgment. As a consequence, the results of an experiment may be projected to a large universe, whereas the results of a test usually are restricted to the areas where the test was conducted.

On the other hand, a test may be less expensive than an experiment. Many companies that cannot afford the cost of an experiment still have some way of finding answers to their problems by conducting tests. Furthermore, tests usually take less time to conduct than experiments. Often there just isn't enough time for an experiment, but something needs to be learned. A test may provide this. Then, too, although the test design promises less than an experiment, often what is promised is enough. For example, a planner may simply want some clues, rather than a complete rationale, for a decision. Finally, a test is analyzed on the basis of relatively simple logic and reasoning that can be understood by everybody. Those who use experiments often err by substituting the elegance of their statistics for good, commonsense reasoning. The formulas of statistics are means to an end—not the end.

Yet both experiments and tests have limitations. For example, neither may be able to detect small changes that have occurred. Furthermore, when testing alternative advertising expenditure levels in a number of markets, the total sales of a brand may decline because a control market has received no advertising for a period of time. Both tests and experiments may also be so visible that competitors not only know they are going on, but they may deliberately foil the research by reducing the price of their own brands or by introducing another product similar to the one being tested. Sometimes, the sales force of a company can ruin either a test or experiment

---

1. Banks, Seymour, "Using Experimental Design to Study Advertising Productivity," in *How Much to Spend for Advertising,* New York: Association of National Advertisers, 1969, p. 77.

by working either for it or against it—rather than letting the research commence naturally. When salespeople deviate from their normal handling of a brand, their actions can distort the outcomes of research.

One final consideration about both testing and experimenting: Neither may produce results that are projectable across the country. As Professor Roy H. Campbell of Arizona State University noted, "Research has shown the projection error from three markets to national market shares ranges from 22 percent over-projection to 22 percent under-projection."[2]

Even an experiment may be inadequate, because it does not take competitive action (or reaction) into consideration, a concern expressed by Benjamin Lipstein, senior vice president for research at the advertising agency Sullivan, Stauffer, Colwell & Bayles:

> There is serious question as to whether this classical experiment is valid in the social and economic sciences. The experimental design inference process implies that we can draw conclusions from the experiment which will have application in the larger world. If we arrive at some optimum level of advertising expenditures from test marketing situations, these results when applied to the larger environment of the total economy could well lead to serious error since they do not anticipate competitive reaction to our presumed optimum level of expenditures. The experiment in no way makes provision for the independent intellectual life of competition.[3]

Lipstein also noted that, although it may be possible to anticipate competitive reactions to a strategy, statistical theory could give no rules on when and how competitors would really react. He concluded that competitive reactions would have to be assessed on the basis of judgment, something the experiment was supposed to have eliminated. Lipstein's alternative to classical experiments was a call for non-manipulative experiments in marketing and advertising, using mathematical model building to estimate what is likely to happen in the real world. These mathematical theories involve the use of nonstationary Markov chains, stability theory, simulation, and adaptive control theory.

What the Media Planner Should Know about Test Marketing

What Is Test Marketing?

Test marketing is the use of controlled tests or experiments (depending on how they are done) in one or more geographical areas to gather certain kinds of information or to gain experience in marketing a brand. In actual practice, test marketing may

---

2. Campbell, Roy H., *Measuring the Sales and Profit Results of Advertising,*" New York: Association of National Advertisers, 1969, p. 54.

3. Lipstein, Benjamin, "Advertising Effectiveness Measurement, Has It Been Going Down a Blind Alley?" in *Papers from the American Association of Advertising Agencies Regional Meetings,* New York, 1969, p. 2.

mean different things to different people. Consultant Alvin Achenbaum pointed out that to research-oriented people, test marketing means a precise method for gaining information or experience.[4] At the other extreme, test marketing can mean to some entrepreneurs: "Let's try something out in the marketplace." Between these two extremes exist many other possibilities.

Test marketing is most often done for new brands in existing product categories or for extensions of a product line. Even in new product testing, the media portion of the test is usually not the first consideration because the brand first has to be developed, packaged, and priced; selling strategies must be determined; and starting dates must be decided upon. In a sense, then, media planning assumes the same relationship in test marketing that it does in an existing brand strategy: Marketing considerations must be decided first.

It is important for a media planner to have a good basic understanding of test marketing because the planner may be involved in it when translating national media plans to a local level. Although it is beyond the scope of this book to provide all the details of test marketing, the following discussion covers the more essential facts for planners.

Purposes of Test Marketing

Because most market testing deals with new products, it should be obvious that the risks of making a wrong decision in introducing a new product could be costly. The number of new products that fail each year always is assumed to be high. Essentially test marketing is conducted to reduce the risk of failure by providing top management with knowledge gained from advertising in a limited geographical area. Management then can project test findings to a larger geographical area. The major objectives of test marketing are to estimate the brand market share that is likely to occur once the brand is introduced nationally and to evaluate alternative marketing and advertising strategies that also may be effective on a national basis.

Specifically, the purpose of test marketing is to help planners work out the mechanics of a market introduction while learning the local market share and effects of various strategies. If problems exist, then it is better to learn them ahead of time and solve them before national introduction. By spending a relatively small amount of money in a local market, one has less to lose than after national introduction. Once top management learns the local brand shares, then it may try to project those findings to the national market, using local shares as a predictive device. At that point, management may decide not to go ahead because there is not enough profit in the brand. In such a case, the investment in the test is considerably less than it would have been had the brand been introduced nationally without test marketing.

Despite the fact that a brand's local share can be learned from test markets, a

---

4. Achenbaum, Alvin A., "Market Testing: Using the Marketplace as a Laboratory," in *Handbook of Marketing Research,* Robert Ferber (ed.), New York: McGraw-Hill, 1974, pp. 4–32.

growing number of marketing experts feel that the data cannot be projected nationally, because a few markets simply cannot accurately reflect the national market. Because the number of test markets used tends to be no more than three, the populations found in those markets may not be representative of the national universe. As a consequence, statistical inference usually cannot be used to analyze results. Furthermore, biases of many kinds tend to creep into test marketing operations. For example, in some tests higher distribution levels are present in test markets than could be expected on a national level. Or extra sales efforts are used locally that could not be expected nationally. Sometimes the expenditure of dollars for advertising is excessive at the local level and could not be duplicated nationally. Finally, markets change, people's attitudes change, and the economy may change so that, by the time a test marketing operation has been completed, the national universe, as well as the local universe, is far different than it was in the initial findings.

One must not conclude, however, that test marketing results can never predict national shares and/or profits. A sizable number of experts still feel that test marketing is here to stay and believe firmly in it underlying concepts. Their attitudes toward test marketing are based on the following arguments.

1. It is possible to improve the projectability of local market shares to national shares if better controls are exercised and more than just a few markets are used.
2. Market testing is better than no testing at all. It helps reduce the odds on failure, and it is the best that is available.
3. It has been successful in predicting market shares many times. The track records for some companies using market testing in predicting national share have been excellent.

A study made by Market Facts, Inc., and reported by Verne B. Churchill, Jr., showed that 52 percent of the respondents said their test marketing results were ''very predictive''; and in controlled test marketing, the percentage saying results were very predictive was even higher.[5] So it would be incorrect to state that test marketing is totally invalid as a means of predicting national share, although almost all marketing experts agree that there is room for improvement in the degree of control that could be exercised to produce more meaningful results.

On the other hand, there is less disagreement about the use of market testing for determining alternative strategies. The test market seems to be a laboratory that can help the planner decide which courses of action to use nationally. However, most of the same limitations that apply to market share prediction should also apply to alternative strategy prediction.

---

5. Churchill, Verne B., Jr., ''New Product Test Marketing—An Overview of the Current Scene,'' an address before the Midwest Conference on Successful New Marketing Research Techniques, March 1971, p. 4; report published by Market Facts, Inc., Chicago, 1971.

Number of Test Markets to Use

Although most marketing experts would agree that more markets should be used in testing, few actually are used. In Churchill's research, 67 percent (or 36 out of 54) used no more than three markets.

The reason more markets are not used is the prohibitively high cost. Even though management can be shown that the results of an experiment might be considerably enhanced through the use of more markets, there is still a great deal of reluctance to spend the extra money. Using fewer than three markets could be considered inadequate for predicting national share, but some kinds of information may be learned from two or even one market. But the results usually are not representative of the entire country. Cost and degree of accuracy are considerations in determining the number of markets that should be used. No simple rules exist for deciding on a number of markets.

Kinds of Markets to Include

There are a number of criteria used in selecting test markets. The primary one is that a market should be representative of the universe. Because the markets selected are really samples from the universe, the more they are like the larger area, the better. This would mean that the markets selected should have the same demographic distribution of population as the country (if the universe is the entire country).

Peoria, Illinois, is among those markets that have a population distribution that closely matches the population distribution of the entire country, as shown in Table 16–1. Because of this similarity, Peoria is often used as a single test market. At times, it is used in combination with others. Yet, despite this similarity, there should be some question about the life-style of Peoria inhabitants compared with life-styles in other areas of the country.

Other criteria for a test market are:

1. Its economy should be independent rather than dependent on a nearby market.
2. Competition in the market should be similar to what a brand would expect nationally, and distribution opportunities in the number and kinds of retail outlets should be similar to the national level.
3. There should be diversification of industry in the community, and there should not be a strong franchise for other brands.[6]

Media availability should be investigated to ensure that the market is representative of the average market in the universe. There is one other requirement: Markets should be randomly dispersed so that, in conjunction with large-sized markets, the competitors would find it difficult to disrupt the effects of the test.

---

6. Sederberg, Kathryn, "Anatomy of a Test Market: How It Works in Peoria," *Advertising Age,* Nov. 1, 1971, p. 147.

TABLE 16-1.   Peoria Compared with the National Population (1971)

Population	Metro Peoria	Total U.S.A.
Male	49.2%	49.2%
Female	50.8%	50.8%
Children under 18 yrs. of age	35.5%	35.8%
Age Brackets:		
Under 5 years	11.5%	11.3%
5–19 yrs.	26.6%	27.2%
20–34 yrs.	19.1%	18.7%
35–44 yrs.	13.1%	13.4%
45–64 yrs.	20.4%	20.1%
65 & over	9.3%	9.3%
Employment:		
Employed Males	53.1%	49.2%
Employed Females	21.8%	23.2%
Unemployed Males	46.9%	50.8%
Unemployed Females	78.2%	76.8%
By occupation:		
Business and Professional	9.6%	11.2%
Salaried and Semiprofessional	7.8%	8.4%
Skilled	63.7%	59.6%
Unskilled	18.9%	20.8%
Median Family Income	$5,998	$5,660
Median School Years (males, 25 yrs. & over)	10.2 yrs.	10.6 yrs.
Median Age (total population)	29.4 yrs.	30.3 yrs.

Source: Sederberg, Kathryn, "The Anatomy of a Test Market: How It Works in Peoria," *Advertising Age,* November 1, 1971, p. 147.

Market Sizes

There is a difference of opinion about the optimum market size for test markets. One expert feels that the range should be from 100,000 to 1,000,000 population. Another expert employs a rule-of-thumb that the size should be about 2 percent to 3 percent of the national population. Achenbaum feels that the total population involved in test marketing should be not less than 20 percent of the United States because anything less would affect the amount of statistical sampling variance.[7] Probably the size of each market is not as important as the kinds or numbers of markets used. Size, however, may be an important consideration controlling the cost of the test. Larger markets could be expected to have relatively higher media costs.

What to Test

A number of marketing variables can be tested in addition to sales volume or share at a profitable level. These include tests of advertising media weights, various price levels, store promotion plans, trial and repeat buying rates, creative approaches,

7. Achenbaum, Alvin A., "Market Testing: Using the Marketplace as a Laboratory," in *Handbook of Marketing Research,* Robert Ferber (ed.), New York: McGraw-Hill, 1974, pp. 4–32.

package sizes and assortments, brand names, brand awareness and/or attitude changes, and alternative media strategies.

Research Designs Used in Test Marketing

Research design refers to a plan of actions to be taken in the testing. This plan, or design, is carefully worked out in such a way so as to obtain certain kinds of information. Most often research design refers to experimental situations where the test data results will lend themselves to statistical manipulation.

Research design can be very simple, for example, observing a market, introducing an experimental variable, and then observing it again to learn what effects the variable had on the market. Or, the design can be simple to the extent that two or more markets, presumably similar in demographic characteristics, are tested at the same time, with each one getting a different treatment. However, more complex designs sometimes are used in test marketing experiments.

Use of Control Markets. Before conducting test marketing, the planner must design the test in such a way as to guarantee its validity. *Validity* means that the test measures what it is supposed to measure and not something else. If, for example, advertising is introduced into a test market as an experimental treatment, the planner will want to know to what extent advertising had any effect on the outcome.

One method of assuring the planner of the internal validity of the test is to use a control market along with a test market. A *control market* is one that does not receive any experimental treatment while the test market does. The control market, therefore, must be selected carefully so that it shares all the demographic and economic characteristics of the test market. If the research objective is to measure advertising's effect on sales, then advertising will be used in the test market only. Sales then are measured in both kinds of markets. If sales rise higher in the test market than in the control market, one may conclude that advertising had a significant effect on sales. But if sales rise to about the same degree in both markets, then advertising had little or no effect.

The design of a test and control market for a new brand is shown in Figure 16–1. This kind of test can involve more than a single variable. For example, different spending levels may be tested in different test markets and compared with the control group. In addition, market shares of all groups may be tested simultaneously for the total of all test groups and compared with the control group.

Randomized Block Design. A *randomized block design* is one where subjects to be measured are first grouped together into blocks. Each subject is carefully chosen so that he or she will be much like every other subject in that block. The selection process, however, is done on a random basis so that every person with the same characteristic has an equal chance of being chosen. Randomized blocks are designed to prevent situations in which differences within the sample affect the outcome, rather than differences due to the treatments.

The matching or grouping of subjects can be on the basis of age, for example, people aged 18–34; or income, people earning $15,000 or more a year; or store volume, grocery stores with less than $500,000 income. Once subjects are placed into

FIGURE 16-1.   How Test and Control Markets Are Used

blocks, the experimenter can compare the results of treatments among the blocks. If subjects are not combined into blocks, then the experimenter may not be able to find significant results because the differences might be too small to be measured. This problem may be overcome if the experiment uses a very large number of subjects, but randomized blocks aid the experimenter in reducing the number of subjects to be used in an experiment.

Latin Square Designs

A *Latin square* is a block divided into a number of cells containing coded letters and so arranged that a letter appears only once in each row and column. This design technique is more precise than the randomized block because it helps control the problem of two rather than one source of variation within markets that could not be controlled by careful selection.

An example of a Latin square used in a marketing experiment is shown in Table 16-2, within which two variables were controlled, and three different treatments were applied. The two variables were geographic variation and competitive expenditures. It is assumed in this design that each control or treatment is independent of the others and therefore will not affect the others in any way.

The problem illustrated in Table 16-2 is: If Brand X should spend three varying amounts of money for advertising, which would produce the most sales, or brand awareness, or other marketing variable? In order to make the experiment projectable to the entire country, different expenditure levels were tried in different parts of the country, and also in areas where different competitive spending levels took

TABLE 16-2. A Latin Square Design Applied to a Test Marketing Situation

Degree of Competitive Spending	Regions of the United States		
	East	Central	West
Low spending levels	A	C	B
Medium spending levels	C	B	A
High spending levels	B	A	C

Source: Lipstein, Benjamin, "The Design of Test Market Experiments," *Journal of Advertising Research,* December 1965, p. 6.
Treatments: A = high spending level for Brand X; B = medium spending level for Brand X; C = low spending level for Brand X.

place. By controlling for both variables, the experiment thereby eliminated them as possible reasons for variations in sales that were found through the experiment.

The method of eliminating the effects of both variables is to add the rows and average out the effect of regions. By adding the columns, it is possible to average out the effects of competitive spending levels. By adding the expenditure levels for Brand X (or treatments), it is possible to average out the effects of both regions and competitive activity to obtain a determination which Brand X spending level was best.

Factorial Design. A *factorial design,* based on a factor as an independent variable, is one in which it is possible to measure the effects of different kinds of treatments, with the added value of determining whether the factors interact, or whether they are independent of each other. In conceptual terms, experiments may be designed to determine the influence of two or more independent variables on a dependent variable. *Independent variables* are those which the experimenter controls, manipulates, or varies. *Dependent variables* are the yield, or the effect variables; they vary depending on the independent variable.

An example of differing treatments in an experiment could be the effects of old versus new packaging, or an old package price versus a new price. The goal is to determine whether price and package changes are related to each other or are independent.

Other Test Marketing Designs

Achenbaum suggested a *checkerboard design* as a valid means of obtaining data in test marketing.[8] He described this design as requiring three basic elements:

1. Dividing a universe into groups of markets. These markets should be randomly selected and be about equal in size, for example, select three television market groups from each of Nielsen's ten geographical areas.
2. The use of alternative strategies in groups of three. Perhaps one group would receive 80 percent of a current spending level while the second group would receive 100 percent and the third group might receive 120

---

8. Achenbaum, Alvin A., "Market Testing: Using the Marketplace as a Laboratory," in *Handbook of Marketing Research,* Robert Ferber (ed.), New York: McGraw-Hill, 1974, pp. 4, 47, 48.

percent. Achenbaum would also use local media such as newspapers, spot television, and local magazines as the testing media. Three complete media plans at each spending level would then be produced.

3. Then, through syndicated retail auditing services, measure results over a period of a year. The key to the success of this plan is representativeness, good control, and ease of measurement (because it uses Nielsen areas).

Other testing designs are *minimarkets,* where a test is conducted in a very small area, usually for testing a new product introduction; or *in-store tests*, used to test marketing variables within a store. Stores may be divided into two groups with each group being given a different treatment. And finally, there are Cable TV *tests*, in which two randomly matched groups of homes that have cable television can receive different treatments. At present, about one in two homes have cable television. But if expectations are correct, the number will be significantly larger in the future.

Media Testing

Media play an important role in most test marketing operations. Although the objective of a market test may be to learn whether certain marketing actions will result in a given level of sales or profits, usually other parts of a test are directly related to the selection and use of media. These other parts may have different objectives, such as learning which spending levels or which media mixes to use.

How Planners Test the Plan

A media planner's initial responsibility in test marketing is to create a national media plan, then reduce this plan in size to fit the individual markets that are to be tested. (The reduction process is called *media translation,* and will be explained in detail later.) Meanwhile, the planner may have a number of different objectives to test, which are described in the following sections.

Testing a Complete Media Plan. A national media plan may be developed for a new product that has not been marketed before. While the objective of the marketing part of a test is to learn a brand's sales or the market share that may be developed on a national scale, alternative forms of the national media plan may be tested to see which will best fulfill the brand's media needs later on.

Testing Alternative Spending Levels. A special part of media planning information is testing how much money should be spent on media. The following kinds of spending plans could be tested:

1. High spending versus current spending levels
2. Low spending versus current spending levels
3. High spending versus low spending levels

4. Allocation spending tests to determine how much to allocate, either by dollars or gross rating points, to various geographic markets and/or media. In testing allocation weights, the tester may use various kinds of weighted BDIs and CDIs to help arrive at spending levels.

Testing Alternative Schedules. At times, it is important to know whether a media plan should use flighting, continuity, or pulsing. Although experience provides planners with some basis for judgment, there are times when a test may provide more objective information than that based on experience.

Testing Alternative Media Mixes. One could test the results obtained from any single medium or any combination: television versus magazines, television versus newspapers, national versus local media, etc. Media mix testing could also include the comparison of various dayparts in broadcast media: Should a media plan use an exclusive daypart, such as prime time, or a combination of dayparts, such as daytime and early or late fringe? These are only a few of the possible combinations that could be tested.

Testing Alternative Commercial Lengths or Ad Sizes. In these tests, one could test 60-second versus 30-second commercials, or 30-second versus 15- (or 10-) second commercials, or 60-second commercials versus a full page print ad.

It should be noted that there are times when media tests are made for reasons other than that of predicting sales share. It may be important to learn how media and advertising work, and media may play an integral role in such learning experiences.

Requirements for Media Testing

There are a number of criteria for selecting test markets that apply specifically to media. For example, there should be enough media options available in the test markets to replicate the national media that will be used later. As a result, certain very small markets may be unsuitable for testing purposes. But there are other considerations as well.

Media Availability. A test market must have a balance of media alternatives available. For example, if television is to be part of a national media plan, then there ought to be at least three TV stations in the test market because there probably will be at least three TV stations in most major markets when the plan is implemented nationally. In the same manner, if radio is to be used in the national plan, then one radio station in the test market should not dominate the market, because it is highly unlikely that, when translated nationally, most markets will be dominated by a single radio station.

Spill-in and Spill-out. One of the qualities of a test market medium is the degree to which it is isolated from other markets. Media from markets outside the test area often *spill into* the test market, that is, people in the test market are exposed to media originating from another market. Sometimes it works the other way, when media from the test market *spill out* into adjacent markets.

The degree to which media in a test market spill out messages to markets outside the test area can be a serious problem. Spill-out is generally undesirable for a number of reasons. Consumers who live outside the test market area may hear or see advertising for a product but may be unable to buy it because it does not yet have national distribution. These consumers may become irritated at their inability to buy the advertised brand, and may not respond to later advertising because of their annoyance at not being able to find the brand on store shelves during the testing period.

A marketer can attempt to avoid the problem by distributing the brand in the broader spill-out area, but this in turn may cause another problem: Will the supply of the brand be adequate? At times, only a limited amount of a brand is available for testing purposes, perhaps just enough for the test, but not for spill-out.

There is another way to get around the problem of poor distribution in spill-out areas: Print and broadcast advertisements can specifically tell consumers where to purchase the brand, thereby averting the animosity that could occur when there is no distribution in a spill-out area.

The reverse problem to spill-out is *spill-in*, which occurs when media originating in another market spill into the test market. The more that people in the test market are exposed to media from another market, the greater is the variation in the reach and frequency pattern from the pattern ordinarily expected. For example, if a schedule of 100 GRPs produces a 50 reach and a 2.0 frequency in an *average* market, it will produce lower reach and higher frequency in a market where there is a proportionately high level of spill-in.

Some areas of the United States have more spill-in markets than others. Markets in the Northeast, for example, tend to have large spill-in (although Portland, Maine, is an exception). Meanwhile, Phoenix and Tucson (southwestern markets) have relatively little spill-in.

Recently, the growth of cable TV has added a complicating factor to the problem of solving spill-ins and spill-outs in testing. Adjustments for cable TV should be made by using local cable systems or over-the-air stations to deliver proper test weight.

Media Costs. When a market becomes known as a good test area, the local media may sometimes raise their advertising rates to take advantage of their popularity, making it more expensive to test media in such a popular area. Some experts feel that persons responsible for the media portion of testing should not worry about higher media costs in certain markets because there are other more important considerations to watch for—spill-in, spill-out, quality, availability, etc. In translating a national media plan to a test market, the objective should be not to translate costs downward from a national plan, but to translate the delivery (e.g., reach and frequency) into the test market regardless of the cost. If a test market cannot generate the kinds of reach and frequency effects that are necessary, then some other market should be selected.

Test Area Coverage. In selecting test markets for media planning, enough markets (whether ADIs or DMAs) should be used to cover at least 95 percent of the test areas (sales districts, territories, etc.) that the company typically uses. This assumes that the test is being made to correspond to a specific company's sales area. At times, this correspondence is not necessary, depending on what the client wants to learn from the test.

Network Delivery. Another consideration for test market selection, especially when the test is supposed to represent the entire United States, is that the daypart usage in the test market should closely match the planned national daypart usage of television or radio.

Number of Markets. As discussed previously, the number of markets used in testing should be more than two or three. Yet despite consensus that as many as five, six, or more are desirable, only one is often used. When a single market is used, it is assumed that the "one" is a Little U.S.A. market (to be discussed later). Dangers of projecting from one market are well recognized.

Some advertisers find it advantageous to test in very large markets such as New York, Los Angeles, or Chicago, on the assumption that these markets are more representative of the United States than smaller markets. A marketer might also try a test in an entire geographic region, such as the West Coast, where a number of various-sized population centers exist. The regional approach could be much easier to use than a single isolated market because the planner can more easily simulate the national media plan in the area. Regional editions of national magazines may be available, whereas in a single market no local editions of a national magazine may exist. The regional test would be less likely to be affected by local strikes, bad weather, or high competitive reactions to the test. Sometimes network buys in a region such as the West Coast may be relatively inexpensive and flexible, but for most regions regional network buys may be difficult, if available at all, especially with the advent of satellite-delivered network programs to affiliates.

Other reasons why regional test markets may be preferred to individual and isolated markets are that it may be easier to obtain distribution in a region as well as easier to compare market data with media coverage. In local test markets, the media coverage may far exceed market coverage measurements. Finally, in auditing sales, it may be easier and less costly to audit sales in large regions than in isolated markets.

On the other hand, there are three good reasons for not using regional tests: the cost may be prohibitive; there could be a large amount of wasted media impressions because not everyone in the region is being tested; and a regional test is not really a laboratory or sample test, but a small-scale introduction. If the product is not well accepted, the risks of large-scale failure have not been eliminated in the testing procedure.

Sometimes media considerations are not an important part of test marketing. Although media usually are an important part of test marketing, there are occasions where the purpose of the test does not involve media. As one media planner noted, "our client was interested only in finding out if he could sell the product to the trade. In this instance, the actual media schedules were not important."[9]

---

9. Yovovich, B. G., "Quality of Local Media Can Be a Determining Factor," *Advertising Age*, Feb. 4, 1980, p. S-2.

Media Translations

Media translation was defined earlier as a process for reducing national media plans to fit the needs of individual test markets. This is an adjustment technique, and there are several ways to make such adjustments. Each technique is based on a different philosophy of operations.

Little U.S.A. versus As Is (or As It Falls) Philosophy

There are at least two philosophies regarding media translations in test marketing. One is the *Little U.S.A.* concept; the other the *As Is* concept. The *Little U.S.A.* concept is based on the idea that some test markets are so much like the country as a whole, that what one finds in one market can easily be projected to the National market. Therefore, if a media plan calls for the use of one prime-time network minute per week with a 20 national rating, the test market translation would be a 20 rating on some local program, or a number of spot commercials with 20 gross rating points in that market, regardless of the local rating for that network vehicle in the test market. Another way of using the Little U.S.A. concept would be to translate it in direct proportion to the weight that would be delivered on a national basis. The measurement could be the average number of impressions to be delivered per household nationally, translated to a proportion the local market should have received.

In the *As Is* concept, the exact media weight of the national plan is delivered into specific markets. Using the same example as above, with a prime-time network program rated 20, the planner might find that this program delivers a higher or lower rating in the test market, since national media deliver varying levels of advertising weight from market to market. If the prime-time program happens to deliver, for example, an 18 rating in the chosen test market, then 18 GRPs should be purchased in the test market.

The decision to use Little U.S.A. or As Is is generally related to how representative the test area is relative to the national plan. If the As Is translation method would result in delivering an abnormally high (or low) level of media weight, some adjustment toward the Little U.S.A. should be considered.

Table 16–3 shows how a Little U.S.A. media translation would be made. A national media plan has been devised in which network and spot television and national magazines would be the only media used. The spot television plan covers markets that include 60 percent of U.S. households. In order to make a Little U.S.A. translation, average delivery is scheduled in local test markets as shown in Table 16–3.

Using the same data, the As Is translation would first require the planner to determine how many GRPs were to go into individual markets. Whereas the Little U.S.A. technique used the average delivery, this technique requires much more detail planning in order to know what local delivery might be. In making this translation it may not be possible to buy GRPs precisely as planned, so some media get more and others less than the national plan, as shown in Table 16–4.

TABLE 16–3.   National Media Plan—Little U.S.A. Method

Media Used	Spot Markets (Women GRPs)	Total U.S. (Women GRPs)	Test Market Translation (Women GRPs)
Network TV		400	400
Magazines		100	100
Spot TV (60% of U.S. covered)			
Average spot*	100	60**	60 (National average)
Total		560	560

*A markets received 150 GRPs, B markets 100 GRPs, and C markets 50 GRPs, but the average for all markets is 100.
**Average calculations are as follows: 100 GRPs in 60% of U.S. = 60
0 GRPs in 40% of U.S. = 0
Weighted average = 60

Note that, under the As Is approach, only 380 GRPs were purchased in network TV while 120 GRPs were purchased in magazines in the test market. The reason is that this combination of national media delivers the desired levels of GRPs in the test market. Although the difference between the two-translation techniques may not seem like much, it is the difference between average and actual plan deliveries.

Translations in Radio and Television

There are a number of ways to translate a national media plan in radio and television. One way is the *cut-in,* in which a local commercial is inserted in a network or transcribed program in place of some other commercial originally scheduled in a market for the same advertiser. This is possible when the client already has purchased a commercial on a network, and simply replaces it with the test market commercial by cutting in only in the test market. The remainder of the country would see the national commercial. A cut-in is considered an excellent way to translate for broadcast media because it keeps the program environments the same as in the national plan, and it provides the exact national weight in a local market. Local stations, however, charge high fees for mechanically inserting substitute commercials. Also, national advertising for some other product may suffer because it was replaced with the cut-in.

If a cut-in is not feasible, then the planner will have to substitute local an-

TABLE 16–4.   National Media Plan—As Is Method

Media Used	Spot Markets (Women GRPs)	Total U.S. (Women GRPs)	Test Market Translation (Women GRPs)
Network TV		400	380
Magazines		100	120
Spot TV (60% of U.S. covered)			
Average spot*	100	100	
A markets	150		
B markets	100		
C markets*	50		50
Total		600	550

*The GRPs of C markets were used because test markets were C markets in character.

nouncements for the network commercials. This may be a problem because the spot announcement times chosen must provide the same kind of target audience and the same audience sizes that the network program in that market would provide. In order to use spot television, the only times available at a reasonable cost may be fringe times. Although fringe time spots do not produce as high ratings as would prime-time network programs, some kind of compensation might be used. Planners add gross rating points to those of the theoretical plan level as a form of compensation. The degree of additional spot weight over the theoretical plan level is usually determined by the research experience of each advertiser. There is no single set of industry standards that applies to such translation methods.

When a prime-time spot is used (instead of a prime-time network program) then the additional gross rating point compensation may not be as high as the amount of compensation used with fringe spot. In deciding on any compensation, two factors should be considered: compensation for loss of reach, and compensation for loss of program environment. Of course, it is assumed that any spots used will aim for a selected target audience.

Compensations will vary in different markets, depending on the relationship of audience sizes between prime-time and fringe times. Daytime spots, on the other hand, may be used in lieu of daytime network programs without compensation since they may be purchased either within or next to the kinds of network programs used in the national media plan.

When a national media plan calls for spot television, no compensation may be necessary; spots are simply scheduled in the same number, same number of gross rating points, length, placement, reach, and frequency called for in the national plan.

In translating network radio, the method is identical to that used for translating daytime network television. For spot radio, the translation method would be identical to spot television.

Translations in Print

Translation of newspapers is direct and simple, because the national media plan would spell out all details for local markets.

Magazines may or may not require special translations. If regional, metropolitan, or special test market editions of a magazine exist, then there is little difficulty in making a translation.

But if a national magazine has none of the above editions, three alternatives exist for translation: using Sunday supplements adjusted to deliver the same number of impressions in a local market that a national magazine would have delivered, using local magazines that are similar to those in the national plan and adjusting differences through compensation, and using ROP color in newspapers with some kind of compensation. The last alternative may be the poorest choice because the reproduction of ROP color in newspaper advertisements is not the same as color printed in most national magazines. But it would be possible to make some kind of compensation for the differences if that were the only viable alternative.

The first alternative, using Sunday supplements in lieu of national magazines,

TABLE 16-5. Translation of National Magazine Impressions to Sunday Supplements

Problem:	How many Sunday supplement ads are needed to deliver the same number of national magazine impressions that would be delivered by a national magazine in Test Market X?
Solution:	1. Find the number of target audience members of a national magazine delivered into Test Market X (either from published data or by estimate). Suppose the magazine delivers 100,000 readers in Market X.
	2. Assume that the national media plan called for 6 national ads in that market for a year. Find the total number of impressions in Market X: (100,000 impressions × 6 ads = 600,000).
	3. Find the number of target audience members delivered by one ad in a Sunday supplement in Market X. Assume it would be 75,000 readers.
	4. Calculate the number of Sunday supplement ads that would be needed to deliver 600,000 target impressions: 600,000 ÷ 75,000 = 8 ads.
	5. If the media planner judges that supplements have a lower "value" than magazines, the number of insertions needed in the test market can be increased to compensate: For example, scheduling 9 or 10 insertions in supplements rather than 8.

may be relatively easy to translate. An example of how this could be done is shown in Table 16-5. If the data on target audience delivery is not known in any given market, it could be estimated by working from known data. The number of circulation units delivered into Market X can usually be obtained from the publisher, who also can furnish the national number of readers per copy for the magazine. Multiply circulation by readers per copy to find the readers in Market X. However, these would be total audience readers, not target audience members. The same could be done for readers of Sunday supplements or similar magazines, and a translation then could be worked out. At times, the audience data could be further reduced by multiplying it by known recognition scores for a product category and comparing it with the substitute medium's noted score projection.

If a national media plan calls for Sunday supplements in a select group of test markets, then translation is easily done by using the local supplement or test insertions in the nationally syndicated supplements. On the other hand, if there is no Sunday supplement in a given market, then one could buy ROP color ads in the local newspaper. In the latter situation, some form of compensation would be required. In some markets, syndicated national supplements make test market breakouts available.

In summary, whenever a direct translation can be made, it is preferable to simulating a national medium in a local market. Almost any simulation will require some kind of compensation based at times on arbitrary rather than empirical means.

Conclusions

Testing and experimenting to find the best media strategy is a reasonable and relatively objective way of finding answers, as opposed to using simple judgment and experience. Yet there are countervailing forces that work against them. The high cost of research, the pressure of time, and the failure to control extraneous factors that could bias the outcomes all affect the continued use of these methods. But it is likely that as time progresses, more companies will pay the cost, take the time, and place competent persons who understand experimental research in positions of authority so that experiments will be used more for solving problems. At present, the number of persons engaged in this kind of research is not large compared with the number of companies for whom media strategies are being devised in a single year.

QUESTIONS FOR DISCUSSION

1. Generally, what are the values of testing and experimenting?
2. What are the differences between a test and an experiment?
3. Does an experiment, even if carefully designed and conducted, guarantee an answer that will solve a problem? Briefly explain.
4. Why do some marketing experts feel that the results of test marketing may not be projectable to the entire country?
5. Although Peoria, Illinois, may have demographics similar to the demographics of the entire country, why is there still some question that it may not be representative of the country?
6. What is the value of using statistical inference in market testing?
7. What is the main difference between the Little U.S.A. and the As Is philosophies of media translation?
8. What are the main reasons for not using an entire geographic region, such as the West Coast, for a media translation?
9. Why may it be important to test in very large metropolitan centers such as New York, Los Angeles, or Chicago, apart from other testing?
10. Explain how one can translate a network television program to a local area.
11. Explain the purposes of compensation in media translations.

SELECTED READINGS

Achenbaum, Alvin A., "Market Testing: Using the Marketplace as a Laboratory," *Handbook of Marketing Research*, Robert Ferber (ed.), New York: McGraw-Hill, 1974, pp. 4–47.

Advertising Age, "Test Marketing Full of Inconclusive, Contradictory Evidence, Berdy Says," November 16, 1964, p. 37.

Advertising Age, "Test Marketing," February 4, 1980, pp. S-1, 5–28.

Banks, Seymour, *Experimentation in Marketing*, New York: McGraw-Hill, 1965.

Banks, Seymour, in "Using Experimental Design to Study Advertising Productivity," *How Much to Spend for Advertising?* Malcolm A. McNiven (ed.), New York: Association of National Advertisers, 1969, pp. 72–89.

Becknell, James C., Jr., "Use of Experimental Design in the Study of Media Effectiveness," *Media/Scope*, August 1962, pp. 46–49.

Brown, George H., "Measuring the Sales Effectiveness of Alternative Media," *Advertising Research Foundation, 7th Conference Report*, 1961, pp. 43–47.

Campbell, Roy H., *Measuring the Sales and Profit Results of Advertising*, New York: Association of National Advertisers, 1969.

Canter, Stanley, "The Evaluation of Media through Empirical Experiments," *Advertising Research Foundation, 11th Conference Report*, 1965, pp. 39–44.

Casey, Richard F., "Tests for Test Marketing," *Papers from the 1962 Regional*

Conventions, American Association of Advertising Agencies, Western Region Meeting, October 22, 1962.

Cohen, R. J., "Computer Enhanced Qualitative Research," *Journal of Advertising Research,* June/July 1985, pp. 48–52.

Edwards, Allen L., *Experimental Design in Psychological Research,* New York: Holt, Rinehart and Winston, 1960.

Giges, Nancy, "Advertisers Take Harder Look at Test Market Ways," *Advertising Age,* October 12, 1972, p. 3.

Hajek, F., "Testing," *Marketing and Media Decisions,* July 1987, p. 132.

Hardin, David K., "A New Approach to Test Marketing," *Journal of Marketing,* October 1966, pp. 28–31.

Honomichl, Jack J., "Market Facts' Success with Controlled Market Tests Attracts Nielsen," *Advertising Age,* October 8, 1973, p. 3.

Keshin, Mort, "Media Planners' Role in Test Marketing," *Media/Scope,* December 1967, pp. 14–17.

Kroeger, Albert R. (ed.), "Test Marketing: The Concept and How It Is Changing," Part I, *Media/Scope,* December 1966, p. 63; Part II, January 1967, p. 51.

Lasman, L. L., "Determining the Proper Advertising Mix for a Consumer Product," *NAEA 1964 Summer Meeting Digest,* pp. 21–25.

Lipstein, Benjamin, "The Design of Test Marketing Experiments," *Journal of Advertising Research,* December 1965, pp. 2–7.

Lipstein, Benjamin, "Advertising Effectiveness Measurement: Has It Been Going Down a Blind Alley?" *Papers from the 1969 American Association of Advertising Agencies Annual Meeting,* April 25, 1969, White Sulphur Springs, W. Va.

Marketing Insights, "Test Marketing, The Most Dangerous Game in Marketing," published by *Advertising Age,* October 9, 1967, pp. 16–17.

Media Decisions, "The Media Testers," September 1971, p. 52.

Orman, Allen, "Which Marketing Alternative Should We Test in the Market?" *Marketing Insights,* published by *Advertising Age,* January 22, 1968.

Ribstein, D. J., "Overcontrol in Advertising Experiments," *Journal of Advertising Research,* June/July 1984, pp. 37–42.

Sederberg, Kathryn, "Anatomy of a Test Market: How It Works in Peoria," *Advertising Age,* November 1, 1971, p. 144.

Sherak, Bud, "Controlled Sales and Marketing Tests," paper delivered to the Advertising Research Foundation Conference, March 15, 1967.

Sponsor, "Testing! Anywhere, U.S.A.," March 8, 1965, pp. 28–34.

17

Use of the Computer
in Media Planning

In the early 60s, predictions were widespread that computers were going to dramatically change the practice of media planning. It was predicted that computers would be able to do complex media data analysis, create improved media schedules, determine which media and strategies were the best, and in general, raise the level of media planning operations. After more than two decades of use, computers have not quite lived up to the predictions, even though large amounts of money, time, and effort have been expended on them. Why were these predictions for the most part incorrect? More importantly, what is the role of the computer in the future of media planning? Explanations of the answers to these and other questions about the use of computers are the purpose of this chapter. The main objective, however, is to place the use of computers in a proper perspective for the media planner by showing not only its best potential uses, but some of the continuing problems that need solutions.

What Does a Computer Do?

A computer is essentially an electronic calculator that can add, subtract, multiply, and divide with lightning-like speeds. It can also store information in its memory units, and when this information is called forth, it can be manipulated arithmetically in many ways. Because the four arithmetic functions are part of many formulas needed to solve complex mathematical problems, the computer, if fed the correct data and programmed correctly, can solve the problem quickly.

Specifically in media planning, a computer can do a number of things that help the planner.

Construct media schedules. Through special programming, the computer can create a schedule showing the names of vehicles, gross number of exposures delivered, and the amount of money spent by time period.

Assess alternative media plans. A computer can be given alternative media plans that were either created by computer or by hand and evaluate them in terms of reach and frequency, and/or cost-per-thousand. The planner then can either select the best of available alternatives or improve one or more.

Analyze marketing and/or media data. The computer can scan a great deal of marketing and/or media data quickly and organize them into a meaningful arrangement. It can compute index numbers of demographic segments of a market and then arrange the data in rank order and quickly calculate reach and frequency of any given number of media combinations. It can analyze media expenditures by competitors into percentage of dollars spent in various media by various brands in a given market.

Control billing and management. A computer can be used to tabulate bills and/or payments and analyze other operations within the agency or media department.

Media planning, therefore, posses a special kind of problem that requires the use of the four arithmetic functions. Theoretically, the computer should be able to devise media strategy and solve media problems if the correct data and programs are fed into it. At the heart of the problem, however, is the question of whether it is possible to first create a mathematical model that can solve media strategy problems.

Media Models

A *model* is a simplified representation of reality, or in the case of media planning, a description of a process. But it is more than a simple description because it must explain logical relationships, both quantitative and qualitative, between parts of the process and the whole. In order to help the model builder better perceive the relationships, models are usually expressed in symbolic or mathematical form. These symbols make it relatively easy to see at a glance the entire spectrum of actions and their relationships.

In media planning, most models are predictive, in the sense that if a planner uses the model, certain outcomes should result. Therefore, the model can be used to predict and control the outcomes. Other than simply describing or predicting what happens, a model's value is based on helping one understand a process or reality. This occurs because a good model builder should spell out the relationships, state underlying assumptions on which the model is based, and trace the logic of relationships through parts of the model.

Three Well-Known Media Models

There are a number of media models in existence. Three of the most popular models are *linear programming, simulation,* and a formula model called *beta binomial.* Each model has a number of different variations.

Linear programming is an optimizing model, while simulation is nonoptimizing. Beta binomial is a formula model. On one hand, an *optimizing model* is one created to search for and find an optimum solution to a media problem. Given the costs of media and other requirements for selection, the model can, through the use of a computer, compile a list of vehicles that meet the constraints. The *nonoptimizing model,* on the other hand, assesses media plans that already have been conceived. Each kind of model has its advantages and limitations.

Linear Programming

A *linear programming* model can be used to deliver a list of media vehicles that represent the best of all alternatives subject to certain requirements or constraints. Typically, the model maximizes the total number of exposures subject to a cost constraint or minimizes costs subject to an exposure constraint for each vehicle on a recommended list.

The model is based on a mathematical technique developed by economist Wassily W. Leontief in the 1920s. Further developments were made by George B. Dantzig, who is credited with devising the simplex method of linear programming that is used in media models today. In essence, the model allocates a scarce resource, the budget, to alternative media.

To use the model in computer planning, the planner must set up specific constraints that become a criterion function for making selections. For example, this function gives a set of weights to each vehicle based on its ability to deliver large numbers of targets. However, other constraints usually are added to help the computer decide which media to recommend, such as a set of weights that accounts for qualitative differences between vehicles. Some vehicles have a better image, are more believable, or have more authority than others. Still another set of weights is usually applied to different ad forms, such as a half-page print ad versus a thirty-second TV commercial. The three weights are all part of the criterion function called by such names as rated exposure units (REU) or rated exposure values (REV). Another important constraint is the advertising budget. Obviously the planner cannot accept a decision that costs more money than is available. Still another constraint could be derived from marketing / media objectives, such as an objective to reach at least 70 percent of all women, or planning for year-round continuity, or using at least two different programs, etc. The computer output can be either an analysis of alternative media in terms of REUs, or a schedule, or a summary of a schedule. With linear programming, a media planner can have a computer print out a summary of the media plan, then change one or more of the constraints, and have the computer print out alternative schedules.

Some of the major advantages of linear programming are:

1. It provides a mathematical basis for what otherwise is a subjective decision.
2. It requires the planner to state assumptions and quantify them, a practice not usually required in noncomputerized planning. Such a practice forces one to establish written relationships. If they are wrong, then they should be immediately visible and can be changed.
3. It allows the user to feed audience data that was obtained from different sources into a computer, thus saving time and money.
4. It delivers alternative decisions quickly because it allows the user to examine a number of schedules based on varied constraints.
5. It allows the planner to scan thousands of alternatives quickly.
6. Finally, the computer can find and accumulate many more rated exposure units from among a list of media vehicles than can a group of individuals doing the same thing by hand.

Major disadvantages can outweigh linear programming's advantages:

1. The model does not take reach and frequency into account.
2. It cannot handle the myriad of discount structures one finds in the real world where some rates are determined only by negotiation.
3. It requires a great deal of data that must be constantly updated. The results do not conform to reality.

Simulation

A *simulation model* attempts to reproduce, or simulate, the probable reading or viewing of individuals in the real world to such an extent that it is possible to predict how they will be exposed to media in the future. The model is quite different from linear programming in that it is nonoptimizing, and it contains relatively few, if any, algorithms. The simulation model measures the reading or viewing habits of individuals in a sample population, yielding data in the form of reading and viewing probabilities.

In addition, the model takes into consideration the value of each individual in the marketplace. Obviously some persons are more likely to buy a brand of product than others. Therefore, media vehicles that have large numbers of prospects in their audiences are more heavily weighted than those media with smaller numbers of prospects.

Essentially, then, when programmed through a computer, the model provides the planner with an estimate of exposure delivery of specific media vehicles that have already been chosen and scheduled by time periods. The computer also can rank each vehicle in terms of its ability to deliver target audiences at the lowest unit cost. But the model does not produce a media schedule nor can it answer the question of how good a media plan is. If a planner devises two or more media plans and uses the model, the computer will print out the reach and frequency and cost per thousand for each plan. But the ultimate decision about which is better rests on the planner's judgment.

Elaborate simulation models have been made that do more than simply provide basic reach and frequency data. In some models, the data are modified by impact evaluation variables. One such variable is vehicle appropriateness. This model assumes that some vehicles are more appropriate for carrying advertisements than others. Perhaps television is more appropriate than newspapers to carry dishwasher detergent ads. Television then might be assigned a weight of 1.10 while newspapers might be assigned a weight of 0.75. The determination of how much weight to assign each media class is usually decided by a consensus vote of experts, because there is little objective data on which to base weights.

Another impact variable might be to weight ad forms differently. A sixty-second TV commercial, therefore, would be given a different weight than a thirty-second commercial, or a full-page, black-and-white newspaper ad. The assignment of weights to different ad forms is another area where there is little objective evidence, so decisions on how much weight to give each form are usually done by consensus vote.

Other simulation models take the value of repetition into consideration. A model created by Dennis Gensch required six repeat exposures of an ad in a given vehicle before that ad could have maximum impact. In addition, Gensch's model allowed for memory decay of ad messages.[1] The decision on how to draw a decay curve usually is based on subjective judgment, plus any objective evidence that is available.

Some people believe that the simulation model generally has a number of advantages over a linear programming model. They feel that the simulation model usually includes fewer simplifying assumptions which, when converted into mathematics, tend to emasculate the media selection problem. As Simon Broadbent noted, the linear programming model may solve a problem, but it may not be the correct problem, while simulation models may come closer to the real problem. Simulation models also are more flexible, theoretically, so that they may be extended into time, if suitable data become available.

Simulation models, nevertheless, have some disadvantages. Broadbent noted that they "suffer because they are restricted to only one heuristic method of obtaining a solution."[2] To overcome this problem, Gensch recommended that a simulation model assessment of a schedule be followed by a hueristic program. Because the simulation model may include judgmental weights applied to impact variables, the media planner could use the same data bank to first evaluate a schedule and then, through heuristic programming, find a number of alternative schedules that are better. But the simulation does not find the best schedule, and this is one of its

1. Gensch, Dennis H., *Advertising Planning,* Amsterdam: Elsevier Scientific Publishing Company, 1973, pp. 94–95.

2. Broadbent, Simon, "Media Planning and the Computer by 1970," in *Thomson Medals and Awards for Advertising Research, 1965,* Report, London: Thomson Organization Ltd., p. 68.

limitations. Finally, many simulation models devised in the past do not have an effectiveness function, though some of the newer ones do.

Formula Models

At present, neither linear programming nor simulation models are used very much in media planning. Rather models based on formulas are used almost exclusively for calculating the reach, frequency, and frequency distributions of any number of media vehicles. The planner generally preselects a number of alternative media vehicles that could deliver the target demographics, and then uses the computer to calculate the reach and other information via the formulas. At times, the planner may even have a computer do an optimization run in which the computer will compare all vehicles submitted and rank them according to optimum reach, frequency, etc.

There are a number of different kinds of formula models available for doing the above calculations. A media planner who wants to know the net reach of a combination of media vehicles could, theoretically, have their audiences measured directly, but at great expense of time, effort, and money. Planners have sought for some kind of formula that could be used to estimate the reach and frequency of alternative vehicles using as few measurements as possible. If, for example, the duplications of every combination of two vehicles being considered were measured, it would be possible to project reach for those two and extend them to a large number of insertions. To validate such formula use, planners have compared observed measurements with estimated measurements to see how large an error results. The best formulas have relatively small degrees of error. Some of the observed measurement data used for comparisons have come from old research such as Alfred Politz's measurement of audience accumulation of *Life* magazine in 1952.

Perhaps the best known and most widely used formula is the *beta binomial model,* which comes from the area of probability statistics. Although a typical binomial curve looks much like the curve in a normal distribution, a beta curve closely approximates a typical reach curve. Through the use of the beta function in statistics, it is possible to make survey measurements of audiences of two media vehicles and extend the data to more issues of the same two. In addition, it is possible to calculate a frequency distribution using the beta function.

Richard A. Metheringham devised an early formula for estimating the reach and frequency of vehicles using the beta function, but his version contained a problem: It was possible for the reach level to decline after a certain number of vehicles and insertions had been calculated. At that point, the addition of just one more insertion might result in a decrease of reach, something that does not happen in real life where reach continues to increase, if only by a very small amount.

Newer formulas have resolved the problem of declining reach and reproduce data that corresponds fairly well with observed measurements. The beta binomial model, with varying kinds of modifications, is now being used widely.

The advantages of formula models over others are two-fold: They do not promise as much and therefore less can go wrong in using the results for planning; they estimate reach and frequency fairly well. Disadvantages center around the use of different versions of these models that sometimes produce different results.

Use of Microcomputers in Planning. One of the major changes in media operations has been the increased use of microcomputers for planning purposes. In fact, the major syndicated research companies such as Nielsen, Arbitron, Telmar, and Interactive Marketing Systems, to name only a few, have special programs for microcomputers. Research done by IMS in 1986 reported that 80 percent of advertising agencies surveyed were using micros for media planning purposes.

Programs written for micros cover many different planning operations—from manipulating rates for buying radio and television advertising to calculating reach and frequency distributions, cost per thousands, or preparing flowcharts. (See Figures 17–1, 17–2 for examples.) In addition, there are many market-related programs available for media analysis. The kinds of programs that are available are conjoint analysis, SIC references and coding, cross-tabulation tables, PRIZM target marketing, perceptual mapping, and statistical tests such as ANOVA, correlation, and multiple regression.

Problems with Computers Used for Planning Purposes. Almost everyone who uses mainframe and micros for media planning agrees that they are wonderful tools that help planners do their jobs. Their main advantage is saving time in handling quantitative data.

But they cannot be used to produce finished media plans. In the early days of computer usage, predictions were made that planning was going to be totally automated. Even today, there are people who think that it can be done.

The truth of the matter is that we are a long way from planning media by using computers alone, and there is some doubt about whether we ever will reach that state.

One of the main reasons why planning may never be totally computerized is that numerical data must be interpreted by judgment based on experience. This is difficult to program. Furthermore, there are so many different marketing situations for so many different brands, that it would be difficult if not impossible to create a computer program that took every possible strategy variable into consideration.

Another reason, and perhaps the most important, is that the formulas used for making major decisions such as reach and frequency are relatively poor. There isn't one formula, but many alternatives. They provide rough estimates rather than accurate representations of reality.

A number of different studies have shown that different models of estimating reach and frequency produce different results. Some slight differences may be expected, but when the differences are large, the formulas are suspect. Bernard Guggenheim, vice president of support operations at the Campbell-Ewald advertising agency in Detroit, points to an experiment using different formula models in which he found differences in answers that were too great to be acceptable. His findings using one of these models compared with a standard analysis is shown in Table 17–1 (p.366). Guggenheim called for validation of computer formula models by the Advertising Research Foundation—something that has not been done as yet.

Another researcher who found the same problems with these formulas was Roger Baron, media research director of Foote, Cone & Belding, Chicago, who compared people meter data with formulas on reach and frequency. He found different

FIGURE 17-1.   Multi-Media Reach and Frequency Analysis Adults 25-54

```
TAPSCAN MULTI-MEDIA REACH AND FREQUENCY ANALYSIS
         ADULTS 25-54 -- CITYNAME METRO
                   CLIENT NAME
               CAMPAIGN DESCRIPTION
```

SCHEDULE DESCRIPTIONS

RADIO -- WEEKLY SCHEDULE   (WEEKS: 4)

STATION	----- MONDAY-FRIDAY ------				-------- SATURDAY --------				-------- SUNDAY ---------				M-FRI AM+PM	M-FRI 6A-7P	M-FRI 6A-MD	WKEND 6A-MD	M-SU 6A-M
	6-10	10-3	3-7P	7-MID	6-10	10-3	3-7P	7-MID	6-10	10-3	3-7P	7-MID					
KMMM	6	6	5	....	....	....	....	....	....	....	....	....	....	....	....	....	....
KCCC A-F	6	6	5	....	....	....	....	....	....	....	....	....	....	....	....	....	....
KZZZ	6	6	5	....	....	....	....	....	....	....	....	....	....	....	....	....	....

TELEVISION -- WEEKLY SCHEDULE   (WEEKS: 4)

DESCRIPTION	DAYTIME		EARLY FRINGE		PRIME TIME		LATE FRINGE		MULTI-DAYPART	
	SPOTS	GRP'S	SPOTS	GRP'S	SPOTS	GRP'S	SPOTS	GRP'S	SPOTS	GRP'S
KABC,KCBS,KNBC	2	15.0	2	20.0	1	20.0	1	10.0		

NOTE: ESTIMATES WERE ENTERED BY THE USER.

NEWSPAPER -- WEEKLY SCHEDULE   (WEEKS: 4)

NEWSPAPER NAME	= DAYS =	==FULL PAGE== -ADS---RATE--	== 3/4 PAGE== -ADS---RATE--	==HALF PAGE== -ADS---RATE--	== 1/4 PAGE== -ADS---RATE--	== 1/8 PAGE== -ADS---RATE--	==UNDER 1/8== -ADS---RATE--	ADS PER
CITYNAME JOURNAL	MON-FRI	....	....	....	2 $1000	....	....	2
MORNING DAILY	SATURDAY	....	....	....	....	....	....	
	SUNDAY	....	....	1 $3000	....	....	....	1
PERCENT NOTING ADJUSTMENTS ----->		41 %	38 %	33 %	27 %	24 %	15 %	

NOTE: ESTIMATES WERE ENTERED BY THE USER. PERCENT NOTING ADJUSTMENTS REFLECT THE ESTIMATED PERCENTAGE OF THE AVERAGE-ISSUE
      READERSHIP NOTING EACH AD.

SCHEDULE COMPUTATIONS
ADULTS 25-54   (POPULATION -   894,800)

MEDIUM	SPOTS/ADS WKLY TOT	GRP'S	GROSS IMP	REACH	FREQ	EFF RCH	--CPM--	--CPP--	CPM NR	CPM EF RCH	TOTAL COST
RADIO	51 204	483.9	4,329,600	40.6%	11.9	34.7%	$4.63	$41.46	$55.16	$64.67	$20,060
TELEVISION	6 24	260.0	2,326,480	73.3%	3.5	44.7%	$8.60	$76.92	$30.51	$49.96	$20,000
NEWSPAPER	3 12	122.2	1,093,248	41.3%	3.0	19.5%	$18.29	$163.70	$54.17	$114.61	$20,000
TOTALS		866.0	7,749,328	90.7%	9.6	70.9%	$7.75	$69.35	$74.02	$94.62	$60,060

NOTE: THE EFFECTIVE REACH COMPUTATIONS REFLECT THE PERCENTAGE OF THE POPULATION EXPOSED TO THE MESSAGE 3 OR MORE TIMES.
====> NET REACH COMPUTATIONS ARE BASED UPON THE BETA-BINOMIAL STATISTICAL EXTENSION FORMULA

Source: Multi-Media Reach and Frequency Analysis is reprinted with permission of Tapscan, Inc.

FIGURE 17–2.   Theoretical Media Plan Flowchart

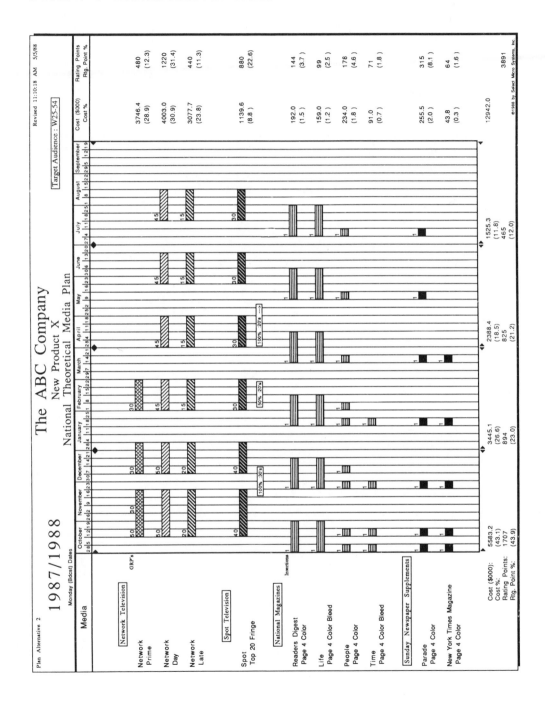

Source: FlowMaster Chart is reprinted with the permission of Select Micro Systems, Inc.

TABLE 17-1.   Differences in the Reach of Women Aged 18–49

	291 GRPs Late Fringe	245 GRPs Prime, Plus Day
Reach of standard spot system	67.0%	59.3%
Reach of Version B	55.4	67.9
Difference between versions	– 11.6%	– 8.6%

Source: Guggenheim, Bernard, ''My Black Box Is Better than Your Black Box,'' *Marketing and Media Decisions,* November 1979, p. 88.

results using formula models. Not only that, but frequency distributions also did not match reality. As Baron said in a talk to the Media Research Club of Chicago:

> The lesson here is that shifting between models can produce markedly different estimates for the same media plan. To avoid this problem, advertisers with several agencies should decide on one standard, and then require that it be used for evaluating all media plans.[3]

Table 17–2 is an example of a printout of a formula-derived estimation of reach, frequency, and frequency distribution.

TABLE 17-2.   An Example of Reach and Frequency Calculations Based on a Formula Model

Reach and Frequency of Three Vehicles

Targets: Upscale adults

Vehicles: 3 insertions in CCC
4 insertions in BBB
5 insertions in AAA

Total Population	Gross Impressions	Net Reach	Avg. Frequency	Median Frequency	Coverage (%)	CPM Gross Impressions	CPM Net Reach
29,356	81,726	20,643	3.96	3.80	70.32	$5.32	$21.07

Total cost is $434,900.

Frequency	Number	Number in Group plus All Higher Frequency Levels	Population (%)
0	8,713		
1	3,285	20,643	70.32
2	2,277	17,358	59.13
3	3,170	15,081	51.37
4	5,322	11,911	40.57
5	2,588	6,589	22.45
6	1,106	4,001	13.63
7	1,210	2,895	9.86
8	687	1,685	5.74
9	699	998	3.40
10	121	299	1.02
11	91	178	0.61
12	87	87	0.30

Source: Interactive Market Service (IMS).

---

3. Baron, Roger, ''Ex Machina Veritas'' Speech given to the Media Research Club of Chicago, November 10, 1987.

Other Uses for Computers in Media Planning

While estimating reach and frequency is certainly one of the most important functions that computers can fulfill for media planners, it certainly is not the only one. Computers are used for many other media planning activities and new uses are continually being found, meaning that computers will probably be used more rather than less in the future. Some of the new computer uses fall directly within the area of media planning, while others may affect marketing and/or creative planning.

Many advertising agencies do not own a computer outright, but rather work with on-line, time-sharing companies such as Telmar and IMS. An agency may have one or more terminals in its offices which can connect to a central computer in some other city. Recently, time-sharing companies have produced small, desk-top, hand computers with special media programs built into them that can calculate some of the same things that the larger computers can. But these small hand computers cannot handle very complex media planning problems.

What follows is a partial list of some of the general uses for a computer as an aid in media planning.

Helping the planner evaluate alternatives. One media planning principle widely accepted today is that the media vehicles selected should represent the best of all alternatives. But the planner cannot very well examine many alternatives by hand. Through the use of a computer, the planner can expand the number of alternatives to be explored at relatively low cost and with minimum effort. The organization of data by a computer also helps the planner study the output with less effort than if it had to be done by hand. Evaluations are made on the basis of reach, frequency, cost per thousand, and frequency distributions both of vehicles and ads in vehicles.

Helping the planner find alternatives to be evaluated. Through the use of heuristic programming, the computer can develop many alternative schedules quickly. These then may be analyzed by the computer through the simulation process.

Saving time and effort in media analysis. The best use of computers at this time is in the area of media analysis. There are so many computations that must be made that huge quantities of time must be allotted for this task if it is done by hand. The computer prints out many kinds of analyses quickly and in convenient order for the media planner. Perhaps one of the major unrealized values in this area is that if the inputs into the computer are correct, then the output is likely to be free from computational or recording errors.

Serving as a learning tool. If planners continue to use computers for media planning they will be forced to be more thoughtful about the underlying assumptions under which they operate. If the initial outputs of computers are wrong, the model builder or planner modifies the assumptions and discards erroneous ones. The use of a computer motivates the planner to reevaluate assumptions continually and learn as a result.

Simulating test markets. Another, but limited, use of computers in media planning has been test market simulations in which media strategy plays a role. The test market simulation model is much like the media simulation model, but the former is more comprehensive. It not only attempts to predict consumer exposure to media, but also probable purchase rates, brand-switching rates, attitude changes, and, eventually, market share. Because media play a role in these models, the planner may want to see what responses could be obtained from changes in advertising in much the same way a test marketing experiment allows investigation of advertising changes.

Finding targets with automatic interaction detection (AID). Computers have been used to find the best prospective market segments. The automatic interaction detector technique is one means of dividing a market into subgroups on the basis of product usage until the best targets appear.

The method starts with a national sample of individuals chosen because they are representative of the universe, or the entire United States. Then, through an analysis of purchase rates and demographics, the computer is programmed to determine the average product-buying rate for each person, identify the most powerful demographic predictor of usage, divide the universe into high and low purchase groups on the basis of the predictor, and continue to subdivide each group until no more meaningful subdivisions can be made.

Henry Assael, professor of marketing at New York University, explained how the process works:

> In operation, the program splits the sample into two subgroups to provide the largest reduction in the unexplained sum of squares of the dependent variable. This is accomplished as follows: group means are determined for each classification of all independent variables, and all dichotomous groupings of each variable are examined. . . . The division will take place at the point of greatest discrimination in group means.[4]

The result looks like a decision tree. Figure 17–3 shows that the best target market, other things being equal, would be females, living in the North Central states, who are heavy users of Brand X, and whose annual income is $12,500 and under. A second group, much larger in number, would be females in the remainder of the U.S., who are homemakers or executives under 55 years of age.

Cross tabulation of demographic market segments. In the past, media planners were handicapped in analyzing marketing data because few cross tabulations were possible. Probably the most frequent cross tabulation was for age and sex. Beyond that, few data were available. The computer, however, makes it possible to obtain multiple cross tabulations to whatever extent the planner would like. As a result, the planner now can look at the relationships of a number of demographic variables at one time. This technique, in addition to AID, provides better opportunities to find the most precise target to whom to direct media.

Other specific examples of computer uses in media planning are shown in Case Studies 17–1 through 17–11. These examples by no means represent all computer planning systems used today. Most of the larger agencies have developed their own proprietary systems for specific uses in planning media for their clients.

---

4. Assael, Henry, ''Segmenting Markets by Group Purchasing Behavior: An Application of the AID Technique,'' *Journal of Marketing Research,* May 1970, pp. 153–54.

FIGURE 17–3. Use of AID to Find Best Target Markets

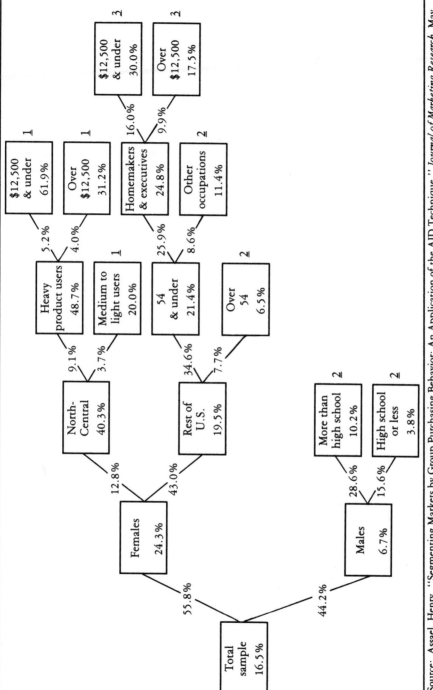

Source: Assael, Henry, "Segmenting Markets by Group Purchasing Behavior: An Application of the AID Technique," *Journal of Marketing Research,* May 1970, p. 154.

Stopping rules invoked:
$\underline{1}$ = Sample size too small
$\underline{2}$ = Split eligibility criterion not met
$\underline{3}$ = Split reducibility criterion not met

CASE STUDY 17-1
Analysis of Sales Related to Advertising per Market

Description. This is a breakout of sales or shipments to various markets and advertising dollars spent in those markets. Various ratios are calculated in the form of index numbers that relate population to sales, population to advertising dollars, and advertising dollars to case shipments.

How the analysis is used in planning. This analysis may be used to determine market weights for allocating dollars to markets proportionately. Markets that have the largest percentage of sales (relative to population) usually are assigned higher advertising weights than others.

Example

District	U.S. Pop. (MM)	U.S. Pop. (%)	Shipments (M)	Shipments (%)	Shipments Index	Advertising $(M)	Advertising (%)	Adv.$/M Pop. $	Adv.$/M Pop. Index	Adv. $/Case $(M)	Adv. $/Case Index
Boston	11.5	5.3	36.2	3.6	68	150.3	3.9	13.12	73	4.15	107
New York	17.6	8.1	49.2	4.9	60	240.2	6.2	13.68	76	4.88	126
Philadelphia	7.5	3.5	10.7	1.1	31	105.7	2.7	14.17	78	9.88	254
Syracuse	3.7	1.7	16.8	1.7	98	59.2	1.5	16.08	89	3.52	91
Buffalo	3.2	1.5	7.1	0.7	47	44.9	1.2	13.91	77	6.33	163
***Division	43.4	20.1	120.0	12.0	60	600.3	15.4	13.84	77	5.00	129
Baltimore	5.4	2.5	10.2	1.0	41	75.3	1.9	14.05	78	7.38	190
Wash. DC	7.1	3.3	28.0	2.8	85	103.5	2.7	14.56	81	3.69	95
Charlotte	8.5	3.9	80.5	8.0	204	236.3	6.1	27.85	154	2.94	76
Atlanta	8.8	4.1	64.0	6.4	157	200.7	5.1	22.91	127	3.14	81
Jacksvle	8.9	4.1	10.4	1.0	25	117.3	3.0	13.14	73	****	290
Louisville	4.7	2.2	60.3	6.0	276	169.5	4.3	36.07	200	2.81	72
***Division	43.3	20.1	253.4	25.2	126	902.5	23.1	20.82	115	3.56	92
Pittsburgh	4.7	2.2	14.6	1.5	67	70.8	1.8	15.07	83	4.85	125
Cleveland	5.1	2.3	12.7	1.3	54	76.2	2.0	15.05	83	6.00	154
Detroit	9.4	4.3	11.2	1.1	26	130.7	3.4	13.96	77	****	300
Cincinnati	6.1	2.8	35.6	3.5	125	117.5	3.0	19.12	106	3.30	85
Indianapolis	4.7	2.2	28.3	2.8	131	92.4	2.4	19.85	110	3.27	84
Chicago	8.8	4.1	22.4	2.2	55	114.5	2.9	12.99	72	5.11	132
Milwaukee	4.7	2.2	17.4	1.7	80	64.5	1.7	13.74	76	3.71	95
***Division	43.4	20.1	142.2	14.2	70	666.7	17.1	15.35	85	4.69	121
St. Louis	5.7	2.6	37.8	3.8	142	120.5	3.1	21.10	117	3.19	82
Kansas City	4.8	2.2	42.3	4.2	190	127.9	3.3	26.70	148	3.02	78
Okla. City	5.7	2.7	65.3	6.5	244	186.4	4.8	32.42	180	2.85	73
Dallas	5.1	2.4	52.4	5.2	220	154.3	4.0	30.08	167	2.95	76
Houston	6.8	3.2	34.4	3.4	109	117.9	3.0	17.30	96	3.43	88
Memphis	4.5	2.1	59.2	5.9	283	166.0	4.3	36.91	204	2.80	72
New Orleans	5.2	2.4	54.4	5.4	226	159.6	4.1	30.81	171	2.93	76
***Division	37.9	17.5	345.8	34.5	196	1032.7	26.5	27.27	151	2.99	77
Mpls.	5.4	2.5	11.6	1.2	46	67.6	1.7	12.46	69	5.83	150
Omaha	4.6	2.1	28.1	2.8	131	91.5	2.3	19.89	110	3.26	84
Denver	8.3	3.9	45.4	4.5	117	146.7	3.8	17.60	97	3.23	83
Seattle	6.5	3.0	35.8	3.6	119	116.2	3.0	17.99	100	3.25	84
San Fran	8.6	4.0	14.3	1.4	36	102.9	2.6	12.01	67	7.19	185
Los Angeles	14.6	6.7	7.0	0.7	10	170.6	4.4	11.70	65	****	627
***Division	48.0	22.2	142.2	14.2	64	695.4	17.8	14.50	80	4.89	126
*Total U.S.	216.0	100.0	1003.6	100.0	100	3900.0	100.0	18.06	100	3.89	100

Source: J. Walter Thompson.

CASE STUDY 17–2
Allocation of Network Delivery on a Market-by-Market Basis

Description. This is an analysis of network delivery on a market-by-market basis. It shows how a number of network television shows deliver an audience locally. In the example below, the network shows are listed at the top and analyzed. Then a market by market delivery analysis is shown.

How the analysis is used in planning. The media planner does not know how much of each program's audience is delivered into any particular market unless this kind of analysis is done. The planner does know each market's sales potential, however. With this analysis, it is possible to learn whether good markets are being underdelivered and poor markets are overdelivered. The planner may use spot television on top of network to balance weights in some markets.

Example

Actual Program		Comml.	Cost/Comml.	Total	Estimated Program Rating	
Name	Net.	Units	Unit	Sched. Cost	Avg.	GRP
All in Family	C	4	25,000	100,000	16.5	66.0
Waltons	C	4	25,000	100,000	18.5	74.0
Rhoda	C	2	150,000	300,000	17.4	34.8
Bob Newhart	C	2	150,000	300,000	11.1	22.2
Totals		12		800,000		197
Average			66,666		16.4	

Audience Analysis

Pro Rata: % TV Households
Ranked on: % TV Households

Rank	Market Name	% US TVHH	% Target Mkt	Pro Rata Cost/ Market	Gross Aud. Total (000)	Comml. Delvy. Sched. (%)	GRPs Schedule Wkly	GRPs	Index
1	New York	8.90	8.70	71,192	5,464	5.8	16	130	66
2	Los Angeles	5.19	5.05	41,535	3,148	3.3	16	129	65
3	Chicago	3.89	3.92	31,121	3,343	3.5	22	177	90
4	Philadelphia	3.25	3.28	26,018	3,288	3.5	26	208	106
5	Boston	2.41	2.46	19,265	2,136	2.2	23	180	91
6	San Francisco	2.36	2.34	18,872	1,850	1.9	21	164	83
7	Detroit	2.18	2.35	17,429	2,209	2.3	24	195	99
8	Washington, DC	1.83	2.04	14,667	1,931	2.0	25	196	99
9	Cleveland	1.77	1.85	14,172	1,724	1.8	24	193	98
10	Pittsburgh	1.54	1.50	12,331	1,658	1.7	29	230	117
Subtotal		33.33	33.50	266,602	26,752	28.2	20	166	84
Remainder		66.67	66.50	533,398	68,260	71.8	27	213	108
Total		100.00	100.00	800,000	95,012	100.0	24	197	100

Source: Interactive Market Systems (IMS).

CASE STUDY 17–3
Demographic Analysis of a Brand's Users

Description. This is a breakdown of data normally found in Simmons Market Research Bureau reports. Usually, the data are cross-tabulated as in the example following, which has degree of usage (in columns) cross-tabulated with age and income classes.

How the analysis is used in planning. The planner may want to study close-at-hand the most significant data about a brand's users. The planner may have found that age and income are the most important demographics (from SMRB data), but wants to have a closer look at these demographics and their relationship with usage. The ultimate aim is to select a precise target market.

Example

Demographic Analysis of Users of Product A

	Total	Total Users	Heavy Users	Medium Users	Light Users
Total	68,386	9,161	3,202	4,101	1,857
% Table	100.0	13.4	4.7	6.0	2.7
% Col.	100.0	100.0	100.0	100.0	100.0
Age 18–34	23,923	4,274	1,406	1,819	1,049
% Table	35.0	6.2	2.1	2.7	1.5
% Col.	35.0	46.7	43.9	44.4	56.5
Age 35–49	18,305	2,352	904	1,096	353
% Table	26.8	3.4	1.3	1.6	0.5
% Col.	26.8	25.7	28.2	26.7	19.0
Age 50+	26,158	2,534	892	1,187	455
% Table	38.3	3.7	1.3	1.7	0.7
% Col.	38.3	27.7	27.9	28.9	24.5
Income $0–8	24,480	2,943	847	1,572	524
% Table	41.6	4.3	1.2	2.3	0.8
% Col.	41.6	32.1	26.5	38.3	28.2
Income $8–10	9,086	1,297	536	490	271
% Table	13.3	1.9	0.8	0.7	0.4
% Col.	13.3	14.2	16.7	11.9	14.6
Income $10+	30,820	4,921	1,819	2,040	1,062
% Table	45.1	7.2	2.7	3.0	1.6
% Col.	45.1	53.7	56.8	49.7	57.2

Source: Telmar.

CASE STUDY 17–4
Magazine Reach and Frequency Calculations
for Various Numbers of Issues

Description. This is an analysis of magazine alternatives to show reach over a number of differrent issues. Also cost-per-thousand data for four color and/or black-and-white ads may be shown (as in the example following).

How this analysis is used in planning. This kind of analysis is useful in planning where it is important to know how many target audience members may be reached. Typically, media plans are made on a month by month basis where the reach is known for any given month, but not for a number of months combined. These data, therefore, provide the longer range time element for decision-making purposes.

Example

Magazine		Total Audience*								
		1 Issue	3 Issue	4 Issue	12 Issue	15 Issue	18 Issue	36 Issue	45 Issue	52 Issue
AAA	Reach(%)	17.20	28.53	31.56	42.51	44.57	46.20	52.04	53.79	54.90
	Gross (000)	10,433	31,299	41,732	125,196	156,495	187,794	375,588	469,485	542,516
	GRPs	17	52	69	206	258	310	619	774	895
	4C CPM GI	5.63	5.63	5.63	5.63	5.41	5.32	5.18	5.07	4.96
	BL CPM GI	6.48	6.48	6.48	6.48	6.22	6.12	5.96	5.83	5.70
BBB	Reach (%)	14.88	23.85	26.23	34.91	36.58	37.91	42.76	44.24	45.18
	Gross (000)	9,023	27,069	36,092	108,276	135,345	162,414	324,828	406,035	469,196
	GRPs	15	45	60	179	223	268	536	670	774
	4C CPM GI	4.61	4.61	4.61	4.61	4.42	4.36	4.24	4.15	4.07
	BL CPM GI	5.30	5.30	5.30	5.30	5.09	5.01	4.88	4.77	4.69
CCC	Reach (%)	14.62	25.75	28.85	40.36	42.55	44.30	50.54	52.41	53.59
	Gross (000)	8,666	26,598	35,464	106,392	132,990	159,588	319,176	398,970	461,032
	GRPs	15	44	58	175	219	263	526	658	760
	4C CPM GI	2.27	2.27	2.27	2.27	2.18	2.13	2.09	2.04	2.00
	BL CPM GI	2.61	2.61	2.61	2.61	2.50	2.45	2.40	2.35	2.29
DDD	Reach (%)	4.84	8.95	10.18	15.08	16.09	16.91	20.00	20.97	21.60
	Gross (000)	2,934	8,802	11,736	35,208	44,010	52,812	105,624	132,030	152,568
	GRPs	5	15	19	58	73	87	174	218	252
	4C CPM GI	9.82	9.82	9.82	9.82	9.42	9.28	9.03	8.83	7.61
	BL CPM GI	11.29	11.29	11.29	11.29	10.84	10.67	10.39	10.16	8.75

Source: Interactive Market Systems (IMS).
*Age 18–34; Population (000) = 60643; Unweighted Pop. = 5433.

CASE STUDY 17–5
Reach and Frequency of Alternative Media Packages

Description. This is a report of the reach and frequency of a number of alternative vehicle packages. The example below shows that the first package consisted of six insertions of vehicle AAA, four of FF, six of BBB, and two of GGG. The package developed a net reach of 76.21 percent and a frequency of 4.7. Other data such as cost per thousand, gross impressions, and total cost are also shown. This package, then, may be compared with other packages.

How this analysis is used in planning. The planner usually selects a number of vehicles that he or she feels will best reach the target audience. The planner uses audience analysis data from the syndicated services to determine which package group will reach the largest number of targets at the lowest unit cost. This analysis is a help in making vehicle selection decisions.

Example*

Schedule		Total Uses	Total Cost	Net Reach	% Net Reach	CPM Net	Gross Imprs.	CPM Gross	Avg. Freq.
6 AAA	6 BBB								
4 FF	2 GGG	18	593,000	38,739	76.21	15.31	182,084	3.26	4.7
6 AAA	6 BBB								
2 E	4 FFF	18	595,000	38,406	75.55	15.49	174,678	3.41	4.5
6 AAA	2 GGG								
6 H	4 BBB	18	586,000	38,338	75.42	15.28	174,148	3.36	4.5
6 AAA	6 BBB								
4 CC	2 EEE	18	599,000	38,112	74.97	15.72	177,406	3.38	4.7
6 AAA	6 BBB								
4 CCC	1 DDD	17	595,000	37,903	74.56	15.70	181,194	3.28	4.8
6AAA	4 FFF								
2 GGG	6 HHH	18	578,000	32,341	63.62	17.87	123,092	4.70	3.8

Source: Telmar.
*Population-50,833.

CASE STUDY 17–6
Optimization of Reach and Frequency

Description. This analysis takes a number of media vehicle alternatives and calculates all possible combinations of them until those with the highest reach (optimum) for a given budget are found. This is done in a series of steps by the computer.

How this analysis is used in planning. The media planner may have found, through poor planning, a number of media vehicles that reach the target audience very well. However, some of these vehicles in combinations with selected others may produce more reach at a lower unit cost than others. The computer does the calculations and prints out the optimum combination. The planner then must decide whether this combination meets all other objectives before deciding to use it.

Example

Master Optimization

271 Schedules Evaluated

Schedule: Known Optimal
8 insertions cost $243,250

Total Population	Gross Impr.	Net Reach	Average Frequency	%–Cover	CPM–GI	CPM–NR
17,711	36,043	11,470	3.1422	64.7655	6.75	21.21
1 DDD						
1 BBB						
5 AAA						
1 CCC						

Other Schedules (Not Optimal)
8 insertions cost $242,250

Total Population	Gross Impr.	Net Reach	Average Frequency	%–Cover	CPM–GI	CPM–NR
17,711	32,577	11,373	2.8645	64.2137	7.44	21.30
1 EEE						
1 DDD						
1 BBB						
4 AAA						
1 CCC						

Source: Interactive Market Systems (IMS).

CASE STUDY 17-7
Reach and Frequency and Frequency Distribution

Description. This is a basic analysis of a package of media vehicles to show reach, frequency, and frequency distribution. The frequency distribution is shown in two forms: the first is an incremental form that shows, for each insertion, the number and percentage exposed individually; the second is cumulative, showing the number and percentage of targets exposed for all levels up to the one in question.

How this analysis is used in planning. In order to make decisions about which media to use and how the media attains objectives, this analysis is necessary. The frequency distribution is especially useful for demonstrating how many people will be exposed to a given number of advertising impressions. Frequency distributions are also necessary to calculate "*effective* reach and/or frequency."

Example

Media Name	Number of Uses		Unit Cost	Average Audience	CPM	Percent Coverage
AAA	4		35,000	12,894	2.71	25.37
BBB	3		36,500	14,662	2.49	28.84
CCC	2		16,500	2,580	6.40	5.08
DDD	1		26,000	5,538	4.69	10.89
		Total Cost		$308,500		
		Total Uses		10		
		Net Reach		34,159		
		Percent Net Reach		67.20		
		CPM Net Reach		9.03		
		Gross Impressions		106,260		
		CPM Gross Impressions		2.90		
		Average Frequency		3.11		

Insertion Level	Exposed (%)	Exposed (000)	Exposed at Least (%)	Exposed at Least (000)
0	32.80	16,673	100.00	50,833
1	19.39	9,854	67.20	34,160
2	13.88	7,054	47.82	24,306
3	10.36	5,266	33.94	17,252
4	7.77	3,952	23.58	11,986
5	5.76	2,927	15.80	8,033
6	4.14	2,103	10.05	5,107
7	2.83	1,437	5.91	3,004
8	1.77	902	3.08	1,567
9	0.95	484	1.31	665
10	0.36	181	0.36	181

Source: Telmar.

CASE STUDY 17–8
Magazine Audience Analysis wth In-Home, Out-of-Home Weighting

Description. This analysis shows magazine audience delivery broken down by in-home and out-of-home and total audience segments. In addition, it is possible to weight the out-of-home segment (or in-home) as desired.

How this analysis is used in planning. Many planners feel strongly that out-of-home magazine audiences should be given less weight than in-home audiences because the former do not have an opportunity to see a given magazine regularly. This analysis helps the planner see just what a list of magazines actually delivers on a weighted basis (out-of-homes weighted 50 percent in sample).

Example*

In-Home	Cost	Weight	(000)	% Covg.	% Comp.	CPM
Magazine AAA	21,300	100.00	134*	1.8	13.3	158.96
Magazine BBB	41,590	100.00	1,024	14.0	17.5	40.62
Magazine CCC	49,750	100.00	149*	2.0	6.6	333.89
Magazine DDD	13,390	100.00	23**	0.3	6.8	582.17
Magazine EEE	20,670	100.00	101*	1.4	17.5	204.65
Magazine FFF	13,440	100.00	452	6.2	24.0	29.73
Total (With Out-of-Home Discounted 50%)						
1. Magazine AAA	21,300	100.00	247	3.4	13.8	86.23
2. Magazine BBB	41,590	100.00	1,347	18.5	16.8	30.88
3. Magazine CCC	49,750	100.00	159	2.2	6.4	312.89
4. Magazine DDD	13,390	100.00	31	0.4	7.2	431.94
5. Magazine EEE	20,670	100.00	175	2.4	17.7	118.11
6. Magazine FFF	13,440	100.00	529	7.3	19.7	25.41
Total Audience						
Magazine AAA	21,300	100.00	361	4.9	14.1	59.00
Magazine BBB	41,590	100.00	1,671	22.9	16.5	24.89
Magazine CCC	49,750	100.00	169*	2.3	6.3	294.38
Magazine DDD	13,390	100.00	39**	0.5	7.4	343.33
Magazine EEE	20,670	100.00	250	3.4	17.9	82.68
Magazine FFF	13,440	100.00	606	8.3	17.3	22.18

Source: Interactive Market Systems (IMS).
*Target Market: Men 18–34; Household Income $15,000+ ; A counties;
Population = 7295 (000); Percent of Base = 10.07.

CASE STUDY 17-9
Reach and Frequency Table

Description. This is a table showing the reach, frequency, and effective reach for a given level of GRPs for prime time in network television programs. The effective reach shown in the example is of two different levels: from 3 to 8 and from 9-plus.

How this analysis is used in planning. Early in the planning process, the person in charge may want some quick analyses of how many GRPs will deliver various kinds of reaches and frequencies. Such a table is a handy method for finding the answers quickly. By analyzing more or fewer GRPs, it is possible to increase or decrease reaches or effective reaches quickly.

Example

Prime Network Average 4/Week Reach Table

4/Week GRPs	Average Frequency	Total Reach	3–8 Reach	9+ Reach
50	1.1	44	0	0
100	1.7	58	10	0
150	2.2	68	22	0
200	2.7	74	34	0
250	3.1	80	42	1
300	3.6	83	50	2
350	4.1	86	54	4
400	4.5	88	56	8
450	5.0	90	57	13
500	5.6	90	58	17

Source: J. Walter Thompson.

CASE STUDY 17-10
Spot TV Planning Guide

Description. An analysis of the ability of spot TV to reach various target markets at different levels of coverage. In the example below, the top analysis shows coverage of 50 percent of the U.S. and the bottom, 100 percent. Note also that this analysis can show network TV delivery in conjunction with spot television and the delivery of various dayparts.

How this analysis is used in planning. A media planner usually considers a number of alternative strategies before settling on a final decision. In order to make the wisest decision, it must be known how various alternatives would affect delivery results. This analysis helps in such a respect.

Example

Plan: 1
Spot Universe 50.0%

	W 18+				W 18–34				W 18–49			
	Reach	Freq.	GRPs	Adj.	Reach	Freq.	GRPs	Adj.	Reach	Freq.	GRPs	Adj.
Grand Total	92	21.4	1970	1003	93	17.4	1621	835	93	19.1	1774	909
Total Network	85	6.9	587	360	89	5.9	527	326	90	6.2	560	344
Tot. Nite Net.	83	5.6	466	305	88	4.9	431	282	89	5.1	452	295
Total Spot	84	16.5	1383	643	88	12.4	1094	509	90	13.5	1214	565
Day Network	33	3.7	121	55	30	3.2	96	44	32	3.4	108	49
Prime Network	77	4.6	354	258	82	4.0	326	238	85	4.0	338	247
Late Nite Net.	45	2.5	112	47	59	1.8	105	44	57	2.0	114	48
Day Spot	63	15.5	977	472	85	9.3	787	380	92	9.6	880	425
Early Fringe	71	5.7	406	171	67	4.6	307	129	69	4.8	334	140

Total U.S. 100.0%

	W 18+				W 18–34				W 18–49			
	Reach	Freq.	GRPs	Adj.	Reach	Freq.	GRPs	Adj.	Reach	Freq.	GRPs	Adj.
Grand Total	89	14.4	1279	681	91	11.8	1075	580	92	12.7	1167	627
Total Network	85	6.9	587	360	89	5.9	527	326	90	6.2	560	344
Tot. Nite Net.	83	5.6	466	305	88	4.9	431	282	89	5.1	452	295
Total Spot	42	16.5	692	321	44	12.5	548	254	45	13.5	607	283
Day Network	33	3.7	121	55	30	3.2	96	44	32	3.4	108	49
Prime Network	77	4.6	354	258	82	4.0	326	238	85	4.0	338	247
Late Nite Net.	45	2.5	112	47	59	1.8	105	44	57	2.0	114	48
Day Spot	32	15.3	489	236	43	9.2	394	190	46	9.6	440	213
Early Fringe	36	5.6	203	85	34	4.5	154	64	35	4.8	167	70

Source: Interactive Market Systems (IMS).

CASE STUDY 17–11
Weekly Radio Planning Guide

Description. This analysis shows a typical radio buy delivery for one week in a given market. It shows the number of stations, commercials, reach, and frequency ranked by amount of reach per station.

How this analysis is used in planning. This analysis would most likely be requested by the radio buyer as he or she contemplates the amount of delivery to be achieved in a given market. In the example below, a reach goal of 40 percent of the market is given. The analysis therefore should tell the buyer how many stations he needs to achieve the 40 percent goal level.

Example

Rad-Buy Radio Planning System (1 Week)

Metro Anytown   Total 18+
ARB Jan.–Feb.   Target Pop. (00): 115,476

Schedule: 3 spots Mon.–Fri. 6 am–7 pm
Buy Schedule: Until 60.0% of each station's cume is reached

Station Order: Rank by Reach
Market Goal: Reach 40.0% of Target

| | By Station | | | | Cumulative | |
	No. of Spots	Gross Imps. (00)	% Net Reach	Average Frequency	Net Reach	Average Frequency
WAAA-AM	18	31,014	11.53	2.33	11.53	2.33
WBBB-AM	21	29,484	11.11	2.30	21.67	2.42
WCCC-AM	12	26,928	10.53	2.22	29.96	2.53
WDDD-AM	18	25,866	9.54	2.35	36.41	2.69
WEEE-AM	15	14,775	5.58	2.29	39.73	2.79
WFFF-FM	9	14,616	5.54	2.28	42.87	2.88

Source: Telmar.

Thoughts on the Use of Computers in Media Planning

Few people would disagree that computers are playing an increasingly important role in the media planning process. The use of computers saves time and frees the planner from a great deal of lengthy hand-computations and routine paperwork that was formerly required. This freedom, theoretically, should mean that the planner would have more time to concentrate on making judgments and evaluating the quantified data. It should allow the planner more time to make creative, rather than mechanical, decisions. If such is the case, then computers help planners do a better job.

Some experts, however, are concerned about the possibility that planners could develop a blind acceptance of computerized data to such an extent that it could lessen the amount of judgment that goes into planning. These experts point out that no matter how valid formula models are, they do not justify uncritical acceptance of the data without being modified by experience and judgment. They fear that computer printouts may carry an aura of unwarranted credibility. The sight of page after page of computerized numbers printed in neat columns on computer paper could have a numbing effect on a planner.

Part of this problem exists because media models usually are not the concern of most media planners. The evaluation of such models is usually left to a few persons in an advertising agency, such as a research director or department head. The planner may assume that because someone has justified the use of the computer model, then it must be valid.

Other experts, however, feel that there is little cause for concern. Richard C. Anderson, former director of media resources at Needham, Harper & Steers, Chicago, pointed out that there are at least four problems that a computer cannot answer in the media planning process. Therefore, planners will *always* have to modify computer printouts with a great deal of personal judgment. The four unanswerable problems are:

1. A computer cannot tell the planner which medium is most suitable for the message. Such a decision has to be made by the planner in cooperation with creative strategists.
2. The computer cannot analyze environments of media and tell which is best for the message being disseminated. Although attempts have been made to quantify qualitative media values, there are few persons who accept such numbers as being valid in the planning process.
3. The computer cannot tell the planner when to switch to some other medium. This is a decision that has to be made by watching marketing results and synthesizing a great deal of other information before making a decision.
4. The computer cannot tell the planner how to reach the consumers with an unexpected message in an unexpected place. Anderson said that there is a time to take a leap into the unknown and this decision is more a matter of gut feeling than fact.

No one can tell you when to make this judgment call, but when it works, you have a final bit of assurance that the computer cannot dominate you. It could be a decision to take a TV maker's $4 million budget, which is struggling to be seen on the tube against competitors with far more dollars to spend, and taking the same money and putting it all into one, single print medium with frequency and merchandising events to help it along.[5]

Other experts agree with Anderson. The computer will not eliminate judgment in media planning because the numbers must be interpreted first before they can be used. As long as one of the major requirements for good planning is subjective judgment added to quantifiable computer data, there will be no danger of developing media planning automatons.

The computer can aid in the planning process. But it should not be the only contributor to planning. As the price of media space and time rises, and as clients spend more money in media, there will be a need for more and better media plans. The computer should be an important aid in this process. Planners might better use computers if they could spend more time learning about programmed models. They should learn the underlying assumptions on which the models are based as well as their strengths and limitations. As clients ask for more accountability for decisions, a valid model will help explain those decisions that are based on computer usage. Computers will never replace planners, but they will certainly help them more than they have in the past.

---

5. Anderson, Richard C., "Do Computers Leave Room for Judgment?" *Advertising Age,* Jan. 14, 1980, pp. 47–48.

QUESTIONS FOR DISCUSSION

1. What value is there in creating a model of media planning?
2. What is the main advantage of using the beta binomial formula in estimating the reach and frequency of vehicles?
3. Why would AID data be better than using a single demographic variable in target identification?
4. Briefly explain the purpose of a computer optimization run.
5. Explain some of the major concerns about the use of computers in media planning.

SELECTED READINGS

Abelson, Robert P., and Bernstein, Alex, *The Simulation of a Test Market,* New York: Simulmatics Corporation, 1962.

Alpert, Lewis, "Measuring Effects of Simulation," *Advertising Research Foundation 18th Annual Conference Proceedings,* 1972, pp. 48–50.

Assael, Henry, "Segmenting Markets by Group Purchasing Behavior: An Application of the AID Technique," *Journal of Marketing Research,* May 1970, pp. 153–58.

Atwater, H. B., Jr., "Mathematical Models to Improve Advertising Decisions," *Perspectives in Advertising Management,* Association of National Advertisers, April 1969, pp. 75–88.

Bass, Frank, M., and Lomsdale, Robert T., "An Exploration of Linear Programming in Media," *Journal of Marketing Research,* May 1966, pp. 179–88.

Broadbent, Simon, "A Year's Experience of the LPE Media Model," *Advertising Research Foundation 1965 Conference Proceedings,* pp. 51–56.

Broadbent, Simon, "Media Planning and the Computer by 1970," *Thomson Medals and Awards for Advertising Research,* London, 1965, pp. 63–86.

Brown, Douglas B., "A Practical Procedure for Media Selection," *Journal of Marketing Research,*, August 1967, pp. 262–69.

Brown, Douglas B., and Warshaw, Martin R., "Media Selection by Linear Pro-

gramming," *Journal of Marketing Research,* February 1965, pp. 83–88.

Charles, A., Cooper, W. W., DeVoe, J. K., Learner, D. B., and Reinceke, W., "A Goal Programming Model for Media Planning" and "Note on Goal Programming Model for Media Planning," *Management Science,* April 1968, pp. 423–36.

Day, Ralph L., "Linear Programming in Media Selection," *Journal of Advertising Research,* June 1962, pp. 40-44.

Dobbins, Robert, and Shiffman, Philip, "What Kind of Mathematical Models, if Any, Are Useful for Day-to-Day Activity or Long-Range Planning?" *Media Decisions,* January 1972. p. 52.

Ferguson, Robert D., and Sargent, F., *Linear Programming,* New York: McGraw-Hill, 1958.

Fleck, Robert A., Jr., "How Media Planners Process Information," *Journal of Advertising Research,* April 1973, pp. 14–18.

Friedman, Lawrence, "Constructing a Media Simulation Model," *Journal of Advertising Research,* August 1970, pp. 33–39.

Gensch, Dennis H., "Computer Models in Advertising Media Selection," *Journal of Marketing Research,* November 1968, pp. 414-24.

Gensch, Dennis H., "A Computer Simulation Model for Selecting Advertising

Schedules," *Journal of Marketing Research,* May 1969, pp. 203–14.

Gensch, Dennis H., "Media Factors: A Review Article," *Journal of Marketing Research,* May 1970, pp. 216–25.

Gensch, Dennis H., *Advertising Planning,* New York: Elsevier Scientific Research Publishing Company, 1973.

Headen, R. S., Klompmaker, J. E., and Teel, J. E., "TV Audience Exposure," *Journal of Advertising Research,* 1976, pp. 49–52.

Jaffe, A., "New Katz, Reach/Frequency Media Mix System Labeled Breakthroughs," *Television/Radio Age,* November 1987, p. 30.

Jones, P. I., "The Future Use of Computers in Media Planning—Research and Planning, a Dichotomy?" *Thomson Medals and Awards for Advertising Research,* London, 1965, pp. 103–24.

Kaplan, R. S., and Shocker, A.D., "Discount Effects on Media Plans," *Journal of Advertising Research,* June 1971, pp. 37–43.

Keshin, M., Lyman, R. F., Ross, K., and St. Georges, J., *Some Important Things I Believe a Young Account Executive Should Know about Electronic Data Processing,* American Association of Advertising Agencies, January 1969.

Knowlton, Arch, "Using the Computer to Select and Appraise Media," *Perspectives in Advertising Management,* Association of National Advertisers, April 1969, pp. 178–84.

Kotler, Philip, "Toward an Explicit Model for Media Selection," *Journal of Advertising Research,* March 1964, pp. 34–41.

Kotler, Philip, "Computerized Media Planning: Techniques, Needs and Prospects," *Occasional Papers in Advertising,* Urbana, Ill.: American Academy of Advertising, 1965.

Landis, Jack B., "Improving Media Schedules via Computers," *Computer Operations,* January–February 1968, pp. 22–25.

Learner, D., and Godfrey, M., "Mathematical Methods of Media Selection," *A Report of the Sixth Meeting of the Advertising Research Foundation Operations Research Discussion Group,* New York, December 1961.

Liebman, L., and Lee, E., "Reach and Frequency Estimating Services," *Journal of Advertising Research,* 1974, pp. 23–25.

Little, John D., and Lodish, L. M., "A Media Planning Calculus," *Operations Research,* February 1969, pp. 1–35.

Maneloveg, Herbert, "A Year of Linear Programming Media Planning for Clients," *Advertising Research Foundation 8th Annual Conference Report,* New York, October 1962.

Maneloveg, J., "Microcomputer's Role in Advertising," *Marketing and Media Planning,* May 1984, pp. 140–42.

Moran, William T., "Practical Media Models: What Must They Look Like?" Paper presented at the Midwest Conference of the Advertising Research Foundation, Chicago, November 1962.

Oshoff, C., "The Ten Commands (for Using Computers in Agency Media Departments)," *Marketing and Media Decisions,* November 1987, pp. 90ff.

Schreiber, Robert J., "A Practical Procedure for Media Selection: Comments," *Journal of Marketing Research,* May 1968, pp. 221–24.

Schreiber, Robert J., "Instability in Media Exposure Habits," *Journal of Advertising Research,* April 1974, pp. 13–17.

Zahradnik, R., "Media's Micro Age," *Marketing and Media Decisions,* August 1986, pp. 34–50.

18

The Future

Everything you have read in the preceding chapters applies to the state of the art of advertising as it now exists. The future of advertising is shaping up as something quite different from what we have been accustomed to. There will be enormous changes in the years ahead—in our society as a whole, in media availability, and in media consumption patterns. Moving at great speed is technological evolution that will affect how people consume various media and how advertisers reach consumers with their advertising.

Former New York Yankee manager Casey Stengel once said, "Predictions are a very tricky business. Especially if they involve the future." But predictions must be made so that advertisers and media planners can cope with change and pave the way for a better understanding of what might happen. All media plans are written for the future, even if that future is only three months to a year away. The astute media planner is constantly trying to foretell what will happen—what costs will be, which TV programs will be viewed and at what levels, which radio stations will garner what kinds of audiences, which magazines will perform as they have in the past, and on and on. Therefore, attempting to predict what media will be like ten years hence can only be an aid to the media planner, so the planner can take advantage of the change and harness the opportunities it might present.

Population Changes

Let's first make some predictions about people. America is undergoing substantial changes. Inflation, roller-coastering energy costs, unemployment, and the continuing international skirmishes in which our government finds itself embroiled are making people wonder what kind of future they and their children face. All of these events affect the fundamental values of Americans, and to a great extent affect the demographic composition of the population.

The U.S. Census indicates that the population will not grow much in numbers

TABLE 18-1.   U.S. Population Projections by Age (millions)

Age	1980	1990	2000	Increase from 1980	
				Millions	Percent
Total	228	250	268	40	18
65+	26	31	35	9	35
45–64	45	46	61	16	36
25–44	64	81	80	16	25
Under 25	93	90	92	− 1	− 1

in the decade of the 1980s, but it will grow older. The total U.S. population will increase by only 23,000,000 from 1980 to 1990—a 10 percent increase, compared with 13 percent from 1960 to 1970. Table 18–1 compares today's population bulges with those expected in 1990. Hardly any change is expected in the number of people under the age of 25. With a decreasing birth rate and people living longer, the population profile will be older. The 1970 median age was 28. For 1980 it was 30.3, and for 1990 the projected median age is 32.7.

In coming years, there will be smaller family units, but more of them. While the total population will not increase much, and the number of persons per household will actually decline (from more than 3 to close to 2.5), the number of people living alone will grow. The percentage of single-person households will grow from 23 percent now, to 26 percent ten years from now.

Minority populations will increase, especially the Hispanic population. The United States is now experiencing a wave of immigration from Mexico, the Caribbean, and South America. According to the U.S. Census, there are now over 18,000,000 Hispanic Americans. Their number has grown at an even faster rate than that of black Americans—three times as fast in the past eight years and almost ten times as fast during the 1970s. Furthermore, these census estimates only include a portion of the illegal population which is conservatively estimated to include more than 4,400,000 undocumented Hispanic immigrants. It's possible that by the end of the decade, Hispanics will represent 12–15 percent of the U.S. population—and a much higher proportion in certain geographic centers, such as the Southwest.

The population will continue to shift geographically. More and more Americans are moving to the Sunbelt states. During the 1970s, two-fifths of the U.S. population growth occurred in three states: California, Florida, and Texas. There is no evidence that this trend will change. Big, overcrowded, cold northern cities will lose population to the warmer climate cities.

The economic pie will be sliced differently in the years ahead. The 1980s will usher in a period of economic extremes. The now comfortable middle class will have to strive to ''stay ahead'' . . . staying ahead of inflation and the tax collector. Disposable income will erode as income and sales taxes continue to inch up. And the real income left after these deductions will buy less and less as inflation raises prices at a faster rate than real income increases. Although the tax reform of the mid–1980s has paralleled an easing of the country's inflation rate, history indicates that income and sales taxes will probably start to rise as 1990 approaches, with a corresponding erosion of disposable income. However, if the inflationary spiral continues to abate, we will see an easing that should stimulate the economy.

TABLE 18–2. The Market Segmentation of 1990

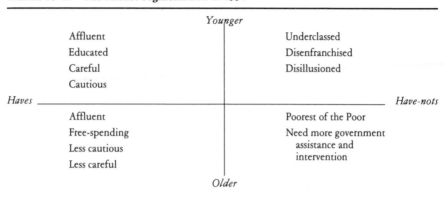

Energy costs will take a bigger bite. How big, no one knows. But the past trend is indicative: In 1970, the average fuel cost per BTU was 30.4 cents; in 1973, it was 41.9 cents; in 1977, $1.08. Energy costs have a ripple effect on much of the economy: industrial production, home heating, and transportation are all effected. Food scientists at Cornell University estimate that the 240 percent increase in American corn yields between 1946 and 1970 was accompanied by a 310 percent increase in the cost of energy used to produce that corn.

So, in the coming years we will see an older population, smaller family units, a higher percentage of minority population, a continuing geographic movement to the Sunbelt, and less disposable income for the masses. All of these factors will have a marked effect on what people will be like, and the population will move from a *basically* poor/middle-class/upper-class structure to a new market segmentation.

Table 18–2 provides a picture of what American consumers will be like at the beginning of the 1990s. People will fit into one of four segments.

The younger haves. These are people who are essentially now in college—for the most part the readers of this textbook. The college student today is looking at a world in which it will be far more difficult to make a living—especially one that is considered a good living. "Me" is becoming increasingly more important: my career, my future, my possessions, my body, my health. The younger haves, skeptical of tomorrow, will favor going into debt today for what they want tomorrow. They will expect more from life, from relationships, and from themselves. And this demand for more will make this group very careful—reading the specs, looking for performance and value.

The younger have-nots. This group exists now. It is the same group that challenges the economic and social status quo. It is a group that will live in a society with moral and political commitments to social welfare programs. The younger have-nots will continue to be an underclassed, disenfranchised, and disillusioned segment of the population. There could well be negative social consequences as a result of this group's actions.

The older haves. The focus on "me" will not be limited to the younger haves. The older haves will be more concerned with themselves than with their children and grandchildren. They will not especially be concerned with building an estate for their heirs and retiring into a moderate-expense way of life.

In 1990, those aged 50 and older will be the same people who were the free spirits of the 1960s. Their outlook on life was formed in a relatively optimistic social environment. The older haves will be self-indulgent spenders, less cautious about spending than the younger haves. This assumes that those now approaching this age category are preparing for it. If the economy sputters there could be a dramatic change in how the "older haves" view money.

The older have-nots. This group will be the most economically disenfranchised in America.

Advertising after 1990

Advertising and marketing will confront a changed consumer, and increasingly complex, specialized, and expensive media. The great technological advances now becoming operational, especially in television, coupled with changes in the family, the economy, and society as a whole, will usher in a decade of media selectivity never known before. The remainder of this chapter will explore the changes in the major media (magazines, newspapers, out-of-home, radio, and television) and demonstrate how media planning must adapt to these changes.

Magazines

It is predicted that magazines will grow after 1990 at a slow but steady pace. Circulation, in general, will keep pace with population increases. Right now the average adult spends about half an hour a day reading magazines. There is no evidence that time spent reading will decline. But *what* is read will change.

The greatest growth in magazines is expected in special interest magazines and special editions of existing magazines. We've seen much evidence of this already. Magazines such as *Omni, Money, American Health, Country Living, Southern Accents,* and *Self* have debuted in just the last few years. These, and other "lifestyle" publications, are cutting a unique slice from the total circulation pie. Mass audience publications are losing circulation. Many large circulation publications are producing more and more demographic and geographic editions that appeal to specific segments of the population. The result of all of this change is an increasingly fragmented medium in which a specific publication will reach only a specific, and oftentimes small, audience.

Costs are increasing. Production and editorial costs, ink, paper, and postage are problems that all publishers must deal with. Publishers have the advantage of being able to increase advertising costs and cover prices to offset production costs. Cover and subscription prices will continue to increase. By the end of the decade it will not be uncommon for single issue cover prices to reach $5 and even $6, which appears extraordinarily high relative to today's family income level, but which will be commonplace in the 1990s. The higher prices will limit circulation levels.

In the last decade, in order to maintain a more competitive edge over broadcast media, publishers did not increase advertising costs in the same proportion as production costs. Readers helped absorb a substantial amount of the production cost. But advertisers will see a change in this pattern. In order to maintain circulation at a level that allows the publication to be a viable alternative for advertisers, publishers will have to balance carefully the cost of advertising and the cost to the reader. Advertisers will be in a better position than readers to absorb most of the cost. (Remember, inflation is biting into consumers' real income and consumers must make careful decisions about their discretionary income and how much they will pay for the privilege of reading magazines.)

The 1985 Russell Hall editorial reports show that the average national magazine has an advertising to editorial ratio of about 50/50. This ratio reflects a 5 percent change from 1980 when the ad/edit ratio reached 55/45. It is believed that this ratio will remain fairly constant in the future.

There is no research showing the perceived value of a magazine with a preponderance of advertising. Some magazines, such as *Seventeen* and *Vogue*, are in fact often purchased by readers very much for their advertising. But whether or not readers think they are getting a better, or worse, value when advertising makes up the majority of pages is not important. What is important is the idea of "clutter." Will an advertisement be read in a cluttered environment? If readership of advertising declines, will more pages of advertising in a given magazine be necessary to effectively communicate with the reader? These questions have not been answered, and unfortunately, there is no research on the drawing boards right now that addresses the issue. The astute media planner, however, must keep these questions in mind when evaluating magazines in the future.

Newspapers

As with magazines, consumers spend about half an hour a day reading a newspaper. This will continue. Circulation will increase in a fairly direct proportion to population increases. And as people move around geographically, newspaper circulation will follow—from the central city to the suburbs to the Sunbelt.

Newspaper publishers will continue to develop special interest and geographic sections. The *Chicago Tribune* coined the phrase "Sectional Revolution" to describe all the new sections of many large daily newspapers that were created to attract new readers, to better serve the readers' interests in specific subjects, and to offer advertisers an opportunity to position ads in a specific editorial environment.

By the year 2000, it is probable that major newspapers will develop regular suburban editions. The editing would occur on location in suburbs and be relayed to the center city operations for make-up. The totally made-up newspaper would then be relayed back to the suburban printing facility using cathode ray equipment. The suburban editions (suburban section plus the center city portions) would then be printed and distributed in the outlying areas. Big city news would be incorporated into suburban editorial. These localized sections and editions will serve to target consumers in an even more precise manner than now—and, of course, will also fragment audiences further.

Newspapers will also be troubled by the rising costs of paper, printing, distribution, and editorial. Publishers will continue to raise advertising rates to pay for these increased production costs, and they will also increase cover prices to the readers.

Newspapers will continue to be an important medium for advertisers, because of their immediacy in delivering advertising, their retail orientation, and schedule flexibility. They are now the second most local of major media (out-of-home being the most local) and with the advances in sectional and geographic editions, newspapers will become more local in nature and therefore more efficient in reaching small segments of the population.

In addition, the emergence of *USA Today* has added a fresh element to the newspaper advertising industry for national advertisers. Traditionally, national advertisers have been charged higher rates than local advertisers, and they found local newspaper advertising too expensive and difficult to execute. *USA Today* now offers an efficient, one-buy, four-color newspaper medium for national advertisers desiring to reach a national audience.

The printed newspaper is now available on your TV set. Two techniques, now in test operation, make this possible.

Teletext printed messages are carried along with the normal broadcast signal. The subscriber is supplied with a key-pad and a decoder attached to the TV set. This equipment enables the user to access the Teletext signal and receive specifically requested data, such as classified advertising, airline schedules, theater reviews, restaurant listings, etc.

Viewdata or **Videotex** takes Teletext a step further and allows the viewer to interact with the TV set (not unlike QUBE). With Viewdata, the subscriber requests specific information (using specialized equipment), such as a catalog listing, and then can order the merchandise directly from the TV set by punching certain codes on the TV attachment. The advertiser then sends the merchandise and the invoice directly to the consumer.

Clearly, the viewer who subscribes to the Teletext or Viewdata systems can preempt programming or commercials at any time to use the systems—a real threat to broadcasting.

The Electronic Newspaper

Such publishers as the *New York Times* and the *Wall Street Journal* have been supplying professional and business customers with data electronically through news-retrieval services. As the cost for computers declines, general-interest newspapers are testing the viability of having all their news broadcast on TV. Many newspapers have already converted their production operations to electronics, with computers and display screens in newsrooms and press rooms. Extending the technology to delivering news to homes would be relatively simple.

There were a number of experiments in operation in the United States during the late 1970s and early 1980s. The *Ledger & Times* in Murray, Kentucky, fed its text onto a cable TV screen that could be seen by any cable viewer tuning in. *Knight-*

Ridder newspapers aggressively tested Viewtron, a Viewdata system. Gannet Company, the nation's largest circulation newspaper chain, planned to establish a satellite network to transmit new information services. The *New York Times* and the *Times Mirror* were among the publishers buying cable TV systems—for investment and for possible transmission of news directly to viewers.

In early 1986, there were four major operational electronic information service systems. The Source and Compuserve provide on-line access to a large variety of data bases and shopping services, geared mainly to the computer innovators. Knight-Ridder's Viewdata service, Viewtron, rolled out on a national basis after operating in Southern Florida for several years, and Gateway, a Viewdata service being tested by the *Times Mirror,* was also functional. Recently, both Gateway and Viewtron discontinued operation.

Electronic newspapers and information services are obviously in a volatile market primarily due to the players involved and the assessment of future consumer needs and ready acceptance of information services. In the near future, several expert companies in the areas of retail, computers and computer communications, finance, and entertainment/publishing will enter the electronic information service market. New services in the research and development stage have been announced by IBM, Sears, and CBS (Trintex); by RCA, NYNEX, and Citicorp (venture unnamed to date); and by AT&T, Chemical Bank, Bank of America, and Time, Inc.

Currently, Viewdata is available in less than 1 percent of households. With the entrance of such big players in the marketplace, Viewdata's growth could follow the growth of computers; it could be available in 50 percent of U.S. homes by the year 2000. Its success, however, will depend on how well it meets a given consumer need at an affordable cost and/or its ability to demonstrate its usefulness.

In general, Americans are increasingly more video conscious, but it would appear that the newspaper (in the printed form) will continue to be published and read at breakfast and on the commuter train. Any reduction in printed circulation probably will not surface until cable penetration reaches extraordinarily high levels, and the consumer becomes accustomed to ''reading'' TV.

Out-of-Home Media

Several facts suggest that demand for out-of-home media will increase in the 1990s. Advertisers will continue to feel the pressures of government restrictions on broadcast copy. There will be lower billboard capacity due to attrition. Land development and construction will eliminate some portion of existing locations, while local zoning laws will limit deployment of new boards. The result of all this interplay will be a net loss of available units.

Some new technology will make out-of-home more attractive and more effective. Computerized painting of painted boards, for example, will serve to speed up production, ensure uniformity of design across multiple showings, and help control production costs. Panographics, which are billboards illuminated from behind the design, will be available on a broadscale basis. In addition, outdoor big screen video boards, health club boards, and restroom advertising are available.

Other forms of outdoor in existence today show signs of significant growth. Advertising displays in shopping malls, at bus shelters, on trash cans, on top of taxi cabs and the sides of buses, and around stores and other gathering places are all increasing in number.

The out-of-home media are changing and will continue to change, shifting from the traditional billboard medium to a great variety of unique and localized options. This fragmentation of the creative unit will provide new opportunities for reaching very selective markets with even greater effectiveness.

Radio

People will have a continuing need for radio, especially when TV viewing is impractical, such as when getting ready in the morning, going to and from work and the store, while working, studying, relaxing. But, as stated earlier, the population is getting older, and this graying of the population could have an adverse effect on overall radio listening levels. The heaviest listening segment is comprised of people under 30 years old, and this segment is declining as a percentage of the population.

Broadcasters will have to adapt to the population changes in order to retain the nearly three and a half hours a day each individual spends with radio. Different formats must be developed to hold the 30- to 40-year-olds. The possibility of specialized programming for those over 50 also exists, as does possible programming for the sick and those with poor vision.

Radio is now the most fragmented of the major media. To reach large numbers of people, it is necessary to purchase a long list of stations in a given market. This is considered by some media planners as a disadvantage. Planners often characterize radio as a frequency medium (as opposed to reach) because budgets are often too slim to purchase a significant number of announcements on each radio station *and* a long list of stations to increase reach. But what now works for radio will work even harder in the future. What works is radio's fragmentation—its ability to attract very selective audiences that have specific demographic and life-style patterns.

Advertising rates will increase, but at a slower rate than the other major media. This will give radio a relative cost advantage over other major media forms.

Television

The most dramatic changes in media are happening in television. The popular TV medium that was born in the 1950s has matured considerably. Currently, nine out of ten people have color sets. More than half of all homes have two or more sets and almost 20 percent of homes have three or more sets. It is conceivable by the end of the century that half of all homes will have three or more TV sets—75 percent of homes will have two or more sets.

The television public appears to have an insatiable appetite for more and better viewing options. It is this hunger for programming that is encouraging the development of imaginative systems for delivering greater diversity and choice. Syndication, new independent networks, cable, the VCR as well as new technologies like stereo television and remote control devices offer the viewer more choice of programming and more control over viewership.

TABLE 18-3.   Historical Network Prime-time Ratings and Shares

Year	Average Three-Network Prime-time Rating	Index to 1978–79	Three-Network Share	Index to 1978–79
1978–79	17.2	100	89	100
1979–80	16.8	98	86	97
1980–81	16.5	96	83	93
1981–82	15.5	90	80	90
1982–83	15.3	89	77	87
1983–84	15.0	87	75	84
1984–85	14.6	85	73	82
1985–86	14.9	87	73	82

The lesson learned in the 1970s is that consumers are willing to pay to satisfy their appetite. The emergence of pocket-size units has made television a portable medium making it reasonable to project that, like Dick Tracy, the comic book detective, we could have TV sets the size of a watch snapped to our wrists.

Network Decline. Historically, the three networks have held a dominant share of the television audience and continue to hold over 70 percent of all television viewers. However, network ratings and shares have experienced a steady decline. Table 18–3 details the 20 percent decrease in average prime-time ratings and shares the networks have experienced since the 1978–79 broadcast year.

The decline in network ratings and shares is largely attributable to the rapid changes that have occurred in the television environment over the past several years. Four major events have accounted for the changing network television environment. First, the 1970 FCC decision which ended network-controlled program production and re-run syndication, fostered the development of independent program producers, independent syndicators, and local independent stations without network affiliation. Second, the 1974 FCC Prime Access Rule which prohibited network originated programming in the 7:00 P.M.–8:00 P.M. time slot further encouraged independent re-run and first run syndication and gave local independent stations an opportunity to compete with off-network re-runs. Third, the emergence of satellite delivery systems during the mid–70s enabled the rapid growth of pay cable (HBO, Showtime), superstations (WTBS, WGN), and basic cable networks (ESPN, CNN). Fourth, and finally, the emergence of VCR technology at ever-decreasing prices allows viewers to take control of the TV schedule and watch non-commercialized tapes instead of over-the-air network programming.

In summary, although television viewing is becoming more fragmented and the choices offered increase, the networks continue to hold the dominant, albeit declining, share of viewing. As illustrated in Table 18–4, it is estimated that network shares of viewing will continue to decline from 66 percent of prime-time viewing in 1985 to 56 percent in 1995.

Syndication and Independent Stations. Many of the same factors that contributed to the decline in network shares have also contributed to the growth of syndication and independent television stations. Syndication evolved in the 1970s and has boomed in the 1980s. The number of syndicators increased from 143 in 1975 to 226 in 1985, with the greatest increase, +51% from 1980 to 1985. Major companies

TABLE 18–4.   Prime-time Viewing Shares

	1985	1995
Network	66%*	66%
Independent	10	15
PBS	3	3
Superstations	5	5
Basic cable	11	11
Pay cable	17	14

*Figures add to more than 100 percent due to multiset viewing.

such as Columbia, Paramount, 20th Century Fox, and Disney Studios now offer quality syndicated programming. The number of syndicated properties has also shown a steady increase. For example, in 1975 approximately 306 properties were available; by 1985, the number of properties available had increased to over 345.

Along with the increase in the number of syndicators and the number of syndicated properties has come a dramatic increase in the amount of advertiser's dollars in syndication. All of the top 100 advertisers use syndication. Further, syndication generally consists of more than 10 percent of a major advertiser's network budget. Table 18–5 details the dollar growth syndication has experienced since the early 1970s. As more and more quality syndicated properties and original programming become available, it is likely that the advertiser commitment will increase to an estimated one billion dollars by the year 2000.

The number of local independent television stations and their percentage of U.S. coverage has also increased dramatically. In 1975, there were seventy-two independent stations that provided 63 percent U.S. coverage. By 1985, there were 294 independents with 82 percent U.S. coverage. By 1990, the Association of Independent Television Stations projects there will be 400 independents providing 90–95 percent coverage of U.S. TV households. Independent television stations are also increasing share in almost all dayparts at the expense of network affiliate shares. However, the greatest competition for share in most markets is between the independent stations within that market, not between independents and networks.

One of the most interesting recent developments in independent television is the emergence of the "Fourth" network, Fox Broadcasting Company. Under the control of Rupert Murdoch, the Fox Broadcasting Company is trying to establish a fourth network slot. The initial offering of Murdoch's fourth network was a late night talk show originally starring Joan Rivers which premiered in October of 1986. Original prime-time programming followed in the spring of 1987. Fox network pro-

TABLE 18–5.   Advertising Dollars in Syndication

	Dollar Amount (thousands)	Percent of Increase
1972–73	30	—
1981–82	300	+1000
1982–83	400	33
1983–84	600	25
1984–85	720	20
2000	1,000	—

gramming is sold as syndication and Murdoch has enough independent stations under contract to provide 80 percent coverage of U.S. TV households.

Cable Television. Let's review the history of cable TV. Community Antenna Television (CATV, now referred to simply as *cable*) began in the late 1940s as a means of providing a television signal, or an improved signal, to households in areas unable to receive "over-the-air" signals. These households were generally located in mountainous regions where the topography interfered with normal transmission. The cable operator built a high antenna designed to receive signals from the closest television stations. These signals were then transmitted via coaxial cable to households subscribing to the service. One cable system was capable of transmitting a maximum of twelve channels (approximately 70 percent of the systems in operation today still offer no more than twelve channels).

Early cable operators were rarely involved in television programming. They were entrepreneurs and engineers who seized the opportunity to provide a needed service and enjoy a handsome return on their investment. Some of the more innovative cable operators broadcast local community events. Nearly all systems provided a twenty-four-hour weather channel. Advertising on the weather channel took the form of a printed reminder to shop at the local grocery store or drug chain.

In November 1975, Home Box Office (HBO) began using a satellite to transmit first-run movies to cable operators across the U.S. Cable operators received the signal via a disc antenna ("Earthstation") and retransmitted it to their subscribers. The cable industry learned that satellites could be used to distribute quality programming over great distances faster and more efficiently than transmitting the same program over land. The ready accessibility of quality programming was rapidly changing the cable industry from a transmitter of signals (with an emphasis on engineering) to a transmitter of television programming (with an emphasis on entertainment and information).

This change in industry emphasis stimulated growth in the number of cable systems and cable subscribers. As shown in Table 18–6, households subscribing to cable represented seven percent of households in 1970. In 1980, the percentage of households with cable TV has more than tripled. By 1990, it is anticipated that approximately six out of ten homes will have cable capacity. (Technology employing fiber optics permits each household to receive a limitless number of channels. Of course, each household pays for this chance to view additional channels, and most of these homes pays an extra subscription fee for at least one pay channel.)

Cable programming can be divided into two basic segments: basic programming and pay programming. Basic programming is the standard service available at the normal subscription rate. In addition to installation charges, there is a basic monthly rate each subscriber pays to the cable operator. Basic programming consists of local television signals and two types of additional programming:

News/Community Programming. This programming consists of 24-hour national and international news, state news, community news, live coverage from the House of Representatives, stock market reports, coverage of the local school system, comparative shopping information, and classified advertising.

TABLE 18-6.   Growth of Cable Television

Year	Cable Systems	Total Subscribers (thousands)	U.S. TV Households (%)
1952	70	14	—
1970	2,490	4,500	7
1975	3,506	9,800	12
1979	4,150	14,100	18
1981	4,375	29,300	36
1990	8,000 +	46,900–56,300	50–60

Source: *Television Digest's Cable & Station Coverage Atlas;* A. C. Nielsen; Turner Communications; Leo Burnett Media Costs and Coverage.

Information / Entertainment Programming. This programming includes sports, "superstation" news, children, special audience, and religious programs.

Pay programming is an option available to subscribers for an additional monthly fee—on top of the basic fee. It normally consists of movies, specials, and sports. Pay networks do not currently accept advertising. Table 18–7 lists the fifty-eight cable networks in operation in 1987, all of which are transmitted to cable operators via satellite, and which are, in turn, transmitted to television households subscribing to basic and/or pay programming. (All this increased programming availability, especially recently released movies, could have an adverse effect on the local movie theatre. It's conceivable that movie house attendance will decline, or change in demographic composition to exclude many of those able to afford a pay cable package.)

Once HBO and its competitors began generating ratings at the expense of the networks and WTBS succeeded in getting distribution all over the U.S., many observers adopted a "pie-in-the-sky" perspective on the growth of cable. They expected that cable network shares would eventually overtake the networks, creating a ratings free-for-all among a wide variety of program outlets. Many thought most minority tastes would be served by 100 or more cable networks, and that interactive cable systems would become the norm, facilitating all sorts of two-way communications like polling, security monitoring, and fire alarms.

The reality of cable in the late 1980s has turned out to be considerably less grand than what was anticipated. Only a few operators went as far as to build 100 channel systems, and they are full of unused channels. As noted, only about sixty networks exist today, and while new ones are coming on board all the time, network failures occur just as fast. No single cable network has come close to catching any of the networks in the ratings race—only HBO approaches a 10 household rating, which is only about 2 percent of total U.S. homes in its universe. Two-way services have also fallen by the wayside as costs relative to the demand have not been efficient enough to ensure their survival.

Nonetheless, a number of networks will survive and continue to grow, albeit in a limited fashion. Pay services that offer uninterrupted movies will probably survive in the long term, despite inroads made by the release of movies on videotape and disc immediately after their theater release. Basic services—those supported by advertising—will also survive, but only a few will be successful over the long term. The hoped-for narrowcasting phenomenon will not materialize in any major way— the goal of most cable networks is to maximize audience appeal. Some, like WTBS

TABLE 18–7.   Cable Networks

Network	Systems	Homes (000)	Percent of U.S. TV HH	Percent of U.S. Cable HH	Advertiser Supported
Basic Services					
ACTS Satellite Network	236	4,600	5.2	11.1	Yes
Alternate View Network	206	2,500	2.9	6.0	Yes
Arts & Entertainment (A&E)	2,200	19,700	22.5	47.6	Yes
Black Entertainment Television (BET)	717	11,400	13.0	27.6	Yes
Cable News Network (CNN)	9,386	33,100	37.9	80.1	Yes
Cable Value Network	500	10,000	11.4	24.2	Yes
C-SPAN	2,300	25,250	28.9	61.1	Yes
C-SPAN II	286	7,600	8.7	18.4	Yes
CBN Cable Network	7,318	32,338	36.9	78.3	Yes
CNN	7,215	35,834	40.9	86.7	Yes
Consumer Discount Network	N/A	1,000	1.1	2.4	Yes
Country Music Television	438	6,200	7.0	15.0	Yes
Discovery Channel	1,034	10,100	11.5	24.4	Yes
ESPN	14,260	38,500	44.0	93.2	Yes
Eternal Word Television Network (EWTN)	334	6,100	6.9	14.8	Yes
Financial News Network (FNN)	1,434	23,300	26.6	56.4	Yes
Headline News	2,222	29,760	34.0	72.0	Yes
Hit Video USA	41	1,700	1.9	4.1	Yes
Home Shopping Network	517	9,774	11.2	23.7	Yes
Innovations to Living (HSN2)	176	5,322	6.0	12.9	Yes
International Television Network	5	622	*	1.5	Yes
Learning Channel	800	7,200	8.2	17.4	Yes
Liberty Broadcasting Network	90	1,300	1.5	3.1	Yes
Lifetime	3,050	27,100	30.9	65.6	Yes
Music Television (MTV)	4,269	30,700	35.1	74.3	Yes
Nashville Network	3,770	26,600	30.4	64.4	Yes
National Jewish Television (NJTV)	247	5,569	6.4	13.5	Yes
Nickelodeon	4,501	29,000	33.1	70.1	Yes
Nostalgia Channel	350	300	*	*	Yes
PTL: Inspirational Network	1,300	13,000	14.9	31.5	Yes
QVC Network	450	10,500	12.0	25.4	Yes
Score	1,020	19,000	21.7	45.9	Yes
Rock Christian Network	9	886	1.0	2.1	Yes
Silent Network	206	6,800	7.8	16.4	Yes
SIN Television Network	383	33,673	38.5	81.5	Yes
Sky Merchant	N/A	N/A	—	—	Yes
Sweepstakes Channel	N/A	N/A	—	—	Yes
TelShop	650	10,200	11.7	24.7	Yes
Tempo Television	640	12,500	14.3	30.3	Yes
Trinity Broadcasting Network	444	6,304	7.2	15.2	Yes
USA Network	6,500	33,000	37.7	79.8	Yes
Video Hits One	1,189	14,100	16.1	34.1	Yes
Video Shopping Mall	N/A	N/A	—	—	Yes
Weather Channel	2,200	12,000	25.2	53.2	Yes
WGN-TV	9,254	22,180	25.4	53.7	Yes
WOR-TV	1,999	8,669	9.9	20.9	Yes
WPIX-TV	254	2,434	2.7	5.9	Yes
WTBS-TV	8,373	37,582	43.0	90.9	Yes

Source: Cablevision, January 19, 1987. Reprinted by permission.
*Less than 1%.

(*continued*)

TABLE 18–7.   (continued)

Network	Systems	Homes (000)	Percent of U.S.		Advertiser Supported
			TV HH	Cable HH	
Pay Services					
American Movie Channel	350	2,000	2.2	4.8	No
Bravo	285	350	*	*	No
Cinemax	3,300	3,700	4.2	8.9	No
Disney Channel	4,300	3,000	3.4	7.6	No
Gala Vision	234	183	*	*	No
Home Box Office (HBO)	6,900	14,600	16.7	35.3	No
Home Theater Network (HTN)	350	300	*	*	No
Movie Channel	3,250	3,250	3.7	7.8	No
Playboy Channel	580	732	*	1.7	No
Showtime	3,200	5,400	6.2	13.0	No

and USA, function more like a broadcast station or network, offering a smorgasbord of programming for all demographics. Others, like CNN or the Weather Channel, break out the same program type around the clock in hope that everyone will tune in for at least a short time. There are a few true "narrowcast" cable networks, like MTV (rock video), Nickelodeon (kids), and the various religious networks, that do target a particular audience segment with custom-tailored programming, but it is the broad-appeal networks that have been the most successful to date.

Years of speculation about direct satellite-to-home broadcasting (DBS) resulted in several companies' aborted development of such a service. The widening availability of cable, the discount pricing of VCRs, and proliferation of backyard satellite receiving dishes designed to receive cable-only signals spelled doom for one company (USCI) that actually marketed a DBS service, and scared several others away from start-up. In fact, the easy availability of satellite dishes in rural areas led to a sort of de facto DBS; essentially, the dish owner was pirating pay and basic cable feeds. This led to computerized scrambling of pay and some basic signals, which resulted in direct marketing of descrambling devices and collection of program fees from dishowners not unlike the fees cable customers pay.

VCRs.   The biggest news in the 1980s has been the advent of the low-priced VCR, and the resultant proliferation of video software which is available in video rental stores, record stores, bookstores, supermarkets, and convenience marts. By 1995, 65 percent of all homes will have VCRs. Many will have their own video cameras, and many will have digital audio/video disc technology which will enable them to record and play back audio and video software.

The impact of all this on the media plan is already being felt. The popularization of VCRs has introduced remote control, and these remote controls are being used to, among other things, avoid commercials while watching television (zapping), and to fast-forward through commercials while replaying taped television programs (zipping). These phenomena are expected to increase as penetration of remote controls increases. By 1995, 75 percent of homes are expected to have remote controlled television sets and/or remote controlled VCRs.

New Technologies. In addition to the many changes the television environment has already experienced, new and better technologies that will change the face of the television medium have been and will continue to be developed. Stereo television, satellite technology, and the home computer are but a few of the technologies that we know will contribute to the changes in media.

Stereo television. Currently, over 200 television stations broadcast in stereo, covering 75 percent of U.S. homes. General Electric's purchase of RCA, and its subsidiary NBC, sparked the growth of stereo television. NBC became the first network to broadcast in stereo, and RCA introduced its deluxe line of stereo television sets. ABC began transmitting in stereo shortly thereafter, but to date, CBS has remained reluctant to follow suit. Although the sale of stereo television receivers has been slow (due primarily to $100 difference between mono and stereo), it is estimated that stereo will soon be available to all homes, and that 33 percent of color sets will be stereo by 1990.

Satellite technology. Since 1975, when SATCOM I, the first domestic communications satellite, was launched, satellite technology has changed the communication paths between senders and receivers. It is estimated that well before the end of the century, all network audio and video signals (radio, broadcast, and cable) will be delivered via satellite. This would eliminate all land-line distribution and facilitate stereo sound.

In addition, satellite technology is and will continue to be used by the print media. National print editorial and advertisements are being sent by satellite uplinks and downlinks to regional and local printing plants to improve the timeliness of content and delivery. In addition, clients and their agencies may use satellite transmission to beam copy executions from office to office, reducing time spent on the road and in meetings.

Home computers. Estimating home computer penetration is more difficult than estimating VCR penetration. SMRB states that 8.4 percent of all adults own home computers; other industry estimates range from 5 percent to 10 percent of U.S. homes. Although initial home computer sales were sluggish, advances in technology will lower prices and the maturing of a new generation of computer-literate children should increase sales. By the end of the century, at least 50 percent of all homes should have a computer. Ultimately, home computer usage for business and pleasure may impact on TV viewing.

Summary

The 1990s will offer advertisers both opportunities and obstacles. A more fragmented media world results in greater audience selectivity, and greater selectivity results in less waste. In light of the increasing cost of media, the less waste in a media plan the better.

More viewing, reading, and listening options should inevitably lead to higher interest, deeper involvement, and higher attentiveness—to both the media and the advertising within the media. There is a good chance that if advertisers react to this segmentation with personalized and localized advertising messages, their media budgets can be used with greater discrimination and far more effectiveness. The key to all is research. With more precise research, the media planner can make better decisions.

Over the next twenty-five years, technology will continue to grow and provide the media environment with more choices, more consumer control as well as the capability to interact with information and entertainment sources. Satellites, video recorders, and computers will dominate the media world. Consolidation will be a key trend, not only in the ownership of media sources themselves, but in the technologies which access them. Electronic component systems, which incorporate TV monitors, cable tuners, videocassette players and recorders, computer keyboards, stereo receivers and speakers, compact disc players, and computer modems are available now. Stereo sound will be commonplace. Video enhancements, such as digital signal transmission, will make the channel switcher's life easier by displaying two channels simultaneously. More people, with more leisure time, will spend that time at home in their "media rooms"; they will have more opportunities to work at home, and more reasons to be there.

Media Planning

Media planners will have their hands full trying to come to grips with a bigger total audience that will be more and more splintered. As an outgrowth of rapidly developing marketing sophistication and an increasingly personalized media environment, marketing and media planning goals will become more precise, with consumers being defined in much greater detail than we have today.

In addition to more and better traditional consumer data, research will have to provide a greater understanding of who the best prospects are and how to reach them. For example, women aged 25–54 who are working and in a household with a total income of $25,000 are good prospects if they characterize current Brand Z users. But women currently using a category brand, or intending to buy, are even more descriptive of a prime prospect. Research will provide greater insight into media usage patterns to reach these individuals and others who will influence a purchase.

An increasingly fragmented audience, coupled with a media inflation spiral that appears to have no end, will make it more important than ever to get every ounce of effectiveness out of each advertising dollar by developing new media techniques and applications. A vast amount of testing and trial of new media will occur in the 1980s. The new technologies will enable advertisers and agencies to measure alternatives and concepts with greater precision than ever. Two-way systems such as QUBE and its successors can be employed for many purposes. Measurements of attitudes or actual purchases could occur instantaneously.

Each component of a media plan might be scheduled as part of a unique pattern to achieve a designated effective reach goal against each specialized segment of the target audience. The average media plan could have a very unorthodox appearance

TABLE 18-8. Late Fringe TV—Kansas City

Station	DMA/HH Rating
WDAF	7
KCTV	6
KMBC	5
KSHB	2
KZKC	1
Total	21
Average	4.2

when it includes some daytime serials, pay cable adult movies, sports cable network, demographic editions of magazines and newspapers, and some syndicated network radio.

A new generation of sophisticated computerization will permeate media planning and media buying. There will be more research, more media outlets, more complex analyses to conduct, more extensive tracking of results—more details than ever. All media professionals will have to have a greater understanding of computer technology, while not losing touch with basic tools and responsibilities.

Changing Dynamics

The first important consideration is that current solutions to the problems of the future will not work. All media dynamics must be reassessed: reach, frequency, frequency distribution, audience accumulation, target audience, etc.

Average Rating

If you buy Kansas City spot TV in late fringe now, you will be purchasing one or more of the five TV stations in the market and delivering, on average, a 4.2 household rating, as shown in Table 18-8.

Now consider the ratings report of the future. As Table 18-9 shows, it will contain many more stations.

The media planner in 1995 might find eighteen different stations broadcasting in the Kansas City market. Perhaps ten to fifteen of these stations will accept advertising. The planner will have to choose among programs that will be delivering an average of a 1.4 rating. Four programs (or announcements) will have to be purchased to equal the 4.2 gross rating points one can now buy with one program.

Reach/Frequency

If 400 gross rating points are planned today, it can be anticipated that it would be necessary to purchase twenty-five announcements with an average of a 16 rating each. These twenty-five announcements, on the average, will reach 87 percent of the designated audience an average of 4.6 times each. In the future, that viewing audience will be splintered across 10, 20, 30, or more channels with each channel

TABLE 18–9.   Representative TV Market in the Future

Station	DMA/HH Rating
A	0.1
B	3.1
C	1.3
D	1.3
E	2.2
F	0.5
G	0.1
H	0.7
I	1.2
J	1.8
K	2.3
L	0.7
M	0.9
N	1.7
O	0.4
P	3.2
Q	2.0
R	2.7
Total	26.2
Average	1.4

delivering a smaller average rating than today. To deliver 400 gross rating points, more announcements will have to be purchased, and probably more stations, as shown in Tables 18–9 and 18–10.

This raises the following questions:

• Will the reach/frequency be the same?
• Is it conceivable that reach could be higher because new programming will attract light and non-TV viewers?
• Is it possible that reach will be lower because there will be more viewers watching pay TV?

Audience Accumulation

When one thinks of audience accumulation, one generally thinks of magazines because it takes time for magazines to build their total readership through pass-along. Television and radio are now thought of as "instantaneous" media vehicles. This will probably change. Reach accumulation in the future could be the same over a long period of time, but it is possible that it could take longer to accumulate a total broadcast audience because many people will record a program for later viewing. If

TABLE 18–10.   Reach/Frequency

	Now	Future
Number announcements	25	200
Average rating	16	2
Gross rating points	400	400
Reach/frequency	87/4.6	87/4.6 (?)
		90/4.4 (?)
		80/5.0 (?)

TABLE 18-11.   Audience Accumulation in TV—100 GRPs per Week

Week	Now	Future Same (?)	Future Longer (?)
1	59	59	50
2	78	78	65
3	85	85	75
4	87	87	80
5	—	—	85
6 Mos. later	—	—	87

the advertiser plans a sale that ends June 30, it should anticipate that some viewers will see the commercials in July, August, or even later. Table 18–11 illustrates the problem.

Target Audience

Many advertising people subscribe to a viewing theory that might be called "least objectionable program"—viewers first decide to watch TV, then tune in a specific program. In the future, the program might be the first decision made. People will seek out programs they really want to watch, and there will be many more programs available. Programs will appeal to very specific segments of the population based both on demographic characteristics and life-style orientation. When broadcast media are purchased now, audience information is available only for certain demographic breaks. In the future, research will have to provide not only narrower demographic breaks, but also life-style and, quite possibly, product consumption information.

Direct Response

Another media/marketing vehicle that has received increased attention by national advertisers is direct response or direct mail advertising. As noted in an earlier chapter, direct response is a very selective, targeted, personal medium that offers great geographic and production flexibility and response is easily measurable. Direct mail promotions, catalogs, and home shopping vehicles are receiving increased usage by both national advertisers and their agencies. According to the Direct Marketing Association, marketers who utilize catalogs most frequently express positive feedback regarding their intent to continue utilizing direct mail/catalog advertising. More importantly, these catalog leaders reported strengthened unit sales and higher profits as a result of their direct mail/catalog efforts.

The emergence of home shopping television broadcasts (such as Home Shopping Network) have also contributed to the increase in interest in direct response advertising. Advertisers now have the ability to sell product directly to the consumer simply by providing a toll-free phone number and an operator standing by to take the credit card number and the order. If the popularity of this medium increases, it is conceivable that media planners will utilize direct response advertising as an integral part of their media plans.

TABLE 18-12.   Possible New Media Jargon

Today	Future
RTG – Rating	APR – Accumulated Program Rating
HUT – Homes Using TV	HUEM – Homes Using Electronic Media
CPM – Cost per Thousand	CPC – Cost per Hundred
R – Reach	ER – Eventual Reach
RWN – Reach When Needed	F – Frequency
IF – Initial Frequency	
	EF – Eventual Frequency
RF – Repeat Frequency	IMP – Impressions
IWN – Impressions When Needed	
	ITL – Impressions Too Late
Circ – Circulation	ED – Electronic Delivery
Rdrs – Readers	RL – Reader/Listeners

New Media Jargon

Media planners certainly will have new challenges in the decades to come. There will be bigger audiences, but they will be more splintered. *When* a person will be exposed to advertising will become as important as *what* they are exposed to. There will be greater selectivity in television, magazines, newspapers, radio, out-of-home, and direct response.

Media jargon will have to keep pace with these changes. Planners will have to shift from *average quarter hour rating* to *accumulated program rating*. *Homes using TV* will be antiquated and eventually will be replaced by *homes using electronic media*. *Cost per thousand* may change to *cost per hundred* because there will be smaller target audiences to reach. *Reach* will change to *eventual reach* and eventually to *reach when needed*. *Frequency* will become divided into *initial frequency* (when the commercial is first seen), *eventual frequency*, and *repeat frequency* (for those who record a program and view it a second time). Will part of a newspaper's or magazine's delivery be called *electronic delivery* for those subscribers who view the periodical on their TV screen? If *Time* magazine's experiment of creating a "talking magazine," which uses an electronic device reacting to an electronically treated page, is successful, will these readers need to be called *reader/listeners*? Table 18-12 lists some of the potential new terms.

Summary

The late 1980s offer advertisers both opportunities and obstacles. A more fragmented media world results in greater audience selectivity, and greater selectivity results in less waste. In light of the increasing cost of media, the less waste in a media plan the better.

More viewing, reading, and listening options should inevitably lead to higher interest, deeper involvement, and higher attentiveness—to both the media and the advertising within the media. There is a good chance that if advertisers react to this segmentation with personalized and localized advertising messages, their media budgets can be used with greater discrimination and far more effectiveness.

The key to all is research. With more precise research, the media planner can make better decisions.

SELECTED READINGS

Frank, Betsy, ''When VCR Meets NBC,'' *Marketing and Media Decisions,* October 1986, pp. 106–10.

Heeter, Carrie, and Greenberg, Bradley S., ''Profiling the Zappers,'' *Journal of Advertising Research,* April/May 1985, pp. 15–20.

Kaplan, Barry M., ''Zapping—The Real Issue Is Communication,'' *Journal of Advertising Research,* April/May 1985, pp. 9–14.

Glossary

A **A.B.C. (Audit Bureau of Circulations)**—An organization that provides certified statements of net paid circulations of magazines and newspapers, supported jointly by advertisers, agencies, and media.

A.B.P. (Associated Business Publications)—A trade association of business (industrial, trade, and technical) publications.

Accordion Insert—An advertisement not printed by the publisher, but inserted in a magazine, folded in such a way as to appear as an accordion fold.

Accumulation—A method of counting audiences wherein each person exposed to a vehicle is counted once, either in a given time period such as four weeks for broadcast, or for one issue in print.

A Counties—As defined by A. C. Nielsen Company, all counties belonging to the 25 largest metropolitan areas. These metro areas correspond to the *MSA (Metropolitan Statistical Area)* and include the largest cities and consolidated areas in the United States.

ADI (Area of Dominant Influence)—Geographical market definition wherein each county is assigned exclusively to only one television market as defined by Arbitron.

Adjacencies—The specific time periods that precede and follow regular television programming, usually two minutes. These are commercial break positions between programs that are available for local or spot advertisers. There is no such thing as a network adjacency; only spot adjacencies are available.

Adnorm—A term used by Daniel Starch & Associates to indicate readership averages by publication, by space size and color, and by type of product for ads studied by Starch in a two-year period. It is used to provide a standard of comparison for individual ads against averages of similar types of ads.

Advertising Allowance—Money paid under contract by the manufacturer or his representative to a wholesaler or a retailer for the express purpose of being spent to advertise a specified product, brand, or line. Usually used for consumer advertising. (See *Cooperative Advertising, Promotion Allowance*.)

Advertising Appropriation—A company's estimated dollar figure for an advertising effort of a short-term flight, seasonal campaign and/or total marketing year. Usually reflects general categories for media, production, promotion, and reserve and is based on projected business volume.

Advertising Checking Bureau (ACB)—A service organization that supplies advertisers and agencies with tearsheets of advertisements run in publications and with other information, in order that client and competitor advertising impact can be assessed.

Advertising Impression—One person or home exposed to a single advertisement: on a gross basis, the sum of all impressions to the ads in a schedule. This includes duplication, for some of those exposed may be exposed more than once. In some instances, advertising impression refers to those persons or homes that are exposed to a media vehicle (magazine, television show, etc.) and is developed by multiplying the audience of each vehicle (on a household or person basis) by the number of advertisements or commercials carried by each vehicle and obtaining the total. In other cases, it refers to the number of persons or homes exposed to an advertisement or commercial within the carrier. In these cases, data on ad/commercial exposure are applied to the carrier audiences.

Advertising Page Exposure (APX)—A measurement of physical opportunity to observe a print ad. Defined as the act of opening a spread of facing pages wide enough to glance at any advertising.

Advertising Weight—The amount of advertising planned for, or used by, a brand. Although it is not limited to a particular measurement, it is most frequently stated in terms of the number of messages or impressions delivered or broadcasts / insertions placed over a period of time.

Afternoon Drive—Radio daypart between 3:00 P.M. and 7:00 P.M.

Agate Line (usually simplified to Line)—A unit of space by which newspaper and other print advertising space is sold. One agate line represents a space 1 column wide and $^1/_{14}$ of an inch high. This is a measure of area, not shape—a 210 line ad can be 1 column × 210 lines, 2 columns × 105 lines, or 3 columns × 70 lines.

Agency of Record—An agency that purchases media time or space for another agency or a group of agencies serving the same client.

Aided Recall—A measurement technique in which respondents are helped to remember portions or all of ads by having an interviewer provide clues. (See *Unaided Recall*.)

Algorithm—A computer term referring to processing rules: a defined process that leads to an assured development of a desired output from a given input.

Alternate Week Sponsor—An advertiser who purchases full or participating sponsorship every other week of a network program for a full fifty-two-week broadcast year. Each sponsor purchasing at least two minutes in a given program episode will receive billboard commercial time on his week of sponsorship.

AM (Amplitude Modulation)—AM is the standard broadcast transmission system used by the majority of licensed radio stations. The term is commonly used to differentiate between AM and FM radio.

Animatic—(a) Noting or pertaining to mechanical animation. (b) A television commercial produced from semifinished artwork, generally used only for test purposes.

Announcement—A commercial message between or within programs. Announcements may be live, or recorded, or a combination of both. Common lengths in television are 60, 30, 20, 15, and 10 seconds.

Arbitron—A television and radio rating service used to measure viewing / listening audiences. Arbitron publishes both a monthly radio network rating report and TV and radio reports for selected individual markets (no network TV).

Area of Dominant Influence (ADI)—An exclusive cluster of counties in which the originating or home market station reflects the largest share of total viewing hours. This term is used by Arbitron.

Audience—The number of people or households who are exposed to a medium. Exposure measurements indicate nothing about whether audiences saw, heard, or read either the advertisements or editorial contents of the medium.

Audience Accumulation—The total net audience exposed to repeated periodical, outdoor, television, or radio advertising.

Audience Composition—The demographic makeup of people represented in an audience with respect to income group, age, sex, geography, etc.

Audience Duplication—In broadcast, a measurement of the number of listeners or viewers reached by two or more programs, or by the same program over repeated telecasts, sponsored by the same advertiser. In print, the measurement of the overlap of potential exposure between different issues of the same magazine or among issues of different magazines.

Audience Flow—Changes in audience of broadcast programs. May be reported on a minute-by-minute basis, by five-minute intervals, or from show to show.

Audience Holding Index—A measurement of the retentive power or audience loyalty of a given program. A. C. Nielsen, for thirty-minute programs, uses an index based on the percentage of homes tuned to the same program twenty-five minutes after the first measurement. It is a simple measure of the ratio of average audience rating to total audience rating of a given program.

Audience, Potential—In broadcasting, the number of sets in use in the time period to be studied, or the number of set owners. In print, the total audience of an issue.

Audience, Primary—In a study of audience accumulation, the noncumulative potential audience of an advertising message. In print, all readers who live in households where someone subscribes to, or purchases, the magazine. May be called primary readership.

Audience Profile—The characteristics of the people who make up the audience of a magazine, TV show, newspaper, radio show, etc., in terms of age, family size, location, education, income, and other factors.

Audience, Secondary—Pass-along readers who read a publication they did not purchase. These readers should be taken into account in determining the total number of readers of a particular publication.

Audience Turnover—The average number of times that a television program receives new audience members in a four-week period. Calculated by dividing reach by the average rating.

Audilog—The diary that members of Nielsen's local rating panels fill out to show what they are viewing on television.

Audimeter—An electronic device developed by the A. C. Nielsen Company that records set usage and tuning on a minute-by-minute basis. Nielsen used a national sample of approximately 1,200 Audimeter homes which are used to measure television usage and program audiences.

Audit Bureau of Circulations (ABC)—A tripartite, nonprofit, self-regulatory organization of advertisers, agencies, and magazine and newspaper publishers, which verifies the circulation figures of publishers and members and reports these data to advertiser and agency members.

Audit Report (White Audit)—Official document issued by the A.B.C. detailing its findings as a result of an audit. (Printed on white paper to differentiate it from semiannual publisher's statements printed on colored paper.) Audit reports are issued annually covering the twelve-month period of the two previous publisher's statements. (See *Publisher's Statement*.) If the auditor's findings differ from the information in the publisher's statements, the discrepancies are reported and explained in the audit report.

Availability—A specific period of broadcast commercial time offered for sale by a station or network for sponsorship.

Average Audience (AA)—In broadcasting, the number of homes/persons tuned in to a TV program for an average minute (a Nielsen network TV measurement). In print, the number of persons who looked into an average issue of a publication.

Average Frequency—The number of times the average home (or person) reached by a media schedule is exposed to the schedule. This is measured over a specific period of time, e.g., four weeks in broadcast media.

Average Net Paid—Average circulation per issue arrived at by dividing the sum total paid circulation for all the issues of the audit period by the total number of issues.

B   **Back of Book**—The section of a magazine following the main editorial section.

Back-to-Back Scheduling—Two or more commercials run one immediately following the other.

BAR (Broadcast Advertisers Reports)—An organization that monitors network and spot TV activity and spending by brand as well as non-network activity in selected markets and reports to subscribers the position, length, and advertised brand of all announcements broadcast during a given week. Also reports network radio.

Barter—Acquisition by an advertiser of sizable quantities of spot time or free mentions at rates lower than card rates from broadcast stations in exchange for operating capital or merchandise. Although direct negotiation between the advertiser and station is possible, it is more common for barter to be arranged through a middleman, a barter agency, or a film producer or distributor, who may have procured the time through an exchange of film or taped shows.

Base Rate—See *Open Rate*.

Basic Cable—A service that transmits television signals by wire (cable) instead of through the air. This allows for improved reception and increased availability of retransmitted local and distant stations. Available at a basic monthly subscription fee.

B Counties—As defined by A. C. Nielsen Company, all counties not included under A that are either over 150,000 population or in a metro area over 150,000 population according to the latest census.

BehaviorScan—A technique for measuring product and brand purchased through use of Universal Product Code at checkout counters.

Best Food Day—A day on which a newspaper runs editorial material on food, making that day's edition the most advantageous for retail grocers' advertising and hence, for the advertising of food manufacturers; usually Wednesday evening or Thursday editions.

Billboard—An identifying announcement of sponsorship at the beginning, end, or breaks of radio and television sponsored programs. Billboards are not sold, but usually are a bonus, based on the advertiser's volume or commitment with the program or the broadcaster. Usually 5 to 10 seconds in length. Also, an outdoor poster.

Billing—(a) A charge made to an advertiser by an advertising agency, based on the listed or gross charges of the media from which space or time has been purchased, along with any other charges and fees incurred by the agency that are passed on to the advertiser. (b) Loosely, the money spent by an advertiser through an agency. (c) The actual charge made by a medium of communication to an advertising agency; the gross charge less the agency discount.

Black & White (B&W, B/W)—Printing with black ink on white paper (or vice versa); no color. Also known as monotone.

Blanket Coverage—Total coverage by television and radio of a given geographic area.

Bleed—An advertisement in which part or all of the illustration or copy runs past the usual margins out to the edge of a page. Bleed insertions are generally sold at a premium price, usually 15 percent over the basic rate.

Bonus Circulation—Circulation delivered by a publication that is above and beyond the circulation on which an advertiser's rate is based.

Brand Development Index (BDI)—The number of cases, units, or dollar volume of a brand sold per 1,000 population. It is calculated by dividing the percentage of sales in a market by the population percentage in the same market.

Broadsheet—A newspaper size approximately 15 inches wide and 22 inches high.

Broadside—A promotion piece consisting of one large sheet of paper, generally printed on one side only.

Brochure—An elaborate booklet, usually bound with a special cover.

Bulk Circulation—Sales in quantity lots of an issue of a magazine or newspaper. The purchases are made by individuals or concerns and the copies are usually directed to lists of names supplied by the purchasers. In the A.B.C. report, bulk circulation is listed separately from single-copy sales.

Bulk Sales—Sales of copies of a publication in quantity to one purchaser to be given free by him. Many advertisers do not consider bulk sales to be a valuable part of a publication's circulation.

Bulldog Edition—An edition that is issued and on sale earlier than regular editions. Usually applies to morning newspapers. There are also Bulldog Sunday editions that go on sale Saturday night.

Burke Test—A test service of Burke Marketing Research, Inc., that measures recall of an advertisement among those persons exposed to it the preceding day.

Business Building Test—A test run by a specific brand designed to determine if a marketing or advertising plan change will produce enough additional business for the brand to pay the required costs of the change.

Business Paper—A publication directed to a particular industry, trade, profession, or vocation. A *horizontal* business paper is designed to reach all groups in a broad trade or industry regardless of location or occupational title. A *vertical* publication is for a specific profession, trade, or occupational level within or across various industries.

Buyout—A one-time payment to television or radio talent for all rights to performance.

C **CATV**—Community Antenna (or cable) TV services that deliver high-quality TV signals to homes via coaxial cable. Also called *cable television*.

C.C.A. (Controlled Circulation Audit)—An organization that audits the circulation statements of publications that are sent free to selected lists.

Cable TV—A system of broadcasting television whereby programs are first tuned-in by a Community Antenna and then distributed to individual homes by cables. Cable operators often receive programs transmitted by satellites and then transmit by cable to their subscribers.

Cancellation Date—The last date on which it is possible to cancel advertising. Such dates occur for print, outdoor, and broadcasting.

Cannibalize—To draw sales away from another product of the same manufacturer in a manner diminishing the maker's profit; said of new products, flanker items, or line extensions.

Car Card—A standard 11-inch-high siderack card, generally with posterlike design, placed in buses, street cars, and subways. Common sizes are $11'' \times 28''$, $11'' \times 42''$, and $11'' \times 56''$.

Card Rate—The cost of time and space quoted on a rate card.

Case Allowance—An allowance or discount a manufacturer or wholesaler gives to a retailer on each case of product purchased in return for which the retailer is to use the money to advertise the product.

Cash Discount—A deduction allowed by print media (usually 2 percent of the net) for prompt payment (e.g., within 15 to 30 days), generally passed along by the agency to the advertiser to encourage collections.

Cash Refund Offer—A type of mail-in offer used by a brand, or group of brands, which offers cash to the consumer upon providing proof of purchase.

Category Development Index (CDI)—Means the same as *Marketing Development Index*. Essentially, the percentage of total U.S. sales of a product category related to population percentage in a geographical market.

C Counties—As defined by A. C. Nielsen Company, all counties not included under A or B that either have over 40,000 population or are in a metropolitan area of over 40,000 population according to the latest census.

Center Spread—An advertisement appearing on the two facing center pages of a publication.

Chain Break—(a) The time between network programs during which a station identifies itself. (b) A commercial appearing in a chain break.

Checking Copy—A copy of a publication sent to an advertiser and agency as proof that the advertisement appeared as ordered.

Circulation—In print, the number of copies of a vehicle distributed based on an average of a number of issues. In broadcast, the number of television or radio households that tune in to a station a minimum number of times within a specified time period (such as once a week or once a day). In outdoor, the total number of people who have an opportunity to see a given showing of billboards within a specified time, such as a twenty-four-hour period.

City Zone—A geographic area that includes the corporate limits of the central city of the market plus any contiguous areas that have substantially the same built-up characteristics of the central city. This provides a method of reporting newspaper circulation according to A.B.C. standards.

Class A, B, C Rates—Rates for the most desirable and costly television time, usually between 6 P.M. and 11 P.M., are called Class A rates; the next most costly is Class B; and so on. Each station sets its own time classifications.

Class Magazine—A publication that reaches select high-income readers in contrast to magazines with larger circulations, generally referred to as *mass magazines*.

Clear Channel Station—An AM radio station allowed 50,000 kilowatts, the maximum power allowed, and priority in the use of frequency band. At sunset, other stations on this frequency sign off, because broadcasting range is extended after dark and stations on the same frequency tend to interfere with one another.

Clear Time—Process used by an advertiser to reserve a time period with a local station and by a network to check with its affiliates on the availability of a time period.

Clearance—Obtaining a time period for a program or commercial on a station or obtaining approval to use advertising from clients, legal and/or medical counsel, or network continuity departments.

Clipping Bureau—An organization that examines newspapers and magazines and clips articles from them; references and allusions of interest to its clients are sent to them.

Closed Circuit TV—The transmission of television signals by cable or other nonbroadcast means to connected locations. Often used to transmit special events to theaters or for educational purposes.

Closing Date—The final date to commit contractually for the purchase of advertising space. Generally, cancellations are not accepted after the closing date, although some publications have a separate cancellation date, which may fall before the closing date. Also used in connection with supplying ad material to the publication.

Clutter—Excessive amounts of advertising carried by media vehicles, both print and broadcast. Term refers to both the total amount of advertising time and space and to its scheduling—long strings of consecutive commercials for broadcasting and solid banks of advertisements in print.

Coaxial Cable—Usually abbreviated to *cable*. The mechanical facility used by broadcasters for the transmission of programming from city to city or from a cable organization to individual homes. The cable is actually owned by A.T.&T. and, in turn, is rented to the user. Sometimes, microwave broadcasting operations are utilized instead of these cables. More generally, coaxial cable is any electrical cable capable of carrying large information loads with minimal distortion. (See *CATV, Cable TV.*)

Combination Rate—A discounted rate offered to encourage use of two or more stations, newspapers, magazines, etc., having common ownership. Occasionally, an advertiser has no choice but to buy the combination as space/time may not be sold separately.

Commercial Audience—The audience for a specific commercial as determined by a survey that elicits information about what program viewers were doing just before, during, and after the commercial. The commercial audience is operationally defined as those people who were physically present in the room with the TV set at the time the commercial was on.

Commercial Break—In broadcasting, an interruption of programming in which commercials are broadcast.

Commercial Delivery—That part of the audience actually exposed to a particular commercial.

Commercial Pool—The selection of television or radio commercials that an advertiser has available for airing at any one time.

Commercial Protection—The amount of time that a network or station provides between the scheduling of competitive commercials.

Commission—Compensation to a salesperson, agency, etc., as a percent of their sales. (See *Agency of Record.*)

Concentration Campaign—One in which a small number of media vehicles is used to carry a relatively heavy amount of advertising.

Confirmation—Broadcast media statement that a requested time slot is available to a prospective client.

Consecutive Weeks Discount—A discount granted to an advertiser who uses a minimum number of weeks of advertising on a station or network without interruption.

Consumer Magazine—A magazine whose editorial content appeals to the general public, or a specific segment or layer of the public. Differentiated from trade or business magazines.

Contemporary Format—The format of radio stations which play mostly single records (usually country, pop, or middle-of-the-road styles) currently being sold at record stores, rotating them on the basis of popularity. Also called top-40 and rock formats.

Continuity—A method of scheduling advertising so that audiences have an opportunity to see ads at regular intervals. There are many patterns that could be used, from advertising once each day of the year to once a month.

Controlled Circulation Publications—Publications that confine or restrict their distribution to special groups on a free basis. Some controlled circulation is solicited, although most is nonsolicited.

Cooperative Advertising—Advertising run by a local advertiser in conjunction with a national advertiser. The national advertiser usually provides the copy and/or printing material and also shares the cost with the local retailer. In return, the national advertiser receives local promotion for its product. The name of the local advertiser and its address appear in the ad.

Co-Sponsorship—The participation of two or more sponsors in a single broadcast program where each advertiser pays a proportionate share of the cost.

Cost Efficiency—The effectiveness of media as measured by a comparison of audience, either potential or actual, with cost and expressed as a cost per thousand.

Cost per Point—In broadcast, the cost of one household or demographic rating point in a given market. Used in media planning and evaluation, it is calculated by dividing the cost per spot by the rating, or, in the cost of a number of spots, their total cost by the total ratings or GRPs.

Cost per Thousand (CPM)—A figure used in comparing or evaluating the cost efficiency of media vehicles. CPM is the cost to deliver 1,000 people or homes and is calculated by dividing the cost by the audience delivery and multiplying the quotient by 1,000.

Cost Ratio—Term used by Daniel Starch & Associates. The cost ratio is an adjustment made to the score obtained on each readership measure. The score is translated into per dollar terms (based on the magazine's reported primary circulation and the cost of the ad in terms of size, color, etc.) and then stated as a percentage of the average per dollar scores of all ads studied in the same issue. (See *Noted, Starch Method.*)

Counterprogramming—A technique used by networks to regulate audience flow by offering a program of a different type from that broadcast by a strong competitor in the same time period.

Coupon Insert—An IBM-type coupon attached to a carrier unit that is bound into the subscription copies of a magazine much like a normal page is inserted. Several configurations are available depending on the size of magazine, the manner in which it is bound, and the number of coupons to be carried.

Couponing—Distribution of coupons by a manufacturer through the mail, by household calls, or through media, offering a price reduction at the store on a product.

Coverage—A term used to define a medium's geographical potential. In newspapers, the number of circulation units of a paper divided by the number of households in a given area. In magazines, the percentage of a given demographic market reached by a magazine. In radio/television, the percentage of television households that can tune in to a station (or stations) because they are in the signal area. In outdoor, the percentage of adults who pass a given showing and are exposed in a thirty-day period. In previous years, coverage meant the same as reach. Today, the meaning will depend on which medium is being discussed.

Cover Positions—Premium-priced cover space for magazine or business publication advertisements: 1st cover—outside front cover; 2nd cover—inside front cover; 3rd cover—inside back cover; 4th cover—outside back cover. The first cover of consumer publications is seldom used for advertising.

Cowcatcher—A commercial occurring at the beginning of, and forming a part of, a television or radio program, advertising a product of the sponsor that is not mentioned again in the program.

Cume—A broadcast term that is Nielsen's shorthand for net cumulative audience of a program or of a spot schedule (radio or TV) in four weeks' time. Based on total number of unduplicated TV homes or people reached.

Cumulative Audience—The net unduplicated audience of a campaign, either in one medium or a combination of media. Sometimes called *reach* or *cume*.

Cut-In—Different broadcast copy or format that is used to replace an originating commercial in a network program in a specific market or region. Frequently used in test markets.

Cycle—An interval within a contract year at the end of which, upon proper notice, an advertiser may cancel network stations and/or facilities. Weekly and multiweekly program cycles usually are thirteen weeks in length, while co-sponsored program cycles usually encompass thirteen major broadcasts. Also refers to the thirteen-week periods used as a base for talent and use fee payments.

D   **Daily Rate**—The rate a newspaper charges for space in its weekday editions as opposed to the rate for the Sunday or weekend editions.

Day-After Recall—Probably the most common method used to test television commercials. Test commercials are shown on the air in the normal fashion. Approximately twenty-four hours later people are phoned and asked about their previous day's viewing. Only those who viewed the program carrying the test commercial are further questioned. The test score consists of that proportion of the commercial audience who are able to provide specific correct audio or video details from the test commercial. (See *Burke Test, Commercial Audience*.)

Daypart—A part of the broadcast day, so designated for analytical purposes. In TV, the dayparts are usually daytime (morning and afternoon), early fringe, prime time, and late fringe. In radio, they are morning, daytime, afternoon, evening.

D Counties—Essentially rural counties in the Nielsen classification system of A, B, C, D counties.

Demographic Characteristics—Physical characteristics, such as sex, age, education, occupation, used to describe a population. Standard definitions, established by the 4A's, are used by many research companies.

Designated Marketing Area (DMA)—Nonoverlapping TV market coverage as defined by the A. C. Nielsen Company. (ADI is the equivalent term used by Arbitron.)

Differential (Newspaper)—The difference in newspaper rates charged local and national advertisers. Most newspapers continue to charge higher rates to national advertisers.

Direct Broadcast Satellite (DBS)—A satellite transmission system that delivers a signal directly to a home via an earth station or a receiver dish.

Direct Mail Advertising—Letters, folders, reprints, or other material sent through the mails directly to prospective purchasers.

Direct Response Advertising—Advertising material reproduced in quantity and distributed directly to prospects, either by mail, house-to-house delivery, bag stuffers, magazines and newspapers, or television. Allows prospect to respond directly to the advertiser rather than going through a retailer or other middleman.

Directory Advertising—Advertising in a directory. Popularly used to signify any advertising that consumers may deliberately consult, i.e., department store or food advertisements.

Discount—A reduction from regular rates when an advertiser contracts to use quantities of advertising. Discounts in print may consider amount of space bought and frequency of insertion. Discounts in network broadcasting may be based upon number of dayparts used, frequency or weight, and length of contract; in local broadcasting, discounts will consider number of spots per week, length of contract, or purchase of plans or packages.

DMA (Designated Market Area)—Geographical market definition wherein each county is assigned exclusively to only one television market as defined by Nielsen.

Double-Carding—A transit advertising term specifying two displays in each vehicle.

Double Truck—A two-page spread in newspapers where the editorial or advertising runs across the gutter of the spread.

Downlink—Programming delivered from a satellite to the ground.

Downscale—A general description of a medium's audience of lower socioeconomic class members.

Drive Time—The times of day (both morning and afternoon) when most people drive to or from work (about 6 to 10 am and 3 to 7 pm).

Duplication—The number or percentage of people in one vehicle's audience who also are exposed to another vehicle. Also audiences who are counted more than once in measurements, such as those who view the same TV program more than once a month.

Dutch Doors—In magazines, vertical half-page gatefolds which fold inward on both sides of a two-page spread.

E   **Earned Rate**—The rate that an advertiser has earned based on volume or frequency of space or time used to obtain a discount.

Earth Station—Communications station used to send or receive electronic signals from or to a satellite (seldom both). Usually employs one of a variety of dish-type antennas used by television stations and cable operators.

Effective Reach / Frequency—The reach of a medium or media schedule at a predetermined level of frequency (as opposed to total reach).

Efficiency—See *Cost Efficiency*.

Eight-Sheet Poster—See *Junior Panel*.

Electronic Newspaper—The use of a home CRT to receive newspaper-type textual material such as news, stock listings, and sports.

Entertainment and Sports Programming Network (ESPN)—An advertiser-supported twenty-four-hour cable service covering professional and amateur sporting events and sports talks. The primary owner is Getty Oil.

Ethnic Media—A catch-all term for those newspapers, magazines, and radio and television stations that direct their editorial and/or language to specific ethnic groups.

Exclusivity—Freedom from competing advertising within a given communications medium enjoyed by one advertiser; requires major space or time purchases.

Expansion Plan—An outline of the media to be used and timing thereof for a brand that plans to apply a theoretical national plan to portions of the country subsequent to testing and prior to actual national application. The expansion areas are the geographical units in which the product is to be sold.

Exposure—"Open eyes facing a medium." Practically, however, measurements are based on respondents who either say with assurance that they have looked into a given magazine, or that, after looking at a list of magazines, say that they have looked into those they checked on the list. In broadcast, those who are sitting in the room while a television or radio program is being broadcast.

Exposure, Depth of—The value credited to an increased number of broadcast commercials or multipage spreads in the form of heightened consciousness of an advertisement. While the audience for such media usage generally does not increase proportionally with the amount of additional investment made, the depth of exposure tends to provide adequate compensation.

Exposure, Opportunity of—The degree to which an audience may reasonably be expected to see or hear an advertising message.

F **Facing**—Used in outdoor advertising to refer to the number of billboards used in one display. A single facing is one billboard. A double facing is two billboards either joined or with less than twenty-five feet between them. A triple facing is three billboards, etc. Also, the number of packages in a store facing out from the front row of a shelf.

Farm Publication—A publication devoted to general agricultural topics edited for farm families or farmers.

Field Intensity Map—A broadcast coverage map showing the quality of reception possible on the basis of signal strength. Sometimes called a *contour map*.

Field Intensity Measurement—The measurement of a signal delivered at a point of reception by a radio transmitter in units of voltage per meter of effective antenna height, usually in terms of microvolts or millivolts per meter.

Fifteen and Two—The same terms on which advertising media is ordered by advertising agencies for their clients, i.e., 15 percent commission is allowed by the media on the gross cost, plus 2 percent discount on the net amount for prompt payment.

Fifty-Fifty Plan—In cooperative advertising, the equal sharing by a manufacturer and a dealer of the cost of a manufacturer's advertisement appearing over a dealer's name.

Fixed Position—A specific period of station broadcasting time reserved for an advertiser and sold at a premium rate.

Fixed Rate—Station's price for a time slot which guarantees that the advertiser's announcement will run in that position without preemption.

Flat Rate—An advertising rate that does not include any discounts.

Flighting—A method of scheduling advertising for a period of time, followed by a period of no advertising, followed by a resumption of advertising.

Float—In periodical advertising, to run an advertisement within a space which is larger than the ad.

Flowchart—A system-analysis tool, either computerized or manual, that provides a graphical presentation of a procedure. Such charts present data flows, procedures, growth, equipment, methods, documents, machine instructions, etc.

FM (Frequency Modulation)—FM is a radio broadcast band in the broadcast spectrum different from that used by AM stations. There is no static in FM radio reception.

Folio—(a) A size of paper measuring 17" by 22". (b) A book with signatures formed of a single sheet of paper folded once, and thus of four pages each. (c) Loosely, any book with very large pages. (d) Any of the numbers that identify the successive pages of a book.

Forced Combination—Morning and evening newspapers owned by the same publisher that are sold to national advertisers only in combination. Some forced combinations are morning and evening editions of the same newspapers.

Four-Color (4/C)—Black and three colors (blue, yellow, red). Standard color combinations used by practically all publications offering color advertising.

Fractional Showing—In outdoor, a showing of less than 25, offered in certain areas.

Franchise Position—A specified position in a publication (e.g., back cover, inside front cover) for which an advertiser is granted a permanent franchise (or right to use) as long as he continues to use it. Franchise positions are sometimes specific locations such as "opposite punched hole recipe page" in *Better Homes & Gardens*. Some positions are negotiated for specific issues, while others may be granted by frequency of use (i.e., six out of twelve issues). If a given position is not used one year, it usually must be renegotiated to regain it.

Free Publication—A publication sent without cost to a selected list of readers. Circulation may or may not be audited by C.C.A., but cannot qualify for A.B.C. audit unless at least 70 percent of circulation is paid.

Free-Standing Insert (FSI)—A preprinted advertisement in single or multiple page form that is inserted loose into newspapers, particularly Sunday editions.

Frequency—The average number of times an audience unit is exposed to a vehicle. Usually referred to as *average frequency*.

Frequency Discount—A discount given for running a certain number of insertions irrespective of size of advertisement within a contract year. Similar discounts are available in broadcasting, but may be of two types: frequency per week as well as total number of announcements in a contract year.

Frequency Distribution—An array of reach according to the level of frequency delivered to each group.

Fringe Time—Time periods preceding and following peak set-usage periods and adjacent network programming blocks. Usually represents for television, Class B or C time—4:30–7:30 P.M. or after 11 P.M. EST.

Full Position—Preferred position for a newspaper advertisement, generally following and next to reading matter, or top of column next to reading matter. When specifically ordered, it costs more than a run-of-paper (ROP) position.

Full-Program Sponsorship—A regular program sponsored by only one advertiser.

Full-Showing—In car card advertising, usually denotes one card in each car of a line in which space is bought. In New York subways, a full showing consists of two cards in each car; a half showing is two cards in every other car. In outdoor poster advertising, a full or 100-intensity showing indicates use of a specified number of panels in a particular market.

FY—Fiscal Year.

G   **Gatefold**—A special space unit in magazines, usually consisting of one full page plus an additional page or part of a page that is an extension of the outer edge of the original page and folds outward from the center of the book as a gate.

General Editorial Magazine—A consumer magazine not classified as to specific audience.

Geographic Split Run—A split run where one ad is placed in all of the circulation which falls within a specified geographic area and another ad is placed in other geographic areas or the balance of the country.

Grade A and B Contours—Areas in a television station's coverage pattern in which the transmission signals should have specific levels of strength according to FCC requirements. Grade A service is defined as providing a picture expected to be satisfactory to the median (average) observer at least 90 percent of the time in at least 70 percent of the receiving locations within the contour, in the absence of interfering co-channel and adjacent-channel signals. Grade B service is satisfactory at least 90 percent of the time in at least 50 percent of the receiving locations.

Grid Card—A rate card in which a broadcast station's spots are priced individually, with charges related to the audience delivered.

Gross Audience—The combined audience of a combination of media or a campaign in a single medium. For example, if Medium A and Medium B have audiences of 7 million and 6 million respectively, their gross audience is 13 million. To go from gross audience to net audience, one must subtract all duplicated audiences.

Gross Impressions—The sum of audiences of all vehicles used in a media plan. This number represents the message weight of a media plan. The number is sometimes called the "tonnage" of the plan, because it is so large. (See *Gross Audience*.)

Gross Rate—The published rate for space or time quoted by an advertising medium, including agency commission, cash discount, and any other discounts.

Gross Rating Points (GRP)—A measure of the total gross weight delivered by a vehicle (or vehicles). It is the sum of the ratings for the individual announcements or programs. A rating point means an audience of 1 percent of the coverage base. Hence 150 gross rating points means 1.5 messages per average home. Gross rating points are duplicated ratings. Also, reach times frequency equals GRPs.

Guaranteed Circulation — The circulation level of a print vehicle on which the advertising space rate is based. Similar to *rate base circulation* except that an advertiser is assured of an adjustment if the circulation level is not achieved.

Gutter—The inside margins of facing pages; the point at which a saddle stitched publication is bound.

H   **Half-Page Spread**—An advertisement composed of two half-pages facing each other in a publication.

Half Run—In transportation advertising, a car card placed in every other car of the transit system used. Also called a *half service*. Can also apply to publications that offer advertising in half of their circulation.

Half Showing—One half of a full showing of cards; a 50-intensity showing of outdoor posters or panels.

Hiatus—A period of time during which there is no advertising activity.

Hi-Fi Preprinted Insert—A full-page, four-color gravure advertisement printed by a supplier on coated newsprint and furnished to a newspaper in roll form for insertion in lieu of a page of standard newsprint. As the roll is fed into the newspaper, the newspaper prints normal editorial/advertising matter on the reverse side and, in some cases, a column of type next to the advertisement itself. The advertiser pays the supplier for producing the ad and the newspaper for distributing the ads (usually B&W space rates plus an insertion charge). Generally, the cost is twice as expensive as ROP color. Because there is no accurate cut-off on Hi-Fi pages, the copy and illustration has a repeating "wallpaper" design in order to insure full ad exposure.

High Definition TV (HDTV)—A television system that can provide a sharper picture than the current U.S. standard (or 525 lines per frame).

Hitchhike—An isolated commercial for a sponsor's secondary product (not advertised in the main body of the show) which is given a free ride following the end of the program.

Holding Power—The degree to which a program retains its audience throughout a broadcast. It is expressed in a percentage determined by dividing the average audience by the total audience.

Holdover Audience—The audience a program acquires from listeners or viewers who tuned to the preceding program on the station and remained with the station.

Home Box Office (HBO)—The first pay cable service. Began satellite distribution in December 1975 and ushered in a new era in cable television. Currently programs movies and specials reaches about 25 percent of U.S. households.

Home Service Magazine—A publication with editorial content keyed to the home and home living. Examples of this are *Better Homes & Gardens* and *House Beautiful*.

Horizontal Cume—The cumulative audience rating for two programs in the same time period on different days.

Horizontal Half-Page—A half-page advertisement running horizontally across the page. (See *Vertical Half-Page*.)

Horizontal Trade Publications—A business publication editorially designed to be of interest to a variety of businesses or business functions.

HUT (Households Using TV)—A term used by Nielsen and referring to the total number of TV households using their television sets during a given time period. Can be used for the total U.S. or a local market.

Hyping—Intense activity on the part of a broadcaster to increase rating during a rating survey.

I   **ID**—Any short-length "identification" commercial on radio or TV (i.e., a 10-second ID).

Impact—The extent and degree of consumer awareness of an advertisement within a specific medium, and the degree to which a medium and an ad within that medium affect the ad's audience.

Illuminated Panel—See *Panels*.

Impressions—See *Gross Impressions*.

Impression Studies—Starch provides studies of print ads and TV commercials called, respectively, "Starch Reader Impression Studies" and "Starch Viewer Impression Studies," which try to evaluate the kind of impressions made by the ad.

Imprint—Used in cooperative poster advertising programs. Sometimes the local dealer pays a portion of the cost of the poster space and the parent company pays the remaining portion. The dealer's name—the imprint—is placed on the bottom portion of the poster design (about 20 percent of the total copy area) so that his store is listed as the place to buy the product advertised.

Index—A percentage that relates numbers to a base. Used to show what is above average (101 or greater), average (100), or below average (99 or less).

Industrial Advertising—Advertising of capital goods, supplies, and services directed mainly to industrial or professional firms that require them in the course of manufacturing.

Informercial—A long commercial (2 to 7 or more minutes) that provides more information than thirty-second commercials.

Inherited Audience—The carry-over from one program to another on the same station of a portion of the preceding program's audience. (See *Holdover Audience*.)

In-Home—Refers to that portion of media exposure (reading, listening, or viewing) done in the home.

Insert—A special page printed on superior or different paper stock by the advertiser and forwarded to the publisher to be bound into the publication or to be inserted loose. Usually used for fine color work.

Insertion—An advertisement in a print medium.

Insertion Order—Authorization from an advertiser or agency to a publisher to print an advertisement of specified size on a given date or dates at a definite rate. Copy instructions and printing materials may accompany the order or be sent later.

Instantaneous Rating—The size of a broadcast audience at a given instant expressed as a percentage of some base.

Integrated Commercial—A commercial that features more than one product or service in the form of a single commercial message.

Integration (or Origination or Networking) Charge—An extra cost charged to an advertiser by a TV network for integrating a commercial into a program and for the distribution of the commercial from origination and other points, including the preparation of prints for delayed broadcast.

Intensity—In outdoor advertising, the strength of combinations of poster locations throughout a city in terms of coverage or repetition opportunities. A 100 showing has a 100 intensity. A 100 showing (therefore, a 100 intensity) varies from city to city.

Interconnect—Two or more cable systems joining together to create a larger subscriber base for advertising sales purposes.

Interactive Cable—A system where audience members respond to messages on a TV screen by pushing buttons that send responses back to the station.

Interim Statement—Sworn circulation statement of a publisher made quarterly to the A.B.C. at the publisher's option and issued unaudited but subject to audit. A situation that might call for an interim statement would occur when a community served by more than one newspaper loses one of them through consolidation or discontinuance and its circulation is absorbed by the other newspaper. (See *Publisher's Statement*.)

Island Position—A newspaper or magazine advertisement entirely surrounded by editorial matter or margin.

Isolated 30—A thirty-second commercial surrounded only by programming.

Issue Life—The time during which a publication accrues its total readership. For a weekly, this is generally five weeks; for a monthly, three months.

J **Junior Page**—In print, a page size that permits an advertiser to use the same printing materials for small and large page publications. The ad is prepared as a full-page unit in the smaller publication, appears in the larger publication as a junior page with editorial around it.

Junior Panel—A small-scale version of the thirty-sheet poster. Also called *eight-sheet poster*.

Junior Spread—An advertisement appearing on two facing pages that occupies only part of each page.

K   **Keying an Advertisement**—Identification within an advertisement or coupon that permits inquiries or requests to be traced to a specific advertisement.

Keyline—An assembly of all elements of a print ad pasted on a board. It is camera-ready art that is photographed in order to make the negative that in turn is used to make the printing plate. Also called *mechanical*.

L   **Lead-In**—Words spoken by announcer or narrator at the beginning of some shows to perform a scene-setting or recapitulation function. Also a broadcast program positioned before another program.

Lead-Out—In relation to audience flow, the program following an advertiser's program on the same station.

Limited Time Station—A station that usually shares its channel with another station in the same area.

Linage—A newspaper term denoting the number of (agate) lines in an ad or an ad schedule. Also, amount of total space run by a publication in certain categories, e.g., retail grocery linage.

List Broker—In direct mail advertising, an agent who rents prospect lists, compiled by one advertiser, and sold by the agent to another advertiser. He receives a commission for his services.

List House—In direct mail advertising, an agent who sells prospect lists compiled by the organization to an advertiser.

Listener Diary—Method of TV or radio research whereby audience keeps continuing record of viewing or listening in a diary.

Listening Area—The geographic area covered by a station's signal, usually divided into primary and secondary areas.

Little America (or Little U.S.A.) Concept—A test market media plan translation method that equalizes the media weight in the test area with the weighted average of the media weight that will be delivered by the national plan in all areas of the country.

Live Time—The time that the actual performance of a program is transmitted by interconnected facilities directly to the receiving stations at the moment of performance.

Live Time Delay—A delay that coincides with the local live time. Usually occurs when the station is noninterconnected and thus unable to take a live feed.

Leading National Advertiser-Broadcaster Advertiser Reports (LNA-BAR)—A monthly analysis for network television, national spot TV, local spot TV, TV syndication, cable TV, and network radio. It covers competitive spending in these media, plus other related data.

Lloyd Hall Editorial Analysis (now called Russell Hall)—A study of the number of editorial pages a magazine devotes to various categories of product interest over a period of time. For example, the number of pages a magazine devotes to articles on food, home furnishings, fiction, news. This information is frequently used in analyzing the editorial content of a magazine before advertising is placed in it.

Local Advertising—Advertising by local retailers (as opposed to national advertisers advertising in local markets), usually at a lower rate than that charged national advertisers.

Local Channel Station—A radio station that is allowed just enough power to be heard near its point of transmission and is assigned a channel on the air wave set aside for local channel stations (usually 250 watts).

Local Media—Media whose coverage and circulation are confined to or concentrated in their market of origin. Usually, they offer different sets of rates to the national advertiser and the local advertiser.

Local Rate—Rate charged by a medium to the local retail trade.

Local Time—Availabilities or times of broadcasting quoted in terms of local time rather than Eastern Standard Time.

Locally Edited Supplement—Sunday magazine supplement similar in character to syndicated magazine supplements but owned and edited by the newspaper distributing it. Such supplements are available in most of the larger cities throughout the country. Certain of them have banded together into groups for purposes of more efficient soliciting of national advertising and they offer group rates to advertisers who buy all the papers.

Low Power Television (LPTV)—A mini television station whose broadcast signal is limited to ten to twenty miles to better serve smaller communities.

Loyalty Index—Frequency of listenership to a particular station.

M **Magazine Supplement**—A magazine section of a Sunday or daily newspaper distributed either locally or nationally.

Mail-In Premium—A premium offered at the point of sale in a retail store to be obtained by the consumer by mailing a box top, coin, or label to the manufacturer.

Mail Order Advertising—Type of advertising in which the complete sales transaction is handled through advertising and by mail.

Mail Survey Map—A broadcast coverage map prepared by tabulating cumulative, unsolicited mail received during a certain period or by tabulating listener response to a special order or contest run during a certain period.

Makegood—An announcement or advertisement run as a replacement for one that was scheduled but did not run, or that ran incorrectly.

Market-by-Market Allocation (MBM)—The MBM system of media/marketing planning, which allocates a brand's total available advertising dollars against current and/or potential business on an individual TV market basis. MBM spends all advertising dollars (national and local) available in each market in proportion to current and/or anticipated business in the market. The result of MBM planning is to spend more accurately against anticipated sales and thereby generate greater business for a brand.

Market Development Index—See *Category Development Index, Market Index.*

Market Index—The factor chosen to measure relative sales opportunities in different geographic or territorial units. Any quantitative information that makes it possible to estimate this might be used as a market index. A General Market Index is a factor developed that influences the purchase of a specific product or groups of related products. Sometimes called *Market Development Index* or *Category Development Index.*

Market Outline—The measurement of the share of market based on total purchases of a particular brand or groups of similar brands with a product category during a specific time period.

Market Pattern—The pattern of a product's sales in terms of the relation between the volume and concentration either by total market or by individual market. A *thick market pattern* is one in which a high portion of all people are prospects for a product. A *thin market pattern* is one in which a low portion of all people are prospects for a product.

Market Potential—That portion of a market that a company can hope to capture for its own product.

Market Profile—A demographic description of the people or the households in a product's market. It may also include economic and retailing information about a territory.

Market Share—A product's share of an industry's sales volume.

"Marriage" Split—Occurs when more than one advertiser buys the total circulation of a magazine and each of the advertisers runs its ad in only a portion of that circulation. For example, an advertiser with distribution in the western U.S. and one with distribution in the eastern U.S. may split an ad in a magazine that permits this. In this case, the advertiser with distribution in the West would use only that part of the magazine's circulation which reaches the West and the other advertiser would use the remainder.

Masked Identification Test—A method of assessing an ad's effectiveness by finding the percentage of respondents who can identify the advertiser or brand when all identifying marks are concealed.

Mass Magazine—Magazine of a general nature that appeals to all types of people in all localities.

Maxiline—The maximum milline rate for a newspaper. (See *Miniline*.)

Maximil / Minimil—Milline rates for newspapers offering sliding scale discounts. The maximil is the milline computed on the maximum line rate. The minimil is computed on the lowest line rate available.

Mechanical—See *Keyline*.

Mechanical Requirements—The physical specifications of a publication that must be met by advertising material to be reproduced in the publication. Such requirements are brought about by the physical requirements of the vehicle and the characteristics of its printing process. Broadcast media have similar requirements governing the physical characteristics of material acceptable for broadcast.

Media Records—A detailed report of advertising volume by selected brands in selected daily and Sunday newspapers in selected cities.

Media Strategy Statement—Prepared by an agency, outlining the specific media that it believes best accomplish the brand's marketing objectives (as outlined in the market strategy statement) within the funds available.

Media Translation—The process of reducing a national advertising media plan to local level in order to test a product or campaign locally. It also can mean the expansion of a local advertising campaign to a national level.

Media Weight—The total impact of an advertising campaign in terms of number of commercials, insertions, reach and frequency, advertising dollars, etc.

Medium—Any media class used to convey an advertising message to the public, such as newspapers, magazines, direct mail, radio, television and billboards.

Metropolitan Statistical Area (MSA)—An area that consists of one or more entire counties meeting specified criteria pertaining to population, metropolitan character, and economic and social integration between outlying counties and the central county, determined by the Bureau of the Budget with the advice of the Federal Committee on Standard Metropolitan Areas composed of representatives of major federal government statistical agencies.

Message Weight—Refers to the gross number of advertising messages delivered by a vehicle or group of vehicles in a schedule.

Metro Area—A well-defined county or group of counties comprising the central core of a geographical market (usually based on governmental lines).

Microwave—A way of interconnecting cable systems with a series of high-frequency receiving antenna transmitters mounted on towers spaced up to fifty miles apart.

Middle Break—Station identification at about the halfway point of a show.

Milline Rate—A means of comparing rates of newspapers. It is the cost of one agate line per million circulation. The milline rate is computed by multiplying the line rate by 1 million and then dividing by the circulation. The factor of 1 million is used merely to provide an answer in convenient terms of dollars and cents rather than in fractions of a cent.

Miniline—The milline rate for a newspaper at its minimum rate. (See *Maxiline.*)

Minimil Rate—This represents the minimum cost of one line of advertising per million circulation at the lowest rate available after deducting all space or frequency discounts. (See *Maximil/Minimil.*)

Minimum Depth—Most newspapers have minimum depth requirements for advertising. In general, an ad must be at least one inch high for every column it is wide. For example, if an advertiser wants an ad to run that is eight columns wide, it must be at least eight inches high.

Minute-by-Minute Profile—Nielsen minute-by-minute program audience data. Used to study audience gains and losses during specific minutes of the program and to aid in placing commercials at times in which they receive maximum audiences.

Monitor—To check timing, program, and commercial content of individual broadcasts of radio and/or television shows.

Morning Drive—Radio daypart from 6:00 A.M. to 10:00 A.M.

MRI—Mediamark Research, Inc. A company that measures magazine audiences using the recent-reading technique.

Multichannel Multipoint Distribution System (MMDS)—A wireless (over-the-air) cable network providing entertainment, information, and sports for a fee.

Multi-Network Area Rating—This rating, which is tabulated by Nielsen, measures a program's performance in seventy cities with three or more TV stations.

Multipoint Distribution Systems (MDS)—A pay television system that transmits programming via microwave for short distances to subscribers who pick them up with special equipment.

Multistation Lineup—Buying more than one station in a market.

N   **NAB Code**—The National Association of Broadcasters promulgates radio and television codes to assist its members to meet their mandatory obligation to serve the American public. Such codes deal with both program and advertising standards. Included in the advertising standards are sections dealing with presentation techniques, contests, premiums and offers, and time standards. These codes are extended by other documents dealing with interpretations and guidelines, e.g., Children's Television Advertising Guidelines and Alcoholic Beverage Advertising Guidelines. Disbanded in 1982.

Narrowcasting—Describes a cable system's service to a small community. It is the delivery of programming that addresses a specific need or audience.

National Advertising Rates—Rates for newspaper space charged to a national advertiser as distinguished from local rates applying to local retailers. National advertising rates are generally higher than local rates.

National Media—Media that are national in scope.

National Plan—A media plan that is national in scope, as opposed to a local plan covering less than the entire U.S.

National Rating—A rating of all households or individuals tuned in to a program on a national base. Sometimes the base is all television or radio households in the country. Other times, the base is only those households that can tune in to the program because they are in the signal area of a station carrying the program.

Net Controlled Circulation—The number of purchased and unpurchased copies of a controlled-circulation publication that are actually distributed to its intended readership.

Net Paid Circulation—A term used by A.B.C. audit reports and publishers' statements referring to circulation that has been paid for at not less than 50 percent of the basic newsstand or subscription price.

Net Plus—The net cost of a print ad, commercial, or program with an earned discount added on.

Net Unduplicated Audience—The combined cumulative audience for a single issue of a group of magazines or broadcasts.

Net Weekly Audience—In broadcast research, the number of families tuned in at least once to a program aired more than once a week.

Network—Two or more stations contractually united to broadcast programs, e.g., network programs.

Network Affiliate—A broadcast station that is part of a network and therefore offers network programs.

Network Franchise—A brand's right to retain the sponsorship of a program at the sponsoring brand's discretion. This right is acquired by agreeing to sponsor a program on a continuing basis.

Network Identification—Acknowledgment of a network affiliation at the end of a network broadcast.

Network Option Time—Time on network affiliates for which the network has selling priority. Also called *network time*.

Newspaper Distributed Magazine—A supplement inserted into a Sunday newspaper.

Newspaper Syndicate—A business concern that sells special material (columns, photographs, comic strips) for simultaneous publication in a number of newspapers.

Newsstand Circulation—Copies of publications which are purchased at outlets selling copies. May include hotels, vending machines, newsboys, drug stores, and supermarkets in addition to the traditional newsstand or kiosk.

Nielsen—The A. C. Nielsen Company is the world's largest research company, with worldwide operations. It operates a wide variety of syndicated services: NTI—a national television rating service using people meters to collect set-tuning data; Food & Drug Index—a service collecting information on retail sales movement by means of store audits; NMS—a service collecting audience data by personal interview and diaries for television programs, publications (magazines and newspapers); NSI—a local television rating service. Nielsen is a division of Dun & Bradstreet.

Nielsen Clearing House (NCH)—A company that handles the administrative work associated with processing coupons.

Nielsen Coverage Service (NCS)—This provides broadcast station coverage and circulation information rather than program audience measurements. The data are reported for each station in terms of total daytime and total evening audiences over the span of the day, week, and month, on a county-by-county basis.

Nielsen Market Section Rating—A Nielsen report on television ratings by zone breakdowns. The rating breakdowns are: Territory; County-size Groups; Age of Housewife; Age of Household Head; Size of Family; Time Zone.

Nielsen Rating—TV program rating that uses set-tuning data from Audimeters. The Nielsen rating is used to refer to households who have viewed a program five or more minutes. This audience definition is to the *average audience*, which is the audience of the average minute of a program.

Ninety-Day Cancellation—All poster advertising is cancellable on ninety days' notice to the plant. This means that the advertiser or his agency must notify the poster plant owner of cancellation ninety days prior to the contract posting date.

Noted—The basic measure of the Starch method for testing print ads. The Noted Score represents the percentage of respondents (claimed readers of the issue) who say they saw the ad when they first read or looked into the magazine issue, i.e., claimed recognition of the ad.

O   **O & O Station**—A station owned and operated by a network. The FCC allows networks to own five VHF stations and two UHF stations.

Obtained Score—This is a Gallup-Robinson term for the actual percentage of respondents who prove recall of a print ad before the score is adjusted for color and size or converted to an index score. It is the basis for the final score.

Off Card—The use of a special rate not covered by a rate card.

Offensive Spending—Advertising activity intended to secure new business.

One-Time Rate—The highest rate charged by a medium not subject to discounts. Sometimes called *open* or *transient rate*.

Open End—A broadcast that leaves the commercial spots blank to be filled in locally.

Open End Transcription—A recorded program usually sold on a syndicated basis in various cities and produced so that local commercial announcements may be inserted at various points throughout the show.

Open Rate—In print, the highest rate charged to an advertiser on which all discounts are placed. Also called *base rate*, or *one-time rate*.

Option Time—Network option time is that time reserved by the networks in contract with their affiliates and for which the network has prior call under certain conditions for sponsored network programs. Station option time is that time reserved by the local stations for local and national spot shows.

Orbit—A scheduling method used by stations that consists of rotating an advertiser's commercial among different programs and/or time periods.

O.T.O.—One-time-only, a spot that runs only once; bought outright or as a makegood.

Outdoor Advertising—Display advertising (billboards, posters, signs, etc.) placed out-of-doors, along highways and railroads, or on walls and roofs of buildings.

Outdoor Advertising Plant—A company that builds, maintains, and sells space on outdoor displays consisting of painted bulletins and/or poster panels.

Out-of-Home Audience—Listeners to auto and battery-operated radios outside their homes. Also the audience of a publication derived from exposure that occurred outside the reader's own home. (See *In-Home Audience*.)

Overlapping Circulation—Duplication of circulation when advertising is placed in two or more media reaching the same prospects. Sometimes desirable to give additional impact to advertising.

Overnights—Nielsen household ratings and shares provided to NSI Metered Market clients the morning following the day or evening of telecast.

P   P4C—Abbreviation for Page/Four-Color. Other abbreviations are P2C (Page/Two-Color), PB&W (Page/Black and White), 3/5P4C (3/5 Page/Four-Color), 2C (Second Cover), BC (Back Cover), etc.

Package—A combination of programs or commercials offered by a network for sponsorship as an entity at one price. Spot TV is sometimes sold as a package. Also, a program property in which all elements from script to finished production are owned and controlled by an individual or organization, commonly known as a *packager*.

Packaged Goods—Mostly food, soap, and household products that are marketed in the manufacturer's package, wrapper, or container.

Package Enclosure—A premium enclosed in a package.

Package Insert—Separate advertising material included in packaged goods.

Package Plan—A plan by which an advertiser purchases a certain number of TV or radio announcements per week, in return for which he receives a lower rate per announcement from the station. The advertiser agrees to run the specific number of announcements each week and cannot split them up over a period of time.

Package Plan Discount—In spot television, a discount based upon frequency within a week, e.g., "5-plan," "10-plan."

Packager—An individual or company producing a broadcast program or series of programs that are sold as complete units.

Painted Bulletin—This structure is approximately 48' long by 14' high with the copy message painted on the face of this structure as contrasted to the poster panel.

Painted Display—In outdoor, a display painted on a bulletin structure or wall, which may be illuminated, and sold as an individual unit. The standard size is 48' × 14'.

Painted Wall—An outdoor advertising unit, purchased individually, usually situated on a high-traffic artery or in a neighborhood shopping area.

Panel—A fixed sample of respondents or stores selected to participate in a research project who report periodically on their knowledge, attitudes, and activities. This is in contrast to the technique of using fresh samples each time. (See *Store Panel*.) Also a master TV or radio control board, usually in a master control room.

Panels—Regular and illuminated units of outdoor advertising. A *regular panel* is a billboard that is not lighted at night. An *illuminated panel* is a billboard that is lighted from dusk until midnight.

Panographics—An outdoor bulletin that is lit from behind the display.

Pantry Audit—A consumer survey to tabulate brands, items, and varieties of grocery store products in the home.

Parallel Location—An outdoor advertising location in which the poster panel is parallel to the road.

Participation—A station or network may program a segment of time to carry *participation announcements* sold to various advertisers for commercial use. The announcements are usually :10, :30, or :60, but may be longer. Participations are announcements inside the context of programs as opposed to sponsorship or to chain or station breaks which are placed between programs.

Participation Program—A commercial program co-sponsored by a number of advertisers. Or, a program in which the audience participates, e.g., a quiz show.

Pass-Along Reader—A person who reads a publication that he or a member of his family did not purchase. These readers must be taken into account in determining the total numbers of readers of a particular issue or a particular publication. (See *Audience, Secondary*.)

Pay Cable—Any of a number of program services for which cable subscribers pay a monthly charge in addition to the basic cable subscription fee.

Pay-per-View Television—Pay TV for which subscribers pay on a program basis rather than on a monthly subscription basis.

Pay TV—A television system providing programs available only to subscribing homes. Signals are generally transmitted via coaxial cables or telephone lines, and the subscriber is usually charged on a sliding scale for the number of channels the subscriber can receive.

Penalty Costs—In test market and expansion operation, this refers to the premium paid for local replacement media compared with the national media that the brand would be using under their national plan.

Penetration—The percentage of total homes in a specified area owning at least one TV set.

Penetration Study—The study of the effectiveness of advertising on the public.

People Meter—An electronic device that measures viewership of a given program. Present meters require TV audiences to push buttons when they are viewing. Passive meters may not require button pushing.

Percent Composition—The percentage of a medium's total audience that is part of a specific demographic group. Example: If there are 10 million women who read Magazine A, and 5 million are 18–34 years old, then 50 percent of the total audience is composed of women 18–34.

Percent Coverage—In print media: the total audience of a publication as a percent of the total population. Or, the circulation of a publication as a percent of total homes. In broadcast media: the number of homes that are able to receive a signal of specific strength, but which do not necessarily tune to the station(s). Or, all homes in counties which meet a minimum circulation criterion (e.g., 50 percent).

Per Inquiry Advertising (P.I. Advertising)—An agreement between a media owner and an advertiser in which the owner agrees to accept payment for advertising on the basis of the number of inquiries or completed sales resulting from advertising, soliciting inquiries, or direct sales.

Persons Using Radio (PUR)—The percentage of an area's population (over age 12) listening to a radio at any given time.

Piggyback—The back-to-back scheduling of two or more brand commercials of one advertiser in network or spot positions.

Pilot (Pilot Film)—A sample of a proposed TV series used for demonstration.

Plan Rate—The rate paid by an advertiser who purchased a TV or radio package plan. The rates are lower than if the spots were purchased individually since the advertiser agreed to run a specific number of spots each week.

Plant Operator—The company that owns and maintains poster panels in any given market. The plant operator rents space on its poster panels to advertisers in thirty-day units. It leases or owns the land on which the poster panel is erected.

Pod—A commercial position within a network television program whose length varies according to daypart and program. A pod is usually comprised of more than one commerical.

Position—An advertisement's place on a page and the location of the page in the publication. A preferred position is an especially desirable position obtained by paying an extra charge, or granted to an advertiser who has placed a heavy schedule in a publication, occasionally rotated among advertisers who have contracted for space above a specified minimum. In broadcast, programs or time spots considered most desirable by advertisers.

Posttest—Study of the response to finished advertising after it has been published and telecast in media. Posttests rely on normal patterns of behavior to expose respondents to advertising.

Poster—A product sign intended to be displayed on a store window, or on an inside wall, large enough to be legible at a reasonable distance.

Poster Frame—In point-of-purchase advertising, a frame holding a blowup of an advertisement or poster. Layers of advertisements may be mounted on one frame, and the top one torn off to reveal a new one.

Poster Panel—A standard surface on which outdoor advertisements are mounted. The poster panel is the most widely used form of outdoor advertising. The standard panel measures 12' × 25' long, is usually made of steel with a wood, fiberglass, or metal molding around the outer edges. The twenty-four-sheet poster is actually posted on this structure.

Poster Plant—The company that builds and services poster panels and hangs poster sheets on them displaying illustration and/or message of advertiser.

Poster, Regular—A nonilluminated poster.

Poster Showing—Poster advertising is sold in packages called *showings*. A 100 showing (synonymous with *Gross Rating Points*) produces an advertiser circulation in one day that is equivalent to the total population in the market.

Potential Audience—See *Audience, Potential*.

Preemption—Recapture by the station network of an advertiser's time in order to substitute a special program of universal value. For example, when the President speaks, the show regularly scheduled at that time is preempted.

Preemptible Spot—A spot announcement sold at a reduced rate because the station has the option to sell that same spot to another advertiser willing to pay full rate.

Preferred Position—A position in a magazine or newspaper which is regarded as excellent in terms of its ability to generate a large readership. Preferred position is usually located next to editorial material that has a high interest among the publication's readers.

Preprint—A reproduction of an advertisement before it appears in a publication.

Pretest—Study of advertisements or commercials prior to distribution via regular media channels. Advertising may be studied in rough or finished form; pretesting relies on some special means of exposing respondents to the advertisement other than the regular media planned—portfolios, dummy magazines, etc.

Primary Audience—See *Audience, Primary*.

Primary Households—Households into which a publication has been introduced by purchase, either at the newsstand or by subscription, rather than by pass-along.

Primary Readers—The readers of a publication who reside in primary households.

Primary Service Area—In AM or standard broadcasting, the area in which a station signal is strongest and steadiest. Defined by Federal Communications Commission rules as the area in which the ground wave (the primary wave for broadcast transmission) is not subject to objectionable interference or objectionable fading. No similar term is officially used in TV broadcasting, although television engineering standards recognize three zones of signal service existing in concentric rings from the transmitting tower: City Grade Service, A Contour, B Contour.

Prime Time—The period of peak television set usage—between 7:30 P.M. and 11 P.M. in Eastern and Pacific Time zones and 6:30 P.M. to 10 P.M. in the Central and Mountain Time Zone.

Prime Time Access Rule (PTAR)—The Federal Communications Commission has mandated television stations to put on a required amount of their own programming during prime time. Under PTAR III, regular network programming starts at 8 P.M. NYT Monday through Saturday and 7 P.M. on Sunday.

Product Protection—Protection that an advertiser wants and sometimes gets against adjacency in a medium to advertising of a competitive product. Has special interest in television advertising.

Program Basis—A Nielsen cost estimate of a television show that takes into consideration the length-of-commitment discount as determined by whether the program is normally telecast every week, less-than-weekly, more-than-weekly, or one-time-only. This discount is determined by the number of telecasts of the show and not the number used by a specific advertiser. Also, this basis disregards other programs sponsored by an advertiser that affect its discount structure.

Program Coverage—The number (or percentage) of television households that can receive a program over one or more stations, because they are in the signal area of some station carrying the program.

Program Delivery (Rating)—Percentage of sample contacted who tuned to a particular program at a particular time.

Program Lineup—A listing of stations carrying a program either on a live or delayed basis. Stations are as supplied by the network or as received directly from their affiliates.

Program Station Rating—A rating based on the television homes located in the area in which a program was telecast that permits an unbiased comparison of different programs regardless of variation in the number of homes capable of receiving the programs.

Promotion Allowance—Money received by a wholesaler or a retailer from a manufacturer or his representative for sales promotion other than advertising. (See *Advertising Allowance*.)

Psychographic—A term that describes consumers or audience members on the basis of some psychological trait, characteristic of behavior, or life-style.

Public Access—FCC rule that requires any cable system with 3,500 or more subscribers to have at least one noncommercial channel available to the public on a first come non-discriminatory basis.

Public Broadcasting Service (PBS)—Distributor and representative organization of public TV. Similar to network but does not produce programs or have control over station schedules.

Publisher's Information Bureau, Inc. (PIB)—PIB Service is a monthly analysis of both advertising space and revenue in general magazines, national farm magazines, and newspaper sections. It is designed to give convenient summaries of national advertising expenditures by advertisers and by media.

Publisher's Statement—A notarized statement made by the publisher regarding total circulation, geographic distribution, methods of securing subscriptions, etc. These are often issued between audited statements, especially when market conditions have changed.

Pulsing—A media scheduling technique which produces alternating periods of heavy activity followed by lower activity periods.

Pure Program Ratings—A measurement of audience size in which estimates are made excluding program preemptions that have occurred during the survey period.

Q   **Qualified Issue Reader**—A respondent who qualifies to be interviewed about advertisements in a magazine on the basis of having read the study issue of a magazine. Requirements for such qualification vary: for Starch interviews, readers have merely to claim they looked into the issue when shown the cover; for Gallup & Robinson studies, respondents must prove reading by correctly describing some article when shown the cover and Table of Contents.

Qualified Viewer—Respondent who has demonstrated viewing of a TV program (on the basis of recall of at least one part of the episode), thus becoming eligible or qualified for interview about commercials aired on that show.

Quantity Discount—A graduated discount on quantity purchases scaled to the number of cases in a single order; or, a periodic refund based upon the value of purchases over a period of time.

Quintile—The division of any sample of respondents into five equal-sized groups ranging from the heaviest to the lightest amount of exposure to the medium. Samples may also be divided into tertiles, quartiles, deciles, etc.

Quota—A predetermined media goal in a market. Goals can be established in dollars spent, number of spots to be purchased, or GRPs to be achieved. Used as a target for the agency time buyer in implementing a media plan.

R   **Radio Rating Point**—One percent of the homes in the measured area whose sets are tuned to a station, used for making comparisons of spot stations.

Rate Base—The circulation level of a print vehicle used in setting rates for advertising space charge.

Rate Card—A listing put out by a medium containing advertising costs, mechanical requirements, issue dates, closing dates, cancellation dates, and circulation data. Rate cards are issued by both print and broadcast media.

Rate Class—In broadcast media, the time charge in effect at a specified time.

Rate Differential—Among newspapers, the difference between the national and the local rates.

Rate Holder—A minimum sized advertisement placed in a publication during a contract period to hold a time or quantity discount rate. Also, an ID spot bought by the advertiser for the same reason.

Rate Protection—A guarantee that an advertiser's current rate under the old rate card will be protected for a period, usually from three to six months, should a new rate be introduced.

Reach—The number of different persons or homes exposed to a specific media vehicle or schedule at least once. Usually measured over a specific period of time, e.g., four weeks. Also know as *cume, cumulative, unduplicated,* or *net audience.*

Reach, Cumulative—The total number of homes reached by a medium during a specific time period.

Reader Impression Studies—Studies carried out by Starch over and above their regular Readership Study to find out something of what the advertisement meant to respondents who "noted" the ad.

Reader Interest—Expression of interest by readers in advertisements they have read. Sometimes evaluated by unsolicited mail. Sometimes evaluated by the numbers of people who can remember having read material with interest. Also, an evaluation of the relative level of general interest in different types of products.

Reader Traffic—The movement from page to page by readers of a publication.

Readers—People who are exposed to a print vehicle.

Readers per Copy—The average number of readers of a magazine per copy of circulation. When multiplied by a magazine's circulation, the result equals its audience.

Readership—The degree to which print vehicles have been seen (not necessarily read) by members of the publication's audience.

Readership or Audience—The total average number of persons who are exposed to a publication as distinguished from the circulation or number of copies distributed.

Read Most—Starch ad readership measurement term referring to magazine or newspaper readers who read 50 percent or more of the copy of a specific advertisement.

Rebate—A refund that reduces the contract price for merchandise. A term frequently used for advertising allowances. Also given to advertisers by a certain media vehicle as a result of an advertiser's exceeding the contract minimum and earning a greater discount.

Recent Reading—A measurement technique for magazines in which survey respondents check a list of magazines they have read recently.

Recognition—The technique used to determine whether a person saw or heard a given print advertisement or broadcast commercial by actually showing the ad or commercial (or playing it) and inquiring whether he or she saw or heard it at a previous date in a specific medium. This technique was pioneered and is still being used by Starch.

Recordimeter—An electromechanical device utilized by the A. C. Nielsen Company in conjunction with the *Audilog.* It measures the amount of time that a radio or TV set is turned on during the day, but cannot distinguish among stations as does the *Audimeter.*

Regional Edition—A geographical section of a national magazine's circulation that can be purchased by an advertiser without having to purchase the rest of the magazine's circulation (as is required in a split run). A higher premium is usually paid for regional editions and demographic editions.

Regional Network—A network of stations serving a limited geographic area.

Regular Panel—See *Panels*.

Remnant Space—Magazine space sold at reduced price to help fill out regional editions.

Remote—A broadcast originating outside the regular studio. Also called *remote pickup*.

Remote Control—Broadcasting a program from a point removed from the regular studios of the station.

Renewals—In print: refers to magazine or newspaper subscriptions which people extend past their expiration dates. In outdoor advertising: extra posters over and above the quantity actually needed to post the exact number of panels in a showing. They are shipped to the plant operator and, if one of the posters on display is damaged, the plant operator has a complete poster design on hand to replace immediately the damaged poster.

Representative (or Rep)—A general term used to describe sales representatives for media vehicles. A representative firm usually handles several vehicles, serving as their sales agent and taking commissions on the sales they make; salespersons may also be directly employed by stations or publications.

Replacement Media—Local media that are being used to replace national media in a test market or expansion area, e.g, local rotogravure supplements, comic sections, black-and-white daily newspapers.

Response Function—An effect of an ad in a medium, sometimes called *impact*. These effects may be attitude change, degrees of brand awareness, or sales.

Retail Trading Zone—The area beyond the city zone whose residents regularly trade to an important degree with retail merchants in the city zone. These are defined by the Audit Bureau of Circulation.

Returns per Thousand Circulation—A gauge of the effectiveness of media used in support of promotions computed by dividing the total number of returns by the circulation of the publication to which the returns are attributable. (See *Keying an Advertisement*.)

Roll-Out—A marketing strategy technique in which a brand is introduced in a limited geographical area. If it succeeds in that area, it is then introduced in adjacent areas and, if successful, in other adjacent areas until the entire country is covered.

Roster Recall—Method of research in which a list of radio or TV programs is submitted to respondents for recall.

Rotating Painted Bulletins—Moving the advertiser's copy from one painted bulletin to another, usually every sixty days. This service is available in most major cities. Offers advertiser an opportunity to cover a large area or a given market (over a long period of time) with a limited number of painted bulletins.

Rotation—The practice in store management of moving the older stock forward when restocking shelves or cases. The practice, in retail advertising, of scheduling a branded product or group of products to be featured at intervals throughout the year to maintain a desired stock balance. Also, the process of continuing a series of advertisements over and over again in a regular order.

Rotogravure (Roto or Gravure)—Printing process where an impression is produced by sunken or deep etched letters or pictures in a copper printing plate. The ink is held in indentation in the plates, not on the surface as in offset, or on the tops of dots or letters as in letterpress.

Run of Press (ROP)—A newspaper advertisement for which a definite position is not specified is inserted as run of press (or run of book), but usually in the general news sections. The term is also used in connection with color newspaper advertising to distinguish color advertising in the main portion of the paper from that placed in the magazine section (*Sunday supplement*).

Run of Schedule (ROS)—A broadcast commercial for which a definite time is not specified. For example, a nighttime commercial during prime time may be run at any time during this period. Also, the time at which an announcement runs may vary from week to week, depending upon other requirements.

Runs—In television film syndication, the number of times a film has been telecast in a given area. The number of times a film may be run according to an advertiser's lease. A rerun among television film syndicators is an available program previously telecast in an area.

Russell Hall—See *Lloyd Hall*.

S **Sales Promotion**—Those sales activities that supplement both personal selling and advertising, coordinate the two, and help to make them effective, for example, sales incentives.

Satellite-Fed Master Antenna Television (SMATV)—A small cable system for apartment buildings which provides video for many viewers within the buildings.

Satellite Station—A station that rebroadcasts the signal of the parent television station to an area that would not otherwise be covered. Also it may originate some local programming of its own.

Saturation—A level of advertising weight several times above normal coverage and frequency levels standard for the market or product involved. Saturation implies simultaneous achievement of wide coverage and high frequency designed to achieve maximum impact, coverage, or both.

Saturation Showing—In outdoor, a showing of maximum intensity, designed to surpass complete coverage (the 100 showing) with repeat impressions. Often a 200 showing.

Scatter Plan—The placing of announcements in a number of different network TV programs.

Schedule—A list of media to be used during an advertising campaign. A list of a product's advertising to be included in a media vehicle during a specific time. The chronological list of programs broadcast by a station. Also called a *flowchart*.

Secondary Audience—See *Audience, Secondary*.

Secondary Service Area—The distant area in which a broadcast station's signal is subject to interference or fading, but can still be received.

Sectional Magazine—A magazine that is distributed only sectionally and not nationally (such as *Sunset*, which is confined to the western states). Also called a *regional magazine*.

Selective Magazine—A magazine which, because of its nature and editorial content, appeals only to a certain type of audience.

Self-Liquidating Point-of-Purchase Unit—One for which the retailer wholly or partially pays.

Self-Liquidating Premium—A premium whose total cost is recoverable in the basic sales transaction.

Self-Mailer—A folder, booklet, or other direct mail piece that provides space for addressing, postage, and sealing, and therefore requires no separate envelope for mailing.

Semi-Liquidator—Premium offered to the consumer whose cost is partially recovered by the manufacturer or merchant offering the inducement.

Sets in Use—The total number of sets tuned in to some program at a given time of day and day of week. At one time sets in use was equivalent to HUT, but today, its meaning is limited to sets, not households. (See *HUT*)

Share or **Share of Audience**—The audience for a program as a percentage of all households using the medium at the time of the program's broadcast.

Share of Market—The percentage of the total sales of a specified class of products that is held by or attributed to a particular brand at a given time.

Share of Mind—The percentage of relevant population (or a sample of that population) who indicate awareness of, or preference for, the various brands within a product group. Specific meaning varies considerably with the method of measurement. It may be a test of salience or a test of total recall, aided or unaided. Usually refers to consumer awareness of brands in comparison with like measures of awareness for competing brands.

Share of Voice—A brand's share of the total advertising for a product or commodity classification.

Shelter Magazines—Magazines dealing editorially with the home such as decorating, maintenance, gardening, etc. Additionally, these magazines carry a considerable amount of food editorial matter. An example is *Better Homes & Gardens*.

Shopper—A newspaper published in a local community and containing mainly local news, shopping hints and suggestions, and advertisements. Sometimes called a *shopping newspaper*.

Short Rate—The additional charge incurred when an advertiser fails to use enough media time or space to earn the contract discount envisaged at the time of the original order.

Showing—In outdoor advertising, the number of posters offered as a unit in terms of 100 intensity and variations thereof. In transit advertising, the number of cards included in a unit of sale. (See *Poster Showing*.)

Significantly Viewed—According to the FCC definition, a station is "significantly viewed" in a given county if (a) it is a network affiliate and achieves among noncable households a share of total viewing hours of at least 3 percent, and a net weekly circulation of at least 25 percent; or (b) it is an independent station and achieves among noncable households a share of total viewing hours of at least 2 percent and a net weekly circulation of at least 5 percent. A station which is significantly viewed becomes "local" for regulatory purposes, that is, it can demand carriage on cable systems, and the systems are no longer required to delete the duplicate programming of a significantly viewed station at the request of a higher priority (local) station.

Simmons Data—Print and broadcast media audience exposure and product-usage data reported by the Simmons Market Research Bureau.

Simmons Market Research Bureau (SMRB)—A media and marketing research firm providing syndicated data on audience size, composition, turnover, and duplication of approximately 100 publications using the "through the book" technique to determine readership for selected types. Also provides broad measures of broadcast exposure and data on ownership and usage of consumer products.

Sliding Rate—A space or time rate in a medium that decreases as the amount of space or time used by an advertiser increases over a period of time.

Space Position Value—In outdoor, an estimate of the effectiveness of a particular poster location. The factors considered are the length of approach, the speed of travel, the angle of the panel to its circulation, and the relation of the panel to adjacent panels.

Space Schedule—A schedule sent to the advertiser by the agency, showing the media to be used, the dates on which advertising is to appear, size of advertisements, and cost of space.

Special—A one-time TV show generally employing known talent and usually running an hour or longer. Also called *spectacular*.

Spectacular—(a) Can be a large and elaborate outdoor advertising display with vivid color, special lighting effects, animation, or the like. (b) A television, motion picture, or stage show elaborately cast and produced.

Spill-In (or Spill-Out)—The degree to which programming is viewed in adjacent ADI (or DMA) areas. Depending on the perspective, this is either spill-in or spill-out. Milwaukee television programming spills out of the Milwaukee DMA and spills into the Madison, Wisconsin, area, and vice versa.

Split Run—The running of two or more versions of an ad in alternate copies of the same magazine or newspaper. There are also split runs in which one version of the ad appears in newsstand copies and one in mail subscription copies. Splits may also occur geographically.

Split Run Test—Research designed to test the effectiveness of various copy elements, prices, or types of offers by placing them in alternate copies of an issue. The various forms of the advertisement are evaluated by means of coupon or inquiry returns, or by orders placed for trial offers.

Sponsor Identification (SI)—The extent to which a program's sponsor is identified or its product or service remembered. The percentage of listeners or viewers who correctly associate a program with the sponsor or his product is the Sponsor Identification Index (SII).

Sponsor Rating—A rating determined by applying the Sponsor Identification Index to the total audience rating.

Sponsor Relief—Occurs when an advertiser on a regular television program wishes to suspend activities for an off-season period, and requests contractual relief from the TV networks.

Sponsorship—The purchase of more than one announcement in a program (usually a majority of commercials) by one advertiser.

Spot—A time period filled entirely by a commercial or public service message and sold separately from the adjacent time periods. Such announcements may be placed between network programs or within local programs. Also, to buy time (programs and/or announcements) on a market-by-market basis from stations through their representatives.

Spot Announcement—Commercial placed upon individual stations, radio and TV. Often referred to as *spots*. Technically, spots should be referred to as *announcements*.

Spot Programming—The process by which an advertiser secures the rights to a television program and places it on stations in selected markets without regard to network affiliation. The advertiser may own the television program outright, have rights to the program for a specific length of time, or have the rights to the program in only a certain part of the country.

Spot Radio—The use of stations in selected markets without regard to network affiliation. May involve spot announcements or complete programs.

Spot Schedule—A local spot announcement buy or a standard form that agencies submit showing specific times, adjacencies, etc., of a brand's current spot announcements in a market.

Spot Television—The use of stations in selected markets without regard to network affiliation. May involve spot announcements or complete local programs.

Spread—An advertisement appearing on any two facing pages of a publication.

Staggered Schedule—Several advertisements scheduled in two or more publications, arranged so that the dates of insertion are alternated or rotated.

Standard Activity Unit (SAU)—The fifty-six advertising units in broadsheet, and thirty-three units in tabloid newspapers that are fixed sizes in depth and width and are measured in standard column inches.

Standard Industrial Classification (SIC)—A classification system set up by the U.S. Bureau of the Budget to define business establishments by type of activity. Used to facilitate the analysis of business paper markets.

Standard Rate & Data Service, Inc. (SRDS)—A service that publishes the rates and discount structures of all major media. It also publishes market research studies, often on media or market areas.

Standby Space—An order accepted by some magazines to run an advertisement whenever and wherever they wish, at an extra discount. Advertiser forwards plate with order. Helps magazine fill odd pages or spaces.

Starch Method—A term that refers to the recognition method used by Daniel Starch & Associates in their studies of advertising readership.

Station Break—A time period between two programs when a station announces the call letters, channel number, and also broadcasts commercials.

Station Log—The official, chronological listing of a radio or television station's programming and commercial announcements throughout the day.

Station Rep—A sales organization or person representing individual stations to national advertisers. Short for station representative.

Store Check—An in-the-field personal review of merchandise movement conducted in retail outlets by nonstore personnel.

Store Distributed Magazine—Any one of several magazines (e.g., *Family Circle*, *Woman's Day*) whose primary channel of distribution is retail grocery stores.

Store Panel—A selected sample of stores used repeatedly for market research to collect data on retail sales movement, e.g., A.C. Nielsen Company's food store panel. (See *Panel*.)

Strip Programming—(a) Running of a television or radio series at the same hour on each weekday. (b) Similar but different programs telecast at the same time throughout the week. (c) The same program, but different episodes, broadcast several times weekly at the same time.

Subscription TV (STV)—A pay television system by which programming is transmitted over the air and must be picked up by a special unscrambling decoder apparatus.

Sunday Newspaper Supplement—Any printed matter that is inserted in a Sunday edition of a newspaper on a continuing basis and is not part of the newspaper itself. Two main publications fitting into this category are magazine supplements and comic sections. A supplement may be either syndicated nationally or edited locally.

Superstation—A term originally coined for and copyrighted by WTCG (later WTBS) Channel 17, Atlanta. Now generically, a station whose signal is available to cable systems across the country via satellite transmission. Other superstations currently "on the bird" are WWOR-TV, New York, and WGN-TV, Chicago.

Sweeps—Both Arbitron and Nielsen survey all television local markets four times yearly (November, February, May, and July). These are called *sweep months.*

Syndicated Program—A method of placing a TV or radio program on a market-by-market basis as opposed to the line interconnected network system of program transmission.

Syndicated Sunday Magazine Supplement—A magazine supplement that is distributed through a group of newspapers and is owned by a single publisher. The distributing newspapers pay the publisher for the privilege of distributing the supplement which in turn helps to build circulation for the distributing newspapers. There are only two nationally syndicated supplements: *Parade* and *U.S.A. Weekend.*

T **Tabloid**—A smaller than standard-sized newspaper, with five columns and about 1000 lines per page.

Tag Line—A final line of dramatic scene or act that is treated to give point or impact to the preceding dialogue.

Target Audience—The desired or intended audience for advertising as described or determined by the advertiser. Usually defined in terms of specific demographic (age, sex, income, etc.), purchase, or ownership characteristics.

Targetcasting—Another term for narrowcasting, where cable programing is created to meet special demographic audience interests.

Tear Sheets—Actual pages of advertising as they appear in an issue of any publication, used to serve as proofs of insertion.

Telecast—A broadcast, program, or show on television.

Teleconferencing—Live conferences involving participants in two or more separate locations, with audio, video, and data transmission via satellite to television monitors at each location.

Telephone Coincidental Survey—In research, the interview method in which telephone calls are made while a particular activity, usually a broadcast program, is in progress.

Teletext—A transmission system of text information, by which viewers with special adapters can retrieve wanted signals such as news, weather, etc.

Test Market—A given marketing area, usually a metropolitan census region, in which a market test is conducted. Sometimes used as a verb to refer to introduction of a new product.

Test Market Translation—The use of local media that are available in a specific market to replace the national media included in a brand's national plan. The theoretical national plan must be reproduced as carefully and as accurately as possible in the test market since sales results will be used by company management to determine whether or not the product should be expanded to national distribution.

Thirty-Sheet Poster—An outdoor poster that is approximately 12' by 25'. In the early days of advertising, the poster consisted of twenty-four individual panels pasted together to form an advertisement. Today about ten to twelve panels are used, depending on the type of artwork and copy used.

Through-the-Book—A technique of determining a print medium's audience size by having respondents go through a stripped-down issue with an interviewer to learn which articles are most interesting. After this preliminary examination, respondents are asked whether they are sure they looked into the magazine. Only those who answer positively are counted as readers.

Tie-In—Advertisement run by retail outlets in a newspaper referring to or associating with another ad in the same newspaper. Tie-ins are paid for by the retail outlets running them.

Tiering—Different amounts or levels of cable services that can be ordered by subscribers at different fees.

Time Shifting—Programming that is copied off the air and played back at a different time.

Total Audience—Audience viewing all or any part of a program in excess of five minutes. For programs of less than ten minutes duration, households viewing one minute or more are included. Also total number of unduplicated readers of a magazine.

Total Audience Rating—The sum of all exposures to several issues of the same publication or several issues of different publications.

Total Net Paid—Total of all classes of a publication's circulation for which the ultimate purchasers have paid in accordance with the standards set by the Audit Bureau of Circulations' rules. Includes single copy sales, mail subscriptions, and specials.

TPT (Total Prime Time)—A television research project of Gallup & Robinson evaluating all paid commercials aired during the evening period when national network programming is shown, i.e., both program commercials and station breaks. Offers data both on percentage of commercial audience able to recall the commercial, plus an estimate of actual audience in station coverage. At date of report, such operations were confined to the Philadelphia metro area.

Traceable Expenditures—Published reports on advertising expenditures by media for different advertisers. Currently, traceable expenditures are available for consumer magazines, farm publications, supplements, newspapers, spot TV, network TV (gross time only), and outdoor.

Trade Advertising—Advertisements of consumer items directed to wholesalers and retailers in the distribution channel.

Trade Magazine—See *Business Paper*.

Trade Paper—Publication covering the commercial activities of wholesale and retail outlets, but many reach the sales departments of manufacturers. Trade papers include all publications that offer a manufacturer the opportunity to reach those who will sell the product for him, either from the standpoint of the retail or wholesale level.

Trading Area—The area surrounding a city set up by the Audit Bureau of Circulations whose residents would normally be expected to use the city as their trading center.

Traffic Audit Bureau (T.A.B.)—An organization sponsored by outdoor advertising plants, advertising companies, and national advertisers for the purpose of authenticating circulation as related to outdoor advertising.

Traffic Count—The evaluation of outdoor poster circulation by an actual count of traffic passing the poster.

Traffic Flow Map (Outdoor)—An outline map of a market's streets scaled to indicate the relative densities of traffic.

Traffic Pattern—Comparisons of customer count to establish averages. How customers behave as to shopping time, hour of day, day of week, frequency.

Transient Rate—Same as *one-time rate* in buying space.

Transit Advertising—Advertising on transportation vehicles such as buses, subways, street cars, etc. Uses poster-type ads.

Translator—An independent TV station that picks up programs from a given station and rebroadcasts them to another area on the upper 13 UHF channels (chs. 70–83). Translators serve from several hundred to, in several instances, up to 50,000 TV homes.

Truline Rate—A rate concept sometimes used at the local level. It is computed by multiplying the agate line rate by 1,000,000 circulation and dividing it by the retail trading zone circulation.

Turnover—The ratio of a weekly rating to a four-week reach. This ratio serves as an indication of the relative degree to which the audience of a program changes. The greater the turnover in the audience, the higher the ratio.

TVAR (TV Advertisers Report)—A bimonthly report from Trendex that gives indices of TV audience characteristics in three categories: audience composition, program selection, and sponsor identification.

Two-Sheet Posters—Outdoor posters placed at transit or train stops. They are 60" × 46".

U **UHF (Ultra High Frequency)**—Television channels 14–74.

Unaided Recall—The process of determining whether a person saw or heard a given ad or commercial or brand sometime after exposure with only minimal cueing such as mention of product class (not brand).

Upscale—A general description of a medium's audience indicating upper socioeconomic class membership.

V **VCR**—Video tape recorder that copies programming off the air.

Vehicle—A particular component of a media class, e.g., a particular magazine or broadcast program.

Vertical Cume—In broadcast research, a cumulative rating for two or more programs broadcast on the same day.

Vertical Discount—Broadcast media discount earned through maintenance of specified frequency during given time period, e.g., six spots per week.

Vertical Half-Page—A half page where the long dimension of the ad is vertical. (See *Horizontal Half-Page*.)

Vertical Publication— A business publication that appeals to a specific trade, industry, business, or profession.

VHF (Very High Frequency)—Television channels 2–13. Generally, VHF stations have the greatest range of coverage, whereas UHF stations cover a much smaller area.

Video Discs—A machine that plays pre-recorded programming from a special disc to a special player. It cannot record programming.

Videotex—A two-way interactive cable system that can be retrieved on home TV screens through special terminals. Audiences can request information or data.

Viewer Impression Studies—A service of Daniel Starch & Associates that provides qualiative data about TV commercials. It is based on interviews with respondents who have seen a commercial in the context of normal at-home viewing. Viewers are asked probing questions about the communication of the commercial and its meanings.

Viewers per Set (VPS)—The average number of persons watching or listening to a program in each home.

Volume Discount—A discount given for running a certain volume of space in a publication. An advertiser might use many small insertions to make up the required number of pages.

W **Waste Circulation**—The audience members of a magazine or newspaper who are not prospects for a particular advertised product. Circulation in an area where an advertiser does not have distribution of his product.

Women's Service Magazine—Magazine appealing directly to women (housewives specifically), and whose editorial contents are designed to further their knowledge as homemakers.

Z **Zapping**—Using a remote control device to change television channels from across the room. This technique is usually applied to commerical avoidance.

Zipping—Using a remote control device to skip ahead of any portion of a television or VCR program. Usually applied to skipping over commercials.

Index

A

Achenbaum, Alvin, 91, 347–48
Ad sizes, testing alternative, 349
Advertising
    clutter, 218–19, 391
    communication, 25
    copy checking by media, 219
    creative strategy, 7–8, 110–11, 259
    effectiveness, measuring, 18, 28. *See also*
        Effective frequency
    exposure. *See* Exposure to measure
        media audiences
    future of, 387–407
    goals, long- and short-term, 326–27
    in high-sales versus low-sales markets,
        146–47
    measurement of responses to, 27–28, 174
    after 1990, 390–402
    perception, 25
    relationship between media, consumers,
        and, 21–29
    spending strategy, 314–15
    targets. *See* Target audiences
    task, assessing the, 326
    threshold of responses to, 95–96, 175
    timing of, 159–61
Advertising Age, market and media data
    in, 130
Advertising campaign(s)
    lack of sound selling strategy as weakest
        part of many, 105
    wear-out, 94, 96
Advertising expenditures, increase in, 3
Advertising Research Foundation (ARF),
    18, 175
    Audience Concepts Committee, 70

printed advertising rating methods,
    study by, 214
Adweek, market and media data in, 130
AGB Research (Audits of Great Britain), 3
Aging of the American population, 387–88
Anderson, Richard C., 382–83
Anheuser-Busch budgeting method, 321–22
ANOVA statistical test software for
    personal computers, 365
Appel, Valentine, 92, 96
Arbitron
    area of dominant influence conceived by,
        149
    Product Target AID geodemographic
        media measurements, 69
Area of dominant influence (ADI) defined,
    149–52
Art directors, responsibilities of, 7
As Is (As It Falls) concept of media
    translation, 352–53
Association of National Advertisers (ANA), 18
Associations, market / media data from, 130
Audience(s)
    accumulation, 40–42, 404–5
    actual versus potential size of, 35
    demographics. *See* Demographics
    increasingly fragmented, 16
    measurement, 22, 25–28, 31–40
    media mix to reach different kinds of,
        207
    research data, 11
    secondary, 214–16. *See also* Pass-along
        readers
    size, 8
    total, 40

Audit Bureau of Circulation (ABC), 35,
    40, 151
  circulation figures by, 219
Audits and Surveys Research Company,
    Inc.
  data service, 128
  primary and secondary audiences study
    by, 214, 216
Audits of Great Britain (AGB) Company,
    61, 62, 67–69
Automatic interaction detection (AID), 69,
    370
Average audience rating
  difference between share of audience
    rating and, 50, 52
  through people meters, 49–50

                    B

Banks, Seymour, 339
BAR/LNA Multimedia Service, 116, 118
Baron, Roger, 365, 368
Beta binomial model for media planning,
    364–65
Billboards, 6. *See also* Outdoor media
  attrition, 393–94
  media coverage, 46–47, 198
Brand(s)
  advertising timed for goals of the, 160
  awareness, building, 88, 186
  distribution channels, 104
  evaluation, 24
  frequency levels vary according to, 94
  image, 258–59
  important elements in selling a, 24
  perceived value of a, 176
  position related difficulty of achieving
    advertising goals, 315
  postpurchasing evaluation, 24
  roll-outs, tracking new, 126
  situation analysis, 103–4
  switching, 93, 97, 323
  threat of competing, 114
  use, audience measurement of, 34

Brand development index (BDI), 154–56,
    167–68, 169–71
Broadbent, Simon, 363
Broadcast Advertising Reports (BAR), 119,
    122–24
Broadcast media. *See also* Radio *and*
    Television
  audience accumulation in, 41–42
  circulation, 45–46
  differences between print media and,
    190, 302
  frequency measured in, 79–83
  gross rating points (GRPs) on, 52–53, 99
  reach measured in, 73–78
Broadcast ratings, 8
  means of reporting, 49–51
Broadcasting, market and media data in,
    130
Brown, George H., 322
Budget constraints
  on advertising, 160, 187
  on media objectives, 232–33
  strategies to address media objectives
    under, 241
Budget(s)
  difficulty in determining, 313
  experimental methods for setting,
    321–22
  media allocation prorated for
    advertiser's, 262–64
  most common methods of setting,
    325–26
  newer methods of setting, 321–25
  Ogilvy & Mather's approach to setting,
    314–15
  pro-rata (proportional), 330
  relationship between advertising, profits,
    and market share for determining,
    323–24
  size, factors in determining, 325–28
  theoretical methods of setting, 325
  traditional methods of setting, 315–21
Budget allocations, advertising
  geographic, 328–29
  by medium, 262–64, 329–31
  payout planning technique for, 331–34

Burnett Company, Inc., Leo, 8
Business publications, 5
   sample media plan flowchart for, 252
Buying
   guides, mass media selected because of
      advertising as, 22
   power indices, 156–57
   process, steps of the product, 24–25

C

Cable television. *See also* Television
   advantages of advertising on, 200–1
   advertisers' use of, 4–6
   basic networks (ESPN, CNN), 395
   disadvantages of advertising on, 201–2
   electronic newspapers on, 392–93
   growth of, 398
   history of, 397
   information and entertainment
      programming, 398
   media expenditures, collecting data on,
      118–19, 122
   network list, 399–400
   new opportunities of, 3
   news and community programming, 397
   pay. *See* Pay cable television *and*
      Subscription television (STV)
   people meters to monitor viewing of, 64
   spill-ins and spill-outs in testing on, 350
   tests, 348
C.A.C.I. Company's ACORN
      geodemographic media
      measurements, 69, 128
Campbell, Roy H., 340
Canter, Stanley D., 322–23
Car cards, 5
   advantages of advertising on, 199–200
   costs, 306
   disadvantages of advertising on, 200
   intermedia comparisons for, 205–6
   media coverage, 46–47, 199
Case rate budgeting method, 320–21
Catalogs, 5–6, 405
Category development index (CDI),
      154–56, 167–68, 169–71

Census Bureau
   data for situation analyses, 129
   nine geographic divisions and four
      regions of the, 148
Checkerboard design used in test
      marketing, 347
Churchill, Verne B., Jr., 342
City zone defined, 151
Closing date for buying magazine ads,
      309–10
Color
   high-fidelity, 10, 191
   media best suited to, 110, 191, 192, 198
   quality as a measure of a medium's
      value, 220–21
   run of press or run of paper (ROP), 191,
      304
Commercials, testing alternative lengths
      for, 349
Community Antenna Television (CATV),
      397
Competitive spending budgeting method,
      320
Competitors
   activity impact on advertising budget,
      328
   advertising timing of, 160
   frequency level set by most serious, 176
   media expenditures of, 12, 24, 104, 320.
      See also Media expenditure analysis
   media planner's concerns with, 240–41
   media selection based on those used by,
      114–15
   media strategies of, 238
   product's relative strength for market
      compared with, 315
CompuServe data bases and services, 393
Computer use in media planning, 359–85
   to analyze marketing or media data, 360,
      369
   to assess alternative media plans, 360,
      369
   to construct media schedules, 360
   to control billing and perform
      management tasks, 360

to cross tabulate demographic market segments, 370

to find targets with automatic interaction detection, 370

judgment required to supplement, 382–83

as learning tool, 369

to simulate test markets, 369–70

time-sharing, 369

Consolidated Metropolitan Statistical Area (CMSA), 150

Consumer(s)

choice, 21–22

information processing, 22–23

profile necessary for media planner to devise plan, 104

relationship between media, advertising, and, 21–29

Consumer Bulletin, market and media data in, 130–31

Consumer Reports, market and media data in, 130

Continuity of advertising (straight-through advertising)

as an advertising scheduling technique, 181–84, 349

defined, 160

factor in setting media objectives, 233–34

reach, frequency, and number of markets related to, 185

Convention exhibits, 6

Copy strategy described in media plan, 258–59

Copywriters, responsibilities of, 7

Cost efficiency

of media, 211–13, 294

of premium positions in media, 227

specified in media objectives, 234–35

Cost efficiency measurements

cost per rating point (CPRP), 57

cost per thousand (CPM), 55–56, 164, 170–71, 211, 213, 234–35, 294

Coverage

defined, 42–46, 212

market, 43

modified by HUT data, 47

of newspaper supplements, 193

of outdoor vehicles, 198

reach versus, 76

stated in media objectives, 234

test area, 350–51

Creative constraints in setting media objectives, 233

Creative strategy. *See* Advertising creative strategy

Cut-in commercial, 353

Cut-off point for dropping markets, 157

D

Dantzig, George B., 361

Dayparts

assessing popularity of television viewing by, 68

frequency levels related to, 94

local television, 302

media plan use of, 268–69, 276–77

reach curves for different, 78

recall rates affected by, 226–27

television costs based on, 299–300

usage in test markets of, 351

DDB Needham Worldwide media selection criteria, 207–8

Dealers, media selection to communicate with, 111–12

Delivery

allocated on a market-by-market basis, 373

comparing media for cost and, 294–97

defined, 10

estimated for a media budget, 294

goals described in media plan, 264–67

media plan description of, 258–59

network, 351

Demographic analysis of a brand's users, 374

Demographic targets versus users, 212–13

Demographic universe used for coverage analysis, 42

Demographic variables, 7

Demographics
  audience measurement data to learn
    vehicle, 33
  based on geography, 69
  composite analyses of, 212–13
  delivery in terms of, 258
  magazine special editions geared to, 217,
    390
  personal consumer, 104, 256–57
  sales or product usage related through
    index numbers to, 134
  strategy planning involving, 133–46,
    260–61
Designated market area (DMA) defined,
  150
Diary measurements
  of store purchases, 127
  of television ratings, 62, 64, 66
Direct Broadcast Satellites (DBS), 5, 400
Direct mail, 5–6, 110
  advantages of advertising in, 197
  disadvantages of advertising in, 198
  future trends, 405
  selectivity of, 197
Direct Marketing Assocation, 405
Directories, 5
Disposable income, projected decline in,
  388
Distribution, creating demand to "force,"
  146
Dollar allocation weighting technique,
  164–66

                          E

Editor & Publisher Market Guide, 129
Editor & Publisher, market and media data
  in, 130
Effective frequency, 28
  copy factors that affect, 179, 180
  current standing of, 98–100
  defined, 88
  essence of, 88–90
  frequency distributions necessary to
    calculate, 378
  history of, 91–92

impact of alternative media plans
    assessed with, 99–100
  marketing factors that affect, 178–79,
    180
  media factors that affect, 179–80
  media vehicle frequency required for
    advertising exposure frequencies
    determined by, 97
  need for, 87
  numbers, 90
  problems with, 95–98
  relationship between good advertising
    and, 96
  research behind, 92–95
  response curves and, 89–90
  setting, 177–81
Effective rating points (ERPs), 91
Effective reach, 28
  defined, 90
  frequency distributions necessary to
    calculate, 378
  goal, 256–57, 264
  table of reach, frequency, and, 380
Electronic information service systems, 393
Elliott, Jeremy, 93
Energy costs, expected rise in, 389
Engel/Kollats model of buying process, 24
Expenditure per unit budgeting method,
  320–21
Experiment
  advantages and disadvantages of the,
    339–40
  costs, 339
  defined, 337
  difference between test and, 338–39
  as part of planner's decision making,
    337–38
Exposure(s)
  advertising, 97, 174
  delivery of specific vehicles measured
    with linear programming, 362
  to measure media audiences, 25–26
  required for advertising effectiveness, 94.
    See also Effective frequency
  "three hit theory" of, 89, 92
  vehicle, 97–98, 174

F

Factor defined, 157
Factorial design used in test marketing, 347
Family units, trend toward smaller, 388
FCC Prime Access Rule, 395
Films, 6
Flights
  as an advertising scheduling technique,
    182–84
  defined, 160
  media plan's use of, 269, 349
  television, 126
Foley, William, 325
Formula models of media planning,
  364–68
Four-plus coverage, 94
Freestanding inserts (FSI), 5–6, 110
Frequency, 73–85. *See also* Effective
    frequency
  of billboards, 198
  of car cards, 199
  computer calculation of, 362–63, 366
  defined, 26
  direct measurement of, 64
  distribution, 80–83, 99–100, 207, 265,
    270–71, 368, 378
  estimated exposures patterned to
    maximize, 233
  formula, 79–80
  future trends for, 403–4
  gross, 99
  levels and purchasing, 93, 174–76
  media mix to flatten the distribution of,
    207
  optimum number measurement use of,
    34
  reach, continuity, and number of
    markets related to, 185
  reach relationship to, 83–85
  soap operas to develop more, 82, 84–85
  strategy planning for, 172–77, 256–57
  table of reach, effective reach, and, 380
  vehicle versus advertising, 176–77

Frequency of purchase, advertising budget
    size impacted by, 327

G

Gallup-Robinson (Aided Recall) Measuring
    Technique, 214–15
Gateway Viewdata service, 393
Gensch, Dennis, 363
Geodemographic measurements of media
    audience, 69, 256–57
Geographic areas
  classifying, 148–51
  population shifts in U.S., 388
Geographic divisions or territories for sales,
    147–48
Geographic editions of magazines, 217,
    390
Geographic weighting, 163–72
  case studies, 168–72
  defined, 163
  forms, 164–66
  guidelines, 167–68
  strategies, 262–64
Gerber, Philip, 16
Glossary, 409–44
Goldin, Alan, 15–17
Grass, Robert C., 92, 96
Gross circulation, 46
Gross impression weighting, 164–65
Gross impressions, 51–52, 53–55, 165–67
  analysis, 272–73
  calculating cost per thousands on basis
    of, 294
  media mix to add, 207
Gross rating points (GRPs)
  in broadcast media, 52–53, 99
  conversion of spot TV dollars to, 286
  defined, 51
  effective rating points (ERPs) as
    replacement for, 91
  formula for calculating, 83
  in magazines, 53
  to measure media weight, 113
  in newspapers, 53

out-of-home media purchased on basis of daily, 46, 53
   planning for, 176
   uneven distribution of, 163–64
   women, 269, 275–76
Guggenheim, Bernard, 365

H

Hendbills, 5–6
Hendry method of budgeting, 322
Home Box Office (HBO) satellite transmissions, 397
Home computers, 5, 365, 401
Home shopping vehicles, 405
Households using television (HUT), 47, 51

I

Impact, concept of, 111–12
IMS time-sharing computer services, 369
In-store tests, 348
Index numbers to analyze markets, 133–37
Index of responses, 99–100
Information Resources, Inc. (IRI), 4, 67–69
Intermedia comparisons, 189–210
Intramedia comparisons, 189

J

Jacobovits, L., 92, 96

K

Kaatz, Ron, 70
Kershaw, Andrew, 323–25
"Kid TV," 300
Krugman, Herbert, 89, 92
Kuehn, Alfred A., 320

L

Latin square designs used in test marketing, 346–47
Leading National Advertisers (LNA), 116, 118–19

Leontief, Wassily W., 361
Life-style research, 143–44
Line-extension planning, 126
Linear programming model, 361–62
Lipstein, Benjamin, 340
Little U.S.A. concept, 53
LNA Outdoor Advertising Service, 119–20
Low power TV (LPTV), 5

M

McDonald, Colin, 92–98
Magazine(s)
   advantages of advertising in, 192
   audience accumulation, 40–41
   audience analysis calculated by computer, weighted, 379
   buying ads in, 309–10
   circulation, 192, 390
   for color advertising, 110, 112
   computer used to calculate reach and frequency for different issues of, 375
   consumer, 6
   copy splits, 310
   costs for advertising, 295–96, 302–4
   coverage, 43–44
   disadvantages of advertising in, 193
   general interest, 303
   geographic and demographic editions for limited markets produced by, 217, 390
   gross rating points (GRPs) in, 53
   home, 303–4
   imperatives, 218
   media plan flowchart for, 251
   new product editorials, 219
   position practices, 126, 226
   production costs, 390–91
   rate concessions, 310
   reach, 78
   recent-reading technique for measuring audiences of, 32–33
   responses to thick versus thin, 94
   special interest, 390
   suitability for advertisements, 4–5

through-the-book technique for
  measuring audiences of, 32–33
translations in, 354–55
trends for the 1990s, 390–91
women's service, 303
Magazine, market and media data in, 130
Maneloveg, Herbert D., 313–14
Market(s)
  control, 345
  coverage, 43
  defined, 148–49
  dropping a, 157–58
  history part of marketing situation
    analysis, 103
  profile, 135–36
  reach, frequency, and continuity related
    to, 185
  recommended for test marketing, 343
  segmentation for 1990s, 389–90
  sizes for test marketing, 344
  test market number of, 351
  value, advertising weighting on the basis
    of, 170–72
Market Facts, Inc., test marketing
    effectiveness study, 342
Market Research Corporation of America
    (MRCA) data service, 127
Marketing and Media Decisions, market
    and media data in, 130
Marketing background described in media
    plan, 258–59
Marketing Communications, market and
    media data in, 130
Marketing concept, rise of the, 2
Marketing data sources
  inexpensive, 128–31
  major data services as, 127–28
Marketing mix, 112
Marketing objectives, 106, 108–9, 114,
    232, 260–61
Marketing plan, 7
  key to success of a, 106
  to unify and organize marketing and
    advertising activity, 105–6, 114
Marketing problem, media planning arises
    from, 6–7, 106

Marketing research people, responsibilities
    of, 7
Marketing strategy, 7–8, 103–32
  media plan as outgrowth of the, 106,
    114
  statement, 106–8
Marketing strategy plan
  budget, 109–10
  creative strategy, 110–11
  overall sales strategy, 112–13
  purpose, 104–6
  test marketing, 113–14
Marketing variables
  in-store tests of, 348
  media strategy variables affected by
    certain, 231
  tested in test markets, 344–45
Marshak, Seymour, 214–16
Mass media. *See also* Magazine(s),
    Newspaper(s), Radio, *and* Television
  advertising effectiveness of, 4–6
  most advertising delivered by, 21
Matthews, Leonard, 8
Matthews, William E., 14
Measurements in media planning. *See*
    Advertising, measurement of
    responses to; Audience meaurement;
    and Media measurement
Media
  allocation, 262–64, 329–31
  availability, 349
  broadcast. *See* Radio *and* Television
  buyers, 295, 307
  as buying guides, 22
  classes, 4–6, 189–210
  decisions, 8, 15–17
  discounts, 220, 362
  effectiveness, 25, 242
  expenditures, 12, 114–31, 317–19,
    324–25
  flexibility, 220, 241–42, 264–65
  flowchart or schedule, 248–52, 266,
    268–69, 367
  imperatives, 218
  jargon, current and future, 406
  measurement, 31–33

measuring tools, 61–71
new, 3
packages, reach and frequency of
    alternative, 376
pattern of delivery of, 248
qualitative values of, 221–25
rationale, 274–77
relationship between advertising,
    consumers, and, 21–29
response functions of, 28
schedules, 360
selection principles, 10, 189–210
specialized. *See* Business publications;
    Catalogs; Directories; Handbills;
    Membership listings; Professional
    journals; Programs, event; *and* Yellow
    pages
spending levels, testing alternative,
    348–49
studies of special markets, 129–30
translations, 352–55
used for advertising, most common, 5
values, 176, 211, 214–21
weight, 113, 148
Media cost, 3, 257, 293–312
assumptions, 295
comparisons, 297–306
relation of delivery to, 294
Media expenditure analysis. *See also*
    Competitors *and* Media expenditures
on an annual basis, 122, 125
best use of, 126
data analysis, 125–26
data collection for, 122, 125
on a market-by-market basis, 125
sources of information for, 114–22
using, 126–27
Media mix(es)
learned from media expenditure
    analysis, 126
reasons to use a, 206–7
testing alternative, 349
Media models
defined, 360
three types of, 361–68
Media objectives, 7, 9

defined, 230–31
examples of, 235–36, 256–57
factors, 232–35
Media plan(s)
annotated sample, 255–91
assembling elements of, 242–47
as blueprint for selection and use of
    media, 2
checklists, 243–47
compared with effective frequency data,
    99–100
compared with media strategies, 278–80
cost of advertising estimates for, 293
"creative," 15–17, 238
customized, 11–12
description of the, 266–67
frequency distribution of a, sample, 82
mechanics of preparing a, 229–54
media decisions behind the, 229
testing a complete, 348
Media planners
ad positions selected by, 225
background of marketing effort of a
    brand essential for, 103–4
changing role of, 2–3
competitors' activities considered by,
    240–41
consumer profile required by, 104
experiments and tests used by, 337–38
product history required by, 104
response levels increased by, 27
responsibilities of, 3
sales promotions' significance to, 43
sales volume figures used by, 264–65
Media planning
authority and prestige factors in, 242
computers for. *See* Computer use in
    media planning
defined, 1–2
general procedures for, 6–18
goals, 229–30
gross impressions used in, 54–55
industry changes, 3–4
insufficient information for, 13–14
introduction to, 1–19

marketing strategy and situation analysis
  as starting point in, 103–32
objectivity in, 17–18
problems in, 13–18
purchasing cycle basis for, 98
steps in, 230
testing, experimenting, and, 337–57
time pressures in, 14–15
trends in the 1990s, 402–3
variables, 231
Media preplanning activities, 8
Media Records reports on newspaper media
  expenditures, 116–17
Media selection, 109, 110. *See also* Media
  classes
based on competitors, 114–15
criteria, 207–8
Media strategies
best, 12
creative, 238–39
defined, 7
determining, 236–38
examples of, 256–58
judging, 237
media objectives corresponding to, 9
media plan compared with, 278–80
planning process for, 133–62, 163–88,
  240–42
priorities of, 187
sample, 260–67
Media testing, 348–51
Media vehicle(s)
audience measurement, purposes of,
  33–34
client pressure on selection of, 17
consumer loyalty to particular, 21
defined, 1
editorial environments of, 216–17
exposure, 97–98, 174
need for good measurement of, 23–25
selecting, 10–11, 211–28
Mediamark Research, Inc. (MRI), 33, 67
data service, 128
place of reading analyzed by, 41
Medium defined, 1
membership listings, 5

Memory. *See also* Recall
of advertisements, 26
short- and long-term, 22
Meskill, John J., 206–7
Message weight
distribution, 166–67
measurements of, 51–52, 69
Metropolitan Statistical Area (MSA)
compared to ADI, 151–52
defined, 150
Microcomputers, 5, 365, 401
Minimarkets, 348
Minority populations, expected growth of
  U.S., 388
Movies to develop more reach than
  frequency, 84
Multipoint Distribution System (MDS), 5
Music, media selection based on need for,
  110

N

Naples, Michael J., 92–96, 98
Neisloss, Kathy, 15–17
New products. *See* Product introductions
Newspaper(s)
advantages of advertising in, 190–91
buying ads in, 310–11
circulation, 391
color advertising in, 110, 191
costs, 304–5, 392
coverage, 42–44
custom insert costs, 304–5
disadvantages of advertising in, 191–92
electronic, 392–93
gross rating points (GRPs) in, 53
media expenditures, collecting data on,
  116–18
positions of ads in, 226
special sections, 310–11, 391
suitability for advertisements, 4–5
translations in, 354
trends for the 1990s, 391–92
yesterday-reading technique for
  measuring audiences of, 33
Newspaper designated markets, 151–52

Newspaper supplements. *See* Supplements, newspaper
Nielsen, A. C.
  basic ten territories, 148–49
  correlation of purchasing with television viewing by, 67–69
  county size consumption index, 282
  data service, 127
  designated market area (DMA) used by, 150
  ERIM (Electronic Research for Insights into Marketing) service, 4
  Media Research Group (MRG), 3
  Monitor-Plus, 122
  NTI PRIZM technique using zip codes for geodemographic measurements, 69, 128, 365
  people meters used by, 3, 49, 61–63, 65
  Storage Instantaneous Audimeters, 32
  VCR usage assessments, 203
Nielsen Television Index, 49, 51–52, 66
Nonoptimizing model for media problems, 361

O

Objective and task budgeting method, 320
Ogilvy & Mather's approach to budgeting, 314–15
One-for-one policy, 111
Opportunities to see (OTS), 26, 93
Optimization of reach and frequency, 377
Optimizing models for media problems, 361
Optimum number defined, 34
Ostrow, Joseph, 177–81
Outdoor media, 5
  advantages of advertising on, 198–99
  disadvantages of advertising on, 199
  measurement of audience for, 33
  media expenditures, collecting data on, 119–20
  trends for the 1990s, 303–94
Out-of-home media. *See* Billboards; Car cards; Outdoor media; Poster(s);

Programs, event; *and* Terminal and station displays

P

Panographics for billboards, 393
Pass-along readers
  defined, 40
  magazines with great number of, 192
  media vehicles examined in terms of, 214–16
  newspapers have small number of, 192
  newspaper supplements have small number of, 194
Pay cable television
  advantages of advertising on, 200
  advertisers' use of, 4–6
  rapid growth of, 395, 398
Payout planning budgeting, 331–34
Penetration
  of newspaper supplements, 194
  of video cassette recorders, 202, 204
People meters
  advantages of, 64
  companies vying for adoption of, 61
  defined, 61
  evaluation of, 66–67
  format of, 61–63
  need for, 62, 64
  passive, 67
  potential problems with, 65
  practical problems with, 65–66
  used by A. C. Nielsen, 3, 49, 61–63, 65
Percentages to analyze markets, 133
Percent-of-Sales method for determining advertising budgets, 316–20
Percy Company, R. D., 67
Personal computers, 5, 365, 401
Picturephones, 5
Pipeline defined, 156
Plummer, Joseph T., 143
Points of purchase, car cards to advertise to consumers on way to, 200
Politz, Alfred, 214, 222–23, 364
Population trends in America, 387–90, 394
Positions of ads

cost considerations of, 227
effects of, 226–27
in magazines, 126, 226
media planners' selection of, 225
in print media related to media value, 218
research about, 225–26
on television, 226–27
Poster(s)
costs, 305–6
junior panel or eight-sheet, 305
media coverage, 46–47
panel, 305–6
sales, 53
standard or thirty-sheet, 305
two-sheet, 305
Potential circulation, 46
Priemer, Gus, 95, 174
Primary Metropolitan Statistical Area (PMSA), 150
Primary readers defined, 40
Print measurements
audience (readers per copy), 40
circulation, 35
Print media
circulation trends, 219
differences between broadcast media and, 190
frequency measured in, 79–83
impact, 224
page openings of, 224
positions within, 218
pricing for, 295
qualitative values of, 223–24
reach measured in, 78–79
reading days of, 223
reading time of, 223–24
reputation to advertisers of, 223
satellite technology used by, 401
types, 5
Product
availability a factor in advertising timing, 160
distribution a factor in media decision making, 111–12

history required for media planner to develop plan, 104
protection, 218–19
Product category
frequency effects differ according to, 95
noise level, 176
overspending on advertising by a, 324
Product introductions, 95
budgeting for, 327
expenditure data in, 126–27
payout planning for, 331
Product usage
budget size impacted by level of, 327
groups, selecting, 142–43
habits, 8
heavy, data about, 153–54, 206
index numbers to related demographic segments to, 134
potential, determining, 140–42
strategic impressions examination of, 213
targets selected by, 137–40
Production costs, 256–57
Professional journals, 5
Profit margin impact on budget size, 327
Profit maximization, 324
Profit profile, 323–24
Programming, television. See also Dayparts
advertising revenues to cover the cost of, 308
for children, 299–300
daytime, 299
fringe time, 302, 354
late night, 299
prime time, 299–300
syndicated. See Syndicated television
weekend, 299
Programs, event, 5
intermedia comparisons for, 205–6
Promotion
reach maximized for a special, 113, 186
requirements a factor in advertising timing, 161
Prospects. See Target audience(s)
Psychographics of consumers, 104, 142–46
Publisher's Advertising Reports (PAR), 119

Publisher's Information Bureau
(PIB/LNA), 119, 121
Pulsing as an advertising scheduling
technique, 182, 184, 349
Purchase cycle
media planning based on, 98, 187
optimum exposures during a, 94

Q

Qualitative values of media
defined, 221
guidelines for using, 224
measuring, 222–23
problems of, 222
using, 223–25
QUBE, 5, 392, 402

R

Radio
advantages of advertising on, 195–96
audience accumulation, 41
audience measurement, 32
buying ads on network, 311
buying ads on spot, 311
costs, network, 305
costs, spot, 305
disadvantages of advertising on, 196
media expenditures, collecting data on,
118–19, 122
planning guide, computer to prepare a
weekly, 381–82
product demonstrations using, 110
station rotation, 126
suitability for advertisements, 4–6
translations in, 353–54
trends for the 1990s on, 394
Radio coverage
local, 43–45, 196
spot, 43, 45
Randomized block design used in test
marketing, 345–46
Rate cards for newspaper and magazine ad
costs, 302
Rated exposure units (REU), 361

Rated exposure values (REV), 361
Ratings report of the future, 403–4
Raw numbers to analyze markets, 133–35
Reach, 73–85. *See also* Effective reach
broadcast media, 73–78
cable television, 200–201
combined, 74
computer calculation of, 362–63, 366
cost effective, 211–13
curve, 76–78
defined, 26
direct measurement of, 64
estimated exposures patterned to
maximize, 233
four-week, 74, 82
frequency, continuity, and number of
markets related to, 185
frequency relationship to, 83–85
future trends for, 403–4
gross, 99
magazines' slow building of, 193
media mix to extend, 207
movies or drama to develop, 82, 84
net, 75
newspapers' mass, 191
optimum number measurement use of,
34
print media, 78–79
radio's selective, 195
roadblocks and scatter plans to build, 83,
85
special promotions require maximum,
113
strategy planning for, 172–73
summary of, 80
table of frequency, effective reach, and,
380
television's mass and selective, 194–95
types of, 74–76
Readers
in-home versus out-of-home, 41, 379
primary versus pass-along, 40–41. *See
also* Pass-along readers
Readers per copy, 40
Recall. *See also* Memory
daypart effects on, 226–27

of in-program commercials better than between-program commercials, 227

low for outdoor vehicles, 199

primary versus secondary audience, 214–16

scores for intermedia comparisons, 205–6

types of television programs affect, 226

Records

photograph, 6

vinyl, as magazine inserts, 110

Response(s) *See also* Advertising

to coupons, information, or recipes, 219–20

curves and effective frequency, 89–90

curves, ''convex-shaped'' versus S-curved, 89–90, 96

functions of media, 28

measurement of, 27–28

media planner's role in increasing the size of, 27

Retail trading zone, 149, 151

Roadblocks to build reach, 83, 85

Russell Hall editorial reports, 391

S

Sales

analysis, 151–53, 159–60

analysis related to advertising per market, 372

brand versus category, 159–60

budget determinations based on, 316–20

factors contributing to, 23–24

index numbers to relate demographic segments to, 134

potential, advertising weighting on the basis of, 168–69

promotion, significance to media planners of, 113

proving advertising's effects on, 4

strategy, overall, 112–13

Sales volume

impact on production costs, 327

tested in test marketing, 344

used by media planners for budget allocation, 264–65

Sales & Marketing Management Survey of Buying Power, 129, 156–57

San Augustine, André J., 325

Satellite network for information services, 393

Satellite technology, 401

Satellite-Fed Master Antenna TV (SMATV), 5

ScanAmerica (Arbitron), 3

ScanAmerica (Arbitron and Time, Inc.), 61, 62, 67–69

Scatter

plan to build reach, 83, 85

on syndicated television, 300

Seasons

media performance differences among, 242

television viewing varies among, 47–48

Selective attention, 23

Selectivity percentage, 212. *See also* Coverage

Selling Areas-Marketing, Inc. (SAMI), data service, 128

Selling strategy of an advertising campaign, 105

Share of audience rating

difference between average audience rating and, 50–52

formula, 50–51

Share of market

of competitors' key to devising countering strategies, 114, 125

marketing objectives calling for increased, 109, 258–59

maximum profits do not arise from maximum, 324

tested in test marketing, 344

Share of voice weighting, 166–67

Shoppers, 5

Simmons Market Research Bureau (SMRB)

data prepared by computer, 374

demographic information gathered by, 137–39, 144–45

media imperatives research by, 218

place of reading analyzed by, 41

Simmons Market Research Bureau (SMRB) Report, 33
Simulation model for media problems, 361, 362–64
Single source data of television viewing and purchasing, 67–69
Situation analysis. *See* Marketing strategy *and* Marketing strategy plan
Skew of a frequency distribution, 80–81
Source, The, 393
Specialty publications, sample media plan flowchart for, 252
Spot television. *See also* Television coverage
   buying, 309
   buying strategy, sample, 290–91
   flexibility of, 276–78
   market list, sample, 288–89
   market selection methodology sample for, 282–87
   planning guide, computer to prepare a, 380–81
Standard advertising units (SAUs), 116
Standard Metropolitan Statistical Area, 150
Standard Rate and Data Service (SRDS), 129
Stengel, Casey, 387
Straight-through advertising. *See* Continuity of advertising (straight-through advertising)
Strategic impressions, 213–14
Strategy planning. *See* Media strategies
Study of Printed Advertising Rating Methods, A, 214
Subjective budgeting method, 321
Subscription television (STV), 5. *See also* Pay cable television
Superstations (WTBS, EGN), 395, 398
Supplements, newspaper, 5
   advantages of advertising in, 193–94
   color in, 193, 194, 304
   costs, 304
   disadvantages of advertising in, 194
   translations in, 354–55
Syndicated television
   advertising dollars in, 396
   buying, 309

   cash, 300
   defined, 300
   FCC decisions encouraging, 395
   growth of, 395–97
   part barter/part cash, 300
   scatter, 300
   straight barter, 300
   top programs for, 301

T

Tactics defined, 8
Target audience(s), 23
   budget impacted by difficult-to-reach, 327
   computer ranking of vehicles in ability to deliver, 362
   defining, 139–40, 256–57, 260–61
   determining, 7
   media expenditure analysis to reveal how competitors view their, 126
   of the 1990s, 405
   reach. *See* Reach
   selecting, 137–42
   specified in media objectives, 234
Tatham, Arthur, 105
Telephone coincidental survey, 22
Teletext of newspapers, 392
Television
   advantages of advertising on, 194–95
   audience accumulation, 41–42
   audience measurement, local, 32
   audience measurement, network, 32–33
   building of reach for, 76–78
   costs, local, 300–302
   costs, network, 298–300
   disadvantages of advertising on, 195
   flighting, 126
   imperatives, 218
   media buying problems, 306–9
   media expenditures, collecting data on, 116, 118–19, 123–24
   media plan flowchart for, 250
   network decline, 395
   network scheduling changes, 307
   opportunistic buying on, 308

positions of ads on, 226–27
program cancellations, 307
scatter buying on, 308
stereo, 401
suitability for advertisements, 4–6
suitability for color, 110
translations in, 353–54
trends in the 1990s on, 394–401
upfront network buy on, 308
viewing correlated with purchasing, 67–69
viewing variations by daypart and season for, 47–48
Television Attentiveness and Special Events Study (SMRB), 227
Television coverage
local, 43–45
network, 43, 45–46
spot, 43, 45, 164
Television/Radio Age, market and media data in, 130
Television stereo broadcasts, 401
Telmar time-sharing computer services, 369
Terminal and station displays
advantages of advertising on, 199–200
costs, 305–6
disadvantages of advertising on, 200
Test
advantages and disadvantages of the, 339–40
area coverage, 350–51
defined, 337
difference between experiment and, 338–39
as part of planner's decision making, 337–38
validity, 345
Test marketing, 88, 113–14, 174–75
computer simulations, 369–70
criteria, 343
defined, 340–41
markets to include, 343–44
media costs in, 350
number of markets to use in, 343
purposes of, 341–42
research designs used in, 345–48

samples, measuring, 338–39
spill-in and spill-out in, 349–50
Thompson, J. Walter, research on effective frequency by, 92–94
"Three hit theory," 89, 92
Trade shows, 6
Traditional media. *See* Direct mail, Freestanding inserts (FSI), Handbills, Magazine(s), Newspaper(s), Shoppers, *and* Supplements, newspaper
Transit media. *See* Car cards *and* Terminal and station displays
Tveter, T. Norman, 111

U

Unbalanced frequency distributions, 81
Universe defined, 73
UPC scanners, 4
used by consumers to measure recent purchases, 68
Usage groups. *See* Product usage
USA Today, efficient one-buy medium for national advertisers in, 392

V

Vehicle. *See* Media vehicle(s)
Video cassette recorders
advantages of advertising on broadcasts or cassettes for, 202–3
disadvantages of advertising on broadcasts or cassettes for, 203–4
impact of, 400
planning opportunities of, 3
usage measurement, 203
viewer control of TV schedule through, 395
Video discs, 5
Videotape players, 5
Videotex (two-way television), 3, 392
Viewdata televised merchandise, 392, 393
Viewtron electronic newspaper system, 393

W

Weighted BDIs and CDIs, 155–56
Weilbacher, William, 221–22
Weinblatt, Lee, 69
Weinblatt measurements for media, 69–70
Working women, media plans taking into
    account, 16

Y

Yellow Pages, 5–6
    intermedia comparisons for, 205–6

Z

Zapping of commercials
    defined, 202
    impact on media plan of, 400
    profile of viewers who use, 203–4
Zeltner, Herbert, 106
Zip code marketing, 128
Zipping of commercials
    defined, 202
    impact on media plan of, 400
    profile of viewers who use, 204